Using Proper Proof Marks

D0161382

When I was ten and living in florida, I learned that dogs may not be man's best friend. *always*

I liked to descover new places, and one afternoon, while riding a bycicle on the out skirts of my neighborhood, I *bicycle* discovered a train station. As I was leisurely rolling by the wherehouses, I noticed three large dogs about fifty *warehouses* yards infront of me. Since I had a dog of my own, and he wouldn't without a reason bother anyone, I passed not attention to these Canines. But, as I got closer, the dogs started to approch me with menaceing growls and barks. At *a* this point I began to feel uneasy, so I turned around to ride in the other direction. As soon as I turned, all three dogs started to chase me and nip at my heals. I tried to pick up speed in order to create some distance between me and these malign creatures, but to no avial. One of the dogs sank his teeth into my leg deeply and would not let go, no *a* *not* matter how hard I pulled. Only when I gave a violent yank he did finally let go. At this point, I didn't think about pain; I only though about riding for my life. *t*

SECOND EDITION

Rewriting Writing

A Rhetoric, Reader, and Handbook

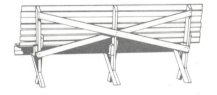

SECOND EDITION

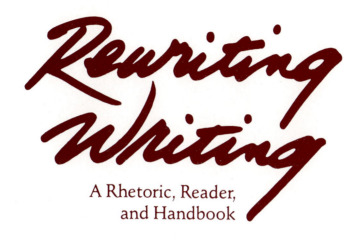

Rewriting Writing

A Rhetoric, Reader,
and Handbook

Jo Ray McCuen

Glendale Community College

Anthony C. Winkler

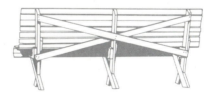

HARCOURT BRACE JOVANOVICH, PUBLISHERS

San Diego   New York   Chicago   Austin   Washington, D.C.
London   Sydney   Tokyo   Toronto

Cover: Lance A. Lavenstein, Lavenstein Studios.

Copyright © 1990, 1987 by Harcourt Brace Jovanovich, Inc.

All rights reserved. No part of this publication may be reproduced or
transmitted in any form or by any means, electronic or mechanical,
including photocopy, recording or any information storage and retrieval
system, without permission in writing from the publisher.

Requests for permission to make copies of any part of the work should
be mailed to: Copyrights and Permissions Department, Harcourt Brace
Jovanovich, Publishers, Orlando, Florida 32887.

NOTE: This work is derived from *Rhetoric Made Plain*, Fourth Edition, by
Anthony C. Winkler and Jo Ray McCuen, copyright © 1984, 1981, 1978, 1974
by Harcourt Brace Jovanovich, Inc., and *Rewriting Writing: A Rhetoric* by Jo Ray
McCuen and Anthony C. Winkler, copyright © 1987 by Harcourt Brace
Jovanovich, Inc.

ISBN: 0-15-576721-6

Library of Congress Catalog Card Number: 89-85891
Printed in the United States of America

Preface

The second edition of *Rewriting Writing* is based on the same premise as the first, namely, that most good writing has been rewritten, and that all rewriting is better done if done systematically and with conscious forethought. We continue to assume that the techniques and methods writers use to make final drafts better than first ones can be covered in a textbook such as this and carefully taught. In important emphasis and principle this second edition of *Rewriting Writing* is, therefore, the same as the first.

In overall content and packaging, however, it is vastly different. To begin with, this new edition now contains readings grouped under four recurring cross-curriculum categories—Humanities, Social Sciences, Sciences, and Business and Technology—for a total of 36 selections. The readings come from a wide range of disciplines such as sociology, psychology, history, biography, marketing, criminology, and business management. Our chosen authors range from such old favorites as Isaac Asimov, James Joyce, and William Golding, to such engaging newcomers as Nicole Duplaix ("Plague," under Epidemiology) and Barbara Lippert ("Send in the Wimps," under Advertising). Every reading is prefaced with a biographical headnote about the author and followed by two categories of questions, "Critical Inquiries," and "Rhetorical Inquiries."

To add these readings, we have had to expand the number of chapters as well as make other changes to the basic structure of the book. We have gone from a first edition total of fourteen chapters to a second edition total of nineteen chapters, not counting the handbook. We no longer group the rhetorical modes two to a chapter but, instead, devote a separate chapter to each one. All other changes made in the chapter sequences are based on reviewer's comments, experience with the text, and organizational logic.

Numbered among the specific topics we now cover that were glossed over or omitted in the first edition are the following: in Chapter 1, we make a clear distinction between personal and objective writing and give examples of each; in Chapter 2, we cover the reaction notebook as a guide to finding and narrowing a topic; in Chapter 4, we look at the intricacies involved in composing both the form and content of a first draft. To the research paper chapter, now Chapter 19, we have added a sample paper, "The Mind and Body: Do They Interact?" documented according to the APA style. This chapter now features two student papers—one exemplifying the MLA style, the other the APA style. To all chapters we have added many new exercises, as well as writing assignments that draw on the students' reactions to the anthologized readings. As before, *Rewriting Writing* comes in two versions—a hardback that contains a grammar handbook, and a paperback that does not.

In preparing this new edition, as with the original book, we have benefited greatly from the many helpful comments and suggestions offered by our colleagues. Our thanks to them all, and especially to Joyce S. Fisher, Henry Ford Community College; Joseph LaBriola, Sinclair Community College; Linda Palmer, California State University, Sacramento; and Gary Roseman, DeKalb College, South Campus. We would also like to thank the people at Harcourt Brace Jovanovich who helped make this book possible: Marlane Miriello, acquisitions editor; Julia Ross, manuscript editor; Ann Smith, designer; Sarah Randall, production manager; Paulette Russo, art editor; Eleanor Garner, permissions editor; and Sandy Steiner, marketing manager.

Anthony C. Winkler and Jo Ray McCuen

Contents

Part

1

Prewriting the Whole Essay

Chapter

1

Writing and Rewriting

Writing and rewriting are a constant search for what it is one is saying.

JOHN UPDIKE (b. 1932)

At 37,000 feet the Lockheed L-1011 was flying from Chicago to Atlanta through a violent thunderstorm. Crammed into the center aisle of seats was a nervous instructor of English and, beside him, a student on her way back to school after a long weekend. Oblivious to the shuddering of the aircraft in the dark night, the student coolly took out a yellow legal pad, neatly outlined an essay, and began to write.

She was finished by the time the L-1011 had shaken itself loose of the storm and was rocking gently in the night sky seven miles above a speck of light the captain had identified as Louisville. Casting her eyes around the cabin at her fellow passengers, the student noticed the instructor watching her and struck up a conversation with him. It was plain to the instructor that she was proud of her freshly composed work and wanted to share it with someone, and since he was fascinated that anyone could even dream of writing under such nerve-wracking conditions, he eagerly accepted the invitation to read her essay.

When he was done, the instructor decided that produced under unthinkable conditions—in bad light aboard a crowded aircraft bouncing through a thunderstorm—the essay was a brilliant effort. But read on the good earth during a placid hour, it would rate at best a "C." Its main point was clear enough but supported only by weak generalizations and trite details. Its paragraphs seemed choppy, being held together neither by a strong narrative thread in the writing nor by smooth transitions. While the language occasionally sparkled with the personality of the writer, for the most part it was drab and obvious. In short, the essay was glib but not at all convincing.

"Do you like it?" the student asked, looking hopefully at her fellow passenger who, so far as she knew, could have been anyone from a plumber to a househusband.

Seven miles up in a stormy night sky aboard a crowded aircraft, the instructor reflected, was no place for academic criticism (prayer struck him as a better use of the time), so he said politely that it seemed like a "good first draft." The student heaved a heavy sigh at this faint praise.

"I'm in premed," she said with disappointment, putting the essay away. "I'm not a writer. It's the best I can do."

In fact, it was not her best effort, and only the belief in a mistaken theory of composing could have made the student think so. She seemed to think that writing an essay required little more than pen, paper, and fifteen

3

makeshift minutes, even in a thunderstorm. She had made no attempt at re-writing, but had merely glanced at the finished work, made a spelling correction here and there, and then sat back radiating an expression of premature contentment. It struck the incredulous instructor, who was occasionally used to struggling for hours over a single paragraph, that a gifted writer working this way could hardly have done better. The student's essay was not badly written; but it had been written badly.

And so we come to the premise of this book, which is a simple one: if you write, you should rewrite. If you do not rewrite, you most likely will not write well. If you do rewrite, you will almost certainly write better than if you don't.

Why Rewrite?

Writers revise and edit their work for the simple reason that experience has taught that doing so will almost always make it better. You begin with a rough idea. You put it down on paper, perhaps in an explosion of inspiration. But if you then think you are done, you're mistaken: you've merely taken an exhilarating plunge on the tram down into the mine shaft. Hours of hard work still lie ahead. That is the labor of rewriting which nearly all writers who wish to perfect their work must practice.

Testimony to the truthfulness of this observation is common in literary history. Somerset Maugham, the English essayist and novelist, said of his style, which is regarded by many as effortlessly graceful, that "nature seldom provides me with the word, the turn of phrase, that is appropriate without being farfetched or commonplace." Maugham admitted that he attained the effect of ease, if at all, "only by strenuous effort." Hemingway rewrote parts of *The Sun Also Rises* some seventeen times. The French writer Colette confessed to often spending an entire morning working on a single page. Then there is this poignant anecdote by Mark Twain, a writer whose homespun prose often strikes our ear as unaffectedly natural:

> I began a story which was to turn upon the marvels of mental telegraphy. A man was to invent a scheme whereby he could synchronize two minds, thousands of miles apart, and enable them to freely converse together through the air without the aid of wire. Four times I started it in the wrong way and it wouldn't go. Three times I discovered my mistake after writing about a hundred pages. I discovered it the fourth time when I had written four hundred pages—then I gave it up and put the whole thing in the fire.
> —*The Autobiography of Mark Twain,* ed. by Charles Neider.

The hard fact is this: Even for the gifted, writing is neither automatic nor easy. A writer's work may read with an effortless grace, but it is wrong to assume that the style cost no effort. What you read on the page as you lounge in a cushioned chair is hardly ever what the writer composed at one sitting. Most good writing is as laboriously cultivated as any drought-stricken farmer's crop and just as dependent on ceaseless labor mixed in with an occasional rain of inspiration.

We bring this up because beginning writers, like the one on the plane, often give up too quickly on their work. Appearing in all its polished glory, the printed page too glibly conveys the mistaken impression that it sprang untouched from the writer's pen. Some such pages no doubt have sprung from writers' pens, but from our own have come no more than one or two in decades of writing. In the more ordinary course of events, a writer begins with a very rough first draft, which is made better only after repeated stabs at rewriting. Yet many students share the universal delusion that if they cannot write a flawless essay at one sitting it means that they cannot write at all. But the truth is that writers can no more be judged by their first drafts than books by their covers. Typically, almost all first drafts are insipid and unpublishable.

For example, here is a good student paragraph. It is clearly written and carries out a sharp sense of purpose with an unfaltering touch. As an experiment, we asked the student who wrote it as part of a paper on Arthur Conan Doyle—the creator of Sherlock Holmes—to save her successive drafts for us. Here is the paragraph as it finally appeared in her paper.

```
From the first, Conan Doyle tried to give

his characters their own idiosyncrasies,

strengths and weaknesses that would make them

react humanly in all their adventures.  The

creation of Dr. John Watson, the narrator for

all of Sherlock Holmes's adventures, gives us a

classic example of how the author succeeded in

his attempt.  Watson was actually a composite of

two men Doyle had known during his service in

the South Seas.  The first was a Dr. James H.

Watson, who had been a close friend and whose

slightly modified name became the character of
```

```
whom Doyle wrote, "Good old Watson! You are the

one fixed point in a changing age!" Before

lending his narrator the name of the real Dr.

Watson, Doyle had called him "Orman Sacker,"

which he later rejected because he sensed that

it "smacked of dandyism." The second person

contributing to the fictional composite of Dr.

Watson was another close friend of Doyle's from

his South Seas days.  His name was Major Wood,

and it was from him that Doyle took his physical

description of Watson with, "the square jaw,

thick neck, moustache, burly shoulder and

indeterminate bullet wound." Although Wood later

became Conan Doyle's secretary, he is remembered

today mainly for the image he gave the

redoubtable Dr. Watson, the most famous of

narrators in the annals of the detective story.
```

The writer who can produce such a compact and clear paragraph on a first try without even a marginal scribble or erasure smudge deserves our admiration. But for this particular student, this was not a first try but a second. Here is her first draft, along with the corrections she made to it. The heavy editing provides more effective diction, adds vivid details, and prunes deadwood.

```
    From the first, Conan Doyle's aim was to

give his characters their own idiosyncrasies,

strengths and weaknesses that would make them

react realistically and humanly in their
              , the narrator for all of Sherlock Holmes' adventures,
adventures.  The creation of Dr. Watson gives us
                                succeeded in his attempt.
a classic example of how he accomplished this.
    Watson
This main character, who was the narrator for
```

~~all of Sherlock Holmes' adventures~~, was actually a
composite of two men ~~Conan~~ Doyle had ~~met~~ known during
his ~~stay~~ service in the South Seas. The first was a Dr.
James H. Watson, who had been a ~~comrade, doctor,~~ close friend
~~and friend~~, and whose slightly modified name
became the character of whom Doyle wrote, "Good
old Watson! You are the one fixed point in a
changing age." Before ~~borrowing~~ lending his narrator the name of ~~his~~ the
~~friend of the South Seas' days,~~ real Dr. Watson Doyle had ~~named~~ called him
~~Watson~~ "Orman Sacker," ~~but~~ which he later rejected ~~this~~ because
he sensed that it "smacked of dandyism." The
second ~~character of whom the composite~~ person contributing to the fictional, composite of
Dr. Watson ~~was made~~, was another ~~a Major Wood, and a~~
close friend of Doyle's ~~in the~~ from his South ~~seas~~ S days. ~~It~~
His name was Major ~~was from~~ Wood ~~that Doyle~~ and it was from him that Doyle took his ~~famous~~
physical description of Watson with, "the square jaw,
thick neck, moustache, burly shoulder and
indeterminate bullet wound." although Wood later became
Conan Doyle's secretary, ~~but posterity~~ he is remembered
~~him~~ today mainly for the image he gave the ~~good~~
redoubtable ~~doctor,~~ Dr. Watson the most famous of narrators in
the annals of the detective story.

This gradual reworking of a blurry first draft into crisp final copy is, very simply, the way most writers work. And if you wish to improve your own writing, it is a process you must master and practice as your own. You learn to be philosophical about first drafts, to greet them not with harsh judgment, but with hope. Before you had nothing, but now you have something, even if only a few pages. Granted they may strike you as scruffy and ill-expressed, but that is the nature of all first drafts. Now you can set about tidying up your language, clarifying your purpose, making your ideas sharper. And if anything about your prose should strike you as especially bad, that is the best sign of all. It means you are seeing your own weaknesses and can begin amending them. It is the unnoticed flaw in style — the overuse of certain phrasings, the doting over a particular construction — that bedevils all writers, not the one that can be flushed out in a single rereading.

The Writing and Rewriting Process

Writing is a creative process that results in a symbolic product, be it book, story, play, report, essay, memo, letter, or paragraph. The related acts of *writing* and *rewriting* are inseparable parts of this process. When you write, you invent. When you rewrite, you better your invention.

The writing process is said to be *recursive,* meaning that it tends to proceed in a circular, back and forth way rather than in a straight line. Figure 1.1 gives a diagrammatic instance of this recursiveness. The figure represents the writing process as a large circle in which smaller circles are embedded, indicating that a writer is just as likely to return to an earlier part of the composing process as to forge straight ahead. For example, one typically does not research and then simply write without ever again researching. More usually, the writer will research, write, and then discover the need for further research. Most writers engage in much the same hopping about implied in the diagram, the same constant changing and rechanging, advancing and retreating between later and earlier parts of the writing process and written work. You jump from a middle paragraph back to the start of the essay because a better word, a sharper image, a less-crooked sentence, occurs to you. While writing the fifth paragraph, you spot a flaw in your reasoning and pause to rethink the premise of your topic. This sort of editorial jumping about is characteristic of the writing process.

In fact, the writing process is generally indivisible, continuous, and ongoing. Usually it is hardly possible to say where writing ends and rewriting begins, since most writers constantly do both during composition. Nevertheless, for the sake of discussion, we will assume that writing and rewriting may be divided into separate, conveniently labeled stages.

Drafting

The first draft is simply an initial effort that usually only vaguely resembles the final work. It is here that a writer will plainly see all the shortcomings, failings, and promises in a project. It is also on the first draft that the writer should ruthlessly unleash the editorial pen — move paragraphs, rewrite sentences, even delete pages. Given the treatment it deserves, your first draft will invariably look as marked up and scribbled over as the one on pages 6–7. First drafts are supposed to wear these marginal marks of editorial discontent. It is, of course, possible to get the words, sentences and ideas so

Figure 1-1   The Recursive Process of Writing and Rewriting

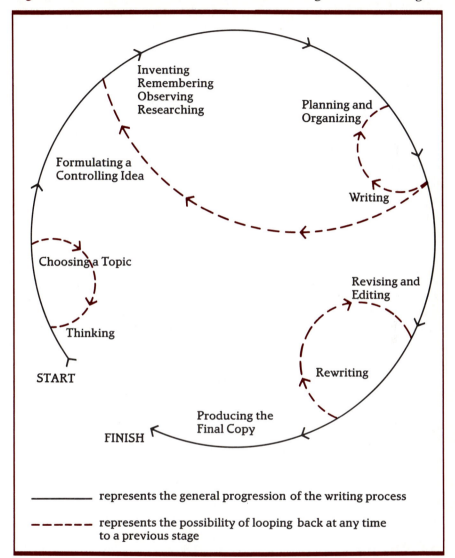

_____ represents the general progression of the writing process

– – – – – – represents the possibility of looping back at any time
to a previous stage

absolutely right the first time that you end up with an untouched first draft. But that outcome occurs with the frequency of pedestrian deaths from falling meteorites.

For working on a first draft, word processors are a godsend because they allow a writer to freely change the text without enduring the drudgery of retyping. Our own preference is to print out a first draft, revise it with a pencil, and then transcribe our changes on the screen. Doing so allows us to reinstate any change that might seem, on further rereading, to have been made for the worse.

Revising

Revising means making gross changes mainly to the content but also to the form of a work. This means you change not only what you say but also how you say it. Our model reviser is the Scottish professor at Oxford who reportedly used to say to his students, "Did ye remember to tear up that fir-r-st page?" For the reviser makes wholesale changes: tears up pages, alters paragraphs, inserts material where the text seems drab or threadbare of meaning. Figure 1-2, for example, is a facsimile page of the beginning of this book showing initial revisions made to the text. As you can see, we started out with an entirely different beginning than the one we finally used. Of some ten beginnings of this book, nine perished in the revision process.

Editing

Editing means making alterations mainly in form rather than content. Changes are made to smooth out a sentence, sharpen an expression, tone down a passage, all with the general aim of improving readability and style. Figure 1-3, for example, is a facsimile page of the manuscript of Mark Twain's *Autobiography* showing some of the writer's editing. Although Twain struck out some redundant words and inserted a clause here and there to round out an idea, little of substance was altered by his editing.

Proofreading

This is the final stage in the rewriting process. Here you read your work for literal correctness. You pore over the page looking for the misspelled word, the grammatical slip, the misplaced comma, and when you come across these venial flaws, you make the correction either by erasure or retyping. Your focus should be microscopic since your aim is to produce clean copy.

For the writer lucky enough to work with a word processor, the drudgery of proofreading has become largely mechanized. Spelling-checker programs are available that can scan a text, identify misspelled words, and correct them at the touch of a key. But whether you use a computer or not, proofreading depends on your own keen eyes and judgment. No program can spot misuses such as "there" in place of "their," and none can replace the writer's own sense of appropriateness for a word or expression. Revision requires that you make changes in the structure of the text.

Figure 1-2   Facsimile Manuscript Page of This Text Showing Rewritten Changes

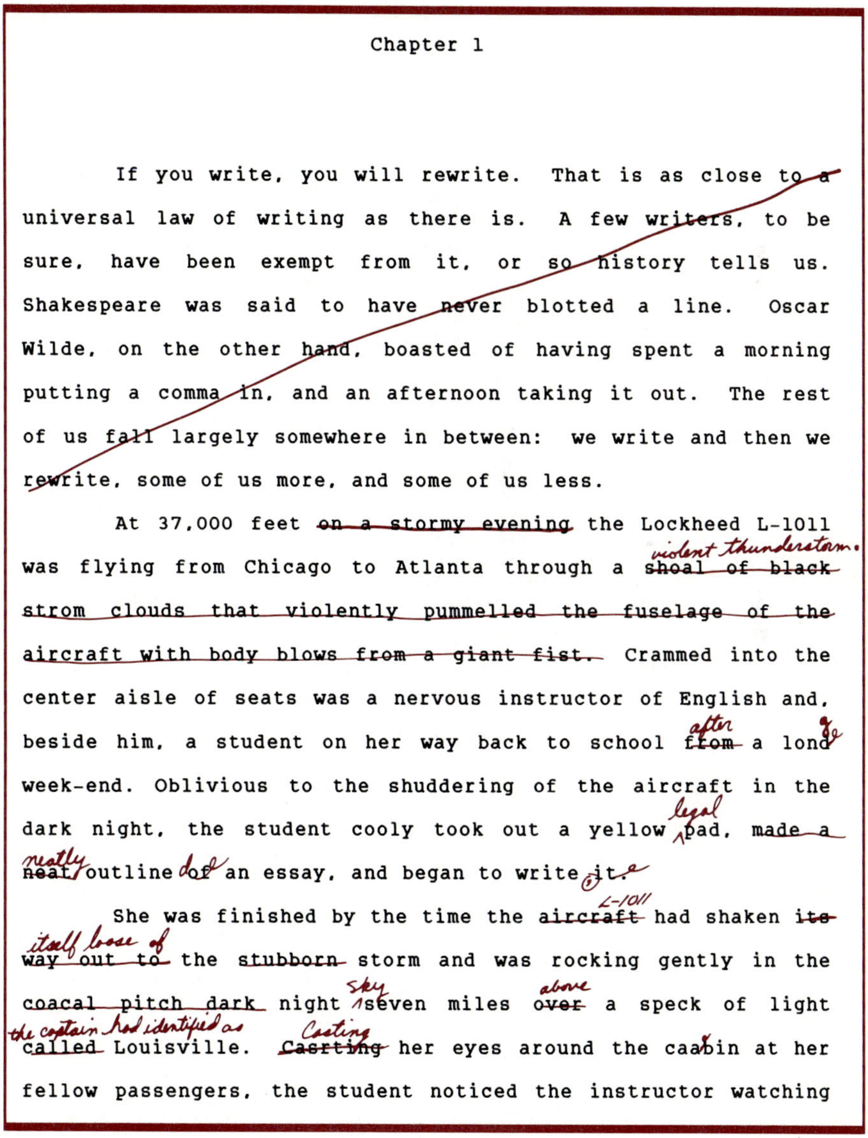

Chapter 1

If you write, you will rewrite. That is as close to a universal law of writing as there is. A few writers, to be sure, have been exempt from it, or so history tells us. Shakespeare was said to have never blotted a line. Oscar Wilde, on the other hand, boasted of having spent a morning putting a comma in, and an afternoon taking it out. The rest of us fall largely somewhere in between: we write and then we rewrite, some of us more, and some of us less.

At 37,000 feet ~~on a stormy evening~~ the Lockheed L-1011 was flying from Chicago to Atlanta through a ~~shoal of black~~ *violent thunderstorm.* ~~strom clouds that violently pummelled the fuselage of the aircraft with body blows from a giant fist.~~ Crammed into the center aisle of seats was a nervous instructor of English and, beside him, a student on her way back to school ~~from~~ *after* a long week-end. Oblivious to the shuddering of the aircraft in the dark night, the student cooly took out a yellow *legal* pad, ~~made a~~ *neatly* outline ~~of~~ an essay, and began to write ~~it~~.

She was finished by the time the ~~aircraft~~ *L-1011* had shaken ~~its~~ *itself loose of* way out to the ~~stubborn~~ storm and was rocking gently in the ~~coacal pitch dark~~ night, *sky* seven miles ~~over~~ *above* a speck of light *the captain had identified as* ~~called~~ Louisville. ~~Casting~~ *Casting* her eyes around the caabin at her fellow passengers, the student noticed the instructor watching

Figure 1-3 A Page of Mark Twain's Manuscript Showing Corrections in His Own Hand

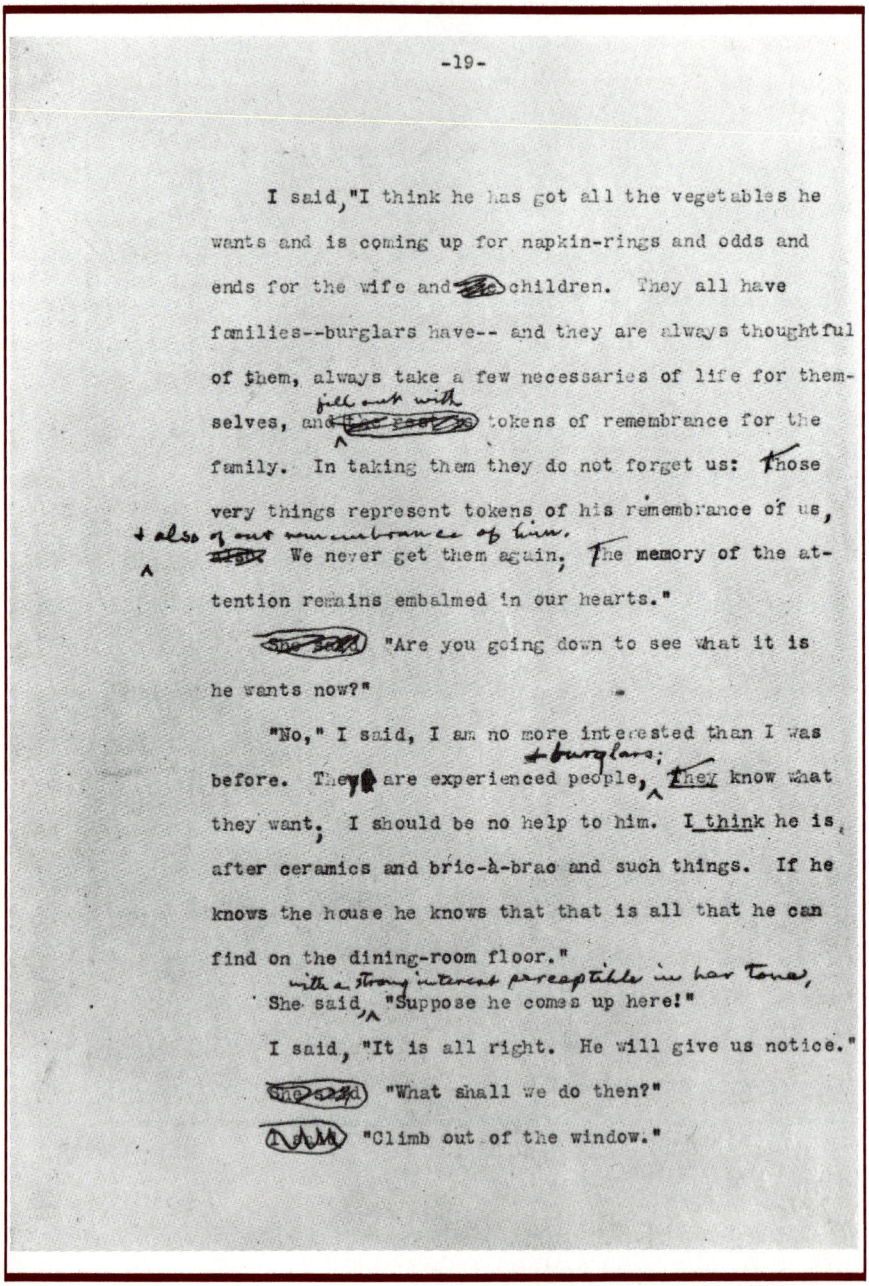

-19-

I said, "I think he has got all the vegetables he wants and is coming up for napkin-rings and odds and ends for the wife and children. They all have families--burglars have-- and they are always thoughtful of them, always take a few necessaries of life for themselves, and fill out with tokens of remembrance for the family. In taking them they do not forget us: those very things represent tokens of his remembrance of us, & also of our remembrance of him. We never get them again; the memory of the attention remains embalmed in our hearts."

"Are you going down to see what it is he wants now?"

"No," I said, I am no more interested than I was before. They are experienced people, & burglars; they know what they want; I should be no help to him. I think he is after ceramics and bric-à-brac and such things. If he knows the house he knows that that is all that he can find on the dining-room floor."

She said, with a strong interest perceptible in her tone, "Suppose he comes up here!"

I said, "It is all right. He will give us notice."

"What shall we do then?"

"Climb out of the window."

Editing means making changes mainly in style. Proofreading is the final cleanup. But all three are as indispensable to writing as the act of composition itself.

Goals of Rewriting

One of the arguments that regularly rages among teachers of writing is whether or not one ever writes entirely for oneself. Does the diarist write for anyone else's eyes? What about the secret keeper of journals who pours out heart and soul onto the unanswering page? Some say no, that all writing is done for an eventual reader. Others argue that it is just as possible to write for oneself as to talk to oneself.

However, nearly everyone would agree that expository prose is written to be read. *Expository* prose is writing done mainly for the purpose of explaining. Under this heading falls the vast majority of writing in the workaday world, from the simple sales memo to the complicated legal brief. Expository prose is not meant to entertain or distract nor to be imaginative and fictional. At its very best it is straightforward, forceful, and clear. It is the language of business, law, commerce, science, researchers, and students. It is the prose taught in composition classes, and the kind of writing mainly covered in this book. While we will not teach the business memo nor the sales presentation, the expository skills we do cover in our chapters on essay writing are exactly the same you will later use to write memos, notes, letters, and reports for your chosen profession. And we may lay down a single principle behind all expository prose: it is always *audience directed*.

This idea is simplicity itself but easily overlooked. As a general rule, writers do not make changes in their writing for the infamous sake of change itself. They make changes for the more purposeful end of expressing their ideas better. But "better" can only be defined by the effect the writing is expected to have on its audience. It follows that you cannot intelligently write or rewrite without having an audience in mind. If you are writing for an audience of laypeople, your style should be appropriately simple and to the point. On the other hand, if you are doing a sociological paper intended to be read by a sociology professor, you should use the jargon of the trade and write in a style of suitable scientific detachment. The intended audience of a work is a writer's only yardstick for writing and rewriting it.

Let us take an example close to home: the book you are now reading. It is written to be used in composition classes attended mainly by freshmen. The need for clarity and directness we had uppermost in mind as we wrote and rewrote. We wanted to get to the point, make it cleanly, and move on briskly to the next idea. To this end, we write mainly in short sentences and with an informal diction. Occasionally, we make a stab at levity or underscore an idea with an anecdote. But mainly we attend to the business at hand and hold asides to a minimum.

Rewriting the manuscript has chiefly meant pruning irrelevancies, substituting plainer words for more complex ones, and chopping in two the occasional serpentine sentence that wiggled out during the heat of composing. This is not the only style we could have used; but it was, however, the style we judged most appropriate for the audience and purpose of this book.

In the chapters that follow, we will focus on specific matters of tone, substance, and style that writers must weigh as they address their prose to particular audiences. We will give general advice about revising, editing, and proofreading, and specific advice about treating this or that item of grammar and style. But the anticipated effect of the work on your audience is the final court of appeal for every word you write and every change you make.

Procedure and Sequence for Rewriting

Rewriting has no fixed procedure, no hard and fast sequence. Neither has writing. Creative processes tend to defy prescription, and writers and their working habits are often wildly individualistic. Writing and rewriting are two halves in the continual process of composing which we will cover in this book. But for now, we will talk in generalities about the procedure you might follow in your rewriting.

Proceed at a Steady Pace

If writing is like eating, rewriting is like nibbling. No one ever rewrites in one big bite. Give yourself at least a good week to peck away at the text, to return to it periodically. When you do come back to the work, begin by rereading it from start to finish. During these rereading sessions, use a pencil or pen and make any changes that occur to you (and they will). One cannot overstate the importance of the pause in rewriting.

In successive attempts at rewriting, the logical progress will be from the big change to the little one: from revising to editing to proofreading. But it is not necessarily always so. On your third pass at the manuscript, for example, you might find some glaring structural defect you had previously overlooked. If that happens, don't talk yourself out of making the necessary corrections (self-delusion is the writer's Satan for avoiding extra work). Buckle down and do what you have to even if it means starting over again from scratch (Twain did that four times).

Maintain an Impersonal Stance

It is written that "if thy right hand offends thee, cut it off." A similarly merciless precept must apply to your efforts at rewriting. Your aim is to be critical without being faultfinding, to look for weaknesses in your own prose with a cool and dispassionate eye. Admittedly, this is as difficult for a writer to do as it is for a parent to criticize a beloved child. Yet it must be done if your rewriting efforts are to be fruitful. Maintain the fiction, if you must, that you are editing not your own brainchild, but the work of a stranger.

Occasionally, you will even find it necessary to cut a perfectly wonderful sentence because sober reflection tags it as unsuitable for either your reader or your purpose. Everyone who has ever set pen to paper has had the horrible experience of watching a vivid but inappropriate image swirl down the revision drain. But if you cling too tenaciously to the fanciful over the appropriate, your work will end up blazing with the occasional "purple patch." This term, commonly defined as the occurrence in the text of an overworked piece of writing, is intended in a derogatory sense. It means that the writer has been caught huffing and puffing at the pen. Here is an example:

```
    It is important to remember that poetry by

itself cannot solve all problems or cure all

illnesses.  Poetry does, however, do more than

many other forms of therapy because as Time

states, "it encourages verbalization, the

life--blood of psychotherapy." There is no doubt

that this language of Parnassus, though it is

rarefied and scented with the dulcet tones of

the immortals--the primal rhythms of

Shakespeare, the Delphic warnings of Milton, the

prurient sighs of Sappho--can help the ordinary,

troubled soul of our time.  Dr. Peter Luke

emphasized this when he said that a poem comes

from a patient's unconscious mind and brings

with it his deepest feelings.  "Poetry and
```

```
medicine," according to poet-physician William

Carlos Williams, "are the two parts of a whole."
```

The underlining in this paragraph—from a paper on poetry therapy—marks where the writer suffered a momentary lapse, forgot her audience and context, and got carried away with her own words. That aptness of expression must always win out over richness is the hardest lesson for all writers to learn.

Don't Become Bogged Down

As you go over a manuscript, you may occasionally find a flaw in it you simply cannot correct. Perhaps there is a page or two that you know doesn't work but somehow you can't rewrite it. If that should happen, proceed to a page that you can rewrite and work on it. Keep coming back to the offending section but don't allow yourself to become bogged down in it. Often, a solution will hit you when you are working on some other part of the manuscript.

Reread, Reread, Reread

Rereading your work can be pure torture after a while, but it is a cleansing lesson in humility and good for rewriting. The next time around you will almost always find minor infelicities you overlooked before. It is also helpful to have a fresh pair of eyes read your work. **Peer editing,** a method of teaching English in which students working in small groups mutually critique the writing of each other, is based on the commonsense notion that two or more heads are better than one. And often they are. Get a friend to read your manuscript and make suggestions for improving it.

Follow Your Hunches

Finally, we come to the hunch, which some may dismiss outright as mumbo jumbo. But as working writers we know that the hunch exists, for it has guided us faithfully through many a torturous exercise in rewriting.

Sometimes, for some inexplicable reason, a passage or page will strike us as simply wrong. We cannot say what offends us about it and have to grope to try and make it better. But still, something about it doesn't seem right.

If that should ever happen to you, as it has to us, we advise you to treat this feeling of dissatisfaction with respect. Your subconscious is trying to tell you something, and since it is by far a larger part of your brain than your conscious, you should listen. We always go on the assumption that if the text doesn't feel right, it probably isn't right. And in such cases, our answer has always been to rewrite until we've gotten rid of that nagging feeling. Usually, we end up with better text than we had before.

Kinds of Writing: Personal and Objective

Expository prose may be broadly classified into two types: personal and objective. Personal writing is writing that expresses an individual in the role of a private person. It is the kind of writing you do when you scribble a letter to a dear friend, jot down an entry in your diary, or recall a summer adventure in a narrative essay. You call yourself "I," vent your opinions on various topics, and are as chatty and intimate as you please, since your primary aim is to say how you feel or think or what befell you personally. Here is a typical example, taken from a student paper:

> There were two things I learned in Karate before I learned to fight. The first thing was respect. I was told that I must salute and bow to the Korean, United States, and our martial arts flag before entering or leaving the training hall. To acknowledge my teacher and elders such as Black Belts, I must also bow to them. Whenever asked a question, I must reply "Yes, sir," or "No, sir," in a confident tone. The second thing I learned was how to execute defensive movements—how to block a punch or a kick, or how to escape a pinning hold. This training made me very unhappy because I wanted to learn immediately how to fight, not how to block. But later I came to see that the

```
emphasis on defense is in keeping with the prime

principle of Karate, namely, that it is a

discipline for self-protection and defense, not

for aggression.
```

Objective writing, on the other hand, is writing that expresses your viewpoint not as an individual, but in some more formal role: a biology student voicing an opinion on a laboratory experiment, a marketing strategist arguing for a certain campaign, an experimenter interpreting data. Conventionally, in these formal roles writers should not refer to themselves as "I," interject excessive personal opinion into the text, or write in slangy language. The emphasis is neither on the writer nor the writer's style, but purely on the content of the writing. Here is an example:

```
Most bats are insectivorous and make a

contribution to human welfare.  Even the vampire

bat, which does not live in the United States,

is not a threat to humans.  With their dynamic

sonar system, bats can detect small flying

insects on a moonless night.  One bat can

consume up to 3,000 insects per night, thus

reducing the depredation of such insects as corn

borer moths, grasshoppers, and locusts on

crops.  In the tropics, many plants depend on

nectar-feeding and fruit-eating bats for

pollination and seed dispersal.  Avocado, mango,

breadfruit, and guava come from plants that are

believed to have been originally dependent on

bats for pollination.
```

Most of us are natural personal writers, if we are at all natural in any branch of writing. Dashing off a letter to mother or brother comes easily enough. Seldom, if ever, do we develop "writer's block" over a diary entry or a message scribbled on a refrigerator note pad. On the other hand, objective writing strikes us as more troublesome to master because it requires us to assume an unfamiliar role and write in an unaccustomed seriousness. Yet, it is the one kind of writing that students will be asked to do not only in school but throughout their careers. Objective writing is therefore heavily emphasized throughout this book.

Our other emphasis will be on writing across the curriculum, meaning writing done for a variety of courses and subjects. Student writers most often write papers in disciplines far afield of their own natural interests and inclinations. Whether the subject is mathematics or anthropology, all the techniques of writing and rewriting taught in this book will certainly apply. But every discipline also has its own vocabulary, technical jargon, and scholarly quirks that the beginner must learn. We have therefore anthologized throughout this book sample pieces from various academic disciplines, our aim being to make this text—and consequently this course—practical and useful to the real-world tasks that all student writers must daily complete.

Exercises

1. Before you can practice the process of rewriting taught in this book, you need to become aware of your present methods of writing. Keep a journal on the next essay you write. Log the amount of time you spend actually writing it. Read the material on pages 10–13 and decide whether your rewriting, if any, consisted of revising, editing, or merely proofreading. Make a note of the time you spent doing each. When you are through, you should have an idea of (a) how much you rewrite (b) exactly what you do when you rewrite.

2. Find any old essay already graded by your teacher and make an attempt at rewriting it. If possible, submit the rewritten version to the teacher and ask for a trial grading. If not, compare the new version with the old.

3. In what sequence do you compose your own essays? Do you work strictly from beginning to middle and end? If so, on your next essay, try writing it as inspiration dictates rather than in strict sequence.

4. How do you react when you get stuck in composing? Do you stare at the wall or chew on the end of a pen? Try doing what professional writers do: reread what you have written from the beginning to the point at which you are stuck. Continue rereading until your pen budges and you begin writing again.

5. Find an old essay written for any science class—geology, chemistry, or biology—and compare it with one written for speech, English, or his-

tory. Is there a difference in the style and diction of each essay? What is this difference, and what does it tell you about your adaptation to different audiences? (If there is no difference, then perhaps you are stubbornly sticking to a single style rather than making an effort to adapt your writing to your audience.)

Writing Assignments

1. Take the final draft of the student paragraph on Doyle's characters on pages 5–6, and try to improve at least two sentences of it. Compare your version with the student's and say why you think yours is better.

2. Select any paragraph from this first chapter, and rewrite it for an audience of a lower grade. What did you find yourself doing to make it easier to read and understand?

3. This is the first sentence from the prologue of *I Never Played The Game,* by Howard Cosell:

> I am writing this book because I am convinced that sports are out of whack in the American society; that the emphasis placed upon sports behavior distorts the real values of life and often produces mass behavior patterns that are downright frightening; and that the frequently touted uplifting benefits of sports have become a murky blur in the morass of hypocrisy and contradiction that I call the Sports Syndrome.

Make at least two, possibly three, simpler and easier to understand sentences of it.

4. Rewrite this brief passage in a style that would be considered appropriate in our own day:

> The appointment of death by the agency of carnivora, as the ordinary termination of animal existence, appears therefore in its main results to be a dispensation of benevolence; it deducts much from the aggregate amount of the pain of universal death; it abridges, and almost annihilates, throughout the brute creation, the misery of disease, and accidental injuries, and lingering decay; and imposes such salutary restraints upon excessive increases of numbers, that the supply of food maintains perpetually a due ratio to the demand.

5. Bertrand Russell once wrote:

> It is clear that for every man and every woman there is a degree of open-mindedness, which is desirable; more than this, or less than this, leads to bad results. A completely open mind is either a disease or a pretense; a completely closed mind is a useless assemblage of indefensible prejudices.

Write a brief essay either agreeing, disagreeing, or simply commenting on this opinion. Produce at least three successive drafts. Label and submit all three to your instructor.

Chapter

2

Prewriting Strategies

Very young writers often do not revise at all. Like a hen look-
ing at a chalk line, they are hypnotized by what they have written.
"How can it be altered?" they think. "That's the way it was written."
Well, it has to be altered.

DOROTHY CANFIELD FISHER (1879–1958)

It is midnight in a dimly lit garret. Suffering a creative itch in the soul that only the pen can scratch, a tormented writer begins to write. Muses whisper and words of wisdom pour in a torrent from the writer's pen while a neglected lover sulks in a corner.

This picture of a working writer is brought to you courtesy of the movies.

Of course, it is narrow, incomplete, and gives a totally false impression. Some lucky few writers may indeed work under the goad of an otherworldly itch, but for the rest writing is strictly a practical art done to satisfy a superior, meet a deadline, and earn bread and board (or a grade). We do not write in a romantic garret, but in a noisy office or busy kitchen, and usually on a subject dropped on us from above like a brick.

Under such workaday circumstances, how do real writers work?

Choosing a Topic

They begin by narrowing the subject into a topic. The subject is the general assignment you are given. It is usually not specific enough for you to leap in and begin writing about it straightaway. Ordinarily, it is fraught with implicit choices and requires you to whittle it down to a narrower option called the **topic.** An instructor, for example, may ask you to write an essay about an environmental problem and leave it at that. But you might as well hope to swallow a Thanksgiving turkey whole as to write about such a subject. It needs carving, paring down, portioning out. So the very last thing you will do is write. But the first thing you will do is make an acceptable topic of your large subject.

One way to do this is through a process of Socratic narrowing. Socrates was a Greek philosopher who taught by asking questions. His questioning was directed at erring listeners who were gradually and firmly led to the truth. You can use this questioning technique to narrow a subject down to a topic you care about.

Here is an example. Your instructor assigns a paper on some environmental problem. You sit down, pen and pad in hand, and begin the questioning:

First Narrowing

Question: What environmental problem do you care about anyway?
Answer: Hardly any. Not enough to write about, anyway.
Question: Do you care about any environmental place at all?
Answer: Yes, I do. I like Wickiup Canyon. I like to go swimming there.

Second Narrowing

Question: So what's the environment of Wickiup like these days?
Answer: Pretty terrible. The ATC riders have really torn up the surrounding landscape.

Final Narrowing

Question: So what'd you think ought to be done?
Answer: If it were my choice, I'd ban all ATCs from wilderness canyons.
Question: Why would you do that?
Answer: Because ATCs are motorized vehicles that belong on paved roads. They're noisy, smelly, and poison to the watershed.

Now you have your topic: the effects of rampant ATCs (all-terrain cycles) riding on the environment of Wickiup Canyon.

Narrowing a Subject through Reflection and Research

Socratic narrowing can help to narrow the subject of a personal essay but is less likely to work with an objective writing assignment. The hard fact is that, no matter how talented and inventive they are, writers rarely write convincingly about an unfamiliar subject without first learning about it. *Write about what you know*—the standard advice urged on all writers—turns out to be thoroughly impractical for most objective writing assignments. The applicable doctrine for such assignments is, *know about what you write.* Dig into sources on the subject before you try to write even the first word about it. Invariably, this digging will steer you to a narrowed topic.

What kind of sources should you consult? Basically, the sources available to a writer on any subject are either *internal* or *external*. An internal source is the writer's own personal experience or background. An airline pilot, for example, in writing an essay about airspace control, can draw largely on personal experience. A student who has worked for many summers as a

camp counselor is in the same enviable position if assigned an essay on recreational camps.

While internal sources play a considerable role in personal writing
assignments, they are not as important in writing objective essays. Few of us
have had any personal encounter that could contribute significantly to a biology essay on the reproduction of amoeba. Rare is the writer who has had
a personal brush with impeachment that could help with the focus of a political science essay. Objective writing assignments—whether in art, biology, psychology, political science, or any other field—require a writer to diligently dig through external sources such as books, magazines, references,
and the testimony and opinion of expert witnesses. In doing this digging,
you will not only learn about your subject but you will inevitably narrow it
into a writing topic.

Let us say, for example, that your computer science instructor assigns an essay on Computer-Assisted Instruction. You not only know little
or nothing about the subject but have no opinions on it and not even a clue
about how to begin. You trek to the library and look up Computer-Assisted
Instruction (CAI) in the various periodical catalogs. And here you discover,
to your astonishment, hundreds of articles about CAI that detail scores of
debates currently raging over it. A scan of the *Reader's Guide To Periodical Literature*, for instance, turns up these entries: "New Computing in Higher Education;" "Instructional Design Flaws in Computer-Assisted Instruction;" "Is
CAI Cost Effective?" "CAI Can Be Made Doubly Effective."

Several topic possibilities are plainly suggested by these titles. *Is* CAI
cost effective or is it just another technological myth? Here is a topic you can
certainly sink your teeth into. What about the new computing in higher
education? What was the old computing like? What makes the new one
better? And for that matter, what advantages does CAI have over traditional
teaching based on lecture and recitation? Answering any of these questions
is likely to lead you to a specific and narrowed topic.

When you do begin digging into external sources, don't expect the
first turn of the spade to immediately unearth a topic. It is just as likely that
you may have to scan several articles and books before some topic catches
your fancy. That is more or less the point of writing assignments. One learns
as one writes; one writes as one learns. Actual writing technique often has
less to do with producing a quality essay than sheer grasp of the subject. If
you find yourself blundering aimlessly about as you begin to write the essay,
don't be quick to blame your imagined lack of technique or talent. More realistically, you probably need to read and learn more about the topic.

Books and magazines will make up most of the external sources you
consult, but they are not the only ones. Most campuses are awash with specialists willing to lend a hand to the student researcher. A recent example

comes to mind. A student of ours was assigned an essay on Afghanistan by a political science instructor. We suggested that he interview a professor of Eastern history on campus, who in turn gave him a minilecture on Afghanistan dynasties. As a result, the student settled on Mahmud of Ghazni, a great Afghan ruler of the eleventh century, as his topic. The professor was also able to direct the student to key reference works on Afghan history, which saved him the usual spade work.

Generating ideas

You have an assigned subject, a preliminary topic, and a blank mind about what to write. With any writer, seasoned or beginner, a blank mind is the standard symptom of a new assignment. It is also a rather hopeful sign, for it is often better to begin with a blank mind than with a bias. What you need to do now is to think creatively about the topic in order to generate ideas for inclusion in your paper. Freewriting, clustering, talking writing, and note-taking are some of the prewriting strategies that might help you think.

Freewriting

This colorful word means an intense thinking session in which you generate and quickly jot down as many ideas as you can. Your aim is to throw open the floodgates of creativity and undam a raging surge of ideas. Sit with pen and paper in a place to your liking. Think intently about your subject. Make a note of every idea, every fragment of thought that swirls down the stream of consciousness. Freewriting on the topic of stress might produce a list such as this:

```
Stress, stress, what is stress?

Anxiety

Panic

Feeling pressure

Needless worry

Causes?

Who knows?

pressure from job

peer pressure

high expectations
```

effects of stress

Can't think of any

heart palpitations

sleeplessness

biofeedback helps

vacation helps

friends are stressful

parents too

What to do?

fight stress

meditation helps

a drink can relax you

thinking too much is bad

Ban brains

do animals suffer stress?

rats do, in psych labs

monkeys go bananas over stress

I can't think

this is stressful

stress affects health

physical health

mental health, too

I wish I lived on an island

think about stress

THINK!

stress causes insomnia

studying causes stress

fretting brings on stress

Christmas stress

```
overwork

holiday stress

type A personality

Am I one?

No

This is tough

type A suffers stress

heart attacks—stress causes them

high blood pressure

Help! I can't think

high blood pressure

wanting to get good grades—that's stress

I'm stressed out on this

Think!

stress is everywhere

fight or flight response

modern life and stress
```

A list produced by freewriting should be strewn with the debris of random, even haphazard, thinking. But as you sift through the litter, you will most likely find some promising ideas that can be used in the essay.

Clustering

Clustering is a technique for associating a large idea with its smaller and related parts. It is the diagrammatic equivalent of freewriting, but done systematically and with more editorial control. You are trying to break down the topic into its constituent parts about which you can write paragraphs and pages. Figure 2–1 is an example of the topic "The Liberal Arts in Colleges Today" rendered in a cluster.

Clustering and freewriting are both useful for generating ideas to be included in an essay, but they are certainly not mutually exclusive. Indeed, it is often helpful to render the best ideas from a freewriting list into a cluster. One way to do this is to cull ideas from your list and arrange them logically under interrogatives such as "What?" "Why?" "Who?" "When?" Figure 2–2 is an example. The freewriting list on the topic of stress is rendered into a

Figure 2–1   Clustering Example of "The Liberal Arts in
Colleges Today"

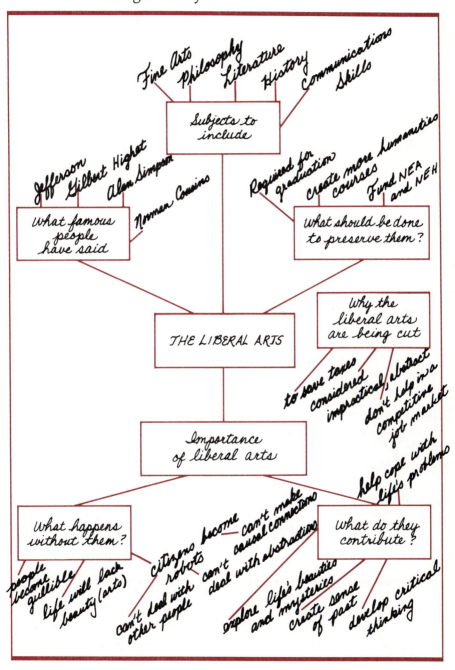

Figure 2–2   Clustering and Freewriting Example

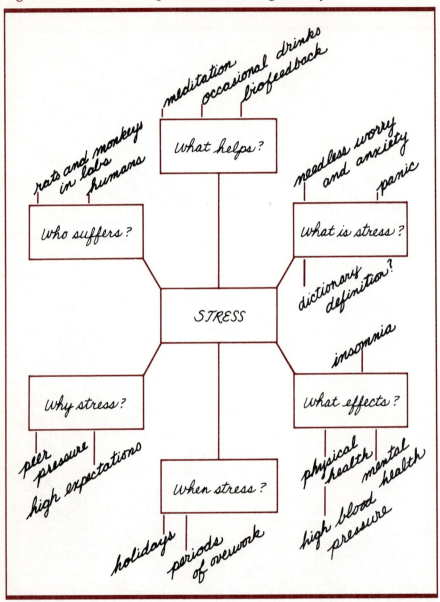

cluster. Your list of randomly generated ideas is now refined into a graphic outline of your essay.

Clustering teaches us an added lesson: writing is never focused on the whole, but always on its parts. We cannot write about the Pacific Ocean, although that may be our intent. What we can write about is this island or that archipelago in the Pacific Ocean. And if we cover enough islands and mention enough archipelagos, we will do justice to our ocean. Just as the sentence is made of individual words and paragraphs of separate sentences, a topic is also necessarily treated in pieces and parts, which clustering (and freewriting) can help us find and identify.

Talking writing

Mark Twain tells this story about how talking helped him write:

> In the course of twelve years I made six attempts to tell a simple little story which I knew would tell itself in four hours if I could ever find the right starting point. I scored six failures; then one day in London I offered the text of the story to Robert McClure and proposed that he publish that text in the magazine and offer a prize to the person who should tell it best. I became greatly interested and went on talking upon the text for half an hour, then he said: "You have told the story yourself. You have nothing to do but put it on paper just as you have told it."
>
> I recognized that this was true. At the end of four hours it was finished, and quite to my satisfaction. So it took twelve years and four hours to produce that little bit of a story, which I have called "The Death Wafer."
>
> —*The Autobiography of Mark Twain,* ed. by Charles Neider.

Twelve years is, of course, a bit long to spend on a freshman essay, but Twain's experience is otherwise applicable.

You can hold a monologue with yourself or talk about your work with someone else. For example, this exchange was overheard between an instructor and a student. The student approached the instructor claiming to be baffled by the assignment to write an essay about his hometown:

Teacher: Which place do you consider your "hometown?"
Student: Kalamazoo, Michigan.
Teacher: Was it a good town to grow up in?
Student: Oh, yes, it was. I was happy there. In fact, I think it is the best town in the world to grow up in.
Teacher: Give me one major reason why.
Student: Well, it was wonderfully . . . safe.

Teacher: How do you know it was safe?

Student: It just was.

Teacher: Give me some specific examples of how it was safe.

Student: Well, for instance, we never had to lock our houses, cars, or any-thing—yet no one ever really got robbed. We wandered freely over the neighborhood, just walking into each other's houses without fear. Little kids played in the streets without fear of being kidnapped or abducted. I had to walk a mile to school every day, but I never worried about it, not even when the snowdrifts hid me from passing cars.

Teacher: O.K. Great! You're flowing. Now, can you think of another reason why your hometown was so great?

Student: Yeah, we always had things to do, fun things! My friends always tell me how bored they were in their hometowns, but I was never bored.

Teacher: Why? Name some things you did for entertainment.

Student: Let me see. We flew kites in the vacant lot in our neighborhood. We explored all the nearby housing developments. We'd pretend to be detectives and follow an adult through the streets and write down everything we saw him do. That was hilarious. In the winter we rode sleds and went ice skating on the ponds.

Teacher: I'm sure you could elaborate even more on that, but let's move on. Give me another general reason why you liked your hometown.

Student: I liked it because I was never lonely there. Everybody played together. Sure, we had our occasional fights, but we usually got over them quickly. Actually, the adults were often just as much fun as the kids. There was an old widowed woman, for example, who lived on our street. One day she called us into her kitchen and showed us how to make an angel cake.

Teacher: So far so good. You have the basis of a good essay. Now, can you express your three reasons in a single sentence?

Student: I'll try. Kalamazoo, Michigan, was a wonderful town to grow up in because it was safe, there was always something to do, and there was always someone to play with.

Teacher: That's the beginning of a good thesis. It just needs tightening.

You can also talk to yourself about your own work, asking yourself how you really feel about this, what your opinion is about that, until you arrive at a conclusion usable as a thesis for your essay. One of the authors of this book, for example, is a great believer in the power of talking writing. When he gets stuck and is in a place where he can talk aloud to himself without fear of the butterfly net, he asks himself bluntly, "What the devil are you trying to say?" and then tries to answer himself in plain language. Often it requires only a transcription of the answer, and a deleting of expletives, for him to get unstuck.

Note-taking

Note-taking is one prewriting strategy whose usefulness varies with the individual writer. Some writers definitely benefit from systematically taking notes on what they think about, and plan to do with, the topic. Others prefer to plunge straight into the writing, once they have completed the necessary reading and scribbled down points that they intend to work into the body of the essay. We will briefly suggest two methods of note-taking: the jot-list and the reaction notebook.

The jot-list

As the name implies, the jot-list is a brief list of main points and important facts to be covered in the essay. Used only by the individual writer and never submitted with the paper, jot-lists may be messy, neat, haphazard, or methodical. Naturally, they work best if they are legible and conform to some known order, even if understandable only to the writer. Here is an example of a jot-list for a history essay written on the famous Scopes trial:

> <u>Scopes Trial</u>
> Mention when and where the trial was held.
> Find out about the defense team.
> Do research on the judge and his conduct of the trial.
> Explain why the trial generated such intense publicity.

This particular list merely includes the main points the writer feels compelled to cover. It contains no specific details that the writer will include nor suggests any particular focus for the essay. At best, it will be only minimally useful since the writer will still have to rummage through sources for facts and list them elsewhere. Instead of dipping into two bins—one for a list of main points, another for your facts—you are better putting them together, as in the example below:

Scopes Trial

When did trial take place?
Dayton, Tenn., beginning July 19, 1925

Defense team? Clarence Darrow, famous
trial lawyer and agnostic; Bainbridge
Colby, eminent corporation lawyer and
former Secretary of State; Dudley
Field Malone, Catholic layman
and popular barrister; and Arthur
Garfield Hays, counsel to the ACLU.

Judge? John T. Raulson. Rulings
prejudicial to the defense; expert
testimony was barred from the
jury. The testimony was read
into the record after Darrow
threatened to release it to the
press.

Why all the publicity? Because of
the temper of the times.
Fundamentalism, under the leadership
of William Jennings Bryan, had
organized in some 20 states. Bills
banning the teaching of evolution
had passed in Tennessee and
Mississippi and were pending in
6 other states.

Now you have both your main queries as well as the facts that answer them
on the same list.

The reaction notebook

This kind of note-taking is not for the fainthearted, for it takes work and a determined disposition. What you do is this: take a notebook and draw a line down the middle of the page, yielding two equal columns. In the left column, jot down the facts, details, or researched opinions that you intend to cite in your essay. In the right column, jot down your reactions, questions, or ideas inspired by the material. Here is an example of notes taken for an essay on earthworms:

Controlling idea: Earthworms in the diet can provide a healthy and abundant source of protein.

Facts	Reactions
Earthworms belong to the class Oligochaeta. 2,700 known species. Abundantly distributed over the globe.	Widespread availability of earthworms makes them an ideal source of protein.
Earthworms are hermaphroditic, but they do cross fertilize. There is no larval stage. The young hatch as miniature adults.	Hermaphroditic nature of earthworms would make them easy to rear and reproduce in worm farms.
Earthworms contain a circulatory system; the blood contains hemoglobin.	How does the protein composition of the earthworm compare with the chicken's or with the fish's?
The Maoris consider certain species of earthworm a delicacy.	Which just proves that no ill-effects are occasioned by eating earthworms.

The advantage of this kind of note-taking is that it gives you not only the raw details but also a glimmer of how you might embed them in your paper, as well as what else you might need to look up. In the example shown, the writer notes in the righthand column her reactions to facts about the distribution and reproduction of earthworms noted in the left. The third entry in the lefthand column suggests to her a possible comparison between the protein of chicken and earthworm, which she might later work into the essay.

What is the best time for note-taking? The answer will vary with the individual writer as well as the method of composition. Common sense, however, tells us that the best time to take notes is after you have definitely settled on a topic and while you are scanning books, magazines, tracts, and pamphlets about it. Indeed, note-taking is apt to continue even during the actual writing of the essay when you are likely to be occasionally struck by random ideas, phrasings, concepts, and twists. In any event, the aim of all your prewriting efforts is to stoke your creative fire, give you something to write about, and discover how you really feel about the topic. These feelings, when you finally ferret them out, will evolve naturally into the *controlling idea* and *thesis* of your essay.

Exercises

1. Freewrite on one of the following:
     The violence in motion pictures today
     The end of the sexual revolution
     Methods of transmitting AIDS
     War memorials and the public good
     Systems of psychological therapies
     Dieting fads and systems
     Inflation

2. For any one of the above subjects, jot down any appropriate personal memories and experiences you might profitably include in an essay.

3. Make a jot-list of classroom teaching techniques you have personally found to be most effective in helping you learn.

4. What makes history so interesting (or dull)? Make a notebook on this preliminary topic. On the left side of the page, record your classroom experiences with history. On the right, how you might possibly incorporate these in an essay on this subject.

5. Use any prewriting strategy covered in this chapter on one of these broad subjects to extract a narrowed topic appropriate for an essay.
     Reading
     Racial problems

Keeping a pet
Professional sports
Fish farming
Social interaction between the sexes
Geography as a discipline

Writing Assignments

1. In an essay, explain the methods of prewriting and actual composition that work best for you.

2. Write a paragraph explaining why freewriting is definitely suited/unsuited to your own style of prewriting and composing.

3. Use the self-questioning process to narrow one of the following subjects into a specific topic. Write out your actual questions and answers and show how they led you to a possible topic.
   Vacations
   Methods of science
   Careers
   Romantic love
   Celibacy
   Money in modern life
   Insanity
   Uses of religion
   Household chemicals

4. Using the techniques of clustering, break down one of the above subjects into a series of smaller ideas you might cover in an essay.

5. Write a paragraph or two about the most successful essay you have ever written, detailing the prewriting and writing techniques you used to create it.

Chapter

3

The Controlling Idea
and the Thesis

Delightful task! To rear the tender thought, To teach the young idea how to shoot.

JAMES THOMSON (1700–1748)

At the end of the last chapter we left you with a topic and a feeling toward it. Let us say that you are writing an essay on the subject of urban anthropology. You have whittled down the topic to the anthropological value of searching garbage. And your reading has left you with a strong feeling that the contemporary researcher can learn much about a neighborhood from rummaging systematically through its garbage bins.

Where do you go from here? We assume that in your reading you have uncovered material enough to prove your case—that garbage searches are anthropologically valuable. If so, you have come far, because not only do you have the topic for your essay but you also have its *controlling idea.*

Unless it is completely frivolous, every essay will be based on a controlling idea. In the writer's mind, the controlling idea will be the stand taken on the topic of the essay. In the reader's mind, the controlling idea, even if not openly stated in a *thesis,* will still be inferable from the writer's presentation and organization of opinions and facts. If someone should wander past and ask your reader, "What's that essay about?" the likely reply will be more or less a thumbnail sketch of your controlling idea. "This writer says that garbage searches are anthropologically valuable."

Every essay needs a similar controlling idea, an angle or approach that the writer adopts towards the narrowed topic. Whether or not the controlling idea is plainly stated as a *thesis* or remains discreetly in the background, it is decidedly there exercising control and direction over the essay. This book, for example, is based on the controlling idea that rewriting is essential to the improvement of writing. Whenever we feel the itch to wander off or stray, our controlling idea looms before us like a stop sign. We break off and sally back to our real work.

The *thesis statement* is your controlling idea made explicit. It is an announcement of exactly what you intend to oppose, propose, suppose, or depose in the essay. Setting down clearly what your essay is about will solidify your purpose and consequently help you write it. For example, your opposition to ATCs in wilderness canyons must be grounded in some substantial facts about the damage they cause, the noise they make, the pollution they spread, and exactly which of these harmful effects your essay intends to document. All of this should be summed up in one thesis statement.

Naturally, the topic, the controlling idea, and the thesis statement are related as progressively narrowed parts of the same subject. A mathematician would say that each is a subset of the other. So if the subject is "environmental problems," your controlling idea must reflect a particular approach to that topic, which your thesis statement must carefully spell out. Here are four examples of a subject reworked into a narrowed topic, controlling idea, and thesis statement:

> **Subject:** Write an essay about an environmental problem.
> **Topic:** Wickiup Canyon.
> **Controlling idea:** The destructive effect of unrestricted ATC use on the environment of Wickiup Canyon.
> **Thesis statement:** Allowing Wickiup Canyon to be used by all-terrain vehicles has unleashed noise and emission pollution that threatens the fragile beauty of this lovely wilderness area.
> **Subject:** Write an essay about a mammal.
> **Topic:** The common shrew.
> **Controlling idea:** The effect of its metabolism on the life of the common shrew.
> **Thesis statement:** The shrew is a furious, reckless mammal whose life is tyrannized by its tiny body and voracious metabolism.
> **Subject:** Medical care in the United States
> **Topic:** Preventative medical care.
> **Controlling idea:** The role of the federal government in preventative medical care for children under 16.
> **Thesis statement:** The federal government should provide free preventative medical care for children under 16 because in the long run this is the most economical way to control medical cost and ensure a healthy and productive workforce.
> **Subject:** Foreign languages.
> **Topic:** Techniques for learning a foreign language.
> **Controlling idea:** The best technique for learning a foreign language.
> **Thesis statement:** Total immersion in culture and everyday life is the best way to learn a foreign language since it teaches not only everyday idioms but also culture.

Do not expect a controlling idea to pop automatically onto the page once you have a topic. But as you gather material on the topic from books and interviews, you will inevitably find yourself inching towards a certain slant, a decided emphasis in your thinking. This movement, gradual though it may be, is the sign of your own emerging opinions, which will eventually crystallize into your controlling idea on the topic. Later, this controlling idea, expressed as a coherent and forceful sentence, will become your thesis.

Exercises

1. Rewrite one of the following controlling ideas into a thesis statement:
   a. The cinema often turns excellent novels into third-rate movies.
   b. Children should be reared to have opinions.
   c. Smoking is a bad habit.
   d. Consumer education belongs in college.
   e. Sex education is appropriate in high schools.

2. Write a paragraph clarifying the distinction between a controlling idea and a thesis.

3. Write (T) beside any of the following that you think possibly usable as theses. Mark (C) beside any you think usable only as controlling ideas.
   a. The Central Intelligence Agency and its charter.
   b. *Ki* is an invisible force developed by the martial artist through fasting, meditation, exercise, and breathing techniques.
   c. The sacraments of the Catholic church.
   d. Humane-society volunteers educate pet owners, screen the adopters of animals, and maintain animal shelters.

Purpose and Thesis

While all essays have a controlling idea, many do not express it in an explicit thesis. Here is an example. Can you find a thesis in this opening paragraph, where one would be expected to occur unfailingly in a student essay?

> Now here is a strange and very likely a wonderful thing: The people who watch chimpanzees in the wild—and that has become a scientific specialty since Jane Goodall made it famous twenty years ago—say that it appears the animals practice herbal medicine.
>
> —Tom Teepen, "Man's Arrogance, and Humility," *Atlanta Constitution,* January 2, 1986.

This paragraph makes an observation about chimpanzees but asserts no overall point that could be called a thesis. And if you inferred from it that the essay is about the habits of chimpanzees, you would be wrong. The author's controlling idea, expressed partly by his title, "Man's Arrogance, and Humility," is to argue for the preservation of animals in the wild because of the lessons about nature that they can teach us. That chimpanzees seem to know instinctively which herbs to chew for certain illnesses is simply one example he uses to shore up this argument.

The undeniable fact is that many professional writers do not write with an explicit thesis. But all write with a controlling idea—some major emphasis that ties their ideas together into a single coherent point. It is harder to write an essay from a background controlling idea than from an explicit thesis, and many beginning writers simply cannot do it well. For that reason, most instructors follow the convention of teaching students always to use an explicit thesis in their essays. As you grow as a writer, your reliance on the formulaic use of an explicit thesis will naturally lessen. But in the meantime, stating the major point of your essay in an explicit thesis is a requirement of most composition instructors. This explicit thesis is conventionally the final sentence of the first paragraph.

For the beginner, then, the entire structure and logic of a writing assignment should spring from its thesis—from the opening statement that commits the essay to one or another of the three aims already listed. The thesis is your declaration of purpose to the reader, a manifest of the cargo contained within your essay's pages. What the reader expects to find in the essay is no more or less than what your thesis has declared will be there. Consequently, the first major efforts at revision should be directed at the thesis statement.

Besides telling the reader what you are up to, your thesis statement can also give you an editorial sense for the kind of details that should go into the essay and the kind that should be left out. Consider, for example, this thesis:

```
Moving from Vietnam to this country gave me

a wrenching sense of loneliness and isolation

that I had never in my life experienced before.
```

An essay written on this thesis will be an exercise in **self-expression,** with its details being drawn chiefly from the writer's personal experiences and memories. If you were writing on this thesis and found yourself pumping dry statistical details into the essay from the unlikely source of an encyclopedia, you should suspect that you had strayed badly from your point.

Here is a thesis of an entirely different kind:

```
Many college graduates become underemployed

as the jobs available to them require highly

technical skills never learned in colleges

stressing a liberal education.
```

The aim of any essay written on this thesis is to *inform,* to paint the picture of suffering experienced by the "many." We expect the air to be drier here and more laden with a cloud of facts and case histories. We do not expect a wealth of personal anecdotes since they would overly particularize the proof.

Here is a third thesis, which makes an entirely different promise:

```
The government should assist historical

societies to preserve our nation's graceful old

homes because the history of architecture is

written on them.
```

"Should" is a call to *argument* and implies the coming of reasons and evidence. We expect to see opponents brought to trial and refuted, to hear expert testimony, to be led by the hand of logic. Persuasion is the strongest single element in an argumentative essay, but it is also implicitly present in essays written for self-expression and to inform. If we are not persuaded by what writers tell us, we are unlikely to be swayed by their stories or informed by their facts.

Revising the thesis for clarity of purpose

If you could know exactly how your writing would affect a reader, you would be a writer of unparalleled ability. But no writer completely knows that. Nevertheless, you probably have a vague idea which of the three purposes your effort comes under—to express yourself, to inform, or to argue. From formulating your controlling idea, you also know what you are trying to say in the essay. In short, you have a clear enough notion of the assignment to describe the content as well as the formal purpose of the essay in the thesis statement.

There is, we think, a decided advantage in wording your thesis statement to do both. The thesis statement that says what you are going to do while simultaneously committing you to a clear aim not only sets the table for the reader, but it also provides a menu for the cook. Here are some examples of what we mean, showing both the original thesis and its revision:

Original: Churches and youth can be incompatible.

This is an aimless thesis, an empty promise that asks no commitment of the writer and evokes no anticipation in the reader. What is the writer trying to do here? Express the self? Inform? Argue? We cannot tell.

Revision: `At an early age I rebelled against the stultifying`

`conformity and orthodoxy of belonging to a church.`

Now the thesis statement clothes the essay in the overall purpose of *self-expression*. It tells the writer what to do—tell a story—while alerting the reader on what to expect.

Original: `American attention has recently been focused on the`

`famine in Africa.`

This thesis reads like a preliminary topic and has neither certainty nor intention to recommend it. A reader cannot know what to expect in an essay written about it; worse yet, neither can a writer.

Revision: `The recent focus of world attention on the African`

`famine has resulted in three major U.S.`

`organizations contributing large sums of money and`

`quantities of food to Ethiopia.`

The aim of this essay is now clear: *to inform* the reader of the work of three charitable organizations to relieve the African famine.

Original: `Why should colleges have honor courses as part of`

`their curriculum?`

As a declaration of a writer's intention and agenda, the thesis should answer the initial question of every reader, namely, "What is this about?" It should not answer this implicit question with another question.

Revision: `A truly democratic college should not allow honor`

`classes in its curriculum because they create a`

`subtle snobbery and elitism that belittle the`

`average student.`

Or, the argument may be just the opposite:

Revision: `Honor courses should be established in every college`

`to challenge, motivate, and bring out the best in`

`talented students.`

Now the writer's purpose is plainly spelled out: it is *to argue* the merits of the thesis.

Revising the thesis for unity

There are many kinds and causes of bad writing, but the recipe for good writing is still somewhat a mystery. One unarguable cause of the badly written essay is the wavering purpose, which is usually found in the forked or split thesis statement. The forked thesis is one that, embodying a split proposition, tugs in different directions and threatens to sunder the essay into two irreconcilable parts.

Original: `Hemingway's fictional women fall into two major`

`categories, the nurturing mother and the bitch`

`goddess, and his men seem to be flawed.`

Buried within this forked thesis are two separate writing assignments: Hemingway's categories of women, and the weakness of his men. The solution to the forked thesis is either entirely to discard one of the propositions or subordinate it to the other. For more on subordination, see Part 5. Basically, subordination in this sense means making one proposition clearly inferior to, or dependent on, another. For example, the Hemingway thesis may be revised through subordination this way:

Revision: `Because of flaws in their nature, Hemingway's men`

`often fell victims to one of two types of women:`

`the nurturing mother or the bitch Goddess.`

The thesis now proposes a cause-and-effect relationship between Hemingway's flawed men and his two types of women.

The danger of the forked thesis is that it wrenches the writer's attention both this way and that. It is simply very difficult to write plainly about two competing topics, especially when there is established between them no clear and logical relationship. Somewhere in the body of the essay the writer is likely to become muddled and spread bewilderment to the reader. Faulty grammatical construction is one common cause of the forked thesis, with the writer typically asserting a relationship between two ideas that should be logically subordinate. Here is an example: "Antony neglected the business of Rome *and* was a self-indulgent general." Better to unite these two propositions in a subordinate relationship: "Antony neglected the business of Rome because he was a self-indulgent general."

Revising the thesis for coherence

Coherence is a word overshadowed in the popular understanding by its opposite. Nearly everyone understands what is meant by, say, "The driver of the car was incoherent and therefore plainly drunk." But it is not as universally clear what is meant by "The essayist writes with coherence."

Coherence in this sense means that the words, sentences, paragraphs, and ideas of the essay are held together not only by sequence on the page but also by logical and syntactic necessity. Sentences following one another on the page may be as sequential as ducks waddling in a row but not necessarily any more coherent. It is a writer's careful use of linking words, phrases, and repeated key terms, that makes words and sentences cohere.

Later, in the chapter on paragraph writing, we will take this up again. But for now we want to emphasize the importance of a coherent thesis statement, one that specifies the writer's purpose and agenda with the utmost clarity. Here is an actual example of an incoherent thesis:

Original: In actuality lobbying the legislature is not always unethical because of desirable political action whereas most people think in terms of negativism, which shows a lack of knowledge about how the system works.

The writer may have known what she was trying to say, but we have only what she has actually said, and it is a perplexing stew. Part of the problem comes from her inappropriate use of the linking words "because," and "whereas." The larger part, however, is caused by muddled thinking. Here is the rewritten thesis:

Revision: Whereas many politically naive citizens think of lobbying the legislature as unethical, in actuality

```
lobbying is a practical system that often results in
desirable political action.
```

"Say what you think" is advice often given in rhetoric books of this kind. "Think about what you say" is, in our view, a better prescription. This means reading and rereading your thesis again and again, trying to fathom the writing through a reader's eyes. Think of the sentences of your essay as poles along which your ideas are to be transmitted like electricity. You must provide the connections, the junction boxes, the relays, the wiring. You do so by carefully linking concepts and ideas together so that they follow with logical necessity.

Revising the thesis for specificity

Every thesis should have one or two pivotal words that encapsulate the essential part of your theme and commit your essay to some specific task. As an example, consider this weak thesis: "The rule of Indira Gandhi was important." The pivotal word here is "important." Demonstrating the importance of Indira Gandhi's rule is what you have committed your essay to do.

But the word "important" is too general, too spongy a term on which to base an essay. If you meant that her rule was characterized by a growing sense of Indian nationalism, or by a policy of nonalignment, you should come out and plainly say so in your thesis. Either point is discussable in itself. "Important," while it may point to discussable matters, is not.

Here is another example. A student tried without success to write an essay on this thesis:

Original: ```A real American is one who is loyal, patriotic,

proud, and thankful to live in the United States of

America.```

After vainly struggling with empty bromides about "real Americans," the writer turned to the instructor for help, who suggested this narrower thesis and redirected focus:

Revision: ```Citizenship in the United States falls essentially

into two categories, each with its own legal```

```
        protections and opportunities:  citizenship by birth

        and by naturalization.
```

This is a discussable and specific thesis. Moreover, it is one that hints help-fully of structure. Later we will see that a thesis, properly worded, can often make the writer's job easier by predicting the structure of the essay. In this case, for example, the writer knows that her main task is to compare and contrast the protections and opportunities offered by the two kinds of citi-zenships (see comparison/contrast, Chapter 13.).

Revising the thesis for wordiness

Of all the sentences in your essay, the thesis is the one that should never be wordy. If it is, you are probably confused about your purpose and should sit down and rethink what you are trying to do.

There are three common kinds of wordiness, each equally ungainly and ugly. The first is *padding.*

```
Original: In my honest opinion, the U.S.  government should

          stop promoting the questionable process of

          affirmative action because, as can be clearly seen,

          it is beginning to have the reverse effect of

          denying school entrance and jobs to middle-class

          whites, who are becoming the disadvantaged minority.
```

The horticultural word used to describe the flaw of this sentence is *deadwood.* It includes all introductory qualifiers such as "in my honest opin-ion," "it is my sincere view," "I think," "I believe." If you express a thought, the world takes it as your own unless you deed it in a footnote to another writer. You do not have to say "I think" or "this is my opinion." That affirmative action is a process is already common knowledge, so it is unnecessary to further say so. The thesis is calling affirmative action into question, which makes the "questionable" superfluous. Also, it is not at all clearly seen that affirmative action is as the writer alleges; that is what the essay must make us clearly see. Here is the revised thesis:

```
Revision: The U.S.  government should stop promoting

          affirmative action because it is beginning to have
```

```
the reverse effect of denying school entrance and

jobs to middle-class whites.
```

Many students tend to overqualify their opinions because of insecurity or out of deference to the instructor. Knowing your topic well is the antidote to insecurity. To express yourself plainly and emphatically insults no one, least of all your instructor, who is hoping to inspire exactly that kind of self-confidence. In any case, hedging in your opinions only makes you sound as if you haven't done your homework.

Repetition is the second kind of wordiness. Here is an example from a student paper:

Original:
```
Traditionally, the southern funeral of past times

was not so much a ritual comforting the bereaved,

who had lost a loved one, as a reminder of man's

immortality and a warning not to lose the faith or

church belief.
```

"Past times" needlessly repeats the idea already summed up in "traditionally." A "bereaved" person is someone who has "lost a loved one"; "the faith" already contains the idea of "church belief." Here is the revision:

Revision:
```
Traditionally, the southern funeral was not so much

a ritual comforting the bereaved as a reminder of

man's immortality and a warning not to lose the

faith.
```

The third kind of wordiness is *roundaboutness*. Writers guilty of it commit the sin of circularity in their sentences. Rather than get to the point cleanly, they circle it like a merry-go-round. Here is an example:

Original:
```
Beginning sometime between 1970 and 1980, automobile

insurance companies began to impose surcharges on

individual drivers who are prone to have accidents,

so as to achieve some form of fairness in assessing

insurance premium rates for drivers in general.
```

"Automobile insurance companies" could be made "auto insurers"; "individual drivers who are prone to have accidents" could become "accident-prone drivers." The phrases are not wrong, but any of them could have been more elegantly and compactly put:

Revision: Since the 1970s auto insurers have used surcharges

on accident—prone drivers to achieve equity in the

overall assessment of automobile insurance premiums.

Sometimes padding is done intentionally so that the essay will meet a minimum word count. But this remedy is wrongheaded and futile. If you are truly interested in your topic, if your are immersed in your sources, if you have a substantial thesis, your efforts should be in the other direction, namely, to rein in your essay before it gallops over the allowed maximum. But if you catch yourself straining to stuff every additional word or two you can in a sentence to satisfy a minimum length, you are either disenchanted with your topic and your thesis, or you do not know your subject well. If so, you should leave off the compositional huffing and puffing and go back to thinking and reading about your subject until you can narrow it into a topic that suits you better.

Following a thesis statement through successive drafts

The example below shows the successive rewriting of a thesis statement to make it sharper and more clearly expressive of the writer's purpose. It also demonstrates what every veteran writer knows: that the distance from first draft to final product is measurable only by persistence and effort.

First draft: Some countries, where class distinctions still

exist, create a bad social atmosphere.

Some countries, where *a* class distinctions still

exists, create a bad social atmosphere, *between the rich and the poor in which two sets of inhabitants are bred totally ignorant of each other.*

This thesis statement does not sufficiently spell out the writer's purpose. Will it express the writer's feelings? Inform us about the effects of class distinctions? Argue against the distinctions of class? A clearer aim is needed.

Second draft: Some countries, where a class distinction still

exists between the rich and the poor, create a

```
social atmosphere in which two sets of

inhabitants are bred totally ignorant of each

other.
```
a country that allows too big a gulf
~~Some countries,~~ where a class distinction still
                    is in danger of becoming like two
~~exists~~ between the rich and the poor, ~~create a~~
countries on different planets, where the
~~social atmosphere in which two sets of~~
                    made what they are by different
inhabitants are ~~bred totally ignorant of each~~
breeding, different food, and different laws
~~other.~~
that control them.

The focus of this thesis statement is sharpened in the second draft with its emphasis on the gap between the rich and the poor. But the writer is still not committed to a specific structure.

Third draft: A country that allows too big a gulf between the
```
         rich and the poor is in danger of becoming like

         two countries on different planets, where the

         inhabitants are made what they are by different

         breeding, different food, and different laws that

         control them.
```
         nation
         A ~~country~~ that allows too big a gulf between the

         rich and the poor is in danger of becoming like
                         separate
         two countries on ~~different~~ planets, where the
                          formed
         inhabitants are ~~made what they are~~ by different
         fed by   *controlled by*
         breeding, different food, and different laws ~~that~~

         ~~control them.~~

The third draft gives the essay structure by limiting the writer to three effects of the gulf between rich and poor: breeding, food, and laws. But the statement could still be further tightened.

Final draft: A nation that allows too big a gulf between the
```
         rich and the poor is in danger of becoming like
```

> two countries on separate planets, where the
>
> inhabitants are formed by different breeding, fed
>
> by different food, and controlled by different
>
> laws.

In this revision, "nation" is substituted for "country," restricting the discussion to formal political entities. "Separate planets" emphasizes the idea of gulf between rich and poor. Repetition of the past participles—"formed," "fed," and "controlled"—gives the statement coherence and symmetry.

Bear in mind that some thesis statements will require many more revisions than are shown here. We do not mean to suggest that you limit your rewriting efforts to three or four passes. We often make a dozen or more passes at our own passages before we are satisfied with them.

Exercises

1. The following thesis statements are poorly written. Correct their flaws in a revision.
   a. Terrorism is often poorly handled by various agencies.
   b. The compact disk player (CD) is flooding the consumer market.
   c. People on vacation try to avoid a heavy intellectual fare when they read.
   d. Francis Bacon is a controversial modern painter.
   e. During its final phase, the Roman Empire declined rapidly, and the Christian church quickly took on a dominant role.
   f. In my opinion, writing with a computer, although some people might find it useful, will only hasten our spreading dependence on high technology while weakening some of our hard-earned literary skills.
   g. Bilingual education may win some short-term gains whereas being offsetted heavily by the divisiveness too many languages can be blamed even in a pluralistic society such as our own.

2. Choosing three topics from the list that follows, compose for each a thesis statement free of all the errors discussed so far in this chapter:
   a. body consciousness
   b. wilderness preservation
   c. private versus public education
   d. fads or fashions
   e. a major government scandal (anywhere in the world)
   f. promiscuity in our society
   g. the developing nations
   h. the effects of romantic love

Revising for Better Structure

The structure of an essay is often implied in its thesis statement, which can be worded to commit the writer to a certain pattern. Here, for example, is the first paragraph of a student essay:

```
Like most people I love to eat and eat and

eat.  If I had just one wish, it would be to be

able to cook.  Being able to cook my own meals

would keep my stomach full, my body healthy, and

my bank account in the black.
```

The structure of this essay is implicit in its thesis: it will be based on a pattern of enumerating the effects being able to cook will have on this student's life. The first would be the effects on his stomach; the second, the effects on his body; and the third, the effects on his bank account. This pattern is known as *simple enumeration* and is especially well suited for any essay that describes a process (see "Process Analysis," Chapter 11).

In planning the overall structure for your essay, then, you should first examine its thesis for any implicit pattern. Sometimes simple enumeration will be the most obvious. But there are other patterns that writers can use in an essay, depending on the particular wording of its thesis.

Structure by order of importance

Thesis: Elderly parents have basic needs that either their children or society must provide.

An essay on this thesis may be structured to present its ideas in either ascending or descending order of importance. For example, you could cover the needs of elderly parents in this descending order:

1. Regular visits from children and other loved ones
2. Good medical care, including proper diet
3. Occasional appropriate recreation
4. Help with grooming
5. Help with housekeeping chores

The first item is, in the writer's opinion, the most important need of an elderly parent; the last item is the least.

Structure by space orientation

An essay may also be based on movement in space: from top to bottom, from left to right, from inside to outside, and so on. A description of a Japanese teahouse, for example, could be structured according to this spatial pattern:

Thesis: The formal Japanese teahouse is a place of solemn ceremony and peace.

1. The stone path leading to the teahouse
2. The low lintel to force a humble bow
3. The starkly furnished one-room interior
   a. The mat on the floor in the middle of the room
   b. The gridiron and the teakettle in front of the mat
   c. One simple flower arrangement on the shelf at the back of the room
   d. A porcelain tea service near the flower arrangement
   e. One painting on the wall above the flower arrangement

The movement of the description is from the outside to the inside of the tearoom. Once begun, the essay should stick to this orderly flow.

Structure by time orientation

Thesis: The English language traces its origins to prehistoric time and has been influenced by many cultures.

This structure is based on a chronological listing of the main points of the essay. The lapse may be over the course of a day, week, month, year, decade, or century. For example, below is the pattern that might be used in an essay on the history of the English language:

1. Celtic influence (earliest recorded time)
2. Roman influence (43 A.D.)
3. Anglo-Saxon influence (449)
4. Norman influence (1066)
5. Influence of northern, midland, and southern dialects (1100)
6. Fixation of standard English as influenced by Oxford and Cambridge universities and by Dr. Johnson's dictionary (1650)

Naturally, once you have begun to use an obviously chronological sequence, you should stay with it consistently to the end.

Structure by logic

Thesis: Taxpayers need not pay millions of dollars to support presidential libraries in order to gain the benefit of the memoirs and recollections of former presidents.

To structure an essay by logic is to use some predictable pattern of reasoning: a discussion of cause and effect, a recounting of examples to support a main point, a listing of reasons why something should be done or not done, a series of questions and answers. For example, here is the pattern that might be used in an essay arguing against perks for presidents leaving office:

1. Thomas Jefferson died so poor that his personal property had to be sold off to satisfy his debtors; yet he left us a brilliant legacy of writings.
2. U.S. Grant left office with a few thousand dollars and later went bankrupt, but he wrote his valuable memoirs without the help of a presidential library.
3. Harry S. Truman typed his own letters once he left office, but these letters are now a historical treasure.

A series of examples supporting the author's overall conclusion is the logical pattern implicit in this outline.

Whichever of these patterns you follow in an essay, it is helpful to spell out your intent somewhere in an opening paragraph. Expository prose is easier to read when one knows what to expect; it is also easier to write once the writer has made a commitment in the thesis statement to some specific pattern.

The following first draft of an essay is annotated to show the thrust of the student's rewriting. A second draft is also included, showing how the student cleaned up some of the lapses in structure. Notice that the revision often entailed the shifting of paragraphs or blocks of sentences that either had been misplaced or became more effective elsewhere.

Original:

Move this opening paragraph to the second sentence of paragraph 3.

What Is Piety?

① In 1535, Sir Thomas More defied King Henry VIII and put his head on the chopping block because of dedication and duty to his religion. When he publicly refused to subscribe to the Act

It can be the first example in the historical sequence. Substitute a new introductory paragraph.

of Supremacy, which made the British king head of the Church instead of the pope, he was imprisoned and eventually beheaded. More had been admired throughout England for his legal decisions in favor of the poor, the weak, and the oppressed. One of his famous works was a treatise comforting people experiencing great tribulation. More's piety gave him the courage to obey his conscience, do his duty, and accept his tragic fate on earth. Such faithfulness to the duties owed to God is called <u>piety</u>.

② The word <u>piety</u> derives from two Latin words—<u>piete</u>, meaning "pity," and <u>pietas</u>, meaning "dutiful ness." Back in the 12th century, when the word first became popular, it was associated exclusively with the first meaning, <u>pity</u>, but then it evolved from pity to a sense of duty concerning one's elders or family. From that meaning it eventually came to be linked primarily with religious matters, as it still is today. In our world, if a person is considered pious, he is devout and obeys the rules of his church.

③ Examples of how piety has affected history are scattered throughout the centuries. *Insert paragraph 1* America was settled by men and women who were persecuted in Europe for their religious convictions. The Plymouth settlers left England for America because they could no longer tolerate neighbors who mocked them, threw bricks at them, burned

their Bibles, or treated them as clowns.   Their
sense of duty to God and Church was strong
enough to let them abandon their homeland and
embark on a journey to an unknown world, where
they could fulfill the dream of freely
practicing their religion.   An important part of
the pilgrims' creed was to have pity on people
in trouble and to share the bounty of their
harvests with neighbors who had fallen on ill
times. The Crusades and Spanish Inquisition are
striking examples of piety run amuck.   In both
instances, the overzealous duties of those
bringing "the true religion" to others consisted
of torture, looting, rape, and murder—hardly
pious means.   These corrupt movements
demonstrate what happens when duty and pity part
ways.

Move this paragraph to follow paragraph 5. It should follow the examples of true piety to indicate a contrast. Piety can be counterfeit. Supply a transition for better coherence.

④ Our present age offers numerous examples of
piety.   For instance, the Moral Majority's quest
to influence governmental policy in the United
States stems from the pious belief that abortion
is wrong and that youth must be kept from moral
decay.   Although the methods of this Moral
Majority may be questioned, still the movement
itself is obviously spurred on by a sense of
religious duty and a concern for fellow man,
which form the essence of piety.

⑤ Nobel Peace Prize recipients Mother Teresa
and Bishop Desmond Tutu have been recognized on
a global scale for their pious behavior.   As

servants of the Church, they both are committed
to doing God's work by helping others. Bishop
Tutu's fight against the injustices of apartheid
in South Africa and Mother Teresa's caring for
the sick and hungry children of India and other
parts of the world are carried on under the
dictates of the Church. As representatives of
their religion, these two humanitarians are
duty—bound to manifest the doctrines of their
faith. In 1985 Bishop Tutu risked his own life
by speaking out for human rights during the
bloody riots of Johannesburg. That same year
Mother Teresa selflessly confronted the
disease—ridden refugee camps of Ethiopia to help
distribute food to starving children. *Insert the section about the Crusades and Spanish Inquisition here.*

(6) Quite clearly, piety is exhibited in its
purest and most admirable form when it reveals
aspects of both its earliest and later meanings.
When a person combines pity with duty and makes
these qualities the fuel for a passionate
involvement with humanity, he or she is living
the highest form of piety. *Add a statement about what happens when the element of pity is lacking.*

Revision:

What Is Piety?

"And I would wish my days to be
Bound each to each by natural piety."
These are lines penned by William Wordsworth, the
great Romantic poet, who longs for piety as a

desirable character trait.   On the other hand,
another noted Romanticist, Edmund Burke, warned
that "religious persecution may shield itself
under the guise of a mistaken over-zealous piety."
It seems then that piety is a Janus: it can be
malevolent as well as benevolent. Since the term is
so loaded, what are its true roots?

   The word piety derives from two Latin
words—piete, meaning "pity," and pietas, meaning
"dutifulness." Back in the 12th century, when the
word first became popular, it was associated
exclusively with the first meaning, pity, but then
it evolved from pity to a sense of duty concerning
one's elders or family. From that meaning it
eventually came to be linked primarily with
religious matters, as it still is today.   In our
world, if a person is considered pious, he is devout
and obeys the rules of his church.

   Examples of how piety has affected history are
scattered throughout the centuries.   In 1535, Sir
Thomas More defied King Henry VIII and put his head
on the chopping block because of dedication and
duty to his religion. When he publicly refused to
subscribe to the Act of Supremacy, which made the
British king head of the church instead of the pope,
he was imprisoned and eventually beheaded. More
had been admired throughout England for his legal
decisions in favor of the poor, the weak, and the
oppressed. One of his famous works was a treatise

comforting people experiencing great tribulation. More's piety gave him the courage to obey his conscience, do his duty, and accept his tragic fate on earth. Such faithfulness to the duties owed to God is called piety.

America was settled by men and women who were persecuted in Europe for their religious convictions. The Plymouth settlers left England for America because they could no longer tolerate neighbors who mocked them, threw bricks at them, burned their Bibles, or treated them as clowns. Their sense of duty to God and Church was strong enough to let them abandon their homeland and embark on a journey to an unknown world, where they could fulfill the dream of freely practicing their religion. An important part of the pilgrims' creed was to have pity on people in trouble and to share the bounty of their harvests with neighbors who had fallen on ill times.

Our present age offers numerous examples of piety. For instance, the Moral Majority's quest to influence governmental policy in the United States stems from the pious belief that abortion is wrong and that youth must be kept from moral decay. Although the methods of this Moral Majority may be questioned, still the movement itself is obviously spurred on by a sense of religious duty and a concern for fellow man, which form the essence of piety.

Nobel Peace Prize—recipients Mother Teresa and Bishop Desmond Tutu have been recognized on a global scale for their pious behavior. As servants of the Church, they both are committed to doing God's work by helping others. Bishop Tutu's fight against the injustices of apartheid in South Africa and Mother Teresa's caring for the sick and hungry children of India and other parts of the world are carried on under the dictates of the Church. As representatives of their religion, these two humanitarians are duty-bound to manifest the doctrines of their faith. In 1985 Bishop Tutu risked his own life by speaking out for human rights during the bloody riots of Johannesburg. That same year Mother Teresa selflessly confronted the disease-ridden refugee camps of Ethiopia to help distribute food to starving children.

But piety has its dark side. Hideous crimes have been committed in the name of a distorted piety, a piety consisting of duty without pity. The Crusades and Spanish Inquisition are striking examples of piety run amuck. In both instances, the overzealous duties of those bringing "the true religion" to others consisted of torture, looting, rape, and murder—hardly pious means. These corrupt movements demonstrate what happens when duty and pity part ways.

Quite clearly, piety is exhibited in its purest and most admirable form when it reveals aspects of both its earliest and later meanings.

In fact, robbed of the element of pity, piety can

turn into a devilish fanaticism. Only when a

person combines pity with duty and makes these

qualities the fuel for a passionate involvement

with humanity, does he or she live the highest form

of piety.

Exercises

1. Which structure would you likely use in writing on the topics below? Your choices are (a) simple enumeration (b) order of importance (c) space orientation (d) time orientation (e) logic.

   a. The Pilgrims, a group of religious separatists who founded Plymouth Colony, were formed in 1606 to express their opposition to the rites and jurisdiction of the Church of England. In 1607 and 1608 the sect migrated to Amsterdam, Holland. Unhappy with life in Amsterdam, some members of the group sailed in 1620 for America aboard the *Mayflower.* They landed at Plymouth harbor in December, 1620, where the settlers established a colony.

   b. A Mongolian "yurt" (home), such as the ones found in the foothills of the High Altai Mountains, consists of a round wooden lattice-work frame covered with canvas or camel-hair felt. The organization of the interior is dictated by the circularity of the structure.

   c. There are important reasons why child pornography should be banned from bookstores and magazine stands.

   d. Saving energy has several effects, from saving money to saving your life. Let us consider the effects according to how each influences human activities.

   e. Some grownups believe that children should not be encouraged to read fairy tales because they are often cruel and frightening. This attitude is based on lack of understanding. In reality, children already know about evil, fear, and bogey. Fairy tales are not responsible for producing fear in children. That is in them already because it is already in the world. In actuality, fairy tales give children the clear possibility of defeating evil and bogey.

2. Identify the flaws in the following thesis sentences. Then correct the flaw by revision:

a. Soccer playing is good.

b. Horror movies offer a threat to the young viewers based on the susceptibility to suggestions of macabre and frightening occurrences and desensitizing their sense of revulsion to violence.

c. Mandatory gun control is necessary and gun violence is escalating all over America.

d. Poetry has been successfully and beneficially employed and used in therapy sessions on patients suffering from psychological maladies of the mind ranging from and running the gamut from manic-depression to schizophrenia.

e. Romantic love conquers all.

Writing Assignments

1. Use a prewriting strategy to find a topic and controlling idea for writing an essay on one of the following subjects. Submit evidence of the prewriting method you used—whether a page of freewriting, a jot-list, a cluster diagram or any other—as well as written justification for your choice of the narrowed topic.

   a. Medical uses of illicit drugs
   b. Geological phenomena and their causes
   c. Modern cartoonists
   d. Exercise
   e. Television news
   f. Newspaper columnists

2. Do the reading or research necessary to devise a thesis for your above chosen topic. Submit at least three drafts of the thesis, showing successive attempts at revision. Write a paragraph explaining and justifying the changes you made.

3. Write an opening paragraph on the above topic of your choice, submitting at least two drafts to the instructor, with your revision changes plainly marked. Be sure to make the final sentence of the paragraph your thesis.

4. Write a paragraph explaining how you generally arrive at structure for your essays. If you have no conscious method, sit down and think about the method you have been unknowingly using.

5. Using the principles covered in this chapter, revise the thesis from any of your old essays. Submit at least three drafts to the instructor.

Chapter

4

The Whole Essay: Organization and Logic

All things began in order, so shall they end, and so shall they begin again.

Sir Thomas Browne (1605–1682)

You have your topic. You've done your freewriting, inventing, reading, have your controlling idea and thesis, and are teeming with ideas. Now you're ready to begin writing. Here we are squarely in the capricious realm of individual differences.

The truth is that some writers do not, cannot, or will not organize any piece ahead of actually writing it. One member of this writing team, for instance, never organizes before writing; the other never writes before organizing. Individual differences are obviously at work here, and it is plainly a waste of time to force anyone to use a composing method antagonistic to his or her personal temperament.

The section that follows explains various processes for organizing, but you would do well if you find and stick to the degree of organizing that matches your working and thinking style. If that means plunging headlong into the sea of disorganized notes flooding your desktop, so be it.

Create a Model of the Essay

A model is a rough sketch of the major parts of your essay. Like a formal outline, it sketches the essay in a sequential listing of abbreviated subtopics. But unlike the formal outline, it is constructed without strict obedience to indenting.

To make a model, you begin by writing down your thesis statement:

```
The legendary cruelty of Moslem forms of

legal punishment is in reality less sadistic

than legal punishment in our own country.
```

Since the aim of the writer is to contrast the Moslem penal system with our own and to argue that ours is the more cruel, the heart of the essay will consist of paragraphs that weigh the dissimilar penalties meted out by the two systems for the same offense. Here is the model:

```
In several Moslem countries, public

flogging is the punishment for drunkenness;
```

```
however, in the U.S. we throw drunks in jail.

     In several Moslem countries, amputation of

the right hand is the punishment for theft; in

the U.S. thieves are sent to prison.

     In several Moslem countries, murder is

punished by public execution; however, in the

U.S. murderers are sent to prison.

     U.S. prison sentences are the ultimate

cruelty because they are indeterminate and place

the criminal in institutions filled with

violence and rampant with serious diseases.
```

At a glance, the model provides an agenda of subtopics along with a sketch of their main points. Not so obvious, however, is that it also prescribes a developmental pattern for writing the essay (for more on developmental patterns, see Chapter 5). The writer knows that this particular essay must be developed as a contrast because that pattern is implicit in the ordering of topics.

Make an Outline

If you were educated in the western hemisphere, chances are good that you have either been taught, seen someone use, or actually used an outline yourself. Essentially, the outline is a numbered system of indented shelves in which a multitude of topics, subtopics, and minor parts of a work may be filed.

The basic numbering system of the outline is this: main topics are designated by Roman numerals such as I, II, III, IV, and V. Subtopics are designated by capital letters: A, B, C, D, and so on. Subtopics may be further divided into smaller units designated by Arabic numerals such as 1, 2, and 3. A further subdivision may be designated by lower case letters: a, b, c, d, and so on. Here are the empty shelves of an outline:

```
Thesis

I.  Main topic
```

```
   A.  Subtopic

      1.  Subdivision of a subtopic

         a.  Further subdivision of a

            subtopic
```

An outline may be either simple or complex. The simplest is a one-level outline—named for its single level of entries—which is especially useful for brief and uncomplicated writing assignments. Here is an example:

```
Thesis: College students are returning to a

          pre-1960 level of academic success.

   I.  They are achieving higher SAT scores.

  II.  They are spending more time in

       libraries.

 III.  They are partying less.

  IV.  They are spending less time on

       politics.
```

All the statements of the outline are extensions of the thesis, which they are intended to prove. Notice that the indenting and the parallel phrasing of the main topics make for easy scanning.

More complex assignments require outlining in greater detail, as in this example:

```
Thesis: Modern science and technology have

          had good as well as bad effects on

          our society.

I. Many scientific and technological

   advances have dramatically improved

   human life.

   A. The ability to communicate worldwide

      has made people less isolated and

      less provincial.
```

    1. National radio and television keep
      Americans in touch with each other.

    2. Communications satellites keep for-
      eign nations in touch with each
      other.

    3. Air travel allows people to study so-
      cieties other than their own.

B. Effective contraception has given
   societies a new sense of freedom.

    1. Women are having small families
      in order to pursue professions.

    2. Men live under a regimen of
      sexual freedom less binding than
      that of the Victorian era.

C. The latest advances in biomedical
   research have cured major
   life—threatening diseases.

    1. Virulent diseases have been
      curbed.

      a. Syphilis is now easily cured.

      b. Typhoid practically no longer
        exists.

      c. Tuberculosis is rare.

      d. Polio has vanished.

    2. Nonvirulent diseases have been
      curbed.

      a. Open heart surgery has
        replaced weakened arteries
        with stronger ones.

       b. Certain forms of cancer are
          forced into remission through
          radiology and chemotherapy.

       c. Genetic research is on the
          verge of preventing genetic
          diseases such as cystic
          fibrosis and Down's syndrome.

II. Many scientific and technological
    advances have endangered human life.

    A. The pollution of our oceans is a
       threat to human food supplies.

       1. Oil tankers and off-shore
          drilling works are causing oil
          slicks that kill fish and plant
          life.

       2. Sewage waste from industrial
          plants is poisoning our beaches.

    B. Pollution of our atmosphere is a
       threat to human health.

       1. Aerial sprays poison the
          atmosphere and destroy its ozone
          layer.

       2. Smog from factories and
          automobiles infects the air and
          causes lung diseases.

    C. World security is being threatened
       by the constant emphasis on improved
       nuclear arsenals.

       1. We have enough megatonnage on

```
         land, at sea, and in the air to

         blast mankind into oblivion.

     2. Competition between the USSR and

        the United States for nuclear

        dominance threatens global

        destruction.
```

The entries of an outline may consist of full sentences, as in the previous examples, or they may consist of words and phrases that merely summarize the intended topics and subtopics. Here is an example of a topic outline:

```
Thesis: Remote sensing of electromagnetic

        radiation (EMR) has proven useful

        in meteorology, geology, and

        archaeology.

    I. Use of remote sensing in meteorology

       A. Remote sensing in short—term

          weather forecasting

       B. Remote sensing in hurricane

          warnings

   II. Use of remote sensing in geology

       A. Use in watershed management

       B. Use in mineral exploration

  III. Use of remote sensing in archaeology

       A. Use in locating cultural deposits

       B. Use in archaeological mapping
```

The choice of sentence or topic outline will be dictated by the complexity of your essay. Use a sentence outline for a complex topic, a topic outline for a simple topic.

Outlines are meant to highlight only the principal points of an essay and do not include introductions, materials, transitions, and details. One page of an outline will usually translate into five pages in the essay.

The most common mistake found in outlines is a lack of parallelism between the entries. Parallelism simply means expressing equivalent ideas in similar phrasing. Properly observed, it is a convention that makes the outline easier to read than one whose entries are randomly worded. Here is an example. The entries in this excerpt from an outline on astrology are not parallel:

```
Thesis: Astrology is based on so-called

        natal signs.

   I. Each person has a sun sign.

  II. Rising signs also play a part.

 III. Signs are ruled either by fire, air,

        earth, or water.
```

Contrast this with the excerpt from the following parallel outline:

```
Thesis: Astrology is based on so-called

        natal signs.

   I. Each person has a sun sign.

  II. Each person also has a rising sign.

 III. Each person is ruled by a sign of

        either fire, air, earth, or water.
```

The difference is decisive: with the parallel outline, the writer can see at a glance the sequence of topics in the essay. With the outline whose entries are not parallel, the structure of the essay is not as immediately apparent.

Faulty subordination of topics is the second most common error found in outlines. The accurate outline should give equal billing only to topics of equal importance in the essay. Consider this excerpt of an outline on the consequences of divorce:

```
Thesis: Divorce has a decisive effect on

        the life of the entire family

   I. The individual marriage partners are

        affected.

  II. Children are affected.
```

III. In-law relationships are affected.

IV. Family pets are affected.

It is plainly warped logic to equate the suffering of the family pet in a divorce with that of the human participants. This kind of error, however, is not strictly one of outlining, but of illogical thinking that is merely reflected in the outline.

Why are outlines so persistently popular with a certain kind of writer? One reason is that writing tends to be a grubby, involved, subterranean act somewhat akin to tunnelling. One's nose often gets too close to the ground to get an overhead view of exactly where all the digging is leading. The outline, however, shows the view from above. It points out glaringly visible defects of structure, logic, and incompleteness. Here is an example:

Controlling idea: People own handguns for

several reasons.

I. People own handguns to commit crimes.

A. Handguns can easily be concealed.

B. Knives are also popular weapons of criminals.

C. Handguns are lethal.

II. People own handguns to defend themselves against criminals.

A. They want to defend their homes.

B. They want to defend themselves while traveling.

C. Too often the homeowner himself gets killed.

III. People own handguns for sport.

A. They feel macho when carrying a handgun.

B. They target shoot with handguns.

C. They hunt animals with handguns.

D. <u>Small-caliber handguns are more</u>

<u>likely to wound than to kill.</u>

  The underlined entries do not follow the heading under which they appear. For example, I B is not a reason for owning a handgun; neither is II C. Likewise, III A and III D do not logically follow under the main point, "People own handguns for sport." These lapses, glaringly visible in the outline, are harder to spot in the essay itself.

Exercises

1. Create a model of one of the following theses:
    a. The tradition of Halloween is a waste.
    b. The tradition of Halloween is an important ritual of childhood.
    c. Providing women with the luxury of a fur coat involves cruelty to animals.
    d. Having married couples share household responsibilities is an excellent new trend.
    e. Having married couples share household responsibilities undermines the traditional family.
    f. Sometimes it is rewarding to take risks.
    g. Living in a big city has decided advantages.
2. Create an appropriate two-level outline for one of the following theses, using full sentences for each entry.
    a. Private ranting—throwing pillows, yelling at the wall, or screaming at an imaginary antagonist—can be an excellent psychological release for pent-up anger.
    b. The recent emphasis on ecology encourages a beneficial respect and love for all forms of life that will help with the preservation of our fragile ecosystems.
    c. Fly casting is a demanding sport that requires patience, guile, and a respect for the most wily adversary a fisherman can stalk—the brown trout.
    d. The relationship between a stepparent and child is often an ambivalent and psychologically troublesome one.
3. Find and correct the flaw in the following outline excerpts:

Thesis: Conspiracy theories on the

assassination of public figures are

frequently unbelievable.

I. They depend on hearsay testimony.

II. Crucial witnesses are usually
    deceased.

III. Our paranoid fears are fueled by them.

Thesis: The movie is an inferior,
        collaborative art form.

  I. It often dazzles the viewer with
     vistas while resorting to
     psychological implausibilities.

 II. It often resorts to <u>deus ex machina</u>
     resolutions.

III. Ticket prices have simply gotten too
     high.

Thesis: Travel is a broadening experience
        that can teach graphic lessons
        about foreign cultures and lands in
        the way that no book can.

I. Travel teaches about foreign customs and
   cultures.

II. Travel teaches intimate lessons on
    geography and history.

III. Seeing the grandeur of the Roman
     Colosseum teaches an unforgettable
     lesson about the Christian martyrs.

Revising for Logical Progression and Thought

Three indispensable characteristics are required of logical arguments: that their arguments be *focused,* cite only *verifiable* evidence, and consist of *visible* reasoning.

To develop a thesis logically, your argument should focus unwaveringly on the supporting evidence and facts. It should not splatter your opponent's reputation over the stones, make appeals that tug at the heartstrings, or trumpet facts that are bogus or irrelevant. It should concentrate only on the available evidence, which must be publicly verifiable and therefore cannot come from the unnamed sources of journalism. Your reasoning must show all the intermediate calculations in your thinking that led from proposition to conclusion. Nothing can be hidden, concealed, masked, or disguised in a logical argument, and its outcome is never dependent on secret testimony or unique gifts. With logic, what you see is what you get.

In fact, a great deal of what makes an argument logical comes from fair play and common sense. Playing fair with the evidence, being willing to listen to the reasoning of an opponent, ignoring irrelevant issues of personality—these are traits universally associated with logic. To argue logically, you need only focus on the question in dispute, cite verifiable evidence, and make your reasoning visible to a listener or reader.

Below are some of the common departures from logic often committed by speakers and writers along with suggestions for editing them out of your own arguments.

Avoid hasty generalizations

A hasty generalization is a rash conclusion based on too few examples, on atypical examples, or on the omission of examples that attest to the contrary. For instance, if because of a newspaper story about two TWA crashes you were to assert that travel on TWA is dangerous, you would be making a hasty generalization utterly unjustified by the scant evidence. A similar charge could be made against you for concluding that small towns such as Santa Fe, New Mexico, produce the best grand opera. Santa Fe has exceptional opera, but that distinction is unshared by thousands of other small towns. Or, if your thesis argued that Japanese students in the United States were unimaginative writers, you would be generalizing hastily since you probably have not had contact with a large enough number of Japanese students to infer any sweeping truth about their writing.

Some generalizations may be accurately deduced from a single example, especially those based on experience or natural law. For example, one fall from a tree is enough to teach a true and accurate lesson about gravity. But to lose money in one transaction in the stock market does not make that institution a den of thieves. Everyone who falls from a tree is taught more or less the same lesson by nature. But not everyone who invests in the stock market has the same experience and learns the same lesson.

Part of growing up is to come to a painful awareness that personal experience, cherished as it may be to us, is not always the best doorway to truth. It is simply our personal experience. One man might hate dentists because he was roughly drilled by an unfeeling quack. But another may have had just the opposite experience, having spent serene moments in a dental chair listening to music and being afterwards told that he hasn't a single cavity in his mouth. Neither experience teaches anything universal about dentists.

Before you make such sweeping pronouncements as "All American cars are poorly engineered," "No woman can bear as much stress as a man," or "The best motion pictures are foreign made," ask yourself how you came to these opinions and what support you have for them. If it turns out that you once owned an American-made lemon, that you once were stuck in an elevator with a hysterical woman, that you once saw a wonderfully made foreign film, be mature enough to realize that your sampling is based entirely on personal experience that, while justifying your feelings, is insufficient to proclaim a truth.

Here are some examples of hasty generalizations, followed by acceptable revisions:

Original: `All commencement speakers parrot the same old advice`
`about gaining society's respect, finding a`
`fulfilling career, and living an altruistic life.`

Revision: `Some commencement speakers parrot the same old`
`advice about gaining society's respect, finding a`
`fulfilling career, and living an altruistic life.`

Some commencement speakers are plainly windbags who hurl about a good deal of mush and bombast at graduation ceremonies. But other speakers on these occasions have made eloquent and memorable speeches.

Original: `Since no one can stem the tide of illegal drugs`
`flowing into this country, they might as well be`
`legalized for everybody.`

Revision: `Unless a way can be found soon to stem the tide of`
`illegal drugs flowing into this country, we might as`
`well opt to legalize them in order to control their`
`use.`

The idea of legalizing drugs to control them at the source has been proposed by serious thinkers (the American writer Gore Vidal, for example, wrote a perceptive essay on that very subject). Advocating this view, however, is not the same as arguing for legalization of drugs because no one can stem their influx into the country (that smacks of specious negativism).

Original: `Marriage is an unworkable institution in which two`

       `people are trapped for life by humdrum convention`

       `and boredom.`

This is clearly a rash overstatement: all marriages are obviously not bad, nor would all married people consider themselves trapped by humdrum convention.

Revision: `Although the divorce rate in America remains high,`

       `marriage is an institution that has worked well for`

       `some people who have worked hard at it.`

Double check your evidence

An argument is very much like a teeter-totter on which two propositions sit. If the weight of evidence is preponderantly on one side over the other, the balance will tip in its favor, leaving the opposing side up in the air. In judging whether or not your assertion is based on strong evidence, ask yourself these basic questions.

What is the weight of the evidence?

The weight of evidence is its sheer quantity and preponderance. The evidence of ten eyewitnesses who positively identify a bank robber is weightier than the evidence of one person who claims the suspect was home at the time minding the baby. If virtually all medical experts regard a disease as having a certain cause, their opinion outweighs the contrary claims of two dissenting experts. The idea is not to practice a slavish adherence to popular thought, but to carefully sift and weigh the evidence.

That the majority is often wrong is, as a matter of fact, the paradox to be learned from history. But that is as it should be in a society which lives by the impartiality of evidence and marches progressively closer to the truth. For example, in earlier centuries a standard treatment for disease was to bleed the victim by making a small incision in a vein and suctioning off blood in a cup. The father of England's Queen Victoria was treated with this remedy for a fever, with some 120 fluid ounces of blood being drained from his shivering body during a 24-hour period. It is still unclear whether he died from his illness or his treatment. Fever was thought to be caused by an imbalance of "humors" in the blood, which the bleeding was believed to correct. Today, medical science knows better, and therapeutic bleeding is often cited in textbooks on medical history as an example of a misguided theory that did more harm than good. No doubt some of the medical beliefs of our own day will seem just as nonsensical and bizarre to a distant generation.

Nevertheless, in the light of present knowledge, a belief supported by the testimony of large numbers of experts is more convincing than one that enjoys little or no backing. While its value is always relative to what is known and accepted, evidence is still the best available support in a logical argument. A classic example of how the weight of evidence leads to a reliable conclusion can be found in the death of Josef Mengele, the notorious Nazi concentration camp doctor. It was only after all the evidence had been carefully weighed—the dental charts checked, the bone samples exhumed and compared with known injuries suffered by Mengele—that an official consensus was reached confirming his death.

What is the source of the evidence?

Whether in a court of law, a family dispute, or a written argument, the value of a source depends on its credibility. Quoting your Uncle Louis as supporting testimony for the belief that Uganda has an atomic arsenal and is planning to attack the United States will brand your argument as empty— unless, of course, your uncle is a big shot in the CIA. (Even so, one would wonder about an uncle who would leak such confidential information to a chatty relative.) Sources stand or fall on the world's judgment of their expertise, and making this judgment is part of the writer's job.

As a beginning writer, you may feel overawed by this task. Yet it is an exercise in free thinking you are called upon to do every day. If a shadowy figure beckons to you in a parking lot and offers to sell you a gold watch for $10, you are certain to pass internal judgment on the source before plunking down the money or walking away. (If you would buy a gold watch under such circumstances, we'd like to interest you in a good used bridge.) Much of the thinking that is required by logic is simply a more elaborate exercise of common sense.

The trick in citing expert opinion is to stay with impeccable sources, the ones roosting in the pages of major encyclopedias and enjoying tenure at such recognized institutions as Harvard, Johns Hopkins, M.I.T., or Yale. A glance at the various volumes of *Who's Who* will help you get a feel for what's what. Certainly, few instructors will question articles by experts printed in newspapers like the *New York Times,* the *Chicago Tribune,* and the *Christian Science Monitor.* Reasonable men and women also give due honor and credit to evidence culled from established magazines such as *Time, Newsweek, National Geographic,* and the like.

What is the worth of the evidence?

Good evidence is timely, impartial, and relevant. Annual statistics about the number of criminals released from prison in 1975 no longer bear on our own time. The racial speculations and findings of a person known to

be a committed racist must be held suspect. Statistics on newspaper reporting have little relevance in an argument directed against television news. Perhaps we are not all equally equipped to judge evidence for its timeliness, impartiality, and relevance, but most of us are at least adequate to the task.
Can you, for example, spot the flaws in the following assertions?

Original: The evidence proves incontrovertibly that aliens

have made contact with humans and have even

occasionally abducted them for study.

Rare indeed is the reputable writer who would attach "incontrovertible" to
this opinion. Many allegations have been made about the abduction and
study of humans by alien creatures, and many books have been written on
the subject. But the evidence is, for the most part, anecdotal and unverifiable.
Here is a more cautious contention on this controversial subject:

Revision: The stories about the abduction and study of humans

by alien creatures share inexplicably similar

features.

Original: Indians are the poorest people in our country: They

die early; they live in squalor; they have no work;

they go to their graves uneducated; and no one

cares.

As an argumentative thesis statement, this assertion could lead to a provocative essay. But now it is only an assertion, not evidence or proof. Here is
the kind of evidence it would need:

Revision: According to Peter Collier, Walter Daniels, and

Edwin Embree, who have written widely on the plight

of the American Indian, the American Indian suffers

one of the most serious economic and cultural

deprivations of any minority in our country. His

average yearly income is $1,500, below the poverty

level. The Indian's average age at death is 44,

much lower than that of the national average, which

```
is 72.5.  The median number of school years
completed by Indians is 8, and between 15 and 20
percent have never been to school at all.  About 70
percent of Indian housing is substandard.  A 50
percent unemployment rate is not considered high.
Yet, the government has done very little to improve
the Indian's plight.
```

Original:
```
An alarming health problem in our country is the
recent growth in numbers of preteen youths who have
taken to chewing tobacco and dipping snuff.  If
parents would instruct their children in the
religious principles set forth in the Bible, where
it is clearly stated that man's body is the temple
of God, this terrible habit could be stopped.  But
going to church and reading the Bible in order to
find a pure way of life is distasteful to many
parents, who themselves indulge in evil
habits. . . .
```

The evidence behind this assertion is based on moral belief not hardhearted facts and figures. Evidence based on belief is no evidence at all; it is merely belief. The revision correctly sticks to relevant evidence concerning health:

Revision:
```
An alarming health problem in our country is the
recent growth in the number of preteen youths who
have taken to chewing tobacco and dipping snuff.
Although these youngsters claim that this smokeless
tobacco is healthier than smoking cigarettes,
doctors disagree vehemently, pointing out that in a
relatively short span of time chewing and dipping
can cause gums to recede, teeth to loosen, biting
```

surfaces to be worn off, and even cancer to appear.
Some users may well require gum grafts or radical
mouth surgery. Recent medical research by the
National Cancer Institute and the University of
North Carolina points to a direct link between oral
cancer and the use of smokeless tobacco.

Avoid non sequiturs

A **non sequitur** is an assertion or conclusion that does not logically
follow from the statements preceding it. For example, here is a syllogism
whose conclusion is a non sequitur:

> Large cars use a lot of gas.
> Harry Smith's car uses a lot of gas.
> Therefore, Harry Smith's car must be large.

That Harry's car must be large because it uses a lot of gas is not necessarily
true. Instead, it could be a *small* sports car with an engine designed for speed
and performance rather than economy. This fallacy, elegantly known to lo-
gicians as "the undistributed middle term," fails to account for exceptions. A
more valid version follows:

> Large cars use a lot of gas.
> Harry Smith's car is large.
> Therefore, Harry Smith's car must use a lot of gas.

The premise of this syllogism says that if a car is large, it uses a lot
of gas. That Harry Smith's car is large is admitted in the second statement. It
therefore logically follows that Harry Smith's car must use a lot of gas. On
the face of it, this is all very logical. But only on the face of it; for the assertion made by the premise of a syllogism could be dubious or untrue. Here is
an example:

> Blonds have more fun.
> So-and-so is a blond.
> Therefore so-and-so has more fun.

This nonsense has a logically intact look to it if we take its initial
premise to be true. But is it necessarily true that blonds have more fun? In

the whole world, are there no blonds who are also chronic, joyless grumps? Even if you have never met a blond sourpuss, common sense should tell you that some must exist and that having fun can bear no logical relationship to the color of one's hair. Logical propositions, even if accurately reasoned, are valid only when they are founded on assertions of truth.

Another kind of non sequitur is the **post hoc ergo propter hoc** fallacy—from the Latin meaning "after this therefore because of this." It occurs when precedence and causation are confused, with an earlier occurrence being mistaken as the cause of a later one. For example, we once saw a man angrily shoo his wife away from a blackjack table in a Las Vegas casino because he started to lose after she arrived. (He continued to lose at an even greater pace when she left, which made us wonder why he didn't stem the tide by bringing her back.) A man walks under a ladder and shortly afterwards suffers an accident, so walking under ladders is assumed to be the accident's cause.

Many medieval fears and superstitions were often founded on post hoc fallacies. A certain planetary conjunction immediately preceding the bubonic plague was taken as its cause. Much later, microbes were found to be the carriers. Ringworm was treated by washing the scalp with a boy's urine, gout by applying a plaster of goat dung mixed with rosemary and honey. Both remedies were probably based on rumors about the recovery of some fortunate soul on whom they were applied, but who would have gotten better anyway.

Here is a typical post hoc fallacy, followed by a revision for improved logic:

Original: Ever since Mayor Bryan was elected, the traffic situation in Boom City has become intolerable. We must get rid of the mayor before it is no longer possible to drive in our city.

Revision: Ever since Mayor Bryan was elected, a new influx of industry and people has caused an enormous increase in traffic snarls and accidents. However, the mayor does not seem willing to deal with the problem; therefore, he should be replaced.

The second version makes the mayor answerable for the heavy traffic, but does not blame him for causing it.

Faulty condition is another common fallacy of the non sequitur variety. This fallacy is based on an erroneous "if this, then that" equation. Here is an example:

Original: If students are allowed to question their teachers' lectures or assignments, soon the whole educational system will come under the rule of immature and capricious students.

Revision: While students should be encouraged to ask questions about their teachers' lectures or assignments, those in charge of school administration cannot uncritically accept all student judgments about teachers since these judgments are often immature and capricious.

It is a faulty condition to assume that the rule of the immature and capricious must automatically result if students are allowed to question their teachers' lectures and assignments. The revision more reasonably sees this questioning as useful if done in the right spirit.

Closely related to the faulty condition is the fallacy of the **faulty alternative,** which stews an issue down to two simplistic and equally inedible alternatives. To insist, for example, that a person is either against abortion or a supporter of murder is to exclude those who regard life as precious but approve of abortions under extenuating conditions. To argue that recruits join the police force because they are either sadistic or have an inferiority complex is to ignore the attractions of adventure and good pay. Here is an example of an either/or argument:

Original: Either our government must legislate socialized medicine, or Americans by the millions will die of serious illnesses because they cannot afford hospitalization and doctor's care.

Revision: Because of the soaring costs in medical care, it is time for the government to make it possible for all U.S. citizens to have some form of low-cost

compulsory insurance, such as Kaiser, Ross–Loos, or
a similar form of health maintenance organization.

"Sink or swim" is the motto of those who see issues as divisible into only two alternatives. Generally, it is more prudent to clamber onto the high middle ground rather than to take the plunge with them.

Finally, there is the non sequitur of circular reasoning, also known as "begging the question." This argument "begs" the reader or listener to accept a debatable assumption as if it were already proved or disproved. This is the classic exchange of circular reasoning:

> The Bible is the word of God.
> How do you know this?
> Because the Bible says so.

In effect, this proposition asserts that "the Bible is the word of God because the Bible is the word of God." To write, "Everyone knows that prison reform is a big waste of taxpayers' money," is to beg that question, which everyone does not know. Here is another example of circular reasoning:

Original: Prostitution should be legalized because both men
and women have strong sexual drives which they are
now forced to unlawfully satisfy through contacts
with prostitutes.

Revision: Legalization of prostitution has been undertaken in
some states, for example, Nevada, with none of the
consequences of moral doom and wholesale promiscuity
that opponents have claimed were bound to occur.

The original argument states that prostitution should be legalized because otherwise people will break the law against prostitution.

Avoid irrelevancies

An irrelevance is any assertion or allegation that has no bearing on the issue in dispute and therefore does not belong in the argument. The **ad hominem** argument (Latin, "against the man"), which directs its venom at the character of an opponent rather than at the opponent's ideas, is the most common example. For instance, to mention that the sponsor of a mass transit bill you are against is a three-time divorcee is to engage in an ad hominem argument. Here is another example:

Original:

> Some unthinking people applaud Richard
> Nixon's foreign policy, placing a veneer on his
> diplomatic efforts in China. They claim that he
> made inroads into a renewed friendship between
> the United States and the regime of Mao Tse-tung
> by using extreme tact in upholding our American
> democracy with its attendant capitalistic system
> while also praising China for its advances in
> literacy and help for its starving millions. But
> isn't it the height of hypocrisy to engage in
> hero worship of a man who created the greatest
> governmental scandal since Teapot Dome? Nixon's
> memoirs should be taken off the shelves of
> bookstores because a President who committed the
> crimes that Nixon did should not be given credit
> for advancing a creative foreign policy.

This argument is directed against Nixon the man, not Nixon the maker of foreign policy. Here is a possible revision of the passage:

Revision:

> During his term as U.S. President, Richard
> Nixon administered a strong foreign policy,
> beginning the phased withdrawal of U.S. troops
> from South Vietnam, achieving a cease-fire
> accord with North Vietnam, and initiating
> strategic arms limitation talks with the Soviet
> Union. However, his greatest achievement in

foreign policy came as a result of his 1972

visit to the People's Republic of China, where

he effected a change in the chilled relationship

between Chinese and Americans by talking with

Mao Tse-tung personally and promising to have

cultural and economic exchanges with China but

not to interfere in its internal politics.

Another fallacy of irrelevance is the **ad populum** argument, which appeals to prejudices, slogans, and cliches beloved by the populace. The debater's views are therefore stroked with the brush of "Mom," "flag," and "apple pie," while the opposition's are tarred with "Communism," "dictatorship," and "bureaucratic red tape." Since every country has its stock of favorite virtues, ad populum arguments are appeals of cultural relativism. "Communism" carries the same diseased association in our culture that "capitalism" must have in the Soviet Union. Here is a typical ad populum argument:

Original:

Recently the papers have been filled with

editorials promoting the idea of clearing up the

slum area of our city and building brand-new

facilities for the poor. Who would bear the

gigantic financial burden of this project? The

faithful middle class, who always ends up paying

for the extravagant ideas wild-eyed liberals

think up. This particular brainstorm is

especially odious because the health and welfare

types whom these new buildings would house are

irresponsible and dedicated to the perpetuation

of crime. They will not maintain the new

buildings properly and thus more and more money

will be drained from law-abiding citizens, who

are already carrying an excessive tax burden.

Our wonderful democratic system is based on
individual responsibility, not socialistic
reform. In the days of our pilgrim fathers every
American was on his own. Big Brother was not
responsible for him. Let's keep it that way.

Hidden in this murky ad populum argument is the issue of whether or not
the redevelopment of slum areas is good or bad. The writer's side on the
issue is propped up by such righteous pillars as "faithful middle class," "law-
abiding citizens," "individual responsibility," "our pilgrim fathers," "every
American on his own." The opposition is gored with negative epithets such
as "wild-eyed liberals," "welfare types," "irresponsible," and "dedicated to
the perpetuation of crime."

Revision:

Our city council is debating the
possibility of redeveloping the downtown slum
area in order to build adequate housing for
people with low incomes. While the project
appears an excellent one on the surface, certain
admonitions are in order. First, we must make
sure that all residents of this tax-supported
project are truly needy and not just taking
advantage of a handout. Second, we must
establish a system of rewards that will motivate
residents to maintain the buildings and keep
them from deteriorating into the kind of slum
they became in the first place. Finally, since
the area in question has always had a high crime
rate, the police department should organize a
workable district watch program in order to
assure a safe new neighborhood.

In the fallacy of the **red herring,** a writer or speaker introduces a luridly emotional side issue to disguise the weakness of an argument. The term comes from a ruse practiced by escaping prisoners who dragged a bleeding fish across their trail to confuse tracking bloodhounds. Many arguments on controversial issues of our day often use the red herring to disguise the trail of evidence and truth. Here is an argument containing a red herring:

Original:

> The unisex clothing fashion that has been
> occasionally proposed by designers is an
> international attack on the nuclear family.
> Traditionally, father and mother dressed
> differently, were brought up differently, and
> were expected to perform different roles in the
> family setting. Father was supposed to go out
> into the world and earn a living for his family,
> while mother was expected to stay home and take
> care of the children. Now comes unisex clothing
> which many international designers are pushing
> on the American public. The fashion has not yet
> caught on, but when and if it does, it will
> drive a stake through the heart of the American
> family. Father and mother will not only look
> alike, eventually they will become alike. The
> role separation on which all families are based
> will dim and then disappear. And so will the
> family.

Common sense tells us that fashion designers are motivated not by hatred of the family, but by a desire for profit and popular acceptance of their styles. In any event, clothes do not the person make, and it is rash to assume that the differences between the sexes must automatically vanish if they dress alike. It is also untrue that the structure of the family must be ruined if its traditional male and female roles are in any way modified. In many families today, the wife is the breadwinner while the husband is the homemaker. (One popular newspaper cartoon, *Adam,* depicts exactly that situation.) The red herring nature of this argument was pointed out to the student, who was asked to recast the paragraph's opposition to unisex clothing in more reasonable terms. In the revision, the student took a more humorous approach:

Revision:

> Unisex clothing is sexless ugliness. Rather
> than highlight the endearing differences that
> exist between the sexes, this style covers them
> both in the same burlap sack. The physique of
> the male, the figure of the female, are hidden
> under baggy cloth. Femininity is smothered, and
> so is masculinity. One would think that the
> style was designed for an organism like the
> amoeba that reproduces by fission. But our
> species and its reproductive existence depends
> on attraction between the sexes. The female
> cannot go into a hospital and split herself into
> two halves, nor can the male. Thank goodness
> that the unisex clothing fashion has not caught
> on, for what it could do to our species not even
> Darwin himself could have anticipated.

Note that it is a legitimate ploy to make a measured emotional appeal in an argument. Here, for example, is an emotional appeal used in an essay arguing for stronger air pollution laws. The student has already made a stirring factual and statistical argument for stronger mandatory control on automobile emissions. Now she winds up her paper with an emotional appeal:

> There is a condition in Los Angeles known
> as the "School Smog Alert." When the ozone

concentration is high enough, this alert is
issued by the public health authorities, and
schools are asked to keep children in the
classrooms and away from the playgrounds. The
oxygen they need to breathe and play is poisoned
by ozone, carbon monoxide, and traces of
cyanide. At this level of alert, older people
are warned to remain indoors and not to exert
themselves. Age has already made their lungs
liable to disease, but now the air itself has
become an enemy that would further weaken, and
even kill. The healthful oxygen they need for
life has already been inhaled by automobiles and
exhaled back into the atmosphere as poisons. Is
this the sort of world we want to live in? And
is the convenience of family automobiles worth
the bad air we suffer? On sober thought, most
of us would have to say it is not.

Although such appeals can be moving if they are carefully used, they cannot entirely replace evidence, testimonial opinion, and hardheaded reasoning.

Finally, there is the irrelevance of **faulty analogy,** which asserts a false resemblance between two situations and then draws a conclusion from it. Instead of addressing real issues, the faulty analogy fusses over bogus metaphors. For example, here is one writer's view of the lot of the American farmer: "The American farmers are like the Jews of Hitler's World War II concentration camps: they are mistreated, neglected, and left to survive on their own." This analogy is laughably farfetched. Hitler set out to systematically exterminate the Jews. No administration, however uncompromising its attitude toward farm subsidies, would even think of exterminating farmers. Analogies are useful in making complex issues understandable, but they seldom prove anything. Here is an argumentative statement based on a faulty analogy, followed by an improved revision:

Original:

> Teaching sex education in the high schools
> is like teaching a terrorist how to use
> explosives. Teenagers do not have self-control
> to prevent them from getting into trouble.
> Giving them the techniques for having sex will
> not make things better, but worse. What they
> need to learn is the moral discipline and
> restraint, and these cannot be taught or learned
> from a manual or textbook on sexual practices.
> Yet everywhere we hear that more education is
> the answer. This is like saying, "Give the
> terrorist a bigger gun. Teach the terrorist how
> to use the A-bomb." It used to be said that
> ignorance is bliss. This remains true when it
> comes to high school teenagers and sex.

Enough absolute differences exist between teenagers and terrorists to make this analogy inapplicable. Note that what is wrong with this argument is not the stand it takes on sex education, but the farfetched analogy it uses to make it. The writer was asked to recast the argument without resorting to the false analogy:

Revision:

> Teaching sex education in the high schools
> is a wrong idea because it seems to show the
> approval of society for sexual experimentation
> among teenagers. Teenagers do not have the
> self-control to prevent them from getting into
> trouble over sexual matters. Teaching them the
> techniques for having sex and practicing birth

control will not make things better, but worse.
What they need to learn is moral discipline and
restraint, and these cannot be taught or learned
from a manual or textbook on sexual practices.
Yet everywhere we hear that more sex education
is the answer because teenagers will experiment
anyway. That may be true, but it may also be
untrue. Some experiments will occur among
teenagers, no matter how little or much they
know about sex. But more sophisticated
experiments are going to occur among teenagers
who are taught sexual techniques without at the
same time being taught moral restraint.

Whether or not you agree with this, it is now plainly a more reasoned and logical opposition than before.

To sum up, what distinguishes the logical writer from the illogical one is not the presence or absence of belief, but the grounds on which belief is based. Stick to the issue, play fair with the evidence, explain your reasoning, avoid hysterical appeals, and your own writing will be distinguished by its logic.

The following brief student argument contains some logical fallacies. Study the essay, along with the editor's marginal comments. Then notice how the rewritten version corrects the fallacies.

Original:

Next to sleeping, the typical American
child spends most of his time watching
television. Of course, all of the major networks
proclaim that television can instruct these
children in amusing and captivating ways that
parents and teachers cannot. On the battlefield
of television ratings, where viewing points are

the bullets used to kill the enemy competitor, children function as important hostages. Programs like <u>Sesame Street</u> or <u>Mr. Wizard</u> seem to bear out the contention that all knowledge becomes delectably fascinating when proffered via the boob tube. Indeed, viewed superficially, persuasive reasons exist for encouraging children to broaden their intellectual and emotional horizons by watching television. Nevertheless, subtle signals alert us to a greater truth: Far from broadening children emotionally or intellectually, television contributes to their mental and social stagnation. Here are some proofs:

First, children who watch television do not read. The reason they do not is obvious: It is easy to sit in mesmerized passivity while a steady dose of cartoons, movies, or live dramatizations bombard the child's psyche. Watching the Pink Panther or Mickey Mouse escape the conniving enemy by diving off a cliff or leaping across mountain tops with aerial magic is far less strenuous than trying to read a child's edition of Greek mythology or American history. Watching a program about Tarzan swinging from tree to tree above the flora and fauna of a phony T.V. jungle certainly titillates the emotions of a child more than does visiting a museum and reading the

inscriptions describing endangered animal
species in their natural habitats. But the
romance of watching television will not help the
child to become an accomplished student. In
fact, it will probably have the opposite effect
of slowing down his reading skills by blunting
intellectual curiosity and preempting the
precious time needed to develop proper reading
skills at an age when these skills are the
easiest to acquire.

Evidence needed for this assertion.

Second, children who watch television do
not interact socially. A child sitting
cross-legged on the carpet, munching from a bag
of chocolate chip cookies while following the
vicissitudes of Charles and Caroline Ingalls in
some episode from Little House on the Prairie,
is not going to want to play with little brother
or answer Dad's humdrum queries about school.
Why bother with a lackluster real family life
when one can be involved with the fictional
Ingalls, who have just discovered that an
unethical tycoon is taking over the town of
Walnut Grove? Here is the excitement of a
romanticized farm life and the glamour of youth
combatting evil powers to achieve heroism. Some
children become so entranced with television
that if a parent dares call them away from the
screen, they stage temper tantrums. Children who
no longer want to interact with the family

evidence needed

evidence needed

become isolated and estranged. Families whose main source of recreation is watching television don't really know each other well because they have forfeited the chance to share each other's hearts and minds. Later on, this same kind of isolation and estrangement can cause the adult to suffer serious problems in relating to colleagues and to friends. He may actually become a social outcast. How can a child who has spent so much time silently staring at a T.V. screen grow into a man or woman capable of holding an interesting conversation with a

faulty analogy between T.V. and heroin addiction

friend or colleague? A child who watches television is like a heroin addict. All he cares about is his next fix. He withdraws from the world around him and merely exists in his foggy world of fantasies, adventures, and escapades, accompanied by appropriate background music.

Last, children who watch television develop a distorted view of reality. Even though this medium has the uncanny ability to catch life in crucial moments of truth, such as Robert Kennedy's 1968 assassination in the rear exit of the Ambassador Hotel in Los Angeles, it ignores truth for the most part in favor of the sensational, the romantic, or the occult. Most programs children watch teach them totally false ethical values. They may grow up believing that violence is an acceptable means for social reform or that sex is the way to personal happiness. After all, the _A-Team_'s Mr. T becomes a hero by knocking people unconscious or by machine-gunning storefronts and factories. If violence works for him, why not for the average person? The most successful cops on _Hill Street Blues_ are constantly seen dallying in bed with incomparably sensual sex goddesses. Erotomania seems the agenda for all their evenings. Surely a young boy watching this series will be tempted to judge the good life as one in which lust plays a leading role. A little girl who is allowed to watch _Charlie's Angels_ may grow up believing that only women who combine perfect figures with lovely faces and brilliant minds will attract fame, fortune, and happiness. After all, everyone knows that as the twig is bent, so the tree grows. In one way or another, most T.V. programs typically watched by children give a slanted, biased view of life. Additionally, many top actors and actresses lead utterly debauched personal lives. Celebrities like Stacy Keach, John Belushi, and Madonna--reputed either to be on drugs, to promote pornography, or generally to live (and, in the case of Belushi, die) in the fast lane--should never be allowed to appear on television, where minors can see them and use them as role models.

ad populum argument

ad hominem attack

Television is a double-edged sword in that

it is capable of influencing the young for bad
as well as for good. And although staring at the
tube seems far more mentally stimulating than
sleeping, there are times when for children a
nap would be better than watching T.V.

Revision:

   Next to sleeping, the typical American
child spends most of his time watching
television. Of course, all of the major networks
proclaim that television can instruct these
children in amusing and captivating ways that
parents and teachers cannot. On the battlefield
of television ratings, where viewing points are
the bullets used to kill the enemy competitor,
children function as important hostages.
Programs like Sesame Street or Mr. Wizard seem
to bear out the contention that all knowledge
becomes delectably fascinating when proffered
via the boob tube. Indeed, viewed superficially,
persuasive reasons exist for encouraging
children to broaden their intellectual and
emotional horizons by watching television.
Nevertheless, subtle signals alert us to a
greater truth: Far from broadening children
emotionally or intellectually, television
contributes to their mental and social
stagnation. Here are some proofs:

   First, children who watch television do not
read. The reason they do not is obvious: It is

easier to sit in mesmerized passivity while a
steady dose of cartoons, movies, or live
dramatizations bombard the child's psyche.
Watching the Pink Panther or Mickey Mouse escape
the conniving enemy by diving off a cliff or
leaping across mountain tops with aerial magic
is far less strenuous than trying to read a
child's edition of Greek mythology or American
history. Watching a program about Tarzan
swinging from tree to tree above the flora and
fauna of a phony T.V. jungle certainly
titillates the emotions of a child more than
does visiting a museum and reading the
inscriptions describing endangered animal
species in their natural habitats. But the
romance of watching television will not help the
child to become an accomplished student. In
fact, it will have the opposite effect of
slowing down his reading skills by blunting
intellectual curiosity and preempting the
precious time needed to develop proper reading
skills at an age when these skills are the
easiest to acquire. "A Nation at Risk," the
significant report presented to Ronald Reagan
and the Secretary of Education in 1981 by a
special task force appointed by the President to
analyze trends in education, is an alarming
analysis of how the ability to read has declined
since television came to dominate children's

lives. The report states that 13 percent of all 17-year-olds in the United States are functionally illiterate. Functional illiteracy among minority youths may be as high as 40 percent. Since 1960, when watching television became the national pastime, there has been an unbroken decline in the average verbal scores of students trying to enter college. The report indicates that many teenagers do not possess the "higher order" intellectual skills expected of them. Nearly 40 percent cannot draw inferences from written material; only one-fifth can write a persuasive essay. In short, learning to become educated is a difficult, demanding enterprise for which television viewing does not prepare children.

Second, children who watch television do not interact socially. A child sitting cross-legged on the carpet, munching from a bag of chocolate chip cookies while following the vicissitudes of Charles and Caroline Ingalls in some episode from Little House on the Prairie, is not going to want to play with little brother or answer Dad's humdrum queries about school. Why bother with a lackluster real family life when one can be involved with the fictional Ingalls, who have just discovered that an unethical tycoon is taking over the town of Walnut Grove? Here is the excitement of a

romanticized farm life and the glamour of youth
combatting evil powers to achieve heroism. Some
children become so entranced with television
that if a parent dares call them away from the
screen, they stage temper tantrums. Children who
no longer want to interact with the family
become isolated and estranged. Families whose
main source of recreation is watching television
don't really know each other well because they
have forfeited the chance to share each other's
hearts and minds. The Pulitzer Prize—winning
author, Daniel Boorstin, warns against the
"segregation from one another" caused by too
much television. He points to the fact that
with "more and more two—T.V. families, a
member of the family can actually withdraw and
watch in complete privacy," thus breaking all
ties with other people. How can a child who has
spent so much time silently staring at a T.V.
screen grow into a man or woman capable of
holding an interesting conversation with a
friend or colleague? A child addicted to
watching T.V. runs the risk of becoming a social
misfit.

Last, children who watch television develop
a distorted view of reality. Even though this
medium has the uncanny ability to catch life in
crucial moments of truth, such as Robert
Kennedy's 1968 assassination in the rear exit of

the Ambassador Hotel in Los Angeles, it ignores
truth for the most part in favor of the
sensational, the romantic, or the occult. Most
programs children watch teach them totally false
ethical values. They may grow up believing that
violence is an acceptable means for social
reform or that sex is the way to personal
happiness. After all, the A-Team's Mr. T becomes
a hero by knocking people unconscious or by
machine-gunning storefronts and factories. If
violence works for him, why not for the average
person? The most successful cops on Hill Street
Blues are constantly seen dallying in bed with
incomparably sensual sex goddesses. Erotomania
seems the agenda for all their evenings. Surely
a young boy watching this series will be tempted
to judge the good life as one in which lust
plays a leading role. A little girl who is
allowed to watch Charlie's Angels may grow up
believing that only women who combine perfect
figures with lovely faces and brilliant minds
will attract fame, fortune, and happiness. In
one way or another, most T.V. programs typically
watched by children give a slanted, biased view
of life. As Daniel Boorstin comments, "A new
miasma—which no machine before could
emit—enshrouds the world of T.V. We begin to be
so accustomed to this foggy world, so at home
and solaced and comforted within and by its

```
blurry edges, that reality itself becomes

slightly irritating."

     Television is a double-edged sword in that

it is capable of influencing the young for bad

as well as for good. And although staring at the

tube seems far more mentally stimulating than

sleeping, there are times when for children a

nap would be better than watching T.V.
```

The revision has added the weight of evidence by quoting an important study and an authority on the influence of television on the lives of children. It has deleted the faulty analogy, the ad populum argument, and the ad hominem attack, replacing these with more measured commentary.

Exercises

1. Find and correct the logical fallacy in each of the following assertions:
   a. The most feared disease of our time is cancer. It is a known truth that a Pollyanna personality can prevent, postpone, and cure cancer. Most psychiatrists agree that there is a strong connection between the mind and the body.
   b. Benjamin Franklin once wrote that executive officers in the federal government should not be salaried lest profit and avarice become motivations for serving in government posts. What was true of Franklin's day is still true today. If only the wealthy would become senators, representatives of congress, or heads of departments, they would not be tempted to make decisions based on bribes and other temptations.
   c. Old people become crotchety and selfish. Mr. Smith, the city councilman, is a terrible grouch and refuses to spend money to improve the city. It is obvious that Mr. Smith is getting old.
   d. Enacting stringent teenage curfew laws will reduce juvenile crime because it provides the steps to make teenagers more law abiding.
   e. There is no such creature as a juvenile criminal. As Judge Tom Clark pointed out long ago, "Every boy in his heart would rather steal second base than a car." Juveniles are capable of continuous moral improvement.
   f. If we are not vigilant, the computer will force teachers out of business the way the car forced horses and mules out of business.
   g. What does it matter whether or not import tariffs are economically

sound? Willis Hawley, one of the original senators who sponsored the Tariff Act, was in league with labor bosses and was therefore beholden to organized crime.

Writing the First Draft: Finding Content and Form

Once you have your topic, controlling idea, and thesis, and have done the necessary research, you are ready to begin the actual writing. How should you proceed? With expository prose the safest course is to begin at the beginning. Express your controlling idea as a thesis and jot it down on a sheet of paper. For example, one student planned to write an essay about bats. She arrived at this controlling idea:

```
     Bats have been given an undeservedly bad

name.
```

After considerable research into the reputation and habits of bats, she refined the controlling idea into the following thesis:

```
     Bats are extraordinarily shy and harmless

     animals that significantly contribute to human

     welfare through insect reduction and pollination

     of crops.
```

Then she made this preliminary model of her essay:

```
     Bats have been the subject of numerous

     myths.  They are generally pictured as

     bloodsucking animals that are likely to attack

     humans.  This is a false picture.

     Bats are insectivores and consequently help

     control the numbers of potentially harmful

     insects.  Bats are also a part of nature's

     pollination system.
```

```
        Bats do not spread rabies.  They are no
   more liable to parasites than dogs or cats.
        Bats are an endangered species whose
   extinction would be devastating to nature as
   well as to humans.
```

At this stage she faced, as any writer would, an array of choices. She could choose to cite one fact instead of another, to quote this expert opinion over that, or to include this anecdote and omit that one. These choices will affect the *content* of her essay—the ideas, data, arguments, opinions, and so on that actually go into work. But she must also make choices that will affect the *form* of the essay—how these various ideas, data, arguments, and opinions are organized and expressed. For example, how much ink should she give to debunking the misconception about bats and parasites? Should she refer to herself in the paper as "I," and use contractions such as "I've" or "We'll" or more formal equivalents? Writing expository prose always requires a writer to exercise choice among elements that will affect both the content and form of a work.

But it ought never to be a choice exercised in a vacuum. Indeed, this is where your knowledge of your audience enters the equation. You know that yours is to be an objective essay written on a researched subject. Perhaps you know that your instructor (your only audience that counts) discourages the use of contractions or excessive personal references in objective writing and that she prefers essays written in five paragraphs, each briskly devoted to a single purpose. If so, your choices are refreshingly narrowed, for you know exactly what to do in order to please.

As for the writer of the essay about bats, she began her essay with this paragraph:

```
     In the shape of a sneaky bat, Dracula zooms
   through the window of the crenellated castle,
   lands on the neck of the sleeping mistress of
   the house, and begins to suck blood from her
   artery.  A hiker stumbles into a cave, rouses a
   colony of bats, and is forced to flee for his
   life as they swarm over him.  Neither story is
   true.  Vampire bats do not attack humans.  Bats
```

```
do not swarm over hikers.  In fact, contrary to

the popular myths about them, bats are

extraordinarily shy and harmless animals that

significantly contribute to human welfare

through insect reduction and pollination of

crops.
```

And she was off to a fine start.

Notice, by the way, that her thesis is the final sentence of the opening paragraph. The traditional slot for the thesis sentence is always the last sentence of the first paragraph, and many teachers insist on this placement in student essays. Indeed, putting the thesis here benefits both reader and writer. The reader gets a snapshot of the writer's intent; the writer, an early reminder of the agenda on which the essay must focus.

Writing Assignments

1. Choose a thesis from the list on pages 36–37. Create an outline of it using one of the organizing patterns taught in this chapter.

2. Organize the following facts into a logical outline. If necessary, delete or add appropriate heads. Write an essay of 300–500 words based on the outline:

   Multiple-choice examinations have replaced the essay.
   Students no longer have to think.
   Homemakers no longer use creativity in housework.
   Students use calculators for simple arithmetical problems.
   Precooked or frozen food has replaced food made from scratch.
   High technology is keeping people from using creative mindpower.
   To drive a car, you just put the gear level in "drive."
   Factory workers have become like robots.
   Robots have replaced factory workers.

3. Write an essay of 300–500 words using appropriate evidence on one of the following topics:
   a. Fantasies are good for one's mental health.
   b. The space program has given us many useful technological spin-offs.
   c. Funeral rites and customs are a rip-off for most consumers.
   d. Preservatives in food serve a useful function.

4. Write an essay analyzing the logic (or lack of it) in many popular television commercials.

5. Write an essay describing the tastes and preferences of a past instructor in any discipline who once served as an audience for your essays.

6. Take an article from any issue of *Reader's Digest*, find the original source from which it was condensed, and write an essay specifying the differences in form and content between the two. Comment on the implied differences in their audiences.

Part

2

Writing and Rewriting Strategies

Chapter

5

The Paragraph: Structure and Rhetoric

A sentence should contain no unnecessary words, a paragraph no unnecessary sentences, for the same reason that a drawing should contain no unnecessary lines and a machine no unnecessary parts.

WILLIAM STRUNK, JR. (1869–1946)

The paragraph may be a nearly universal convention of writing, but it is still subject to a wide range of inconsistent practices. Most newspapers and popular magazines use short paragraphs, whereas scholarly journals and serious books use long ones. Writers use new paragraphs mainly to change topics, to move a discussion to a different angle, to make a transition between ideas, to shift rhythm, or even to alter emphasis. While logic dictates many of these usages, the individual practice is largely based on personal style. Indeed, paragraphs can be so mystifyingly varied that beginning writers often find the principle behind their writing utterly bewildering. So we will begin by saying what a paragraph is not.

A paragraph is not a chunk of words randomly framed into a rectangular segment. It is not on the page mainly to relieve the monotony of a compact block of print. It is not merely an ornamental form to which all prose writing must capriciously adapt. Primarily, the paragraph is a division of thought, a subtopic of your subject, one room in the house of your essay. The foundations of your paragraphs are laid when you break the subject into a series of smaller topics, which you will do as you map out the organization of your essay. (See Chapter 4 for more on doing this.) If you paragraph badly, you are most likely failing to perceive the presence of the big subject among the fragments of smaller topics.

Parts of the Paragraph

In its simplest formulation, a paragraph consists of a topic sentence that makes a general assertion and of supporting details that prove it. The topic sentence is usually but not necessarily the first sentence of the paragraph. Sometimes it is the last sentence, and sometimes it is not even stated but merely understood.

In any case, the topic sentence should contain some discussable issue or assertion. It should not be the plain statement of a dead-end fact, such as "My eyes are blue," or you will leave yourself with nothing further to say. (A seasoned and clever writer may indeed write a paragraph on such a skimpy sentence, but it is tricky and difficult to do.) Instead, the topic sentence should contain some idea or proposition in need of support or proof

Figure 5-1   The Structure of a Typical Paragraph

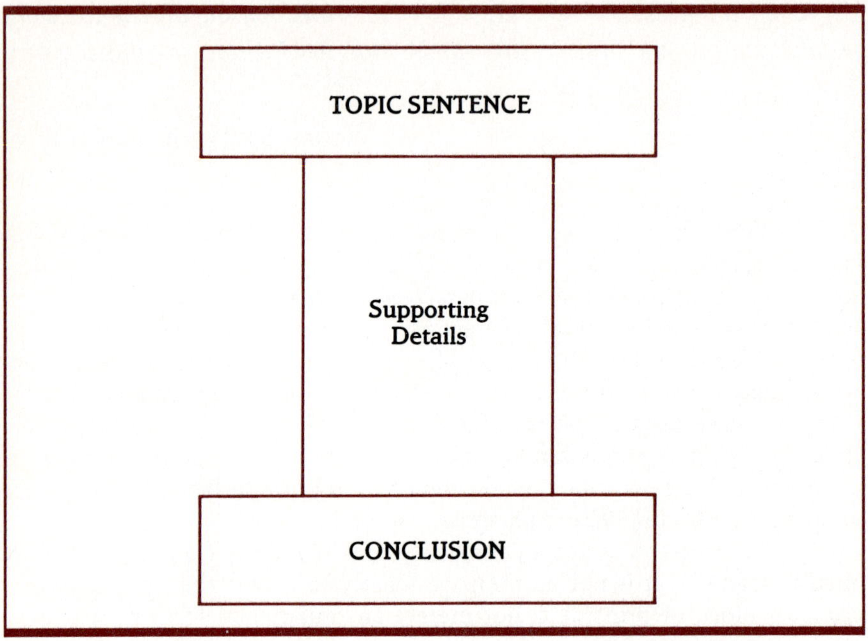

```
┌─────────────────────────────────────────────────┐
│          ┌───────────────────────────┐          │
│          │      TOPIC SENTENCE        │          │
│          └───────────────────────────┘          │
│                  │            │                  │
│                  │            │                  │
│                  │ Supporting │                  │
│                  │  Details   │                  │
│                  │            │                  │
│                  │            │                  │
│          ┌───────────────────────────┐          │
│          │        CONCLUSION          │          │
│          └───────────────────────────┘          │
└─────────────────────────────────────────────────┘
```

as, for example, "I have always wanted to have blue eyes." Picture your reader as an impudent doubting Thomas who challenges your every topic sentence with, "Oh, yeah? Prove it!" or, "Oh, yeah? Show me!" If you have nothing to show or prove in your topic sentence then you have nothing to write a paragraph about.

The second part of a paragraph consists of its supporting details—those facts, data, evidence, testimony, and opinions that prove the assertion made by the topic sentence and satisfy your doubting reader. What you include here will depend on the topic sentence. For example, if your topic sentence was "No time of the day is more serene and lovely in the tropics than sunset" (Oh, yeah? Show me!), you must pack your paragraph with details of serenity and loveliness found in a tropical sunset. On the other hand, if your topic sentence was "My Aunt Agatha was an unconscionable witch who plagued me throughout my childhood" (Oh, yeah? Prove it!), your details must show her in the act of cackling and tormenting you.

In addition to having the principal parts of a topic sentence and supporting details, paragraphs are also subject to two universal conventions of style: unity and coherence.

Writing Unified Paragraphs

The principle of writing unified paragraphs is a simple one. Plainly put, it says, stick to the point. Don't introduce irrelevant issues or details that have no bearing on your topic sentence. Here is an example of a paragraph that has unity:

A <u>good</u> <u>example</u> <u>of</u> <u>this</u> <u>disguising</u> <u>of</u> <u>the</u> <u>female</u> <u>figure</u> <u>is</u> <u>the</u> <u>unique</u> <u>ruff</u> <u>of</u> <u>the</u> <u>Elizabethan</u> <u>era.</u> In those days women were not satisfied with the necks created for them by God, so they began to wear the ruff. The ruff is an immense collar with ruffle piled on ruffle, starched and wired, to give the famous strangulating effect much sought after by women at court. A woman appeared to be stretching her neck like a ruffled ostrich. (These "neck braces" would have served well for whiplash had whiplash been popular then.) When looking at pictures of an Elizabethan woman wearing a ruff, one finds it easy to imagine her head being detached from her body and remaining with the collar when it is taken off at night.

On the other hand, here is a paragraph that lacks unity.

Another <u>example</u> <u>of</u> <u>women's</u> <u>desire</u> <u>to</u> <u>disguise</u> <u>their</u> <u>natural</u> <u>appearance</u> <u>is</u> <u>the</u> <u>Victorian</u> <u>bustle.</u> Apparently Victorian women disagreed with God's construction of their rumps, so they took the Elizabethan barrel, cut it in half, and attached it to their backsides. This contraption was called the bustle, a wire

cage shaped like a big bump and worn under the
back of the dress. No prehistoric monster was
shaped any funnier. A bustle could be as much
as a foot deep, giving the wearer the silhouette
of an "h." A woman wearing a bustle looked as if
some little prankster were hovering under her
skirt. <u>The bustle, as bizarre as it may seem,</u>
<u>does not win the prize for the most absurd</u>
<u>fashion. This honor belongs to the leg-</u>
<u>o'-mutton sleeve. The sleeve was tight from the</u>
<u>wrist to the elbow, but from the elbow on it</u>
<u>looked like a gigantic balloon waiting to be</u>
<u>popped. Although a leg of mutton would look</u>
<u>flattering on most sheep, the same could not be</u>
<u>said of the Victorian women wearing it.</u>

The last four underlined sentences break the unity of the paragraph by straying to a discussion of the "leg-o'-mutton sleeve," an irrelevance not required by the topic sentence. These details should either be dropped or the topic sentence reworded to predict them: "Further examples of women's desire to change their natural appearance are the Victorian bustle and leg-o'-mutton sleeve."

Paragraphs written with unity are more believable than those without it for the same reason that the speaker who sticks to the point is more believable than the one who doesn't. The writer whose mastery of a topic is artfully demonstrated in focused paragraphs tends to be convincing. The one who cannot make a point and stick to it tends to be boring.

Writing Coherent Paragraphs

The incoherent paragraph, like the incoherent essay we discussed in Chapter 3, is one whose sentences and ideas do not logically follow. The coherent paragraph, on the other hand, is one whose ideas do follow and whose sentences make sense. Here is an example of an incoherent paragraph:

Owning a home is far more satisfying than
The homeowner can   to his heart's content; the
renting a place. ~~Remodeling by renters is out~~
renter cannot and ^ is compelled to
~~of the question since all money expended brings~~
                    the property
~~no return. Most renters~~ live in ~~their living~~
exactly   he   it
~~quarters just~~ the way ~~they~~ found ~~them when they~~
              it happens to suit his
~~moved in,~~ whether or not ~~they are convenient~~.
particular taste. know
^Home owners ~~experience a feeling of deep~~

~~satisfaction~~ each time they make their mortgage
        that   *indirectly*
payments ~~because they know that~~ they are ~~inching~~
enriching themselves. Renters know each time
~~closer to the time when they will own their~~
they make their rent payments that they are
~~homes outright.~~ Each ~~month hundreds or even~~
directly enriching only the landlord.
~~thousands of dollars go into rent. The canceled~~

~~check among the stack received is the only~~
Moreover,
~~reward.~~ ^Every April, when income tax is due,

homeowners realize a decided financial boon

because all interest payments are tax
        whereas the renter's   not being deductible,
deductible, ^ ~~Rent~~ money, ~~disappears forever into~~
is gone forever.
~~the pockets of the landlords.~~

A beleaguered reader might possibly grasp what this writer is trying to say, but only after repeated reading and tiring effort. The problem is that the sentences seem to have no logical and compelling connection with one another other than succession on the page. Some rhetorical glue, some careful patching together of the successive ideas, is badly needed.

How can you write coherent paragraphs? First, fulfill the promise made in your topic sentence. In the paragraph above, for example, the writer promises in the topic sentence to demonstrate that owning a home is more satisfying than renting one, but fails to follow through as he erratically hops from point to point. Second, use the following techniques to logically link your sentences into a coherent whole:

1. Repeat key words or their synonyms and pronouns. This repetition will intermittently remind the reader what the paragraph is about.
2. Use transitions and pointers to keep the ideas flowing smoothly.

These include such handy phrases as, "For example," "Moreover," "Nevertheless," "First, second," and so on.
3. Use parallel structures to create a sense of rhythm and harmony.

Here, for example, is a revision of the paragraph above, using these techniques:

> Owning a home is far more satisfying than renting. The <u>home owner</u> can remodel to his heart's content; the <u>renter</u> cannot and is compelled to live in the property exactly the way he found it, whether or not it happens to suit his particular taste. <u>Home owners</u> know each time they make their mortgage payments that they are indirectly enriching themselves. <u>Renters</u> know each time they make their rent payments that they are directly enriching only the landlord. <u>Moreover</u>, every April, when income tax is due, <u>home owners</u> realize a decided financial boon because all interest payments are tax deductible, <u>whereas</u> the <u>renter</u>'s money, not being deductible, is gone forever.

This rewritten paragraph makes generous use of repetition and transition pointers to ensure the coherence of its ideas. For example, "home owner" and "renter" are repeated several times; the transitions, "moreover" and "whereas," are used to knit together sentences and ideas. The sentences, "*Home owners* know each time they make their mortgage payments that they are indirectly enriching themselves," and "*Renters* know each time they make their rent payments that they are directly enriching only the landlord," create a sense of continuity with their parallel structures (for more on parallelism, see Part 5). We can easily follow the ideas of the revised paragraph because the writer has carefully linked them together with these mechanical techniques.

Of the three techniques, modern writers are more apt to use mechanical transitions and repeated key terms over parallelism, a proportion which holds true in our own writing. Parallelism is a nice occasional touch, but it confers an air of ceremonial formality to writing. If you cannot think of appropriate transitions to use, consider the following options:

1. When an example is to follow:
   as an illustration, for instance, for example, in other words, specifically, that is
2. When a comparison is to follow:
   in comparison, likewise, similarly, also, as
3. When a contrast is to follow:
   in contrast, yet, but, although, however, nevertheless, on the contrary, on the other hand, otherwise
4. When an additional comment is to follow:
   furthermore, further, then, besides, also, and, first, second, next, last, moreover, and then, yet another
5. When a result is to follow:
   therefore, as a consequence, consequently, as a result, accordingly, then
6. When a concession is to be granted:
   admittedly, granted that, naturally, of course, one must admit, after all
7. When a summary is to follow:
   finally, all in all, on the whole, last, in conclusion, as has been stated, to summarize

If you find our suggestions here too mechanical for your taste, we will leave you with this ancient and intuitive suggestion for ensuring paragraph coherence: *make sure each sentence of your paragraph begins with old information and ends by adding new.* Indeed, this commonsense advice is exactly what the sentences of a paragraph should do. Each should begin by directly or obliquely serving up some information contained in the sentence before; each should end by adding a little to it. If you make a point of faithfully practicing this advice, your paragraphs will automatically be coherent. Here is an example:

> Samuel Johnson has fascinated more people than any other writer except Shakespeare. Statesmen, lawyers, and physicians quote him, as do writers and scientists, philosophers and farmers, manufacturers and leaders of labor unions. For generations people have been discovering new details about him and re-examining and correcting old ones. Interest in Johnson is by no means confined to the English-speaking world, though naturally it is strongest there. In Asia, Africa, and South America, groups of Johnsonians

meet every year to talk about every aspect of him. The reason why Johnson has always fascinated so many people of different kinds is not simply that Johnson is so vividly picturesque and quotable, though these are the qualities that first catch our attention. The deeper secret of his hypnotic attraction, especially during our own generation, lies in the immense reassurance he gives to human nature, which needs—and quickly begins to value—every friend it can get.

—From *Samuel Johnson,* W. Jackson Bute

The sentences of this paragraph follow this advice: each begins with the old and ends by adding something new. For example, the first sentence tells us that Samuel Johnson has fascinated many people. The second opens with this fascination and ends by enumerating the kinds of people who feel it. Sentence number three tells us that this fascination has been carried on for generations and adds that it has resulted in new discoveries about Johnson. The fourth sentence begins with the fascination for Johnson in the English speaking world and ends by extending it elsewhere on the globe. And so it goes.

The basic function of a sentence is to deliver an increment of meaning; the basic function of the paragraph, to organize this increment into a serving. Paragraphs, in turn, make up pages, sections, parts, or chapters, which are even larger portions of meaning. Writers impart meaning in essays and longer works through successive paragraphs written with thematic or mechanical connections between them. (For more on the connection between paragraphs and how to ensure it, see Chapter 6 on "The Beginning, Middle and Ending.") The paragraph is sometimes used in isolation, as is the sentence. But both sentence and paragraph will most typically form part of a larger work and must rhetorically and grammatically reflect that fact.

Exercises

1. Draw a line through any sentence in the following paragraph that weakens its unity:

> In Henrik Ibsen's play *Hedda Gabler,* the major contributing factors to Hedda's confusion and inability to accept her new life with her husband are her notions of aristocracy and superiority, which she considers her birthright as the daughter of the late General Gabler. In this respect, she reminds one of Faulkner's Miss Emily, who likewise came from an aristocratic background but fell in love with one not of her own class. Hedda's father, even in death, is Hedda's controlling force. This fact is evident if one considers the title of the play. A title is often an important clue to the action and theme of a play. Consider Shakespeare's *The Taming of the Shrew* or

Much Ado About Nothing. In both cases the title tells us what the message of the play is. In a letter, Ibsen wrote: "The title of the play is *Hedda Gabler.* My intention in giving it this name was to indicate that Hedda, as a personality, is to be regarded rather as her father's daughter than as husband's wife." The audience is introduced to the venerable gentleman in the opening scenes of the play, and his portrait is a dominating factor of the set throughout. Indeed, Hedda's sense of security and control is seen in terms of her physical proximity to the portrait at several points in the play. Inevitably some critics tried to read into the play statements about social issues. For instance, one critic saw it as a strong attack on conformist respectability. But it really is a play about human beings and their destinies.

2. Identify the most obvious techniques used in the following paragraph to achieve coherence:

> Enormous amounts of time, money, and talent go into commercials. Technically they are often brilliant and innovative, the product not only of the new skills and devices but of imaginative minds. A few of them are both funny and endearing. Who, for instance, will forget the miserable young man with the appalling cold, or the kids taught to use—as an initiation into manhood—a fork instead of a spoon with a certain spaghetti? Among the enlightened sponsors, moreover, are some who manage to combine an image of their corporation and their products with accuracy and restraint.
> —Marya Mannes, "Television: The Splitting Image."

Using the Thesis as a Guide to Paragraph Development

The wording of a thesis statement can often predict the topics of an essay and, therefore, of its paragraphs. Here is an example:

```
    Like most young men I love to eat and eat
and eat.  If I had just one wish it would be to
be able to cook.  Being able to cook my own
meals would keep my stomach full and give me a
pleasant taste in my mouth, keep my body
healthy, and keep my bank account in the black.
```

It is evident from this thesis statement (underlined) not only what the writer must do, but also more or less what the topic sentences of the successive paragraphs should be. Here are the topic sentences that the writer actually used:

First paragraph: To be able to cook like Mom would keep my stomach full and give me a pleasant taste in my mouth.

Second paragrah: Not only would my stomach be full and my taste buds happy, but the rest of my body would also be content and healthy.

Third paragraphs: My life would not be the only thing on cloud nine; my bank account would be there too.

The example teaches two lessons. First, that writing an essay requires a sense of **connection** between the thesis statement and the paragraphs that are its necessary subtopics. This should seem a matter of common sense, but it is a point often ignored by beginning writers who tend to set down one agenda in the thesis and carry out another in the paragraphs.

The second lesson is that as a literary form the paragraph serves two masters. It is the subtopic of an essay; but it is also a group of individual sentences logically connected to make a single point. This single point, in turn, must enlarge on the thesis. For example, here is the first paragraph the student wrote about how being able to cook would help keep his stomach full:

Like most young men I enjoy only one type of cooking: Mom's. To be able to cook like Mom would keep my stomach full and give me a pleasant taste in my mouth. I would be able to enjoy eating a satisfying and filling meal at one gorgeous sitting, instead of incessantly snacking every 20 minutes as I now do. I would be able to savor every morsel of every course,

```
and my stomach would tingle with happiness as
every mouthful went down.  I could make all of
my favorite dishes:  enchilada, lasagna, and
quiche.  Of course, I would also cook all the
fabulous desserts:  all the apple pies, cheese
cakes, and Danish pancakes I crave today but
seldom get.  Just thinking about being able to
cook like my Mom makes me and my stomach
deliriously happy.
```

Notice the dual purpose served by the paragraph. On the one hand, its individual details support its topic sentence. But on the other hand, the paragraph as a whole backs up and adds to the thesis statement, "Being able to cook my own meals would keep my stomach full and give me a pleasant taste in my mouth, keep my body healthy, and keep my bank account in the black."

The Organizing Principle Behind Paragraphs

In planning what to say in your paragraphs, you can use the thesis statement to predict your subsequent topics, especially if you have properly worded it. But the thesis statement can do even more: it can also help you determine the abstract structure of your individual paragraphs.

The abstract structure of a paragraph results from the organizing strategy the writer has used to write it. All paragraphs have an organizing strategy, some purposeful intent the writer has used to meld its sentences into a single unit of meaning. Depending on the temperament of the writer, this intent may be deliberately thought out ahead of time or devised on the spur-of-the-moment during the actual composition. The most common strategies are *narration, description, definition, example, process, classification, comparison/contrast, causal analysis,* and *argumentation.* A paragraph developed by narration, for example, uses the techniques of that strategy to organize and relate a story. Similarly, a paragraph developed by comparison/contrast uses the techniques of that strategy to make clear the similarities and differences between two items.

Ideally, the rhetorical strategy used to develop a paragraph should be the most natural expression of its main idea. Grasping which strategy to use in developing a paragraph is largely a matter of common sense, as the following examples show:

Topic sentence: On my fourteenth birthday a tragedy hit my family that taught me the value of respecting one's elders.

Rhetorical strategy: <u>Narration.</u> The writer will narrate an experience.

Topic sentence: The Statue of Liberty has a virtuous, noble bearing.

Rhetorical strategy: <u>Description.</u> The writer will describe the statue.

Topic sentence: The word <u>gay</u> as applied to homosexuals has an ambiguous history.

Rhetorical strategy: <u>Definition.</u> The writer will do an etymological study of the word <u>gay.</u>

Topic sentence: Women and men today are obsessed with looking young.

Rhetorical strategy: <u>Example.</u> The writer will provide some appropriate examples of how women and men reveal their obsession with looking young.

Topic sentence: Improving one's reading ability involves five major steps.

Rhetorical strategy: <u>Process.</u> The writer will explain the five steps in appropriate order.

Topic sentence: Literature can be divided into four genres: short story, drama, poetry, and novel.

Rhetorical strategy: <u>Classification.</u> The writer will describe and explain each genre in turn.

Topic sentence: The pastime of nineteenth-century dueling was different in France than it was in Austria.

Rhetorical strategy: <u>Comparison/ contrast.</u> The writer will contrast the French and Austrian practices of the duel.

Topic sentence: Human laughter, according to the French philosopher Henri Bergson, has a surprising and simple cause.

Rhetorical strategy: <u>Causal analysis.</u> The writer will cite Bergson's view of what causes human beings to laugh.

Topic sentence: All mothers should be encouraged to breast-feed their infants.

Rhetorical strategy: <u>Argumentation.</u> The writer will try to convince the reader of the rightness of this proposition. (This mode of development will be treated in Chapter 12.)

In deciding which rhetorical strategy to use, be guided by your controlling idea or purpose. Ask yourself, what are the logical divisions of my thesis statement? What should I do and say first, what second? Sometimes the answer will be obvious. For example, the student who wrote the essay about longing to be able to cook developed all its paragraphs by the pattern of cause/effect implicit in the thesis. Every paragraph detailed the good *effects* learning to cook was expected to have on different aspects of his life (see pages 118–19).

But how would you develop this thesis statement and with what kind of paragraphs?

In a matter of mere years, the personal computer revolution has gone from boom to bust

```
mainly because the expected usefulness of the
machines did not live up to the hype.
```

You begin by putting yourself in your reader's shoes and by asking those commonsense questions that immediately come to mind. First, what do you mean by the "computer revolution"? Your opening paragraph, then, might *define* that term. Second, what do you mean when you say that computers have gone from boom to bust? What you mean is that sales of computers have levelled off and are declining, several manufacturers have gone broke, and computer retailers have closed in droves. A paragraph organized by *example* could efficiently convey these facts. Third, you now have to account for the decline in the popularity of the personal computer, which will require a paragraph organized by *cause and effect*.

There is, as you can see, nothing especially mystifying in this process. What you are doing is asking yourself questions about your thesis statement that would logically occur to any interested reader, and then answering them in appropriately organized paragraphs. For that matter, your answer could take the form of a paragraph written in a mixed strategy, where you do two or three different things at once. Be warned, however, that because the mixed strategy paragraph is one of shifting purpose, writing it well requires a strong sense of transition. (See pages 140–42, for the use of transitions.) Seasoned writers can and do write mixed paragraphs because they know how to move gracefully from doing one thing to doing another without leaving the reader behind. This comes with practice and experience. Beginners are better off staying with pure forms until they have acquired this knack.

The chapters that follow contain a detailed discussion of the various rhetorical modes, with explanations of the patterns and techniques behind them. (Argumentation is treated separately in Chapter 12 since it tends to be a hybrid.) Rhetorical strategies can help you organize your thoughts by focusing your paragraphs, and if you should ever tumble into that "I-don't-know-what-to-say" ditch, knowing how to use them can help you to clamber out. Do not, however, regard them as absolutes into which every idea you have must necessarily be crammed or never committed to paper. The rhetorical strategies are nothing more than convenient patterns for expressing your ideas and thoughts; consequently, their usefulness will vary from writer to writer.

Exercises

1. Explain what mode of development would be most appropriate for the following topic sentences:

a. In terms of expense, time, and convenience, the microwave oven is far superior to the conventional oven.

b. Let me explain the easiest way to make a kite that will, on a windy day, soar like a bird.

c. For peculiarly economic reasons, many young adults are choosing to live at home rather than venture out on their own.

d. Chicago is populated by three types of denizens.

e. I was nine years old and living in the Bronx, New York, when I learned a memorable lesson about class differences from witnessing a conflict between a commuter and a bag lady.

f. Love is an often used term whose meaning is seldom clearly understood.

g. The lobbying combination of religion and politics on some issues has produced a clear threat to certain constitutionally guaranteed freedoms.

h. My dog Napoleon is so emaciated that he can hardly walk and so weathered that he looks as if he might die at any minute.

2. The late sociologist Margaret Mead once observed: "The family is the toughest institution we have." Assuming the use of Mead's statement as a topic sentence for a unified paragraph, delete any sentence in the list below that would break its unity:

a. Families are capable of undergoing considerable change and stress without being destroyed.

b. History has witnessed the decay and destruction of numerous families—even entire dynasties.

c. Sometimes what we normally think of as destructive forces may strengthen the family.

d. Despite the present high rate of divorce, most couples want to get married (or remarried) and want to have children.

e. It is difficult to assess just how many couples will have children who are either retarded, handicapped, or socially delinquent.

f. Married couples have obviously not rejected parenthood.

g. According to a recent article in the *New York Times,* cohabitation without being married is mostly a period of experimentation before moving on to conventional marriage and family life.

h. Most women work hard to combine their careers with devotion to family life.

i. Some careers held by women make a good family life impossible.

j. At the present time, and into the foreseeable future, households with married couples directing their families remain the predominant social arrangement.

k. There is good reason to believe that the family is under siege, but it may survive.

3. All the transitions and pointer phrases such as, "for example," "more-over," "however," and so on have been deleted from the following paragraphs. Restore them where you think they should go, using whatever words or phrases you think suitable.

   (1) Most words have at least two meanings—a denotative meaning and a connotative meaning—and this duality is partly responsible for their frequent ambiguity. The denotation of a word is its direct, explicit meaning. It is what the word literally stands for. *Lion* is a word denoting the mammal that biologists classify as *Penthera Leo.* The connotation of a word consists of the cluster of implications associated with it. To be called a lion is generally accepted as a compliment; to be called a sheep is not.

   (2) Today's popular groups have opened up punk rock to more than a select few individuals. It has become a trendy, diverse, and widely accepted type of music. Punk rockers play in various places, ranging from daytime outdoor park concerts to the chic clubs that come alive with the setting of the sun. The clubs in The Village are geared towards the wealthy and vogue clientele, concentrating on the quality of sound and atmosphere. Most clubs offer a large dance floor in front of the stage which creates a "dance concert" influence on the audience. Performers like the audience to get involved with the music and react in dance-type movements.

   (3) "Women's language" shows up in all levels of English. Women are encouraged and allowed to make far more precise discriminations in naming colors than men do. Words like *mauve, beige, ecru, aquamarine, lavender,* and so on, are unremarkable in a woman's active vocabulary, but largely absent from that of most men. I know of no evidence suggesting that women see a wider range of colors than men do. It is simply that fine discriminations of this sort are relevant to women's vocabularies, but not to men's; to men, who control most of the interesting affairs of the world, such distinctions are trivial—irrelevant.

   (4) The trouble is that with everything on earth (and off, too) being quantified, micro and macro, the world is becoming woefully littered with numbers that defy human comprehension. Biology estimates that the human brain contains some 1 trillion cells. But can any imagination get a practical hold on such a quality? It is easy to picture the symbolic numerals: 1,000,000,000,000. Who can comprehend that many individual units at one time? The number teases, dazzles the mind and even dizzies it, but that does not add up to understanding. Biology ought to find out what happens to the brain when it tries to visualize 1 trillion.

Writing Assignments

1. Drawing specific details from your own observations and personal experiences, write a paragraph on one of the topics below:
   a. A description of my favorite relative
   b. Causes of poor grades in school
   c. Steps in writing an essay
   d. My definition of respect
   e. A friend compared to an acquaintance

2. Compose a topic sentence suitable for use in a paragraph that would include the supporting details listed below. Then write the paragraph, inserting whatever transitions or pointers are necessary to make it coherent.
   (1) A girl may be described as "lively" or "vivacious."
   (2) "Lively" is a native formation from the familiar English noun *life.*
   (3) "Vivacious" is a Latin derivative with exactly the same meaning as "lively."
   (4) "Lively" is a popular word usually learned from family and friends in casual chats.
   (5) "Vivacious" is a learned word that we usually first got from reading or a grown-up.

3. Find the supporting details necessary to adequately back one of the topic sentences below. Write the paragraph using the chosen topic sentence and your supporting details. Use whatever technique is necessary to achieve coherence.
   a. Earthquakes can cause widespread devastation and inflict untold numbers of casualties.
   b. The year 1968 was ruinously marked by political upheaval and assassination.
   c. Diabetes is far more prevalent and debilitating than is generally recognized.
   d. Home computers are widely used to serve a variety of useful functions.

Chapter

6

The Beginning, Middle, and Ending

*'B*egin at the beginning,' the King said gravely, 'and go on till you come to the end: then stop.'

LEWIS CARROLL (1832–1898)

The first law of incisive beginnings is a simple one: Begin at the beginning. This is no Oriental paradox. Many essays typically begin too soon, too distant from the point of contention and waste the first few sentences on needless fluff. Generally, this is exactly the sort of flaw to correct in revision. Here is an example of what we mean. The assigned topic was, "Our society expects us to play many difficult and confining roles." One student began thus:

```
     Roles are what we all play, or so
sociologists tell us.  Many definitions of roles
have been given, but the one that seems to fit
sees the role as the equivalent of psychological
clothes.  Thus, an understanding of role playing
is important to the individual's maturing
process.  We may wear the uniform of the service
station attendant at work, but what we do not
know is that we are also dressed in a
psychological uniform.  Mostly, we play at being
what we are supposed to be at the moment.  Roles
are confining by definition, since they force a
mask over one's true face.  But it is my belief
that this mask, and the wearing of it, is not
necessarily bad.  Without the comforting mask of
roles, we would be thrown back on improvising on
every occasion, and many of us would do badly.
It is better that we have the part already
```

```
written out for us by the role, and that we
merely speak the lines from the script.
```

This is not a fatally bad beginning. The writer has some good ideas, and the analogy between role playing and the theater is cleverly put. What troubled her peer editing group about this beginning, however, is that it serves up a needless definition and unnecessary commentary before telling where the writer stands or what position towards roles she intends to take. Many in the group felt that editing and revision would result in a stronger beginning. This is what the writer did in her revision:

```
    ~~Roles are what we all play, or so
sociologists tell us.   Many definitions of roles
have been given, but the one that seems to fit
sees the role as the equivalent of psychological
clothes.   Thus, an understanding of role playing
is important to the individual's maturing
process.   We may wear the uniform of the service
station attendant at work, but what we do not
know is that we are also dressed in a
psychological uniform.   Mostly, we play at being
what we are supposed to be at the moment~~.   Roles
are confining by definition, since they force a
mask over one's true face.   But it is my belief
that this mask, and the wearing of it, is not
necessarily bad.   Without the comforting mask of
roles, we would be thrown back on improvising on
                        which
every occasion, ~~and~~ many of us ~~would~~ do badly.
It is better that we have the part already
written out for us by the role, and that we
~~merely~~ speak the lines from the script.
```

Her opening paragraph now reads:

```
     Roles are confining by definition, since

they force a mask over one's true face.  But it

is my belief that this mask, and the wearing of

it, is not necessarily bad.  Without the

comforting mask of roles, we would be thrown

back on improvising on every occasion, which

many of us do badly.  It is better that we have

the part already written out for us by the role,

and that we speak the lines from the script.
```

With the revision, the essay now begins at the beginning, the point of contention, the opening theme of the essay. Imagine your reader as an inquisitive person and your paragraph a stranger met at a bus stop. "What are you about?" is what the reader is most likely to ask. If your personified paragraph has any manners, it will state its business but not press on a stranger its full range of opinions too early. And that is exactly what the newly edited paragraph now does: it states the essay's business, the writer's attitude, and then politely ends. Later, the writer will tell us how roles have affected her life and give examples of how comforting and liberating she has sometimes found them to be. But that is later. For now, her opening paragraph does its job without flourish, curlicue, or ado.

As the example demonstrates, your real beginning may be buried several sentences, even paragraphs, into the essay and can be coaxed out only by the editorial blade. We have occasionally found a beginning pages into a chapter. If you are unhappy with your beginning, do not be faint-hearted about revising and editing it until you are completely satisfied. It is commonplace for writers to repeatedly revise and rewrite their beginnings long after they have arrived at the essay's ending.

Take a Stand

Since the essay is basically a brief literary form, it is always best to get down to brass tacks early, to tell your reader where you stand, how you feel, what you think. And the first paragraph is exactly the place to make this declaration. Yet many writers often begin their essays by proverbially beating about the bush, not coming to the point, not declaring their opinions or attitudes. Here is one such example. The assigned topic was, "Why do some couples choose to live together without marrying?"

Living together without being married is no
longer a taboo. Millions of Americans are
presently enjoying this state of being. Could
this be because of the divorce rate? Many
people are getting divorced rather than married
because divorces last longer. Whatever the
reason, the fact remains that some couples
choose to live together without getting
married.

Do you see what's wrong with this? It is faltering, wimpy, and wishy-washy. The author has no position, takes no stand, commits to no cause. Paradoxically, the essay in which a writer gives no opinion or takes no stand is the hardest of all to write. If you take a stand on the topic, you are likely to be fired up with the zeal of proving your case or defending your point. But if you haven't decided how you feel or what you want to say, you are in for trouble. The best thing to do under such circumstances is not to write more, but to think more. Examine how you really feel about the topic. That is what this student did, at the urging of her peer editing group. She decided, after some soul-searching, that she altogether disapproved of couples' living together. Then she rewrote her entire essay, including its beginning. Here is her new opening paragraph:

Living out of wedlock is a fashionable and
trendy arrangement today practiced by couples of
nearly every age group. It is said to be a less
complicated alliance than marriage, to ease the
complications when the day of separation finally
comes, and to more fairly split the expenses and
chores of housekeeping. But it is still an
arrangement that makes a virtue out of
convenience and temporariness in relationships,
and that is exactly why it is morally and
socially bankrupt.

Do you feel your hackles rising? Or conversely, do you find yourself nodding vigorously? If you have either reaction, good! The opening paragraph has done its job—it's gotten your interest, and whether it has done that by riling you to a fury or sending you into a thunder of applause is beside the point. The point is that you want to read on, and that is exactly what a first paragraph should make you want to do.

Do you have no opinion on the topic? Then change your topic (and reread the chapter on finding the thesis). Find an opinion! There is no magic formula for doing this, but reading decidedly helps. Read magazine articles, newspaper stories, books, and even cartoons, and soon you will find yourself reacting with agreement or opposition to an author's point of view. That reaction is the beginning of opinion.

Use Various Kinds of Openings

Your essay does not have to lurch off with an introductory preamble patently intended as an usher for its thesis. And even if you intend to seat your thesis in the same pew every time—as the final sentence of the opening paragraph—you can at least lead it there by a different aisle.

You can, for example, begin with an **anecdote.** This example comes from a student paper in psychology that attempts to define *normal:*

```
One cold winter afternoon Fumiko Kimura

calmly walked into the turbulent Pacific Ocean

holding her four-year-old son and six-month-old

daughter by the hand.  She meant to take her

life and the lives of her two children after

discovering that for the last three years her

husband had secretly kept a mistress.  The

children drowned, but Fumiko herself was rescued

and tried for murder.  To the general American

public her actions appeared bizarrely abnormal,

but in the Japanese community, where seppuku

(ritual suicide) has been traditional in cases

of tarnished honor, the action appeared normal.

What, then, is normal?  The term normal . . . .
```

You can open with what journalists call a **bullet lead**—a short, punchy sentence that clouts the reader on the side of the head and says, "pay attention." Admittedly, bullet leads are not easy to think up, but they reward the effort in effectiveness. Here is an example from a student paper:

```
     Your spouse can give you lung cancer.  And

so can your boyfriend, your girlfriend, your

grandmother.  Anyone who smokes regularly and

heavily around you can give you lung cancer.

Scientists are discovering that passive smoking

is deadlier than they had imagined.
```

This opening grabs your attention right away by being direct, blunt, and unequivocal.

Also effective is the **spotlight opening,** which begins in the middle of things with an image, a scene, or description that dramatizes the topic. You get the chance to insert catchy details and create an impression of reportorial immediacy before launching your thesis. Here is another student writer's use of the spotlight opening:

```
     The victim, a woman in her mid-twenties,

was found slumped on the living room floor, the

side of her head partly bashed in by the blow

from an ashtray.  The house had been ransacked,

the furniture overturned, clothes strewn over

the bed.  For all his cruelty, the thief earned

blood wages of $20, which the victim had hidden

in a vanity drawer.  Ten years later, as the

recovered victim was shopping in downtown

Chicago, she came face to face with her

attacker, screamed for the police, and had him

arrested.  But the charges were dropped because

the statute of limitations on the crime had

expired.  This unexpected outcome seemed to the
```

```
victim a grave injustice.  But although it

allows an occasional criminal to get away with a

crime, the statute of limitations is a

worthwhile curb that does more good than harm.
```

Of course, one should not invent such details, but should uncover them by honest research. Do your homework, find the details you need, and you are ready to create a spotlight opening that will add drama to your thesis.

Finally, you may open with a **quotation.** If the quotation is apt and neatly sums up some essential element of your thesis, it can be an effective beginning. On the other hand, if the quotation is blurry or irrelevant, you could be off to a bad start. Here is an example of a good start from a student essay extolling the benefits of travel:

```
    Francis Bacon, the English sixteenth-

century philosopher, once wrote:  "Travel, in

the younger sort, is a part of education; in the

elder, a part of experience.  He that travelleth

into a country before he hath some entrance into

the language, goeth to school, and not to

travel." Indeed, for centuries the English

regarded travel as so essential to a young

person's education that the English gentleman

always ended his formal schooling with an

extensive trip to the European continent known

as the "grand tour." Travel is a broadening

experience which teaches lessons about foreign

countries and people that you cannot learn from

any book.
```

It is possible to write an essay with a bad beginning but a good middle. Many have done so, claiming that they were cold at the start but progressively warmed to the topic as they went on. One answer to this complaint is to wait until you are loose and thoroughly warmed up before rewriting your beginning.

Exercises

1. From the following paired openings, choose the one with greater reader appeal. Be prepared to give reasons for your choice.

   a.(1) Shakespeare's *King Lear* has often been hailed by critics as Shakespeare's greatest play because the main character vividly dramatizes important truths about life. The play is filled with plots and counterplots that underscore the complexities of life and its sorrows. It is a play that reaches magnificent tragic heights. All of the main characters are three-dimensional and therefore believable. No wonder the popularity of this play has lasted for over three centuries.

   (2) He disowned the only daughter who truly loved him. He spoiled the two daughters who flattered him to get his money and power. He was a vain old man with a mammoth craving for monopolized attention. But in the end he is more sinned against than sinning when, bereft of his kingdom and his sanity, he is pushed out into a raging storm and left to rant and rage on the weather-beaten heath. Few other plays in any language portray more vividly the wretchedness of human life than does *King Lear.*

   b.(1) Ulysses S. Grant, the man who won the Civil War, represents one of history's typical paradoxes—the mediocre person who, through some mysterious combination of circumstance, achieves momentary splendor. Despite the many sleazy facts associated with his life (his drinking, his swindles, and his lower-class tastes), he stumbled onto history's center stage to thrill the audience for a scene or two. He made the American dream come true by becoming a successful military commander and gaining two terms in the White House. Grant has become the symbol of the extraordinary possibilities contained within the ordinary.

   (2) Ulysses Simpson Grant, who lived from 1822 to 1885, became commander in chief of the Union Army during the Civil War and eighteenth president of the United States. Grant was in many ways not a spectacular man. For instance, before joining the army, he was a simple clerk selling cordwood in St. Louis and Galena. He was even forced to resign from the army in 1854 because of excessive drinking. He failed in his attempts to become a farmer and a businessman. His presidency was a national disgrace because of considerable corruption. Yet, Grant made a lasting name for himself.

2. Identify the kinds of leads used in the following opening paragraphs:
   a. It began just the way a good spy story should. Early in 1981 an un-named Frenchman walked into the Paris headquarters of the Direc-tion de la Surveillance du Territoire, the French counterintelligence agency, carrying a letter that he said he had been asked to smuggle out of Moscow. . . .
      —"Secret Admirer," *Time,* January 20, 1986.

   b. For some, it was like being told chocolate cures cancer. A study re-cently released by a Johns Hopkins researcher showed that moderate beer drinkers were sick 25 percent less often than teetotalers or those who drink stronger spirits.
      —"Beer Drinkers Grab onto Study Results with Gusto," *Atlanta Constitution,* January 14, 1986.

   c. I once had a gutsy English teacher who used a drugstore paperback called *Word Power Made Easy* instead of the insipid fare officially available. It contained some nifty words and she would call upon us in turn for definitions. . . .
      —Stephen Jay Gould, "Agassiz in the Galapagos."

3. Choose one of the following controlling ideas and find a quotation that could be used as a suitable opening:
   a. Total dependency on someone of the opposite sex is destructive.
   b. People exaggerate when they apply for a job.
   c. Chicago (or New York, or Los Angeles, or any other major city) is a fascinating city.
   d. Punctuality is a good habit to cultivate.

The Middle

Problems of careless, frail, or nonexistent transitions between para-graphs are typical middle essay weaknesses. It is a mistake to think that be-cause paragraphs are sequential their ideas must follow logically. Logical continuity between the ideas of different paragraphs is the result of some deliberate bridging by the writer—mainly through the use of transitions. Your aim in the middle of the essay should therefore be to caulk the seams between your paragraphs until their separate topics and ideas dovetail with the continuity and smoothness of watertight planking.

How do you accomplish this? First, you master some common tech-niques for making paragraph transitions. Second, you put them to use in your essay. Transitions between paragraphs have two functions: they signal an end to the present discussion; they announce a new beginning. Indirectly, they say to a reader, "We've done with this now; we're about to take up that."

In a few instances, when paragraphs succeed one another with a clear and obvious sameness of purpose, no formal transitions between them is necessary. Here is an example:

> Next to Hitler, Goring was the most popular Nazi leader in the country and the most powerful. As prime minister and minister of the interior of Prussia, he had a great deal of power in the most important and largest part of Germany. He had control of the Prussian police and of most of the rest of the government apparatus. He set up the Gestapo, the secret police, to terrorize any lurking opposition and founded the concentration camps in which to incarcerate any who defied the Nazi authority or who were Communists, Socialists, liberals, pacifists, and/or Jews. He was president of the Reichstag. He was boss of German aviation, both civil and now military. He would soon be given more titles by Hitler that would make him pretty much the czar of the economy.
>
> He got things done. He also loved luxury and opulence and already had begun to acquire several castles and to build a fantastic showplace outside Berlin which he called Karin Hall, after his deceased Swedish wife. He was also said to be a morphine addict, though he would kick the habit for fairly long periods only to fall back into it when the strain of life got him down. Goring was an authentic war hero, the last commander of the famed Richthofen Fighter Squadron, one of the rare holders of Germany's highest war decoration, *Pour le Merite,* though he was only an army captain when he was mustered out.
>
> —William L. Shirer, *The Nightmare Years: 1930–1940.*

The writer uses no formal transition between the paragraphs because they are both focused on the common purpose of describing the Nazi war criminal Hermann Goring.

Instances like this aside, it is usually necessary to join paragraphs by some formal transitions of varying strength, depending on the degree of difference between the linked paragraphs' contents. Where there is an obvious similarity in the ideas of two paragraphs, or even in their purpose, little or no transition is needed. But where there is a gaping difference in idea and purpose, some obvious bonding between the paragraphs will be necessary or your essay will seem disjointed. Here are some ideas for linking paragraphs together with smooth transitions.

Repeat key words at the beginning of each new paragraph

Repeating key words from the thesis statement at the beginning of each new paragraph is a good transitional technique for short essays. The repetition holds the reader's attention on the subject while cementing the paragraphs together with a common theme. Here is an example from a student essay:

Social pressure is an ever present force. Whether it is experienced in small or large degrees, social pressure affects all of us. We get it from the people at work, from friends, and even from our parents.

At my own job I am under constant <u>social pressure</u> to do well. Being a bank teller, I am graded each week by a merit system which reviews overages and shortages in my money drawer and my relationship with my customers. I have also found that fellow workers can exert a great deal of pressure. For example, every year the bank has a number of parties. Being a nondrinker and a nonsmoker I prefer not to go to the parties. Even though I have explained my reasons for not attending, there is still the ever present <u>pressure</u> from co-workers for me to attend the parties, usually with a few added "goody-two-shoes" remarks.

Friends also have a way of exerting <u>social pressure,</u> though it is usually very subtle. During my last year in high school my best

```
friend's personality began to change, and our
friendship slowly dwindled.  A few months ago
she told me that she had gotten involved with
the wrong crowd during our senior year, and
before she realized what was happening she had
let herself be persuaded into all sorts of
trouble.
```

The underlined key words serve as a kind of thematic glue between the paragraphs, enabling a reader to follow the writer's reasoning easily.

Begin the new paragraph by restating the idea that ended the old

Restating an idea is a subtler and more complicated transition used mainly in long essays. Here is an example:

```
     A revolution within our society has been
raging for over a decade, causing radical
changes to occur in the roles of the female.  A
concept of individualism without regard to sex
has evolved into the American ethic with
dramatic results.  Women have gained a greater
sense of worth that has led to increased sexual
freedom and career potential.  Women have also
gained a greater equality in the home, becoming
breadwinners with a more mutual sharing of the
housework.  They have been released both in the
job market and in styles from the traditional
female roles of the past.  But what of the
male's freedom?  If the female has the right to
```

break with the old norms, why does the male
still have to perform within strict masculine
guidelines? <u>While the female has been able to
assume new roles, the male has been only further
imprisoned in his old ones.</u>

    <u>The imprisonment of the male is partly
social and partly self-imposed.</u> Society has long
dictated the roles of the sexes and even with
the advent of women's liberation, not much has
dramatically changed for the male . . . .

Notice that the idea that ended the first paragraph is restated at the beginning of the second, resulting in a smooth transition.

Ask a rhetorical question

    A question that sums up and extends the note on which the previous paragraph ended can also serve as a strong transition. Here is an example taken from a student essay on sailboats:

    There are three main types of rigs among
small pleasure sailing craft with keels. The
first is the sloop. This rig consists of a
single mast and two sails, a main and a jib.
The second is the cutter. This rig uses a main
and usually two small jibs. Cutters have the
advantage of having two smaller and more
manageable jibs in place of a large and unwieldy
one. The third is the ketch, and its variation,
the yawl. This rig uses two masts and usually
three sails: the mizzen, the main, and a jib.

    <u>What prevents the keel sailboat from</u>

> capsizing? The answer is grounded in the laws of
>
> physics and in the design of keel boats. When
>
> the boat heels, its rudder . . . .

Naturally, the question must not only be to the point, it must nudge the discussion into the topic of the new paragraph.

Use transition phrases

Many writers have and use a stock of favorite transition words and phrases to lash together paragraphs. These include such faithful standbys as "besides," "however," "in that case," "also," "needless to say," and "on the other hand." These phrases help the reader by pointing out the new path that the writing intends to take; they also help the writer to alter course. Here is an example from a student essay contrasting love and lust:

> One of the main differences between love
>
> and lust is the length of time that the feeling
>
> lasts. Lust is an immediate reaction towards a
>
> person, and it can fade rather quickly with the
>
> prospect of another relationship. A common
>
> example of a feeling of lust is when a young
>
> student develops an interest in a teacher, often
>
> referred to as a "crush."
>
> On the other hand, love is not nearly as
>
> easy to get over as lust and lasts a great deal
>
> longer. When two people are really in love, the
>
> relationship between them could easily last a
>
> lifetime. Love is also not affected by
>
> newcomers or new prospects, but seems to feed on
>
> and grow with the intimacy between the lovers.

"On the other hand," warns the reader that a contrast is upcoming in the new paragraph while setting the stage for the new business at hand. The suitability of a transition phrase or word depends on what your new paragraph will do and the direction it will take. See Chapter 5 for a listing of some common transition terms and their meanings.

Use an initial summarizing sentence

Magazine writers love this one, which students seldom use: You simply open your new paragraph with a sentence that refers to and sums up the meat of the discussion in the old. This gentle reminder of what has already been said becomes a lead-in for your new material. Here is an example from an essay on local governments:

```
    The basic idea of local government is that
it will solve local problems and be responsive
to local citizens.  Some of the pressing
day-to-day requirements of a community can only
be met by immediate and local response.  So
local governments run the schools, pick up the
garbage, and provide police protection for the
community.
    But making the life of its citizens run
smoother is not all local governments do. What
they are mainly supposed to do is give each
citizen the feeling of participation in his own
destiny.  This feeling . . . .
```

When we come to this opening sentence, we immediately think, "Aha! More on what local governments do will follow" and so the two paragraphs are neatly joined by a single suture.

Use a transition paragraph

Finally, there is the transition paragraph, which is a small, specialized paragraph used to shift the focus of writing between major themes. Because they are usually short and centered on a single topic, student essays seldom use transition paragraphs. But if you should need to lever your writing from one major topic to another, the transition paragraph is a handy fulcrum for doing it. Here is an excerpted example from a student paper on the unhappy lives of some European monarchs. The writer wraps up her discussion of Richard II in the first paragraph, then uses a transition paragraph (underlined) to shift her focus to the fate of Marie Antoinette.

> . . . And so Richard, only 33 years old,
> ended his days a prisoner in Pontecraft Castle,
> where Shakespeare tells us he was murdered by
> noblemen loyal to Henry IV. But even this is
> uncertain, and some historians argue that he
> starved himself to death.
>
> But sad as his last years were, Richard was
> at least spared the humiliating fate reserved
> for Marie Antoinette.
>
> Marie Antoinette was born in 1755, the
> daughter of Austrian Archduchess Maria Theresa
> and Holy Roman Emperor Francis I. Her marriage
> to the dauphin, later King Louis XVI of France,
> took place when she was 15 and was intended
>
> . . . .

Since they perform a specialized function, transition paragraphs are typically skimpy, have no topic sentence, no specific details, and no organizing pattern. They are useful only for making major transitions.

A final word on transitions. Should you find yourself stumbling badly between topics and fumbling for ways to stitch your paragraphs together, the best answer may be to rethink what you are trying to do. A well-thought-out essay shows few of its seams, and with a definite mastery of the material and a sound overall plan, a writer should not have to grope desperately for ways to tie together paragraphs. If that is what you find yourself doing, your inability to find the right transitions may be a symptom of something else wrong with your essay. Perhaps you have not yet decided exactly how to break down your subject. Or you may have taken on more than you can handle. Rather than struggling for the right word or phrase, give some thought to what you really are aiming to do and whether or not you have the order of topics properly worked out.

Exercises

1. Explain the transitions used between the following pairs of paragraphs:

a. Most tarantulas live in the tropics, but several species occur in the temperate zone and a few are common in the southern U.S. Some varieties are large and have powerful fangs with which they can inflict a deep wound. These formidable looking spiders do not, however, attack man; you can hold one in your hand, if you are gentle, without being bitten. Their bite is dangerous only to insects and small mammals such as mice; for a man it is not worse than a hornet's sting.

Tarantulas customarily live in deep cylindrical burrows, from which they emerge at dusk and into which they retire at dawn. Mature males wander about after dark in search of females and occasionally stray into houses. After mating, the male dies in a few weeks, but a female lives much longer and can mate several years in succession. In a Paris museum is a tropical specimen which is said to have been living in captivity for 25 years.
—Alexander Petrunkevitch, "The Spider and the Wasp," *Scientific American.*

b. Not that people think that love is not important. They are starved for it; they watch endless numbers of films about happy and unhappy love stories, they listen to hundreds of trashy songs about love—yet hardly anyone thinks that there is anything that needs to be learned about love.

This particular attitude is based on several premises which either singly or combined tend to uphold it. Most people see the problem of love primarily as that of *being loved,* rather than that of *loving,* of one's capacity to love. Hence the problem to them is how to be loved, how to be lovable . . . .
—Erich Fromm, *The Art of Love.*

c. Let us take, first, the plastic arts, sculpture and painting; and to bring into clear relief the Greek point of view let us contrast with it that of the modern "impressionist." To the impressionist a picture is simply an arrangement of colour and line; the subject represented is nothing, the treatment is everything. It would be better, on the whole, not even to know what objects are depicted; and, to judge the picture by a comparison with the objects, or to consider what is the worth of the objects in themselves, or what we might think of them if we came across them in the connections of ordinary life, is simply to misconceive the whole meaning of a picture. For the artist and for the man who understands arts, all scales and standards disappear except that of the purely aesthetic beauty which consists in harmony of line and tone; the most perfect human form has no more value than a splash of mud; or rather both mud and human form disappear as irrelevant, and all that is left for judgment is the arrangement of colour and form originally suggested by those accidental and indifferent phenomena.

In the Greek view, on the other hand, though we certainly cannot say that the subject was everything and the treatment nothing (for that would be merely the annihilation of art) yet we may assert that, granted the treatment, granted that the work was beautiful (the first and indispensable requirement), its worth was determined by the character of the subject. . . .
—G. Lowes Dickenson, *The Greek View of Life.*

d. The word *stress,* like *success, failure,* or *happiness,* means different things to different people, so that defining it is extremely difficult although it has become part of our daily vocabulary. Is stress merely a synonym for distress? Is it effort, fatigue, pain, fear, the need for concentration, the humiliation of censure, the loss of blood, or even an unexpected great success which requires complete reformulation of one's life? The answer is yes and no. That is what makes the definition of stress so difficult. Every one of these conditions produces stress, but none of them can be singled out as being "it," since the word applies equally to all the others.

Yet, how are we to cope with the stress of life if we cannot even define it? The businessman who is under constant pressure from his clients and employees alike, the air-traffic controller who knows that a moment of distraction may mean death to hundreds of people, the athlete who desperately wants to win a race, and the husband who helplessly watches his wife slowly and painfully dying of cancer, all suffer from stress. The problems they face are totally different, but medical research has shown that in many respects the body responds in a stereotyped manner, with identical biochemical changes, essentially meant to cope with any type of increased demand upon the human machinery. . . .
—Hans Selye, *Stress Without Distress.*

Ending the Essay

There are many ingeniously bad ways to end an essay, with new ones being daily invented. But there is one astoundingly bad ending that enjoys nearly universal popularity, and we intend to do our best to persuade you against using it. To demonstrate, we will use it as a hypothetical ending to this chapter:

```
    And so as you can see from our examples and

from what we have said before, you should try to

give your essay an inviting beginning, a solid

middle, and a crisp ending.  These are the

reasons why we think students who pay attention

to their beginnings, middles, endings, and

writing voice will write better essays.
```

The "as-you-can-see-these-are-the-reasons" ending is the weakest imaginable and is the one note you should never, never strike in your ending. This is a bad ending because it insultingly implies that your reader cannot understand your reasons nor infer what you mean without being pointedly told. Bad writers often feel compelled to point out the obvious; good writers assume that their readers are clever enough to fathom the moral of an essay or tale for themselves. Your reader can obviously grasp your reasons and already knows that they are your own and why you think them important. It is therefore unnecessary to rehash the point further. End abruptly, capriciously, even prematurely if you must; but never end with the "as-you-can-see-these-are-the-reasons" refrain.

Aside from this single principle, our message on endings is necessarily abstract. We cannot tell you how to end your essay without looking over your shoulder as you write it. What we can say is that endings, like beginnings and middles, are frequently improved by editing. Here, as an example, is the unedited ending of the essay on male and female roles:

```
    Altogether, the pressure of peers and

reverse reaction to women's liberation have

brought man even closer to the traditional male

role.  He still must represent the strong,

dominant type on the outside while keeping

sensitivity and weakness buried deep inside.

Man must remain a contradiction to his real
```

```
needs as long as society keeps the keys.  For
that reason, I believe that men will not be free
for a long time.  Men need to have their own
male revolution before they can break out of the
macho shell.  From what I have already said, I
don't know if this will ever happen.
```

Look at what happens to this ending when the student pared away the last three sentences:

```
Altogether, the pressure of peers and
reverse reaction to women's liberation have
brought man even closer to the traditional male
role.  He still must represent the strong,
dominant type on the outside while keeping
sensitivity and weakness buried deep inside.
Man must remain a contradiction to his real
needs as long as society keeps the keys.
```

Can you tell the difference between them? The first ending seems to peter out on the halfhearted expression of an opinion; the second comes to a clean and emphatic end. Because you cannot give it the documentation, support, or elaboration it would enjoy in the middle of an essay, the opinion expressed in an ending paragraph is strictly an orphan. Put your opinions in earlier, where you can defend them. Save the last paragraph for conclusions.

Like the example, many essay endings tend to be two or three sentences too long, mainly because of the composing momentum. By the time you are at the end, you've developed a head of steam and hate to stop. But stop you must, when it is time. Here, for example, is the ending paragraph of a research paper on poetry therapy:

```
If poetry therapy continues to be accepted
and practiced at the rate it is now, it could
end up becoming one of the most widely practiced
methods of therapy around.  Then perhaps poets
will finally be recognized for the major role
```

they played and still play in helping to keep
people who live in an insane society at least
partly sane. According to the author of The
Poetry Cure,

> When the day comes that poetry is an
> acceptable means of treatment we will
> understand Ludwig Van Beethoven and his
> statement, "How can we ever sufficiently
> thank that most precious treasure of a
> nation--a great poet?"

not necessary

The author goes on to express the importance of
the continued practice of poetry therapy when he
exclaims, "Not until mankind learns the
importance of creative expression to his health,
shall we have a better moral world."

Gauging the best stopping point requires an experienced ear, and ours tells us that the writer goes one quotation too far. After editing, this is what her ending sounded like:

> If poetry therapy continues to be accepted
> and practiced at the rate it is now, it could
> end up becoming one of the most widely practiced
> methods of therapy around. Then perhaps poets
> will finally be recognized for the major role
> they played and still play in helping to keep
> people who live in an insane society at least
> partly sane. According to the author of The
> Poetry Cure,
>
> When the day comes that poetry is an
> acceptable means of treatment we will

> understand Ludwig Van Beethoven and his
> statement, "How can we ever sufficiently
> thank that most precious treasure of a
> nation—a great poet?"

With removal of the final quotation, which seemed an afterthought, the ending now has more authority. Note also that the improvement is not the result of additional writing, but of editing. Endings, like beginnings, can often be improved by paring down.

Some other obvious observations may be made about endings. First, good endings always touch on their beginnings, but not too blatantly. You do not have to tie an obvious knot between them, merely hint at the existence of a common thread. Here, for example, is the beginning of an essay by Pearl Buck:

> I have long looked for an opportunity to pay a certain debt which I have owed since I was seven years old. Debts are usually burdens, but this is no ordinary debt, and it is no burden, except as the feeling of warm gratitude may ache in one until it is expressed. My debt is to an Englishman, who long ago in China rendered an inestimable service to a small American child. That child was myself and that Englishman was Charles Dickens. I know no better way to meet my obligation than to write down what Charles Dickens did in China for an American child.

It is clear what the author is starting out to do in this essay: pay homage to Dickens. Here is her ending:

> This is what Dickens did for me. His influence I cannot lose. He has made himself a part of me forever.
> —Pearl Buck, "A Debt to Dickens," *Saturday Review,* April 14, 1936.

In this ending paragraph is contained a glimpse of the beginning. But it is only a glimpse. Some business has been transacted in the essay, and the final paragraph concludes it with that quick backward glance to the beginning which is so characteristic of good endings.

Here is another beginning taken from an essay by H. L. Mencken:

> On a winter day some years ago, coming out of Pittsburgh on one of the expresses of the Pennsylvania Railroad, I rolled eastward for an hour through the coal and steel towns of Westmore-

land county. It was familiar ground: boy and man, I had been through it often before. But somehow I had never quite sensed its appalling desolation. Here was the very heart of industrial America, the center of its most lucrative and characteristic activity, the boast and pride of the richest and grandest nation on earth—and here was a scene so dreadfully hideous, so intolerably bleak and forlorn that it reduced the whole aspiration of man to a macabre and depressing joke. Here was wealth beyond computation, almost beyond imagination—and here were human habitations so abominable that they would have disgraced a race of alley cats.

And here in this essay's ending:

> Here is something that the psychologists have so far neglected: the love of ugliness for its own sake, the lust to make the world intolerable. Its habitat is the United States. Out of the melting pot emerges a race which hates beauty as it hates truth. The etiology of this madness deserves a great deal more study than it has got. There must be causes behind it; it arises and flourishes in obedience to biological laws, and not as a mere act of God. What, precisely, are the terms of those laws? And why do they run stronger in America than elsewhere? Let some honest *Privat Dozent* in pathological sociology apply himself to the problem.
> —H. L. Mencken, *A Mencken Chrestomathy.*

Ugliness is thematically present at the beginning of this essay and, with a slight variation, also at the ending. The lesson here is that if your ending is utterly and untraceably distant from your beginning, you may have ventured a paragraph too far.

Second, an ending should not introduce a topic not already thoroughly covered in the essay. The ending is not the place for asides, for additions, for overlooked ideas, for last minute chest-thumping. It should take you to the limit of your thesis and no further. Here, for example, is the beginning of a student essay on social pressure.

```
         Social pressure is an ever present force.

Whether it is suffered in small or large

degrees, each one of us experiences social

pressure from the people we work with, from

friends, and even from parents.
```

Having described the social pressure often exerted by co-workers, friends, and parents, the writer should have been content to stop. Instead, she blundered into a secondary topic in her ending; which she edited out:

> Social pressure can be bad and it can also work some good. The key is learning which pressures are meant for your benefit and which ones are not. How can you do this? First, you should ask yourself whether you are being pressured into something that goes against your conscience. If you are, then the pressure is bad and shouldn't be tolerated. Second, you should ask yourself what your own inclinations are in this matter. If you find that what you truly want is not what the pressure dictates, you should follow your own mind so long as your desires are not immoral or illegal. Live your own life, not the life of your parents or friends. There are also other things you can do to resist social pressure.

not necessary

How to resist social pressure is not part of the essay's thesis. We suggested the student edit it out. Here is what her revised ending looked like:

> Social pressure can be bad and it can also work some good. The key is learning which pressures are meant for your benefit and which ones are not.

This rounds out things nicely, with little fuss and bother.

Primarily, a good ending should bring the essay to a close that is both logical and necessary. It is logical because having done what you said you would do in the thesis statement, the only reasonable course left is to stop.

And it is necessary because anything else you write will stray beyond your thesis and make you seem long-winded. Here are some models of good endings that demonstrate what we mean:

From an essay by Will and Ariel Durant, discussing the contributions of Boris Pasternak, Aleksandr Solzhenitsyn, and Yevgeni Yevtushenko to Russian literature:

> But it may be wise for us of the West to assume that the spirit of Russia today is voiced not by the tender longings of Pasternak, nor by the bitter memories of Solzhenitsyn, but by the ardor and courage of Yevtushenko. "I want to believe," he writes, "that everything is still ahead of me, as it is for my people." Let us heartily wish them well in their internal affairs despite their sins and ours. Perhaps their experiments and their sufferings will bring some costly but precious increment to the frail intelligence of mankind.
> —Will and Ariel Durant, *Interpretations of Life.*

From an article, written by Jack Smith for *Los Angeles Magazine,* gently satirizing modern hostesses who rarely start and end their parties on time:

> Years after the war, when Gen. Smith had retired and was living in a rose-covered cottage at La Jolla, I was sent down with photographer Bruce Cox to interview him. We had an appointment for 1000 hours. I warned Cox that when Gen. Smith said 1000 hours, he didn't mean 1001. We got to the cottage on time, but Cox used up a minute or two getting his gear out of the trunk, and I told him, "I'm going on. I don't want to be late."
> I rang the doorbell. Gen. Smith himself opened the door.
> "Good morning, General," I said. "I hope I'm not late."
> The general looked at his watch and then gave me a remonstrative look.
> "Well," he said, "only a minute."
> Why can't hostesses be like that?
> —Jack Smith, *Los Angeles Magazine,* January 16, 1986.

From a student essay written on the thesis: "My idea of a beautiful woman is a big buxom German opera singer":

> Daily I pray to the great god Odin to send
> me a woman such as this.

From an article, written by Richard Leakey and Alan Walker for *National Geographic,* describing the unearthing, near Lake Turkana in Kenya, of a fossil skeleton belonging to *homo erectus:*

> Only luck, the presence of a supply of underground water, and the scanty shade of a few parched thorn trees first drew us to the Nariokotome River and the skeleton of the boy from Lake Turkana. During the 1985 excavation, we began to uncover the last of the missing bones, adding another page to his biography—and to mankind's.
> —Richard Leakey and Alan Walker, *National Geographic,* November 1985.

Finally, here is the closing paragraph of Eudora Welty's literary biography:

> . . . I am a writer who came of a sheltered life. A sheltered life can be a daring life as well. For all serious daring starts from within.
> —Eudora Welty, *One Writer's Beginnings.*

While there are no pat formulas for writing such good endings, there is a little exercise that often works for us. Write and rewrite the essay to your heart's content: do the preliminary reading and editing, make several passes at the beginning and middle, and then turn your attention to the ending. If you are unhappy with the ending because it seems weak or somehow a let-down, lop off the final sentence. If it is still unimproved, take out another sentence. Continue doing that until you suddenly find yourself at a paragraph or sentence that recaps the promise of your thesis and rounds out what you have already said with a note of finality. That is your true ending.

Exercises

1. Explain which of the following pairs of endings is more effective for each thesis statement and why.
   a. Thesis: Grave differences distinguish the working days of a blue-collar worker from that of a white-collar worker.
   (*1*) The workers leave their jobs in different ways. The blue-collar worker attempts to wash the grit of the day's work from his hands, hands which will never be clean, for dirt has found a permanent hiding place in their tiny creases. He says goodbye to his former enemy, but now his friend, the clock. His only worries are where to go drinking when his work is done. The white-collar worker leaves when his work is done. He may have to turn out

the lights. He heads home with his job on his mind, wondering whether he will make his forecasts, whether he is maximizing his investments.

(2) The workers leave their jobs in different ways. The blue-collar worker attempts to wash the grit of the day's work from his hands, hands which will never be clean, for dirt has found a permanent hiding place in their tiny creases. He says goodbye to his former enemy, but now his friend, the clock. His only worries are where to go drinking when his work is done. The white-collar worker leaves when his work is done. He may have to turn out the lights. He heads home with his job on his mind, wondering whether he will make his forecasts, whether he is maximizing his investments. But he can find peace of mind in an exercise program or some regimen of meditation. These remedies have proven to be effective in many cases for easing the transition from work to home, and are even thought by some authorities to forestall heart attacks.

b. Thesis: Today's American women are discovering that through prepared natural childbirth, they may deliver their babies more safely and easily than with the aid of drugs or surgery and have a beautiful, memorable experience in the process.

(1) Because of these reasons and other factors already discussed in the essay, it is clear that natural childbirth is superior to the drug-assisted version preferred by many hospitals and sponsored by numerous gynecologists. The couple who follows nature's way, as the examples show, will have by far an easier time of delivery than those who allow hospitals to bully them into artificial delivery.

(2) A relaxed, fearless woman can nearly be assured of delivering an alert baby whose head is not banana-shaped from a long second stage or bruised from the use of forceps. She will be proud of her own strength and perseverance, and her husband will have shared the experience with her. A couple who completes childbirth as Mother Nature dictates, but with a confidence stemming from practice and discipline, will have memories to cherish forever.

Writing Assignments

1. Write a 500-word essay arguing against one of the social nuisances listed below. Begin your essay at the *point of contention.* In other words, let your reader know immediately where you stand on the issue.

   a. dealing with people who are habitually late

b. paying the exorbitant interest rates charged by today's credit card companies

c. having to make small talk at social functions

d. buying mechanical devices that immediately break down

e. living with a sloppy roommate

2. Write a 500-word essay describing a social injustice. Begin either with an *anecdote* or with a *spotlight* opening that dramatizes the injustice. Here are some possible subjects:

a. bag ladies forced to sleep out in the open

b. the high cost of funerals

c. cruelty to animals

d. the hard life of migrant farm workers

e. hungry children in third world countries

3. Write a 500-word essay on some aspect of modern life that endangers everyone. Begin with a *bullet lead*. Here are some possible subjects:

a. lack of exercise

b. drugs

c. cigarette smoke (or some other dangerous air pollutant)

d. too much technology

e. lack of respect for the elderly

4. Write a 500-word essay for which one of the following quotations would serve as an excellent opening. Be sure to introduce the quotation:

a. "At 20 years of age, the will reigns; at 30, the wit; and at 40, the judgment."—Benjamin Franklin

b. "Two roads diverged in a wood, and I—
   I took the one less traveled by,
   And that has made all the difference."—Robert Frost

c. "For it is your business, when the wall next door catches fire."—Horace

d. "I think that I shall never see
   A billboard lovely as a tree
   Indeed, unless the billboards fall
   I'll never see a tree at all."—Ogden Nash

e. "Of all the needs (there are none imaginary) a lonely child has, the one that must be satisfied, if there is going to be hope and a hope of wholeness, is the unshaking need for an unshakable God."—Maya Angelou

f. "So, if we must have a draft registration, I would include young women as well as young men. I would include them because they can do the job. I would include them because all women must gain the status to stop as well as to start wars. I would include them because it has been too easy to send men alone.

"I would include them because I simply cannot believe that I would feel differently if my daughter were my son."—Ellen Goodman

5. Write a 300-word essay with two alternative endings on a subject of your choice. Write a paragraph analyzing which is the better ending and why.

6. Using the techniques you have learned in this chapter, rewrite and improve the ending of one of your other essays.

Chapter

7

Narrating

What is written without effort is in general read without pleasure.

SAMUEL JOHNSON (1709–1784)

Narration is an organizing pattern that treats experience in dynamic rather than static terms; people interact, events come to a climax, cause leads to effect, psychological impulses are satisfied. Something always happens. In its largest sense, narration includes history, biography, personal experience, travel, and fiction. Because we all have an instinctive curiosity about the capricious events and occurrences all around us, narration is probably the easiest mode to master. We want to know what happened. Satisfying this craving has made millionaires of many otherwise forgettable novelists.

Behind the narrative is the inevitable clock. Events in a narrative always occur one after another in time, leading to a final climax and outcome. Nor do these events always have to center on individual characters and destinies. A narrative may tell an entirely impersonal story, the tale of a nation, a people, or even a language, as in this example:

The rise of English is a remarkable success story. When Julius Caesar landed in Britain nearly two thousand years ago, English did not exist. Five hundred years later, *Englisc,* incomprehensible to modern ears, was probably spoken by about as few people as currently speak Cherokee—and with about as little influence. Nearly a thousand years later, at the end of the sixteenth century, when William Shakespeare was in his prime, English was the native speech of between five and seven million Englishmen and it was, in the words of a contemporary, "of small reatch, it stretcheth no further than this iland of ours, naie not there over all".

Four hundred years later, the contrast is extraordinary. Between 1600 and the present, in armies, navies, companies and expeditions, the speakers of English—including Scots, Irish, Welsh, American and many more—travelled into every corner of the globe, carrying their language and culture with them. Today, English is used by at least 750 million people, and barely half of those speak it as a mother tongue. Some estimates have put that figure closer to one billion. Whatever the total, English at the end of the twentieth century is more widely scattered, more widely spoken and written, than any other language has ever been. It has become *the* language of the planet, the first truly global language.
—From *The Story of English,* Robert McCrum, William Cran, Robert MacNeil

157

But the narratives most of us have grown to love are those that regale us with the stories of individual characters and give a glimpse into their hearts and minds. Here is a snippet from one such story:

> In the middle of the night I woke up suddenly and my hair was standing on end: I saw a huge black shadow in my window. Mt. Hozomeen (8080) looking in my window from miles away near Canada. I got up from the forlorn bunk with the mice scattering underneath and went outside and gasped to see black mountain shapes gianting all around; and not only that but the billowing curtains of the northern lights shifting behind the clouds. It was a little too much for a country boy. The fear that the Abominable Snowman might be breathing behind me in the dark sent me back to bed where I buried my head inside my sleeping bag.
> —Jack Kerouac, "Alone on a Mountaintop," *Holiday Magazine,* October 1958.

When would you organize an essay around the narrative strategy? The most obvious answer is when your instructor has plainly assigned you to write a narrative. Such famous assignments as, "Write an essay about your summer vacation," or "In an essay, relate a memorable Christmas experience," obviously require the narrative strategy. But if your history instructor asked for an essay on the events leading up to the gunfight at the O.K. Corral, or those climaxing in the Dred Scott Case, you would also have to organize and plot your essay by a narrative strategy—mainly in an ordered sequence governed by the passing of time.

On the other hand, some assignments might be broad enough to give you the option of organizing your essay either by narration or by some other strategy. For example, if you were assigned this subject, "Write an essay on civic responsibility," you could choose to tell the story of the time you served on a jury. Or, if you were asked to write an essay on the extinction of the dinosaurs, you might—as this writer did—organize the material in a narrative fashion:

> At the close of the Cretaceous, 70 million years ago, the earth was devastated. Life was ravaged by one of the worst catastrophes ever to have struck the planet: what it was has always been something of an enigma. After its passing, no large land animal was left in existence, no plesiosaurs or mosasaurs remained in the seas nor pterosaurs in the skies, no ammonites survived in the depths of the ocean, nor chalk-forming plankton at the surface. All were annihilated simultaneously. The forms of life persisting—mammals, birds, a few reptiles, land plants, and so on—saw a drastic reduc-

tion in numbers: they inherited an earth that would have seemed empty.

—Adrian J. Desmond, *The Hot-Blooded Dinosaurs*

Of course, you could also choose an entirely different tack for writing an essay on dinosaur extinction. For example, you could organize such an essay by the strategy of *causal analysis,* focussing on why dinosaurs became extinct. The point is that the narrative mode, though it most often sees use in the personal story, also has a definite place in organizing and planning objective essays.

All good narratives, personal or objective, exemplify three important techniques: the use of a consistent point of view, the use of pacing, and the use of vivid details. Let us look briefly at each.

A Consistent Point of View

Every narration is a story told by someone (or even in bizarre instances of experimental fiction, something) who speaks to the reader in a particular voice and with a certain personality, referred to as the narrative's **point of view.** For example, if you were narrating an incident from your childhood and wished to tell it dramatically, you might use the point of view of a child. This fiction would be for the sake of realistically recreating what the world looked like to you then, even though it no longer looks the same to you now. But should you begin the narrative in language such as a child might use and then suddenly switch to that of a crotchety philosopher, the effect of believability would be instantly ruined. A prime technique of narration, then, is consistency in the use of point of view. Once you have decided who the spokesman, spokeswoman, or spokesthing of your narration is and assigned he, she, or it a certain voice, you must stick with it for the duration of your story.

For example, the following passage consistently reflects the point of view of a young, uneducated black woman:

> I spend my wedding day running from the oldest boy. He twelve. His mama died in his arms and he don't want to hear nothing bout no new one. He pick up a rock and laid my head open. The blood run all down tween my breasts. His daddy say Don't *do* that! But that's all he say. He got four children, instead of three, two boys and two girls. The girls hair ain't been comb since their mammy died. I tell him I'll just have to shave it off. Start fresh. He say bad luck to cut a woman hair. So after I bandage my head best I can and cook dinner—they have a spring, not a well,

and a wood stove look like a truck—I start trying to untangle hair. They only six and eight and they cry. They scream. They cuse me of murder. By ten o'clock I'm done. They cry theirselves to sleep. But I don't cry. I lay there thinking bout Nettie while he on top of me, wonder if she safe.

—Alice Walker, *The Color Purple.*

To make your prose reflect a consistent voice and point of view, you may want to resort to playacting, to temporarily assume the personality or character of the figure from whose point of view the narration is being told. Try to imagine how that person would talk, in what syntactic patterns and with what vocabulary, and then recreate these patterns faithfully in the language. Whatever voice you choose to hide behind—young and uneducated, or old and wise—be sure to stay in character throughout the whole narrative.

For example, here is a paragraph in which a student narrates his experiences with martial arts training. But catching himself in a capricious shift of voice, he edits out the words and sentences that struck him as inconsistent.

There were two things I learned in Karate before I learned to fight. The first thing was respect. I was told that I must salute and bow to the Korean, United States, and our martial arts flags when entering or leaving the room. To acknowledge my teachers and elders such as the Black Belts, I must also bow to them. ~~Deportment and grooming of all participants in karate is mandatory and demanded by meticulous teachers.~~ Whenever asked a question, I am expected to reply "yes, sir," or "no, sir," in a respectful and confident tone. I also *learned to* ~~absorbed~~ *promote* ~~through studious concentration the habit of~~ a friendly atmosphere by always being open and forthright in my manner.

Pacing

Pacing is the technique of selective focus. The well-paced narrative focuses on the details of important events in order to highlight them, but glosses over those events that have little or no bearing on the meaning of the story. Here is a student's example:

By April of 1975, the victory of the
Communists became obvious. Since my family
wanted to live in freedom, we decided to leave
Vietnam forever. The decision was a highly
risky one and involved some terrifying nights in
foreign camps. Finally, after two weeks of
agonized wandering from camp to camp, we were
flown to Camp Pendleton in the United States. I
wept with relief, thinking that now at last life
would be better than it had been at the hot and
arid camps of such places as Guam. The reality
was disappointing. We arrived at Pendleton at
one o'clock in the morning. The weather was
blue cold. We were checked in by uniformed
officials who did not know our language and who
were crisply but uncaringly efficient. I was so
cold that my teeth chattered; consequently, one
of the clerks handed me a thin blanket and
pointed to a tent with three military beds in
it. My mother and I huddled miserably on the
bed while my father filled out papers. A few
hours later, another official signaled us to
head toward the mess hall, where we were to eat
breakfast. The morning darkness was rendered

```
eerie by a thick fog.  I had to walk down a

steep incline to reach the eating area, and on

the way, I stumbled over a rock and broke my

leg.  The pain was numbing and put me in shock.

I was no longer hungry--just cold and afraid.

One month later, when we left the camp, I was

still in my cast.
```

Notice that a mere phrase is devoted to "two weeks of agonized wandering from camp to camp," and a whole month of living at Camp Pendleton is dismissed with a simple "One month later . . . ." What the writer zooms in on is the misery of arriving at camp. That event is highlighted in detail because the point of the paragraph is to narrate how different the reality of moving to the United States was from the dream.

Note that pacing is really another name for the selective inclusion of certain details and the omission of others. Basic to this inclusion is the principle of narrative focus. Time does not pass at an equal rate in a story as on a clockface. One minute on the clock is as long or as short as any other; one minute in a story, if it is a minute of some significance, may consume a hundred pages. Ten insignificant years can pass in a sentence. And although the hundred pages and the sentence will differ in the wealth or absence of details, the guiding principle a writer will use to lavishly cover one minute while curtly dismissing ten years is the value of each period to the story. That judgment, exercised by the writer, is the narrative's *pacing*.

Here, for example, is a paragraph in which the writer realized that she was dallying too long over an insignificant stretch of her story, consequently clogging its movement with unnecessary details. Notice how she revised the paragraph to pace the storyline more briskly. Her essay, "Reunion with Old Neighbors," focussed on a joyful reuniting with former neighbors.

```
    After living in an Atlanta apartment for a

year and a half, my husband and I anxiously

watched the building of our new house.  We could

not wait to have neighbors--the kind to compare

lawns with, visit on a hot summer night, or

house sit for during vacations.  We could not

have hand picked better neighbors than the
```

Carlsons——Bud and Elysia. We got along so
famously that I thought it wonderful and
destined. Elysia and I would go shopping,
leaving Bud and my husband Terry at home working
on the yards. ~~Bud and Terry differed in some~~
~~respects, but their differences didn't affect~~
~~their friendship. For example, Bud was a~~
~~confirmed baseball fan, while my husband loved~~
~~basketball to distraction. Bud drank only~~
~~European beers and made fun of American beers,~~
~~while my husband, being the hard nosed patriot,~~
~~would only drink American beer.~~ We would return
to find them drinking beer and chuckling over
some private joke. We went everywhere
together——to dinner, to parties, to ball
games——and shared celebrations of birthdays and
holidays. Four years of magical friendship
flashed by when our neighbors were notified that
they would be transferred to Florida. It was a
sad day when the moving van arrived at their
house, and even sadder when we had to say
good-bye.

slows the pace of the paragraph

The differences between the narrator's husband and Bud are irrelevant to the
narrative and only slow its pacing. Consequently, the writer deleted them in
editing.

The Use of Vivid Details

All paragraphs, no matter how developed, are made better and more
lively by the inclusion of vivid details. This is especially true of narratives.
Here is an example, taken from a short story in which a young man tells

how he took his aunt to a concert after she had spent 30 years running a farm on a homestead in Nebraska:

> From the time we entered the concert hall, however, she was a trifle less passive and inert, and for the first time seemed to perceive her surroundings. I had felt some trepidation lest she might become aware of her queer, country clothes, or might experience some painful embarrassment at stepping suddenly into the world to which she had been dead for a quarter of a century. But again, I found how superficially I had judged her. She sat looking about her with eyes as impersonal, almost as stony, as those with which the granite Rameses in a museum watches the froth and fret that ebbs and flows about his pedestal. I have seen this same aloofness in old miners who drift into the Brown Hotel at Denver, their pockets full of bullion, their linen soiled, their haggard faces unshaven; standing in the thronged corridors as solitary as though they were still in a frozen camp on the Yukon.
>
> —Willa Cather, *A Wagner Matinée*.

This kind of vivid accounting requires minute observation of one's environment. In your own narrations, be as specific as you can. Say how things looked, smelled, tasted. Don't be satisfied with the approximate, the hazy, the imprecise. Say what you mean as specifically as possible, using as much detail as you can remember.

Bear in mind two points when using details in a narrative essay. The first is that the specific details must fit your narrator. If you are telling a story from a child's point of view, your language must consist of a child's images and details or your storyteller will seem bogus. The second point is that the concrete detail will always be more memorable and vivid than a mere abstraction. Here are some examples of edited sentences in which the writers culled out abstract words and replaced them with more concrete and effective equivalents:

My brother was ~~a big type~~ *an enormous muscular* man ~~with a happy~~ *who always wore a broad smile.* ~~disposition.~~

Nina, an acquaintance of mine, was ~~a~~ *, always gossiping, spreading rumors, and telling hurtful tales.* ~~trouble-maker.~~

She was a ~~nice sailboat.~~ *sleek sloop with graceful lines.*

In every case, the writers substituted concrete words for abstract ones, sometimes fleshing out the passage with vivid details.

The following is the first draft of a student narrative paragraph. In it, the narrator tried unsuccessfully to narrate the coziness he had felt toward a garret apartment he moved into after the breakup of his marriage:

Original:

Not so long ago, I went in search of "La Paix," the place I lived in for two years after my wife and I broke up our marriage. For a long time we had been haggling over money, religion, friends, and lifestyle. We became increasingly hostile toward each other, eventually reaching the point where we could hardly tolerate each other. Then, one day she kicked me out into the streets, and I went in search of a new dwelling. I finally found a small garret on the top of a condemned garage. It was to be my springboard to a new life. Since it had played an important part in my emotional rehabilitation, I wanted to see it again. Standing on the balcony, looking into what was once my home, I saw no connection, no relationship, no bridge between then and now. I was peering into the dark, uninviting interior of an ugly substandard building—now even shunned by winos infecting the area. Nevertheless, I ventured inside to snoop and mess around a little bit. I was scared spitless that the floor might give way beneath me. It was a hideous, dirty place. I found it increasingly difficult to square this squalid reality with my nostalgic remembrances. Tired and dissatisfied,

[margin notes, handwritten:]

Gloss over for better pacing—unimportant to your story.

Lapse in voice.

Language too colloquial

delete for better pacing

Lapse in voice

I drove to my parents' home and sat in their backyard to mull things over. "La Paix" had witnessed the biggest emotional transition of my life so far. I had hidden there for two years, writing gawd awful poetry, trite short stories, and first scenes of a one-act play. The place had symbolized freedom from a restrictive,

Lapse in voice

middle-class lifestyle, and a wife I had succeeded only in making miserable. Heck, for me it had been a tree house with electricity or a Tom Sawyer's island, and realizing that it was gone made me feel like a trapeze artist who has just been told, "Tonight there'll be no net." After a few moments of self-indulgent, morbid introspection, I quietly acknowledged one of life's cruel aphorisms: "You can never go back."

As indicated by the editorial comments in its margin, the original narration was improperly paced, had an inconsistent point of view, and did not include enough vivid details. Notice the improvement with rewriting:

Revision:

One afternoon not so long ago, I went in search of "La Paix," the place I lived in after my wife had kicked me out into the streets following our stormy and unhappy marriage. It was a small garret on the top of a condemned garage—isolated, self-contained, and inexpensive. After christening it "La Paix" for "peace of mind," I had filled it with books, posters, classical music, and irrepressible

optimism. It was to be my springboard into a new
life. But that afternoon, standing on the
balcony, looking into the spooky bowels of what
was once my cozy home, I saw no connection, no
relationship, no bridge between then and now. I
was peering into the dark, uninviting cavity of
a substandard building now even shunned by the
winos that infect the area. I ventured inside as
carefully as an archaeologist enters a tomb,
genuinely afraid that the floor might give way
beneath me. In the main cavity of the dwelling I
noticed subtle traces of human habitation. The
floor was littered with artifacts of a
primitive, transient branch of humanity. Bottles
of cheap wine lay, long empty, nested in beds of
torn newsprint and acrid smelling rags. Standing
in the midst of what seemed several generations
of accumulated filth and debris, I found it
impossible to square this hideous reality with
my beatific reminiscences. I began probing the
heaps of refuse. Surely somewhere amongst the
broken glass and vile leavings, there must be a
trace of my two years of existence! I searched
for over an hour—in vain. I came up with
nothing except a fit of sneezes and some insect
bites. Disillusioned and tired, I stood in front
of a dusty shelf that had housed my books and
mulled over the experience. "La Paix" had housed
the biggest emotional transition of my life. For

two full years I had hidden there, composing
third-rate poetry, trite short stories, and one
hopelessly insignificant play. This place had
symbolized freedom from a restrictive,
middle-class lifestyle and from a wife I had
succeeded only in making miserable. It was my
tree house, my Tom Sawyer's island, and
realizing that it was gone made me feel like a
trapeze artist who has just been told, "Tonight
there'll be no net." After a few moments of
self-indulgent, morbid introspection, I quietly
acknowledged one of life's cruel aphorisms: "You
can never go back."

The revision has improved the pacing by glossing over the narrator's unhappy marriage and by deleting the reference to his trip home. Neither incident is important to the topic sentence of the paragraph, which in this case is the final sentence: "You can never go back." Getting rid of slang expressions like "mess around," "gawd awful," "scared spitless," and "heck," makes the point of view more consistently that of an introspective, mature person looking back. The addition of vivid details also infuses some liveliness into the narrative.

The following essays are all written in the narrative mode. Three of them, "Searching for Roots in a Changing World," "Eating Christmas in the Kalahari," and "History of the Peter Principle," exemplify the personal narrative in which an individual relates his own story. The fourth, "The Birth and Death of Stars," is an objective essay that uses the narrative strategy. All exemplify the principles of narrative writing discussed in this chapter.

BIOGRAPHY

Richard Rodriguez
SEARCHING FOR ROOTS IN A CHANGING WORLD

Richard Rodriquez (b. 1944, San Francisco, Calif.) is a Mexican-American writer who was educated at Stanford University (B.A., 1967) and Columbia University, (M.A., 1969). His Hunger for Memory: The Education of Richard Rodriguez *(1982) was acclaimed by the* New York Times *as an "honest and intelligent account of how education can alter a life." Since 1981 he has been a free-lance writer.*

Today I am only technically the person I once felt myself to be—a Mexican-American, a Chicano. Partly because I had no way of comprehending my racial identity except in this technical sense, I gave up long ago the cultural consequences of being a Chicano.

The change came gradually but early. When I was beginning grade school, I noted to myself the fact that the classroom environment was so different in its styles and assumptions from my own family environment that survival would essentially entail a choice between both worlds. When I became a student, I was literally "remade"; neither I nor my teachers considered anything I had known before as relevant. I had to forget most of what my culture had provided, because to remember it was a disadvantage. The past and its cultural values became detachable, like a piece of clothing grown heavy on a warm day and finally put away.

Strangely, the discovery that I have been inattentive to my cultural past has arisen because others—student colleagues and faculty members—have started to assume that I am a Chicano. The ease with which the assumption is made forces me to suspect that the label is not meant to suggest cultural, but racial, identity. Nonetheless, as a graduate student and a prospective university faculty member, I am routinely expected to assume intellectual leadership *as a member of a racial minority.* Recently, for example, I heard the moderator of a panel discussion introduce me as "Richard Rodriguez, a Chicano intellectual." I wanted to correct the speaker—because I felt guilty representing a nonacademic cultural tradition that I had willingly abandoned. So I can only guess what it would have meant to have retained my culture as I entered the classroom, what it would mean for me to be today a *Chicano intellectual.* (The two words juxtaposed excite me; for years I thought a Chicano had to decide between being one or the other.)

Does the fact that I barely spoke any English until I was nine, or that as a child I felt a surge of *self*-hatred whenever a passing teenager would yell a racial slur, or that I saw my skin darken each summer—do any of these facts shape the ideas which I have or am capable of having? Today, I suspect they do—in ways I doubt the moderator who referred to me as a "Chicano intellectual" in-

Reprinted by permission of Georges Borchadt, Inc., for the author from *Saturdy Review,* Feb. 8, 1975. Copyright © 1975 by Richard Rodriguez.

tended. The peculiar status of being a "Chicano intellectual" makes me grow restless at the thought that I have lost at least as much as I have gained through education.

I remember when, 20 years ago, two grammar-school nuns visited my childhood home. They had come to suggest—with more tact than was necessary, because my parents accepted without question the church's authority—that we make a greater effort to speak as much English around the house as possible. The nuns realized that my brothers and I led solitary lives largely because we were barely able to comprehend English in a school where we were the only Spanish-speaking students. My mother and father complied as best they could. Heroically, they gave up speaking to us in Spanish—the language that formed so much of the family's sense of intimacy in an alien world—and began to speak a broken English. Instead of Spanish sounds, I began hearing sounds that were new, harder, less friendly. More important, I was encouraged to respond in English.

The change in language was the most dramatic and obvious indication that I would become very much like the "gringo"—a term which was used descriptively rather than pejoratively in my home—and unlike the Spanish-speaking relatives who largely constituted my preschool world. Gradually, Spanish became a sound freighted with only a kind of sentimental significance, like the sound of the bedroom clock I listened to in my aunt's house when I spent the night. Just as gradually, English became the language I came not to *hear* because it was the language I used every day, as I gained access to a new, larger society. But the memory of Spanish persisted as a reminder of the society I had left. I can remember occasions when I entered a room and my parents were speaking to one another in Spanish, seeing me, they shifted into their more formalized English. Hearing them speak to me in English troubled me. The bonds their voices once secured were loosened by the new tongue.

This is not to suggest that I was being *forced* to give up my Chicano past. After the initial awkwardness of transition, I committed myself, fully and freely, to the culture of the classroom. Soon what I was learning in school was so antithetical to what my parents knew and did that I was careful about the way I talked about myself at the evening dinner table. Occasionally, there were moments of childish cruelty: a son's condescending to instruct either one of his parents about a "simple" point of English pronunciation or grammar.

Social scientists often remark, about situations such as mine, that children feel a sense of loss as they move away from their working-class identifications and models. Certainly, what I experienced, others have also—whatever their race. Like other generations of, say, Polish-American or Irish-American children coming home from college, I was to know the silence that ensues so quickly after the quick exchange of news and the dwindling of common interests.

In addition, however, education seemed to mean not only a gradual dissolving of familial and class ties but also a change of racial identity. The new language I spoke was only the most obvious reason for my associating the classroom with "gringo" society. The society I knew as Chicano was barely literate—in English *or* Spanish—and so impatient with either prolonged reflection or abstraction that I found the academic environment a sharp contrast. Sharpening the contrast was the stereotype of the Mexican as a mental inferior. (The fear of this stereotype has been so deep that only recently have I been willing to listen to those, like D. H. Lawrence, who celebrate the "noncerebral" Mexican as an alternative to the rational and scientific European man.) Because I did not know how to distinguish the healthy nonrationality of Chicano culture from the mental incompetency of which Chicanos were unjustly accused, I was willing to abandon my nonmental skills in order to disprove the racist's stereotype.

I was wise enough not to feel proud of the person education had helped me to become. I knew that education had led me to repudiate my race. I was frequently labeled a *pocho,* a Mexican with gringo pretentions, not only because I could not speak Spanish but also because I would respond in English with precise and careful sentences. Uncles would laugh good-naturedly, but I detected scorn in their voices. For my grandmother, the least assimilated of my relations, the changes in her grandson since entering school were especially troubling. She remains today a dark and silently critical figure in my memory, a reminder of the Mexican-Indian ancestry that somehow my educational success has violated.

Nonetheless, I became more comfortable reading or writing careful prose than talking to a kitchen filled with listeners, withdrawing from situations to reflect on their significance rather than grasping for meaning at the scene. I remember, one August evening, slipping away from a gathering of aunts and uncles in the backyard, going into a bedroom tenderly lighted by a late sun, and opening a novel about life in nineteenth-century England. There, by an open window, reading, I was barely conscious of the sounds of laughter outside.

With so few fellow Chicanos in the university, I had no chance   12
to develop an alternative consciousness. When I spent occasional
weekends tutoring lower-class Chicano teenagers or when I talked
with Mexican-American janitors and maids around the campus,
there was a kind of sympathy—a sense, however privately held—
that we knew something about one another. But I regarded them
all primarily as people from my past. The maids reminded me of
my aunts (similarly employed); the students I tutored reminded me
of my cousins (who also spoke English with barrio accents).

When I was young, I was taught to refer to my ancestry as Mex-   13
ican-American. *Chicano* was a word used among friends or relatives. It implied a familiarity based on shared experience. Spoken
casually, the term easily became an insult. In 1968 the word *Chicano* was about to become a political term. I heard it shouted into
microphones as Third World groups agitated for increased student
and faculty representation in higher education. It was not long before I *became* a Chicano in the eyes of students and faculty members. My racial identity was assumed for only the simplest reasons:
my skin color and last name.

On occasion I was asked to account for my interests in Renais-   14
sance English literature. When I explained them, declaring a need
for cultural assimilation on the campus, my listener would dis-
agree. I sensed suspicion on the part of a number of my fellow minority students. When I could not imitate Spanish pronunciations
of the dialect of the barrio, when I was plainly uninterested in
wearing ethnic costumes and could not master a special handshake
the minority students often used with one another, they knew I
was different. And I was. I was assimilated into the culture of a
graduate department of English. As a result, I watched how in less
than five years nearly every minority graduate student I knew
dropped out of school, largely for cultural reasons. Often they
didn't understand the value of analyzing literature in professional
jargon, which others around them readily adopted. Nor did they
move as readily to lofty heights of abstraction. They became easily
depressed by the seeming uselessness of the talk they heard
around them. "It's not for real," I still hear a minority student mur-
mur to herself and perhaps to me, shaking her head slowly, as we
sat together in a class listening to a discussion on punctuation in a
Renaissance epic.

I survived—thanks to the accommodation I had made long be-   15
fore. In fact, I prospered, partly as a result of the political movement designed to increase the enrollment of minority students less

assimilated than I in higher education. Suddenly grants, fellow-ships, and teaching offers became abundant.

In 1972 I went to England on a Fulbright scholarship. I hoped   16
the months of brooding about racial identity were behind me. I
wanted to concentrate on my dissertation, which the distractions
of an American campus had not permitted. But the freedom I anticipated did not last for long. Barely a month after I had begun
working regularly in the reading room of the British Museum, I
was surprised, and even frightened, to have to acknowledge that I
was not at ease living the rarefied life of the academic. With my
pile of research file cards growing taller, the mass of secondary materials and opinions was making it harder for me to say anything
original about my subject. Every sentence I wrote, every thought I
had, became so loaded with qualifications and footnotes that it
said very little. My scholarship became little more than an exercise
in caution. I had an accompanying suspicion that whatever I did
manage to write and call my dissertation would be of little use.
Opening books so dusty that they must not have been used in decades, I began to doubt the value of writing what only a few people would read.

Obviously, I was going through the fairly typical crisis of the   17
American graduate student. But with one difference: After four
years of involvement with questions of racial identity, I now saw
my problems as a scholar in the context of the cultural issues that
had been raised by my racial situation. So much of what my work
in the British Museum lacked, my parents' culture possessed. They
were people not afraid to generalize or to find insights in their generalities. More important, they had the capacity to make passionate statements, something I was beginning to doubt my dissertation would ever allow me to do. I needed to learn how to trust the
use of "I" in my writing the way they trusted its use in their
speech. Thus developed a persistent yearning for the very Chicano
culture that I had abandoned as useless.

Feelings of depression came occasionally but forcefully. Some   18
days I found my work so oppressive that I had to leave the reading
room and stroll through the museum. One afternoon, appropriately enough, I found myself in an upstairs gallery containing
Mayan and Aztec sculptures. Even there the sudden yearning for a
Chicano past seemed available to me only as nostalgia. One morning, as I was reading a book about Puritan autobiography, I overheard two Spaniards whispering to one another. I did not hear
what they said, but I did hear the sound of their Spanish—and it

embraced me, filling my mind with swirling images of a past long abandoned.

I returned from England, disheartened, a few months later. My   19
dissertation was coming along well, but I did not know whether I wanted to submit it. Worse, I did not know whether I wanted a career in higher education. I detested the prospect of spending the rest of my life in libraries and classrooms, in touch with my past only through the binoculars nostalgia makes available. I knew that I could not simply re-create a version of what I would have been like had I not become an academic. There was no possibility of going back. But if the culture of my birth was to survive, it would have to animate my academic work. That was the lesson of the British Museum.

I frankly do not know how my academic autobiography will   20
end. Sometimes I think I will have to leave the campus, in order to reconcile my past and present. Other times, more optimistically, I think that a kind of negative reconciliation is already in progress, that I can make creative use of my sense of loss. For instance, with my sense of the cleavage between past and present, I can, as a literary critic, identify issues in Renaissance pastoral—a literature which records the feelings of the courtly when confronted by the alternatives of rural and rustic life. And perhaps I can speak with unusual feeling about the price we must pay, or have paid, as a rational society for confessing seventeenth-century Cartesian faiths. Likewise, because of my sense of cultural loss, I may be able to identify more readily than another the ways in which language has meaning simply as sound and what the printed word can and cannot give us. At the very least, I can point up the academy's tendency to ignore the cultures beyond its own horizons.

February 1974

On my job interview the department chairman has been listening   21
to an oral version of what I have just written. I tell him he should be very clear about the fact that I am not, at the moment, confident enough to call myself a Chicano. Perhaps I never will be. But as I say all this, I look at the interviewer. He smiles softly. Has he heard what I have been trying to say? I wonder. I repeat: I have lost the ability to bring my past into my present; I do not know how to be a Chicano reader of Spenser or Shakespeare. All that remains is a desire for the past. He sighs, preoccupied, looking at my records. Would I be interested in teaching a course on the Mexican novel in translation? Do I understand that part of my duties would require that I become a counselor of minority students? What was

the subject of that dissertation I did in England? Have I read the book on the same subject that was published this month?

Behind the questioner, a figure forms in my imagination: my grandmother, her face solemn and still.   22

Vocabulary

entail (2)   noncerebral (9)
juxtaposed (3)   repudiate (10)
pejoratively (6)   assimilated (10)
antithetical (7)

Critical Inquiries

1. The author writes that the classroom was "so different in its styles and assumptions" from his own "family environment" that to survive he had to make a choice between the two worlds. Is this a choice confronting all students, or just students from minority backgrounds? Justify your answer.

2. What is your view of the popular movement afoot to declare English the official language of the United States? What effect is such a movement likely to have on Chicano students?

3. Is the choice between two cultures based on different languages necessarily as absolutist as Rodriguez implies? What other alternatives, if any, do you think Rodriguez's parents might have pursued to encourage their children to become assimilated into English?

4. The author implies that classroom culture came to be associated in his mind with a certain way of thinking and behaving. What way of thinking and behaving, if any, do you associate with classroom culture? Is this association inevitable and necessary? Why or why not?

5. Rodriguez writes that the society he knew as Chicano was "impatient with either prolonged reflection or abstraction." What kind of Chicano society do you think he means, or do you regard this assertion as accurately descriptive of Chicano society in general?

Rhetorical Inquiries

1. What contrasts does Rodriguez draw between English and Spanish as these languages were used in his daily upbringing? What contrasts does he imply also exist between being a *gringo* and a *Chicano*?

2. What do the rhetorical tone, style and content of this piece ironically contribute to Rodriguez's self-debate about his place as a Chicano in the academic world?

3. What is the purpose of the short paragraph 15?

4. What do you regard as the main rhetorical risk of writing in this confessional vein? How does Rodriguez avoid it?

5. How does the writer manipulate the tense of this narrative for rhetorical effect?

ANTHROPOLOGY

Richard Borshay Lee
EATING CHRISTMAS IN THE KALAHARI

Richard Borshay Lee (b. 1937), a naturalized Canadian anthropologist, was born in New York and educated at the University of Toronto (B.A., 1959; M.A., 1961) and at the University of California at Berkeley (Phd., 1965). Since 1972 he has been a professor of anthropology at the University of Toronto. Among his many published works are Man the Hunter *(1968), and* Kalahari Hunter-Gatherers *(1974). He has also contributed articles to such journals as* Natural History, American Heart Journal, *and* Archives of Sexual Behavior.

The !Kung Bushmen's knowledge of Christmas is thirdhand.   1
The London Missionary Society brought the holiday to the southern Tswana tribes in the early nineteenth century. Later, native catechists spread the idea far and wide among the Bantu-speaking pastoralists, even in the remotest corners of the Kalahari Desert. The Bushmen's idea of the Christmas story, stripped to its essentials, is "praise the birth of white man's god-chief"; what keeps their interest in the holiday high is the Tswana-Herero custom of slaughtering an ox for his Bushmen neighbors as an annual goodwill gesture. Since the 1930's, part of the Bushmen's annual round of activities has included a December congregation at the cattle posts for trading, marriage brokering, and several days of trance-dance feasting at which the local Tswana headman is host.

As a social anthropologist working with !Kung Bushmen, I   2
found that the Christmas ox custom suited my purposes. I had come to the Kalahari to study the hunting and gathering subsistence economy of the !Kung, and to accomplish this it was essen-

Reprinted with permission from *Natural History,* Dec. 1969, vol. 78, no. 10.
Copyright the American Museum of Natural History, 1969.

tial not to provide them with food, share my own food, or inter-fere in any way with their food-gathering activities. While liberal handouts of tobacco and medical supplies were appreciated, they were scarcely adequate to erase the glaring disparity in wealth be-tween the anthropologist, who maintained a two-month inventory of canned goods, and the Bushmen, who rarely had a day's supply of food on hand. My approach, while paying off in terms of data, left me open to frequent accusations of stinginess and hardhearted-ness. By their lights, I was a miser.

The Christmas ox was to be my way of saying thank you for   3
the cooperation of the past year; and since it was to be our last Christmas in the field, I determined to slaughter the largest, meat-iest ox that money could buy, insuring that the feast and trance dance would be a success.

Through December I kept my eyes open at the wells as the cat-   4
tle were brought down for watering. Several animals were offered, but none had quite the grossness that I had in mind. Then, ten days before the holiday, a Herero friend led an ox of astonishing size and mass up to our camp. It was solid black, stood five feet high at the shoulder, had a five-foot span of horns, and must have weighed 1,200 pounds on the hoof. Food consumption calculations are my specialty, and I quickly figured that bones and viscera aside, there was enough meat—at least four pounds—for every man, woman, and child of the 150 Bushmen in the vicinity of /ai/ai who were expected at the feast.

Having found the right animal at last, I paid the Herero £20 ($56)   5
and asked him to keep the beast with his herd until Christmas day. The next morning word spread among the people that the big solid black one was the ox chosen by /ontah (my Bushman name; it means, roughly, "whitey") for the Christmas feast. That after-noon I received the first delegation. Ben!a, an outspoken sixty-year-old mother of five, came to the point slowly.

"Where were you planning to eat Christmas?"   6

"Right here at /ai/ai," I replied.

"Alone or with others?"

"I expect to invite all the people to eat Christmas with me."

"Eat what?"

"I have purchased Yehave's black ox, and I am going to slaughter and cook it."

"That's what we were told at the well but refused to believe it until we heard it from yourself."

"Well, it's the black one," I replied expansively, although won-dering what she was driving at.

"Oh no!" Ben!a groaned, turning to her group. "They were   7
right." Turning back to me she asked, "Do you expect us to eat
that bag of bones?"

"Bag of bones! It's the biggest ox at /ai/ai."

"Big, yes, but old. And thin. Everybody knows there's no meat
on that old ox. What did you expect us to eat off it, the horns?"

Everybody chuckled at Ben!a's one-liner as they walked away,
but all I could manage was a weak grin.

That evening it was the turn of the young men. They came to   8
sit at our evening fire. /gaugo, about my age, spoke to me man-
to-man.

"/ontah, you have always been square with us," he lied. "What
has happened to change your heart? That sack of guts and bones
of Yehave's will hardly feed one camp, let alone all the Bushmen
around /ai/ai." And he proceeded to enumerate the seven camps in
the /ai/ai vicinity, family by family. "Perhaps you have forgotten
that we are not few, but many. Or are you too blind to tell the
difference between a proper cow and an old wreck? That ox is
thin to the point of death."

"Look, you guys," I retorted, "that is a beautiful animal, and I'm
sure you will eat it with pleasure at Christmas."

"Of course we will eat it; it's food. But it won't fill us up to the
point where we will have enough strength to dance. We will eat
and go home to bed with stomachs rumbling."

That night as we turned in, I asked my wife, Nancy: "What did   9
you think of the black ox?"

"It looked enormous to me. Why?"

"Well, about eight different people have told me I got gypped;
that the ox is nothing but bones."

"What's the angle?" Nancy asked. "Did they have a better one to
sell?"

"No, they just said that it was going to be a grim Christmas because there won't be enough meat to go around. Maybe I'll get an
independent judge to look at the beast in the morning."

Bright and early, Halingisi, a Tswana cattle owner, appeared at   10
our camp. But before I could ask him to give me his opinion on
Yehave's black ox, he gave me the eye signal that indicated a confidential chat. We left the camp and sat down.

"/ontah, I'm surprised at you: you've lived here for three years
and still haven't learned anything about cattle."

"But what else can a person do but choose the biggest, strongest
animal one can find?" I retorted.

"Look, just because an animal is big doesn't mean that it has plenty of meat on it. The black one was a beauty when it was younger, but now it is thin to the point of death."

"Well I've already bought it. What can I do at this stage?"

"Bought it already? I thought you were just considering it. Well, you'll have to kill it and serve it, I suppose. But don't expect much of a dance to follow."

My spirits dropped rapidly. I could believe that Ben!a and /gaugo just might be putting me on about the black ox, but Halingisi seemed to be an impartial critic. I went around that day feeling as though I had bought a lemon of a used car. [11]

In the afternoon it was Tomazo's turn. Tomazo is a fine hunter, a top trance performer . . . and one of my most reliable informants. He approached the subject of the Christmas cow as part of my continuing Bushman education. [12]

"My friend, the way it is with us Bushmen," he began, "is that we love meat. And even more than that, we love fat. When we hunt we always search for the fat ones, the ones dripping with layers of white fat: fat that turns into a clear, thick oil in the cooking pot, fat that slides down your gullet, fills your stomach and gives you a roaring diarrhea," he rhapsodized. [13]

"So, feeling as we do," he continued, "it gives us pain to be served such a scrawny thing as Yehave's black ox. It is big, yes, and no doubt its giant bones are good for soup, but fat is what we really crave and so we will eat Christmas this year with a heavy heart." [14]

The prospect of a gloomy Christmas now had me worried, so I asked Tomazo what I could do about it.

"Look for a fat one, a young one . . . smaller, but fat. Fat enough to make us //gom ('evacuate the bowels'), then we will be happy."

My suspicions were aroused when Tomazo said that he happened to know of a young, fat, barren cow that the owner was willing to part with. Was Tomazo working on commission, I wondered? But I dispelled this unworthy thought when we approached the Herero owner of the cow in question and found that he had decided not to sell. [15]

The scrawny wreck of a Christmas ox now became the talk of the /ai/ai water hole and was the first news told to the outlying groups as they began to come in from the bush for the feast. What finally convinced me that real trouble might be brewing was the visit from u!au, an old conservative with a reputation for fierceness. His nickname meant spear and referred to an incident thirty years ago in which he had speared a man to death. He had an [16] intense manner; fixing me with his eyes, he said in clipped tones:

"I have only just heard about the black ox today, or else I would   17
have come here earlier. /ontah, do you honestly think you can serve meat like that to people and avoid a fight?" He paused, letting the implications sink in. "I don't mean fight you, /ontah; you are a white man. I mean a fight between Bushmen. There are many fierce ones here, and with such a small quantity of meat to distribute, how can you give everybody a fair share? Someone is sure to accuse another of taking too much or hogging all the choice pieces. Then you will see what happens when some go hungry while others eat."

The possibility of at least a serious argument struck me as all too   18
real. I had witnessed the tension that surrounds the distribution of meat from a kudu or gemsbok kill, and had documented many arguments that sprang up from a real or imagined slight in meat distribution. The owners of a kill may spend up to two hours arranging and rearranging the piles of meat under the gaze of a circle of recipients before handing them out. And I also knew that the Christmas feast at /ai/ai would be bringing together groups that had feuded in the past.

Convinced now of the gravity of the situation, I went in earnest   19
to search for a second cow; but all my inquiries failed to turn one up.

The Christmas feast was evidently going to be a disaster, and   20
the incessant complaints about the meagerness of the ox had already taken the fun out of it for me. Moreover, I was getting bored with the wisecracks, and after losing my temper a few times, I resolved to serve the beast anyway. If the meat fell short, the hell with it. In the Bushmen idiom, I announced to all who would listen:

"I am a poor man and blind. If I have chosen one that is too old   21
and too thin, we will eat it anyway and see if there is enough meat there to quiet the rumbling of our stomachs."

On hearing this speech, Ben!a offered me a rare word of com-   22
fort. "It's thin," she said philosophically, "but the bones will make a good soup."

At dawn Christmas morning, instinct told me to turn over the   23
butchering and cooking to a friend and take off with Nancy to spend Christmas alone in the bush. But curiosity kept me from retreating. I wanted to see what such a scrawny ox looked like on butchering, and if there *was* going to be a fight, I wanted to catch every word of it. Anthropologists are incurable that way.

The great beast was driven up to our dancing ground, and a shot 24
in the forehead dropped it in its tracks. Then, freshly cut branches
were heaped around the fallen carcass to receive the meat. Ten
men volunteered to help with the cutting. I asked /gaugo to make
the breast bone cut. This cut, which begins the butchering process
for most large game, offers easy access for removal of the viscera.
But it also allows the hunter to spot-check the amount of fat on
the animal. A fat game animal carries a white layer up to an inch
thick on the chest, while in a thin one, the knife will quickly cut to
bone. All eyes fixed on his hand as /gaugo, dwarfed by the great
carcass, knelt to the breast. The first cut opened a pool of solid
white in the black skin. The second and third cut widened and
deepened the creamy white. Still no bone. It was pure fat; it must
have been two inches thick.

"Hey /gau," I burst out, "that ox is loaded with fat. What's this 25
about the ox being too thin to bother eating? Are you out of your
mind?"

"Fat?" /gau shot back, "You call that fat? This wreck is thin, sick, 26
dead!" And he broke out laughing. So did everyone else. They
rolled on the ground paralyzed with laughter. Everybody laughed
except me; I was thinking.

I ran back to the tent and burst in just as Nancy was getting up. 27
"Hey, the black ox. It's fat as hell! They were kidding about it being too thin to eat. It was a joke or something. A put-on. Everyone
is really delighted with it!"

"Some joke," my wife replied. "It was so funny that you were
ready to pack up and leave /ai/ai."

If it had indeed been a joke, it had been an extraordinarily con- 28
vincing one, and tinged, I thought, with more than a touch of malice as many jokes are. Nevertheless, that it was a joke lifted my
spirits considerably, and I returned to the butchering site where
the shape of the ox was rapidly disappearing under the axes and
knives of the butchers. The atmosphere had become festive. Grin-
ning broadly, their arms covered with blood well past the elbow,
men packed chunks of meat into the big cast-iron cooking pots,
fifty pounds to the load, and muttered and chuckled all the while
about the thinness and worthlessness of the animal and /ontah's
poor judgment.

We danced and ate that ox two days and two nights; we cooked 29
and distributed fourteen potfuls of meat and no one went home
hungry and no fights broke out.

But the "joke" stayed in my mind. I had a growing feeling that 30
something important had happened in my relationship with the

Bushmen and that the clue lay in the meaning of the joke. Several days later, when most of the people had dispersed back to the bush camps, I raised the question with Hakekgose, a Tswana man who had grown up among the !Kung, married a !Kung girl, and who probably knew their culture better than any other non-Bushman.

"With us whites," I began, "Christmas is supposed to be the day   31
of friendship and brotherly love. What I can't figure out is why the Bushmen went to such lengths to criticize and belittle the ox I had bought for the feast. The animal was perfectly good and their jokes and wisecracks practically ruined the holiday for me."

"So it really did bother you," said Hakekgose. "Well, that's the   32
way they always talk. When I take my rifle and go hunting with them, if I miss, they laugh at me for the rest of the day. But even if I hit and bring one down, it's no better. To them, the kill is always too small or too old or too thin; and as we sit down on the kill site to cook and eat the liver, they keep grumbling, even with their mouths full of meat. They say things like, 'Oh this is awful! What a worthless animal! Whatever made me think that this Tswana rascal could hunt!'"

"Is this the way outsiders are treated?" I asked.   33

"No, it is their custom; they talk that way to each other too. Go and ask them."

/gaugo had been one of the most enthusiastic in making me feel bad about the merit of the Christmas ox. I sought him out first.

"Why did you tell me the black ox was worthless, when you could see that it was loaded with fat and meat?"

"It is our way," he said smiling. "We always like to fool people   34
about that. Say there is a Bushman who has been hunting. He must not come home and announce like a braggard, 'I have killed a big one in the bush!' He must first sit down in silence until I or someone else comes up to his fire and asks, 'What did you see today?' He replies quietly, 'Ah, I'm no good for hunting. I saw nothing at all [pause] just a little tiny one.' Then I smile to myself," /gaugo continued, "because I know he has killed something big.

"In the morning we make up a party of four or five people to cut   35
up and carry the meat back to the camp. When we arrive at the kill we examine it and cry out, 'You mean to say you have dragged us all the way out here in order to make us cart home your pile of bones? Oh, if I had known it was this thin I wouldn't have come.' Another one pipes up, 'People, to think I gave up a nice day in the shade for this. At home we may be hungry but at least we have nice cool water to drink.' If the horns are big, someone says, 'Did

you think that somehow you were going to boil down the horns for soup?'

"To all this you must respond in kind. 'I agree,' you say, 'this one is not worth the effort; let's just cook the liver for strength and leave the rest for the hyenas. It is not too late to hunt today and even a duiker or a steenbok would be better than this mess.' 36

"Then you set to work nevertheless; butcher the animal, carry the meat back to the camp and everyone eats," /gaugo concluded. 37

Things were beginning to make sense. Next, I went to Tomazo. He corroborated /gaugo's story of the obligatory insults over a kill and added a few details of his own.

"But," I asked, "why insult a man after he has gone to all that trouble to track and kill an animal and when he is going to share the meat with you so that your children will have something to eat?"

"Arrogance," was his cryptic answer.

"Arrogance?"

"Yes, when a young man kills much meat he comes to think of himself as a chief or a big man, and he thinks of the rest of us as his servants or inferiors. We can't accept this. We refuse one who boasts, for someday his pride will make him kill somebody. So we always speak of his meat as worthless. This way we cool his heart and make him gentle." 38

"But why didn't you tell me this before?" I asked Tomazo with some heat.

"Because you never asked me," said Tomazo, echoing the refrain that has come to haunt every field ethnographer.

The pieces now fell into place. I had known for a long time that in situations of social conflict with Bushmen I held all the cards. I was the only source of tobacco in a thousand square miles, and I was not incapable of cutting an individual off for noncooperation. Though my boycott never lasted longer than a few days, it was an indication of my strength. People resented my presence at the water hole, yet simultaneously dreaded my leaving. In short I was a perfect target for the charge of arrogance and for the Bushmen tactic of enforcing humility. 39

I had been taught an object lesson by the Bushmen; it had come from an unexpected corner and had hurt me in a vulnerable area. For the big black ox was to be the one totally generous, unstinting act of my year at /ai/ai, and I was quite unprepared for the reaction I received. 40

As I read it, their message was this: There are no totally generous acts. All "acts" have an element of calculation. One black ox 41 slaughtered at Christmas does not wipe out a year of careful manipulation of gifts to serve your own ends. After all, to kill an animal and share the meat with people is really no more than Bushmen do for each other every day and with far less fanfare.

In the end, I had to admire how the Bushmen had played out   42
the farce — collectively straight-faced to the end. Curiously, the episode reminded me of the *Good Soldier Schweik* and his marvelous encounters with authority. Like Schweik, the Bushmen had retained a thorough-going skepticism of good intentions. Was it this independence of spirit, I wondered, that had kept them culturally viable in the face of generations of contact with more powerful societies, both black and white? The thought that the Bushmen were alive and well in the Kalahari was strangely comforting. Perhaps, armed with that independence and with their superb knowledge of their environment, they might yet survive the future.

Vocabulary

catechists (1)

pastoralists (1)

disparity (2)

rhapsodized (13)

corroborated (37)

ethnographer (38)

viable (42)

Critical Inquiries

1. What American holiday custom comes closest to Bushman celebration of feasting? How does the American custom differ from the Bushman's? How is it similar?

2. What is your view of the morality of anthropologists who live among poorer peoples for the sake of studying them but do not lift a finger to improve the deprivation present in the native culture?

3. What American customs do you think would strike a foreign people as bewildering and odd? Name at least one, and then justify it.

4. What is the American attitude towards the braggart? How does our attitude differ from the Bushman's? If you think it similar, why have we not adopted a similar tactic as the Bushman's for discouraging boasting?

5. How would you characterize the economic relationships that can be inferred as existing between the Bushmen? How do the Bushmen differ from us in this regard?

Rhetorical Inquiries

1. What is the purpose of the information about himself and his situation provided by the author in the first three paragraphs?
2. How does the author suggest the flavor of the !Kung Bushmen's language in his English translations of their speech?
3. What is at least one example in the narrative of the compression of events and activities for the sake of pacing?
4. The narrative is dividing roughly into two parts. What are they, and what is the narrative logic behind this division?
5. What is the function of paragraph 30?

ASTRONOMY

Robert Jastrow
THE BIRTH AND DEATH OF STARS

Robert Jastrow, astronomer, was born in New York and educated at Columbia University. He is the founder and director of NASA's Goddard Institute for Space Studies, Professor of Astronomy and Geology at Columbia, and Professor of Earth Sciences at Darthmouth College. In addition to serving as a popular television commentator on space science, Dr. Jastrow is also the best-selling author of several books, among them Red Giants and White Dwarfs, *and* Until the Sun Dies.

About thirty years ago science solved the mystery of the birth and death of stars, and acquired new evidence that the Universe had a beginning. 1

According to the story pieced together by astronomers, a star's life begins in swirling mists of hydrogen that surge and eddy through space. The Universe is filled with tenuous clouds of this abundant gas, which makes up 99 per cent of all the matter in the Cosmos. In the random motions of such clouds, atoms sometimes come together by accident to form small, condensed pockets of gas. Stars are born in these accidents. 2

Normally the atoms fly apart again in a short time, and the pocket of gas disperses to space. However, each atom exerts a small gravitational attraction on its neighbor, which counters the tendency of the atoms to fly apart. If the number of atoms is sufficiently large, the combined effect of all these separate pulls of 3

Reprinted with permission of the author from *God and the Astronomers,* W. W. Norton, 1978, 105–110. Copyright © 1978 by Robert Jastrow.

gravity will be powerful enough to prevent any of the atoms in the pocket of gas from leaving the pocket and flying out into space again. The pocket becomes a permanent entity, held together by the mutual attraction of all the atoms within it upon one another.

With the passage of time, the continuing attraction of gravity, pulling all the atoms closer together, causes the cloud to contract. The atoms "fall" toward the center of the cloud under the force of gravity; as they fall, they pick up speed and their energy increases. The increase in energy heats the gas and raises its temperature. The shrinking, continuously self-heating ball of gas is an embryonic star.

The ball of gas continues to collapse under the force of its own weight, and the temperature at the center rises further. After 10 million years the temperature has risen to the critical value of 20 million degrees Fahrenheit. At this time, the diameter of the ball has shrunk to one million miles, which is the size of our sun and other typical stars. When the temperature reaches 20 million degrees, a nuclear fire flares up in the center of the star, releasing vast amounts of energy. The release of nuclear energy halts the further collapse of the ball of gas. The energy passes to the surface and is radiated away in the form of heat and light. A new star has been born; another light has appeared in the heavens.

Throughout most of the life of the star, the nuclear fires in its interior burn steadily, consuming hydrogen and leaving behind a residue of heavier elements. These heavier elements are the ashes of the star's fire. Oxygen, iron, copper, and many other elements, ranging up to gold, lead, and uranium, are included among the ashes. According to astronomers, all the elements in the Universe are formed in this way in the interiors of stars, out of the basic building block of hydrogen.

At the end of a star's life, when its reserves of nuclear fuel are exhausted, the star collapses under the force of its own weight. In the case of a small star, the collapse squeezes the entire mass into a volume the size of the earth. Such highly compressed stars, called white dwarfs, have a density of ten tons per cubic inch. Slowly the white dwarf radiates into space the last of its heat and fades into darkness.

A different fate awaits a large star. Its final collapse is a catastrophic event which blows the star apart. The exploding star is called a supernova. Supernovas blaze up with a brilliance many billions of times greater than the brightness of the sun. If the supernova is located nearby in our Galaxy, it appears suddenly as a brilliant new star, visible in the daytime.

The supernova explosion sprays the material of the star out into 9 space, where it mingles with fresh hydrogen to form a mixture containing all 92 elements. Later in the history of the galaxy, other stars are formed out of clouds of hydrogen which have been enriched by the products of these explosions. The sun is one of these stars; it is a recent arrival in the Cosmos, and contains the debris of countless supernova explosions dating back to the earliest years of our Galaxy. The planets also contain the debris; and the earth, in particular, is composed almost entirely of it. We owe our corporeal existence to events that took place billions of years ago, in stars that lived and died long before the solar system came into being.

This beautiful theory allows the Universe to go on forever in a 10 timeless cycle of death and rebirth, but for one disturbing fact. Fresh hydrogen is the essential ingredient in the plan; it is the main source of the energy by which stars shine, and it is also the source of all the other elements in the Universe. The moment a star is born it begins to consume some of the hydrogen in the Universe, and continues to use up hydrogen until it dies. Once hydrogen has been burned within that star and converted to heavier elements, it can never be restored to its original state. Minute by minute and year by year, as hydrogen is used up in stars, the supply of this element in the Universe grows smaller.

Reflecting on this situation, the astronomer turns the clock back 11 in his imagination and asks himself: What was the world like billions of years ago? Clearly there was more hydrogen in the Universe at that time than there is today, and less of the heavier elements. Ten billion years ago, there would have been still more hydrogen and still less of the heavier elements. Turning the clock back still farther, the astronomer comes to a time when the Universe contained nothing but hydrogen—no carbon, no oxygen, and none of the other elements out of which planets and life are made. This point in time must have marked the beginning of the Universe.

Vocabulary

tenuous (2)   embryonic (4)

Critical Inquiries

1. In what way does the author's narrative about the birth and death of stars conflict with the theory of creation proposed by some religions? In what way does it not conflict?

2. As a theory of the first cause, what essential mystery does this astronomical explanation not address? Why?

3. Two contending astronomical theories about the beginning differ in this way: one argues that the universe always was; the other, that the universe had a definite beginning. Which theory are religious believers likely to prefer, and why?

4. How are your religious beliefs affected by scientific theories offering alternative explanations about the beginning?

5. You are a brilliant research scientist who has formulated an experiment that can decisively prove, once and for all, whether or not God exists. Would your experiment necessarily be good for humans and their religious beliefs? Why, or why not?

Rhetorical Inquiries

1. In what way does this article correspond to the narrative form?

2. What technique does the author use in paragraph 3 to ensure its coherence?

3. What do the beginning and ending of this narrative have in common?

4. From whose point of view is the narrative told? Why is that an appropriate point of view?

5. Pacing is the technique of selective focus on a sequence of events, the passage of time, the phases of an act. What sequential factor does the author focus on in his pacing of this narrative?

MANAGEMENT

Laurence J. Peter
HISTORY OF THE PETER PRINCIPLE

Laurence J. Peter (b. 1919 in Vancouver, British Columbia), a psychologist, professor, writer and propounder of the Peter Principle—namely, that everyone has the tendency to rise to his or her level of incompetence—was educated at Washington State University (Ed.D., 1963). He is the author or coauthor of several books, including The Peter Principle: Why Things Always Go Wrong *(with Raymond Hull, 1969);* The Peter Prescription and How To Make Things Go Right *(1972); and* Competencies for Teaching, *(4 vols., 1975).*

Foreword from *The Peter Principle,* by Laurence J. Peter. Reprinted by permission of William Morrow and Co., Inc. Copyright © 1969 by William Morrow and Company, Inc.

It is sometimes difficult for the discoverer of a principle to iden-   1
tify accurately that moment when the revelation occurred. The Peter Principle did not enter my consciousness in a flash of recognition, but I became aware of it gradually over several years of
observation of man's incompetence. It therefore seems appropriate
I should present the reader with a historical account of my discovery.

A Clot for Every Slot

Although some people function competently, I observed others   2
who had risen above their level of competence and were habitually bungling their jobs, frustrating their coworkers and eroding the
efficiency of the organization. It was logical to conclude that for
every job that existed in the world there was someone, somewhere, who could not do it. Given sufficient time and enough promotions he would get that job!

I was not concerned with the oversight, the slip of the tongue,   3
the faux pas, the occasional error which can be an embarrassment
to any of us. Anyone can make a mistake. The most competent
men throughout history have had their lapses. Conversely, the habitually incompetent can, by random action, be right once in a
while. Instead, I was searching for the underlying principle which
would explain why so many important positions were occupied
by persons incompetent to fulfill the duties and responsibilities of
their respective offices.

Rot at the Top

The first public presentation of the Peter Principle occurred at a   4
seminar in September, 1960, when I addressed a group of directors
of federally funded educational research projects. Because each participant had written a successful grant proposal, each had been rewarded by a promotion to a position as director of one or more
research projects. Some of these men actually had research skills,
but this was irrelevant to their acquiring the directorship. Many
others were inept at research design and, in desperation, were simply intending to replicate some oft-repeated statistical exercise.

As I became aware of their plan to spend time and taxpayers'   5
money on rediscovering the wheel, I decided to explain their pre-
dicament by introducing them to the Peter Principle. Their reaction
to my presentation was a mixture of hostility and laughter. A

young statistician in the group convulsed with laughter and literally fell from his chair. Later he confided that his intense reaction
was caused by my humorous presentation of outrageous ideas
while at the same time he was watching the district research director's face turn red, then purple.

Tongue in Both Cheeks

Although case studies were accurately compiled and data realis-   6
tic, I had decided to present the Peter Principle exclusively in satirical form. Therefore, in all lectures from 1960 to 1964, and in the
articles that followed, examples with a humorous connotation
were used and fictitious names were employed to protect the
guilty.

All Rights Reserved

It was in December, 1963, during the intermission of a badly   7
presented play that I explained to Raymond Hull why the actor
playing the lead was saying his lines with his back to the audience
and gesturing into the wings. This formerly competent actor had
found his level of incompetence by attempting to be a combination actor-director-producer. In the conversation that ensued, Mr.
Hull convinced me that I was not doing justice to the Peter Principle by presenting it to only a select few who might attend my lectures. He insisted that it should be available to the world in book
form. He further suggested that without publication and copyright,
someone else might attach his name to my discovery. A collabora-
tion was agreed upon and the manuscript was completed in the
spring of 1965.

Victims of the Peter Principle

The final manuscript was submitted to the editors of a number   8
of major publishing houses. The first returned it with an accompanying letter which stated: "We can see no commercial possibilities
for this work and cannot encourage you to continue with it. Even
with interdivisional sales the publication of this work is not war-
ranted." The next editor wrote: "You should not deal so lightly
with such a serious topic." Another suggested: "If you are writing a
comedy, it should not contain so many tragic case studies." Still
another said: "I will reconsider publication if you will make up
your mind and rewrite this as a humorous book or as a serious sci-

entific work." Fourteen rejection notices and two years later I began to doubt whether the world was ready for my discovery.

A Bit at a Time

It was decided that if the publishing world was not ready for a book then perhaps we might introduce the Peter Principle gradually through several short articles. Mr. Hull completed an article for *Esquire* magazine for December, 1966. Later I wrote about the principle for West Magazine *(Los Angeles Times,* April 17, 1967). The response to this article was overwhelming. Over four hundred letters were received within a few months. Requests for lectures and articles poured in and as many as possible were fulfilled.   9

The Selling of the Principle, 1968

In March, 1968, the President of William Morrow inquired about the possibility of a book about the Peter Principle. I dusted off the manuscript and handed it to a William Morrow editor.   10

The book, released in February, 1969, gradually climbed to the number one position on the nonfiction best-seller list where it stayed for twenty weeks. It remained on the best-seller list for over a year and has now been translated into fourteen languages. The book has been required reading in a number of university courses and has been the subject of discussion for many seminars.   11

The book has also inspired several serious research projects investigating the validity of the principle. Each research supports the correctness of my observations.   12

Quit While You Are Behind

Since publication of the book I have had many opportunities to reach my own level of incompetence in one giant step. I have declined many offers to become a management consultant and to conduct seminars for business administrators. Although these proposals were rejected I have not been protected from the Peter Principle. Recently a school of business administration invited me to give a lecture and then scheduled my appearance in no less than five different rooms at the same time. An association of industrial engineers and systems experts asked me to address their convention but misinformed me regarding the date, the time, and the place. Appliances I have purchased still fail to operate, or break down within thirty days, my car is returned from the service shop   13 with mysterious defects, and the government continues to increase the number of regulations which influence my life, while it ensnares itself in bureaucratic red tape.

Death Is Nature's Warning to Slow Down

As individuals we tend to climb to our levels of incompetence. We behave as though *up* is better and *more* is better, and yet all around us we see the tragic victims of this mindless escalation.   14

We see men in groups, and most of the human race, struggling for status on a treadmill to oblivion, escalating warfare and weaponry to overkill the population of the world, escalating production of power and products while polluting the environment and upsetting the life-supporting ecological balance.   15

If man is going to rescue himself from a future intolerable existence, he must first see where his unmindful escalation is leading him. He must examine his objectives and see that true progress is achieved through moving *forward* to a better way of life, rather than *upward* to total life incompetence. Man must realize that improvement of the quality of experience is more important than the acquisition of useless artifacts and material possessions. He must reassess the meaning of life and decide whether he will use his intellect and technology for the preservation of the human race and the development of the humanistic characteristics of man, or whether he will continue to utilize his creative potential in escalating a super-collosal deathtrap.   16

Man, on occasion, has caught a glimpse of his reflection in a mirror, and not immediately recognizing himself, has begun to laugh before realizing what he was doing. It is in such moments that true progress toward understanding has occurred. This book is intended to be that mirror.   17

Vocabulary

faux pas (3)   convulsed (5)
replicate (4)   artifacts (16)

Critical Inquiries

1. What is flawed about the practice of promoting workers based on their competency at a specific job or task? What is the alternative to this practice, and why do businesses and institutions seem loath to follow it?

2. What, in your opinion, should be the penalty for job incompetence? What, the reward for competence?

3. If the Peter Principle is true, what steps can you take to prevent falling victim to it in your own work?

4. What are at least two other humorous laws to which business and work are commonly said to be subject?

5. What kind of organizational structure is prerequisite for the Peter Principle to function?

Rhetorical Inquiries

1. Upon its publication the Peter Principle enjoyed, and still enjoys, widespread popularity. To what do you think its success can be attributed?

2. What is the effect of the section headings sprinkled throughout this article?

3. What rhetorical advantage does Peter derive from his choice of a satirical, over a serious, presentation?

4. Why do you think the author quotes the critical comments of editors who rejected his manuscript?

5. Read the last three paragraphs. What would an author of today change in the wording of these same ideas and thoughts?

Exercises

1. What kind of person are you—patient, easygoing, nervous, timid, imaginative, jealous? Choose the adjective most characteristic of you and write a narrative paragraph that highlights it. Pace the narration to focus on details that prove what kind of person you are.

2. Using the point of view of either an old man or a young child, write a paragraph about the experience of opening gift packages at Christmas. Be sure to keep your point of view consistent.

3. Write a narrative paragraph or two on one of the following topics:
   a. Experience is the best teacher.
   b. when love turned to hate
   c. a psychic experience
   d. an awakening to books

4. Choose from the following pairs the word or phrase that is more concrete and specific.
   a. They beat him with chairs/furniture; they beat him with sticks/things; they beat him with weapons/guns.

b. After dinner you get out the machine/portable typewriter that you got for a present/high school graduation.

c. His face was leanly composed/serene.

d. He had some objects/statuettes in his study.

e. Five grueling/difficult nights this took, but it was worth it.

f. John is a big/husky boy of eleven.

g. Betty is constantly picked on by the other children for being a bungler/stupid.

h. He walked/swaggered onto the scene.

i. Punishing/Flogging the clients of prostitutes does seem silly.

j. They live under poor/brutal conditions.

Writing Assignments

1. In a 500-word essay, narrate any incident important to our history and culture that occurred within the last ten years. (Examples: the election of George Bush as 41st President of the United States; the space shuttle explosion of January 28, 1986, that killed seven astronauts, including teacher Christa McAuliffe). Pace your narration to make it interesting and use vivid details to capture your reader's imagination.

2. Read the anthologized article, "The Birth and Death of Stars." After doing the necessary research, write a narrative about the end astronomers predict for our solar system.

3. Using "Eating Christmas in the Kalahari" as your guide, write a narrative about some trait or belief of our culture that would strike an alien visitor as utterly inexplicable. Use the alien as your storyteller.

4. Write a narration that dramatizes your own contact or experience with the Peter Principle.

5. Narrate a classroom incident that taught you a lesson about you or your culture.

Chapter

8

Describing

Thy word is a lantern unto my feet: and a light unto my paths.

ENGLISH PRAYER BOOK, 1662

A good description lures the reader into a sensory experience of sight, touch, smell, taste by focusing on a single dominant impression and then supporting it with vivid details. For instance, the dominant impression of the paragraph below is a blinding November snowstorm in Russia:

> On the sixth of November the sky became terrible; its blue disappeared. The army marched along wrapped in a cold mist. Then the mist thickened, and presently from this immense cloud great snowflakes began to sift down on us. It seemed as if the sky had come down and joined with the earth and our enemies to complete our ruin. Everything in sight became vague, unrecognizable. Objects changed their shape; we walked without knowing where we were or what lay ahead, and anything became an obstacle. While the men were struggling to make headway against the icy, cutting blast, the snow driven by the wind was piling up and filling the hollows along the way. Their smooth surfaces hid unsuspected depths which opened up treacherously under our feet. The men were swallowed up, and the weak, unable to struggle out, were buried forever.
> —Count Philippe-Paul de Segur, *Napoleon's Russian Campaign.*

This description of the Russian winter storm that destroyed Napoleon's invading army allows the reader to feel the icy blast of the relentless wind, to see the sinister vagueness of the mist, to experience the mortal despair of the soldiers facing burial in the snowdrifts. The writer, who was an aide-de-camp of Napoleon, practiced in it the two fundamental requirements of all good descriptions: focusing on a dominant impression and appealing to the reader's senses.

Focus on a Dominant Impression

A dominant impression is a representative characteristic of the whole scene that functions as the theme of your description. We do not mean that the scene must resemble your dominant impression in every way. No doubt there were a handful of officers in Napoleon's retreating army who had the luxury of temporary shelter and adequate clothing to shield them from the ferocity of the storm. But if the author had focused on these fortunate few, he would have missed the mark in depicting the ravages of the wintry blast on the majority of the men. What you are after in your description is not photographic accuracy, but concentration of an overall theme that is mainly faithful to the truth. So if you have decided to describe the Ayatollah Khomeini as a stern fanatic, stick to that dominant impression and hammer it home with details. In the following example, the writer caught herself drifting away from the point of her dominant impression and edited out the details that tended to water it down:

> Iran's present leader, the Ayatollah
> Khomeini, is a frighteningly fanatical man, who
> rules without tenderness or mercy. During
> interviews with the press, his piercing black
> eyes send out darts of hatred, especially when
> he refers to the United States as "the great
> Satan." When he orders an execution——"Death by
> hanging!"——he does so without a hint of regret.
> His eyes mist over with gentleness when he is
> caught looking at one of his grandchildren. He
> obviously is a strong family man with a great
> love for his grandchildren.

If your subject does indeed combine cruelty and gentleness and you wish to include details about both traits, then you should word your dominant impression to reflect that odd blend. But given the dominant impression of the above paragraph, the writer was smart to delete the distracting sentences.

Here is yet another example of a descriptive paragraph, written about the German composer Richard Wagner (1813–1883), which focuses unremittingly on its dominant impression.

> He was a monster of conceit. Never for one minute did he look at the world or at people, except in relation to himself. He was not only the most important person in the world, to himself; in his own eyes he was the only person who existed. He believed himself to be one of the greatest dramatists in the world, one of the greatest thinkers, and one of the greatest composers. To hear him talk, he was Shakespeare, and Beethoven, and Plato, rolled into

one. And you would have had no difficulty in hearing him talk. He
was one of the most exhausting conversationalists that ever lived.
An evening with him was an evening spent in listening to a monologue. Sometimes he was brilliant; sometimes he was madden-
ingly tiresome. But whether he was being brilliant or dull, he had
one sole topic of conversation: himself. What *he* thought and what
he did.
—Deems Taylor, "The Monster," *Of Men and Music.*

Every detail supports the dominant impression—namely that "he was a
monster of conceit."

Appeal to the Reader's Senses through Specific Details and Figures of Speech

Specific detail is detail that is exact, representative, precise, and hard-
edged. Its opposite is the generalization made up of offhanded observations
and insipid adjectives. "He walked like a seaman and looked around him as
though he were at sea" is a generalization. "He walked with the stooping,
shuffling gait of a seafarer and squinted at everything about him as though
even the grasslands and trees sparkled with the painful scintillation of the
open sea" is specific. With practice, you will soon get a feel for this difference. Blurry generalizations, vague adjectives, drab details are the first to occur to any writer. Only after hard digging and searching does a writer occasionally strike a vein of crystalline images. Here is a passage from a first draft
filled with generalizations:

```
     The Eagle Rock Plaza is a melting pot of

lonely people.  Here the old people congregate

in the hope that they will find someone who will

listen to their sad tales of woe.  They sit on

one of the center benches, wearing old clothes

and old tennis shoes.  Sometimes, they munch on

food, and occasionally they can be seen

gratefully chatting with a younger person, who

probably reminds them of a son or daughter.

These are society's neglected citizens.
```

This drab description does not fulfill the promise of its opening sentence. Here is the second draft after the writer received some editorial suggestions from a peer group:

> The Eagle Rock Plaza is a melting pot of lonely people. These forlorn citizens migrate toward the center benches, where they sit in various hunched-over positions, their wrinkled eyes, furtively darting up and down the mall, hoping to catch a glimpse of some scene that will allow them to escape their empty lives for a few minutes. For instance, they will smile eagerly at two screaming four-year-olds fighting over a silver balloon, or at a young man spontaneously planting a kiss on his lover's lips. Occasionally, one of them will lick a single-scoop ice cream cone as if it were a gourmet delicacy--each bite savored and made to last as long as possible. Sooner or later, one of the more outgoing types will strike up a conversation with her neighbor: "Yep, my son's in charge of the Main Street post office," one might hear her announce proudly. Or, one of the old men, leaning on his cane, will complain, "The rheumatism is really getting to me today." The plaza is occupied by the same people every day--all suffering identical loneliness, but too proud to let anyone know.

This second draft is superior to the first mainly because it uses more vivid specific details.

The vividness of a description can usually be enhanced by the use of figures of speech. Often, these figures evoke a colorful comparison, as when the young boy from James Joyce's "Araby" falls in love and confesses that "my body was *like a harp* and her words and gestures were *like fingers running upon the wires."* Or, when William Faulkner describes Miss Emily: "She looked bloated, *like a body long submerged in motionless water,* and of that pallid hue. Her eyes, lost in the fatty ridges of her face, looked *like two small pieces of coal pressed into a lump of dough. . . .* "

Similes are comparisons openly linked by the prepositions "like" or "as." **Metaphors** are comparisons made without the use of any linking word as in the following description of May Bartram by Henry James: *"She was a sphinx,* yet with her white petals and green fronds *she might have been a lily too—only an artificial lily,* wonderfully imitated and constantly kept, without dust or stain, though not exempt from a slight droop and a complexity of faint creases, under some clear glass bell." The power of these figures is illustrated by this passage:

> She was a little woman, with brown, dull hair very elaborately arranged, and she had prominent blue eyes behind invisible pince-nez. Her face was long, *like a sheep's;* but she gave no impression of foolishness, rather of extreme alertness; *she had the quick movements of a bird.* The most remarkable thing about her was her voice, high, metallic, and without inflection; it fell on the ear with a hard monotony, irritating to the nerves *like the pitiless clamour of the pneumatic drill.*
> —W. Somerset Maugham, *Rain.*

Figures of speech can add sparkle to your writing, but they should be used cautiously and with a deft touch. Overusing these figures, especially in straight expository writing, can make writing seem ridiculous rather than sublime. There are also some well-known dangers attendant on their use. The first is triteness. It is better to write plain descriptions than colorfully trite ones. Similes such as "white as a sheet," "hungry as a bear," or "sharp as a needle" are shopworn and no longer effective. Other examples of tired images are expressions such as "He threw in the towel"; "They swallowed it hook, line, and sinker"; "There's a fly in the ointment."

The second danger is the mixed figure of speech. Some examples of these, culled from actual student papers, are: "Into every life some rainbows will fall"; "He is a thorn among daisies"; "She tends to sweep all of the perfume of life under the rug." The effect of these twisted images is invariably comical.

Finally, be careful not to create an absurd image through the use of the wrong word or clumsy phrasing. Here are some examples: "Many problems steam throughout the city"; "In many areas of the world people bear the weight of suffrage"; "The movements of break dancing are completely uninhabited;" "Once you have climbed the hill of education, don't throw your knowledge overboard."

A staple of everyday communication, descriptive writing is by no means always devoted to depicting scenes or persons. For example, in the essays at the end of this chapter, a psychiatrist describes a game played by nurses and doctors, while a sociologist describes the corporate top, which is more than just a physical place. The Irish writer James Joyce contributes a stirring description of hell, and a naturalist paints for us the ways and habits of the common shrew.

The student paragraph is devoted to describing a place, the island of Iwo Jima, site of a fierce and bloody battle of World War II between American and Japanese troops. Pay attention to the editorial comments in the margin and to the changes the writer made in revision. Mainly, what the student did in revising the paragraph was to strengthen its dominant impression, eliminate those sentences that detracted from it, and add more specific details.

Original:

Needs a stronger dominant impression
Be more specific

> The island of Iwo Jima is the site where many men have died. As the wind blowing in from the sea tousled my hair, I felt myself deeply moved. Perhaps it was the sight of war wreckage all around me. Not more than three feet from me were the very bunkers that had housed the Japanese guns. These same guns had mercilessly pounded the landing craft at point-blank range

Eliminate cliché

> until the beach was cluttered with craft smashed to smithereens. To my right was another beach

Drop details that don't support your dominant impression.

> the invasion forces attacked as an alternative. The beach was long and sloping, so it provided no cover. Fishing canoes sunned themselves there, accenting a scene of peace and

Add more details about this.

tranquility. The Japanese had defended this calm and beautiful beach with an interlocking network of machine gun emplacements; many lives were lost capturing the beach. No wonder I felt odd, standing here on this plot of death. One could almost hear the screams of a thousand souls caught in the anguish and torment of battle.

Revision:

Looking out over the barren, windswept island of Iwo Jima, I stood on the pinnacle of Mount Suribachi surveying the site where, 39 years before, thousands of men had struggled and died for this barren speck of volcanic ash. As the wind blowing in from the sea tousled my hair, I felt myself deeply moved by an eerie sense of death and foreboding. Perhaps it was the sight of the American landing craft still sitting there, half submerged in the shallows, that made my knees quiver. Their shattered hulks sat there rusting through the years since that fateful day they had met their destruction at the hands of the Japanese defenders. Not more than three feet from me were the very bunkers that had housed the Japanese guns. These same guns had mercilessly pounded the landing craft at point-blank range until the beach was cluttered with wreckage and impassable for the remaining troops. To my right was another beach the invasion forces attacked as an alternative.

The beach was long and sloping, so it provided no cover. The Japanese had defended it with an interlocking network of machine gun emplacements; many lives were lost capturing the beach. No wonder I was ill at ease, standing here on this plot of death. One could almost hear the screams of a thousand souls caught in the anguish and torment of battle.

LITERATURE

James Joyce

HELL

James Joyce (1882–1941), Irish writer, is numbered among the most eminent novelists and writers of this century. Born in Dublin, Ireland, and educated at University College, Dublin, Joyce spent the greater part of his adult life abroad in Paris and Zurich. He is regarded as a master stylist who, in his attempts to recreate on the page the interior life of his characters, pushed language to its outer limit of intelligibility. His major works are Portrait of the Artist as a Young man *(1916),* Ulysses *(published in the United States in 1933 after a lengthy court challenge on grounds of alleged obscenity), and* Finnegan's Wake *(1939). The selection below is taken from* Portrait of the Artist as a Young Man, *an autobiographical account of Joyce's early years at Catholic schools in Ireland.*

Hell is a strait and dark and foulsmelling prison, an abode of demons and lost souls, filled with fire and smoke. The straitness of this prisonhouse is expressly designed by God to punish those who refused to be bound by His laws. In earthly prisons the poor captive has at least some liberty of movement, were it only within the four walls of his cell or in the gloomy yard of his prison. Not so in hell. There, by reason of the great number of the damned, the prisoners are heaped together in their awful prison, the walls of which are said to be four thousand miles thick: and the damned are so utterly bound and helpless that, as a blessed saint, saint

1

From *The Portrait of an Artist as a Young Man,* by James Joyce. Copyright 1916 by B. W. Huebsch, 1944 by Nora Joyce. Copyright © 1964 by the Estate of James Joyce. All rights reserved. Reprinted by permission of Viking Penguin, a division of Penguin Books USA, Inc.

Anselm, writes in his book on similitudes, they are not even able to remove from the eye a worm that gnaws it.

They lie in exterior darkness. For, remember, the fire of hell 2
gives forth no light. As, at the command of God, the fire of the Babylonian furnace lost its heat but not its light so, at the command of God, the fire of hell, while retaining the intensity of its heat, burns eternally in darkness. It is a neverending storm of darkness, dark flames and dark smoke of burning brimstone, amid which the bodies are heaped one upon another without even a glimpse of air. Of all the plagues with which the land of the Pharaohs was smitten one plague alone, that of darkness, was called horrible. What name, then, shall we give to the darkness of hell which is to last not for three days alone but for all eternity?

The horror of this strait and dark prison is increased by its awful 3
stench. All the filth of the world, all the offal and scum of the world, we are told, shall run there as to a vast reeking sewer when the terrible conflagration of the last day has purged the world. The brimstone too which burns there in such prodigious quantity fills all hell with its intolerable stench; and the bodies of the damned themselves exhale such a pestilential odour that as saint Bonaventure says, one of them alone would suffice to infect the whole world. The very air of this world, that pure element, becomes foul and unbreathable when it has been long enclosed. Consider then what must be the foulness of the air of hell. Imagine some foul and putrid corpse that has lain rotting and decomposing in the grave, a jellylike mass of liquid corruption. Imagine such a corpse a prey to flames, devoured by the fire of burning brimstone and giving off dense choking fumes of nauseous loathsome decomposition. And then imagine this sickening stench, multiplied a millionfold and a millionfold again from the millions upon millions of fetid carcasses massed together in the reeking darkness, a huge and rotting human fungus. Imagine all this and you will have some idea of the horror of the stench of hell.

But this stench is not, horrible though it is, the greatest physical 4
torment to which the damned are subjected. The torment of fire is the greatest torment to which the tyrant has ever subjected his fellowcreatures. Place your finger for a moment in the flame of a candle and you will feel the pain of fire. But our earthly fire was created by God for the benefit of man, to maintain in him the spark of life and to help him in the useful arts whereas the fire of hell is of another quality and was created by God to torture and punish the unrepentant sinner. Our earthly fire also consumes more or less rapidly according as the object which it attacks is more or less

combustible so that human ingenuity has even succeeded in inventing chemical preparations to check or frustrate its action. But the sulphurous brimstone which burns in hell is a substance which is specially designed to burn for ever and for ever with unspeakable fury. Moreover our earthly fire destroys at the same time as it burns so that the more intense it is the shorter is its duration: but the fire of hell has this property that it preserves that which it burns and though it rages with incredible intensity it rages for ever.

Our earthly fire again, no matter how fierce or widespread it may be, is always of a limited extent: but the lake of fire in hell is boundless, shoreless and bottomless. It is on record that the devil himself, when asked the question by a certain soldier, was obliged to confess that if a whole mountain were thrown into the burning ocean of hell it would be burned up in an instant like a piece of wax. And this terrible fire will not afflict the bodies of the damned only from without but each lost soul will be a hell unto itself, the boundless fire raging in its very vitals. O, how terrible is the lot of those wretched beings! The blood seethes and boils in the veins, the brains are boiling in the skull, the heart in the breast glowing and bursting, the bowels a redhot mass of burning pulp, the tender eyes flaming like molten balls.

And yet what I have said as to the strength and quality and boundlessness of this fire is as nothing when compared to its intensity, an intensity which it has as being the instrument chosen by divine design for the punishment of soul and body alike. It is a fire which proceeds directly from the ire of God, working not of its own activity but as an instrument of divine vengeance. As the waters of baptism cleanse the soul with the body so do the fires of punishment torture the spirit with the flesh. Every sense of the flesh is tortured and every faculty of the soul therewith: the eyes with impenetrable utter darkness, the nose with noisome odours, the ears with yells and howls and execrations, the taste with foul matter, leprous corruption, nameless suffocating filth, the touch with redhot goads and spikes, with cruel tongues of flame. And through the several torments of the senses the immortal soul is tortured eternally in its very essence amid the leagues upon leagues of glowing fires kindled in the abyss by the offended majesty of the Omnipotent God and fanned into everlasting and ever increasing fury by the breath of the anger of the Godhead.

Consider finally that the torment of this infernal prison is increased by the company of the damned themselves. Evil company on earth is so noxious that even the plants, as if by instinct, withdraw from the company of whatsoever is deadly or hurtful to them. In hell all laws are overturned: there is no thought of family or country, of ties, of relationships. The damned howl and scream at one another, their torture and rage intensified by the presence of beings tortured and raging like themselves. All sense of humanity is forgotten. The yells of the suffering sinners fill the remotest corners of the vast abyss. The mouths of the damned are full of blasphemies against God and of hatred for their fellowsufferers and of curses against those souls which were their accomplices in sin. In olden times it was the custom to punish the parricide, the man who had raised his murderous hand against his father, by casting him into the depths of the sea in a sack in which were placed a cock, a monkey and a serpent. The intention of those lawgivers who framed such a law, which seems cruel in our times, was to punish the criminal by the company of hateful and hurtful beasts. But what is the fury of those dumb beasts compared with the fury of execration which bursts from the parched lips and aching throats of the damned in hell when they behold in their companions in misery those who aided and abetted them in sin, those whose words sowed the first seeds of evil thinking and evil living in their minds, those whose immodest suggestions led them on to sin, those whose eyes tempted and allured them from the path of virtue. They turn upon those accomplices and upbraid them and curse them. But they are helpless and hopeless: it is too late now for repentance.

Vocabulary

conflagration (3)	execrations (6)
prodigious (3)	noxious (7)
pestilential (3)	parricide (7)
noisome (6)	allured (7)

Critical Inquiries

1. What is your attitude towards the possible existence of hell?

2. If God is omniscient and omnipotent, how is the exercise of free will possible in the choice of sinfulness or virtue? If free will is not possible, is damnation predestined even before birth—or the result of personal choice?

3. What is your attitude towards the belief in eternal damnation for a sin that may have been committed only in fleeting moments?

4. Literary accounts and descriptions of hell are always more gripping and vivid than similar attempts at depicting heaven. Why do you think this is so?

5. How can the concept of hell be reconciled with the concept of a forgiving and merciful God?

Rhetorical Inquiries

1. What is the dominant impression behind this description, and where is it stated?

2. What authority support does the author evoke in this description and how is it used?

3. What allusions does the author make in paragraph 2, and how do they add to his description?

4. What other rhetorical mode does the author enlist to the aid of his description in paragraph 5? Comment on the effectiveness of using this other mode.

5. Around what dominant impression is paragraph 3 centered, and to which sense does this impression appeal?

SOCIOLOGY OF MEDICINE

Leonard I. Stein
THE DOCTOR–NURSE GAME

Leonard I. Stein, M.D., is a professor of psychiatry at the University of Wisconsin Medical School and Medical Director of the Dane County Mental Health Center, Madison, Wisconsin. He is the author of numerous professional articles and studies, and of two monographs, Community Support Systems for the Long Term Patient *(1979); and* The Training in Community Living Model: A Decade of Experience *(1985, with Mary Ann Test).*

The relationship between the doctor and the nurse is a very special one. There are few professions where the degree of mutual respect and cooperation between co-workers is as intense as that between the doctor and nurse. Superficially, the stereotype of this relationship has been dramatized in many novels and television serials. When, however, it is observed carefully in an interactional framework, the relationship takes on a new dimension and has a

From *Archives of General Psychiatry,* vol. 16, 1967, 699–703. Copyright 1967, American Medical Association.

special quality which fits a game model. The underlying attitudes which demand that this game be played are unfortunate. These attitudes create serious obstacles in the path of meaningful communications between physicians and nonmedical professional groups.

The physician traditionally and appropriately has total responsibility for making the decisions regarding the management of his patients' treatment. To guide his decisions he considers data gleaned from several sources. He acquires a complete medical history, performs a thorough physical examination, interprets laboratory findings, and at times obtains recommendations from physician-consultants. Another important factor in his decision making is the recommendations he receives from the nurse. The interaction between doctor and nurse through which these recommendations are communicated and received is unique and interesting.   2

The Game

One rarely hears a nurse say, "Doctor, I would recommend that   3
you order a retention enema for Mrs. Brown." A physician, upon hearing a recommendation of that nature, would gape in amazement at the effrontery of the nurse. The nurse, upon hearing the statement, would look over her shoulder to see who said it, hardly believing the words actually came from her own mouth. Nevertheless, if one observes closely, nurses make recommendations of more import every hour and physicians willingly and respectfully consider them. If the nurse is to make a suggestion without appearing insolent and the doctor is to seriously consider that suggestion, their interaction must not violate the rules of the game.

Object of the Game

The object of the game is as follows: the nurse is to be bold,   4
have initiative, and be responsible for making significant recommendations, while at the same time she must appear passive. This must be done in such a manner so as to make her recommendations appear to be initiated by the physician.

Both participants must be acutely sensitive to each other's non-   5
verbal and cryptic verbal communications. A slight lowering of the head, a minor shifting of position in the chair, or a seemingly nonrelevant comment concerning an event which occurred eight months ago must be interpreted as a powerful message. The game requires the nimbleness of a high wire acrobat, and if either participant slips, the game can be shattered; the penalties for frequent failure are apt to be severe.

Rules of the Game

The cardinal rule of the game is that open disagreement be- 6
tween the players must be avoided at all costs. Thus, the nurse
must communicate her recommendations without appearing to be
making a recommendation statement. The physician, in requesting
a recommendation from a nurse, must do so without appearing to
be asking for it. Utilization of this technique keeps anyone from
committing themselves to a position before a subrosa agreement
on that position has already been established. In that way open
disagreement is avoided. The greater the significance of the recommendation, the more subtly the game must be played.

To convey a subtle example of the game with all its nuances 7
would require the talents of a literary artist. Lacking these talents,
let me give you the following example, which is unsubtle but happens frequently. The medical resident on hospital call is awakened
by telephone at 1:00 A.M., because a patient on a ward, not his
own, has not been able to fall asleep. Dr. Jones answers the telephone and the dialogue goes like this:

This is Dr. Jones. 8

(An open and direct communication.) 9

Dr. Jones, This is Miss Smith on 2W—Mrs. Brown, who 10
learned today of her father's death, is unable to fall asleep.

(This message has two levels. Openly, it describes a set of cir- 11
cumstances: a woman who is unable to sleep and who that morning received word of her father's death. Less openly, but just as directly, it is a diagnostic and recommendation statement; i.e., Mrs.
Brown is unable to sleep because of her grief, and she should be
given a sedative. Dr. Jones, accepting the diagnostic statement and
replying to the recommendation statement, answers.)

What sleeping medication has been helpful to Mrs. Brown in the 12
past?

(Dr. Jones, not knowing the patient, is asking for a recommen- 13
dation from the nurse, who does know the patient, about what
sleeping medication should be prescribed. Note, however, his
question does not appear to be asking her for a recommendation.
Miss Smith replies.)

Pentobarbital mg 100 was quite effective night before last. 14

(A disguised recommendation statement. Dr. Jones replies with 15
a note of authority in his voice.)

Pentobarbital mg 100 before bedtime as needed for sleep; got it? 16

(Miss Smith ends the conversation with the tone of a grateful 17
supplicant.)

Yes, I have, and thank you very much doctor. 18

The above is an example of a successfully played doctor–nurse   19
game. The nurse made appropriate recommendations which were
accepted by the physician and were helpful to the patient. The
game was successful because the cardinal rule was not violated.
The nurse was able to make her recommendations without appearing to, and the physician was able to ask for recommendations
without conspicuously asking for them.

The Scoring System

Inherent in any game are penalties and rewards for the players.   20
In game theory, the doctor–nurse game fits the non-
zero-sum-game model. It is not like chess, where the players compete with each other and whatever one player loses the other
wins. Rather, it is the kind of game in which the rewards and pun-
ishments are shared by both players. If they play the game successfully they both win rewards, and if they are unskilled and the
game is played badly, they both suffer the penalty.

The most obvious reward from the well-played game is a doc-   21
tor–nurse team that operates efficiently. The physician is able to
utilize the nurse as a valuable consultant, and the nurse gains self-
esteem and professional satisfaction from her job. The less obvious
rewards are no less important. A successful game creates a doctor–
nurse alliance; through this alliance the physician gains the respect
and admiration of the nursing service. He can be confident that his
nursing staff will smooth the path for getting his work done. His
charts will be organized and waiting for him when he arrives, the
ruffled feathers of patients and relatives will have been smoothed
down, his pet routines will be happily followed, and he will be
helped in a thousand and one other ways.

The doctor–nurse alliance sheds its light on the nurse as well.   22
She gains a reputation for being a "damn good nurse." She is respected by everyone and appropriately enjoys her position. When
physicians discuss the nursing staff it would not be unusual for her
name to be mentioned with respect and admiration. Their esteem
for a good nurse is no less than their esteem for a good doctor.

The penalties for a game failure, on the other hand, can be se-   23
vere. The physician who is an unskilled gamesman and fails to recognize the nurses' subtle recommendation messages is tolerated as
a "clod." If, however, he interprets these messages as insolence and
strongly indicates he does not wish to tolerate suggestions from
nurses, he creates a rocky path for his travels. This old truism "If
the nurse is your ally you've got it made, and if she has it in for

you, be prepared for misery" takes on life-size proportions. He receives three times as many phone calls after midnight as his colleagues. Nurses will not accept his telephone orders, because "telephone orders are against the rules." Somehow, this rule gets suspended for the skilled players. Soon he becomes like Joe Bfstplk in the "Li'l Abner" comic strip. No matter where he goes, a black cloud constantly hovers over his head.

The unskilled gamesman–nurse also pays heavily. The nurse 24 who does not view her role as that of consultant, and therefore does not attempt to communicate recommendations, is perceived as a dullard and is mercifully allowed to fade into the woodwork.

The nurse who does see herself as a consultant but refuses to 25 follow the rules of the game in making her recommendations has hell to pay. The outspoken nurse is labeled a "bitch" by the surgeon. The psychiatrist describes her as unconsciously suffering from penis envy, and her behavior is the acting out of her hostility towards men. Loosely translated, the psychiatrist is saying she is a bitch. The employment of the unbright, outspoken nurse is soon terminated. The outspoken, bright nurse whose recommendations are worthwhile remains employed. She is, however, constantly reminded in a hundred ways that she is not loved.

Genesis of the Game

To understand how the game evolved, we must comprehend 26 the nature of the doctors' and nurses' training which shaped the attitudes necessary for the game.

Medical Student Training

The medical student in his freshman year studies as if possessed. 27 In the anatomy class he learns every groove and prominence on the bones of the skeleton as if life depended on it. As a matter of fact, he literally believes just that. He not infrequently says, "I've got to learn it exactly; a life may depend on me knowing that." A consequence of this attitude, which is carefully nurtured throughout medical school, is the development of a phobia: the overdetermined fear of making a mistake. The development of this fear is quite understandable. The burden the physician must carry is at times almost unbearable. He feels responsible in a very personal way for the lives of his patients. When a man dies leaving young children and a widow, the doctor carries some of her grief and despair inside himself; and when a child dies, some of him dies too.

He sees himself as a warrior against death and disease. When he loses a battle, through no fault of his own, he nevertheless feels pangs of guilt, and he relentlessly searches himself to see if there might have been a way to alter the outcome. For the physician a mistake leading to a serious consequence is intolerable, and any mistake reminds him of his vulnerability. There is little wonder that he becomes phobic. The classical way in which phobias are managed is to avoid the source of the fear. Since it is impossible to avoid making some mistakes in an active practice of medicine, a substitute defensive maneuver is employed. The physician develops the belief that he is omnipotent and omniscient and therefore incapable of making mistakes. This belief allows the phobic physician to actively engage in his practice rather than avoid it. The fear of committing an error in a critical field like medicine is unavoidable and appropriately realistic. The physician, however, must learn to live with the fear rather than handle it defensively through a posture of omnipotence. This defense markedly interferes with his interpersonal professional relationships.

Physicians, of course, deny feelings of omnipotence. The evidence, however, renders their denials whispers in the wind. The slightest mistake inflicts a large narcissistic wound. Depending on his underlying personality structure, the physician may be obsessed for days about it, quickly rationalize it away, or deny it. The guilt produced is unusually exaggerated, and the incident is handled defensively. The ways in which physicians enhance and support each other's defenses when an error is made could be the topic of another paper. The feeling of omnipotence becomes generalized to other areas of his life. A report of the Federal Aviation Agency (FAA), as quoted in *Time* (August 5, 1966), states that in 1964 and 1965, physicians had a fatal-accident rate four times as high as the average for all other private pilots. Major causes of the high death rate were risk-taking attitudes and judgments. Almost all of the accidents occurred on pleasure trips and were therefore not necessary risks to get to a patient needing emergency care. The trouble, suggested an FAA official, is that too many doctors fly with "the feeling that they are omnipotent." Thus, the extremes to which the physician may go in preserving his self-concept of omnipotence may threaten his own life. This overdetermined preservation of omnipotence is indicative of its brittleness and its underlying foundation of fear of failure. 28

The physician finds himself trapped in a paradox. He fervently wants to give his patient the best possible medical care, and being open to the nurses' recommendations helps him accomplish this. 29

On the other hand, accepting advice from nonphysicians is highly threatening to his omnipotence. The solution for the paradox is to receive sub-rosa recommendations and make them appear to be initiated by himself. In short, he must learn to play the doctor–nurse game.

Some physicians never learn to play the game. Most learn in their internship, and a perceptive few learn during their clerkships in medical school. Medical students frequently complain that the nursing staff treats them as if they had just completed a junior Red Cross first-aid class instead of two years of intensive medical training. Interviewing nurses in a training hospital sheds considerable light on this phenomenon. In their words they said:

> A few students just seem to be with it, they are able to understand what you are trying to tell them and they are a pleasure to work with; most, however, pretend to know everything and refuse to listen to anything we have to say and I guess we do give them a rough time.

In essence, they are saying that those students who quickly learn the game are rewarded, and those that do not are punished.

Most physicians learn to play the game after they have weathered a few experiences like the one described below. On the first day of his internship, the physician and nurse were making rounds. They stopped at the bed of a fifty-two-year-old woman who, after complimenting the young doctor on his appearance, complained to him of her problem with constipation. After several minutes of listening to her detailed description of peculiar diets, family home remedies, and special exercises that have helped her constipation in the past, the nurse politely interrupted the patient. She told her the doctor would take care of the problem and that he had to move on because there were other patients waiting to see him. The young doctor gave the nurse a stern look, turned toward the patient, and kindly told her he would order an enema for her that very afternoon. As they left the bedside, the nurse told him the patient has had a normal bowel movement every day for the past week and that in the twenty-three days the patient has been in the hospital she has never once passed up an opportunity to complain of her constipation. She quickly added that *if* the doctor wanted to order an enema, the patient would certainly receive one. After hearing this report the intern's mouth fell open, and the wheels began turning in his head. He remembered the nurse's comment to the patient that "the doctor had to move on," and it occurred to him that perhaps she was really giving him a message. This experience and a few more like it, and the young doctor learns to listen for the subtle recommendations the nurses make.

Nursing Student Training

Unlike the medical student who usually learns to play the game after he finishes medical school, the nursing student begins to learn it early in her training. Throughout her education she is trained to play the doctor–nurse game. 32

Student nurses are taught how to relate to the physician. They are told he has infinitely more knowledge than they, and thus he should be shown the utmost respect. In addition, it was not many years ago when nurses were instructed to stand whenever a physician entered a room. When he would come in for a conference, the nurse was expected to offer him her chair, and when both entered a room the nurse would open the door for him and allow him to enter first. Although these practices are no longer rigidly adhered to, the premise upon which they were based is still promulgated. One nurse described that premise as, "He's God almighty and your job is to wait on him." 33

To inculcate subservience and inhibit deviancy, nursing schools, for the most part, are tightly run, disciplined institutions. Certainly, there is great variation among nursing schools, and there is little question that the trend is toward giving students more autonomy. However, in too many schools this trend has not gone far enough, and the climate remains restrictive. The student's schedule is firmly controlled, and there is very little free time. Classroom hours, study hours, mealtime, and bedtime with lights out are rigidly enforced. In some schools meaningless chores are assigned, such as cleaning bedsprings with cotton applicators. The relationship between student and instructor continues this military flavor. Often their relationship is more like that between recruit and drill sergeant than between student and teacher. Open dialogue is inhibited by attitudes of strict black and white with few, if any, shades of gray. Straying from the rigidly outlined path is sure to result in disciplinary action. 34

The inevitable result of these practices is to instill in the student nurse a fear of independent action. This inhibition of independent action is most marked when relating to physicians. One of the students' greatest fears is making a blunder while assisting a physician and being publicly ridiculed by him. This is really more a reflection of the nature of their training than the prevalence of 35 abusive physicians. The fear of being humiliated for a blunder while assisting in a procedure is generalized to the fear of humiliation for making any independent act in relating to a physician, especially the act of making a direct recommendation. Every nurse interviewed felt that making a suggestion to a physician was equivalent to insulting and belittling him. It was tantamount to questioning his medical knowledge and insinuating he did not know his business. In light of her image of the physician as an omniscient and punitive figure, the questioning of his knowledge would be unthinkable.

The student, however, is also given messages quite contrary to the ones described above. She is continually told that she is an invaluable aid to the physician in the treatment of the patient. She is told that she must help him in every way possible and that she is imbued with a strong sense of responsibility for the care of her patient. Thus she, like the physician, is caught in a paradox. The first set of messages implies that the physician is omniscient and that any recommendation she might make would be insulting to him and leave her open to ridicule. The second set of messages implies that she is an important aspect to him, has much to contribute, and is duty-bound to make those contributions. Thus, when her good sense tells her a recommendation would be helpful to him, she is not allowed to communicate it directly, nor is she allowed not to communicate it. The way out of the bind is to use the doctor–nurse game and communicate the recommendation without appearing to do so.

Vocabulary

stereotype (1)

effrontery (3)

insolent (3)

sub-rosa (6)

nuances (7)

unsubtle (7)

supplicant (12)

inherent (14)

truism (17)

dullard (18)

nurtured (21)

narcissistic (22)

enhance (22)

adhered (27)

promulgated (27)

subservience (28)

inhibit (28)

autonomy (28)

instill (29)

belittling (29)

tantamount (29)

punitive (29)

imbued (30)

Critical Inquiries

1. In his examples, Stein always assumes that the doctor is a male and the nurse a female. To what extent do you think sexism rather than professional necessity might be responsible for the doctor–nurse game?

2. What practical steps do you think might be taken to entirely eliminate the need for the doctor–nurse game?

3. Using techniques of artificial intelligence, many expert medical systems exist that make medical diagnoses with uncanny accuracy. Forecasts are for such systems to become increasingly popular in the future, and possibly even to someday replace physicians. What effect do you think the advent of such computer technology is likely to have on the doctor–nurse game?

4. The writer attributes the origin of the doctor–nurse game to the need many doctors feel to feign omnipotence. What other sociological explanation do you think might explain the origin of the game?

5. What disadvantages can you perceive in the doctor–nurse game as it is presently played?

Rhetorical Inquiries

1. How would you sum up, in your own words, the dominant impression driving the description in this article?

2. What technique for achieving coherence does the writer use in paragraph 6?

3. What is odd about the sentences making up paragraph 13? How might you revise them to add variety to the style?

4. In paragraph 16, what is the author implying by placing the words "damn good nurse" in quotation marks?

5. What is the purpose of paragraph 20? What is the primary rhetorical purpose and mode of the remaining paragraphs that follow it?

ZOOLOGY

Alan Devoe
SHREW—THE LITTLEST MAMMAL

Alan Devoe (1909–1955) was a prolific writer of naturalist essays and books. He contributed widely to numerous magazines, among them the American Mercury, Audubon, *and* Reader's Digest. *He was also the author of many books, including* Phudd Hill *(1937),* Down to Earth *(1940), and* This Fascinating Animal World *(1951).*

The zoological Class to which we human beings belong is the Mammalia. There has been some dispute as to whether we possess immortal souls and the capacity for a unique kind of intellection, but we do possess unquestionably the " . . . four-chambered heart, double circulatory system, thoracic cavity separated from abdominal cavity by muscular diaphragm, and habit of bearing the young alive and nursing them at the breast" which classically establish our membership in that group of warm-blooded animals which are guessed to have come into being on the planet some hundred-odd million years ago.

It is today a large and various group, this mammalian kindred. With some of our fellow-mammals it is not hard to feel relationship: with apes, for instance, or with the small sad-eyed monkeys that we keep for our beguilement as flea-bitten captives in our pet-shops. But with others of the group our tie is less apparent; and the reason, often enough, is disparity of size and shape. It is such disparity, no doubt, that prevents our having much fellow-feeling for the hundred-ton sulphur-bottomed whales that plunge through the deep waters of both Pacific and Atlantic, though whales' blood is warmed as ours is, and the females of their kind have milky teats; and likewise it is doubtless in part because we have two legs and attain to some seventy inches of height that we do not take as much account as otherwise we might of the little animal that is at the opposite end of the mammal size-scale: the little four-footed mammal that is rather smaller than a milkweed pod and not as heavy as a cecropia cocoon.

This tiniest of mammals is the minute beast called a shrew. A man need go to no great trouble to look at it, as he must to see a whale; he can find it now in the nearest country woodlot. Despite its tininess a shrew is still after a fashion a relative of ours; and on that account, even if on no other, should merit a little knowing.

In the narrow twisting earth-burrow dug by a mouse or a mole the least of the mammals is usually born. Its fellows in the litter may number four or five, and they lie together in the warm subterranean darkness of their tiny nest-chamber in a little group whose whole bulk is scarcely that of a walnut. The infant shrew, relative

Excerpt from *Lives Around Us,* by Alan Devoe. Copyright © 1942 by Alan Devoe. Copyright renewal © 1969 by Mary Devoe Guinn. Reprinted by permission of Farrar, Straus and Giroux, Inc.

of whales and elephants and us, is no more than a squirming pink speck of warm-fleshed animal aliveness. Totally defenseless and unequipped for life, it can only nuzzle the tiny dugs of its mother, wriggle tightly against its brothers to feel the warmth of the litter, and for many hours of the twenty-four lie asleep in the curled head-to-toes position of a minuscule foetus.

The baby shrew remains a long time in the birth-chamber. The size of even an adult shrew is very nearly the smallest possible for mammalian existence, and the young one cannot venture out into the world of adult activity until it has almost completely matured. Until then, therefore, it stays in the warm darkness of the burrow, knowing the universe only as a heat of other little bodies, a pungence of roots and grasses, a periodic sound of tiny chittering squeakings when its mother enters the burrow after foraging-trips, bringing food. She brings in mostly insects—small lady-beetles whose brittle spotted wing-covers must be removed before they can be eaten, soft-bodied caterpillars, ants, and worms. The young shrew, after its weaning has come about, acquires the way of taking this new food between its slim delicate forepaws, fingered like little hands, and in the under-earth darkness nibbles away the wing-covers and chitinous body-shells as adroitly as a squirrel removes the husk from a nut.

When at last the time comes for the young shrew to leave its birthplace, it has grown very nearly as large as its mother and has developed all the adult shrew-endowments. It looks, now, not unlike a mouse, save that its muzzle is more sharply pointed, but a mouse reduced in size to extreme miniature. The whole length of its soft-furred little body is only a fraction more than two inches, compared to the four-inch length of even the smallest of the white-footed woods-mice; its tail is less than half as long as a mouse's. The uniquely little body is covered with dense soft hair, sepia above and a paler buffy color underneath—a covering of fur so fine and close that the shrew's ears are nearly invisible in it, and the infinitesimal eyes are scarcely to be discerned. The shrew's hands and feet are white, smaller and more delicate than any other beast's; white also is the underside of the minute furry tail. The whole body, by its softness of coat and coloring and its tininess of bulk, seems far from kinship with the tough strong bodies of the greater mammals. But it is blood-brother to these, all the same; warm blood courses in it; the shrew is as much mammal as a wolf. It sets forth, with its unparalleledly tiny physical equipments, to live as adventurous a life as any of its greater warm-blooded relatives.

The life-adventure of Man, "the medium-sized mammal," is

shaped by such diverse motives and impulsions that it is difficult to say what may be the most powerful of the driving urges that direct it. In the life-adventure of the littlest mammal, the shrew, the driving urge is very plain and single: it is hunger. Like hummingbirds, smallest of the *Aves,* this smallest of the mammals lives at a tremendous pitch of nervous intensity. The shrew's little body quite literally quivers with the vibrance of life-force that is in it; from tiny pointed snout to tailtip the shrew is ever in a taut furor of aliveness. Its body-surface, like a hummingbird's, is maximally extensive in relation to its minimal weight; its metabolism must proceed with immense rapidity; to sustain the quivering nervous aliveness of its mite of warm flesh it must contrive a food-intake that is almost constant. It is possible on that account to tell the shrew's life-story almost wholly in terms of its feeding. The shrew's life has other ingredients, of course—the seeking of its small mate, the various rituals of copulating and sleeping and dung-dropping and the rest, that are common to all mammal-lives—but it is the process of feeding that is central and primary, and that is the distinguishing preoccupation of the littlest mammal all its days.

The shrew haunts mostly moist thick-growing places, the banks of streams and the undergrowth of damp woods, and it hunts particularly actively at night. Scuttling on its pattery little feet among the fallen leaves, scrabbling in the leaf-mould in a frenzy of tiny investigation, it looks ceaselessly for food. Not a rodent, like a mouse, but an insectivore, it seizes chiefly on such creatures as crickets, grasshoppers, moths, and ants, devouring each victim with nervous eagerness and at once rushing on with quivering haste, tiny muzzle incessantly a-twitch, to look for further provender. *8*

Not infrequently the insects discoverable in the shrew's quick scampering little sallies through the darkness are inadequate to nourish it, so quick is its digestion and so intense the nervous energy it must sustain. When this is the case, the shrew widens its diet-range, to include seeds or berries or earthworms or any other sustenance that it can stuff with its little shivering forepaws into its tiny muzzle. It widens its diet to include meat; it becomes a furious and desperate carnivore. It patters through the grass-runways of the meadow-mice, sniffing and quivering; it darts to the nest of a deer-mouse. And presently, finding deer-mouse or meadow-mouse, it plunges into a wild attack on this "prey" that is twice its size. The shrew fights with a kind of mad recklessness; it becomes a leaping, twisting, chittering, squeaking speck of hungering fury. Quite generally, when the battle is over, the shrew has won. Its *9* thirty-two pinpoint teeth are sharp and strong, and the wild fury of its attack takes the victim by surprise. For a little while, after victory, the shrew's relentless body-needs are appeased. For a little while, but only a little; and then the furry speck must go pattering and scuttling forth into the night again, sniffing for food and quivering with need.

That is the pattern of shrew-life: a hunting and a hungering that never stops, an endless preoccupied catering to the demands of the kind of metabolism which unique mammalian smallness necessitates. The littlest mammal is a mammal in all ways; it breathes and sleeps and mates and possibly exults, as others do; but chiefly, as the price of unique tininess, it engages in restless never-ending search for something to eat. 10

The way of a shrew's dying is sometimes curious. Sometimes, of course, it dies in battle, when the larger prey which it has tackled proves too strong. Sometimes it dies of starvation; it can starve in a matter of hours. But often it is set upon by one of the big predators—some fox or lynx or man. When that happens, it is usually not the clutch of fingers or the snap of the carnivorous jaws that kills the shrew. The shrew is usually dead before that. At the first instant of a lynx's pounce—at the first touch of a human hand against the shrew's tiny quivering body—the shrew is apt to shiver in a quick violent spasm, and then lie still in death. The littlest of the mammals dies, as often as not, of simple nervous shock. 11

Vocabulary

beguilement (2)   diverse (7)
disparity (2)   impulsions (7)
minuscule (4)   extensive (7)
chitinous (5)   contrive (7)
adroitly (5)   provender (8)
infinitesimal (6)   sustenance (9)
discerned (6)   exults (10)

Critical Inquiries

1. What other reason can you give, other than membership in a common species, to justify learning about different creatures?

2. What term is applied to the act of attributing human characteristics to

other animals? Is the author guilty of such attribution in his essay? Why or why not?

3. What is the idiomatic meaning of the word "shrew," and how well does it fit the characteristics of the namesake animal?

4. The author asserts a common kinship among whales, monkeys, shrews, and humans. Which of these other animals can you most easily identify with, and why? Which creature of whatever zoological class can you least identify with?

5. What is your attitude towards laboratory experimentation on animals in the Mammalian class, if such experiments are likely to benefit humans?

Rhetorical Inquiries

1. The author cites a quotation in the first paragraph. What is this quotation, and why does he cite it?

2. Sprinkled throughout the essay are specialized terms such as "cecropia cocoon," "chitinous body-shells." What do these terms add to the author's style?

3. What primary pattern of organization does the author use to structure his description of the shrew?

4. In paragraph 6, what other rhetorical mode does the author use to describe the shrew? What makes this use effective?

5. What is the purpose of paragraph 10?

MANAGEMENT

Rosabeth Moss Kanter
HOW THE TOP IS DIFFERENT

Rosabeth Moss Kanter (b. 1943, Cleveland, Ohio) is a professor of Sociology at Yale University. Educated at the University of Michigan (Ph.D., 1967), she is the author of several books and monographs, among them Commitment and Community: Communes and Utopias in Sociological Perspective *(1972), and* Life in Organizations *(1979).*

Corporate headquarters of the company I have called Indsco, oc-   1
cupied many floors in a glass and steel office building in a large

From *Life in Organizations: Workplaces as People Experience Them,* edited by Rosabeth Moss Kanter and Barry A. Stein. Copyright © 1979 by Rosabeth Moss Kanter and Barry A. Stein. Reprinted by permission of Basic Books, Inc., Publishers.

city. The surroundings were luxurious. At ground level was a changing art exhibit in glass cases with displays of awards to Indsco executives for meritorious public service or newspaper clippings about the corporation. There might be piles of company newspapers on a nearby table or special publications like the report by foreign students who spent the summer with Indsco families. Such public displays almost always stressed Indsco's contributions to the welfare of the larger community. Across from gleaming chrome elevators and a watchman's post were doors leading into the employees' dining room. In the morning a long table with coffee, sweet rolls, and bagels for sale was set up outside the dining room; during the day coffee carts were available on each floor. Inside, the dining room was divided into two parts; a large cafeteria for everyone and a small area with already set tables, hostess seating, menus, and waitress service. Those tables were usually occupied by groups of men; the largely female clerical work force tended to eat in the cafeteria. Special luncheon meetings arranged by managers were held in the individual executive dining rooms and conference areas on the top floor; to use these rooms, reservations had to be made well in advance by someone with executive status.

Indsco executives were also likely to go out for lunch, especially if they were entertaining an outside visitor, to any of the numerous posh restaurants in the neighborhoods. At these lunches a drink was a must; at one time it was two extra-dry martinis, but more recently it became a few glasses of wine. However, despite the fact that moderate social drinking was common, heavy drinking was frowned upon. A person's career could be ruined by the casual comment that he or she had alcoholic tendencies. Stories told about men who cavorted and caroused in bars, staying up all night, were told with the attitude that "that was really crazy."   2

The office floors were quietly elegant, dominated by modern design, white walls, and beige tones. At one end, just off the elevators, sat a receptionist who calls on a company telephone line to announce visitors. A secretary would then appear to escort a visitor to his or her appointment. Offices with windows were for higher status managers, and their secretaries were often proud of having drapes. Corner offices were reserved for the top. They were likely to be larger in size, with room for coffee tables and couches, and reached through a reception area where a private secretary sat. Inside offices went to assistants and other lower-status salaried personnel; conference rooms were also found along the inside rim. Secretaries and other hourly workers occupied rows of desks with   3 banks of cabinets and files in the public spaces between. There were few signs of personal occupancy of space, except around the secretaries' desks. Managers might put up a painting or poster on the wall, and they usually had a small set of photographs of their families somewhere on or near their desk. Rarely would more than a few books or reports be visible, and the overall impression was one of tidiness, order, and uniformity from office to office. In fact, it was often true that the higher the status of an executive, the less cluttered was his desk. Office furnishings themselves reflected status rather than personality. There was a clear system of stratification. As status increased, desks went from a wood top with steel frame through solid wood to the culmination in a marble-top desk. Type of ashtray was also determined by the status system; and a former executive secretary, promoted into a management position herself, reported that her former peers were upset that she took her stainless steel file trays with her because a secretary working for her would not be entitled to such luxurious equipment. The rational distribution of furniture and supplies was thought to make the system more equitable and to avoid competition for symbols of status. . . .

The secretary also contributed in minor ways to the boss's status. Some people have argued that secretaries function as "status symbol" for executives, holding that the traditional secretarial role is developed and preserved because of its impact on managerial egos, not its contribution to organizational efficiency. Robert Townsend, iconoclastic former president of Avis, claimed in *Up the Organization* that the existence of private secretaries was organizationally inefficient, as proven by his experience in gaining half a day's time by giving up what he called "standard executive equipment." One writer was quite explicit about the meaning of a secretary: "In many companies a secretary outside your door is the most visible sign that you have become an executive; a secretary is automatically assigned to each executive, whether or not his work load requires one. . . . When you reach the vice-presidential level, your secretary may have an office of her own, with her name on the door. At the top, the president may have two secretaries. . . ." A woman professional at Indsco agreed with the idea that secretaries were doled out as rewards rather than in response to job needs, as she talked about her own problems in getting enough secretarial help.

At Indsco, the secretary's function as a status symbol increased up the ranks as she became more and more bound to a specific boss. "It's his image, his status, sitting out in front," a personnel administrator said. "She's the sign of how important he is." . . .

Physical height corresponded to social height at Indsco, like 6
other major corporations. Corporate officers resided at the very top
on the forty-fifth floor, which was characterized by many people
in Indsco as "a hospital ward." The silence was deafening. The offices were huge. According to one young executive who had
served as an assistant to an officer, "One or two guys are sitting
there; there's not much going on. It's the brain center, but there is
no activity. It's like an old folks' home. You can see the cobwebs
growing. A secretary every quarter mile. It's very sterile." An executive secretary told the story of her officer boss's first reaction to
moving onto the forty-fifth floor. "He was the one human being,"
she said, "who was uncomfortable with the trappings of status.
When he moved up, he had to pick an office." She wouldn't let
him take anything but a corner—it was the secretary who had to
tell him that. Finally he agreed for the sake of the corporate image,
but he was rarely there, and he set up the office so that everything
was in one corner and the rest was useless space.

Some people felt that the physical insulation of top executives 7
also had its counterpart in social insulation. Said a former officer's
assistant, "There are courtiers around the top guys, telling them
what they want to hear, flattering them. For example, there was a
luncheon with some board members. The vice-chairman mentioned that he was looking for a car for his daughter. A courtier
thought, 'We'll take care of it.' He went down the line, and someone in purchasing had to spend half a day doing this. The guy who
had to do it resented it, so he became antagonistic to the top. The
vice-chairman had no idea this was going on, and if he had
known, he would probably have stopped it; but you can't say anything at the top without having it be seen as an order. Even ambiguous remarks may get translated into action. At the top you have
to figure out the impact of all of your words in advance because an
innocent expression can have a major effect. A division president
says, 'It might be a good idea to———.' He's just ruminating, but
that gets sent down to the organization as an ultimatum, and everyone scrambles around to make sure it gets done. He looks
down and says, 'What the hell is happening?' "

At the same time, officers could also be frustrated by their dis- 8
tance from any real action. One remarked, "You get into a position
like mine, and you think you can get anything done, but I shout
down an order, and I have to wait years for any action. The guy in
the plant turns a valve and sees the reaction, or the salesman offers
a price, but I may never live to see the impact of my decisions."

For this reason, it was known that once in a while officers could be expected to leave their protected environment and try to get involved in routine company activities. Some would go down and try to do something on the shop floor. Once in a while one would make a sales call at a very high level or make an appearance at a customer golf outing. It was also a legend that an early president had his own private laboratory outside of his office—his own tinkering room. As a manager put it, "He would close the door and go play. It was almost as though he was babied. He was given a playroom." . . .

Vocabulary

cavorted (2)

stratification (3)

iconoclastic (4)

courtiers (7)

antagonistic (7)

ambiguous (7)

ruminating (7)

Critical Inquiries

1. The segregation of management from workers aside, what other kind of occupational segregation seems evident at Indsco?

2. What disadvantages can you perceive in a corporate system that stratifies its workers and management into rigid ranks? What advantages does such a system offer?

3. Aside from the differences among the executives' offices in furniture and furnishings, what rationed element is used to signal high status at Indsco?

4. Why is it necessary or unnecessary for management to be distinctly separated from workers in the corporate world?

5. What kind of job do you think preferable: one of physical and manual exertion, or one that stresses brainwork and thinking? Why?

Rhetorical Inquiries

1. What dominant impression is used as the basis of the description in paragraph 3?

2. What organizational pattern does the author use to structure her description? (See Chapter 3.)

3. What evidence does the author cite in paragraph 4 to support her contention that the secretary functions as a status symbol in corporations?

4. From what point of view is the article written? How does the author make her point of view so unobtrusive?

5. In paragraph 7, what other rhetorical mode does the author use to amplify on her description?.

Exercises

1. In one sentence, state the dominant impression you might use to describe one of these items:
   a. your bedroom
   b. your favorite restaurant
   c. your car
   d. your best friend
   e. the woman or man of your dreams
   f. any scene in your neighborhood

2. Complete the following sentences with a fresh simile or metaphor:
   a. His voice trembled like a . . . .
   b. Once they were married, they got along as well as . . . .
   c. The train whistled in the distance; it promised . . . .
   d. For him life had become a . . . .
   e. You couldn't see the barren trees and bushes in the dark, but you knew they were there—like . . . .
   f. The street wound its way downhill and across the sand dunes . . . .
   g. I shuddered, for I barely recognized her. The passing months had turned her into . . . .

Writing Assignments

1. Turn the following model into an essay developed by description. Only the skeleton of the model is provided. Some reorganization of the details below may also be necessary:

> In the eleventh grade I was introduced to the infamous and dreaded Miss Sullivan.
> She was then in her late forties and not glamorous.
> She had an unpleasant voice.
> She would stare piercingly at the class from her desk.
> She marked our English essays with a red pencil and returned them to us bleeding from many wounds.
> She always referred to us as, "Now, class . . ." and demanded, it seemed, the impossible.

In the eleventh grade I hated her, but today I revere her as the best teacher I have ever had.

2. Using "Shrew" as your model, write an essay describing the habits and ways of your favorite pet.

3. Write an essay describing game-playing that goes on in your workplace or business.

4. Using "The Doctor–Nurse Game" as a guide, write an essay describing the "Teacher–Student" game.

5. Drawing on your best efforts at imagination, write an essay, or if your prefer, a sermon, describing heaven.

6. Now that we know how the top is different, write an essay describing the bottom of the workplace or corporation.

Chapter

9

Defining

It is very easy to persuade oneself that a phrase that one does not quite understand may mean a great deal more than one realizes. From this there is only a little way to go to fall into the habit of setting down one's impressions in all their original vagueness.

W. SOMERSET MAUGHAM (1874–1965)

What do you mean? In composition, in debating, in nearly every effort of thinking, this is assuredly among the most asked questions. You say that this baseball player is better than that one, but what do you mean by "better"? Do you mean that he had more overall hits? That he had a higher lifetime average? That he scored more runs in his career, or was a better fielder? You argue that capital punishment is not a deterrent, but is it clear what you mean by "deterrent"?

A paragraph or essay organized by definition tells what you mean. It draws a circle of meaning around a word or term; it says what the boundaries include and what they do not. The basic procedure in defining is to place a word into a general category and then specify how it differs from other words in that same category. This is the method employed by dictionaries. Here are some examples:

WORD	GENERAL CATEGORY	DIFFERENCE
NIGHTMARE	DREAM	AROUSING HORROR
TO CLASSIFY	TO ORGANIZE	BY CATEGORY
LOVE	AN EMOTION	OF TENDERNESS

It is also what writers more or less do in defining terms, although not nearly as neatly as our diagram might imply. Placed in full sentences, however, the above terms might read this way:

A *nightmare* [the word being defined] is a *dream* [the category to which nightmare belongs] that arouses horror in the dreamer [the differentiating factor between dreams and nightmares—the nightmare arouses horror].

To classify [the term being defined] means *to organize* [the category to which classification belongs—it is a form of organizing] by category or type [the differentiating factor—classification is not organizing by physical dimensions but by category].

Love [the word being defined] is *an emotion* [the category to which love belongs] of tenderness [it differs from other emotions by being tender, not brutish].

This is basically how writers, scholars, researchers, and others generally draw definitions: they first specify the general category to which the defined term belongs and then differentiate it from others in that category.

In writing an essay, you should define any word crucial to your thesis whose meaning is fuzzy, ambiguous, or disputed. This especially includes any abstract word—such as *sovereignty, intuition, communism, prejudice,* or *economy*—that can be easily misunderstood and misinterpreted. Notice how Joan Didion, the noted writer, carefully defines the word *migraine* before she gets into the full swing of an essay on this disability, from which both she and her husband suffer:

> It was a long time before I began thinking mechanistically enough to accept migraine for what it was: something with which I would be living, the way some people live with diabetes. Migraine is something more than the fancy of a neurotic imagination. It is an essentially hereditary complex of symptoms, the most frequently noted but by no means the most unpleasant of which is a vascular headache of blinding severity, suffered by a surprising number of women, a fair number of men (Thomas Jefferson had migraine, and so did Ulysses S. Grant, the day he accepted Lee's surrender), and by some unfortunate children as young as two years old. (I had my first when I was eight. It came on during a fire drill at the Columbia School in Colorado Springs, Colorado. I was taken first home and then to the infirmary at Peterson Field, where my father was stationed. The Air Corps doctor prescribed an enema.) Almost anything can trigger a specific attack of migraine: stress, allergy, fatigue, an abrupt change in barometric pressure, a contretemps over a parking ticket. A flashing light. A fire drill. One inherits, of course, only the predisposition. In other words, I spent yesterday in bed with a headache not merely because of my bad attitudes, unpleasant tempers and wrongthink, but because both my grandmothers had migraine, my father has migraine, and my mother has migraine.
> —Joan Didion, "In Bed," *The White Album.*

If you were to reduce this paragraph to a one-sentence definition, you would see that it places migraine into the general category of vascular headaches and then differentiates it from other vascular headaches (causes blinding pain). The capsuled definition would read something like this: "Migraine is a vascular headache that is inherited and that causes blinding pain."

By emphasizing that a migraine attack is severe enough to be blinding, Didion also clarifies what it is *not:* the mild and characteristically common headache everyone occasionally experiences.

Here are some other suggestions on how to make sure that your definition really clarifies the word you want to explain: give the etymology of the word; supply examples, functions, and effects of the word; say what the word does *not* mean.

Give the Etymology of the Word

The **etymology** of a word is its linguistic history—where it began, what it originally meant, how it was first formed. An unabridged dictionary is the best source of etymologies, which are usually provided in brackets following the word's entry. Sometimes the etymology of a word is a useful starting point for a discussion of its meaning. For example, it could be significant to find out that the word *hypnosis* comes from the Greek *hypnos,* meaning "sleep," or that the word *simple* originally meant "foolish." To explain that the root of the word *jeopardy* is the French *jeu parti,* meaning "divided play" or "even chance," is to at least show the great shift that has occurred between that original meaning and today's "peril and vulnerability." Sometimes explaining the history of an ambiguous word can help you to anecdotally define it.

Supply Examples, Functions, and Effects of the Word

Words change in meaning, fashion, or usage, and dictionaries are hopelessly behind the times in cataloging these subtle shifts. It is therefore not enough to parrot the dictionary definition of a complex or ambiguous word. You also need to show, through examples and anecdotes, the effect of the word in a living context. For instance, Marya Mannes has written an essay in which she defined the term "sophisticated man." Admitting that the term is at best elusive, the author resorts to using examples:

> Would you recognize this kind of man if you saw him across the room? I think so. He's the one talking with an attractive woman; conservatively dressed, but easy in his clothes. His hair is trimmed close to his head, but not too close. His hands are well-groomed, but not manicured. He does not laugh loudly or often. He is looking directly at the woman he speaks to, but he is not missing the

other attractive women as they enter; a flick of the eye does it. For in all ways this man is not obvious. He would no more appear to examine a woman from the ankles up than he would move his head as he read or form the words with his lips. His senses are trained and his reflexes quick. And how did they get that way? From experience, from observation, and from deduction. He puts two and two together without adding on his fingers. He is educated in life.

—Marya Mannes, "The Sophisticated Man."

Here is another example. The author is defining the meaning of tonnage in 1492. He tells us where the word "tonnage" came from and shows us how the wine tun, which was the original meaning of the word *tonelada,* emerged as a rough index of a vessel's capacity.

What did tonnage mean in 1492? Not weight or displacement of the vessel, or her deadweight capacity; tonnage meant simply her cubic capacity in terms of wine tuns. The Castilian *tonelada,* or the Portuguese *tonel* (both of which I translate "ton"), was really a tun of wine, a large cask equivalent in volume to two *pipas* or pipes, the long, tapering hogsheads in which port wine is still sold. As wine was a common cargo, and both pipe and tun of standard dimensions, a vessel's carrying capacity below decks in terms of *toneladas* became a rough-and-ready index of her size; and so a ship's tonnage in 1492 meant the number of tuns or twice the number of pipes of wine she could stow. The tun, *tonelada* or ton being roughly (very roughly) equivalent to 40 cubic feet, this last figure became in the course of time the unit of burthen (or tonnage or capacity) for English vessels, and was so used in America until the Civil War. From the seventeenth century on, it became customary in every country to fix a vessel's official tonnage by a formula composed of her length, breadth and depth, which gave a rough measurement of her capacity. But in 1492 tonnage meant simply the number of tuns of wine that the ship could stow, as estimated by the owner or verified by common report. It was not a constant but a variable.

—Samuel Eliot Morison, *Admiral of the Ocean Sea*

In this paragraph, a student defines *klutz* by likewise cataloguing examples, functions, and effects of the term:

```
The term klutz has its origin in the

Yiddish term klots, and is applied to males and

females alike as an insult or reproach.
```

Basically, a klutz is someone who cannot get
from here to there without a mishap occurring—
without stumbling, tripping, or falling. For
example, the klutz is the outfielder who drops
the lazy fly ball that soars overhead in a
perfect arc on a clear, cloudless day. The
klutz has room to park but nevertheless runs
into the curb, bumps into the trash can, or
bangs into another car. The klutz handles your
prized Chinese vase only once and then shatters
it on the edge of the hearth. Fathers don't
want their sons to be klutzes; wives don't want
their husbands to be klutzes; daughters don't
want their mothers to be klutzes. Klutziness is
devoutly to be avoided.

In sum, merely to base a defining essay on what the dictionary says about a word is never enough, for dictionaries always lag behind in the shades of meanings that words daily accumulate. Showing these subtle meanings will require you to add to the dictionary with examples and other details.

Say What the Word Does Not Mean

Clarifying what a term does *not* mean can sometimes help a reader understand what it does. For instance, after a writer has defined *felony* as "a serious crime punishable by stringent sentencing," a reader may still not know exactly what kind of crime is considered a felony. One way to clarify the meaning is to say that a felony is *not* a misdemeanor, such as disturbing the peace by getting drunk, stealing someone's purse, or cheating in some small way on income tax. In her essay defining the "sophisticated man," Marya Mannes explains not only what a sophisticated man is but also what he is not:

Now, here we come to the crux of the situation, for I maintain that a man who has never traveled in other countries and been ex-

posed to other societies cannot be sophisticated. I am not speaking of package tours or cruise trips, but of a reasonable familiarity with foreign cities and peoples and arts and customs; an education reading alone cannot provide. For sophistication to me suggests, primarily, a refinement of the senses. The eye that has not appreciated Michelangelo's David in Florence or the cathedral of Chartres is not a sophisticated eye; nor is the tongue that has not tasted the best fettuccine in Rome or the best wine in Paris. The hand that has not felt the rough heat of an ancient wall in Siena or the sweating cold of a Salzburg stein of beer is an innocent hand. So are the fingers that have not traveled, in conscious and specific savoring, over the contours of many different women.
—Marya Mannes, "The Sophisticated Man."

The most important principle, of course, is to keep amplifying on the definition until the term is made so clear that it cannot be misunderstood by the averge reader.

Defining Mistakes

Definitions are based on a straightforward principle: you tell the reader what a certain word, term, or expression means, adding whatever information is necessary to dispel confusion. But there are certain missteps to avoid in penning a definition. Probably the most common is the circular definition as, for example, defining "face" as "visage." Such a definition adds nothing to clarity, "visage" being only a fancier word for "face." Here is an example of a circular definition:

```
A poltergeist is a ghost.  "Ghost" comes

from the Saxon gaste or gest, and in the north

of England guest is sometimes used for ghost.

Poltergeists tend to appear in households with

pubescent children, although no one has been

able to explain why.  Poltergeists have

reportedly appeared in England, Italy, and

America, where they were studied by Cotton

Mather.
```

To define a "poltergeist" as a "ghost" is very much like saying that a student is a pupil or that an instructor is a teacher. A reader needs to know more about what kind of ghost a poltergeist is for the definition to be clear. Here is the writer's revision of the above paragraph that corrected this circularity by supplying more details:

A poltergeist is a ghost that causes a noise or uproar. Poltergeists generally throw objects, move furniture, make loud rapping sounds. Some have even been known to whistle, sing, and talk. "Ghost" comes from the Saxon gaste or gest, and in the north of England guest is sometimes used for ghost. Poltergeists, on the other hand, originated in Germany, where the earliest recorded visitation occurred in the year 355. In that visitation, several villagers complained of being shaken out of bed. Raps and noises were heard throughout the village of Bingen-am-Rhein, where the poltergeist appeared. Poltergeists tend to appear in households with pubescent children, although no one has been able to explain why. Visitations by poltergeists have been reported in England, Italy, and America, where they were studied by Cotton Mather.

The details added in revision are italicized. Circular definitions often occur when a writer places the defined word or term in the larger category but fails to differentiate it from other words and terms found there. "Poltergeist" does indeed belong to the category of "ghosts." But that it is a ghost of a particular kind, not just any run-of-the-mill spook, needs to be clearly specified.

Another common error to guard against is the definition that overuses figurative language. Figurative language—images, metaphors, similes and the like—work well in poetry, drama, and fiction, where the writer's goal is to entertain and amuse. But in expository prose figurative language tends to muddle, rather than clarify, meaning. Here is a fragment of sample paragraph defining "impeachment" in which the writer deleted some unnecessary images:

```
Impeachment is a formal process whereby a

public official is removed from office, usually

by a committee of the legislature.  This

uprooting of bad growth among the forest of

public service is often sadly necessary.

Impeachment originated in fourteenth—century

England as a process for trying and removing

corrupt officials.  In the U.S.  the

Constitution has specific provisions for

impeachment. . . .
```

The writer wisely edited out the metaphorical sentence about uprooting bad growth, since it contributed nothing to the definition.

When to use definition

When should you organize an essay by definition? That depends on the writing assignment. For example if you are asked to write an essay defining "mammal," you have no choice but to do a definition. But if you are asked to write an essay on "mammals," you could organize it by one of several rhetorical strategies. You could, for example, *narrate* the life cycle of a mammal; you could *describe* a mammal; or you could write an essay defining "mammal." Nor are your choices limited to those three, as we saw in Chapter 5. A writer's decision to organize an essay by one rhetorical strategy over another is usually founded on personal preference. You gauge your potential audience, decide what tack you think will most likely appeal to them, and what particular information you wish to convey. Often a rhetorical strategy will emerge naturally as you do the research and learn more about the topic. The upshot is that you cannot know what kind of essay to write or what rhetorical strategy to use until you have actually begun the process of prewriting and writing. Then you should use the strategy you think will work best, given the topic, the audience, and your own particular bent.

Commonly, definition as a strategy is used in entire essays, but as we saw earlier, it can also be the organizing focus of single paragraphs. Indeed, essays organized by some other main strategy often include opening paragraphs that define basic terms in the thesis. But you should use such paragraphs only for defining uncommon, technical, specialized, or rare words and terms. For example, if you were writing an essay on the controlling idea, "Buying a new car requires careful research and purchasing savvy," you can safely assume that your reader knows the meaning of both "buying" and "car" and that it would be tedious and fussy to waste a paragraph defining either. On the other hand an essay on supersonic airliners should, in at least one paragraph, define that term. Use common sense. Ask yourself whether or not the reader is likely to be puzzled by any key word in your thesis. If the answer is yes, then define it.

Anthologized here are four defining essays that exemplify the techniques discussed in this chapter. They successively define *imagination, sociologist, pi,* and *computer virus.* Also included here is an early draft of a paragraph defining *envy.* Notice how the writer considerably improved the second draft through careful revision.

Original:

Envy produces nothing but pain and misery; *[Use examples to show differences between two terms.]* it is a viciously destructive trait. Envy is often confused with jealousy; yet, the two terms *[Give the etymology of envy.]* are quite different one from the other. Envy is *[you really]* wanting what does not by right belong to you whereas jealousy is resenting having something *[don't go much beyond the dictionary definition.]* taken away that by right does belong to you. Thus jealousy is justifiable whereas envy is not. The person who wants to remain psychologically healthy should purge away all feelings of envy. At the root of envy are selfishness and pride. But what envious persons *[You need an anecdote here on the evil effects of envy.]* often fail to realize is that when they harbor strong feelings of envy, they are destroying only themselves. Those who shoot arrows of envy at others, end up wounding only themselves. The surest way to gain victory over jealousy is to

promote the welfare of the one envied. To
conquer this green-eyed monster, the envious
person must show good will to the object of
envy.

Revision:

Envy produces nothing but pain and misery;
it is a viciously destructive trait. Envy is
often confused with jealousy; yet, the two terms
are quite different one from the other. Envy is
wanting what does not by right belong to you
whereas jealousy is resenting having something
taken away that by right does belong to you. For
instance, a wife who flies into a rage because
her husband is having a love affair with another
woman is experiencing jealousy, an emotion quite
appropriate to the situation. On the other hand,
a woman who wants her best friend's husband for
herself is feeling envy, an inappropriate trait.
Consider what The American Heritage Dictionary
says about envy. The roots of this word are
traced back to the Latin invidere, meaning "to
look upon with malice." Envy is seen as
synonymous with begrudging and coveting, which
all Christians and Jews are warned against in
the Decalogue. The person who wants to remain
psychologically healthy should purge away all
feelings of envy. At the root of envy are
selfishness and pride. But what envious persons
often fail to realize is that when they harbor

strong feelings of envy, they are destroying only themselves. An ancient fable tells the story of an eagle who was envious of another eagle who could fly better. One day this envious eagle spied a sportsman with a bow and arrow and said to him, "I wish you would bring down that eagle up there." The sportsman replied agreeably that he would do so gladly if he had some feathers for his arrow. So the envious eagle quickly pulled out one feather from his wings and gave it to the hunter. The arrow was shot, but it did not quite reach the rival bird because he was flying too high. The envious eagle then pulled out another feather, then another, and still another—until he had lost so many feathers that he himself could not fly. The archer took advantage of the situation, turned around, and killed the helpless bird. Here is the lesson from this fable: If you are envious of others, the one you will hurt the most by your envy is you. In shooting arrows of envy at others, you wound only yourself.

The definition uses clarifying examples, etymological information, and even an illustrating fable to explain what the writer means by envy.

Exercises

1. In a brief paragraph, define each of the following items by (1) placing it in a general category, (2) indicating how it differs from others in its class (see page 152), and (3) extending the definition to further explain it.
   a. lawyer   *b.* red

    c. hammer   *e.* ghetto
    d. expressionism   *f.* pinafore

2. Using an example, clarify your definition of one these words:
    a. nonchalance
    b. reverence
    c. desolation

3. Clarify your definition of one of the following words by stating what it is not:
    a. heaven
    b. platitude
    c. genius

4. Supply the etymology for the following words:
    a. anecdote   *e.* lunatic
    b. nausea   *f.* mediocre
    c. clinic   *g.* phlegmatic
    d. dandelion   *h.* xenophobic

MYTHOLOGY

Ursula K. Le Guin
WHY ARE AMERICANS AFRAID OF DRAGONS?

Ursula Kroeber Le Guin (b. 1929 in Berkeley, Calif.) was educated at Radcliffe College (B.A., 1951) and Columbia University (M.A., 1952). She is the author of numerous science fiction and fantasy books, among them, A Wizard of Earthsea *(1968),* The Left Hand of Darkness *(1969),* The Lathe of Heaven *(1971), and* The Compass Rose *(short stories, 1982).*

    This was to be a talk about fantasy. But I have not been feeling very fanciful lately, and could not decide what to say; so I have been going about picking people's brains for ideas. "What about fantasy? Tell me something about fantasy." And one friend of mine said, "All right, I'll tell you something fantastic. Ten years ago, I went to the children's room of the library of such-and-such a city, and asked for *The Hobbit;* and the librarian told me, 'Oh, we keep that only in the adult collection; we don't feel that escapism is good for children.' "   1

    My friend and I had a good laugh and shudder over that, and we agreed that things have changed a great deal in these past ten   2

Reprinted by permission of The Putnam Publishing Group from *The Language of the Night,* by Ursula K. Le Guin. Copyright © 1979 by Susan Wood.

years. That kind of moralistic censorship of works of fantasy is very uncommon now, in the children's libraries. But the fact that the children's libraries have become oases in the desert doesn't mean that there isn't still a desert. The point of view from which that librarian spoke still exists. She was merely reflecting, in perfect good faith, something that goes very deep in the American character: a moral disapproval of fantasy, a disapproval so intense, and often so aggressive, that I cannot help but see it as arising, fundamentally, from fear.

So: Why are Americans afraid of dragons?   3

Before I try to answer my question, let me say that it isn't only   4
Americans who are afraid of dragons. I suspect that almost all very highly technological peoples are more or less antifantasy. There are several national literatures which, like ours, have had no tradition of adult fantasy for the past several hundred years: the French, for instance. But then you have the Germans, who have a good deal; and the English, who have it, and love it, and do it better than anyone else. So this fear of dragons is not merely a Western, or a technological, phenomenon. But I do not want to get into these vast historical questions; I will speak of modern Americans, the only people I know well enough to talk about.

In wondering why Americans are afraid of dragons, I began to   5
realize that a great many Americans are not only antifantasy, but altogether antifiction. We tend, as a people, to look upon all works of the imagination either as suspect, or as contemptible.

"My wife reads novels. I haven't got the time."   6

"I used to read that science fiction stuff when I was a teenager,   7
but of course I don't now."

"Fairy stories are for kids. I live in the real world."   8

Who speaks so? Who is it that dismisses *War and Peace, The Time*   9
Machine, and *A Midsummer Night's Dream* with this perfect self-assurance?[1] It is, I fear, the man in the street—the hardworking, over-thirty American male—the men who run this country.

Such a rejection of the entire art of fiction is related to several   10
American characteristics: our Puritanism, our work ethic, our profit-mindedness, and even our sexual mores.

To read *War and Peace* or *The Lord of the Rings* plainly is not   11
"work"[2]—you do it for pleasure. And if it cannot be justified as "educational" or as "self-improvement," then, in the Puritan value

---

[1]*War and Peace, The Time Machine,* and *A Midsummer Night's Dream:* by Leo Tolstoy, H. G. Wells, and William Shakespeare, respectively.
[2]*The Lord of the Rings:* the trilogy by J. R. R. Tolkien.

system, it can only be self-indulgence or escapism. For pleasure is not a value, to the Puritan; on the contrary, it is a sin.

Equally, in the businessman's value system, if an act does not bring in an immediate, tangible profit, it has no justification at all. Thus the only person who has an excuse to read Tolstoy or Tolkien is the English teacher, because he gets paid for it. But our businessman might allow himself to read a best-seller now and then: not because it is a good book, but because it is a best-seller—it is a success, it has made money. To the strangely mystical mind of the money-changer, this justifies its existence; and by reading it he may participate, a little, in the power and mana of its success. If this is not magic, by the way, I don't know what is.   12

The last element, the sexual one, is more complex. I hope I will not be understood as being sexist if I say that, within our culture, I believe that this antifiction attitude is basically a male one. The American boy and man is very commonly forced to define his maleness by rejecting certain traits, certain human gifts and potentialities, which our culture defines as "womanish" or "childish." And one of these traits or potentialities is, in cold sober fact, the absolutely essential human faculty of imagination.   13

Having got this far, I went quickly to the dictionary.   14

The *Shorter Oxford Dictionary* says: "Imagination. 1. The action of imagining, or forming a mental concept of what is not actually present to the senses; 2. The mental consideration of actions or events not yet in existence."   15

Very well; I certainly can let "absolutely essential human faculty" stand. But I must narrow the definition to fit our present subject. By "imagination," then, I personally mean the free play of the mind, both intellectual and sensory. By "play" I mean recreation, re-creation, the recombination of what is known into what is new. By "free" I mean that the action is done without an immediate object of profit—spontaneously. That does not mean, however, that there may not be a purpose behind the free play of the mind, a goal; and the goal may be a very serious object indeed. Children's imaginative play is clearly a practicing at the acts and emotions of adulthood; a child who did not play would not become mature. As for the free play of an adult mind, its result may be *War and Peace,* or the theory of relativity.   16

To be free, after all, is not to be undisciplined. I should say that the discipline of the imagination may in fact be the essential method or technique of both art and science. It is our Puritanism, insisting that discipline means repression or punishment, which   17 confuses the subject. To discipline something, in the proper sense of the word, does not mean to repress it, but to train it—to encourage it to grow, and act, and be fruitful, whether it is a peach tree or a human mind.

I think that a great many American men have been taught just the opposite. They have learned to repress their imagination, to reject it as something childish or effeminate, unprofitable, and probably sinful.

They have learned to fear it. But they have never learned to discipline it at all.

Now, I doubt that the imagination can be suppressed. If you truly eradicated it in a child, he would grow up to be an eggplant. Like all our evil propensities, the imagination will win out. But if it is rejected and despised, it will grow into wild and weedy shapes; it will be deformed. At its best, it will be mere ego-centered daydreaming; at its worst, it will be wishful thinking, which is a very dangerous occupation when it is taken seriously. Where literature is concerned, in the old, truly Puritan days, the only permitted reading was the Bible. Nowadays, with our secular Puritanism, the man who refuses to read novels because it's unmanly to do so, or because they aren't true, will most likely end up watching bloody detective thrillers on the television, or reading hack Westerns or sports stories, or going in for pornography, from *Playboy* on down. It is his starved imagination, craving nourishment, that forces him to do so. But he can rationalize such entertainment by saying that it is realistic—after all, sex exists, and there are criminals, and there are baseball players, and there used to be cowboys—and also by saying that it is virile, by which he means that it doesn't interest most women.

That all these genres are sterile, hopelessly sterile, is a reassurance to him, rather than a defect. If they were genuinely realistic, which is to say genuinely imagined and imaginative, he would be afraid of them. Fake realism is the escapist literature of our time. And probably the ultimate escapist reading is that masterpiece of total unreality, the daily stock market report.

Now what about our man's wife? She probably wasn't required to squelch her private imagination in order to play her expected role in life, but she hasn't been trained to discipline it, either. She is allowed to read novels, and even fantasies. But, lacking training and encouragement, her fancy is likely to glom on to very sickly fodder, such things as soap operas, and "true romances," and nursy novels, and historico-sentimental novels, and all the rest of the baloney ground out to replace genuine imaginative works by the artistic sweatshops of a society that is profoundly distrustful of the uses of the imagination.

What, then, are the uses of the imagination? 23

You see, I think we have a terrible thing here: a hardworking, 24 upright, responsible citizen, a full-grown, educated person, who is afraid of dragons, and afraid of hobbits, and scared to death of fairies. It's funny, but it's also terrible. Something has gone very wrong. I don't know what to do about it but to try and give an honest answer to that person's question, even though he often asks it in an aggressive and contemptuous tone of voice. "What's the good of it all?" he says. "Dragons and hobbits and little green men—what's the *use* of it?"

The truest answer, unfortunately, he won't even listen to. He 25 won't hear it. The truest answer is, "The use of it is to give you pleasure and delight."

"I haven't got the time," he snaps, swallowing a Maalox pill for 26 his ulcer and rushing off to the golf course.

So we try the next-to-truest answer. It probably won't go down 27 much better, but it must be said: "The use of imaginative fiction is to deepen your understanding of your world, and your fellow men, and your own feelings, and your destiny."

To which I fear he will retort, "Look, I got a raise last year, and 28 I'm giving my family the best of everything, we've got two cars and a color TV. I understand enough of the world!"

And he is right, unanswerably right, if that is what he wants, 29 and all he wants.

The kind of thing you learn from reading about the problems of 30 a hobbit who is trying to drop a magic ring into an imaginary volcano has very little to do with your social status, or material success, or income. Indeed, if there is any relationship, it is a negative one. There is an inverse correlation between fantasy and money. That is a law, known to economists as Le Guin's Law. If you want a striking example of Le Guin's Law, just give a lift to one of those people along the roads who own nothing but a backpack, a guitar, a fine head of hair, a smile, and a thumb. Time and again, you will find that these waifs have read *The Lord of the Rings*—some of them can practically recite it. But now take Aristotle Onassis, or J. Paul Getty: could you believe that those men ever had anything to do, at any age, under any circumstances, with a hobbit?

But, to carry my example a little further, and out of the realm of 31 economics, did you ever notice how very gloomy Mr. Onassis and Mr. Getty and all those billionaires look in their photographs?

They have this strange, pinched look, as if they were hungry. As if they were hungry for something, as if they had lost something and were trying to think where it could be, or perhaps what it could be, what it was they've lost.

Could it be their childhood?   32

So I arrive at my personal defense of the uses of the imagination,   33
especially in fiction, and most especially in fairy tale, legend, fantasy, science fiction, and the rest of the lunatic fringe. I believe that maturity is not an outgrowing, but a growing up: that an adult is not a dead child, but a child who survived. I believe that all the best faculties of a mature human being exist in the child, and that if these faculties are encouraged in youth they will act well and wisely in the adult, but if they are repressed and denied in the child they will stunt and cripple the adult personality. And finally, I believe that one of the most deeply human, and humane, of these faculties is the power of imagination: so that it is our pleasant duty, as librarians, or teachers, or parents, or writers, or simply as grownups, to encourage that faculty of imagination in our children, to encourage it to grow freely, to flourish like the green bay tree, by giving it the best, absolutely the best and purest, nourishment that it can absorb. And never, under any circumstances, to squelch it, or sneer at it, or imply that it is childish, or unmanly, or untrue.

For fantasy is true, of course. It isn't factual, but it is true. Chil-   34
dren know that. Adults know it too, and that is precisely why many of them are afraid of fantasy. They know that its truth challenges, even threatens, all that is false, all that is phony, unnecessary, and trivial in the life they have let themselves be forced into living. They are afraid of dragons, because they are afraid of freedom.

So I believe that we should trust our children. Normal children   35
do not confuse reality and fantasy—they confuse them much less often than we adults do (as a certain great fantasist pointed out in a story called "The Emperor's New Clothes"). Children know perfectly well that unicorns aren't real, but they also know that books about unicorns, if they are good books, are true books. All too often, that's more than Mummy and Daddy know; for, in denying their childhood, the adults have denied half their knowledge, and are left with the sad, sterile little fact: "Unicorns aren't real." And that fact is one that never got anybody anywhere (except in the story "The Unicorn in the Garden," by another great fantasist, in which it is shown that a devotion to the unreality of unicorns may get you straight into the loony bin). It is by such statements as,

"Once upon a time there was a dragon," or "In a hole in the ground there lived a hobbit"—it is by such beautiful non-facts that we fantastic human beings may arrive, in our peculiar fashion, at the truth.

Vocabulary

mana (12)   propensities (20)
repression (17)   inverse (30)
eradicated (20)

Critical Inquiries

1. The author claims that Americans are "afraid of dragons because they are afraid of freedom." What do you think she means by this?
2. What is the difference between self-indulgence and escapism, as the author uses these terms in paragraph 11?
3. The author claims that the American boy and man is forced to define his maleness by rejecting the imagination as "womanish." Given the current emphasis on nonsexist childrearing, how true do you think this assertion is today?
4. In what way may the daily stock market report be said to be a "master-piece of total unreality"?
5. What is the difference between factual and true? How can fantasy not be factual and yet be true?

Rhetorical Inquiries

1. Le Guin's essay is actually the transcript of a talk given before an audience of librarians. In what ways does she acknowledge her audience and try to engage its interest?
2. What meaning does the author intend for the word "dragons" in her title? If you do not think her meaning literal, what figure of speech does she intend in this use of the word?
3. What characteristics of an oral style can you identify in this selection?
4. What technique of argumentation is the author employing in paragraphs 5 through 8 and paragraphs 24 through 28?
5. Le Guin's talk is included in the chapter on definition. What other rhetorical purposes does she follow throughout her speech?

SOCIOLOGY

Peter L. Berger
WHAT IS A SOCIOLOGIST?

Peter Ludwig Berger (b. 1929 in Vienna, Austria) migrated to the United States in 1946. Berger was educated at Wagner College (B.A., 1949), and the New School for Social Research (M.A., 1950; Ph.D., 1954). A professor of sociology at Rutgers University, Berger is also the author of numerous professional articles, monographs, and books, among them The Precarious Vision *(1961);* Invitation to Sociology: A Humanistic Perspective *(1963); and* The Heretical Imperative: Contemporary Possibilities of Religious Affirmation *(1979).*

The sociologist (that is, the one we would really like to invite to our game) is a person intensively, endlessly, shamelessly interested in the doings of men. His natural habitat is all the human gathering places of the world, wherever men come together. The sociologist may be interested in many other things. But his consuming interest remains in the world of men, their institutions, their history, their passions. And since he is interested in men, nothing that men do can be altogether tedious for him. He will naturally be interested in the events that engage men's ultimate beliefs, their moments of tragedy and grandeur and ecstasy. But he will also be fascinated by the commonplace, the everyday. He will know reverence, but this reverence will not prevent him from wanting to see and to understand. He may sometimes feel revulsion or contempt. But this also will not deter him from wanting to have his questions answered. The sociologist, in his quest for understanding, moves through the world of men without respect for the usual lines of demarcation. Nobility and degradation, power and obscurity, intelligence and folly—these are equally *interesting* to him, however unequal they may be in his personal values or tastes. Thus his questions may lead him to all possible levels of society, the best and the least known places, the most respected and the most despised. And, if he is a good sociologist, he will find himself in all these places because his own questions have so taken possession of him that he has little choice but to seek for answers. 1

It would be possible to say the same things in a lower key. We could say that the sociologist, but for the grace of his academic ti- 2

Exerpts from *Invitation to Sociology,* by Peter Berger. Copyright © 1963 by Peter Berger. Reprinted by permission of Doubleday, a division of Bantam, Doubleday, Dell Publishing Group, Inc.

tle, is the man who must listen to gossip despite himself, who is tempted to look through keyholes, to read other people's mail, to open cabinets. Before some otherwise unoccupied psychologist sets out now to construct an aptitude test for sociologists on the basis of sublimated voyeurism, let us quickly say that we are speaking merely by way of analogy. Perhaps some little boys consumed with curiosity to watch their maiden aunts in the bathroom later become inveterate sociologists. This is quite uninteresting. What interests us is the curiosity that grips any sociologist in front of a closed door behind which there are human voices. If he is a good sociologist he will want to open that door, to understand these voices. Behind each closed door he will anticipate some new facet of human life not yet perceived and understood.

The sociologist will occupy himself with matters that others regard as too sacred or as too distasteful for dispassionate investigation. He will find rewarding the company of priests or of prostitutes, depending not on his personal preferences but on the questions he happens to be asking at the moment. He will also concern himself with matters that others may find much too boring. He will be interested in the human interaction that goes with warfare or with great intellectual discoveries, but also in the relations between people employed in a restaurant or between a group of little girls playing with their dolls. His main focus of attention is not the ultimate significance of what men do, but the action in itself, as another example of the infinite richness of human conduct. So much for the image of our playmate.

In these journeys through the world of men the sociologist will inevitably encounter other professional Peeping Toms. Sometimes these will resent his presence, feeling that he is poaching on their preserves. In some places the sociologist will meet up with the economist, in others with the political scientist, in yet others with the psychologist or the ethnologist. Yet chances are that the questions that have brought him to these places are different from the ones that propelled his fellow-trespassers. The sociologist's questions always remain essentially the same: "What are people doing with each other here?" "What are their relationships to each other?" "How are these relationships organized in institutions?" "What are the collective ideas that move men and institutions?" In trying to answer these questions in specific instances, the sociologist will, of course, have to deal with economic or political matters, but he will do so in a way rather different from that of the economist or the political scientist. The scene that he contemplates is the same human scene that these other scientists concern themselves with. But the sociologist's angle of vision is different. When this is understood, it becomes clear that it makes little sense to try to stake out a special enclave within which the sociologist will carry on business in his own right. Like Wesley the sociologist will have to confess that his parish is the world. But unlike some latter-day Wesleyans he will gladly share this parish with others. There is, however, one traveler whose path the sociologist will cross more often than anyone else's on his journeys. This is the historian. Indeed, as soon as the sociologist turns from the present to the past, his preoccupations are very hard indeed to distinguish from those of the historian. [T]he sociological journey will be much impoverished unless it is punctuated frequently by conversation with that other particular traveler.

Any intellectual activity derives excitement from the moment it   5
becomes a trail of discovery. . . . The excitement of sociology is [not always to penetrate] into worlds that had previously been quite unknown . . . for instance, the world of crime, or the world of some bizarre religious sect, or the world fashioned by the exclusive concerns of some group such as medical specialists or military leaders or advertising executives. [M]uch of the time the sociologist moves in sectors of experience that are familiar to him and to most people in his society. He investigates communities, institutions and activities that one can read about every day in the newspapers. Yet there is another excitement of discovery beckoning in his investigations. It is not the excitement of finding the familiar becoming transformed in its meaning. The fascination of sociology lies in the fact that its perspective makes us see in a new light the very world in which we have lived all of our lives. This also constitutes a transformation of consciousness. Moreover, this transformation is more relevant existentially than that of many other intellectual disciplines, because it is more difficult to segregate in some special compartment of the mind. The astronomer does not live in the remote galaxies, and the nuclear physicist can, outside his laboratory, eat, and laugh and marry and vote without thinking about the insides of the atom. The geologist looks at rocks only at appropriate times, and the linguist speaks English with his wife. The sociologist lives in society, on the job and off it. His own life, inevitably, is part of his subject matter. Men being what they are, sociologists too manage to segregate their professional insights from their everyday affairs. But it is a rather difficult feat to perform in good faith.

The sociologist moves in the common world of men, close to   6
what most of them would call real. The categories he employs in

his analyses are only refinements of the categories by which other men live—power, class, status, race, ethnicity. As a result, there is a deceptive simplicity and obviousness about some sociological investigations. One reads them, nods at the familiar scene, remarks that one has heard all this before and don't people have better things to do than to waste their time on truisms—until one is suddenly brought up against an insight that radically questions everything one had previously assumed about this familiar scene. This is the point at which one begins to sense the excitement of sociology.

Vocabulary

demarcation (1)

degradation (1)

sublimated (2)

voyeurism (2)

inveterate (2)

dispassionate (3)

ethnologist (4)

enclave (4)

existentially (5)

truisms (6)

Critical Inquires

1. The author writes that the sociologist "moves through the world of men without respect for the usual lines of demarcation." What does this mean, and how is it possible for a sociologist not to be affected by "lines of demarcation" in the society to which he or she belongs?

2. What differences, if any, exist in methodology and intent between the sociologist and the historian?

3. Do you think "value-free" study of society by sociologists possible? Why or why not?

4. With which end of the political spectrum are sociology and sociologists usually associated, and why?

5. If you were part of a group being studied by sociologists, would your behavior likely be changed by being the focus of that study? If so, how would the change affect the validity of the study?

Rhetorical Inquires

1. Sociology has often been accused of writing the worst English of any discipline. To what do you think can be attributed the notoriously crabbed style of sociology papers?

2. What effect do you think the author's exclusive use of "he" when refer-

ring to a sociologist, and "men" when referring to society, is likely to have on a female reader? How might this essay be rewritten to eliminate this sexist bias?

3. What two techniques for achieving coherence does the author use in paragraph 1?

4. What transition technique does the author use to link paragraphs 1 and 2?

5. Berger is numbered among the better and clearer sociological writers. What characteristics of his style do you think have helped earn him this reputation?

MATHEMATICS

Isaac Asimov
MATHEMATICIANS LOOK FOR A PIECE OF PI

Isaac Asimov (b. 1920 in the U.S.S.R.) was brought to the United States at the age of three, where he has won renown as a prolific writer of science fiction and a masterful explainer of science. A professor of biochemistry at Boston University, Asimov is said to have written one book every six weeks for the past thirty years, and already has over 100 published titles to his credit. His field spans the range from biblical criticism to Shakespeare, although he is best known as the author of such science-fiction classics as I, Robot *(1950), and* The Caves of Steel *(1954).*

There are problems in mathematics that go on and on and on and on—that never have an end. And yet there are mathematicians who willingly pursue such problems on and on and on and on. 1

Consider a circle, for instance, of a certain width or diameter. How much longer is the distance around the circle (or the circumference) than the diameter? 2

Actually, the circumference is a little more than three times the length of the diameter, and this value is called pi (a Greek letter.) It turned out, as mathematicians developed their field over the centuries, that this quantity, pi, turned up in equation after equation, so that people grew very interested in knowing what the exact value of pi might be. 3

It turned out to be fairly close to $3\frac{1}{7}$. In decimals that comes 4

From *Los Angeles Times,* May 6, 1988, part V, pp. 3, 20. Copyright 1989, *Los Angeles Times* Syndicate.

out to 3.142857 . . . which is just a trifle too high. Better still is the value 3 ¹⁶/₁₁₃. In decimals that comes out to 3.14159292.

That's almost right, but not exactly. Of course, in any practical computation, 3 ¹⁶/₁₁₃ would certainly give you an answer that was close enough. If the correct answer to an equation involving pi were 12.5 million, then using 3 ¹⁶/₁₁₃ for pi instead of the absolutely correct value would give an answer of 12,500,001. Anyone would be satisfied with that.

Except mathematicians.

They continued looking for the exact value and, finally, they had to come to the conclusion that there was no fraction—no fraction at all—that would give the exact value of pi.

Any fraction, if expressed as a decimal, either comes to an end, or keeps on repeating. Thus one-eighth is equal to 0.125 exactly. On the other hand, one-third is equal to 0.333333 . . . forever. The number 3 ½ in decimals is 3.142857142857142857 . . . forever.

The value of pi, however, never comes to an end, and it never repeats. The numbers just go on and on and on and on forever and there is never any way of predicting, just by looking at it, what the next number in the series will be. However, the values of pi can be calculated to any number of decimal places, if you wish to go to the trouble.

Mathematicians discovered that there were various series of numbers, each one smaller than the one before, which, if added together, come to a total that equals pi exactly. The only trouble is that the series of numbers goes on and on and on and on and never comes to an end. This means if you add up the first eight numbers of the series you come close to pi; if you add up the first 16 you come closer; if you add up the first 32 you come still closer and so on—but you never get it exactly. What's more, the numbers are mathematically complicated and it takes time to work out exactly what each successive number is.

Even so, mathematicians set to work getting as long a decimal expression as they could, spending more and more time on the painstaking, endless calculations. An English mathematician named William Shanks spent years calculating and calculating until, in 1873, he came up with a value of pi that ran to 707 places! (It eventually turned out, though, that he had made an error in the 528th place and everything after that was wrong.)

No one ever tried to beat Shanks in pen-and-paper calculations; no one had that many years to spare. By the end of World War II, however, computers existed that could be programmed to work out a series that would give the value of pi, and do so much more quickly than a human being could.

In 1949, a computer worked for 70 hours and came up with the 13
value of pi to 2,035 decimal places. In 1955, a faster computer
worked away for 33 hours and came up with a value of pi to
10,107 places.

Since then, computers have continued to become faster, and 14
programming has become more expert.

Early in 1988, a Japanese computer scientist, Yasumasa Kanada 15
of the University of Tokyo, made use of a super computer and, after it had worked for six hours, it came up with a value of pi to
201,326,000 decimal places. He intends to beat that record and figure out a way of getting a computer to give him twice that number
of places in a reasonable amount of time.

There's no end, of course. A trillion trillion places wouldn't 16
help—so why bother, except for the infinite curiosity of the inquiring human mind? Well, for one thing, it offers a perfect way of
testing any advanced computer. Set such a computer to working
out the value of pi. If it makes a mistake, then somewhere there is
a glitch in its workings.

Then, too, mathematicians are interested in the details of the 17
long decimals. Do any digits appear more than any other digits do?
Are there combinations of digits that show up too often or not often enough? Such questions might lead to interesting results.

Critical Inquiries

1. If you were in charge of a supercomputer, would you permit it to be used
   to add further to the endless repeating decimal that represents the un-
   reachable value of pi? Why or why not?

2. Lately, it has been alleged that American students generally do less well
   at mathematics than their counterparts in other countries. To what in our
   system of teaching mathematics, or in our culture, do you think this failure can be attributed?

3. Some mathematics departments of American universities, sensitive to
   charges that their student bodies are dominated by Asian-American students, have begun setting ethnic quotas on admissions. If Asian-American
   students excel at mathematics, why shouldn't they be admitted in dispro-
   portionate numbers to mathematics departments?

4. With what liberal-arts subject is mathematics traditionally allied? Why?

Rhetorical Inquiries

1. What kind of paragraphs does Asimov use in this article? What can you
   deduce about his intended audience from these paragraphs?

2. How does Asimov use parentheses in this article?

3. What objection might an English-language purist raise to paragraph 6?

4. Asimov has a reputation for being the great explainer. Other than his use of short sentences and simple diction, name at least one explaining technique, evident in this piece, that has helped earn him this reputation.

COMPUTER SCIENCE

Philip Elmer-DeWitt
COMPUTER VIRUSES

Philip Elmer-DeWitt, (b. 1949) Time-*magazine staff writer, was born in Boston and educated at Oberlin College (B.A., 1971) and Columbia University Graduate School of Journalism. He began with* Time *as a part-time secretary in 1979 and has been a staff writer with the magazine since 1982.*

Froma Joselow was getting ready to bang out a newspaper story   1
when the invisible intruder struck. Joselow, a financial reporter at the Providence *Journal-Bulletin,* had carefully slipped a disk holding six months worth of notes and interviews into one of the newsroom computers when the machine's familiar whir was pierced by a sharp, high-pitched beep. Each time she tried to call a file to the screen, the warning DISK ERROR flashed instead. It was as if the contents of her floppy disk had vanished. "I got that sinking feeling," recalls Joselow. "Every writing project of mine was on that disk."

In the *Journal-Bulletin's* computer center, where Joselow took her   2
troubled floppy, the detective work began immediately. Using a binary editor—the computer equivalent of a high-powered magnifying glass—Systems Engineer Peter Scheidler examined the disk's contents line by line. "What I saw wasn't pretty," says Scheidler. "It was garbage, a real mess." Looking for a way to salvage at least part of Joselow's work, he began peering into each of the disk's 360 concentric rings of data.

Suddenly he spotted something that gave him a chill. Buried   3
near Sector 0, the disk's innermost circle, was evidence that the glitch that had swallowed six months of Joselow's professional life was not a glitch at all but a deliberate act of sabotage. There,

From "Invasion of the Data Snatchers," Sept. 26, 1988. Copyright 1988 The Time Inc. Magazine Company. Reprinted by permission.

standing out amid a stream of random letters and numbers, was the name and phone number of a Pakistani computer store and a message that read, in part: WELCOME TO THE DUNGEON . . . CONTACT US FOR VACCINATION

Joselow had been stricken by a pernicious virus. Not the kind that causes measles, mumps or the Shanghai flu, but a special strain of software virus, a small but deadly program that lurks in the darkest recesses of a computer waiting for an opportunity to spring to life. The computer virus that struck Joselow had been hiding in the memory of the newspaper's machine and had copied itself onto her data disk, scrambling its contents and turning the reporter's words and sentences into electronic confetti. 4

What was the intruder doing in the newsroom computer? Who had unleashed it and to what purpose? This particular virus was ultimately traced to two brothers who run a computer store in, of all places, Lahore, Pakistan. The brothers later admitted that they had inserted the program into disks they sold to tourists attracted to their store by its cut-rate prices. Their motive: to "punish" computer users for buying and selling bootleg software and thus depriving merchants of potential sales. 5

The Pakistani virus is only one of a swarm of infectious programs that have descended on U.S. computer users this year. In the past nine months, an estimated 250,000 computers, from the smallest laptop machines to the most powerful workstations, have been hit with similar contagions. Nobody knows how far the rogue programs have spread, and the exact mechanism by which they select their innocent victims — resting harmlessly in some computers and striking destructively in others — is still a mystery. 6

What is clear, however, is that a once rare electronic "disease" has suddenly reached epidemic proportions. Across the U.S., it is disrupting operations, destroying data and raising disturbing questions about the vulnerability of information systems everywhere. Forty years after the dawn of the computer era, when society has become dependent on high-speed information processing for everything from corner cash machines to military-defense systems, the computer world is being threatened by an enemy from within. 7

Last week in Fort Worth, a jury heard evidence in what prosecutors describe as the epidemic's first criminal trial. A 40-year-old programmer named Donald Gene Burleson is accused of infecting a former employer's computer with a virus-like program that deleted more than 168,000 records of sales commissions. Burleson says he is innocent, but he was ordered to pay his former em- 8 ployer $12,000 in a civil case based on similar charges. If convicted, he could face ten years in prison.

A virus, whether biological or electronic, is basically an informa-   9
tion disorder. Biological viruses are tiny scraps of genetic code—DNA or RNA—that can take over the machinery of a living cell and trick it into making thousands of flawless replicas of the original virus. Like its biological counterpart, a computer virus carries in its instructional code the recipe for making perfect copies of itself. Lodged in a host computer, the typical virus takes temporary control of the computer's disk operating system. Then, whenever the infected computer comes in contact with an uninfected piece of software, a fresh copy of the virus passes into the new program. Thus the infection can be spread from computer to computer by unsuspecting users who either swap disks or send programs to one another over telephone lines. In today's computer culture, in which everybody from video gamesters to businessmen trades computer disks like baseball cards, the potential for widespread contagion is enormous.

Since viruses can travel from one place to another as fast as a   10
phone call, a single strain can quickly turn up in computers hundreds of miles apart. The infection that struck Froma Joselow hit more than 100 other disks at the *Journal-Bulletin* as well as an estimated 100,000 IBM PC disks across the U.S.—including some 10,000 at George Washington University alone. Another virus, called SCORES for the name of the bogus computer file it creates, first appeared in Apple Macintosh computers owned by Dallas-based EDS, the giant computer-services organization. But it spread rapidly to such firms as Boeing and Arco, and has since turned up in computers at NASA, the IRS and the U.S. House of Representatives.

Many of America's 3,000 electronic bulletin-board systems have   11
suffered some kind of infection, as have hundreds of users groups and thousands of businesses. "It is *the* topic of conversation within the computing society," says John McAfee, head of InterPath, a computer firm in Santa Clara, Calif.

So far, real disaster has been avoided. No killer virus has pene-   12
trated the country's electronic funds-transfer system, which is essential to the operation of the nation's banks. No stock- or commodity-exchange computer centers have crashed. No insurance-company rolls have been wiped out. No pension funds have had their records scrambled. No air-traffic-control systems have ground to a halt. And the U.S. military-defense system remains largely un-

compromised, although there have been published reports of virus attacks at both the FBI and the CIA.

But most experts warn that the worst is yet to come. "The viruses we've seen so far are child's play," says Donn Parker, a computer-crime expert at SRI International in Menlo Park, Calif. Parker fears that the same viruses that are inconveniencing personal-computer users today could, through the myriad links and entry points that connect large networks, eventually threaten the country's most vital computer systems. Agrees Harold Highland, editor of *Computers & Security* magazine: "We ain't seen nothing yet." 13

At last count, more than 25 different viral strains had been isolated, and new ones are emerging nearly every week. Some are relatively benign, like the virus spread through the CompuServe network that causes machines equipped with voice synthesizers to intone the words "Don't panic." Others are more of a nuisance, causing temporary malfunctions or making it difficult to run isolated programs. But some seem bent on destroying valuable data. "Your worst fear has come true," wrote a computer buff in a report he posted on an electronic bulletin board to warn other users about a new Macintosh virus. "Don't share disks. Don't copy software. Don't let anyone touch your machine. Just say no." 14

Who are the perpetrators of this mischief? At first glance they seem an odd and varied lot. The Pakistani brothers are self-taught programmers isolated from the rest of the computer community. Two viruses exported to the U.S. from West Germany, by contrast, were bred in academia and spread by students. Other outbreaks seem to have come directly out of Silicon Valley. Rumor has it that the SCORES virus was written by a disgruntled Apple employee. 15

But some observers see an emerging pattern: the virus writers tend to be men in their late teens or early 20s who have spent an inordinate portion of their youth bathed in the glow of a computer screen. *Scientific American* Columnist A.K. Dewdney, who published the first article on computer viruses, describes what he calls a "nerd syndrome" common among students of science and technology. Says Dewdney: "They live in a very protected world, both socially and emotionally. They leave school and carry with them their prankish bent." 16

Thomas Lunzer, a consultant at SRI, believes the proliferation of microcomputers in schools and homes has exacerbated the problem. A powerful technology became widely available without the development of a code of ethics to keep that power in check. 17

"We're harvesting our first crop of a computer-literate generation," says Lunzer. "The social responsibility hasn't caught up with them."

A case in point is Drew Davidson, a 23-year-old programmer   18
from Tucson, who has achieved some notoriety as the author of the so-called Peace virus, which flashed an innocuous greeting on thousands of computer screens last spring. A study in self-contradiction, Davidson rails against those who would create malignant viruses, calling them "copycats" and "attention seekers." Yet he cheerfully admits that he created his virus at least in part to draw attention to his programming skills. "In the beginning, I didn't think it would have this kind of impact," he says. "I just thought we'd release it and it would be kind of neat."

On March 2, when several thousand Macintosh owners turned   19
on their machines, they were greeted by a drawing of planet earth and a "universal message of peace" signed by Richard Brandow, a friend of Davidson's and the publisher of a Canadian computer magazine. The virus did no harm. It flashed its message on the screen and then erased its own instructions, disappearing without a trace.

But what made this virus special was how it spread. Brandow,   20
who collaborated with Davidson in creating it, inserted the virus into game disks that were distributed at meetings of a Montreal Macintosh users group. A speaker at one meeting was a Chicago software executive named Marc Canter, whose company was doing some contract work for Aldus Corp., a Seattle-based software publisher. Canter innocently picked up a copy of the infected disk, tried it out on his office computer, and then proceeded, on the same machine, to review a piece of software being prepared for shipment to Aldus. Unaware that he had thereby passed on the hidden virus to the Aldus program, Canter sent an infected disk to Seattle. There the virus was unwittingly reproduced by Aldus employees, inserted in several thousand copies of a graphics program called Freehand, and shipped to computer stores around the country. It was the first known case of a virus spreading to a commercial software product.

The Peace virus capped a series of outbreaks that began last December, when a seemingly harmless Christmas greeting appeared   21
mysteriously on terminals connected to a worldwide network owned and operated by IBM. Users who followed the instructions on the screen and typed the word Christmas inadvertently triggered a virus-like self-replicating mechanism, sending an identical

copy of the original program to every name on their personal electronic mailing lists. In a matter of days, clones of the tiny program had multiplied in such profusion that they clogged the 350,000-terminal network like so many hairs in a bathtub drain.

Later that month, scientists at Jerusalem's Hebrew University reported that some of their desktop computers were growing lethargic, as if a hidden organism were sapping their strength. Once again, the problem was traced to a rapidly multiplying program that was consuming computer memory. This program carried something else as well. Within its instructional code was a "time bomb" linked to each computer's internal clock and set to go off on the second Friday in May—Friday the 13th, the 40th anniversary of the State of Israel. Any machine still infected on that date would suffer the instant loss of all its files. Fortunately, the virus was eradicated well before May 13, and the day passed without incident.   22

The alarm caused by the appearance of these three viruses was amplified by two groups with a vested interest in making the threat sound as dramatic as possible. On one side are the computer-security specialists, a small group of consultants who make $100 an hour or more by telling corporate computer users how to protect their machines from catastrophic failure. On the other is the computer press, a collection of highly competitive weekly tabloids that have seized on the story like pit bulls, covering every outbreak with breathless copy and splashy headlines.   23

Meanwhile, entrepreneurs eager to profit from the epidemic have rushed to market with all sorts of programs designed to protect against viruses. In advertising that frightens more than it informs, they flog products with names like Flu Shot +, Vaccinate, Data Physician, Disk Defender, Antidote, Virus RX, Viru-Safe and Retro-V. "Do computer viruses really exist? You bet they do!" screams a press release for Disk Watcher 2.0, a product that supposedly prevents virus attacks. Another program, VirALARM, boasts a telling feature: it instructs an IBM PC's internal speaker to alert users to the presence of a viral intruder with a wail that sounds like a police siren.   24

Comparisons with germ warfare and sexually transmitted diseases were perhaps inevitable. A virus that struck Lehigh University quickly got tagged "PC AIDS." That analogy is both overstated and insensitive, but it stems from a real concern that the computer revolution, like the sexual revolution, is threatened by viruses. At Apple, a company hit by at least three different viral strains, em-   25 ployees have been issued memos spelling out "safe computing practices" and reminded, as Product Manager Michael Holm puts it, "If you get a floppy disk from someone, remember that it's been in everybody else's computer too."

The publicity has triggered a certain amount of hysteria. Systems managers have imposed elaborate quarantines on their companies' machines. Computer columnists have advised readers to put their PCs under lock and key and, in one radical proposal, to disconnect their machines permanently from all data networks and telephone lines. Data-processing managers have rushed to stock up on antiviral programs. "We're seeing panic buying by those who have already been hit," says William Agne, president of Com-Netco, which publishes Viru-Safe. When a virus showed up at the University of Delaware, the assistant manager of academic computing services immediately bought six different pieces of antiviral software. Then she began screening every floppy disk on campus—some 3,000 in all.

In some cases, the threat of a virus is enough to spread panic. When scientists at the Lawrence Livermore National Lab were warned by a Government security center last May that a virus lurking in the lab's 450 computers was set to be activated that day, many users stopped work and began feverishly making backup copies of all their disks. The warning of a virus proved to be a hoax, but in such an atmosphere, says Chuck Cole, Livermore's deputy computer-security manager, "a hoax can be as disruptive as the real thing."

Industry experts are concerned that the publicity surrounding virus infections, like the attention given political kidnapings, could invite more attacks. "When we talk viruses, we create viruses," cautions Robert Courtney, a computer consultant from Kingston, N.Y. "We almost make it a self-fulfilling prophecy."

But the ranks of those who would dismiss the virus threat as a Chicken Little scare are getting smaller with every outbreak. Mitchell Kapor, founder of Lotus Development and now chairman of ON Technology, became a believer when some of his associates were infected. "It isn't the fall of Western civilization," says Kapor, "but the problem is real and the threat is serious." *Scientific American's* Dewdney has had a similar change of heart. "At first I thought these new outbreaks were much ado about nothing," he says. "But I'm now convinced that they are a bigger threat than I imagined."

The idea of an electronic virus was born in the earliest days of the computer era. In fact, it was Computer Pioneer John von Neu-

26

27

28

29

30

mann who laid out the basic blueprint in a 1949 paper titled "Theory and Organization of Complicated Automata." If most of his colleagues found the idea that computer programs might multiply too fantastic to be taken seriously, they can be forgiven, for the paper predated the first commercial electronic computers by several years. But a handful of scientists quietly pursued Von Neumann's ideas, keeping them alive in the scientific literature until they sprang to life ten years later at AT&T's Bell Laboratories, in the form of a bizarre after-hours recreation known as Core War.

Core War was the brainstorm of three Bell Labs programmers 31 then in their early 20s: H. Douglas McIlroy, Victor Vysottsky and Robert Morris. Like Von Neumann, they recognized that computers were vulnerable to a peculiar kind of self-destruction. The machines employed the same "core" memory to store both the data used by programs and the instructions for running those programs. With subtle changes in its coding, a program designed to consume data could be made instead to consume programs.

The researchers used this insight to stage the first Core War: a 32 series of mock battles between opposing armies of computer programs. Two players would write a number of self-replicating programs, called "organisms," that would inhabit the memory of a computer. Then, at a given signal, each player's organisms did their best to kill the other player's—generally by devouring their instructions. The winner was the player whose programs were the most abundant when time was called. At that point, the players erased the killer programs from the computer's memory, and that was that.

These clandestine battles, which took place late at night when 33 computer usage was low, were quietly sanctioned by Bell Labs' bemused managers, many of whom were senior scientists. The fun soon spread to other leading computer-research facilities, including Xerox's Palo Alto Research Center and the artificial-intelligence lab at M.I.T.

In those early days, when each computer was a stand-alone de- 34 vice, there was no threat of a runaway virus. If things got out of control on a particular machine, its keepers could simply shut it down. But all that changed when computers began to be connected to one another. A self-replicating organism created in fun could be devastating if loosed upon the world of interconnected machines. For that reason, the Core War combatants observed an unspoken vow never to reveal to the public the details of their game.

In 1983 the programmers' code of honor was broken. The culprit 35 was Ken Thompson, the gifted software engineer who wrote the original version of Unix, the computer operating system now coming into widespread use. Thompson was being presented the Association for Computing Machinery's prestigious A.M. Turing Award when he gave a speech that not only revealed the existence of the first computer viruses but showed the audience how to make them. "If you have never done this," he told them, "I urge you to try it on your own."

His colleagues were aghast, but the secret was out. And the revelation was further compounded by Dewdney's landmark article in the May 1984 issue of *Scientific American,* which described Core War and offered readers who sent $2 for postage a copy of the guidelines for creating their own viral battlefields.   36

Soon software viruses began appearing in university computer systems and in the widely proliferating desktop computers. A rogue program that made the rounds of Ivy League schools featured a creature inspired by *Sesame Street* called the Cookie Monster. Students trying to do useful work would be interrupted by persistent messages saying "I want a cookie." In one variation, the message would be repeated with greater and greater frequency until users typed the letters C-O-O-K-I-E on their terminal keyboards.   37

But not all viruses are so playful. One particularly vicious program deletes everything stored on the computer and prints the word GOTCHA! on the screen. Another takes the form of a game called "rck.video." It delights unsuspecting users with an animation featuring the singer Madonna before erasing the files on their disks. Then it chortles, "You're stupid to download a video about rock stars."   38

Such pranks enrage the original Core War programmers. McIlroy and his friends took care that their high-tech high jinks did not put other people's programs and data at risk. "I'm amazed at how malicious some of today's players are," says McIlroy, who is now a senior member of the technical staff at Bell Labs. "What was once a friendly, harmless game has deteriorated into something that is neither friendly, harmless, nor a game."   39

So far, the mainframe computers that do much of the most vital information processing in the U.S. remain relatively unscathed. "With mainframes, we've got a whole regimen of quality control and data integrity that we use," says Bill Wright, a spokesman for EDS. But with the rapid spread of PC-to-mainframe linkups, that safety could be compromised. "If the same sorts of standards aren't   40 applied soon to the PC environment," says Wright, "it's going to be a real problem for the whole industry."

In the past, companies that were hit by a virus generally kept it quiet. But the computer-sabotage trial in Fort Worth may be a sign that things are changing. Texas is one of 48 states that have passed new laws against computer mischief, and four years ago President Reagan signed a federal law that spelled out harsh penalties for unauthorized tampering with Government computer data. But most statutes were written before viruses surfaced as a major problem, and none mention them by name. In May an organization of programmers called the Software Development Council met in Atlanta to launch a movement to plug that loophole in the law. Declares Michael Odawa, president of the council: "I say, release a virus, go to jail."   41

Some computer users are not waiting for legal protection. Don Brown, a Macintosh enthusiast from Des Moines, responded to the Peace virus outbreak by writing an antiviral program and giving it away. Brown's Vaccine 1.0 is available free on most national computer networks, including CompuServe, the Source and GEnie. InterPath's McAfee fights viruses from a 27-ft. mobile home known as the Bugbuster. Carrying up to six different computers with him, he pays house calls on local firms and colleges that have been infected, dispensing advice and vaccines and, like a good epidemiologist, taking samples of each strain of virus. Lately he has been averaging more than 30 calls a day. Says he: "You're always trying to stay one step ahead or as close behind as possible."   42

Like a biological vaccination, a vaccine program is a preventive measure—an attempt to protect an uninfected disk from invasion by an uninvited program. Most software vaccines take advantage of the fact that computer viruses usually hide themselves in one of a few locations within the machine's control software. A typical vaccine will surround those memory locations with the equivalent of a burglar alarm. If something tries to alter the contents of one of those cells, the vaccine program is supposed to stop everything and alert the operator. But because there are so many different viral strains out there, vaccines are often ineffective.   43

Once a computer has been hit by a virus, the invader can sometimes be eradicated by a special program that searches out and erases each bit of foreign material. Generally, however, the simplest way to bring an infected computer back to health is to shut it down, purge its memory and all its disks, and rebuild its files from scratch. Programs should be loaded from the original manufactur-   44 er's copy, and new disks should be carefully screened for the presence of an unwanted intruder. There are any number of products that will do this, usually by searching for files that are suspiciously long and may be harboring a virus.

But none of these antiviral programs are foolproof. Virus writers 45 are constantly making end runs around the barricades erected against them. Even a total purge of a computer system is no guarantee against reinfection. McAfee reports that 3 out of 4 of the installations he visits suffer a relapse within a week, usually from disks missed on the first go-round or carried in from the outside. In recent months, a pesky new type of virus has emerged. So-called retroviruses are designed to reappear in systems after their memories have been wiped clean. Other viruses infect a computer's hardware, speeding up a disk drive, for example, so that it soon wears itself out. Particularly dangerous are bogus antiviral programs that are actually viruses in disguise and spread infection rather than stop it.

Where will it end? The computer world hopes that the novelty 46 of software viruses will pass, going the way of letter bombs and poisoned Tylenol. But even if the epidemic eventually eases, the threat will remain. The uninhibited program swapping that made the early days of the computer revolution so exciting may be gone forever. Never again will computer buffs be able to accept a disk or plug into a network without being suspicious—and cautious.

Vocabulary

pernicious (4)   eradicated (22)
syndrome (16)   clandestine (33)
exacerbated (17)   bemused (33)
lethargic (22)

Critical Inquiries

1. What effect do you think the publicity about computer viruses might have on encouraging their spread? What do you think can be done to discourage those who would write virus programs?

2. What punishment should be given to those convicted of infecting computers with a virus?

3. What important differences exist between a human virus and one that infects a computer?

4. In what kind of computers, devoted to what function, do you think a viral infection poses the greatest threat to human welfare?

5. One expert quoted speculated that the computer is a powerful technology that has developed without "a code of ethics to keep that power in check." Are special ethics needed to check the behavior of computer nerds? If so, what should these ethics be?

Rhetorical Inquiries

1. What technique does the author use to initially hook us into the subject?

2. In which paragraph does the author actually define a computer virus? Why does he not do so sooner?

3. What transition does the author use at the beginning of paragraph 5?

4. What obvious technique for achieving coherence does the author practice in paragraph 12?

5. What primary kind of evidence does the author use in this article?

Writing Assignments

1. Turn this model into an essay developed by definition. Only a skeleton of the model is provided. If necessary, go to the library and find your own details. Some reorganization of the model may also be necessary.
   Controlling Idea: Semantics is the study of the meanings of words.

   > The basic principle of semantics is that every word is a symbol.
   > Another principle of semantics is that words have denotative as well as connotative meanings.
   > A third principle is that words are concrete and abstract.

2. With the help of an unabridged dictionary, write an extended definition (300–500 words) of one of the words below. Include an etymology of the word, if necessary, and examples to illustrate its meaning:
   a. mediocrity
   b. monopoly
   c. sophistry
   d. xenophobia
   e. ghost
   f. molecule

3. Read the article, "Why Are Americans Afraid of Dragons?" Then write an essay defining "dragons."

4. Using the essay, "What Is a Sociologist?" as your model, write an essay entitled, "What Is an English Teacher?"

5. Write an essay defining "calculus" for a lay reader.

6. What is a CPU in a computer? Write an essay defining this term, giving examples of its functions and uses.

Chapter

10

Exampling

Example is always more efficacious than precept.

SAMUEL JOHNSON (1709–1784)

    The use of examples to explain or reinforce an idea is a mode of development found in the writings of nearly every profession. Ministers use examples in their sermons to illustrate religious principle; lawyers use them to establish precedents; psychologists infer theories from specialized examples known as "case histories." Much of what we do or refrain from doing is based on the example of those who have preceded us. Selected carefully, examples can clarify a point better than any other rhetorical technique.

    An example is a supportive instance of some larger point: an idea, a state, an allegation. It is not a different kind of detail, but detail used in a particular way. You are giving examples when you are trying to support some larger point by citing details that are contextual and representative of it. Merely writing "for example," does not make an example any more than writing "the fact is" actually creates a fact. Here is an example of what we mean:

```
     Rock and roll music is the greatest music

on the radio.  For example, the Rolling Stones

are my favorite band.  Their music ranges from

hard, solid rock to softer songs.  Rock music is

the best because you do not have to know the

words to enjoy the music.  . . .
```

This is not an example, it is an expression of personal preference. Use the prefacing "for example," only when you are truly giving examples, meaning details that are representative of a larger whole, that are contextual, and that explicate it.

    There are two main kinds of examples. A point may be supported either by many brief exemplifying details or by a single extended example. Here is a paragraph containing a list of brief examples:

    There can be no question about the average American's Americanism or his desire to preserve this precious heritage at all costs. Nevertheless, some insidious foreign ideas have already wormed their way into his civilization without his realizing what was going on. Thus, dawn finds the unsuspecting patriot garbed in pajamas, a garment of East Indian origin; and lying on a bed built on a pattern which originated in either Persia or Asia Minor. He is muffled to the ears in un-American materials: cotton, first domesticated in India; linen, domesticated in the Near East; wool from an animal native to Asia Minor; or silk, whose uses were first discovered by the Chinese. All these substances have been transformed into cloth by a method invented in Southwestern Asia. If the weather is cold enough, he may even be sleeping under an eiderdown quilt invented in Scandinavia.

—Ralph Linton, "The 100% American," *The American Mercury* 40 (April 1937).

And here is a paragraph whose main point—that biographers must carefully investigate quoted writers who have inexplicably changed their views—is supported by a single extended example:

> Sometimes a writer will contradict what he has already written, and in that case the only thing to do is to investigate what has changed his point of view. For instance, in 1608 Captain John Smith issued a description of his capture by Powhatan, and he made it clear that the Indian chief had treated him with unwavering courtesy and hospitality. In 1624 the story was repeated in Smith's *General History of Virginia,* but the writer's circumstances had changed. Smith needed money, "having a prince's mind imprisoned in a poor man's purse," and he wanted the book to be profitable. Powhatan's daughter, the princess Pocahontas, had recently been in the news, for her visit to England had aroused a great deal of interest among the sort of people that Smith hoped would buy his book. So Smith supplied a new version of the story, in which the once-hospitable Powhatan would have permitted the hero's brains to be dashed out if Pocahontas had not saved his life. It was the second story that achieved fame, and of course it may have been true. But it is impossible to trust it because the desire of the writer is so obviously involved; as Smith said in his prospectus, he needed money and hoped that the book would give "satisfaction."
>
> —"Getting at the Truth," Marchette Chute

Either use of examples is fairly straightforward and demonstrates the writer's grasp of representative details.

Here are some other tips for getting the most out of your examples: Make your examples relevant and establish a clear connection between your example and the point being made.

Make Your Examples Relevant

Whether brief or extended, the example must support the point of the paragraph. The following example in a first draft misses the point:

                In fourteenth-century England, a campaign

        of heresy was launched against the Templar

        knights, a monastic order formed to be the right

        arm of the Church, who were accused of sorcery

        and magic. For example, they had become

        immensely rich, since they were tax exempt. As

        a result of their wealth, they became the

        bankers of the Church and preferred living

        lavishly to going on crusades. Also, they

        acquired a sinister reputation because of the

        secrecy of their rituals and because, unlike

        other knighthoods, they supported no hospitals.

The topic sentence requires an example of the campaign of heresy against the Templars for purportedly using sorcery and magic, forbidden by the Catholic church. But instead of an example, the writer provides a general description of the Templars. Here is how the writer edited this paragraph:

                In fourteenth-century England, a campaign

        of heresy was launched against the Templar

        knights, a monastic order formed to be the right

        arm of the Church, who were accused of sorcery

        and magic. For example, ~~they had become~~ *many of the old Templars*

        ~~immensely rich, since they were tax exempt~~ *were racked, thumbscrewed, starved, hung with* As

        ~~a result of their wealth, they became the~~ *weights until joints were dislocated, had teeth*

        ~~bankers of the Church and preferred living~~ *and fingernails pulled one by one, bones broken*

        ~~lavishly to going on crusades~~ *by the wedge, and feet held over flames. In* Also, they *between torture, they would be asked to confess* ~~acquired a sinister reputation because of the~~ *that they had indulged in sorcery or black magic,* ~~secrecy of their rituals and because, unlike~~ *or some other form of Devil worship.* ~~other knighthoods, they supported no hospitals.~~

And here is the final draft as it appeared in the paper.

In fourteenth-century England, a campaign
of heresy was launched against the Templar
knights, a monastic order formed to be the right
arm of the Church, who were accused of sorcery
and magic. For example, many of the old
Templars were racked, thumbscrewed, starved,
hung with weights until joints were dislocated,
had teeth and fingernails pulled one by one,
bones broken by the wedge, and feet held over
flames. In between torture, they would be asked
to confess that they had indulged in sorcery or
black magic, or some other form of Devil
worship.

The example now supports the topic sentence.

Establish a Clear Connection between Your Example and the Point Being Made

Generally, an example should use a brief introduction or preface to make its meaning clear to the reader. The following first draft fails to make a connection:

Old people are referred to as
"chronologically advantaged." Stinky garbage
pits are called "landfills." People who used to
be considered crippled, are now considered

"physically challenged." Even nuclear war has
been diluted to "nuclear exchange." People seem
to feel more comfortable asking for the "powder
room" than for the toilet. It is rather amusing
to consider how often we avoid saying what we
really mean.

These examples lack an introductory context; the reader needs to know what they mean and what they have to do with the topic sentence. Here is the draft with the writer's revision:

The dictionary tells us that a euphemism *is "the substitution of an inoffensive term for an offensive term that would be more accurate." Examples of euphemisms abound in our society. For instance,*

Øld people are referred to as
as if by eliminating the word old
"chronologically advantaged!" Stinky garbage
perhaps age itself will vanish.
pits are called "landfills." People who used to
handicapped now prefer to be called
be considered crippled are now considered
hoping that the new label will encourage employers to treat them more
"physically challenged." Even nuclear war has
respectfully   the much less threatening   Most of the time we use
been diluted to "nuclear exchange." People seem
euphemisms because we do not wish to offend our listeners. Thus we prefer to ask
to feel more comfortable asking for the "powder
room" than for the toilet, It is rather amusing
to consider how often we avoid saying what we
really mean.

and we serve "ragout" rather than stew made from leftover meat and vegetables.

And here is the completely revised paragraph:

```
     The dictionary tells us that a euphemism is

"the substitution of an inoffensive term for an

offensive term that would be more accurate."

Examples of euphemisms abound in our society.

For instance, old people are referred to as

"chronologically advantaged," as if by

eliminating the word old perhaps age itself will

vanish.  People who used to be considered

handicapped now prefer to be called "physically

challenged," hoping that the new label will

encourage employers to treat them more

respectfully.  Even nuclear war has been diluted

to the much less threatening "nuclear exchange."

It is rather amusing to consider how often we

avoid saying what we really mean.  Most of the

time we use euphemisms because we do not wish to

offend our listeners.  Thus, we prefer to ask

for the "powder room" rather than the toilet,

and we serve "ragout" rather than stew made from

leftover meat and vegetables.
```

Use these connective expressions to introduce an example: "for example," "for instance," "to illustrate," "a case in point is," "the following illustration underscores this point."

Occasionally, the point of the example will be unmistakable from its context, in which case no formal connective phrase is necessary. Here is an example:

A dress code signifies that school is a special place in which special kinds of behavior are required. The way one dresses is an indication of an attitude toward a situation. And the way one is *ex-*

pected to dress indicates what that attitude ought to be. You would not wear dungarees and a T-shirt that says "Feel Me" when attending a church wedding. That would be considered an outrage against the tone and meaning of the situation. The school has every right and reason, I believe, to expect the same sort of consideration.

—Neil Postman, "Teaching as a Conserving Activity."

The example of not wearing a T-shirt to a church wedding needs no formal connective because its context is so clear that the reader knows exactly what is exemplified.

Exampling as a Writing Technique

We do not wish to give the impression that examples are used only in essays specifically organized to give examples. In fact, examples are used in essays of every kind whenever a writer wishes to support an abstract point with a specific instance. For example, in the essay "Computer Viruses," included in Chapter 9 as an essay organized to define, we find this paragraph:

> A case in point is Drew Davidson, a 23-year-old programmer from Tucson, who has achieved some notoriety as the author of the so-called Peace virus, which flashed an innocuous greeting on thousands of computer screens last spring. A study in self-contradiction, Davidson rails . . . .

You can find many similar examples sprinkled throughout the essays in other chapters.

Some essays, however, expend a good deal of ink and paper on examples. The writer will no doubt also be trying to do something else—perhaps to describe for us the plight of the homeless as Marin does in "Homelessness," or to show us how size operates as a biological principle as Haldane does in "On Being the Right Size." But achieving this other aim forces the writer to use such a succession of examples that they seem part of the essay's dominant purpose. In "Of What Use?" for example, Asimov cannot persuade us to his thesis—that pure research often turns out to be of inestimable value—without showing us instances where this has been true. Nor can Joyce Carol Oates get us to understand why she loves boxing without stirring us with examples and stories of the best boxers. In short, exampling is used in all kinds of writing. But the predominant use of examples in an essay can also be an organizing strategy.

The following first draft uses examples that are either irrelevant or not clearly connected to the rest of the text. Notice the changes made in the revision:

Original:

The topic sentence that should say that much litigation in the U.S. is intensely personal. At least that seems to be the point of your details.

The United States ranks among the most litigious countries in the world. From 1979–1985 *indicate that examples will follow.* Mary Kling sued Los Angeles County after the University of Southern California Medical Center withdrew her admission to nursing school because she could not pass certain physical tests due to an ileostomy involving the removal of part of her large and small intestines. After five years of court battles, an appeals court ruled in her favor, saying that she had been discriminated *This example seems out of place with the others.* against. A string of airline crashes during the last few years is expected to result in suits for hundreds of millions of dollars in compensation to victims' families. A high school girl in New Jersey sued the school district *Transition needed* because she was not allowed to play on the high school's football team. The Illinois estate of a *Transition?* man who committed suicide in jail sued the prison's architect for "breach of duty" because *your conclusion is weak.* he did not make the jail suicide proof. People *Say what the examples mean.* in our country love to sue.

Revision:

"I've never lived in a country where people sue in court for such strangely personal reasons as they do here in the United States." This is a

comment made by the British Consul General at a
reception in Los Angeles. Indeed, the United
States is the most litigious country in the
world. Lawsuits based on what might strike a
foreign observer as "strangely personal reasons"
are part of our cultural sense of individuality
and freedom. For instance, from 1979 to 1985
Mary Kling sued Los Angeles County after the USC
Medical Center withdrew her admission to nursing
school because she could not pass certain
physical tests due to an ileostomy involving the
removal of part of her large and small
intestines. After five years of court battles,
an appeals court ruled in her favor, saying that
she had been discriminated against. Another
rather eccentric case involved a high school
girl in New Jersey, who sued the school district
because she was not allowed to play on the high
school's football team. In a most extraordinary
move, the Illinois estate of a man who committed
suicide in jail sued the prison's architect for
"breach of duty" because he did not make the
jail "suicide proof." These examples illustrate
how Americans consider it their constitutional
privilege to go to court when they think their
personal rights are in danger of being abridged.

In the revision, the example of the airline lawsuit was deleted because it seemed out of place with the theme of the others. Added were an introduction, some connective phrases linking the examples to the topic sentence, and a conclusion pointing out what the examples mean.

LITERATURE

Joyce Carol Oates
ON BOXING

Joyce Carol Oates (b. 1938, Lockport, N.J.) is a prolific writer whose range encompasses virtually every literary form, from the play to the poem to the essay. She was educated at Syracuse University (B.A., 1960) and at the University of Wisconsin (M.A., 1961). Her published works are numerous and varied and include By the North Gate *(stories, 1963);* With Shuddering Fall *(novel, 1964);* Expensive People *(novel, 1968); and* Anonymous, and Other Poems *(1969).*

They are young welterweight boxers so evenly matched they might be twins—though one has a redhead's pallor and the other is a dusky-skinned Hispanic. Circling each other in the ring, they try jabs, tentative left hooks, right crosses that dissolve in midair or turn into harmless slaps. The Madison Square Garden crowd is derisive, impatient. "Those two! What'd they do, wake up this morning and decide they were boxers?" a man behind me says contemptuously. (He's dark, nattily dressed, with a neatly trimmed mustache and tinted glasses. A sophisticated fight fan. Two hours later he will be crying, "Tommy! Tommy! Tommy!" over and over in a paroxysm of grief as, on the giant closed-circuit television screen, middleweight champion Marvelous Marvin Hagler batters his challenger, Thomas Hearns, into insensibility.)

The young boxers must be conscious of the jeers and boos in this great cavernous space reaching up into the $20 seats in the balconies amid the constant milling of people in the aisles, the smell of hotdogs, beer, cigarette and cigar smoke, hair oil. But they are locked desperately together, circling, jabbing, slapping, clinching, now a flurry of light blows, clumsy footwork, another sweaty stumbling despairing clinch into the ropes that provokes a fresh wave of derision. Why are they here in the Garden of all places, each fighting what looks like his first professional fight? What are they doing? Neither is angry at the other. When the bell sounds at the end of the sixth and final round, the crowd boos a little louder. The Hispanic boy, silky yellow shorts, damp, frizzy, floating hair, strides about his corner of the ring with his gloved hand aloft—not in defiance of the boos, which increase in response to his gesture, or even in acknowledgment of them. It's just something he

Published in *The New York Times Magazine,* June 16, 1985. Reprinted by permission of the author and her agent, Blanche C. Gregory, Inc. Copyright © 1985 by The Ontario Review, Inc.

has seen older boxers do. He seems to be saying "I'm here, I made it, I did it." When the decision is announced as a draw, the crowd's derision increases in volume. "Get out of the ring!" "Go home!" Contemptuous male laughter follows the boys in their robes, towels about their heads, sweating, breathless. Why had they thought they were boxers?

How can you enjoy so brutal a sport, people ask. Or don't ask.   3

And it's too complicated to answer. In any case, I don't "enjoy"   4
boxing, and never have; it isn't invariably "brutal"; I don't think of it as a sport.

Nor do I think of it in writerly terms as a metaphor for some-   5
thing else. (For *what* else?) No one whose interest in boxing began in childhood—as mine did as an offshoot of my father's interest—is likely to suppose it is a symbol of something beyond itself, though I can entertain the proposition that life is a metaphor for boxing—for one of those bouts that go on and on, round following round, small victories, small defeats, nothing determined, again the bell and again the bell and you and your opponent so evenly matched it's clear your opponent *is* you and why are the two of you jabbing and punching at each other on an elevated platform enclosed by ropes as in a pen beneath hot crude all-exposing lights in the presence of an indifferent crowd: that sort of writerly metaphor. But if you have seen 500 boxing matches, you have seen 500 boxing matches, and their common denominator, which surely exists, is not of primary interest to you. "If the Host is only a symbol," the Catholic writer Flannery O'Connor said, "I'd say the hell with it."

Each boxing match is a story, a highly condensed, highly dra-   6
matic story—even when nothing much happens: then failure is the story. There are two principal characters in the story, overseen by a shadowy third. When the bell rings no one knows what will happen. Much is speculated, nothing known. The boxers bring to the fight everything that is themselves, and everything will be exposed: including secrets about themselves they never knew. There are boxers possessed of such remarkable intuition, such prescience, one would think they had fought this particular fight before. There are boxers who perform brilliantly, but mechanically, who cannot improvise in midfight; there are boxers performing at the height of their skill who cannot quite comprehend that it won't be enough; to my knowledge there was only one boxer who possessed an extraordinary and disquieting awareness, not only of his opponent's

every move or anticipated move, but of the audience's keenest shifts in mood as well—Muhammad Ali, of course.

In the ring, death is always a possibility, which is why I prefer to see films or tapes of fights already past—already crystallized into art. In fact, death is a statistically rare possibility of which no one likes to think—like your possible death tomorrow morning in an automobile crash, or in next month's airplane crash, or in a freak accident involving a fall on the stairs—a skull fracture, subarachnoid hemorrhage.

A boxing match is a play without words, which doesn't mean that it has no text or no language, only that the text is improvised in action, the language a dialogue between the boxers in a joint response to the mysterious will of the crowd, which is always that the fight be a worthy one so that the crude paraphernalia of the setting—the ring, the lights, the onlookers themselves—be obliterated. To go from an ordinary preliminary match to a "Fight of the Century"—like those between Joe Louis and Billy Conn, Muhammad Ali and Joe Frazier, most recently Marvin Hagler and Thomas Hearns—is to go from listening or half-listening to a guitar being idly plucked to hearing Bach's "Well-Tempered Clavier" being perfectly played, and that too is part of the story. So much is happening so swiftly and so subtly you cannot absorb it except to know that something memorable is happening and it is happening in a place beyond words.

The fighters in the ring are time-bound—is anything so excruciatingly long as a fiercely contested three-minute round?—but the fight itself is timeless. By way of films and tapes, it has become history, art. If boxing is a sport, it is the most tragic of all sports because, more than any human activity, it consumes the very excellence it displays: Its very drama is this consumption. To expend oneself in fighting the greatest fight of one's life is to begin immediately the downward turn that next time may be a plunge, a sudden incomprehensible fall. *I am the greatest,* Muhammad Ali says. *I am the greatest,* Marvin Hagler says. You always think you're going to win, Jack Dempsey wryly observed in his old age, otherwise you can't fight at all. The punishment—to the body, the brain, the spirit—a man must endure to become a great boxer is inconceivable to most of us whose idea of personal risk is largely ego related or emotional. But the punishment, as it begins to show in even a young and vigorous boxer, is closely assessed by his rivals. After junior-welterweight champion Aaron Pryor won a lackluster fight on points a few months ago, a younger boxer in his weight division, interviewed at ringside, said: "My mouth is watering."

So the experience of seeing great fighters of the past—and great   10
sporting events are always *past*—is radically different from having
seen them when they were reigning champions. Jack Johnson, Jack
Dempsey, Joe Louis, Sugar Ray Robinson, Willie Pep, Rocky Marciano, Muhammad Ali—as spectators we know not only how a
fight ends but how a career ends. Boxing is always particulars, second by incalculable second, but in the abstract it suggests these
haunting lines by Yeats:

> Everything that man esteems
> Endures a moment or a day.
> Love's pleasure drives his love away,
> The painter's brush consumes his dreams;
> The herald's cry, the soldier's tread
> Exhaust his glory and his might:
> Whatever flames upon the night
> Man's own resinous heart has fed.
>   —from "The Resurrection"

The referee, the third character in the story, usually appears to   11
be a mere observer, even an intruder, a near-ghostly presence as
fluid in motion and quick-footed as the boxers themselves (he is
frequently a former boxer). But so central to the drama of boxing is
the referee that the spectacle of two men fighting each other unsu-
pervised in an elevated ring would appear hellish, obscene—life
rather than art. The referee is our intermediary in the fight. He is
our moral conscience, extracted from us as spectators so that, for
the duration of the fight, "conscience" is not a factor in our experience, nor is it a factor in the boxers' behavior.

Though the referee's role is a highly demanding one, and it has   12
been estimated that there are perhaps no more than a dozen really
skilled referees in the world, it seems to be necessary in the intense dramatic action of the fight that the referee have no dramatic
identity. Referees' names are quickly forgotten, even as they are
announced over the microphone preceding a fight. Yet, paradoxically, the referee's position is one of crucial significance. The referee cannot control what happens in the ring, but he can frequently control, to a degree, *that* it happens: he is responsible for
the fight, if not for the individual fighter's performance. It is the
referee solely who holds the power of life and death at certain
times; whose decision to terminate a fight, or to allow it to continue, determines a man's fate. (One should recall that a well-
aimed punch with a boxer's full weight behind it can have an as-

tonishing impact—a blow that must be absorbed by the brain in its jelly sac.)

In a recent heavyweight fight in Buffalo, 220-pound Tim Witherspoon repeatedly struck his 260-pound opponent James Broad, caught in the ropes, while the referee looked on without acting—though a number of spectators called for the fight to be stopped. In the infamous Benny Paret-Emile Griffith fight of March 24, 1962, the referee Ruby Goldstein was said to have stood paralyzed as Paret, trapped in the ropes, suffered as many as 18 powerful blows to the head before he fell. (He died 10 days later.) Boxers are trained not to quit; if they are knocked down they will try to get up to continue the fight, even if they can hardly defend themselves. The primary rule of the ring—to defend oneself at all times—is both a parody and a distillation of life.   13

Boxing is a purely masculine world. (Though there are female boxers—the most famous is the black champion Lady Tyger Trimiar with her shaved head and tiger-striped attire—women's role in the sport is extremely marginal.) The vocabulary of boxing is attuned to a quintessentially masculine sensibility in which the role of patriarch/protector can only be assured if there is physical strength underlying it. First comes this strength—"primitive," perhaps; then comes civilization. It should be kept in mind that "boxing" and "fighting," though always combined in the greatest of boxers, can be entirely different and even unrelated activities. If boxing can be, in the lighter weights especially, a highly complex and refined skill belonging solely to civilization, fighting seems to belong to something predating civilization, the instinct not merely to defend oneself—for when has the masculine ego ever been assuaged by so minimal a gesture?—but to attack another and to force him into absolute submission. Hence the electrifying effect upon a typical fight crowd when fighting emerges suddenly out of boxing—the excitement when a boxer's face begins to bleed. The flash of red is the visible sign of the fight's authenticity in the eyes of many spectators, and boxers are right to be proud—if they are—of their facial scars.   14

To the untrained eye, boxers in the ring usually appear to be angry. But, of course, this is "work" to them; emotion has no part in it, or should not. Yet in an important sense—in a symbolic sense—the boxers *are* angry, and boxing is fundamentally about anger. It is the only sport in which anger is accommodated, ennobled. Why are boxers angry? Because, for the most part, they belong to the disenfranchised of our society, to impoverished ghetto   15 neighborhoods in which anger is an appropriate response. ("It's hard being black. You ever been black? I was black once—when I was poor," Larry Holmes has said.) Today, when most boxers—most good boxers—are black or Hispanic, white men begin to look anemic in the ring. Yet after decades of remarkable black boxers—from Jack Johnson to Joe Louis to Muhammad Ali—heavyweight champion Larry Holmes was the object of racist slurs and insults when he defended his title against the overpromoted white challenger Gerry Cooney a few years ago.

Liberals who have no personal or class reason to feel anger tend   16
to disparage, if not condemn, such anger in others. Liberalism is also unfairly harsh in its criticism of all that predates civilization—or "liberalism" itself—without comprehending that civilization is a concept, an idea, perhaps at times hardly more than a fiction, attendant upon, and always subordinate to, physical strength: missiles, nuclear warheads. The terrible and tragic silence dramatized in the boxing ring is the silence of nature before language, when the physical *was* language, a means of communication swift and unmistakable.

The phrase "killer instinct" is said to have been coined in refer-   17
ence to Jack Dempsey in his famous early fights against Jess Willard, Georges Carpentier, Luis Firpo ("The Wild Bull of the Pampas") and any number of other boxers, less renowned, whom he savagely beat. The ninth of 11 children born to an impoverished Mormon sharecropper and itinerant railroad worker, Dempsey seems to have been, as a young boxer in his prime, the very embodiment of angry hunger; and if he remains the most spectacular heavyweight champion in history, it is partly because he fought when rules governing boxing were somewhat casual by present-day standards. Where aggression must be learned, even cultivated, in some champion boxers (Tunney, Louis, Marciano, Patterson, for example), Dempsey's aggression was direct and natural: Once in the ring he seems to have wanted to kill his opponent.

Dempsey's first title fight in 1919, against the aging champion   18
Jess Willard, was called "pugilistic murder" by some sportswriters and is said to have been one of boxing's all-time blood baths. Today, this famous fight—which brought the nearly unknown 24-year-old Dempsey to national prominence—would certainly have been stopped in the first minute of the first round. Badly out of condition, heavier than Dempsey by almost 60 pounds, the 37-year-old Willard had virtually no defense against the challenger. By the end of the fight, Willard's jaw was broken, his cheekbone split, nose smashed, six teeth broken off at the gum, an eye was bat-

tered shut, much further damage was done to his body. Both boxers were covered in Willard's blood. Years later Dempsey's estranged manager Kearns confessed—perhaps falsely—that he had "loaded" Dempsey's gloves—treated his hand tape with a talcum substance that turned concrete-hard when wet.

For the most part, boxing matches today are scrupulously monitored by referees and ring physicians. The devastating knockout blow is frequently the one never thrown. In a recent televised junior-middleweight bout between Don Curry and James Green, the referee stopped the fight because Green seemed momentarily disabled: His logic was that Green had dropped his gloves and was therefore in a position to be hurt. (Green and his furious trainer protested the decision but the referee's word is final: No fight, stopped, can be resumed.) The drama of the ring begins to shift subtly as more and more frequently one sees a referee intervene to embrace a weakened or defenseless man in a gesture of paternal solicitude that in itself carries much theatrical power—a gesture not so dramatic as the killing blow but one that suggests that the ethics of the ring are moving toward those that prevail beyond it. As if fighter-brothers whose mysterious animosity has somehow brought them to battle are saved by their father. . . .

In the final moment of the Hagler-Hearns fight, the dazed Hearns—on his feet but clearly not fully conscious, gamely prepared to take Hagler's next assault—was saved by the referee from what might well have been serious injury, if not death, considering the ferocity of Hagler's fighting and the personal anger he seems to have brought to it that night. This 8-minute fight, generally believed to be one of the great fights in boxing history, ends with Hearns in the referee's protective embrace—an image that is haunting, in itself profoundly mysterious, as if an indefinable human drama had been spontaneously created for us, brilliantly improvised, performed one time and one time only, yet permanently ingrained upon our consciousness.

Years ago in the early 1950's, when my father first took me to a Golden Gloves boxing tournament in Buffalo, I asked him why the boys wanted to fight one another, why they were willing to get hurt. My father said, "Boxers don't feel pain quite the way we do."

Gene Tunney's single defeat in an 11-year career was to a flamboyant and dangerous fighter named Harry Greb ("The Human Windmill") who seems to have been, judging from boxing literature, the dirtiest fighter in history. Low blows, butting, fouls, holding and hitting, using his laces on an opponent's eyes—Greb was famous for his lack of interest in the rules. He was world middle-weight champion for three years but a presence in the boxing world for a long time. After the first of his several fights with Greb, the 24-year-old Tunney had to spend a week in bed, he was so badly hurt; he'd lost two quarts of blood during the 15-round fight. But as Tunney said years afterward: "Greb gave me a terrible whipping. He broke my nose, maybe with a butt. He cut my eyes and ears, perhaps with his laces. . . . My jaw was swollen from the right temple down the cheek, along under the chin and part way up the other side. The referee, the ring itself, was full of blood. . . . But it was in that first fight, in which I lost my American light-heavyweight title, that I knew I had found a way to beat Harry eventually. I was fortunate, really. If boxing in those days had been afflicted with the commission doctors we have today—who are always poking their noses into the ring and examining superficial wounds—the first fight with Greb would have been stopped before I learned how to beat him. It's possible, even probable, that if this had happened I would never have been heard of again."

Tommy Loughran, the light-heavyweight champion from 1927 to 1929, was a master boxer greatly admired by other boxers. He approached boxing literally as a science—as Tunney did—studying his opponents' styles and mapping out ring strategy for each fight. He rigged up mirrors in his basement so that he could see himself as he worked out—for, as Loughran realized, no boxer ever sees himself quite as he appears to his opponent. But the secret of Loughran's career was that he had a right hand that broke so easily he could use it only once in each fight: It had to be the knockout punch or nothing. "I'd get one shot, then the agony of the thing would hurt me if the guy got up. Anybody I ever hit with a left hook, I knocked flat on his face, but I would never take a chance for fear if my left hand goes, I'm done for." 23

Both Tunney and Loughran, it is instructive to note, retired from boxing before they were forced to retire. Tunney was a highly successful businessman and Loughran a successful sugar broker on the Wall Street commodities market—just to suggest that boxers are not invariably illiterate, stupid, or punchdrunk. 24

One of the perhaps not entirely acknowledged reasons for the attraction of serious writers to boxing (from Swift, Pope, Johnson to Hazlitt, Lord Byron, Hemingway, and our own Norman Mailer, George Plimpton, Wilfrid Sheed, Daniel Halpern et al.) is the sport's systematic cultivation of pain in the interests of a project, a 25 life-goal: the willed transposing of the sensation called "pain" (whether physical or psychological) into its opposite. If this is masochism—and I doubt that it is, or that it is simply—it is also intelligence, cunning, strategy. It is the active welcoming of that which most living beings try to avoid and to flee. It is the active subsuming of the present moment in terms of the future. Pain now but control (and therefore pleasure) later.

Still, it is the rigorous training period leading up to the public appearance that demands the most discipline. In this, too, the writer senses some kinship, however oblique and one-sided, with the professional boxer. The brief public spectacle of the boxing match (which could last as little as 60 seconds), like the publication of the writer's book, is but the final, visible stage in a long, arduous, fanatic, and sometimes quixotic, subordination of the self. It was Rocky Marciano who seems to have trained with the most monastic devotion, secluding himself from his wife and family for as long as three months before a fight. Quite apart from the grueling physical training of this period and the constant preoccupation with diet and weight, Marciano concentrated on only the upcoming fight, the opening bell, his opponent. Every minute of the boxer's life was planned for one purpose. In the training camp the name of the opponent was never mentioned and Marciano's associates were careful about conversation in his presence: They talked very little about boxing.

In the final month, Marciano would not write a letter. The last 10 days before a fight he saw no mail, took no telephone calls, met no new acquaintances. The week before the fight he would not shake hands with anyone. Or go for a ride in a car. No new foods! No envisioning the morning after the fight! All that was not *the fight* was taboo: When Marciano worked out punching the bag he saw his opponent before him, when he jogged early in the morning he saw his opponent close beside him. What could be a more powerful image of discipline—madness?—than this absolute subordination of the self, this celibacy of the fighter-in-training? Instead of focusing his energies and fantasies upon Woman, the boxer focuses them upon the Opponent.

No sport is more physical, more direct, than boxing. No sport appears more powerfully homoerotic: the confrontation in the ring—the disrobing—the sweaty, heated combat that is part dance, courtship, coupling—the frequent urgent pursuit by one boxer of the other in the fight's natural and violent movement toward the "knockout." Surely boxing derives much of its appeal from this mimicry of a species of erotic love in which one man overcomes the other in an exhibition of superior strength.

Most fights, however fought, lead to an embrace between the boxers after the final bell—a gesture of mutual respect and apparent affection that appears to the onlooker to be more than perfunctory. Rocky Graziano, often derided for being a slugger rather than a "classic" boxer, sometimes kissed his opponents out of gratitude for the fight. Does the boxing match, one almost wonders, lead irresistibly to this moment: the public embrace of two men who otherwise, in public or in private, could not approach each other with such passion. Are men privileged to embrace with love only after having fought? A woman is struck by the tenderness men will express for boxers who have been hurt, even if it is only by way of commentary on photographs: the startling picture of Ray (Boom Boom) Mancini after his second losing fight with Livingstone Bramble, for instance, when Mancini's face was hideously battered (photographs in *Sports Illustrated* and elsewhere were gory, near-pornographic); the much-reprinted photograph of the defeated Thomas Hearns being carried to his corner in the arms of an enormous black man in formal attire—the "Hit Man" from Detroit now helpless, only semiconscious, looking precisely like a black Christ taken from the cross. These are powerful, haunting, unsettling images, cruelly beautiful, very much bound up with the primitive appeal of the sport.   29

Yet to suggest that men might love one another directly without the violent ritual of combat is to misread man's greatest passion— for war, not peace. Love, if there is to be love, comes second.   30

Boxing is, after all, about lying. It is about cultivating a double personality. As José Torres, the ex-light-heavyweight champion who is now the New York State Boxing Commissioner, says: "We fighters understand lies. What's a feint? What's a left hook off the jab? What's an opening? What's thinking one thing and doing another . . . ?"   31

There is nothing fundamentally playful about boxing, nothing that seems to belong to daylight, to pleasure. At its moments of greatest intensity it seems to contain so complete and so powerful an image of life—life's beauty, vulnerability, despair, incalculable and often reckless courage—that boxing *is* life, and hardly a mere game. During a superior boxing match we are deeply moved by the body's communion with itself by way of another's flesh. The body's dialogue with its shadow-self—or Death. Baseball, foot-   32 ball, basketball—these quintessentially American pastimes are recognizably sports because they involve play: They are games. One *plays* football; one doesn't *play* boxing.

Observing team sports, teams of adult men, one sees how men   33
are children in the most felicitous sense of the word. But boxing in its elemental ferocity cannot be assimilated into childhood— though very young men box, even professionally, and numerous world champions began boxing when they were hardly more than children. Spectators at public games derive much of their pleasure from reliving the communal emotions of childhood, but spectators at boxing matches relive the murderous infancy of the race. Hence the notorious cruelty of boxing crowds and the excitement when a man begins to bleed. ("When I see blood," says Marvin Hagler, "I become a bull." He means his own.)

The boxing ring comes to seem an altar of sorts, one of those   34
legendary magical spaces where the laws of a nation are suspended: Inside the ropes, during an officially regulated three-minute round, a man may be killed at his opponent's hands but he cannot be legally murdered. Boxing inhabits a sacred space predating civilization; or, to use D. H. Lawrence's phrase, before God was love. If it suggests a savage ceremony or a rite of atonement, it also suggests the futility of such rites. For what atonement is the fight waged, if it must shortly be waged again . . . ?

All this is to speak of the paradox of boxing—its obsessive ap   35
peal for many who find in it not only a spectacle involving sensational feats of physical skill but an emotional experience impossible to convey in words; an art form, as I have suggested, with no natural analogue in the arts. And of course this accounts, too, for the extreme revulsion it arouses in many people. ("Brutal," "disgusting," "barbaric," "inhuman," "a terrible, terrible sport"—typical comments on the subject.)

In December 1984, the American Medical Association passed a   36
resolution calling for the abolition of boxing on the principle that it is the only sport in which the *objective* is to cause injury. This is not surprising. Humanitarians have always wanted to reform boxing— or abolish it altogether. The 1896 heavyweight title match between Ruby Robert Fitzsimmons and Peter Maher was outlawed in many parts of the United States, so canny promoters staged it across the Mexican border 400 miles from El Paso. (Some 300 people made the arduous journey to see what must have been one of the most disappointing bouts in boxing history—Fitzsimmons knocked out his opponent in a mere 95 seconds.)

During the prime of Jack Dempsey's career in the 1920's, boxing 37
was illegal in many states, like alcohol, and like alcohol, seems to
have aroused a hysterical public enthusiasm. Photographs of
jammed outdoor arenas taken in the 1920's with boxing rings like
postage-sized altars at their centers, the boxers themselves scarcely
visible, testify to the extraordinary emotional appeal boxing had at
that time, even as reform movements were lobbying against it.
When Jack Johnson won the heavyweight title in 1908 (he had to
pursue the white champion Tommy Burns all the way to Australia
to confront him), the special "danger" of boxing was also that it
might expose and humiliate white men in the ring. After Johnson's
victory over the "White Hope" contender Jim Jeffries, there were
race riots and lynchings throughout the United States; even films
of some of Johnson's fights were outlawed in many states. And because boxing has become a sport in which black and Hispanic men
have lately excelled, it is particularly vulnerable to attack by white
middle-class reformers, who seem uninterested in lobbying against
equally dangerous but "establishment" sports like football, auto
racing, and thoroughbred horse racing.

There is something peculiarly American in the fact that, while 38
boxing is our most controversial sport, it is also the sport that pays
its top athletes the most money. In spite of the controversy, boxing has never been healthier financially. The three highest paid athletes in the world in both 1983 and 1984 were boxers; a boxer
with a long career like heavyweight champion Larry Holmes—48
fights in 13 years as a professional—can expect to earn somewhere beyond $50 million. (Holmes said that after retirement
what he would miss most about boxing is his million-dollar
checks.) Dempsey, who said that a man fights for one thing
only—money—made somewhere beyond $3,500,000 in the ring
in his long and varied career. Now $1.5 million is a fairly common
figure for a single fight. Thomas Hearns made at least $7 million in
his fight with Hagler while Hagler made at least $7.5 million. For
the first of his highly publicized matches with Roberto Duran in
1980—which he lost on a decision—the popular black welterweight champion Sugar Ray Leonard received a staggering $10 mil-
lion to Duran's $1.3 million. And none of these figures takes into
account various subsidiary earnings (from television commercials,
for instance) which in Leonard's case are probably as high as his
income was from boxing.

Money has drawn any number of retired boxers back into the 39 ring, very often with tragic results. The most notorious example is perhaps Joe Louis, who, owing huge sums in back taxes, continued boxing well beyond the point at which he could perform capably. After a career of 17 years he was stopped by Rocky Marciano—who was said to have felt as upset by his victory as Louis by the defeat. (Louis then went on to a degrading second career as a professional wrestler. This, too, ended abruptly when 300-pound Rocky Lee stepped on the 42-year-old Louis's chest and damaged his heart.) Ezzard Charles, Jersey Joe Walcott, Joe Frazier, Muhammad Ali—each continued fighting when he was no longer in condition to defend himself against young heavyweight boxers on the way up. Of all heavyweight champions, only Rocky Marciano, to whom fame and money were not of paramount significance, was prudent enough to retire before he was defeated. In any case, the prodigious sums of money a few boxers earn do not account for the sums the public is willing to pay them.

Though boxing has long been popular in many countries and under many forms of government, its popularity in the United States since the days of John L. Sullivan has a good deal to do with what is felt as the spirit of the individual—his "physical" spirit—in conflict with the constrictions of the state. The rise of boxing in the 1920's in particular might well be seen as a consequence of the diminution of the individual vis-à-vis society; the gradual attrition of personal freedom, will, and strength—whether "masculine" or otherwise. In the Eastern bloc of nations, totalitarianism is a function of the state; in the Western bloc it has come to seem a function of technology, or history—"fate." The individual exists in his physical supremacy, but does the individual matter?

40

In the magical space of the boxing ring so disquieting a question has no claim. There, as in no other public arena, the individual as a unique physical being asserts himself; there, for a dramatic if fleeting period of time, the great world with its moral and political complexities, its terrifying impersonality, simply ceases to exist. Men fighting one another with only their fists and their cunning are all contemporaries, all brothers, belonging to no historical time. "He can run, but he can't hide"—so said Joe Louis before his famous fight with young Billy Conn in 1941. In the brightly lighted ring, man is *in extremis,* performing an atavistic rite or agon for the mysterious solace of those who can participate only vicariously in such drama: the drama of life in the flesh. Boxing has become America's tragic theater.

41

Vocabulary

derisive (1)

paroxysm (1)

prescience (6)

disquieting (6)

distillation (13)

quintessentially (14)

disparage (16)

subsuming (25)

oblique (26)

quixotic (26)

celibacy (27)

homoerotic (28)

felicitous (33)

analogue (35)

prodigious (39)

atavistic (41)

agon (41)

solace (41)

vicariously (41)

Critical Inquiries

1. What emotional reason might be inferred from the author's childhood to account for her consuming fondness for boxing?

2. What does the author mean when she says that great sporting events always exist in the past?

3. Why is it important that the referee of a boxing match have no identity?

4. What assumption does the author make about "liberals" in paragraph 16? Is this a fair assumption or a stereotype?

5. In paragraph 26, the writer asserts a kinship between boxing and writing based on the mutual subsuming of the present to the future by participants in either activity. What are at least three ways in which boxing and writing entirely differ?

Rhetorical Inquiries

1. What is the strategy behind the opening paragraph?

2. What essential information about herself does the author manage to assert in the skimpy paragraph 3?

3. The writer asserts in paragraph 5 that she does not accept boxing as a writerly metaphor for anything else. How does she subsequently treat boxing, metaphorically or literally? What is the rhetorical purpose behind her disclaimer?

4. What transitional lead-in to the examples in paragraph 13 does the writer use?

5. By what rhetorical mode, directed to what purpose, is paragraph 40 developed?

SOCIOLOGY

Peter Marin
HOMELESSNESS

Peter Marin (b. 1936, Brooklyn, N.Y.), a contributing editor for Harper's
*magazine, is a free-lance man of letters and occasional college teacher. He
was educated at Swarthmore College (B.A., 1955) and Columbia University (M.A., 1958). The essay printed below is condensed from a longer
work on homeless people, which Marin researched for two years by sleeping on the streets and spending nights in the public shelters of New Or-
leans, Portland, and Seattle. Marin is the author of several works, among
them* In a Man's Time *(novel, 1972);* Divided Conscience *(poems,
1973); and* Margins *(scheduled for publication in 1990.)*

Homelessness, in itself, is nothing more than a condition visited   1
upon men and women (and, increasingly, children) as the final
stage of a variety of problems about which the word *homelessness*
tells us almost nothing. Or, to put it another way, it is a catch ba-
sin into which pour all of the people disenfranchised or marginalized or scared off by processes beyond their control, those that lie
close to the heart of American life. Here are the groups packed into
the single category of "the homeless":

Veterans, mainly from the war in Vietnam. In many American   2
cities, vets make up close to 50 percent of all homeless males.

The mentally ill. In some parts of the country, roughly a quarter   3
of the homeless would, a couple of decades ago, have been institu-
tionalized.

The physically disabled or chronically ill, who do not receive   4
any benefits or whose benefits do not enable them to afford permanent shelter.

The elderly on fixed incomes whose funds are no longer suffi-   5
cient for their needs.

Men, women, and whole families pauperized by the loss of a   6
job. Some 28 percent of the homeless population is composed of
families with children, and 15 percent are single women.

Single parents, usually women, without the resources or skills to   7
establish new lives.

Runaway children, many of whom have been abused.   8

From "Helping and Hating the Homeless," by Peter Marin. Copyright ©
1987 by *Harper's Magazine.* All rights reserved. Reprinted from the January
issue by special permission.

Alcoholics and those in trouble with drugs (whose troubles often   9
begin with one of the other conditions listed here).

Traditional tramps, hobos and transients, who have taken to the   10
road or the streets for a variety of reasons and who prefer to be
there.

You can quickly learn two things about the homeless from this   11
list. First, you can learn that many of the homeless, before they
were homeless, were people more or less like ourselves: members
of the working or middle class. And you can learn that the world
of the homeless has its roots in various policies, events and ways
of life for which some of us are responsible and from which some
of us actually prosper.

We decide, as a people, to go to war, we ask our children to kill   12
and to die, and the result, years later, is grown men homeless on
the street.

We change, with the best intentions, the laws pertaining to the   13
mentally ill and then, without intention, neglect to provide them
with services; and the result, in our streets, drives some of us crazy
with rage.

We cut taxes and prune budgets, we modernize industry and   14
shift the balance of trade, and the result of all these actions and
errors can be read, sleeping form by sleeping form, on our city
streets.

The liberals cannot blame the conservatives. The conservatives   15
cannot blame the liberals. Homelessness is the sum total of our
dreams, policies, intentions, errors, omissions, cruelties, kind-
nesses, all of it recorded, in flesh, in the life of the streets.

The homeless can be roughly divided into two groups: those   16
who have had homelessness forced upon them and want nothing
more than to escape it; and those who have at least in part chosen
it for themselves, and now accept it, or in some cases embrace it.

I understand how dangerous it is to introduce the idea of choice   17
into a discussion of homelessness. It can all too easily be used to
justify indifference or brutality toward the homeless, or to argue
that they are only getting what they "deserve." And yet it seems to
me that it is only by taking choice into account, in all of the intricacies of its various forms and expressions, that one can really understand certain kinds of homelessness.

The fact is, many of the homeless are not only hapless victims   18
but voluntary exiles, "domestic refugees," people who have turned
not against life itself but against us, our life, American life. Look
for a moment at the vets. The price of returning to America was to

forget what they had seen or learned in Vietnam, to "put it behind them." But some could not do that, and the stress of trying showed up as alcoholism, broken marriages, drug addiction, crime. And it showed up too as life on the street, which was for some vets a desperate choice made in the name of life—the best they could manage.

We must learn to accept that there may indeed be people, and   19 not only vets, who have seen so much of our world, or seen it so clearly, that to live in it becomes impossible. Here, for example, is the story of Alice, a homeless middle-aged woman in Los Angeles, where there are perhaps 50,000 homeless people, a 50 percent increase over the previous year. It was set down last year by one of my students at the University of California at Santa Barbara, where I taught for a semester. I had encouraged them to go find the homeless and listen to their stories. And so, one day, when this student saw Alice foraging in a dumpster outside a McDonald's, he stopped and talked to her:

"She told me she had led a pretty normal life as she grew up and   20 eventually went to college. From there she went on to Chicago to teach school. She was single and lived in a small apartment.

"One night, after she got off the train after school, a man began   21 to follow her to her apartment building. When she got to her door she saw a knife and the man hovering behind her. She had no choice but to let him in. The man raped her.

"After that, things got steadily worse. She had a nervous break-   22 down. She went to a mental institution for three months, and when she went back to her apartment she found her belongings gone. The landlord had sold them to cover the rent.

"She had no place to go and no job because the school had ter-   23 minated her employment. She slipped into depression. She lived with friends until she could muster enough money for a ticket to Los Angeles. She said she no longer wanted to burden her friends, and that if she had to live outside, at least Los Angeles was warmer than Chicago.

"It is as if she began back then to take on the mentality of a   24 street person. She resolved herself to homelessness. She's been out West since 1980, without a home or job. She seems happy, with her best friend being her cat. But the scars of memories still haunt her, and she is running from them, or should I say, him."

This is, in essence, the same story one hears over and over again   25 on the street. You begin with an ordinary life; then an event occurs—traumatic, catastrophic; smaller events follow, each one deepening the original wound; finally, homelessness becomes inevitable, or begins to seem inevitable to the person involved—the only way out of an intolerable situation.

Every government program, almost every private project, is geared as much to the needs of those giving help as it is to the needs of the homeless.   26

Santa Barbara is as good an example as any. There are three main shelters in the city—all of them private. Between them they provide fewer than 100 beds a night for the homeless. Two of three shelters are religious in nature: the Rescue Mission and the Salvation Army. In the mission, as in most places in the country, there are elaborate and stringent rules. Beds go first to those who have not been there for two months, and you can stay for only two nights in any two-month period. No shelter is given to those who are not sober.   27

Even if you go to the mission only for a meal, you are required to listen to sermons and participate in prayer, and you are regularly proselytized. There are obligatory, regimented showers. You go to bed precisely at 10: lights out, no reading, no talking. After the lights go out you will find 15 men in a room with double-decker bunks. As the night progresses the room grows stuffier and hotter. Men toss, turn, cough, and moan. In the morning you are awakened precisely at 5:45. Then breakfast. At 7:30 you are back on the street.   28

The town's newest shelter was opened almost a year ago by a consortium of local churches. Families and those who are employed have first call on the beds—a policy that excludes the congenitally homeless. Alcohol is not simply forbidden in the shelter; those with a history of alcoholism must sign a "contract" pledging to remain sober and chemical-free. Finally, in a paroxysm of therapeutic bullying, the shelter has added a new wrinkle: If you stay more than two days you are required to fill out and then discuss with a social worker a complex form listing what you perceive as your personal failings, goals and strategies—all of this for men and women who simply want a place to lie down out of the rain.   29

We are moved either to "redeem" the homeless or to punish them. Perhaps there is nothing consciously hostile about it. Perhaps it is simply that as the machinery of bureaucracy cranks itself up to deal with these problems, attitudes assert themselves automatically. But whatever the case, the fact remains that almost every one of our strategies for helping the homeless is simply an attempt to rearrange the world cosmetically, in terms of how it looks and smells to us. Compassion is little more than the passion for control.   30

The central question emerging from all this is, What does a soci- 31
ety owe to its members in trouble, and how is that debt to be
paid? It is a question that must be answered in two parts: first, in
relation to the men and women who have been marginalized
against their will, and then, in a slightly different way, in relation
to those who have chosen (or accept or even prize) their marginal-
ity.

Vocabulary

marginalized (1)   congenitally (29)
stringent (27)   paroxysm (29)
proselytized (28)

Critical Inquiries

1. If some people simply choose to live on the streets rather than in a permanent dwelling, what, if anything, should society do? Why?
2. What is "deinstitutionalization?" (Look up the term in your library.) What
   effect has this policy had on homelessness?
3. Marin writes that "every government program, almost every private
   project, is geared as much to the needs of those giving help as it is to the
   needs of the homeless." What kind of needs might a government program have? How might these needs result in attitudes of "blaming the
   victim?"
4. What should be done about Alice, the homeless woman whose story was
   told to the University of Santa Barbara student?
5. What is your opinion of shelters who proselytize homeless people before
   giving them sleeping space?

Rhetorical Inquiries

1. Based on the style and paragraphing of this article, for what kind of outlet
   and audience do you think it was originally written?
2. What stylistic feature of paragraph 11 would many English instructors object to?
3. What common feature for ensuring coherence do paragraphs 12, 13, and
   14 share?
4. What is the purpose and rhetorical strategy implicit behind paragraph 25?
5. In paragraph 28, Marin writes about a shelter for the homeless: "You go

to bed precisely at 10: lights out, no reading, no talking. After the lights go out you will find 15 men in a room with double-decker bunks. . . . "Why does he use "you" instead of "the homeless" or "the inhabitants?"

ZOOLOGY

J. B. S. Haldane
ON BEING THE RIGHT SIZE

John Burton Sanderson Haldane (1892–1964), English biologist, physiologist, and geneticist, was born in Oxford, England, and educated at New College, Oxford University. Haldane, a worldwide authority on heredity and inherited diseases who formulated a mathematical theory of natural selection, migrated to India in 1957 and became a naturalized Indian citizen in 1960. He was a prolific writer who published numerous works on science and biology, among them Daedalus; or, Science and the Future *(1924);* Animal Biology *(1927);* Possible Worlds, and Other Essays *(1927); and* The Philosophy of a Biologist *(1955).*

The most obvious differences between different animals are differences of size, but for some reason the zoologists have paid singularly little attention to them. In a large textbook of zoology before me I find no indication that the eagle is larger than the sparrow, or the hippopotamus bigger than the hare, though some grudging admissions are made in the case of the mouse and the whale. But yet it is easy to show that a hare could not be as large as a hippopotamus, or a whale as small as a herring. For every type of animal there is a most convenient size, and a large change in size inevitably carries with it a change of form.

Let us take the most obvious of possible cases, and consider a giant man sixty feet high—about the height of Giant Pope and Giant Pagan in the illustrated *Pilgrim's Progress* of my childhood. These monsters were not only ten times as high as Christian, but ten times as wide and ten times as thick, so that their total weight was a thousand times his, or about eighty to ninety tons. Unfortunately, the cross sections of their bones were only a hundred times those of Christian, so that every square inch of giant bone had to support ten times the weight borne by a square inch of human bone. As the human thighbone breaks under about ten times the

"On Being the Right Size," from *Possible Worlds* by J. B. S. Haldane. Copyright 1928 by Harper & Brothers. Reprinted by permission of Harper & Row, Publishers, Inc.

human weight, Pope and Pagan would have broken their thighs every time they took a step. This was doubtless why they were sitting down in the picture I remember. But it lessens one's respect for Christian and for Jack the Giant Killer.

To turn to zoology, suppose that a gazelle, a graceful little creature with long thin legs, is to become large—it will break its bones unless it does one of two things. It may make its legs short and thick, like the rhinoceros, so that every pound of weight has still about the same area of bone to support it. Or it can compress its body and stretch out its legs obliquely to gain stability, like the giraffe. I mention these two beasts because they happen to belong to the same order as the gazelle, and both are quite successful mechanically, being remarkably fast runners.   3

Gravity, a mere nuisance to Christian, was a terror to Pope, Pagan, and Despair. To the mouse and any smaller animal it presents practically no dangers. You can drop a mouse down a thousand-yard mine shaft and, on arriving at the bottom, it gets a slight shock and walks away. A rat is killed, a man is broken, a horse splashes. For the resistance presented to movement by the air is proportional to the surface of the moving object. Divide an animal's length, breadth, and height each by ten; its weight is reduced to a thousandth, but its surface only to a hundredth. So the resistance to falling in the case of the small animal is relatively ten times the driving force.   4

An insect, therefore, is not afraid of gravity; it can fall without danger, and can cling to the ceiling with remarkably little trouble. It can go in for elegant fantastic forms of support like that of the daddy-long-legs. But there is a force which is as formidable to an insect as gravitation to a mammal. This is surface tension. A man coming out of a bath carries with him a film of water of about one-fiftieth of an inch in thickness. This weighs about a pound. A wet mouse has to carry about its own weight of water. A wet fly has to lift many times its own weight, and, as everyone knows, a fly once wetted by water or any other liquid is in a very serious position indeed. An insect going for a drink is in as great danger as a man leaning out over a precipice in search of food. If it once falls into the grip of the surface tension of the water—that is to say, gets wet—it is likely to remain so until it drowns. A few insects, such as water-beetles, contrive to be unwettable; the majority keep well away from their drink by means of a long proboscis.   5

Of course tall land animals have other difficulties. They have to pump their blood to greater heights than a man and, therefore, require a larger blood pressure and tougher blood vessels. A great   6 many men die from burst arteries, especially in the brain, and this danger is presumably still greater for an elephant or a giraffe. But animals of all kinds find difficulties in size for the following reason: A typical small animal, say a microscopic worm or rotifer, has a smooth skin through which all the oxygen it requires can soak in, a straight gut with sufficient surface to absorb its food, and a simple kidney. Increase its dimensions tenfold in every direction, and its weight is increased a thousand times, so that if it is to use its muscles as efficiently as its miniature counterpart, it will need a thousand times as much food and oxygen per day and will excrete a thousand times as much of waste products.

Now, if its shape is unaltered its surface will be increased only a hundredfold, and ten times as much oxygen must enter per minute through each square millimeter of skin, ten times as much food through each square millimeter of intestine. When a limit is reached to their absorptive powers, their surface has to be increased by some special device. For example, a part of the skin may be drawn out into tufts to make gills, or pushed in to make lungs, thus increasing the oxygen-absorbing surface in proportion to the animal's bulk. A man, for example, has a hundred square yards of lung. Similarly the gut, instead of being smooth and straight, becomes coiled and develops a velvety surface, and other organs increase in complication. The higher animals are not larger than the lower because they are more complicated. They are more complicated because they are larger. Just the same is true of plants. The simplest plants such as the green algae growing in stagnant water or on the bark of trees are mere round cells. The higher plants increase their surface by putting out leaves and roots. Comparative anatomy is largely the story of the struggle to increase surface in proportion to volume. 7

Some of the methods of increasing the surface are useful up to a point but not capable of a very wide adaptation. For example, while vertebrates carry the oxygen from the gills or lungs all over the body in the blood, insects take air directly to every part of their body by tiny blind tubes called tracheae which open to the surface at many different points. Now, although by their breathing movements they can renew the air in the outer part of the tracheal system, the oxygen has to penetrate the finer branches by means of diffusion. Gases can diffuse easily through very small distances, not many times larger than the average length traveled by a gas molecule between collisions with other molecules. But when such vast journeys—from the point of view of a molecule—as a quarter of an inch have to be made, the process becomes slow. So the 8 portions of an insect's body more than a quarter of an inch from the air would always be short of oxygen. In consequence, hardly any insects are much more than half an inch thick. Land crabs are built on the same general plan as insects, but are much clumsier. Yet, like ourselves, they carry round oxygen in their blood, and are therefore able to grow far larger than any insect. If the insects had hit on a plan for driving air through their tissues instead of letting it soak in, they might well have become as large as lobsters, though other considerations would have prevented them from becoming as large as man.

Exactly the same difficulties attach to flying. It is an elementary principle of aeronautics that the minimum speed needed to keep an airplane of given shape in the air varies as the square root of its length. If it is four times as big each way it must fly twice as fast. Now the power needed for the minimum speed increases more rapidly than the weight of the machine. Of the two airplanes considered above, the larger weighs sixty-four times as much as the smaller but needs one hundred and twenty-eight times its horsepower to keep up. Applying the same principles to the birds, we find that the limit to their size is soon reached. An angel whose muscles developed no more power weight for weight than those of an eagle or pigeon would require a breast projecting for about four feet to house the muscles engaged in working its wings, while to economize in weight, its legs would have to be reduced to mere stilts. Actually a large bird such as an eagle or kite does not keep in the air mainly by moving its wings. It is generally to be seen soaring, that is to say balanced on a rising column of air. But even soaring becomes more and more difficult with increasing size. Were this not the case eagles might be as large as tigers and as formidable to man as hostile airplanes.

But it is time that we passed to some of the advantages of size. One of the most obvious is that it enables one to keep warm. All warm-blooded animals at rest lose the same amount of heat from a unit area of skin, for which purpose they need a food-supply proportional to their surface and not to their weight. Five thousand mice weight as much as a man. Their surface and food, or oxygen consumption, are about seventeen times a man's. In fact a mouse eats about one-quarter of its own weight of food every day, which is mainly used in keeping it warm. For the same reason small animals cannot live in wild countries. In the arctic regions there are no reptiles or amphibians, and no small mammals. The smallest mammal in Spitzbergen is the fox. The small birds fly away in the winter, while the insects die, though their eggs can survive six months or more of frost. The most successful mammals are bears, seals, and walruses.

Similarly, the eye is a rather inefficient organ until it reaches a   11
large size. The back of the human eye on which an image of the outside world is thrown and which corresponds to the film of a camera, is composed of a mosaic of "rods and cones" whose diameter is little more than the length of an average light wave. Each eye has about half a million, and for two objects to be distinguishable their images must fall on separate rods or cones. It is obvious that with fewer but larger rods and cones we should see less distinctly. If they were twice as broad, two points would have to be twice as far apart before we could distinguish them at a given distance. But if their size were diminished and their number increased we should see no better. For it is impossible to form a definite image smaller than a wave-length of light. Hence a mouse's eye is not a small-scale model of a human eye. Its rods and cones are not much smaller than ours, and therefore there are far fewer of them. A mouse could not distinguish one human face from another six feet away. In order that they should be of any use at all, the eyes of small animals have to be much larger in proportion to their bodies than our own. Large animals on the other hand require only relatively small eyes, and those of the whale and elephant are little larger than our own.

For rather more recondite reasons the same general principle   12
holds true of the brain. If we compare the brain-weights of a set of very similar animals such as the cat, cheetah, leopard, and tiger, we find that as we quadruple the body-weight the brain-weight is only doubled. The larger animal with proportionately larger bones can economize on brain, eyes, and certain other organs.

Such are a very few of the considerations which show that for   13
every type of animal there is an optimum size. Yet although Galileo demonstrated the contrary more than three hundred years ago, people still believe that if a flea were as large as a man it could jump a thousand feet into the air. As a matter of fact the height to which an animal can jump is more nearly independent of its size than proportional to it. A flea can jump about two feet, a man about seven. To jump a given height, if we neglect the resistance of the air, requires an expenditure of energy proportional to the jumper's weight. But if the jumping muscles form a constant fraction of the animal's body, the energy developed per ounce of muscle is independent of the size, provided it can be developed quickly enough in the small animal. As a matter of fact an insect's muscles, although they can contract more quickly than our own, appear to

be less efficient, as otherwise a flea or grasshopper could rise six feet into the air.

And just as there is a best size for every animal, so the same is   14
true for every human institution. In the Greek type of democracy all the citizens could listen to a series of orators and vote directly on questions of legislation. Hence their philosophers held that a small city was the largest possible democratic state. The English invention of representative government made a democratic nation possible, and the possibility was first realized in the United States, and later elsewhere. With the development of broadcasting it has once more become possible for every citizen to listen to the political views of representative orators, and the future may perhaps see the return of the national state to the Greek form of democracy. Even the referendum has been made possible only by the institution of daily newspapers.

To the biologist the problem of socialism appears largely as a   15
problem of size. The socialists desire to run every nation as a single business concern. I do not suppose that Henry Ford would find much difficulty in running Andorra or Luxembourg on a socialistic basis. He has already more men on his payroll than their population. It is conceivable that a syndicate of Fords, if we could find them, would make Belgium Ltd. or Denmark Inc. pay their way. But while nationalization of certain industries is an obvious possibility in the largest of states, I find it no easier to picture a completely socialized British Empire or United States than an elephant turning somersaults or a hippopotamus jumping a hedge.

Vocabulary

proboscis (5)   optimum (13)
recondite (12)

Critical Inquiries

1. If fairytale writers were scrupulously true to zoological reality, what would a giant such as the one Jack killed look like?

2. Haldane says that there is an intrinsic and limiting relationship between size and form. In what way does a similar biological limitation also apply to human communities?

3. Name at least two most obvious differences, size and form excepted, that also differentiate all organisms.

4. What role in fostering human affection and affinity for a species does physical appearance seem to play?

5. Haldane's objections to socialism are based on limitations imposed by size. What kinds of limitations do you think size would disadvantageously impose on socialism?

Rhetorical Inquiries

1. What is Haldane's thesis, and where is it stated?

2. What are some of Haldane's lead-ins to the successive examples?

3. What is the topic sentence of paragraph 7, and where can it be found?

4. What transition technique is used at the beginning of paragraph 6?

5. In paragraph 7 Haldane writes: "Now, if its shape is unaltered its surface will be increased only a hundred-fold, and ten times as much oxygen must enter per minute through each square millimeter of skin, ten times as much food through each square millimeter of intestine. When a limit is reached to their absorptive powers, their surface has to be increased by some special device." To what does the "their" refer? How might this passage be rewritten and made clearer?

HISTORY OF TECHNOLOGY

Isaac Asimov
OF WHAT USE?

Isaac Asimov (b. 1920 in the U.S.S.R.) was brought to the United States at the age of three where he has won renown as a prolific writer of science fiction and a masterful explainer of science. A professor of biochemistry at Boston University, Asimov is said to have written one book every six weeks for the past thirty years, and already has over 100 published titles to his credit. His field spans the range from biblical criticism to Shakespeare, although he is best known as the author of such science-fiction classics as I, Robot *(1950), and* The Caves of Steel *(1954).*

It is the fate of the scientist to face the constant demand that he   1
show his learning to have some "practical use." Yet it may not be of any interest to him to have such a "practical use" exist; he may feel that the delight of learning, of understanding, of probing the Universe is its own reward entirely. In that case, he might even

"Of What Use," by Isaac Asimov from *The Greatest Adventure,* © 1974 published by Rockefeller University Press. Reprinted by permission of the author.

allow himself the indulgence of contempt for anyone who asks more.

There is a famous story of a student who asked the Greek phi- 2
losopher Plato, about 370 B.C., of what use were the elaborate and abstract theorems he was being taught. Plato at once ordered a slave to give the student a small coin so that he might not think he had gained knowledge for nothing, then had him dismissed from the school.

The student need not have asked, and Plato need not have 3
scorned. Who would today doubt that mathematics has its uses? Mathematical theorems which seem unbearably refined and remote from anything a sensible man can have any interest in turn out to be absolutely necessary to such highly essential parts of our modern life as, for instance, the telephone network that knits the world together.

This story of Plato, famous for two thousand years, has not 4
made the matter plainer to most people. Unless the application of a new discovery is clear and present, most are dubious of its value.

There is a story of the English scientist Michael Faraday that il- 5
lustrates this. He was in his time an enormously popular lecturer as well as a physicist and chemist of the first rank. In one of his lectures in the 1840s, he illustrated the peculiar behavior of a magnet and a spiral coil of wire which was connected to a galvanometer that would record the presence of an electric current.

There was no current in the wire to begin with, but when the 6
magnet was thrust into the hollow center of the spiral coil, the needle of the galvanometer moved to one side of the scale, showing that a current was flowing. When the magnet was withdrawn from the coil, the needle flipped in the other direction, showing that the current was now flowing the other way. When the magnet was held motionless in any position within the coil, there was no current at all, and the needle was motionless.

At the conclusion of the lecture, one member of the audience 7
approached Faraday and said, "Mr. Faraday, the behavior of the magnet and the coil of wire was interesting, but of what possible use can it be?"

And Faraday answered politely, "Sir, of what use is a newborn 8
baby?"

It was precisely the phenomenon whose use was questioned so 9
peremptorily by one of the audience which Faraday made use of to develop the electric generator, which, for the first time, made it possible to produce electricity cheaply and in quantity. That, in turn, made it possible to build the electrified technology that sur-

rounds us today and without which life, in the modern sense, is inconceivable. Faraday's demonstration was a newborn baby that grew into a giant.

Even the shrewdest of men cannot always judge what is useful   10 and what is not. There never was a man so ingeniously practical in judging the useful as Thomas Alva Edison, surely the greatest inventor who ever lived, and we can take him as our example.

In 1868, he patented his first invention. It was a device to record   11 votes mechanically. By using it, congressmen could press a button and all their votes would be instantly recorded and totaled. There was no question but that the invention worked; it remained only to sell it. A congressman whom Edison consulted, however, told him, with mingled amusement and horror, that there wasn't a chance of the invention's being accepted, however unfailingly it might work.

A slow vote, it seemed, was sometimes a political necessity.   12 Some congressmen might have their opinions changed in the course of a slow vote where a quick vote might, in a moment of emotion, commit Congress to something undesirable.

Edison, chagrined, learned his lesson. After that, he decided   13 never to invent anything unless he was sure it would be needed and wanted and not merely because it worked.

He stuck to that. Before he died, he had obtained nearly 1300   14 patents—300 of them over a four-year stretch, or one every five days, on the average. Always, he was guided by his notion of the useful and the practical.

On October 21, 1879, he produced the first practical electric   15 light, perhaps the most astonishing of all his inventions. (We need only sit by candlelight for a while during a power breakdown to discover how much we accept, and take for granted, the electric light.)

In succeeding years, Edison labored to improve the electric light   16 and, mainly, to find ways of making the glowing filament last longer before breaking. As was usual with him, he tried everything he could think of. One of his hit-and-miss efforts was to seal a metal wire into the evacuated electric light bulb, near the filament but not touching it. The two were separated by a small gap of vacuum.

Edison then turned on the electric current to see if the presence   17 of a metal wire would somehow preserve the life of the glowing filament. It didn't and Edison abandoned the approach. However, he could not help noticing that an electric current seemed to flow from the filament to the wire across that vacuum gap.

Nothing in Edison's vast practical knowledge of electricity ex-   18
plained that, and all Edison could do was to observe it, write it up
in his notebooks, and, in 1884 (being Edison), patent it. The phenomenon was called the "Edison effect" and it was Edison's only
discovery in pure science.

Edison could see no use for it. He therefore pursued the matter   19
no further and let it go, while he continued the chase for what he
considered the useful and practical.

In the 1880s and 1890s, however, scientists who pursued "use-   20
less" knowledge for its own sake discovered that subatomic parti-
cles (eventually called "electrons") existed, and that the electric current was accompanied by a flow of electrons. The Edison effect
was the result of the ability of electrons, under certain conditions,
to travel, unimpeded, through a vacuum.

In 1904, the English electrical engineer John Ambrose Fleming   21
(who had worked in Edison's London office in the 1880s in connection with the developing electric light industry) made use of the
Edison effect and of the new understanding which the electron
theory had brought, and devised an evacuated glass bulb with a filament and wire which would let current pass through in one direction and not in the other. The result was a "current rectifier."

In 1906, the American inventor Lee De Forest made a further   22
elaboration of Fleming's device, introducing a metal plate which
enabled it to amplify electric current as well as rectify it. The result
is called a "radio tube" by Americans.

It is called that because it was only such a device that could han-   23
dle an electric current with sufficient rapidity and delicacy to make
the radio a practical device for receiving and transmitting sound
carried by the fluctuating amplitude of radio waves.

In fact, the radio tube made all of our modern electronic devices   24
possible, including television.

The Edison effect, then, which the practical Edison shrugged off   25
as interesting but useless, turned out to have more astonishing
results than any of his practical devices. In a power breakdown,
candles and kerosene lamps can substitute (however poorly) for
the electric light, but what substitute is there for a television
screen? We can live without it (if we consider it only an entertainment device, which does it wrong), but not many people seem to
want to.

In fact, the problem isn't a matter of showing that pure science   26
can be useful. It is much more difficult a problem to find some
branch of science that *isn't* useful. Between 1900 and 1930, for
instance, theoretical physics underwent a revolution. The theory

of relativity and the development of quantum mechanics led to a new and more subtle understanding of the basic laws of the universe and of the behavior of the inner components of the atom.

None of it seemed to have the slightest use to mankind, and the 27 scientists involved, a brilliant group of young men, had apparently found an ivory tower for themselves which nothing could disturb. Those who survived into later decades looked back on that happy time of abstraction and impracticality as a Garden of Eden out of which they had been evicted.

For out of that abstract work, there unexpectedly came the nu- 28 clear bomb, and a world that lives in terror, now, of a possible war that could destroy mankind in a day.

But it did not bring only terror. Out of that work, there came 29 radioisotopes which have made it possible to probe the workings of living tissue with a delicacy otherwise quite impossible, and whose findings have revolutionized medicine in a thousand ways. There are also nuclear power stations which, at present and in the future, offer mankind the brightest hope of ample energy during all his future existence on Earth.

There is nothing, it turns out, that is more practical, more down- 30 right important to the average man, whether for good or for evil, than the ivory tower researches of the young men of the early twentieth century who could see no use in what they were doing and were glad of it, for they wanted only to revel in knowledge for its own sake.

The point is, we cannot foresee the consequences in detail. 31 Plato, in demonstrating the theorems of geometry, did not envisage a computerized society. Faraday knew that his magnet-born electric current was a newborn baby, but he surely did not foresee our electrified technology. Edison certainly didn't foresee a television set when he puzzled over the electric current that leaped the vacuum, and Einstein, when he worked out the equation $E = mc^2$ from purely theoretical considerations in 1905, did not sense the mushroom cloud as he did so.

We can only make the general rule that through all of history, an 32 increased understanding of the Universe, however out-of-the-way a particular bit of new understanding may seem, however ethereal, however abstract, however useless, has always ended in some practical application (even if sometimes only indirectly).

It cannot be predicted what the application will be in advance, 33 but we can be sure that it will have both its beneficial and its uncomfortable aspects. (The discovery of the germ theory of disease by Louis Pasteur in the 1860s was the greatest single advance ever made in medicine and led to the saving of countless millions of lives. Who can quarrel with that? Yet it has also led, in great measure, to the dangerous population explosion of today.)

It remains for the wisdom of mankind to make the decisions by   34
which advancing knowledge will be used well and not ill, but all the wisdom of mankind will never improve the material lot of man unless advancing knowledge presents it with the matters over which it can make those decisions. And when, despite the most careful decisions, there come dangerous side effects of the new knowledge—it is only still further advances in knowledge that will offer hope for correction.

And now we stand in the closing decades of the twentieth cen-   35
tury, with science advancing as never before in all sorts of odd, and sometimes apparently useless, ways. We've discovered quasars and pulsars in the distant heavens. Of what use are they to the average man? Astronauts have brought back Moon rocks at great expense. So what? Scientists discover new compounds, develop new theories, work out new mathematical complexities. What for? What's in it for you?

No one knows what's in it for you right now, any more than   36
Plato knew in his time, or Faraday knew, or Edison knew, or Einstein knew.

But *you* will know if you live long enough; and if not, your chil-   37
dren or grandchildren will know. And they will smile at those who say, "But what is the use of sending rockets into space?" just as we now smile at the person who asked Faraday the use of his demonstration.

In fact, unless we continue with science and gather knowledge,   38
whether it is seemingly useful on the spot or not, we will be buried under our problems and find no way out.

It is up to you, then, and up to everyone, to support science and,   39
where possible, to keep abreast of it, for today's science is tomorrow's solution—and tomorrow's problems, too—and most of all, mankind's greatest adventure, now and forever.

Vocabulary

peremptorily (9)   ethereal (32)
chagrined (13)

Critical Inquiries

1. Asimov's examples of the unexpected usefulness of ethereal inventions all come from science or the practical arts. Of what use are such subjects as poetry and literature?

2. What justification exists for forcing a student who merely wants to become, say, a baker to take courses in the humanities and the liberal arts?

3. In what way does this essay apply, or not apply, to the stand of animal-rights activists against the so-called "uselessness" of animal experiments?

4. Which publicly funded projects today are most likely to be challenged on grounds of their supposed uselessness?

5. Are there limits to knowledge beyond which, in your view, science should never venture? If so, what are these limits, and what dangers can you foresee if science exceeds them?

Rhetorical Inquiries

1. What implicit bias towards scientists and science does Asimov seem to reflect in his chosen examples? How might this bias be written out of the article?

2. Asimov leads into his first example, in paragraph 2, without any formal prefacing phrase such as "for example." Why?

3. Compare the paragraph transitions used at the beginning of paragraphs 14 and 25. What different transition techniques does Asimov use in these two paragraphs?

4. Asimov's cites several examples to support his main point about the unexpected usefulness of pure science. What different kinds of introductions to his examples does he use?

5. What is the rhetorical purpose of paragraph 31?

Exercises

1. Support each of the following statements with three appropriate examples:
   a. The wedding ceremony has become a sham.
   b. Newspapers focus on bad news.
   c. Fraternities and sororities promote snobbery.
   d. Some people substitute love of a pet for love of human beings.
   e. Old people can be fascinating.

2. Give a typical example of each of the following:
   a. government fraud
   b. words that come from people's names (Example: *Machiavellian* comes from "Nicolo Machiavelli" [1469–1527], the Florentine writer who wrote *The Prince*.)
   c. a utopian society
   d. discrimination
   e. new slang expressions

3. Choose one of the concepts listed below. After defining it in one sentence, list some examples you would use to develop a paragraph amplifying your definition. (*Note:* If you are unsure about the concepts, look them up in a good dictionary.)
   a. Moorish architecture
   b. euphemistic expression
   c. archetypal symbol
   d. Freudian slip
   e. military camouflage

Writing Assignments

1. Turn this model into an essay developed by examples. Only the skeleton of the model is provided. If necessary, go to the library and find additional details and examples. Some reorganization of the model might also be necessary:

   Thesis: Some foods, long thought to be wholesome, contain unhealthy ingredients.
   Carrots contain carotaroxin, a potent nerve gas.
   Avocados contain the chemicals *pressor amines,* which elevate the blood pressure.
   Milk contains *galactose,* a component of milk sugar that has caused cataracts in animals when given in large doses.
   Shrimp contains a significant amount of arsenic.

2. Write an essay on your favorite sport, giving specific examples of some climactic events and spectacular plays that have made you come to love it.

3. Following the suggestion Marin made to his students in his essay on "Homelessness," interview at least two homeless people and use their stories as examples in an essay on the cause of homelessness.

4. Haldane says in his essay "On Being the Right Size," that socialism is un-

workable because it defies naturally imposed limitations on size. Write an essay giving examples of the inefficiency and bungling that large bureaucracies often commit because of unwieldy size. Use the newspaper and magazine section of your library to uncover the details about such mishaps by the Social Security Administration, the Postal Service, the IRS, and so on.

5. Asimov says about Thomas Alva Edison that "there never was a man so ingeniously practical in judging the useful." After researching the life of Edison, write an essay supporting this statement with three specific examples.

Chapter

11

Explaining Process

Less is more in prose as in architecture.

DONALD HALL (b. 1928)

To develop by **process** is to give a step-by-step explanation of something. The explanation may be of a concrete process—writing a research paper, hoisting a boat sail, performing a chemistry experiment—or it may be of an abstract process—how a U.S. president is elected, how a medieval Catholic atoned for their sins, or how the Japanese economy has come to be among the world's most powerful. Much of this chapter, especially those parts that explain how to write in the different modes, is developed by process.

Clearly written processes are crucial to many of the daily tasks performed in the workaday world. Yet, as anyone knows who has ever tried to follow instructions for assembling a chair, installing an electric garage door, or weatherproofing a window, process manuals are among the most bedevilling products of our time. In them, simple tasks become mystifying, ordinary jobs nightmarishly perplexing.

In spite of this widespread deficiency, the process essay is regarded by many instructors as too simple for college students. Indeed, it is the easiest essay to write if the student observes five basic steps.

Begin with a Clear Statement of Purpose

In plain language, tell your reader what process you are explaining. A simple "Here are the directions for planting pansies in a clay pot" will do. Or, "Let me explain the steps involved in researching and establishing a family tree." Or, "The purpose of this paper is to demonstrate the simplest way to organize your home library." This initial summary tells your reader what to expect while providing a usefully limiting context for your explanations.

Here, for example, a student revises her paragraph to insert a more complete statement of what process her essay intends to explain:

The aim of this paper is to teach students the steps ~~It is not easy to file one's income tax~~ *involved in filing the long form federal income tax return. Although* ~~return, especially it is not easy for students~~ *most students do not have to file the long form since* ~~who often work only part time and have~~ *their returns tend to be uncomplicated, the occasional* ~~transitory habits and living conditions.~~ *student who works full-time or nearly full-time can definitely* ~~Moreover, many students only file the short form~~ *benefit from taking the trouble to file a long form.* ~~tax return, because their returns are basically~~

312

~~simple.~~ ~~But~~ *t*o file a successful tax return
requires you to gather up your papers showing
expenses and income. You should also get the
forms you need from the tax office. Then you
should find a quiet place to work with paper and
a calculator.

Notice how much clearer the intent of the rewritten paragraph becomes once the student has included a clear statement of purpose:

The aim of this paper is to teach students
the steps involved in filing the long-form
federal income-tax return. Although most
students do not have to file the long form,
since their returns tend to be uncomplicated,
the occasional student who works full-time or
nearly full-time can definitely benefit from
taking the trouble to file the long form. To
file a successful tax return requires you to
gather up your papers showing expenses and
income. You should also get the forms you need
from the tax office. Then before you begin, you
should find a quiet place to work with paper and
a calculator.

Know Your Process Thoroughly

You should know your process extraordinarily well or you will be unable to anticipate the reader's occasional mystification. This mastery may well mean extra work, more time spent in the library, but that is what writing a clear process takes. For example, if your political science instructor asks for an essay explaining the process of a presidential veto, be prepared to consult sources other than the textbook. Aim to collect the information you need not merely to understand, but to explain as well.

It is impossible for us to overemphasize the importance of thoroughly mastering a process before trying to explain it. As we said at the outset, virtually every reader of this book will have had the frustrating experience of wrestling with a perplexing manual, or trying to assemble some simple toy from a set of exasperating instructions. Usually the author of the knotty manual or instruction booklet is a professional writer who earns a living by the pen but does not completely understand the process. Perhaps the engineer did not give the writer enough information. Or perhaps the writer was too lazy to go through the written instructions step-by-step to see if they actually worked. Grammar and rhetoric are usually innocent bystanders in such unhappy instances. But the good news is that you can avoid this chief pitfall of the process essay simply by thoroughly mastering any process you intend to explain.

Work Out the Correct Order of Your Steps

Don't start too soon or too late. Begin at the beginning, assuming that your reader is a kindly ignoramus on this particular subject and badly in need of your clarifying advice. After you have found your opening, place the rest of the steps in their exact order. A practical way to do this is to create an outline of all major and minor steps necessary for a full understanding of the process. Here is an example of such an outline:

```
Topic sentence: When people fast, their
                bodies take certain steps
                to adjust.
    I.  Tissues supplement their glucose
        supplies.
        A.  Fat is used.
        B.  The brain gets energy from ketone
            bodies.
   II.  The body tries to protect vital
        organs.
        A.  The metabolic rate drops.
```

        B.   The pulse slows.

        C.   The blood pressure lowers.

        D.   The body's thermostat cranks
              down.

III.   If the fast continues, the body
        consumes itself.

        A.   Muscles are consumed.

        B.   Protein reserves are consumed.

A detailed outline of this sequence makes either confusing the steps or omitting a step less likely.

Make Sure That the Details of Each Individual Step Are Clear and Complete

Number and explain every step in the process. For example, a process analysis of Richard Nixon's transformation from a hard-liner in the cold war with the Soviet Union to the architect of a policy of peaceful coexistence would probably list the following major stages: (1) From World War II to 1952, when he was elected vice-president of the United States, Nixon was a hard-liner who often denounced the Soviet Union as evil and dangerous. (2) From 1952 to 1969 Nixon was suspicious of Russian moves but ended the period with a changed attitude and an attempted easing of cold-war tensions. (3) Beginning with 1969 to August 9, 1974, Nixon initiated his policy of peaceful coexistence known as détente. These major stages in Nixon's foreign policy towards the Soviet Union also include some minor stages that should be mentioned. For example, the period of détente can also be subdivided into smaller stages of the SALT agreement to limit nuclear weaponry, the Paris peace talks to end the war in Vietnam, and the new trade and cultural agreements with Russia.

Similarly, to explain how to assemble the equipment needed for snow skiing, you might divide the process into two main steps, both of which would also include minor parts: (1) preparing the clothes (2) preparing the skis. Preparing the clothes means getting a waterproof parka and pants, warm gloves, a hat that covers the ears, light but warm underwear, and a pair of goggles. Preparing the skis includes getting the ski bindings adjusted, filling and waxing the bottoms and tops of the skis, sharpening their steel edges, and tending to the poles. Both the major and minor parts of the entire process should be covered.

Use Transitions to Indicate When You Are Moving from One Step to the Next

The easiest and simplest way to emphasize the correct sequence of a process is to number each step, either by using terms like "first," "second," "third," or by placing each step under a sequential heading such as (1) "choosing a subject," (2) "narrowing the subject," (3) "formulating a thesis statement," and so on. Clear headings can be exceedingly helpful to anyone who must follow a complicated explanation.

Often it is also helpful to specify in your opening paragraph the steps you intend to cover. For example, here is how the student revised her paragraph on income-tax preparation to clearly numerate the steps in the process:

```
          The aim of this paper is to teach students

     the steps involved in filing the long-form

     federal income-tax return.  Although most

     students do not have to file the long form,

     since their returns tend to be uncomplicated,

     the occasional student who works full-time or

     nearly full-time can definitely benefit from

     taking the trouble to file the long form.  To

     file a successful tax return requires you to
perform at least three steps. First you should
     ∧ gather up your papers showing expenses and
              Second,
     income. ∧ You should also get the forms you need
                          Third,
     from the tax office. ∧ Then before you begin, you

     should find a quiet place to work with paper and

     a calculator.
```

The result was this opening paragraph in her successful and clearly written essay:

```
          The aim of this paper is to teach students

     the steps involved in filing the long-form

     federal income-tax return.  Although most
```

```
students do not have to file the long form,

since their returns tend to be uncomplicated,

the occasional student who works full-time or

nearly full-time can definitely benefit from

taking the trouble to file the long form.  To

file a successful tax return requires you to

perform at least three steps.  First, you should

gather up your papers showing expenses and

income.  Second, you should get the forms you

need from the tax office.  Third, you should

find a quiet place to work with paper and a

calculator.
```

Most process essays either aim to teach us some specific thing or to inform us about some general process. The essays anthologized at the end of this chapter fall primarily into the second category. For example, "How the Supreme Court Makes Decisions" tells us how this court of last resort decides cases. "Literature, Writing, and Economics" focuses on the generalized process of writing and rewriting, while "The Spider and the Wasp" inches us, step by gruesome step, through one of nature's deadly rivalries. On a more commonplace note, "Fitting New Employees into the Company Culture" shows us how companies initiate new employees into the organization's official ways of thinking, doing, and being. Finally, the student essay acquaints us with the steps involved in a "special circumstances" murder trial in California. As before, we have included the instructor's editorial suggestions along with the student's revisions.

Original:

```
    In 1978 California adopted a death penalty

law that requires execution or life imprisonment

without possibility of parole for first-degree

murder committed under what are termed "special

circumstances," such as murder for financial

gain, multiple or torture murder, murder by a
```

hidden bomb, murder of a police officer, or
murder to avoid arrest. Here are the steps
involved in the trial of such an alleged
murderer: (First,) the suspect is apprehended and
charged with the murder. Second, a jury is
chosen to listen to the testimony of the
prosecution and defense and to find the
defendant either guilty or innocent, and, if the
defendant is found guilty, to decide whether
"special circumstances" were involved. Third, if
the defendant is convicted of murder with
special circumstances, then the jury must decide
whether to impose the death sentence or life
imprisonment without the possibility of parole.
Fourth, the law requires that in determining
punishment, jurors must make a judgment
concerning the aggravating or mitigating
elements affecting the crime, being bound to
impose death if aggravating circumstances
outweigh mitigating ones. In presenting its case
for mitigating circumstances, the defense can
bring up anything, from the defendant's tragic
childhood to mental illness or drug addiction.
Finally, the judge pronounces the sentence.
(Appeal) of a death sentence to the California
Supreme Court is automatic. If the California
Supreme court affirms the sentence, the
defendant may appeal to the U.S. Supreme Court.
If that route fails, the defendant may go the

[handwritten margin note, top:] This step — apprehending and charging — is not part of the trial (as announced in your first sentence.)

[handwritten margin note, bottom:] The appeal is not part of the trial either.

route of <u>habeas</u> <u>corpus</u> proceedings, where any
issue not raised before can be brought up. Aside
from the courts, the governor may commute a
death sentence. It is no wonder that most murder
trials go on for years, completely ignoring the
U.S. Constitution's call for a fair and speedy
trial.

Revision suggestion: reorganize essay into three phases of bringing a murder suspect to justice. Revise the topic sentence to include ① arrest, ② trial, ③ appeal. If needed, add substeps under each heading

Revision:

In 1978 California adopted a death penalty
law that requires execution or life imprisonment
without the possibility of parole for
first-degree murder committed under what are
termed "special circumstances," such as murder
for financial gain, multiple or torture murder,
murder by a hidden bomb, murder of a police
officer, or murder to avoid arrest. The task of
bringing a murder suspect to trial and seeing
that justice prevails is long and complex. The
entire process moves in three stages: The first
stage consists of the <u>arrest</u> in order to set a
court date. The second stage consists of the
<u>trial,</u> which in itself moves in phases: First, a
jury is chosen to listen to the testimony of the
prosecution and defense and to find the
defendant either guilty or innocent, and if the
defendant is found guilty, to decide whether to
impose the death sentence or life imprisonment
without parole. Second, the law requires that in

determining punishment, jurors must make a
judgment concerning aggravating or mitigating
circumstances, being bound to impose the death
sentence if aggravating circumstances outweigh
mitigating ones. In presenting its case for
mitigating circumstances, the defense can bring
up anything, from the defendant's tragic
childhood to mental illness or drug addiction.
Last, the judge pronounces the sentence. Now,
the final stage, the <u>appeal,</u> begins. Appeal of a
death sentence to the California Supreme Court
is automatic. If the California Supreme Court
affirms the sentence, the defendant may appeal
to the U.S. Supreme Court. If that route fails,
the defendant may go the route of <u>habeas</u> <u>corpus</u>
proceedings, where any issue not raised before
can be brought up. The last appeal is to the
governor, who may commute a death sentence. Each
of the three stages mentioned usually takes
months and years to become final. It is no
wonder that most murder trials go on for years,
completely ignoring the U.S. Constitution's call
for a fair and speedy trial.

The original version was badly organized because it did not stick to elaborating on the key word *trial* in the topic sentence. Since the paragraph dealt with such topics as apprehension and appeal, which are technically not part of a trial, the revised version enlarged the purpose of the paragraph to include a process analysis of "the task of bringing a murder suspect to trial and seeing that justice prevails." The process was then divided into three separate stages (arrest, trial, appeal) and explained one step at a time. For visual emphasis, each new stage was underlined when first introduced.

LITERATURE

John Kenneth Galbraith
WRITING, TYPING, AND ECONOMICS

John Kenneth Galbraith (b. 1908, Ontario, Canada) is a well-known economist, Harvard professor, and adviser to presidents. Educated at the University of California (Ph.D., 1934), Galbraith is the author of many notable works, including A Theory of Price Control *(1952);* The Great Crash, 1929 *(1955);* The Affluent Society *(1958); and* Economics and the Public Purpose *(1973).*

All writers know that on some golden mornings they are touched by the wand—are on intimate terms with poetry and cosmic truth. I have experienced those moments myself. Their lesson is simple: It's a total illusion. And the danger in the illusion is that you will wait for those moments. Such is the horror of having to face the typewriter that you will spend all your time waiting. I am persuaded that most writers, like most shoemakers, are about as good one day as the next (a point which Trollope made), hangovers apart. The difference is the result of euphoria, alcohol, or imagination. The meaning is that one had better go to his or her typewriter every morning and stay there regardless of the seeming result. It will be much the same. 1

All professions have their own ways of justifying laziness. Harvard professors are deeply impressed by the jeweled fragility of their minds. More than the thinnest metal, these are subject terribly to fatigue. More than six hours teaching a week is fatal—and an impairment of academic freedom. So, at any given moment, they are resting their minds in preparation for the next orgiastic act of insight or revelation. Writers, in contrast, do nothing because they are waiting for inspiration. 2

In my own case there are days when the result is so bad that no fewer than five revisions are required. However, when I'm greatly inspired, only four revisions are needed before, as I've often said, I put in that note of spontaneity which even my meanest critics concede. My advice to those eager students in California would be, "Do not wait for the golden moment. It may well be worse." I would also warn against the flocking tendency of writers and its use as a cover for idleness. It helps greatly in the avoidance of 3

From *Annals of an Abiding Liberal,* by John Kenneth Galbraith. Copyright © 1979 by John Kenneth Galbraith. Reprinted by permission of Houghton Mifflin Company.

work to be in the company of others who are also waiting for the golden moment. The best place to write is by yourself, because writing becomes an escape from the terrible boredom of your own personality. It's the reason that for years I've favored Switzerland, where I look at the telephone and yearn to hear it ring.

The question of revision is closely allied with that of inspiration. 4 There may be inspired writers for whom the first draft is just right. But anyone who is not certifiably a Milton had better assume that the first draft is a very primitive thing. The reason is simple: Writing is difficult work. Ralph Paine, who managed *Fortune* in my time, used to say that anyone who said writing was easy was either a bad writer or an unregenerate liar. Thinking, as Voltaire avowed, is also a very tedious thing which men—or women—will do anything to avoid. So all first drafts are deeply flawed by the need to combine composition with thought. Each later draft is less demanding in this regard. Hence the writing can be better. There does come a time when revision is for the sake of change—when one has become so bored with the words that anything that is different looks better. But even then it may be better.

For months in 1955–1956, when I was working on *The Affluent* 5 *Society,* my title was "The Opulent Society." Eventually I could stand it no longer: the word opulent had a nasty, greasy sound. One day, before starting work, I looked up the synonyms in the dictionary. First to meet my eye was the word "affluent." I had only one worry; that was whether I could possibly sell it to the publisher. All publishers wish to have books called *The Crisis in American Democracy.* My title, to my surprise, was acceptable. Mark Twain once said that the difference between the right adjective and the next-best adjective is the difference between lightning and a lightning bug.

Next, I would stress a rather old-fashioned idea to those stu- 6 dents. It was above all the lesson of Harry Luce. No one who worked for him ever again escaped the feeling that he was there looking over one's shoulder. In his hand was a pencil; down on each page one could expect, any moment, a long swishing wiggle accompanied by the comment: "This can go." Invariably it could. It was written to please the author and not the reader. Or to fill in the space. The gains from brevity are obvious; in most efforts to achieve brevity, it is the worst and dullest that goes. It is the worst and dullest that spoils the rest.

I know that brevity is now out of favor. The *New York Review of* 7 *Books* prides itself on giving its authors as much space as they want and sometimes twice as much as they need. Even those who have read only Joyce must find their thoughts wandering before the end of the fortnightly article. Writing for television, I've learned in the last year or two, is an exercise in relentless condensation. It has left me with the feeling that even brevity can be carried to extremes. But the danger, as I look at some of the newer fashions in writing, is not great.

The next of my injunctions, which I would impart with even   8 less hope of success, would concern alcohol. Nothing is so pleasant. Nothing is so important for giving the writer a sense of confidence in himself. And nothing so impairs the product. Again there are exceptions: I remember a brilliant writer at *Fortune* for whom I was responsible, who could work only with his hat on and after consuming a bottle of Scotch. There were major crises in the years immediately after World War II, when Scotch was difficult to find. But it is, quite literally, very sobering to reflect upon how many good American writers have been destroyed by this solace—by the sauce. Scott Fitzgerald, Sinclair Lewis, Thomas Wolfe, Ernest Hemingway, William Faulkner—the list goes on and on. Hamish Hamilton, once my English publisher, put the question to James Thurber: "Jim, why is it so many of your great writers have ruined themselves with drink?" Thurber thought long and carefully and finally replied: "It's this way, Jamie. They wrote these novels, and they sold very well. They made a lot of money and so they could buy whiskey by the case."

Their reputation was universal. A few years before his death,   9 John Steinbeck, an appreciative but not a compulsive drinker, went to Moscow. It was a triumphal tour; and in a letter that he sent me about his hosts, he said: "I found I enjoyed the Soviet hustlers pretty much. There was a kind of youthful honesty about their illicit intentions that was not without charm. And their lives are difficult under their four-party system [a reference that escapes me]. It takes a fairly deft or very lucky man to make his way upward in the worker's paradise." I later heard that one night, after a particularly effusive celebration, he decided to make his way back to the hotel on foot. On the way he was overcome by fatigue and the hospitality he had received and sat down on a bench in a small park to rest. A policeman, called a militiaman in Moscow, came along and informed John, who was now asleep, and his companion, who spoke Russian, that the benches could not be occupied at that hour. His companion explained, rightly, that John was a very great American writer and that an exception should be made. The militiaman insisted. The companion explained again, insisted more strongly. Presently a transcendental light came over the policeman's face. He looked at Steinbeck asleep on the bench, inspected his condition more closely, recoiled slightly from the fumes, and said, "Oh, oh, Gemingway." Then he took off his cap and tiptoed carefully away.

We are all desperately afraid of sounding like Carry Nation. I   10
must take the risk. Any writer who wants to do his best against a deadline should stick to Coca-Cola. If he doesn't have a deadline, he can risk Seven-Up.

Next, I would want to tell my students of a point strongly   11
pressed, if my memory serves, by Shaw. He once said that as he grew older, he became less and less interested in theory, more and more interested in information. The temptation in writing is just the reverse. Nothing is so hard to come by as a new and interesting fact. Nothing is so easy on the feet as a generalization. I now pick up magazines and leaf through them looking for articles that are rich with facts; I do not care much what they are. Richly evocative and deeply percipient theory I avoid. It leaves me cold unless I am the author of it. My advice to all young writers is to stick to research and reporting with only a minimum of interpretation. And especially this is my advice to all older writers, particularly to columnists. As the feet give out, they seek to have the mind take their place.

Reluctantly, but from a long and terrible experience, I would   12
urge my young writers to avoid all attempts at humor. It does greatly lighten one's task. I've often wondered who made it impolite to laugh at one's own jokes; it is one of the major enjoyments of life. And that is the point. Humor is an intensely personal, largely internal thing. What pleases some, including the source, does not please others. One laughs; another says, "Well, I certainly see nothing funny about that." And the second opinion has just as much standing as the first, maybe more. Where humor is concerned, there are no standards—no one can say what is good or bad, although you can be sure that everyone will. Only a very foolish man will use a form of language that is wholly uncertain in its effect. That is the nature of humor.

There are other reasons for avoiding humor. In our society the   13
solemn person inspires far more trust than the one who laughs. The politician allows himself one joke at the beginning of his speech. A ritual. Then he changes his expression, affects an aspect of morbid solemnity signaling that, after all, he is a totally serious man. Nothing so undermines a point as its association with a wisecrack—the very word is pejorative.

Also, as Art Buchwald has pointed out, we live in an age when   14 it is hard to invent anything that is as funny as everyday life. How could one improve, for example, on the efforts of the great men of television to attribute cosmic significance to the offhand and hilarious way Bert Lance combined professed fiscal conservatism with an unparalleled personal commitment to the deficit financing of John Maynard Keynes? And because the real world is so funny, there is almost nothing you can do, short of labeling a joke a joke, to keep people from taking it seriously. A few years ago in *Harper's* I invented the theory that socialism in our time was the result of our dangerous addiction to team sports. The ethic of the team is all wrong for free enterprise. The code words are cooperation; team spirit; accept leadership; the coach is always right. Authoritarianism is sanctified; the individualist is a poor team player, a menace. All this our vulnerable adolescents learn. I announced the formation of an organization to combat this deadly trend and to promote boxing and track instead. I called it the C.I.A.—Congress for Individualist Athletics. Hundreds wrote in to *Harper's* asking to join. Or demanding that baseball be exempted. A batter is on his own. I presented the letters to the Kennedy Library.

Finally, I would come to a matter of much personal interest, intensely self-serving. It concerns the peculiar pitfalls of the writer who is dealing with presumptively difficult or technical matters. Economics is an example, and within the field of economics the subject of money, with the history of which I have been much concerned, is an especially good case. Any specialist who ventures to write on money with a view to making himself intelligible works under a grave moral hazard. He will be accused of oversimplification. The charge will be made by his fellow professionals, however obtuse or incompetent. They will have a sympathetic hearing from the layman. That is because no layman really expects to understand about money, inflation, or the International Monetary Fund. If he does, he suspects that he is being fooled. One can have respect only for someone who is decently confusing. 15

In the case of economics there are no important propositions that cannot be stated in plain language. Qualifications and refinements are numerous and of great technical complexity. These are important for separating the good students from the dolts. But in economics the refinements rarely, if ever, modify the essential and practical point. The writer who seeks to be intelligible needs to be right; he must be challenged if his argument leads to an erroneous conclusion and especially if it leads to the wrong action. But he can safely dismiss the charge that he has made the subject too easy. The truth is not difficult. 16

Complexity and obscurity have professional value—they are the academic equivalents of apprenticeship rules in the building trades. They exclude the outsiders, keep down the competition, preserve the image of a privileged or priestly class. The man who makes things clear is a scab. He is criticized less for his clarity than for his treachery.   17

Additionally, and especially in the social sciences, much unclear writing is based on unclear or incomplete thought. It is possible with safety to be technically obscure about something you haven't thought out. It is impossible to be wholly clear on something you do not understand. Clarity thus exposes flaws in the thought. The person who undertakes to make difficult matters clear is infringing on the sovereign right of numerous economists, sociologists, and political scientists to make bad writing the disguise for sloppy, imprecise, or incomplete thought. One can understand the resulting anger. Adam Smith, John Stuart Mill, John Maynard Keynes were writers of crystalline clarity most of the time. Marx had great moments, as in *The Communist Manifesto.* Economics owes very little, if anything, to the practitioners of scholarly obscurity. If any of my California students should come to me from the learned professions, I would counsel them in all their writing to keep the confidence of their colleagues. This they should do by being always complex, always obscure, invariably a trifle vague.   18

You might say that all this constitutes a meager yield for a lifetime of writing. Or that writing on economics, as someone once said of Kerouac's prose, is not writing but typing. True.   19

Vocabulary

euphoria (1)

orgiastic (2)

spontaneity (3)

unregenerate (4)

injunctions (8)

solace (8)

effusive (9)

transcendental (9)

evocative (11)

percipient (11)

pejorative (13)

authoritarianism (14)

obtuse (15)

Critical Inquiries

1. How applicable to your own experiences as a scribbler do you find Galbraith's observations about revising?

2. Galbraith dismisses the idea of a "golden morning" as a dangerous illusion for writers. What experiences have you had with your own "golden mornings" of inspiration?

3. What characteristics are usually associated with an effect of "spontaneity" in a writer's style?

4. Why should theory be so much easier to write about than fact?

5. Which of Galbraith's several injunctions about writing do you find most applicable to you as a writer? Which, least?

Rhetorical Inquiries

1. How descriptive is Galbraith's title of the content of his article? What might a better title be?

2. Beginning two sentences in a row with the same initial phrasing, unless for deliberate emphasis, can lead to monotonous constructions. Where in paragraph 2 does such a slip occur, and how would you correct it?

3. What process explanation is Galbraith offering? Where is the thesis statement explaining the purpose of his article?

4. What transitional word does Galbraith mainly use to establish links between the steps of his process?

5. In paragraph 7, Galbraith writes: "Even those who read only Joyce must find their thoughts wandering before the end of the fortnightly article." What figure of speech is this, and what is its meaning?

POLITICAL SCIENCE

William Joseph Brennan, Jr.
HOW THE SUPREME COURT ARRIVES AT DECISIONS

William Joseph Brennan, Jr., (b. 1906 in Newark, N.J.) was educated at Harvard University. Before his appointment by President Dwight Eisenhower to the United States Supreme Court in 1956, he served as a judge of the superior court (1949–50), appellate division court (1950–52) and the New Jersey supreme court (1952–56). He is regarded as a liberal justice.

The screening process works like this: when nine Justices sit, it   1
takes five to decide a case on the merits. But it takes only the votes

---

From *The New York Times,* Oct. 12, 1963. Copyright © 1963 by *The New York Times* Company. Reprinted by permission.

of four of the nine to put a case on the argument calendar for argument and decision. Those four votes are hard to come by—only an exceptional case raising a significant federal question commands them.

Each application for review is usually in the form of a short petition, attached to which are any opinions of the lower courts in the case. The adversary may file a response—also, in practice usually short. Both the petition and response identify the federal questions allegedly involved, argue their substantiality, and whether they were properly raised in the lower courts.

Each Justice receives copies of the petition and response and such parts of the record as the parties may submit. Each Justice then, without any consultation at this stage with the others, reaches his own tentative conclusion whether the application should be granted or denied.

The first consultation about the case comes at the Court conference at which the case is listed on the agenda for discussion. We sit in conference almost every Friday during the term. Conferences begin at ten in the morning and often continue until six, except for a half-hour recess for lunch.

Only the Justices are present. There are no law clerks, no stenographers, no secretaries, no pages—just the nine of us. The junior Justice acts as guardian of the door, receiving and delivering any messages that come in or go from the conference.

Order of Seating

The conference room is a beautifully oak-paneled chamber with one side lined with books from floor to ceiling. Over the mantel of the exquisite marble fireplace at one end hangs the only adornment in the chamber—a portrait of Chief Justice John Marshall. In the middle of the room stands a rectangular table, not too large but large enough for the nine of us comfortably to gather around it.

The Chief Justice sits at the south end and Mr. Justice Black, the senior Associate Justice, at the north end. Along the side to the left of the Chief Justice sits Justices Stewart, Goldberg, White, and Harlan. On the right side sit Justice Clark, myself and Justice Douglas in that order.

We are summoned to conference by a buzzer which rings in our several chambers five minutes before the hour. Upon entering the conference room each of us shakes hands with his colleagues. The handshake tradition originated when Chief Justice Fuller presided many decades ago. It is a symbol that harmony of aims if not of views is the Court's guiding principle.

Each of us has his copy of the agenda of the day's cases before him. The agenda lists the cases applying for review. Each of us before coming to the conference has noted on his copy his tentative view whether or not review should be granted in each case.   9

The Chief Justice begins the discussion of each case. He then yields to the senior Associate Justice and discussion proceeds down the line in order of seniority until each Justice has spoken.   10

Voting goes the other way. The junior Justice votes first and voting then proceeds up the line to the Chief Justice, who votes last.   11

Each of us has a docket containing a sheet for each case with appropriate places for recording the votes. When any case receives four votes for review, that case is transferred to the oral argument list. Applications in which none of us sees merits may be passed over without discussion.   12

Now how do we process the decisions we agree to review?   13

There are rare occasions when the question is so clearly controlled by an earlier decision of the Court that a reversal of the lower court judgment is inevitable. In these rare instances we may summarily reverse without oral argument.   14

Each Side Gets Hour

The case must very clearly justify summary disposition, however, because our ordinary practice is not to reverse a decision without oral argument. Indeed, oral argument of cases taken for review, whether from the state or federal courts, is the usual practice. We rarely accept submissions of cases on briefs.   15

Oral argument ordinarily occurs about four months after the application for review is granted. Each party is usually allowed one hour, but in recent years we have limited oral argument to a half-hour in cases thought to involve issues not requiring longer arguments.   16

Counsel submit their briefs and record in sufficient time for the distribution of one set to each Justice two or three weeks before the oral argument. Most of the members of the present Court follow the practice of reading the briefs before the argument. Some of us often have a bench memorandum prepared before the argument. This memorandum digests the facts and the arguments of both sides, highlighting the matters about which we may want to question counsel at the argument.   17

Often I have independent research done in advance of argument   18
and incorporate the results in the bench memorandum.

We follow a schedule of two weeks of argument from Monday   19
through Thursday, followed by two weeks of recess for opinion
writing and the study of petitions for review. The argued cases are
listed on the conference agenda on the Friday following argument.
Conference discussion follows the same procedure I have described for the discussions of certiorari petitions.

Opinion Assigned

Of course, it is much more extended. Not infrequently discus-   20
sion of particular cases may be spread over two or more conferences.

Not until the discussion is completed and a vote taken is the   21
opinion assigned. The assignment is not made at the conference
but formally in writing some few days after the conference.

The Chief Justice assigns the opinions in those cases in which he   22
has voted with the majority. The senior Associate Justice voting
with the majority assigns the opinions in the other cases. The dis-
senters agree among themselves who shall write the dissenting
opinion. Of course, each Justice is free to write his own opinion,
concurring or dissenting.

The writing of an opinion always takes weeks and sometimes   23
months. The most painstaking research and care are involved.

Research, of course, concentrates on relevant legal materials—   24
precedents particularly. But Supreme Court cases often require
some familiarity with history, economics, the social and other sciences, and authorities in these areas, too, are consulted when necessary.

When the author of an opinion feels he has an unanswerable   25
document he sends it to a print shop, which we maintain in our
building. The printed draft may be revised several times before his
proposed opinion is circulated among the other Justices. Copies are
sent to each member of the Court, those in the dissent as well as
those in the majority.

Some Change Minds

Now the author often discovers that his work has only begun.   26
He receives a return, ordinarily in writing, from each Justice who
voted with him and sometimes also from the Justices who voted
the other way. He learns who will write the dissent if one is to be

written. But his particular concern is whether those who voted with him are still of his view and what they have to say about his proposed opinion.

Often some who voted with him at conference will advise that they reserve final judgment pending the circulation of the dissent. It is a common experience that dissents change votes, even enough votes to become the majority.   27

I have had to convert more than one of my proposed majority opinions into a dissent before the final decision was announced. I have also, however, had the more satisfying experience of rewriting a dissent as a majority opinion for the Court.   28

Before everyone has finally made up his mind a constant interchange by memoranda, by telephone, at the lunch table continues while we hammer out the final form of the opinion. I had one case during the past term in which I circulated ten printed drafts before one was approved as the Court opinion.   29

Uniform Rule

The point of this procedure is that each Justice, unless he disqualifies himself in a particular case, passes on every piece of business coming to the Court. The Court does not function by means of committees or panels. Each Justice passes on each petition, each time, no matter how drawn, in long hand, by typewriter, or on a press. Our Constitution vests the judicial power in only one Supreme Court. This does not permit Supreme Court action by committees, panels, or sections.   30

The method that the Justices use in meeting an enormous caseload varies. There is one uniform rule: Judging is not delegated. Each Justice studies each case in sufficient detail to resolve the question for himself. In a very real sense, each decision is an individual decision of every Justice.   31

The process can be a lonely, troubling experience for fallible human beings conscious that their best may not be adequate to the challenge.   32

"We are not unaware," the late Justice Jackson said, "that we are not final because we are infallible; we know that we are infallible only because we are final."   33

One does not forget how much may depend on his decision. He knows that usually more than the litigants may be affected, that the course of vital social, economic and political currents may be directed.   34

This then is the decisional process in the Supreme Court. It is   35 not without its tensions, of course—indeed, quite agonizing tensions at times.

    I would particularly emphasize that, unlike the case of a Congressional or White House decision, Americans demand of their Supreme Court judges that they produce a written opinion, the collective expression of the judges subscribing to it, setting forth the reason which led them to the decision.   36

    These opinions are the exposition, not just to lawyers, legal scholars and other judges, but to our whole society, of the bases upon which a particular result rests—why a problem, looked at as disinterestedly and dispassionately as nine human beings trained in a tradition of the disinterested and dispassionate approach can look at it, is answered as it is.   37

    It is inevitable, however, that Supreme Court decisions—and the Justices themselves—should be caught up in public debate and be the subjects of bitter controversy.   38

    An editorial in *The Washington Post* did not miss the mark by much in saying that this was so because   39

> one of the primary functions of the Supreme Court is to keep the people of the country from doing what they would like to do—at times when what they would like to do runs counter to the Constitution . . . . The function of the Supreme Court is not to count constituents; it is to interpret a fundamental charter which imposes restraints on constituents. Independence and integrity, not popularity, must be its standards.

Vocabulary

tentative (3)	summarily (14)
exquisite (6)	certiorari (19)

Critical Inquiries

1. What should be the responsibility of the Supreme Court—to enforce the law of the Constitution or to reinterpret the Constitution based on prevailing social practice?

2. On what famous issue has history proven the Supreme Court to have been completely wrong?

3. What remedy does a petitioner whose case has been refused a hearing by the Supreme Court have under our present legal and political system?

4. Which majority group of the United States population is little mentioned by, and has been given short shrift in, the Constitution? What remedy is open to that majority?

5. What effect do you think the sorry under-representation of women and ethnic minorities on the Supreme Court has had on its decision-making?

Rhetorical Inquiries

1. Justice Brennan includes considerable detail about the decor and seating arrangements of the Supreme Court along with information about the job assignments of the various justices. What do these details contribute to the account?

2. What secondary point about the Supreme Court is implicitly made by the description of seating and protocol in paragraphs 7 and 8?

3. What is the function of paragraph 13?

4. Which of the various patterns of organizations discussed in Chapter 3 does this essay rely on as its organizing principle?

5. What basic assumption behind this entire article is belied by the present Supreme Court?

ANIMAL BEHAVIOR

Alexander Petrunkevitch
THE SPIDER AND THE WASP

Alexander Petrunkevitch (1875–1964) is a world authority on spiders. In 1911 he published his first book of scientific research, entitled The Index Catalogue of Spiders of North, Central, and South America, *which is still used as one of the basic works for anyone interested in the classification of spiders. Other works include* Choice and Responsibility (1947) *and* Principles of Classification (1952). *In addition to his scientific work, Petrunkevitch also wrote many translations of poetry in both Russian and English. The essay below first appeared in the August, 1952, issue of* Scientific American.

In the feeding and safeguarding of their progeny insects and spiders exhibit some interesting analogies to reasoning and some   1

From "The Spider and the Wasp," by Alexander Petrunkevitch, *Scientific American,* August, 1952. Reprinted with permission. Copyright © 1952 by *Scientific American,* Inc. All rights reserved.

crass examples of blind instinct. The case I propose to describe here is that of the tarantula spiders and their archenemy, the digger wasps of the genus Pepsis. It is a classic example of what looks like intelligence pitted against instinct—a strange situation in which the victim, though fully able to defend itself, submits unwittingly to its destruction.

Most tarantulas live in the tropics, but several species occur in the temperate zone and a few are common in the southern U.S. Some varieties are large and have powerful fangs with which they can inflict a deep wound. These formidable looking spiders do not, however, attack man; you can hold one in your hand, if you are gentle, without being bitten. Their bite is dangerous only to insects and small mammals such as mice; for man it is no worse than a hornet's sting.

Tarantulas customarily live in deep cylindrical burrows, from which they emerge at dusk and into which they retire at dawn. Mature males wander about after dark in search of females and occasionally stray into houses. After mating, the male dies in a few weeks, but a female lives much longer and can mate several years in succession. In a Paris museum is a tropical specimen which is said to have been living in captivity for 25 years.

A fertilized female tarantula lays from 200 to 400 eggs at a time; thus it is possible for a single tarantula to produce several thousand young. She takes no care of them beyond weaving a cocoon of silk to enclose the eggs. After they hatch, the young walk away, find convenient places in which to dig their burrows and spend the rest of their lives in solitude. The eyesight of tarantulas is poor, being limited to a sensing of change in the intensity of light and to the perception of moving objects. They apparently have little or no sense of hearing, for a hungry tarantula will pay no attention to a loudly chirping cricket placed in its cage unless the insect happens to touch one of its legs.

But all spiders, and especially hairy ones, have an extremely delicate sense of touch. Laboratory experiments prove that tarantulas can distinguish three types of touch: pressure against the body wall, stroking of the body hair, and riffling of certain very fine hairs on the legs called trichobothria. Pressure against the body, by the finger or the end of a pencil, causes the tarantula to move off slowly for a short distance. The touch excites no defensive response unless the approach is from above where the spider can see the motion, in which case it rises on its hind legs, lifts its front legs, opens its fangs and holds this threatening posture as long as the object continues to move.

The entire body of a tarantula, especially its legs, is thickly
clothed with hair. Some of it is short and wooly, some long and
stiff. Touching this body hair produces one of two distinct reactions. When the spider is hungry, it responds with an immediate
and swift attack. At the touch of a cricket's antennae the tarantula
seizes the insect so swiftly that a motion picture taken at the rate
of 64 frames per second shows only the result and not the process
of capture. But when the spider is not hungry, the stimulation of
its hairs merely causes it to shake the touched limb. An insect can
walk under its hairy belly unharmed.

The trichobothria, very fine hairs growing from disklike membranes on the legs, are sensitive only to air movements. A light
breeze makes them vibrate slowly, without disturbing the common hair. When one blows gently on the trichobothria, the tarantula reacts with a quick jerk of its four front legs. If the front and
hind legs are stimulated at the same time, the spider makes a sudden jump. This reaction is quite independent of the state of its ap-
petite.

These three tactile responses—to pressure on the body wall, to
moving of the common hair, and to flexing of the trichobothria—
are so different from one another that there is no possibility of
confusing them. They serve the tarantula adequately for most of
its needs and enable it to avoid most annoyances and dangers. But
they fail the spider completely when it meets its deadly enemy,
the digger wasp Pepsis.

These solitary wasps are beautiful and formidable creatures.
Most species are either a deep shiny blue all over, or deep blue
with rusty wings. The largest have a wing span of about four
inches. They live on nectar. When excited, they give off a pungent
odor—a warning that they are ready to attack. The sting is much
worse than that of a bee or common wasp, and the pain and
swelling last longer. In the adult stage the wasp lives only a few
months. The female produces but a few eggs, one at a time at intervals of two or three days. For each egg the mother must provide
one adult tarantula, alive but paralyzed. The mother wasp attaches
the egg to the paralyzed spider's abdomen. Upon hatching from
the egg, the larva is many hundreds of times smaller than its living
but helpless victim. It eats no other food and drinks no water. By
the time it has finished its single Gargantuan meal and become
ready for wasphood, nothing remains of the tarantula but its indi-
gestible chitinous skeleton.

The mother wasp goes tarantula-hunting when the egg in her
ovary is almost ready to be laid. Flying low over the ground late on

a sunny afternoon, the wasp looks for its victim or for the mouth of a tarantula burrow, a round hole edged by a bit of silk. The sex of the spider makes no difference, but the mother is highly discriminating as to species. Each species of Pepsis requires a certain species of tarantula, and the wasp will not attack the wrong species. In a cage with a tarantula which is not its normal prey, the wasp avoids the spider and is usually killed by it in the night.

Yet when a wasp finds the correct species, it is the other way about. To identify the species the wasp apparently must explore the spider with her antennae. The tarantula shows an amazing tolerance to this exploration. The wasp crawls under it and walks over it without evoking any hostile response. The molestation is so great and so persistent that the tarantula often rises on all eight legs, as if it were on stilts. It may stand this way for several minutes. Meanwhile the wasp, having satisfied itself that the victim is of the right species, moves off a few inches to dig the spider's grave. Working vigorously with legs and jaws, it excavates a hole 8 to 10 inches deep with a diameter slightly larger than the spider's girth. Now and again the wasp pops out of the hole to make sure that the spider is still there.   11

When the grave is finished, the wasp returns to the tarantula to complete her ghastly enterprise. First she feels it all over once more with her antennae. Then her behavior becomes more aggressive. She bends her abdomen, protruding her sting, and searches for the soft membrane at the point where the spider's legs join its body— the only spot where she can penetrate the horny skeleton. From time to time, as the exasperated spider slowly shifts ground, the wasp turns on her back and slides along with the aid of her wings, trying to get under the tarantula for a shot at the vital spot. During all this maneuvering, which can last for several minutes, the tarantula makes no move to save itself. Finally the wasp corners it against some obstruction and grasps one of its legs in her powerful jaws. Now at last the harassed spider tries a desperate but vain defense. The two contestants roll over and over on the ground. It is a terrifying sight and the outcome is always the same. The wasp finally manages to thrust her sting into the soft spot and holds it there for a few seconds while she pumps in the poison. Almost immediately the tarantula falls paralyzed on its back. Its legs stop twitching; its heart stops beating. Yet it is not dead, as is shown by the fact that if taken from the wasp it can be restored to some sensitivity by being kept in a moist chamber for several months.   12

After paralyzing the tarantula, the wasp cleans herself by dragging her body along the ground and rubbing her feet, sucks the   13 drop of blood oozing from the wound in the spider's abdomen, then grabs a leg of the flabby, helpless animal in her jaws and drags it down to the bottom of the grave. She stays there for many minutes, sometimes for several hours, and what she does all that time in the dark we do not know. Eventually she lays her egg and attaches it to the side of the spider's abdomen with a sticky secretion. Then she emerges, fills the grave with soil carried bit by bit in her jaws, and finally tramples the ground all around to hide any trace of the grave from prowlers. Then she flies away, leaving her descendant safely started in life.

In all this the behavior of the wasp evidently is qualitatively different from that of the spider. The wasp acts like an intelligent animal. This is not to say that instinct plays no part or that she reasons as man does. But her actions are to the point; they are not automatic and can be modified to fit the situation. We do not know for certain how she identifies the tarantula—probably it is by some olfactory or chemo-tactile sense—but she does it purposefully and does not blindly tackle a wrong species.   14

On the other hand, the tarantula's behavior shows only confusion. Evidently the wasp's pawing gives it no pleasure, for it tries to move away. That the wasp is not simulating sexual stimulation is certain because male and female tarantulas react in the same way to its advances. That the spider is not anesthetized by some odorless secretion is easily shown by blowing lightly at the tarantula and making it jump suddenly. What, then, makes the tarantula behave as stupidly as it does?   15

No clear, simple answer is available. Possibly the stimulation by the wasp's antennae is masked by a heavier pressure on the spider's body, so that it reacts as when prodded by a pencil. But the explanation may be much more complex. Initiative in attack is not in the nature of tarantulas; most species fight only when cornered so that escape is impossible. Their inherited patterns of behavior apparently prompt them to avoid problems rather than attack them. For example, spiders always weave their webs in three dimensions, and when a spider finds that there is insufficient space to attach certain threads in the third dimension, it leaves the place and seeks another, instead of finishing the web in a single plane. This urge to escape seems to arise under all circumstances, in all phases of life, and to take the place of reasoning. For a spider to change the pattern of its web is as impossible as for an inexperienced man to build a bridge across a chasm obstructing his way.   16

In a way the instinctive urge to escape is not only easier but often more efficient than reasoning. The tarantula does exactly what   17 is most efficient in all cases except in an encounter with a ruthless and determined attacker dependent for the existence of her own species on killing as many tarantulas as she can lay eggs. Perhaps in this case the spider follows its usual pattern of trying to escape, instead of seizing and killing the wasp, because it is not aware of its danger. In any case, the survival of the tarantula species as a whole is protected by the fact that the spider is much more fertile than the wasp.

Vocabulary

progeny (1)

cylindrical (3)

burrows (3)

riffling (5)

membranes (7)

flexing (8)

formidable (9)

pungent (9)

Gargantuan (9)

chitinous (9)

species (10)

antennae (11)

girth (11)

protruding (12)

secretion (13)

qualitatively (14)

olfactory (14)

chemo-tactile (14)

Critical Inquiries

1. In what ways are the tarantula and wasp basically different creatures? How would you apply their differences to human beings? Give examples.

2. How can the species of tarantulas continue to survive the purposeful and systematic destruction wreaked upon it by the wasp? What does this survival say about nature? Can you cite other examples of similar survival?

3. Why is the outcome of the battle between the tarantula and the wasp always the same? How would you characterize the tarantula's response to the wasp's attack?

4. What irony exists in the conflict between the tarantula and the wasp?

5. What lesson about the ethics or morality of nature do you draw from Petrunkevitch's description?

Rhetorical Inquiries

1. The author makes clear that vividly describing a process is not the only purpose of his essay. What is another purpose? Where is it introduced?

2. How is the essay organized? How effective is this organization?

3. Where in the essay does the author use a well-paced narration? Comment on the narrator's technique.

4. What are some examples of figurative language used in the essay? Cite at least three.

5. What is the purpose of the question at the end of paragraph 15?

MANAGEMENT

Richard Pascale

FITTING NEW EMPLOYEES INTO THE COMPANY CULTURE

Richard Pascale (b. 1938, N.Y.) is professor at the Stanford University Business School. In his best seller, The Art of Japanese Management *(1981), Pascale has shown a desire to explain the great success of certain Japanese business firms so that United States companies could profit from Japanese techniques and strategies. The essay below appeared in the May 1984 issue of* Fortune, *preceded by the following subheading: "Many of the best-managed companies in America are particularly skilled at getting recruits to adopt the corporate collection of shared values, beliefs, and practices as their own. Here's how they do it, and why indoctrination need not mean brainwashing."*

What corporate strategy was in the 1970s, corporate culture is 1 becoming in the 1980s. Companies worry about whether theirs is right for them, consultants hawk advice on the subject, executives wonder if there's anything in it that can help them manage better. A strong culture—a set of shared values, norms, and beliefs that get everybody heading in the same direction—is common to all the companies held up as paragons in the best-seller *In Search of Excellence.*

There is, however, one aspect of culture that nobody seems to 2 want to talk about. This is the process by which newly hired employees are made part of a company's culture. It may be called learning the ropes, being taught "the way we do things here at XYZ Corp." or simply training. Almost no one calls it by its precise social-science name—socialization.

To American ears, attuned by Constitution and conviction to 3 the full expression of individuality, socialization tends to sound

Reprinted with permission from *Fortune,* May 28, 1984. © 1984 Time Inc. All rights reserved.

alien and vaguely sinister. Some equate it with the propagation of socialism—which it isn't—but even when it is correctly understood as the development of social conformity, the prospect makes most of us cringe. How many companies caught up in the corporate culture fad will be quite as enthusiastic when they finally grasp that "creating a strong culture" is a nice way of saying that employees have to be more comprehensively socialized?

The tradition at most American corporations is to err in the other direction, to be culturally permissive, to let employees do their own thing to a remarkable degree. We are guided by a philosophy, initially articulated by John Locke, Thomas Hobbes, and Adam Smith, that says that individuals free to choose make the most efficient decisions. The independence of the parts makes for a greater sum. Trendy campaigns to build a strong corporate culture run into trouble when employees are asked to give up some of their individuality for the common good.

The crux of the dilemma is this: We are opposed to the manipulation of individuals for organizational purposes. At the same time we increasingly realize that a degree of social uniformity enables organizations to work better. One need not look to Japan to see the benefits of it. Many of the great American companies that thrive from one generation to the next—IBM, Procter & Gamble, Morgan Guaranty Trust—are organizations that have perfected their processes of socialization. Virtually none talk explicitly about socialization; they may not even be conscious of precisely what they are doing. Moreover, when one examines any particular aspect of their policy toward people—how they recruit or train or compensate—little stands out as unusual. But when the pieces are assembled, what emerges is an awesome internal consistency that powerfully shapes behavior.

It's time to take socialization out of the closet. If some degree of it is necessary for organizations to be effective, then the challenge for managers is to reconcile this necessity with traditional American independence.

Probably the best guide available on how to socialize people properly is what the IBMs and the P&Gs actually do. Looking at the winners company by company, one finds that, with slight variations, they all put new employees through what might be called the seven steps of socialization:

• Step one. The company subjects candidates for employment to a selection process so rigorous that it often seems designed to discourage individuals rather than encourage them to take the job. By grilling the applicant, telling him or her the bad side as well as the good, and making sure not to oversell, strong-culture companies prod the job applicant to take himself out of contention if he, who presumably knows more about himself than any recruiter, thinks the organization won't fit his style and values.

Consider the way Procter & Gamble hires people for entry level 9 positions in brand management. The first person who interviews the applicant is drawn not from the human resources department, but from an elite cadre of line managers who have been trained with lectures, videotapes, films, practice interviews, and role playing. These interviewers use what they've learned to probe each applicant for such qualities as the ability to "turn out high volumes of excellent work," to "identify and understand problems," and to "reach thoroughly substantiated and well-reasoned conclusions that lead to action." Initially, each candidate undergoes at least two interviews and takes a test of his general knowledge. If he passes, he's flown to P&G headquarters in Cincinnati, where he goes through a day of one-on-one interviews and a group interview over lunch.

The New York investment banking house of Morgan Stanley 10 encourages people it is thinking of hiring to discuss the demands of the job with their spouses, girlfriends, or boyfriends—new recruits sometimes work 100 hours a week. The firm's managing directors and their wives take promising candidates and their spouses or companions out to dinner to bring home to them what they will face. The point is to get a person who will not be happy within Morgan's culture because of the way his family feels to eliminate himself from consideration for a job there.

This kind of rigorous screening might seem an invitation to hire 11 only people who fit the mold of present employees. In fact, it often *is* harder for companies with strong cultures to accept individuals different from the prevailing type.

• Step two. The company subjects the newly hired individual to 12 experiences calculated to induce humility and to make him question his prior behavior, beliefs, and values. By lessening the recruit's comfort with himself, the company hopes to promote openness toward its own norms and values.

This may sound like brainwashing or boot camp, but it usually 13 just takes the form of pouring on more work than the newcomer can possibly do. IBM and Morgan Guaranty socialize with training programs in which, to quote one participant, "You work every night until 2 A.M. on your own material, and then help others." Procter & Gamble achieves the same result with what might be called upending experiences—requiring a recent college graduate to color in a map of sales territories, for example. The message is clear: while you may be accomplished in many respects, you are in kindergarten as far as what you know about this organization.

Humility isn't the only feeling brought on by long hours of intense work that carry the individual close to his or her limit. When everybody's vulnerability runs high, one also tends to become close to one's colleagues. Companies sometimes intensify this cohesiveness by not letting trainees out of the pressure cooker for very long—everyone has so much work to do that he doesn't have time to see people outside the company or reestablish a more normal social distance from his co-workers. 14

Morgan Stanley, for instance, expects newly hired associates to work 12- to 14- hour days and most weekends. Their lunches are not the Lucullan repasts that MBAs fantasize about,[1] but are typically confined to 30 minutes in the unprepossessing cafeteria. One can observe similar patterns—long hours, exhausting travel schedules, and almost total immersion in casework—at law firms and consulting outfits. Do recruits chafe under such discipline? Not that much, apparently. Socialization is a bit like exercise—it's probably easier to reconcile yourself to it while you're young. 15

• Step three. Companies send the newly humble recruits into the trenches, pushing them to master one of the disciplines at the core of the company's business. The newcomer's promotions are tied to how he does in that discipline. 16

In the course of the individual's first few months with the company, his universe of experience has increasingly narrowed down to the organization's culture. The company, having got him to open his mind to its way of doing business, now cements that orientation by putting him in the field and giving him lots of carefully monitored experience. It rewards his progress with promotions at predictable intervals. 17

While IBM hires some MBAs and a few older professionals with prior work experience, almost all of them start at the same level as recruits from college and go through the same training programs. It takes about 15 years, for example, to become a financial controller. At Morgan Stanley and consulting firms like McKinsey, new associates must similarly work their way up through the ranks. There is almost never a quick way to jump a few rungs on the ladder. 18

The gains from this approach are cumulative. For starters, when 19

---

[1]Lucullan repasts: luxurious feasts, like the banquets given by the Roman general, Lucius Licinius Lucullus (first century, B.C.).

all trainees understand there is just one step-by-step career path, it reduces politicking. Since they are being evaluated on how they do over the long haul, they are less tempted to cut corners or go for short-term victories. By the time they reach senior positions they understand the business not as a financial abstraction, but as a reality of people they know and skills they've learned. They can communicate with people in the lowest ranks in the shorthand of shared experience.

• Step four. At every stage of the new manager's career, the company measures the operating results he has achieved and rewards him accordingly. It does this with systems that are comprehensive and consistent. These systems focus particularly on those aspects of the business that make for competitive success and for the perpetuation of the corporation's values.   20

Procter & Gamble, for instance, measures managers on three factors it deems critical to a brand's success: building volume, building profit, and conducting planned change—altering a product to make it more effective or more satisfying to the customer in some other way. Information from the outside world— market-share figures, say—is used in the measuring along with financial data. Performance appraisals focus on these criteria as well as on general managerial skill.   21

IBM uses similar interlocking systems to track adherence to one of its major values, respect for the dignity of the individual. The company monitors this with surveys of employee morale; "Speak Up," a confidential suggestion box; a widely proclaimed policy of having the boss's door open to any subordinates who want to talk; so-called skip-level interviews, in which a subordinate can skip over a couple of organizational levels to discuss a grievance with senior management; and informal social contacts between senior managers and lower level employees. Management moves quickly when any of these systems turns up a problem.   22

The IBM culture includes a mechanism for disciplining someone who has violated one of the corporate norms—handling his subordinates too harshly, say, or being overzealous against the competition. The malefactor will be assigned to what is called the penalty box—typically, a fairly meaningless job at the same level, sometimes in a less desirable location. A branch manager in Chicago might be moved to a nebulous staff position at headquarters. To the outsider, penalty box assignments look like just another job rotation, but insiders know that the benched manager is out of the game temporarily.   23

The penalty box provides a place to hold a manager while the   24 mistakes he's made and the hard feelings they've engendered are gradually forgotten. The mechanism lends substance to the belief, widespread among IBM employees, that the company won't fire anybody capriciously. The penalty box's existence says, in effect, that in the career of strong, effective managers there are times when one steps on toes. The penalty box lets someone who has stepped too hard contemplate his error and return to play another day.

• Step five. All along the way, the company promotes adherence   25
to its transcendent values, those overarching purposes that rise way above the day-to-day imperative to make a buck. At the AT&T of yore, for example, the transcendent value was guaranteeing phone service to customers through any emergency. Identification with such a value enables the employee to accept the personal sacrifices the company asks of him.

Placing oneself at the service of an organization entails real costs.   26
There are long hours of work, weekends apart from one's family, bosses one has to endure, criticism that seems unfair, job assignments that are inconvenient or undesirable. The countervailing force making for commitment to the company in these circumstances is the organization's set of transcendent values that connect its purpose to human values of a higher order than just those of the marketplace—values such as serving mankind, providing a first-class product for society, or helping people learn and grow.

Someone going to work for Delta Air Lines will be told again   27
and again about the "Delta family feeling." Everything that's said makes the point that Delta's values sometimes require sacrifices— management takes pay cuts during lean times, senior flight attendants and pilots voluntarily work fewer hours per week so the company won't have to lay off more-junior employees. Candidates who accept employment with Delta tend to buy into this quid pro quo,[1] agreeing in effect that keeping the Delta family healthy justifies the sacrifices that the family exacts.

• Step six. The company constantly harps on watershed events   28
in the organization's history that reaffirm the importance of the firm's culture. Folklore reinforces a code of conduct—how we do things around here.

All companies have their stories, but at corporations that social-   29
ize well the morals of these stories all tend to point in the same direction. In the old Bell System, story after story extolled Bell employees who made heroic sacrifices to keep the phones working.

---

[1]Latin: "something for something"—an equal exchange.

The Bell folklore was so powerful that when natural disaster struck, all elements of a one-million-member organization were able to pull together, cut corners, violate normal procedures, even do things that would not look good when measured by usual job performance criteria—all in the interest of restoring phone service. Folklore, when well understood, can legitimize special channels for moving an organization in a hurry.

• Step seven. The company supplies promising individuals with role models. These models are consistent—each exemplary manager displays the same traits.

Nothing communicates more powerfully to younger professionals within an organization than the example of peers or superiors who are recognized as winners and who also share common qualities. The protégé watches the role model make presentations, handle conflict, and write memos, then tries to duplicate the traits that seem to work most effectively.

Strong-culture firms regard role models as constituting the most powerful long-term training program available. Because other elements of the culture are consistent, the people who emerge as role models are consistent. P&G's brand managers, for example, exhibit extraordinary consistency in several traits—they're almost all analytical, energetic, and adept at motivating others. Unfortunately most firms leave the emergence of role models to chance. Some of the fast track seem to be whizzes at analysis, others are skilled at leading people, others seem astute at politics: the result for those below is confusion as to what it *really* takes to succeed. For example, the companies that formerly made up the Bell System have a strong need to become more market oriented and aggressive. Yet the Bell culture continues to discriminate against potential fast-trackers who, judged by the values of the older monopoly culture, are too aggressive.

Many companies can point to certain organizational practices that look like one or two of the seven steps, but rarely are all seven managed in a well-coordinated effort. It is *consistency* across all seven steps of the socialization process that results in a strongly cohesive culture that endures.

When one understands the seven steps, one can better appreciate the case for socialization. All organizations require a degree of order and consistency. They can achieve this through explicit procedures and formal controls or through implicit social controls. American companies, on the whole, tend to rely more on formal controls. The result is that management often appears rigid, bureaucratic, and given to oversteering. A United Technologies executive laments, "I came from the Bell system. Compared with AT&T, this is a weak culture and there is little socialization. But of course there is still need for controls. So they put handcuffs on you, shackle you to every nickel, track every item of inventory, monitor every movement in production and head count. They control you by the balance sheet."

At most American companies, an inordinate amount of energy   35
gets used up in fighting "the system." But when an organization can come up with a strong, consistent set of implicit understandings, it has effectively established for itself a body of common law to supplement its formal rules. This enables it to use formal systems as they are supposed to be used—as tools rather than straitjackets. An IBM manager, conversant with the concept of socialization, puts it this way: "Socialization acts as a fine-tuning device; it helps us make sense out of the procedures and quantitative measures. Any number of times I've been faced with a situation where the right thing for the measurement system was X and the right thing for IBM was Y. I've always been counseled to tilt toward what was right for IBM in the long term and what was right for our people. They pay us a lot to do that. Formal controls, without coherent values and culture, are too crude a compass to steer by."

Organizations that socialize effectively use their cultures to   36
manage ambiguity, ever present in such tricky matters as business politics and personal relationships. This tends to free up time and energy. More goes toward getting the job done and focusing on external considerations like the competition and the customer. "At IBM you spend 50% of your time managing the internal context," states a former IBMer, now at ITT. "At most companies it's more like 75%." A marketing manager who worked at Atari before it got new management recalls: "You can't imagine how much time and energy around here went into politics. You had to determine who was on first base this month in order to figure out how to obtain what you needed to get the job done. There were no rules. There were no clear values. Two of the men at the top stood for diametrically opposite things. Your bosses were constantly changing. All this meant that you never had time to develop a routine way for getting things done at the interface between your job and the next guy's. Without rules for working with one another, a lot of people got hurt, got burned out, and were never taught the 'Atari way' of doing things because there wasn't an Atari way."

The absence of cultural guidelines makes organizational life ca-   37
pricious. This is so because success as a manager requires managing not only the substance of the business but also, increasingly,

managing one's role and relationships. When social roles are unclear, no one is speaking the same language; communication and trust break down. A person's power to get things done in a company seldom depends on his title and formal authority alone. In great measure it rests on his track record, reputation, knowledge, and network of relationships. In effect, the power to implement change and execute business strategies depends heavily on what might be called one's social currency—as in money—something a person accumulates over time. Strong-culture firms empower employees, helping them build this currency by supplying continuity and clarity.

Continuity and clarity also help reduce the anxiety people feel about their careers. Mixed signals about rewards, promotions, career paths, criteria for being on the "fast track" or a candidate for termination inevitably generate a lot of gossip, game playing, and unproductive expenditure of energy. Only the naive think that these matters can be entirely resolved by provisions in a policy manual. The reality is that many criteria of success for middle- and senior-level positions can't be articulated in writing. The rules tend to be communicated and enforced via relatively subtle cues. When the socialization process is weak, the cues tend to be poorly or inconsistently communicated. 38

Look carefully at career patterns in most companies. Ambitious professionals strive to learn the ropes, but there are as many "ropes" as there are individuals who have made their way to the top. So the aspirant picks an approach, and if it happens to coincide with how his superiors do things, he's on the fast track. Commonly, though, the approach that works with one superior is offensive to another. "As a younger manager, I was always taught to touch bases and solicit input before moving ahead," a manager at a Santa Clara, California, electronics firm says, "and it always worked. But at a higher level, with a different boss, my base-touching was equated with being political. The organization doesn't forewarn you when it changes signals. A lot of good people leave owing to misunderstandings of this kind." The human cost of the failure to socialize tends to go largely unrecognized. 39

What about the cost of conformity? A senior vice president of IBM asserts: "Conformity among IBM employees has often been described as stultifying in terms of dress, behavior, and lifestyle. There is, in fact, strong pressure to adhere to certain norms of superficial behavior, and much more intensely to the three tenets of the company philosophy—respect for the dignity of the individual, first-rate customer service, and excellence. These are the 40 benchmarks. Between them there is wide latitude for divergence in opinions and behavior."

A P&G executive echoes this thought: "There is a great deal of consistency around here in how certain things are done, and these are rather critical to our sustained success. Beyond that, there are very few hard and fast rules. People on the outside might portray our culture as imposing lock-step uniformity. It doesn't feel rigid when you're inside. It feels like it accommodates you. And best of all, you know the game you're in—you know whether you're playing soccer or football; you can find out very clearly what it takes to succeed and you can bank your career on that."

It is useful to distinguish here between norms that are central to the business's success and social conventions that signal commitment and belonging. The former are essential in that they ensure consistency in executing the company's strategy. The latter are the organizational equivalent of shaking hands. They are social conventions that make it easier for people to be comfortable with one another. One need not observe all of them, but one wants to reassure the organization that one is on the team. An important aspect of this second set of social values is that, like a handshake, they are usually not experienced as oppressive. Partly this is because adherence doesn't require much thought or deliberation, just as most people don't worry much about their individuality being compromised by the custom of shaking hands.

The aim of socialization is to establish a base of shared attitudes, habits, and values that foster cooperation, integrity, and communication. But without the natural rough-and-tumble friction between competing coworkers, some might argue, there will be little innovation. The record does not bear this out. Consider 3M or Bell Labs. Both are highly innovative institutions—and both remain so by fostering social rules that reward innovation. Socialization does not necessarily discourage competition between employees. Employees compete hard at IBM, P&G, major consulting firms, law firms, and outstanding financial institutions like Morgan Guaranty and Morgan Stanley.

There is, of course, the danger of strong-culture firms becoming incestuous and myopic—what came to be known in the early days of the Japanese auto invasion as the General Motors syndrome. Most opponents of socialization rally around this argument. But what one learns from observing the likes of IBM and P&G is that their cultures keep them constantly facing outward. Most companies like this tend to guard against the danger of complacency by having as one element of their culture an *obsession* with some facet of their performance in the marketplace. For example, McDonald's has an obsessive concern for quality control, IBM for customer service, 3M for innovation. These obsessions make for a lot of fire drills. But they also serve as the organizational equivalent of calisthenics, keeping people fit for the day when the emergency is real. When, on the other hand, the central cultural concern points inward rather than outward—as seems to be the case, say, with Delta Air Lines' focus on "family feeling"— the strong-culture company may be riding for a fall.

Revolutions begin with an assault on awareness. It is time to be more candid and clear-minded about socialization. Between our espoused individualism and the reality of most companies lies a zone where organizational and individual interests overlap. If we can manage our ambivalence about socialization, we can make our organizations more effective. Equally important, we can reduce the human costs that arise today as individuals stumble along in careers with companies that fail to articulate ends and means coherently and understandably for all employees. 45

Vocabulary

hawk (1)

norms (1)

paragons (1)

crux (5)

recruiter (8)

cadre (9)

substantiated (9)

prevailing (11)

vulnerability (14)

cohesiveness (14)

unprepossessing (15)

immersion (15)

disciplines (16)

comprehensive (20)

interlocking (22)

malefactor (23)

nebulous (23)

capriciously (24)

transcendent (25)

imperative (25)

yore (25)

countervailing (26)

watershed (28)

folklore (28)

legitimize (29)

protégé (31)

constituting (32)

astute (32)

monopoly (32)

explicit (34)

implicit (34)

inordinate (35)

conversant (35)

quantitative (35)

coherent (35)

ambiguity (36)

diametrically (36)

interface (36)

criteria (38)   divergence (40)
articulated (38)   deliberation (42)
aspirant (39)   incestuous (44)
stultifying (40)   myopic (44)
tenets (40)   complacency (44)
benchmarks (40)   espoused (45)
latitude (40)   ambivalence (45)

Critical Inquiries

1. What is "corporate culture"? Define the term in your own words. Do you agree with the author that corporate culture is important to having a successful business? Why or why not?

2. If a company to which you were applying for a position were to insist that you wear business suits to work, that you refrain from drinking any alcoholic beverage while doing company business, and that you join the local country club as a way of meeting the "right people" in town, would you be inclined to refuse the job based on your belief that such rules are an abridgement of your rights as an individual? Or would you accept the company's cultural code? Give reasons for your answer.

3. The author recognizes that the system used to fit new employees into the culture of large successful companies such as IBM is in conflict with traditional ideas about American independence. In your view, can one reconcile company culture with employee independence? Support your answer with appropriate examples from your own experiences or those of people you know.

4. What are the seven steps of socialization described by the author? Summarize each step in one sentence. Which of the steps do you consider the most important? Give reasons for your opinion.

5. Do you agree that role models constitute the most powerful long-term training program available? (See paragraphs 30–32.) Give an example of how someone in your past served as an effective role model.

Rhetorical Inquiries

1. How does the author make sure that his reader will understand what is meant by the term *culture* as used in this essay?

2. Pascale's essay centers on seven steps of a process. What is the purpose of the process? Where is this purpose stated? In what paragraph is the first step of the process introduced?

3. How does Pascale gather strength for his argument in favor of the process he describes? Do you agree with Pascal's view? Why or why not?

4. How is the reference to Delta Airlines different from that to IBM or Morgan Guaranty?

5. What is the purpose of Pascale's final paragraph? What is your response?

Exercises

1. In each of the following processes, cross out the steps that do *not* belong:
   a. How to find a mate:
   (1) Spend time in popular haunts.
   (2) There is an art to catching a mate.
   (3) Wear the right clothes.
   (4) Know what to say.
   (5) Know how to behave.
   (6) A hostile attitude will not help.
   Now write a well-developed paragraph explaining how a person should go about finding a mate.
   b. How crime artists sketch the face of a suspect:
   (1) All available witnesses are asked for descriptions.
   (2) Unreliable witnesses are excluded.
   (3) Young witnesses are the most reliable.
   (4) The artist focuses on descriptions of these features: face, hair, eyes, ears, mouth, and distinguishing features such as scars.
   (5) Witnesses are asked to identify mug shots that resemble the suspect.
   (6) Witnesses are questioned about the suspect's nationality.
   (7) The artist produces a sketch and gets the witness's reaction.
   (8) It is always helpful if the suspect resembles someone famous.
   Now write a paragraph explaining the process a crime artist uses to render the face of a suspect.
   c. How to improve your reading:
   (1) Most of us can read faster than we do.
   (2) Read actively instead of passively.
   (3) Avoid regressions, that is, re-reading the same passage over and over.
   (4) You avoid regressions by forcing yourself to read faster.
   (5) Don't mouth the words with your lips as you read.
   (6) Read in word groups rather than one word at a time.
   (7) Some materials can be read faster than others.
           $16*10n+5q$Now write a paragraph explaining how to read faster.
   Now write a paragraph explaining how to read faster.

2. Make a list of steps for improving some aspect of your life. Here are some possibilities:
   a. neatness
   b. grades in college
   c. relationship with others
   d. physical health
   e. looks
   f. personality

3. List in chronological order the steps you typically follow in reading the Sunday paper.

4. Pretend that you are dealing with a six-year-old child. Explain to this child exactly how to accomplish one of the following processes:
   a. how to peel an orange
   b. how to swim the breaststroke
   c. how to sharpen a pencil
   d. how to sweep the kitchen floor

Writing Assignments

1. In a well-developed paragraph of at least 150 words, explain one of the following processes, or choose one of your own. Be sure to break down the process into clear, separate steps. Do not leave out any step. Introduce the process with a clear purpose statement:
   a. how to study for a typical history exam
   b. how to make a milkshake
   c. how to lose weight and keep it off
   d. how to refuse a date without being rude or hurting anyone's ego
   e. how to set a formal table
   f. how to cook a meal while camping in the mountains
   g. how to balance a checkbook

2. Based on your reading of "The Spider and the Wasp," (pp. 333–38), write a 100-word summary of the process by which the wasp kills her victim and disposes of it. Delineate each step separately.

3. Using "Fitting New Employees into the Company Culture" (pp. 339–49) as background material, write a compact guide to the process of fitting a new employee into any company with which you are familiar. Break the process into clear, separate steps.

Chapter

12

Division and Classification

From shadows and types to the reality.

CARDINAL NEWMAN (1801–1890)

Division and classification is the rhetorical strategy of using a single predetermined principle to divide and separate a subject into its classes, types, or groups. Basically, all division and classification is based on logical thinking. You try to understand the constituent parts of a thing; you try to label and separate these parts into an ordered scheme. Behind this act of thinking is the strong impulse humans have towards organization, structure, and form. We simply understand things better when we know and understand the component parts that make them up. In both a scientific and everyday sense, classification is important to the way we think.

For example, it is nearly impossible to conceive of the biological sciences without its elaborate system of classification that pegs every living organism into a kingdom, class, order, family, genus, and species. Each of these larger categories contains many smaller types. Under the category of "class," are therefore to be found mammals, amphibians, insects, and arachnids. Under arachnids are found spiders, scorpions, mites, and ticks. This mazelike system of classification, which has struck many students as a pointless exercise designed to torment them, is a useful way of grouping living organisms by shared characteristics. It was primarily responsible for the theory of evolution, which was inferred to explain the observed similarities and differences between species.

The real aim of classification is to shield our thinking from the tyranny of uniqueness. We can imagine a time when primitive creatures must have thought every thunderstorm a singular catastrophe, every earthquake a fearfully unique event. But classification lessens our dread of these natural phenomena by enabling us to identify each individual outbreak as predictably part of a larger and known whole. Knowing the type or class to which an event belongs spares us the need to fear or futilely study every individual instance of it. If this were not so, a doctor would have to treat each case of the common cold as if it were absolutely unique. Every infection of polio would be utterly without precedent. Every thunderstorm would send us scurrying under the bed like children.

In our daily lives, informal classification similarly helps us grasp and relate to the people around us. We ask, "What type of person is he?" and the answer we give ourselves will determine whether we are trustful or suspicious, friendly or aloof. The disadvantage of this use of classification is that we sometimes hold false impressions about different types, which we unjustly use to snub or reject blameless individuals. Prejudice is classification that has gone bad. It is the wrong of unfairly smothering an individual under the blanket inaccuracies of a false type.

Dividing and Classifying

There are primarily two steps involved in writing by classification. First, you separate the whole subject into smaller parts. That is the act of *division.* For example, you might pen an essay dividing poetry into three main types: the epic, the dramatic, and the lyric. But if you were to end there, your essay would not only be frustratingly short, but it would also be curiously empty. What do you mean by an epic poem? What, by a dramatic poem? To be clear, you need to cite and discuss various poems as character- istic of your major types. That is the act of *classification.* So under *epic* you place Homer's *Iliad,* which you discuss as a specific example of the type. And under *dramatic,* you put Robert Browning's *My Last Duchess,* and also discuss it as representative of a typical dramatic poem. You do likewise with the category of lyric poetry. Now your reader understands your meaning, for you have divided the whole (poetry) into three parts (epic, dramatic, and lyric), and classified examples under each type.

That is exactly what the writers of the essays anthologized at the end of this chapter do. For example, in "Thinking as a Hobby," William Golding first divides thinking into three principal types—grade one, grade two, and grade three thinking—and then classifies examples under each type. Mr. Houghton, his old teacher, is classified as a grade-three thinker— someone who parrots vaguely conventional ideas but is untrue to them. Un- der grade-two thinking, which is mindlessly reactionary, the author classifies his own adolescent self and relates how he went about blithely destroying the religious beliefs of his friends without offering any consolation in return. Under grade-one thinking he classifies Albert Einstein—a thinker who does not merely react to the ideas of others but, instead, searches hard for his own truth.

To write such a division and classification essay from scratch, you would be smart to prethink your subject before plunging into the compos- ing. Division and classification is not like narration where the storytelling impulse might propel you through hesitation, setback, and doubt. Nor is it like description where you have a mental picture to guide your hand. Our advice, then, is to first find a principle for dividing your subject. For example, below are notes a student took in preparing a rough sketch of a classifying essay on personal computers. She decided to divide personal computers by the principle of physical size:

Dividing principle: types of personal computers based on physical size.

Categories: desktop computers, portable computers, laptop computers.

Second, find examples that belong under your generated categories, types, sorts, or kinds. Our student, for example, classified these examples under her different types of personal computers.

Desktop computers: IBM PC, XT, AT. Compaq. Zenith. IBM clones. IBM OS/2 systems.

Portable computers: NEC APCIV. Compaq I & II. NEC 386 SX.

Laptop computers: Toshiba 1000, FB 1200. Zenith Supersport. Datavue Spark. Compaq LST.

Writing the essay from this point on is simply a matter of filling in the types and examples with appropriate discussion.

As an essay strategy, division and classification is often an intellectual exercise and a way of helping us to better understand the abstract world. And there are some specific suggestions that we may give for helping you to do it well.

Base your classification on a single principle

If you say, "He is that kind of man," you must have some reason for saying so—whether the way he looks, the things he says, or the way he behaves. Classifying by more than one principle is a fundamental breach of logic that can lead to muddled thinking. For example, you may sort beans into two piles based on the classifying principle of whether or not they are edible by humans. If you then decided to also sort by the added principle of color, you could wind up with the right colored but poisonous bean in the edible pile and so kill some hapless diner.

Let us take a less lethal example of this basic error in classification. Your topic sentence promises to classify popular magazines by the kinds of topics they cover. First, you write, there are magazines like *People* that deal in gossip about famous people. Second, there are magazines like *Cosmopolitan* that stress high-powered lifestyles. Third, there are magazines like *Playboy* that appeal to the erotic appetites of their readers. Fourth, there are magazines like *Time* that report the news. Finally, you conclude, there are magazines like *Architectural Digest* that are subscribed to mainly by affluent suburbanites. This last entry is a poisoned bean and does not belong. Your jump from the principle of magazine topic to type of subscriber has broken the logic of the classification.

Note that the principle you use in a classification may not be as arbitrary as we may imply. Logic and common sense may sometimes suggest one principle over the other. For example, if you were asked to classify blocks identical in color, size, and weight but differing only in geometric shape, it is obvious which principle you should use. Similarly obvious principles will occur to you for various informal classifications. For example, if you were classifying the novels of a writer whose works fell into distinct periods, you would be wise to develop your essay by this obvious grouping rather than by some trivial principle.

Keep your categories from overlapping

The individual categories of a divided subject must be kept separate one from the other or they will overlap and your classification will be flawed. Notice the overlapping segments in this attempt to classify "higher education":

universities
four-year colleges
two-year colleges
postsecondary institutions

Obviously, the last category does not belong since the other three are contained within it. To keep each category separate, use transitions that indicate when you are moving from one category to the next: "The first kind is," "The second kind is," and so forth.

Divide the entire topic

Completeness in a division is a requirement of reasonableness and logic. If you were to divide all religions into polytheism (the belief in many gods), dualism (the belief in two gods, one good and the other evil), and monotheism (the belief in one transcendent god), you would be leaving out the important category of pantheism (the belief that the whole universe is god). More obviously, you would not divide a country into north, east, and south—leaving out west.

Whether or not a reader takes your division and classification seriously enough to expect completeness depends on the purpose and tone of your paragraph or essay. As we have said, much of the classification of the essayist is an informal exercise in thinking to which no reasonable reader would apply the exactness of science. For example, Russell Baker, the noted columnist, once wrote an essay classifying inanimate objects into those that don't work, those that break down, and those that get lost. Given the humorous aim of that essay, it would take a singularly dense reader to quibble with Baker for omitting the category of objects that do work. Some classifications are imaginative and cannot be taken literally.

Write approximately the same number of words on each entry

We would feel cheated by an essay that classifies soccer positions into backfield, midfield, and front line, and then spent five pages on the front line and a scant paragraph on the other two. Remember that a well-developed essay keeps the promise of its thesis. If you promise to classify and discuss, that is what you must do, giving equal time and ink to each individual part.

The essays at the end of this chapter faithfully follow these simple guidelines. They range from Golding's essay on kinds of thinking, to Lerner's essay on American types. One essay, by Lewis Thomas, classifies the sounds of nature; another, by Herrmann and Soiffer, classifies people who participate in garage sales. All exemplify the enlightment a well-done classifying essay can bring to a subject.

In the example that follows, a student classifies the techniques used to combat insomnia. While the draft is informative and clearly written, it has some major weaknesses. The margins contain editorial suggestions that were heeded in the revision.

Original:

There are three techniques commonly used in *What are the three techniques?* the battle against insomnia, which some experts *Introduce* say affects more than 30 million Americans every *them.* night. The first of these, medication, may seem to be the most effective, but actually is the

least and may cause the most harm. Doctors write
some 20 million sleep prescriptions each year
for various drugs, including dangerous
barbiturates. The problem with barbiturates like
Seconal and other drugs is that they interfere
with the natural dreaming rhythm of sleep and
can depress respiration. Drug therapy, agree the
experts, works over the short run, but is not
helpful over the long. With transcendental
meditation the insomniac is taught to breathe
deeply with movement of the diaphragm while
slowly reciting a single syllable word known as
a mantra. With self—hypnosis, the patient
visualizes scenes of serenity. These techniques
can help relax the insomniac and may even foster
sleep, but they require a disciplined mind and
may make the process of falling asleep into a
mental struggle rather than one of relaxation.
Adapting to the fact that you may be one of the
people who needs only four or five hours sleep a
night, say scientists, will stop the worry about
insomnia that sometimes aggravates or even
causes it.

[handwritten margin note: Transition needed to second technique if this is it.]

[handwritten margin note: Where is the third technique? Develop it adequately.]

Revision:

There are three techniques commonly used in
the battle against insomnia, which some experts
say affects more than 30 million Americans every
night. They are: medication, relaxation

techniques, and adaptation to one's true sleep
schedule. The first of these, medication, may
seem to be the most effective, but actually is
the least and may cause the most harm. Doctors
write some 20 million sleep prescriptions each
year for various drugs, including dangerous
barbiturates. The problem with barbiturates like
Seconal and other drugs is that they interfere
with the natural dreaming rhythm of sleep and
can depress respiration. Drug therapy, agree the
experts, works over the short run, but is not
helpful over the long haul. Relaxation
techniques comprise the second major weapon in
the fight against insomnia. With transcendental
meditation, for example, the insomniac is taught
to breathe deeply with movement of the diaphragm
while slowly reciting a single syllable word
known as a mantra. With self-hypnosis, the
patient visualizes scenes of serenity. These
techniques can help relax the insomniac and may
even foster sleep, but they require a
disciplined mind and may make the process of
falling asleep into a mental struggle rather
than one of relaxation. Finally, there is what
seems the least likely of all the techniques to
work: adapting to one's sleep schedule. But this
may just be the most effective of all. Experts
say that insomnia is an illusion that is often
grounded in a mistaken idea of how much sleep

one needs. Scientists estimate that one-half the
people who label themselves insomniacs fall
asleep just as fast and stay asleep as long as
normal sleepers. Many people also do not need
eight or even seven hours sleep, but do well on
only four or five. Adapting to the fact that you
may be one of the people who need only four or
five hours sleep a night, say scientists, will
stop the worry about insomnia that sometimes
aggravates or even causes it.

BIOGRAPHY

William Golding
THINKING AS A HOBBY

William Golding (b. 1911) is an English novelist whose highly imaginative and original works became internationally popular. Golding is basically concerned with the eternal nature of man. In his best-selling work, the allegorical Lord of the Flies *(1954), he describes the nightmarish and primitive adventure of a group of English schoolboys stranded on an island, tracing their degeneration from innocence to savagery. His other works include* The Inheritors *(1955),* Pincher Martin, Free Fall *(1959),* The Spire *(1964),* The Pyramid *(1967), and* The Scorpion God *(1971). Educated at Oxford University, Golding once described his hobbies as "thinking, classical Greek, sailing, and archeology." In 1983 he won the Nobel Prize for Literature.*

While I was still a boy, I came to the conclusion that there were 1
three grades of thinking; and since I was later to claim thinking as
my hobby, I came to an even stranger conclusion—namely, that I
myself could not think at all.

I must have been an unsatisfactory child for grownups to deal 2
with. I remember how incomprehensible they appeared to me at
first, but not, of course, how I appeared to them. It was the headmaster of my grammar school who first brought the subject of

From *Holiday Magazine,* Aug., 1961. Reprinted by permission of Curtis Brown, Ltd. Copyright © 1961 by William Golding.

thinking before me—though neither in the way, nor with the result he intended. He had some statuettes in his study. They stood on a high cupboard behind his desk. One was a lady wearing nothing but a bath towel. She seemed frozen in an eternal panic lest the bath towel slip down any farther, and since she had no arms, she was in an unfortunate position to pull the towel up again. Next to her, crouched the statuette of a leopard, ready to spring down at the top drawer of a filing cabinet labeled A–AH. My innocence interpreted this as the victim's last, despairing cry. Beyond the leopard was a naked, muscular gentleman, who sat, looking down, with his chin on his fist and his elbow on his knee. He seemed utterly miserable.

Some time later, I learned about these statuettes. The headmaster had placed them where they would face delinquent children, because they symbolized to him the whole of life. The naked lady was the Venus of Milo. She was Love. She was not worried about the towel. She was just busy being beautiful. The leopard was Nature, and he was being natural. The naked, muscular gentleman was not miserable. He was Rodin's Thinker, an image of pure thought. It is easy to buy small plaster models of what you think life is like. 3

I had better explain that I was a frequent visitor to the headmaster's study, because of the latest thing I had done or left undone. As we now say, I was not integrated. I was, if anything, disintegrated; and I was puzzled. Grownups never made sense. Whenever I found myself in a penal position before the headmaster's desk, with the statuettes glimmering whitely above him, I would sink my head, clasp my hands behind my back and writhe one shoe over the other. 4

The headmaster would look opaquely at me through flashing spectacles. "What are we going to do with you?" 5

Well, what *were* they going to do with me? I would writhe my shoe some more and stare down at the worn rug. 6

"Look up, boy! Can't you look up?" 7

Then I would look up at the cupboard, where the naked lady was frozen in her panic and the muscular gentleman contemplated the hindquarters of the leopard in endless gloom. I had nothing to say to the headmaster. His spectacles caught the light so that you could see nothing human behind them. There was no possibility of communication. 8

"Don't you ever think at all?" 9

No, I didn't think, wasn't thinking, couldn't think—I was simply waiting in anguish for the interview to stop. 10

"Then you'd better learn—hadn't you?"   11

On one occasion the headmaster leaped to his feet, reached up   12
and plonked Rodin's masterpiece on the desk before me.

"That's what a man looks like when he's really thinking."   13

I surveyed the gentleman without interest or comprehension.   14

"Go back to your class."   15

Clearly there was something missing in me. Nature had en-   16
dowed the rest of the human race with a sixth sense and left me
out. This must be so, I mused, on my way back to the class, since
whether I had broken a window, or failed to remember Boyle's
Law, or been late for school, my teachers produced me one, adult
answer: "Why can't you think?"

As I saw the case, I had broken the window because I had tried   17
to hit Jack Arney with a cricket ball and missed him; I could not
remember Boyle's Law because I had never bothered to learn it;
and I was late for school because I preferred looking over the
bridge into the river. In fact, I was wicked. Were my teachers, perhaps, so good that they could not understand the depths of my
depravity? Were they clear, untormented people who could direct
their every action by this mysterious business of thinking? The
whole thing was incomprehensible. In my earlier years, I found
even the statuette of the Thinker confusing. I did not believe any
of my teachers were naked, ever. Like someone born deaf, but bit-
terly determined to find out about sound, I watched my teachers
to find out about thought.

There was Mr. Houghton. He was always telling me to think.   18
With a modest satisfaction, he would tell me that he had thought a
bit himself. Then why did he spend so much time drinking? Or
was there more sense in drinking than there appeared to be? But if
not, and if drinking were in fact ruinous to health—and Mr.
Houghton was ruined, there was no doubt about that—why was
he always talking about the clean life and the virtues of fresh air?
He would spread his arms wide with the action of man who habitually spent his time striding along mountain ridges.

"Open air does me good, boys—I know it!"   19

Sometimes, exalted by his own oratory, he would leap from his   20
desk and hustle us outside into a hideous wind.

"Now, boys! Deep breaths! Feel it right down inside you—huge   21
draughts of God's good air!"

He would stand before us, rejoicing in his perfect health, an   22
open-air man. He would put his hands on his waist and take a tremendous breath. You could hear the wind, trapped in the cavern
of his chest and struggling with all the unnatural impediments. His

body would reel with shock and his ruined face go white at the unaccustomed visitation. He would stagger back to his desk and collapse there, useless for the rest of the morning.

Mr. Houghton was given to high-minded monologues about the good life, sexless and full of duty. Yet in the middle of one of these monologues, if a girl passed the window, tapping along on her neat little feet, he would interrupt his discourse, his neck would turn of itself and he would watch her out of sight. In this instance, he seemed to me ruled not by thought but by an invisible and irresistible spring in his nape.   23

His neck was an object of great interest to me. Normally it bulged a bit over his collar. But Mr. Houghton had fought in the First World War alongside both Americans and French, and had come—by who knows what illogic?—to a settled detestation of both countries. If either country happened to be prominent in current affairs, no argument could make Mr. Houghton think well of it. He would bang the desk, his neck would bulge still further and go red "You can say what you like," he would cry, "but I've thought about this—and I know what I think!"   24

Mr. Houghton thought with his neck.   25

There was Miss Parsons. She assured us that her dearest wish was our welfare, but I knew even then, with the mysterious clairvoyance of childhood, that what she wanted most was the husband she never got. There was Mr. Hands—and so on.   26

I have dealt at length with my teachers because this was my introduction to the nature of what is commonly called thought. Through them I discovered that thought is often full of unconscious prejudice, ignorance and hypocrisy. It will lecture on disinterested purity while its neck is being remorselessly twisted toward a skirt. Technically, it is about as proficient as most businessmen's golf, as honest as most politicians' intentions, or—to come near my own preoccupation—as coherent as most books that get written. It is what I came to call grade-three thinking, though more properly, it is feeling, rather than thought.   27

True, often there is a kind of innocence in prejudices, but in those days I viewed grade-three thinking with an intolerant contempt and an incautious mockery. I delighted to confront a pious lady who hated the Germans with the proposition that we should love our enemies. She taught me a great truth in dealing with grade-three thinkers; because of her, I no longer dismiss lightly a mental process which for nine-tenths of the population is the nearest they will ever get to thought. They have immense solidarity. We had better respect them, for we are outnumbered and surrounded. A crowd of grade-three thinkers, all shouting the same   28 thing, all warming their hands at the fire of their own prejudices, will not thank you for pointing out the contradictions in their beliefs. Man is a gregarious animal, and enjoys agreement as cows will graze all the same way on the side of a hill.

Grade-two thinking is the detection of contradictions. I reached grade two when I trapped the poor, pious lady. Grade-two thinkers do not stampede easily, though often they fall into the other fault and lag behind. Grade-two thinking is a withdrawal, with eyes and ears open. It became my hobby and brought satisfaction and loneliness in either hand. For grade-two thinking destroys without having the power to create. It set me watching the crowds cheering His Majesty the King and asking myself what all the fuss was about, without giving me anything positive to put in the place of that heady patriotism. But there were compensations. To hear people justify their habit of hunting foxes and tearing them to pieces by claiming that the foxes like it. To hear our Prime Minister talk about the great benefit we conferred on India by jailing people like Pandit Nehru and Gandhi. To hear American politicians talk about peace in one sentence and refuse to join the League of Nations in the next. Yes, there were moments of delight. 29

But I was growing toward adolescence and had to admit that Mr. Houghton was not the only one with an irresistible spring in his neck. I, too, felt the compulsive hand of nature and began to find that pointing out contradiction could be costly as well as fun. There was Ruth, for example, a serious and attractive girl. I was an atheist at the time. Grade-two thinking is a menace to religion and knocks down sects like skittles. I put myself in a position to be converted by her with an hypocrisy worthy of grade three. She was a Methodist—or at least, her parents were, and Ruth had to follow suit. But, alas, instead of relying on the Holy Spirit to convert me, Ruth was foolish enough to open her pretty mouth in argument. She claimed that the Bible (King James Version) was literally inspired. I countered by saying that the Catholics believed in the literal inspiration of Saint Jerome's *Vulgate,* and the two books were different. Argument flagged. 30

At last she remarked that there were an awful lot of Methodists, and they couldn't be wrong, could they—not all those millions? That was too easy, said I restively (for the nearer you were to Ruth, the nicer she was to be near to) since there were more Roman Catholics than Methodists anyway; and they couldn't be wrong, could they—not all those hundreds of millions? An awful flicker of doubt appeared in her eyes. I slid my arm round her waist and murmured breathlessly that if we were counting heads, the Buddhists were the boys for my money. But Ruth had *really* 31 wanted to do me good, because I was so nice. She fled. The combination of my arm and those countless Buddhists was too much for her.

That night her father visited my father and left, red-cheeked and indignant. I was given the third degree to find out what had happened. It was lucky we were both of us only fourteen. I lost Ruth and gained an undeserved reputation as a potential libertine.

So grade-two thinking could be dangerous. It was in this knowledge, at the age of fifteen, that I remember making a comment from the heights of grade two, on the limitations of grade three. One evening I found myself alone in the school hall, preparing it for a party. The door of the headmaster's study was open. I went in. The headmaster had ceased to thump Rodin's Thinker down on the desk as an example to the young. Perhaps he had not found any more candidates, but the statuettes were still there, glimmering and gathering dust on top of the cupboard. I stood on a chair and rearranged them. I stood Venus in her bath towel on the filing cabinet, so that now the top drawer caught its breath in a gasp of sexy excitement. "A-ah!" The portentous Thinker I placed on the edge of the cupboard so that he looked down at the bath towel and waited for it to slip.

Grade-two thinking, though it filled life with fun and excitement, did not make for content. To find out the deficiencies of our elders bolsters the young ego but does not make for personal security. I found that grade two was not only the power to point out contradictions. It took the swimmer some distance from the shore and left him there, out of his depth. I decided that Pontius Pilate was a typical grade-two thinker. "What is truth?" he said, a very common grade-two thought, but one that is used always as the end of an argument instead of the beginning. There is a still higher grade of thought which says, "What is truth?" and sets out to find it.

But these grade-one thinkers were few and far between. They did not visit my grammar school in the flesh though they were there in books. I aspired to them, partly because I was ambitious and partly because I now saw my hobby as an unsatisfactory thing if it went no further. If you set out to climb a mountain, however high you climb, you have failed if you cannot reach the top.

I *did* meet an undeniably grade-one thinker in my first year at Oxford. I was looking over a small bridge in Magdalen Deer Park, and a tiny mustached and hatted figure came and stood by my side. He was a German who had just fled from the Nazis to Oxford as a temporary refuge. His name was Einstein.

32

33

34

35

36

But Professor Einstein knew no English at that time and I knew 37
only two words of German. I beamed at him, trying wordlessly to
convey by my bearing all the affection and respect that the English
felt for him. It is possible—and I have to make the admission—
that I felt here were two grade-one thinkers standing side by side;
yet I doubt if my face conveyed more than a formless awe. I
would have given my Greek and Latin and French and a good slice
of my English for enough German to communicate. But we were
divided; he was as inscrutable as my headmaster. For perhaps five
minutes we stood together on the bridge, undeniable grade-one
thinker and breathless aspirant. With true greatness, Professor Einstein realized that any contact was better than none. He pointed to
a trout wavering in midstream.

He spoke: "Fisch." 38

My brain reeled. Here I was, mingling with the great, and yet 39
helpless as the veriest grade-three thinker. Desperately I sought for
some sign by which I might convey that I, too, revered pure reason. I nodded vehemently. In a brilliant flash I used up half of my
German vocabulary. *"Fisch. Ja. Ja."*

For perhaps another five minutes we stood side by side. Then 40
Professor Einstein, his whole figure still conveying good will and
amiability, drifted away out of sight.

I, too, would be a grade-one thinker. I was irreverent at the best 41
of times. Political and religious systems, social customs, loyalties
and traditions, they all came tumbling down like so many rotten
apples off a tree. This was a fine hobby and a sensible substitute
for cricket, since you could play it all the year round. I came up in
the end with what must always remain the justification for grade-
one thinking, its sign, seal and charter. I devised a coherent system
for living. It was a moral system, which was wholly logical. Of
course, as I readily admitted, conversion of the world to my way
of thinking might be difficult, since my system did away with a
number of trifles, such as big business, centralized government,
armies, marriage . . .

It was Ruth all over again. I had some very good friends who 42
stood by me, and still do. But my acquaintances vanished, taking
the girls with them. Young women seemed oddly contented with
the world as it was. They valued the meaningless ceremony with
a ring. Young men, while willing to concede the chaining sordid-
ness of marriage, were hesitant about abandoning the organizations which they hoped would give them a career. A young man
on the first rung of the Royal Navy, while perfectly agreeable to
doing away with big business and marriage, got as red-necked as

Mr. Houghton when I proposed a world without any battleships in it.

Had the game gone too far? Was it a game any longer? In those prewar days, I stood to lose a great deal, for the sake of a hobby.   43

Now you are expecting me to describe how I saw the folly of my ways and came back to the warm nest, where prejudices are so often called loyalties, where pointless actions are hallowed into custom by repetition, where we are content to say we think when all we do is feel.   44

But you would be wrong. I dropped my hobby and turned professional.   45

If I were to go back to the headmaster's study and find the dusty statuettes still there, I would arrange them differently. I would dust Venus and put her aside, for I have come to love her and know her for the fair thing she is. But I would put the Thinker, sunk in his desperate thought, where there were shadows before him—and at his back, I would put the leopard, crouched and ready to spring.   46

Vocabulary

incomprehensible (2)

statuettes (2)

integrated (4)

penal (4)

opaquely (5)

ruinous (18)

draughts (21)

impediments (22)

monologues (23)

detestation (24)

clairvoyance (26)

disinterested (27)

proficient (27)

proposition (28)

solidarity (28)

skittles (30)

flagged (30)

restively (31)

libertine (32)

inscrutable (37)

veriest (39)

revered (39)

amiability (40)

coherent (41)

Critical Inquiries

1. What are the three categories into which Golding divides all thinking? Explain each. Is there a value judgment involved in this classification?

2. How are the descriptions of the author's grade-school teachers related to the purpose of the essay?

3. Would you like to live in world in which everyone were a grade-one thinker? Why or why not?

4. Why is it so difficult to find grade-one thinkers? Describe someone, from past or present society, whom you consider a grade-one thinker.

5. What, if anything, is important about grade-two thinking?

Rhetorical Inquiries

1. From what point of view is much of the essay written? How is this point of view achieved? Refer to specific passages.

2. Paragraphs 24, 25, and 27 repeatedly use the word *neck*. What does the word mean in these contexts?

3. What analogy does Golding use (see paragraph 28) to explain grade-three thinking? How effective is the analogy?

4. What purpose do the allusions to Nehru, Gandhi, and to certain politicians' refusal to join the League of Nations serve?

5. How effective is the author's conclusion? Explain your view.

SOCIOLOGY

Max Lerner
SOME AMERICAN TYPES

Max Lerner (b. 1902, Minsk, Russia) is an author and lecturer. He was educated at Yale and Washington University in St. Louis. In 1927 he received a Ph.D. from the Robert Brookings Graduate School of Economics and Government. His works include Ideas Are Weapons *(1939) and* America As a Civilization *(1957), from which the excerpt below is reprinted. As the title indicates, this essay comments on our society not by describing individual Americans but by classifying them according to general types.*

Seventeenth-century England produced a number of books on   1
Characters depicting English society through the typical personality patterns of the era. Trying something of the same sort for contemporary America, the first fact one encounters is the slighter emphasis on a number of character types than stand out elsewhere in Western society: to be sure, they are to be found in America as

From *America as a Civilization,* by Max Lerner. Copyright © 1957, 1985 by Max Lerner. Reprinted by permission of Simon & Schuster, Inc.

well, but they are not characteristically American. One thinks of
the scholar, the aesthete, the priest or "parson," the "aristocratic"
Army officer, the revolutionary student, the civil servant, the male
schoolteacher, the marriage broker, the courtesan, the mystic, the
saint. Anyone familiar with European literature will recognize
these characters as stock literary types and therefore as social
types. Each of them represents a point of convergence for character
and society. Anyone familiar with American literature will know
that it contains stock portraits of its own which express social
types. I want to use these traditional types as backdrops and stress
some of the social roles that are new and still in process of formation.

Thus there is the *fixer,* who seems an organic product of a soci-   2
ety in which the middleman function eats away the productive
one. He may be public-relations man or influence peddler; he may
get your traffic fine settled, or he may be able—whatever the com-
modity—to "get it for you wholesale." He is contemptuous of
those who take the formal rules seriously; he knows how to cut
corners—financial, political, administrative, or moral. At best there
is something of the iconoclast in him, an unfooled quality far removed from the European personality types that always obey authority. At worst he becomes what the English call a "spiv" or cultural procurer.

Related to the fixer is the *inside dopester,* as Riesman has termed   3
him. He is oriented not so much toward getting things fixed as toward being "in the know" and "wised up" about things that inno-
cents take at face value. He is not disillusioned because he has
never allowed himself the luxury of illusions. In the 1920s and
1930s he consumed the literature of "debunking"; in the current era
he knows everything that takes place in the financial centers of
Wall Street, the political centers of Capitol Hill, and the communications centers of Madison Avenue—yet among all the things he
knows there is little he believes in. His skepticism is not the wisdom which deflates pretentiousness but that of the rejecting man
who knows ahead of time that there is "nothing in it" whatever
the "it" may be. In short, he is "hep."

Another link leads to the *neutral* man. He expresses the devalu-   4
ing tendency in a culture that tries to avoid commitments. Fearful
of being caught in the crosscurrents of conflict that may endanger
his safety or status, he has a horror of what he calls "controversial
figures"—and anyone becomes "controversial" if he is attacked. As
the fixer and the inside dopester are the products of a middleman's
society, so the neutral man is the product of a technological one.
The technician's detachment from everything except effective re-

sults becomes—in the realm of character—an ethical vacuum that strips the results of much of their meaning.

From the neutral man to the *conformist* is a short step. Although he is not neutral—in fact, he may be militantly partisan—his partisanship is on the side of the big battalions. He lives in terror of being caught in a minority where his insecurity will be conspicuous. He gains a sense of stature by joining the dominant group, as he gains security by making himself indistinguishable from that group. Anxious to efface any unique traits of his own, he exacts conformity from others. He fears ideas whose newness means they are not yet accepted, but once they are firmly established he fights for them with a courage born of the knowledge that there is no danger in championing them. He hates foreigners and immigrants. When he talks of the "American way," he sees a world in which other cultures have become replicas of his own.

It is often hard to distinguish the conformist from the *routineer.* Essentially he is a man in uniform, sometimes literally, always symbolically. The big public-service corporations—railroads, air lines, public utilities—require their employees to wear uniforms that will imprint a common image of the enterprise as a whole. City employees, such as policemen and firemen, wear uniforms. Gas-station attendants, hotel clerks, bellhops, must similarly keep their appearance within prescribed limits. Even the sales force in big department stores or the typists and stenographers in big corporations tend toward the same uniformity. There are very few young Americans who are likely to escape the uniform of the Armed Services. With the uniform goes an urge toward pride of status and a routineering habit of mind. There is the confidence that comes of belonging to a large organization and sharing symbolically in its bigness and power. There is a sense of security in having grooves with which to move. This is true on every level of corporate business enterprise, from the white-collar employee to "the man in the gray flannel suit," although it stops short of the top executives who create the uniforms instead of wearing them. Even outside the government and corporate bureaus there are signs of American life becoming bureaucratized, in a stress on forms and routines, on "going through channels."

Unlike the conformist or routineer, the *status seeker* may possess a resourceful energy and even originality, but he directs these qualities toward gaining status. What he wants is a secure niche in a society whose men are constantly being pulled upward or trodden down. Scott Fitzgerald has portrayed a heartbreaking case history of this character type in *The Great Gatsby,* whose charm and energy are invested fruitlessly in an effort to achieve social position.

The novels of J. P. Marquand are embroideries of a similar theme, narrated through the mind of one who already has status and is confronted by the risk of losing it. At various social levels the status seeker becomes a "joiner" of associations which give him symbolic standing.

Vocabulary

aesthete (1)

courtesan (1)

mystic (1)

convergence (1)

organic (2)

contemptuous (2)

iconoclast (2)

procurer (2)

pretentiousness (3)

hep (3)

devaluing (4)

militantly (5)

battalions (5)

replicas (5)

niche (7)

Critical Inquiries

1. How many types of Americans does Lerner describe? Which, if any, important type has he left out?

2. What is Lerner's real purpose in listing and describing certain American types? Is he simply being informative and entertaining, or might he have another purpose?

3. Which type do you admire most? Which least? Give reasons for your answer.

4. What personal dealings have you had with any of the types described by Lerner? What lesson, if any, did you gain from your experience?

5. Which of Lerner's types best describes the following people: a. The Nazis of World War II b. The political lobbyists of Washington, D.C. c. Women who buy designer label clothes or cosmetics?

Rhetorical Inquiries

1. How does Lerner maintain the organization and coherence of his essay?

2. How does Lerner clarify the difference between conformist and routineer?

3. Which of Lerner's types do you consider most effectively described? Give reasons for your answer.

4. What audience is likely to understand Lerner's allusion to *The Great Gatsby* and to J. P. Marquand's novels? Are you among this audience?

5. With which of the European stock literary characters mentioned in paragraph 1 are you familiar? Can you name a novel, play, or poem containing one of these characters?

BIOLOGY

Lewis Thomas
THE MUSIC OF THIS SPHERE

Lewis Thomas (b. 1917, New York) is a physician and scientist who is presently serving as president of the Memorial Sloan-Kettering Cancer Center in New York. He has written numerous essays on scientific subjects, and these have won him popularity and praise for a lucid, charming style. His essays have been published in three widely read collections: The Lives of a Cell *(1974, National Book Award),* The Medusa and the Snail *(1979), and* Late Night Thoughts On Listening to Mahler's Ninth Symphony *(1983). The essay below, reprinted from* Lives of a Cell, *reveals clearly why Dr. Thomas's observations can be appreciated by scientist and layperson alike.*

It is one of our problems that as we become crowded together, the sounds we make to each other, in our increasingly complex communication systems, become more random-sounding, accidental or incidental, and we have trouble selecting meaningful signals out of the noise. One reason is, of course, that we do not seem able to restrict our communication to information-bearing, relevant signals. Given any new technology for transmitting information, we seem bound to use it for great quantities of small talk. We are only saved by music from being overwhelmed by nonsense.

It is a marginal comfort to know that the relatively new science of bioacoustics must deal with similar problems in the sounds made by other animals to each other. No matter what sound-making device is placed at their disposal, creatures in general do a great deal of gabbling, and it requires long patience and observation to edit out the parts lacking syntax and sense. Light social conversation, designed to keep the party going, prevails. Nature abhors a long silence.

Somewhere, underlying all the other signals, is a continual music. Termites make percussive sounds to each other by beating their heads against the floor in the dark, resonating corridors of their nests. The sound has been described as resembling, to the hu-

From *The Lives of a Cell,* by Lewis Thomas. Copyright © 1974 by Lewis Thomas. All rights reserved. Reprinted by permission of Viking Penguin, a division of Penguin Books USA, Inc.

man ear, sand falling on paper, but spectrographic analysis of sound records has recently revealed a high degree of organization in the drumming; the beats occur in regular, rhythmic phrases, differing in duration, like notes for a tympani section.

From time to time, certain termites make a convulsive movement of their mandibles to produce a loud, high-pitched clicking sound, audible ten meters off. So much effort goes into this one note that it must have urgent meaning, at least to the sender. He cannot make it without such a wrench that he is flung one or two centimeters into the air by the recoil.

There is obvious hazard in trying to assign a particular meaning to this special kind of sound, and problems like this exist throughout the field of bioacoustics. One can imagine a woolly-minded Visitor from Outer Space, interested in human beings, discerning on his spectrograph the click of that golf ball on the surface of the moon, and trying to account for it as a call of warning (unlikely), a signal of mating (out of the question), or an announcement of territory (could be).

Bats are obliged to make sounds almost ceaselessly, to sense, by sonar, all the objects in their surroundings. They can spot with accuracy, on the wing, small insects, and they will home onto things they like with infallibility and speed. With such a system for the equivalent of glancing around, they must live in a world of ultrasonic batsound, most of it with an industrial, machinery sound. Still, they communicate with each other as well, by clicks and high-pitched greetings. Moreover, they have been heard to produce, while hanging at rest upside down in the depths of woods, strange, solitary, and lovely bell-like notes.

Almost anything that an animal can employ to make a sound is put to use. Drumming, created by beating the feet, is used by prairie hens, rabbits, and mice; the head is banged by woodpeckers and certain other birds; the males of deathwatch beetles make a rapid ticking sound by percussion of a protuberance on the abdomen against the ground; a faint but audible ticking is made by the tiny beetle *Lepinotus inquilinus,* which is less than two millimeters in length. Fish make sounds by clicking their teeth, blowing air, and drumming with special muscles against tuned inflated air bladders. Solid structures are set to vibrating by toothed bows in crustaceans and insects. The proboscis of the death's-head hawk moth is used as a kind of reed instrument, blown through to make high-pitched, reedy notes.

Gorillas beat their chests for certain kinds of discourse. Animals with loose skeletons rattle them, or, like rattlesnakes, get sounds from externally placed structures. Turtles, alligators, crocodiles, and even snakes make various more or less vocal sounds. Leeches have been heard to tap rhythmically on leaves, engaging the attention of other leeches, which tap back, in synchrony. Even earthworms make sounds, faint staccato notes in regular clusters. Toads sing to each other, and their friends sing back in antiphony.

Birdsong has been so much analyzed for its content of business 9
communication that there seems little time left for music, but it is there. Behind the glossaries of warning calls, alarms, mating messages, pronouncements of territory, calls for recruitment, and demands for dispersal, there is redundant, elegant sound that is unaccountable as part of the working day. The thrush in my backyard sings down his nose in meditative, liquid runs of melody, over and over again, and I have the strongest impression that he does this for his own pleasure. Some of the time he seems to be practicing, like a virtuoso in his apartment. He starts a run, reaches a midpoint in the second bar where there should be a set of complex harmonics, stops, and goes back to begin over, dissatisfied. Sometimes he changes his notation so conspicuously that he seems to be improvising sets of variations. It is a meditative, questioning kind of music, and I cannot believe that he is simply saying, "thrush here."

The robin sings flexible songs, containing a variety of motifs that 10
he rearranges to his liking; the notes in each motif constitute the syntax, and the possibilities of variation produce a considerable repertoire. The meadow lark, with three hundred notes to work with, arranges these in phrases of three to six notes and elaborates fifty types of song. The nightingale has twenty-four basic songs, but gains wild variety by varying the internal arrangement of phrases and the length of pauses. The chaffinch listens to other chaffinches, and incorporates into his memory snatches of their songs.

The need to make music, and to listen to it, is universally expressed 11
by human beings. I cannot imagine, even in our most primitive times, the emergence of talented painters to make cave paintings without there having been, near at hand, equally creative people making song. It is, like speech, a dominant aspect of human biology.

The individual parts played by other instrumentalists—crickets 12
or earthworms, for instance—may not have the sound of music by themselves, but we hear them out of context. If we could listen to them all at once, fully orchestrated, in their immense ensemble, we might become aware of the counterpoint, the balance of tones and timbres and harmonics, the sonorities. The recorded songs of

the humpback whale, filled with tensions and resolutions, ambiguities and allusions, incomplete, can be listened to as a *part* of music, like an isolated section of an orchestra. If we had better hearing, and could discern the descants of sea birds, the rhythmic tympani of schools of mollusks, or even the distant harmonics of midges hanging over meadows in the sun, the combined sound might lift us off our feet.

There are, of course, other ways to account for the songs of whales. They might be simple, down-to-earth statements about navigation, or sources of krill, or limits of territory. But the proof is not in, and until it is shown that these long, convoluted, insistent melodies, repeated by different singers with ornamentations of their own, are the means of sending through several hundred miles of undersea such ordinary information as "whale here," I shall believe otherwise. Now and again, in the intervals between songs, the whales have been seen to breach, leaping clear out of the sea and landing on their backs, awash in the turbulence of their beating flippers. Perhaps they are pleased by the way the piece went, or perhaps it is celebration at hearing one's own song returning after circumnavigation; whatever, it has the look of jubilation.   13

I suppose that my extraterrestrial Visitor might puzzle over my records in much the same way, on first listening. The 14th Quartet might, for him, be a communication announcing, "Beethoven here," answered, after passage through an undersea of time and submerged currents of human thought, by another long signal a century later, "Bartok[1] here."   14

If, as I believe, the urge to make a kind of music is as much a characteristic of biology as our other fundamental functions, there ought to be an explanation for it. Having none at hand, I am free to make one up. The rhythmic sounds might be the recapitulation of something else—an earliest memory, a score for the transformation of inanimate, random matter in chaos into the improbable, ordered dance of living forms. Morowitz has presented the case, in thermodynamic terms, for the hypothesis that a steady flow of energy from the inexhaustible source of the sun to the unfillable sink of outer space, by way of the earth, is mathematically destined to cause the organization of matter into an increasingly ordered state. The resulting balancing act involves a ceaseless clustering of bonded atoms into molecules of higher and higher complexity, and the emergence of cycles for the storage and release of energy. In a   15

---

[1]Bela Bartok (1881–1945), a Hungarian composer.

nonequilibrium steady state, which is postulated, the solar energy would not just flow to the earth and radiate away; it is thermodynamically inevitable that it must rearrange matter into symmetry, away from probability, against entropy, lifting it, so to speak, into a constantly changing condition of rearrangement and molecular ornamentation. In such a system, the outcome is a chancy kind of order, always on the verge of descending into chaos, held taut against probability by the unremitting, constant surge of energy from the sun.

If there were to be sounds to represent this process, they would have the arrangement of the Brandenburg Concertos[2] for my ear, but I am open to wonder whether the same events are recalled by the rhythms of insects, the long, pulsing runs of birdsong, the descants of whales, the modulated vibrations of a million locusts in migration, the tympani of gorilla breasts, termite heads, drumfish bladders. A "grand canonical ensemble" is, oddly enough, the proper term for a quantitative model system in thermodynamics, borrowed from music by way of mathematics. Borrowed back again, provided with notation, it would do for what I have in mind.

Vocabulary

incidental (1)

bioacoustics (2)

gabbling (2)

syntax (2)

percussive (3)

resonating (3)

spectrographic (3)

tympani (3)

mandibles (4)

audible (4)

recoil (4)

sonar (6)

infallibility (6)

ultrasonic (6)

solitary (6)

protuberance (7)

crustaceans (7)

proboscis (7)

reed (7)

discourse (8)

synchrony (8)

antiphony (8)

glossaries (9)

recruitment (9)

dispersal (9)

redundant (9)

meditative (9)

virtuoso (9)

---

[2]By Johann Sebastian Bach, recognized as the greatest concertos ever composed.

harmonics (9)
improvising (9)
flexible (10)
motifs (10)
repertoire (10)
instrumentalists (12)
orchestrated (12)
ensemble (12)
counterpoint (12)
timbres (12)
sonorities (12)
ambiguities (12)
allusions (12)
descants (12)
krill (13)
convoluted (13)
breach (13)
awash (13)

turbulence (13)
circumnavigation (13)
jubilation (13)
extraterrestrial (14)
recapitulation (15)
transformation (15)
inanimate (15)
chaos (15)
thermodynamic (15)
hypothesis (15)
nonequilibrium (15)
postulated (15)
entropy (15)
ornamentation (15)
taut (15)
canonical (16)
quantitative (16)
notation (16)

Critical Inquiries

1. Lewis Thomas has adapted the title of his essay from the medieval theological belief that God is in charge of a cosmic musical instrument made up of the stars and planets. His divine hand plays the strings to produce cosmic balance and harmony through the "music of the spheres"—always heard in heaven and sometimes heard on earth. How does Thomas's essay relate to this medieval notion?

2. What evidence does Thomas present for his theory of "grand canonical ensemble" as presented in the final paragraph of the essay? Is the evidence convincing to you? Why or why not?

3. Of all the types of sounds described in the essay, which to you seem most like traditional music? What importance do these sounds have in your life?

4. According to Thomas, why do human beings not hear the combined music of nature as a concert played by individual instrumentalists? Do you agree with Thomas's view? Why or why not?

5. How do you explain Thomas's final sentence: "Borrowed back again, provided with notation, it would do for what I have in mind"?

Rhetorical Inquiries

1. How strictly does Thomas follow the rules of classification in this essay about nature's sounds? Where is the classification explicitly stated?

2. How does the author bring his classification to life?

3. How many sounds are identified in paragraph 7? What are they?

4. In paragraph 5, Thomas alludes to a visitor from outerspace. In what paragraph is the allusion picked up again? For what purpose?

5. Perusing the vocabulary list following the essay, what do the following words have in common: percussive, tympani, synchrony, antiphony, virtuoso, harmonics, motifs, repertoire, instrumentalists, orchestrated, ensemble, counterpoint, timbres, descants? How are these words related to Thomas's main point?

MARKETING

Gretchen M. Herrman and Stephen M. Soiffer
THE GREAT AMERICAN GARAGE SALE

Gretchen M. Herrman (b. 1948, Buffalo, N.Y.) is Associate Librarian at the State University of New York, in Courtland, New York. For some time, she and co-author, Stephen Soiffer, have made serious inquiry into the unique phenomenon of American garage sales as big business. They have published articles on this subject in the Sociological Review *(1987) and in* Urban Life *(1988), from which the essay below is reprinted.*
Stephen M. Soiffer (b. 1948, New York City, N.Y.) is Director of the Office of Enrollment Management Systems at the University of Rochester in New York.

OVER SIX MILLION GARAGE SALES are held annually throughout the United States, generating nearly one billion dollars in revenues. Perhaps because of the very ubiquity of the event, there has been virtually no serious scholarly work on garage sales. The present article is a small contribution to filling this gap in our understanding of popular culture. . . .

The garage sale arises from American prosperity, from the ability of families to constantly replace domestic items. Yet, the rapid expansion of the garage sale is linked to long-term decline in the spending power of most of the American populace. . . . Thus, the

From "For Fun and Profit: An Analysis of the American Garage Sale," originally published in *Urban Life,* vol. 12, issue 4. Reprinted by permission of the authors.

garage sale occupies the contradictory symbolic space between the culture of consumerism and the necessity of devising strategies for survival in an age of diminishing expectations. . . . Garage sales represent a truly creative cultural response to the extended economic and social crises of life in advanced industrial society. . . .

Garage sales are a part of the vast, undifferentiated category called the "underground economy." That is, garage sale revenues are not recorded in any official economic indicators, hence are not reflected in measures such as the Gross National Product. However, since garage sales are not illegal in and of themselves, and since few garage sales are subject to or evade income tax, it makes no sense to lump them with such activities as drug-dealing or skimming of business profits. . . . The garage sale is part of a subcategory we call the "informal economy." . . . It includes arenas in which a cash nexus prevails, but where other principles offset, or at least modify, a pure businesslike motivation. The garage sale, then, is a part of an important but rarely discussed portion of the underground economy. . . .

We define garage sales as sales in or on the property of a private residence in which are offered a range of items at prices below their retail cost; the sales appear to run for only a few days, although some may in fact be quasi-permanent; the majority of the items for sale are used; the sales are open for people to drop in at their leisure without an appointment. . . . As long as they fit the above-stated criteria, garage sales may carry a wide variety of names: garage sales, lawn sales, porch sales, barn sales, moving sales, house sales, multifamily sales, rummage sales when these are *not* organizational sales, and many others. . . .

We interviewed the proprietors of 45 garage sales in the greater Cortland, New York, area, speaking to 59 people (since there is often more than one proprietor of a multifamily sale), and collected questionnaires from 125 shoppers. . . . On the basis of interviews, newspaper ads, magazine and newspaper articles, discussion with others, and personal experiences, we developed typologies of garage sale proprietors and shoppers. . . .

It is a fairly safe assumption that garage sales grew out of rummage sales by charitable organizations. As part of the affluence of the 1960s, people eventually amassed enough personal goods to hold private sales. . . . The general trend has been from the sale of a small number of large, expensive items to the sale of many smaller and less expensive items. From 1965 through 1981, there was a steady increase in the number of garage sales, but the real "take off" of the event occurred in the early 1970s when magazines and Sunday supplements ran numerous articles on how to hold garage sales "for fun and profit," essentially legitimizing for middle-class Americans the sale of their castoff goods. By the end of the decade, the legitimation and institutionalization of garage sales was firmly established, as indicated by periodicals dubbing them "as American as apple pie and baseball." . . .

Forms of Garage Sale Participation

Our research has led us to construct the following typologies of garage sale proprietors and shoppers. They are not discrete categories, but rather descriptions of principal styles of and motives for participation. The typologies are listed in Figures 40.1 and 40.2. . . . Both typologies present participants in an approximate rank order by the importance of monetary considerations in their garage sale involvement. . . .

Garage Sale Proprietors

(1) Perpetual Sales: The proprietors of these sales are for all practical purposes running retail outlets off-the-books. They are usually open for business during good weather, whether or not they are actively advertising. Selling and buying for resale may well be the single largest economically productive activity in which these individuals engage. Thus, it is understandable that sellers in this category are the most reticent to discuss their proceeds. Proprietors in this category can be divided into two groups:

(a) Semi-Retailers: Proprietors in this group often buy and sell at flea markets, auctions, estate sales and at other garage sales. They are always on the lookout for commercial transactions. One of our first interviews was with an older man, retired from construction work. As he was mechanically competent and had time on his hands, friends began to bring him small appliances, clocks, radios, and so forth to fix. On occasion, he accepted merchandise in place of payment. Over time, through investment and visits to garage sales and flea markets, he accumulated a substantial stock of items. In fact, his garage held an array of them, including considerable duplication of appliances such as irons, toasters, and clock radios.

He quickly learned the benefits of holding garage sales. Since a cranky neighbor checks to see if he is respecting the local garage sale ordinance, he cannot advertise more than four days per

Figure 40.1
Garage Sale Proprietors

1. Perpetual Sales
   a. Semi-Retailers
   b. Rural Vendors
2. Desperate Straits
3. Entrepreneurs
4. Veterans
5. Retired People
6. Struggling Young Folk
7. Movers
8. Event Sales
9. Group Sales
10. Housecleaners
    a. Spring Housecleaners
    b. Life Passage Sellers
    c. Regulars
11. Dabblers

month. However, he said, customers know that he is there and will come shopping when they need an item, whether he is officially "open for business" or not. He has broadened his trade to include flea markets, having recently invested in expensive display cases designed specifically to fit his flea marketeer's van.

(b) Rural Vendors: This describes a much simpler and less profit-   11 able form of sale. Sellers often advertise with no more than signs on the side of the road and depend on passing traffic to produce their clientele. Sales are seasonal, from midspring to late fall. Rather than the carefully arranged and merchandised displays

Figure 40.2
Garage Sale Shoppers

1. Retailers
2. Child-Item Shoppers
3. Habituals
4. Economic Transition Shoppers
5. Specific-Needs Shoppers
6. Movers
7. Collectors
8. Bargain-Hunters, Browsers, Bored
9. Social Buyers
10. Obligees

common to the previous category, here one might expect to see junk in a pile on the side of the road, or in a cart. Culturally these sellers might even be called "American peasants," constructing a marginal existence out of a multistranded labor arrangement including truck and barter, and perhaps even sharecropping. . . .

(2) Desperate Straits: These are people who are in desperate   12
need of money because of difficulties such as loss of a job, illness, or pressing bills. Unlike some Perpetual Sellers, they have very little market resistance. That is, as they must satisfy some immediate need, they have no choice but to take what they can get for the merchandise being offered. One example was a couple selling a wide array of goods, including tools and small appliances. Although their initial assertion was that this sale was merely "spring housecleaning," they later revealed that the husband was out of work and that they were beginning to feel the squeeze. With the proceeds of the garage sale, they intended to visit relatives in Pennsylvania, in part to look for employment. Status honor and shame will probably lead sellers in this category to conceal their motives.

(3) Entrepreneurs: The primary motive of the Entrepreneur is   13
profit. He or she is not desperately in need of the money and is quite aware of the value of the goods being offered. Thus, the Entrepreneur has considerable market resistance. In addition, he/she is constantly on the lookout for underpriced and resalable goods. Although not as voracious as dealers, the Darth Vaders[1] of the garage sale set, Entrepreneurs might well frequent other garage sales looking for items they can resell for a profit. For example, we encountered one young fellow using garage sales to sell the dross from his used goods store. . . .

(4) Veterans: Veterans are people who have been holding garage   14
sales for a considerable period of time, at least four or five years. They probably have at least one sale per year, and may have as many as three. Veterans have built up a reputation, and generally hold large, well-stocked sales of "quality" items. People who frequent garage sales recognize those of Veterans, and sometimes call to inquire when they will be held. These sellers may well have built up an infrastructure for their sales, e.g., shelves, tables and display areas they store specifically for their garage sales. Although their approach to profit is lackadaisical when compared to that of Entrepreneurs or Perpetual Sellers, they are acutely aware of the

---

[1]Popular science fiction character, who played a leading role in the movie *Star Wars*. He represents evil.

pricing system of garage sales. Thus, they will be much less likely to sell an item for considerably below its garage sale value than would be a more casual seller. If the item has some significant value, the Veteran can simply save it for his/her next sale. . . .

(5) Retired People: These are people who definitely have more   15
time than money. There is a great range in motivation. Some retirees may blend into the Perpetual Seller category, especially when the revenue represents a small but necessary supplement to a fixed income. Others will deemphasize the economic motivation, using their garage sale participation as a way to minimize the social isolation of retirement. Most retirees probably combine these two motivations. . . .

(6) Struggling Young Folk: At least one member of such house-   16
holds has more time than can be successfully converted into salary, i.e., is unemployed or underemployed. In most cases, this will be the woman. Her flexible schedule will facilitate her garage sale participation. Most families in this category have young children. Expenses of childrearing may well provide the immediate motivation. In case of the housewife-proprietor, the garage sale also performs an important ideological function. It valorizes her social role comparable to that of the wage-earner. Not coincidentally, many housewives in this category see garage sale participation—as both buyer and seller—as a way to fight domestic boredom. One young woman, wife of an underpaid factory worker and mother of two small children, has a garage sale every year. She sells, among other things, clothing her children have outgrown. With the money she makes, she will shop at garage sales for another year's children's clothing. Without her garage sale participation, children's expenses would put a severe strain on the family's budget.

(7) Movers: This is a diverse category, including students, trailer   17
people, suburbanites, and all sorts of transients. But it also includes people who have found this a profitable way of handling moves, and members of this category may be drawn from all social strata. Both the escalating cost of moving goods from one region to another and the rapid spread of garage sales make this an acceptable way to dispose of household items. Just as in the case of the Struggling Young Folk, garage sale proceeds may well be important to ease financial strain. However, since selling an item for any price at all is better than being obliged to move it, maximizing of income on any particular item is less important than selling the item. Thus, a direct profit motivation is much less pronounced than in the first three categories described above.

(8) Event Sales: This . . . category is easier to recognize than to describe. They are dramatic events, characterized either by some theme, by prominent person(s) involved or by some well-known building. . . . For example, in Ithaca, New York, an ad appeared referring readers to the "1883 barn in Newfield." . . . 18

(9) Group Sales: These may be either a neighborhood grouping, friends, or relatives. In general, these sales include sharing of setup work and of expenses involved in advertising. People share other resources, such as transportation, and divide the labor on the day of the sale. In most cases, group sales will develop a spirit of the group, making the benefits of group participation nearly as important as individual profits. . . . For example, most of the houses on one circular street in Cortland decided to have sales on the same day. One large advertisement was paid for collectively. Children went around distributing yellow ribbons to be displayed on the mailboxes of participating houses. A great deal of attention went into cleaning up the neighborhood, furthering the collective sentiments. One participant said that the sale left an atmosphere of neighborly good feelings that had not previously been there. 19

(10) Housecleaning: The largest single category of sellers are those we call "Housecleaners." They assert, not without justification, that disposing of unwanted items is the most important reason for them to have the sale. . . . Profits are at least counterbalanced by the need to create domestic space, pleasure that others will get utility from their used goods, the enjoyment of the sale itself, and a generally ill-defined notion that it is better for goods to be recycled than discarded. . . . There are three distinct types of Housecleaners: 20

(a) Spring Housecleaners: They are the families, quite possibly with growing children, who realize from time to time that they need to create space, perhaps to store their own garage sale purchases. 21

(b) Life-Passage Sellers: These are individuals who are disposing of items to mark a particular life passage, such as the maturing of their youngest children, a divorce, or a death in the family. This will often mean disposing of major items: bicycles, tools, major appliances. Although some such sales will produce a significant revenue, the central motive of the seller is putting a distinct phase of life behind him- or herself. 22

(c) Regulars: These are people who will clean house via garage sales every few years. Although their orientation to profit is no different from others in this category, they have internalized the notion that they will regularly dispose of unneeded domestic items in 23 this way. Potential sale items will be set aside specifically for that purpose, perhaps in a separate garage sale box. . . .

(11) Dabblers: These are people trying out the garage sale experience for the first time. They have decided to sell unwanted items in a garage sale because others on their block have done it, because they think it will be fun, or because they are taken with the idea that they will make some money by selling items they would otherwise have given to a charity or discarded. They tend to emphasize the social aspect of the sale, to enjoy the contacts it creates. There is no guarantee that Dabblers will enjoy the experience. If they do, they will probably have other sales and move toward other categories. If they do not, they will have an interesting story to tell friends about the weekend they allowed total strangers into their homes.

Garage Sale Shoppers

(1) Retailers: This category includes people making purchases for used-goods stores, perpetual garage salers, and flea marketeers. These people are buying specifically to resell. They show up early and know exactly what they are looking for. They are often disliked by our informants, because it is assumed that they will try to cheat garage sale proprietors. Some sellers even feel harassed by dealers, because they often arrive early at the house of the sale, sometimes days in advance. Some proprietors have mentioned that dealers make it more difficult and costly for deserving shoppers to obtain what they need.

(2) Child-Item Shoppers: These shoppers are satisfying essentially short-term needs through garage sales because of high commercial prices, the rapidity with which children outgrow items, and, quite possibly, economic necessity. One such shopper, from a household with a severely strained domestic budget, was quite concerned with how she would make ends meet after her children passed the age range within which she could easily clothe them at garage sales.

(3) Habituals: These are people who usually purchase at garage sales some significant portion of the commodities they need. Garage sale shopping may represent for them a survival strategy, a cultural style, a quasi-ideological rejection of consumerism, an assumption that older items are of superior quality to what is currently sold, or, most likely, some combination of these attributes.

(4) Economic Transition Shoppers: Often, these are people who are trying to maintain a standard of living beyond what their in-

comes permit. It might well include young people not as yet on the economic level of their parents. They often do their garage sale shopping by labels, looking for things that are "respectable." These may well be the shoppers most conscious of the status of the neighborhood in which the garage sale is held, as they are looking for "quality" items.

(5) Specific-Needs Shoppers: People who are shocked at the prices of Volkswagen bumpers, throw rugs, and other consumer goods may acquire the habit of looking for them at garage sales. This category would also include people who are constantly on the lookout for certain types of items, such as bicycle parts, for which they have an ongoing need. 29

(6) Movers: This category will include both students and others. They could be shopping for a wide range of items to reestablish a household, or for just a very few items. They may well have sold their household items at a garage sale before their move. 30

(7) Collectors: These people are looking for currently popular "collectables," such as Avon jars and bottles, Jim Beam decanters, depression glass, 78 RPM records, Nancy Drew books, or baseball cards. Sometimes these shoppers may be looking for a particular pattern of china, perhaps for a relative or friend. 31

(8) Bargain-Hunters, Browsers, and the Bored: Some few of these people may be semiprofessional, but their primary motivation is entertainment. Bargain hunters are amused with the idea of garage sale prices, rather than actively pursuing purchases. This category will include a large number of retired people, and both men and women with middle-class income levels. One retired schoolteacher told us of her fascination with garage sales. However, she had only begun to shop at them since her retirement, as she now has "time to kill." 32

(9) Social Buyers: These are shoppers who go to sales as a way of socializing with friends and others. This category also includes a large number of retired people. Shoppers in this category will pride themselves on their garage sale expertise because it establishes their social position in the garage sale set. 33

(10) Obligees: These are neighbors, relatives, and friends of people conducting sales. The category is composed of people who for one or another reason are "obliged" to make an appearance, and probably make at least some minimal purchase. In some cases, the sale provides welcome opportunity to socialize with the seller. 34

It must be stressed that these typologies do not define mutually exclusive categories. Group Sales and Housecleaners, for example, frequently overlap. Similar blendings of categories can be seen in 35 other instances, but it is generally possible to identify a single category as most descriptive of each sale. . . . This overlapping nature of some of the categories touches on a major difficulty in analyzing garage sales: They are complex phenomena. They are multifaceted events, blending practical housecleaning and fanciful treasure hunts, community recreation and individual profiteering. It is almost impossible to posit anything about garage sales to which exceptions cannot be found. Consequently, we are forced to speak of garage sales as an ideal-type, in the Weberian[1] sense. That is, we refer to a stylized model of the garage sale, one that captures all characteristics associated with the phenomenon. . . .

Conclusion: The Rise of Garage Sales and the Decline of Expectations

Economists often describe the reduction of real disposable income of most working-class and middle-class Americans since the late 1960s. But, this reduction can be seen in more than statistics. . . . It is also reflected in the widespread mood of shrinking expectations, the common realization that the American Dream has gone awry. The mood is vividly expressed in the following, from a New York housewife, "Something's got to give. The whole bottom is going to fall out soon, and I'm afraid it'll fall on us." . . .   36

In polls people admit to a fear that the future will be less certain and less prosperous than the present. Fears about the environment, about energy costs, about the solvency of the Social Security System, about impending unemployment and social disaster lead people to look for ways to lessen their dependency on the economic system. . . .   37

It is our contention that acute vulnerability obliges people to develop "Survival Strategies," methods to satisfy their socially defined needs in ways that expend as little as possible of their discretionary funds. Survival strategies include a wide range of actions: exchanging goods and services (babysitting, for example) with kin, friends, and neighbors; performing for themselves a range of services (such as lawn care or auto repair) they would previously have paid for; playing fast and loose with consumer credit; learning a wide range of crafts that provide utilitarian and high-status consumption items at relatively low cost (macramé, pottery, home improvement); cultivating vegetable gardens. . . ;   38

---

[1]Max Weber (1864–1920), a German social scientist who devised the concept of "ideal types" as a basis for comparing societies.

satisfying portions of their consumption needs outside of the
formal sector (food-buying cooperatives, purchase of goods and
services off the books; and—most important for our
purposes—shopping at garage sales, auctions, and flea markets).
As economic crisis becomes deeper and more generalized, an
increasing range of Americans, from every higher economic
strata, are induced to develop or to borrow survival
strategies. . . .

As one would expect of informal economic activities in this so-   39
ciety, garage sales combine contradictory elements. They blend the
harsh economic rationalization of the business world with the generalized reciprocity of the world of good neighbors. In the garage
sale, each of these tendencies tempers the other.

Vocabulary

ubiquity (1)	voracious (13)
consumerism (2)	dross (13)
undifferentiated (3)	infrastructure (14)
nexus (3)	deemphasize (15)
quasi-permanent (4)	ideological (16)
typologies (5)	valorizes (16)
legitimizing (6)	transients (17)
institutionalization (6)	strata (17)
clientele (11)	escalating (17)
marginal (11)	internalized (22)
sharecropping (11)	informants (24)
entrepreneur (13)	posit (34)
	discretionary (37)

Critical Inquiries

1. As suggested by the authors, what paradox attends the reasons for the
   success of garage sales? What other reasons might be given?

2. What is your opinion of the value in garage sales? Do you approve of
   them? Why or why not?

3. How valid do you consider the authors' study? Is it based on personal
   experience, or do the authors take a scientific approach? Support your answer with specific evidence from the text.

4. In the category of proprietors, do you consider all members legitimate, or would you delete any member? Support your answer with reasons.

5. Of the several threats suggested in paragraph 36, which do you consider the most dangerous? What survival strategies can you suggest to lessen the danger?

Rhetorical Inquiries

1. How does the rhetorical strategy used help to achieve the purpose of the essay?

2. In the opening paragraph the authors assert that no serious scholarly work has been pursued on garage sales. Do you consider this essay a serious scholarly work? Why or why not?

3. What does paragraph 34 contribute to the essay? What would happen if the paragraph were deleted?

4. What meaning does the title of the essay connote? Is the essay related to the title?

5. By what means do the authors make the classification easy to follow?

Exercises

1. List the natural groups into which the following topics can be divided:
   a. geological eras
   b. government
   c. fanaticism
   d. letters
   e. sins

2. Name the major category to which the following items belong. Delete any inappropriate term in each group; then write a paragraph discussing them in the groups to which they naturally belong.
   a. metaphor, simile, semicolon, apostrophe, personification, allusion
   b. dog, wolf, coyote, leopard, fox
   c. centaur, unicorn, Medusa, dinosaur, minotaur, Cerberus
   d. Elijah, Tiresias, Cassandra, Isaiah, Hannibal
   e. incisors, files, canines, premolars, molars

3. Divide the contents of your local newspaper into logical major headings. Be sure that your principle of division is clear.

4. Think of some notorious criminals in history, and place them in separate categories based on a single principle of division. List at least two criminals in each category.

Writing Assignments

1. Using "Some American Types" as your model, write a 500-word essay entitled "Some College Types," in which you classify the kinds of students you have observed on campus. You may be serious or satirical, whichever suits your purpose best.

2. Study "The Great American Garage Sale" (pp. 379–89); then, write an essay in which you either praise or discredit garage sales. Provide specific reasons for your attitude.

3. Using a single principle of division, write a 500-word essay in which you classify one of the subjects listed below. Your classification should have a purpose and make a point.
   Example thesis for *c:* "Regardless of whether they are fought to expand a territorial border, to recapture lost lands, or to exact revenge, all wars are barbaric."
   a. professions
   b. politicians
   c. wars
   d. house pets
   e. television serials
   f. computer software

4. Turn the following model into an essay developed by classification. Only the skeleton of the model is provided. If necessary, go to the library and find your own details. Some reorganization of the listed details may also be necessary:
   Thesis: India's caste system divides the population into four distinct types.
   The *Brahmans* are the priests and scholars.
   The *Kshatrias* are the warriors and rulers.
   The *Vaisyas* are the farmers and merchants.
   The *Sudras* are the peasants and laborers.
   Each of these castes has its own rules and traditions and is hierarchically organized. The lifestyles of the upper-class castes differ markedly from those of the lower class. The Brahmans live in luxury whereas the Sudras often suffer in terrible poverty.

Chapter

13

Comparing and Contrasting

Have ideas that are clear, and expressions that are simple.

MME. DE CHARRIERE (1740–1805)

The paragraph or essay developed by comparison/contrast (often the word "comparison" is used to mean both) focuses on finding likenesses and unlikenesses between two people, ideas, objects, events, or items. For writers of expository prose, this is a routine assignment, and many essays begun with an entirely different purpose will be found to have at least one paragraph developed by comparison/contrast. For instance, let us assume that you are writing an essay for a political science class on the importance of free speech. Your thesis statement is "Argumentation is a fundamental aspect of any healthy society." But since you want to make it clear that arguing is not the same as quarreling, you decide to write a paragraph drawing a contrast between them. You begin your paragraph with the following topic sentence: "Arguing must never be confused with quarreling since the former is wholesome for society whereas the latter is pernicious." So far so good, but how to proceed from here?

Declare the Bases of Your Comparison

Every comparison or contrast has an implicit basis. For example, if you say that so-and-so is more handsome than what's-his-name, the basis of that comparison is physical looks. If you declare that Mr. Moneybags has more money than Mr. Skinflint, your comparison is based on wealth. Before you can write a paragraph or essay comparing or contrasting any two items, you must have in mind the bases against which you intend to successively match them up. In the case of quarreling versus arguing, you might construct the following bases:

1. the reasoning involved
2. the mood created
3. the aims to be achieved

You will then show how arguing and quarreling differ in reasoning, mood, and aims.

In selecting the bases for comparing or contrasting, you should always choose those likely to reveal significant, not trivial, likenesses and differences. For example, if you are writing an essay contrasting jogging with tennis as forms of exercise, you might profitably cover their differing health benefits, risks, and expenses. But it would be trivial to focus your contrast on such secondary and inconsequential differences as which sport offers more exposure to fresh air or which is more fashionable in your hometown.

393

As with other writing strategies, it is usually helpful to lead off a paragraph or essay developed by comparison/contrast with a straightforward declaration of your purpose. Here, for example, a writer plainly tells us in a paragraph that she is going to compare reading with television viewing on the basis of differing pace.

> A comparison between reading and viewing may be made in respect to the pace of each experience, and the relative control a person has over that pace, for the pace may influence the ways one uses the material received in each experience. In addition, the pace of each experience may determine how much it intrudes upon other aspects of one's life.
> —Reading and Television, Marie Winn

But you do not have to be that blunt about your purpose. It is enough to merely hint at it so the reader knows where you are going. Here, for example, is a paragraph in which the writer's contrasting purpose is amply implied, though not directly stated.

> Our pace of life has quickened so that women's features now reflect the frenzied, insecure age in which they live. Women's eyes used to be wistful. Today few possess serene eyes; they do not mind creases in their brows and often wear a frown on their foreheads. Young girls are proud of their high cheekbones and a flat hollow in their cheeks, whereas fifty years ago cheeks were fully rounded. Latterly the rather prehensile mouths have replaced the rosebud of yesterday. Whereas make-up was used only by *cocottes* in the Victorian and Edwardian heydays (ladies used to slap their cheeks and bite their lips before entering a ballroom to obtain a higher colour), any woman without lipstick today appears anaemic. Hair dyeing has become so general that it is not kept a guarded secret. Eyebrows, instead of being arched or wearing the old-fashioned startled look or the look of pained surprise, are slightly raised towards the outer edges, even acquiring a mongolian look. After twenty years of eyebrow plucking, eyebrows do not grow as thickly as they did.
> —"Women's Features in an Insecure Age," Cecil Beaton

By the time we have read a sentence or two we understand that the writer is comparing how women look today with how they used to look.

Complete the Comparison by Dealing with Both Sides

There are two sides to every comparison/contrast, and an honest essay or paragraph will cover both equally. However, a common weakness of some comparison/contrasts is the tendency to magnify on the differences of one side while ignoring those on the other. To avoid this lopsidedness, use the topics to be compared/contrasted as headings for separate columns, the bases as headings for separate rows, and then simply list the supporting facts under the appropriate row and column. Here is an example:

	Arguing	*Quarreling*
1. reasoning:	rational	emotional
	factual	embellished
	fair	biased
	consistent	contradictory
2. mood:	calm	turbulent
	reasonable	angry
	objective	subjective
	mature	childish
3. aims:	discover truth	win points
	knowledge	status
	opponent's respect	opponent's defeat

This chart is a visual outline showing exactly what you must cover in the paragraph. Follow it and you are bound to give equal billing to each topic.

Here is a student-written paragraph that covers all the points in the above list. Notice the back and forth movement between arguing and quarreling, making for a fair and evenhanded treatment of both sides:

Compared in reasoning, mood, and aims,
arguing and quarreling are significantly
different modes of discourse. Arguing can be
<u>rational</u> and <u>factual</u>, with arguers exchanging
points in a <u>fair</u> and <u>consistent</u> give-and-take.
Quarreling, on the other hand, is usually
dominated by <u>emotional</u> dialogue and <u>embellished</u>

claims. The quarreler is typically <u>biased</u> and
<u>contradictory</u>, seeing only the right of his
position while ignoring the equally just claims
of his opponent. In mood, arguers are often
<u>calm</u> and <u>reasonable</u>. Yes, arguments can be
occasionally heated, but the prevailing mood can
still be <u>objective</u> and <u>mature</u>. In contrast, the
usual mood during quarreling is <u>turbulent</u> and
<u>angry</u>, with participants frequently becoming
<u>subjective</u> and <u>childish</u>. A key difference is
that arguers are generally trying, however
indirectly, to <u>discover</u> <u>truth</u> and expand
<u>knowledge</u>. Frequently, they earn and return
their <u>opponent's</u> <u>respect</u>. Quarrelers, however,
are just the opposite. Their intent is to <u>win</u>
<u>points</u> from whatever makeshift audience is
present, to achieve <u>status</u> at the expense of the
other, and to revel in their <u>opponent's</u> <u>defeat</u>.

Use Appropriate Transitions to Stress either Likeness or Difference

Transitions, as we saw previously, are an important element in
paragraph coherence. But in a paragraph that strictly compares or contrasts,
they are often crucial. Here is a passage from a comparison/contrast draft
that uses no transitions:

Arguing and quarreling differ sharply in
the type of reasoning each uses. An argument is
based on the rational presentation of ideas.
The one arguing presents the facts without

distorting or exaggerating them beyond
recognition. Throughout the argument, he
remains fair and maintains a consistent
attitude, much the way a good sport calls fair
line shots when playing tennis. A quarrel is an
emotional bombast in which the two sides ignore
facts and fairness. The quarreler loads down
all statements with emotion and embellishes the
truth to the point where it cannot be
recognized. Argument is the calm presentation
of the debater's facts. Quarreling typically
screams out only biased or contradictory
information.

Without transitions, the back and forth movement of the contrast is too abrupt. Notice the writer's transitions:

Arguing and quarreling differ sharply in
the type of reasoning each uses. ~~An~~ *Whereas an* argument is
based on ~~the~~ rational ~~presentation of ideas~~ *behavior buttressed by factual evidence, a quarrel is an emotional bombast in which the two sides ignore facts and fairness.*
In an argument, the arguer ~~The one arguing~~ presents the facts without
distorting or exaggerating them beyond
recognition. ~~Throughout the argument, he~~
He remains fair and maintains a consistent
attitude, much the way a good sport calls fair
line shots when playing tennis. ~~A quarrel is an~~
~~emotional bombast in which the two sides ignore~~
~~facts and fairness.~~ *Typically, the* ~~The~~ quarreler loads down
all statements with emotion and embellishes the
truth to the point where it cannot be

recognized. *While* Argument *involves* ~~is~~ the calm presentation
of the debater's facts/, Quarreling typically
screams out only biased or contradictory
information.

Here is the rewritten paragraph, appropriately edited:

Arguing and quarreling differ sharply in
the type of reasoning each uses. <u>Whereas</u> an
argument is based on rational behavior,
buttressed by factual evidence, a quarrel is
emotional bombast in which the two sides ignore
facts and fairness. <u>In an argument,</u> the arguer
presents the facts without distorting or
exaggerating them beyond recognition. He
remains fair and maintains a consistent
attitude, much the way a good sport will fairly
call line shots when playing tennis. <u>No such</u>
<u>fairness, however, is to be found in most</u>
<u>quarrels. Typically,</u> the quarreler loads down
all statements with emotion and embellishes the
truth to the point where it cannot be
recognized. <u>While argument involves the calm</u>
<u>presentation of the debater's facts,</u> quarreling
typically screams out only biases or
contradictory information.

For a listing of transitions useful for comparison/contrasts, turn to pages
140-41.

Organize Your Comparisons either within or between Paragraphs

A comparison may be organized either within or between paragraphs, depending mainly on the length and emphasis of the essay. If you are writing an essay based on a complex and extended comparison, you may wish to successively write about the compared items in separate paragraphs. On the other hand, for shorter and less emphatic comparisons, a single paragraph whose sentences are linked by appropriately strong transitions will do. Here is an example of self-respect and respectability compared within a single paragraph.

```
        Self-respect and respectability are not to

be confused.  To have self-respect means to like

yourself, to be comfortable about your values

and the way you practice them in your life.  It

is entirely an inner judgment you make of

yourself, which no one else can make of you.

Respectability, on the other hand, is a judgment

others make of you.  The person with

respectability is one who, in the eyes of

others, adheres to conventional and accepted

values.  For example, the man with

respectability will most likely be a churchgoer,

a family man, someone who does not drink, does

not go out at night, and is not mean to the

family pet.  The woman with respectability may

be regarded as a good mother, a faithful wife,

or a conscientious career woman.  It is

possible, however, to have respectability but

not self-respect.  For example, the man

considered respectable may belittle himself for
```

sticking to a job he does not like. The
respectable woman may despise herself for
staying with a husband she no longer loves. Of
the two judgments, self-respect is the
psychologically healthier.

Here is a similar comparison by the same student organized over three paragraphs.

Self-respect and respectability are not to
be confused. To have self-respect means to like
yourself, to be comfortable about your values
and the way you practice them in your life. It
is entirely an inner judgment you make of
yourself, which no one else can make of you.
The person with self-respect thinks he is
basically good and worthwhile and has made this
judgment of himself by his own values and not by
the values of the world.

Respectability, on the other hand, is a
judgment others make of you. The person with
respectability is one who, in the eyes of
others, adheres to conventional and accepted
values. For example, the man with
respectability will most likely be a churchgoer,
a family man, someone who does not drink, does
not go out at night, and is not mean to the
family pet. The woman with respectability may
be regarded as a good mother, a faithful wife,
or a conscientious and ambitious worker.

However, it is possible to have
respectability but not self-respect. For
example, the man considered respectable may
belittle himself for sticking to a job he does
not like. The respectable woman may despise
herself for staying with a husband she no longer
loves. It is also possible to have self-respect
but no respectability. For example, the
conscientious objector who is sent to prison for
that stand is robbed of respectability by his
opposition, but not of his self-respect. If he
had gone to fight in a war he regarded as wrong,
the world might confer "respectability" upon
him, but it would be at the cost of his
self-respect.

Which of the two organizing patterns should you use? That depends on the emphasis of your essay and the complexity of your comparison. As a general observation, complex and lengthy comparisons work better between paragraphs; shorter comparisons, on the other hand, work better within a paragraph. No hard and fast rule exists, however, nor can one be given to cover every possible assignment in which writers might use comparison. Whichever pattern you do use, be sure to link your successive points of similarity or difference with strong and effective transition words and phrases. Some common examples of these words and phrases are listed below:

FOR COMPARING	FOR CONTRASTING
similarly	whereas
likewise	in contrast to
a likeness between	on the other hand
may be compared to	unlike
is likened to	while
also	instead of
much in common	however
both	

And here is an example of a classic comparison/contrast paragraph that specifically explores first the differences and then the similarities between two subjects while effectively using transition words and phrases.

> Lenin, with whom I had a long conversation in Moscow in 1920, was, superficially, very unlike Gladstone, and yet, allowing for the difference of time and place and creed, the two men had much in common. To begin with the differences: Lenin was cruel, which Gladstone was not; Lenin had no respect for tradition, whereas Gladstone had a great deal; Lenin considered all means legitimate for securing the victory of his party, whereas for Gladstone politics was a game with certain rules that must be observed. All these differences, to my mind, are to the advantage of Gladstone, and accordingly Gladstone on the whole had beneficent effects, while Lenin's effects were disastrous. In spite of all these dissimilarities, however, the points of resemblance were quite as profound. Lenin supposed himself to be an atheist, but in this he was mistaken. He thought that the world was governed by the dialectic, whose instrument he was; just as much as Gladstone, he conceived of himself as the human agent of a superhuman Power. His ruthlessness and unscrupulousness were only as to means, not as to ends; he would not have been willing to purchase personal power at the expense of apostasy. Both men derived their personal force from this unshakable conviction of their own rectitude. Both men, in support of their respective faiths, ventured into realms in which, from ignorance, they could only cover themselves with ridicule—Gladstone in Biblical criticism, Lenin in philosophy.
> —"Lenin and Gladstone," Bertrand Russell

The essays at the end of the chapter illustrate the variety of comparison/contrast assignments and topics. "Diogenes and Alexander" brings together two men of utterly different backgrounds and fates. "Pain Among Patients of Jewish and Italian Origin" examines how men from two major ethnic groups cope with pain, while "Beauty Is in the Eye of the Beholder" draws a contrast between mind and brain. Finally, "Send in the Wimps" takes us on a humorous exploration of the contrasting images of men in advertising then and now. The student essay gives us successive drafts of a paragraph comparing two master composers—Beethoven and Chopin.

Original:

> Although Beethoven's music is different from Chopin's, both of these artists created

make clear the basis of your contrast.

some of the most thrilling music ever performed.)
In fact, most people, when asked what classical
music they listen to, will include works by
Beethoven and Chopin. When the ear is tuned to
Beethoven's music, one can hear that it is
perfectly proportioned, like an Athenian temple.
In an era when people valued the classical Greek
ideals of form and rationality, Beethoven
responded by composing within the classical
rules of harmonization. [Chopin, like an untamed
stallion, broke away from all of the precise
melodies of the classical era. He was a
harbinger of the Romantic era, composing
melodies that rang out with the dreams and
hidden longings of the Polish people, to whom he
belonged.] When analyzing Beethoven's method of
composing, one sees clearly that he always
adhered to the classical style, choosing
traditional chords, which through variation he
formed into pure, immaculate, untainted
masterpieces. His "Pathetique," "Moonlight
Sonata," and numerous symphonies are considered
by critics to reveal perfect architectonics.
Chopin composed music that seemed to break all
of the classical rules. He created chords that
swelled into intensely dramatic, but often
strangely unfamiliar, tonal combinations,
bringing music to new heights through his
nocturnes, scherzos, ballads, waltzes, mazurkas,

seems out of place make clear connection between Chopin and the basis of your contrast.

Transition needed to stress contrast.

and fantasies. Chopin's music was so unorthodox
that many critics of his time considered it
distastefully unruly and refused to call it
music.

Revision:

Beethoven and Chopin, two of the world's
greatest composers, differed completely as to
the rules of composition they observed. When the
ear is tuned to Beethoven's music, one can hear
that it is perfectly proportioned, like an
Athenian temple. In an era when people valued
the classical Greek ideals of form and
rationality, Beethoven responded by composing
within the classical rules of harmonization.
When analyzing Beethoven's method of composing,
one sees clearly that he adhered to the
classical style, choosing traditional chords,
which through variation he formed into pure,
immaculate, untainted masterpieces. His
"Pathetique," "Moonlight Sonata," and numerous
symphonies are considered by critics to reveal
perfect architectonics. Unlike Beethoven, Chopin
seemed to abandon all of the classical rules of
composition. He created chords that swelled into
intensely dramatic, but often strangely
unfamiliar, tonal combinations. Through his
nocturnes, scherzos, ballads, waltzes, mazurkas,
and fantasies, he brought music to

```
unprecedented, novel heights. Chopin's music was

so unorthodox that many critics of his time

considered it distastefully unruly and refused

to call it music.
```

The revision improves the organization of the essay by declaring the base of the contrast before cleanly drawing it. Some initial sentences that blurred the focus of the topic sentence were eliminated. Transitions were also inserted as needed to smooth out the back and forth movement between Beethoven and Chopin.

HISTORY

Gilbert Highet
DIOGENES AND ALEXANDER

Gilbert Highet (1906–1978) was born in Glasgow, Scotland, was educated at the University of Glasgow and at Oxford University, and became a naturalized citizen of the United States in 1951. A revered professor, who taught classical literature for over a decade at New York's Columbia University, Highet was also known for his scholarly and critical writing, including The Classical Tradition *(1949),* The Art of Teaching *(1950) and* The Anatomy of Satire *(1962). The essay below first appeared in the March, 1963, issue of* Fortune *magazine and draws sharply contrasting portraits of two famous persons.*

Lying on the bare earth, shoeless, bearded, half-naked, he looked like a beggar or a lunatic. He was one, but not the other. He had opened his eyes with the sun at dawn, scratched, done his business like a dog at the roadside, washed at the public fountain, begged a piece of breakfast bread and a few olives, eaten them squatting on the ground, and washed them down with a few handfuls of water scooped from the spring. (Long ago he had owned a rough wooden cup, but he threw it away when he saw a boy drinking out of his hollowed hands.) Having no work to go to and no family to provide for, he was free. As the market place filled up with shoppers and merchants and gossipers and sharpers and slaves and foreigners, he had strolled through it for an hour or two. Everybody knew him, or knew of him. They would throw   1

From *Horizon Magazine,* Spring 1963. Reprinted by permission of Curtis Brown, Ltd. Copyright © 1963 by Gilbert Highet.

sharp questions at him and get sharper answers. Sometimes they threw jeers, and got jibes; sometimes bits of food, and got scant thanks; sometimes a mischievous pebble, and got a shower of stones and abuse. They were not quite sure whether he was mad or not. He knew they were mad, each in a different way; they amused him. Now he was back at his home.

It was not a house, not even a squatter's hut. He thought everybody lived far too elaborately, expensively, anxiously. What good is a house? No one needs privacy; natural acts are not shameful; we all do the same things, and need not hide them. No one needs beds and chairs and such furniture: the animals live healthy lives and sleep on the ground. All we require, since nature did not dress us properly, is one garment to keep us warm, and some shelter from rain and wind. So he had one blanket—to dress him in the daytime and cover him at night—and he slept in a cask. His name was Diogenes. He was the founder of the creed called Cynicism (the word means "doggishness"); he spent much of his life in the rich, lazy, corrupt Greek city of Corinth, mocking and satirizing its people, and occasionally converting one of them. 2

His home was not a barrel made of wood: too expensive. It was a storage jar made of earthenware, something like a modern fuel tank—no doubt discarded because a break had made it useless. He was not the first to inhabit such a thing: the refugees driven into Athens by the Spartan invasion had been forced to sleep in casks. But he was the first who ever did so by choice, out of principle. 3

Diogenes was not a degenerate or a maniac. He was a philosopher who wrote plays and poems and essays expounding his doctrine; he talked to those who cared to listen; he had pupils who admired him. But he taught chiefly by example. All should live naturally, he said, for what is natural is normal and cannot possibly be evil or shameful. Live without conventions, which are artificial and false; escape complexities and superfluities and extravagances: only so can you live a free life. The rich man believes he possesses his big house with its many rooms and its elaborate furniture, his pictures and his expensive clothes, his horses and his servants and his bank accounts. He does not. He depends on them, he worries about them, he spends most of his life's energy looking after them; the thought of losing them makes him sick with anxiety. They possess him. He is their slave. In order to procure a quantity of false, perishable goods he has sold the only true, lasting good, his own independence. 4

There have been many men who grew tired of human society   5
with its complications, and went away to live simply—on a small
farm, in a quiet village, in a hermit's cave, or in the darkness of
anonymity. Not so Diogenes. He was not a recluse, or a stylite, or
a beatnik. He was a missionary. His life's aim was clear to him: it
was "to restamp the currency." (He and his father had once been
convicted for counterfeiting, long before he turned to philosophy,
and this phrase was Diogenes' bold, unembarrassed joke on the
subject.) To restamp the currency: to take the clean metal of human life, to erase the old false conventional markings, and to imprint it with its true values.

The other great philosophers of the fourth century before Christ   6
taught mainly their own private pupils. In the shady groves and
cool sanctuaries of the Academy, Plato discoursed to a chosen few
on the unreality of this contingent existence. Aristotle, among the
books and instruments and specimens and archives and research-
workers of his Lyceum, pursued investigations and gave lectures
that were rightly named *esoteric* "for those within the walls." But
for Diogenes, laboratory and specimens and lecture halls and pupils were all to be found in a crowd of ordinary people. Therefore
he chose to live in Athens or in the rich city of Corinth, where
travelers from all over the Mediterranean world constantly came
and went. And, by design, he publicly behaved in such ways as to
show people what real life was. He would constantly take up their
spiritual coin, ring it on a stone, and laugh at its false superscription.

He thought most people were only half-alive, most men only   7
half-men. At bright noonday he walked through the market place
carrying a lighted lamp and inspecting the face of everyone he met.
They asked him why. Diogenes answered, "I am trying to find a
man."

To a gentleman whose servant was putting on his shoes for him,   8
Diogenes said, "You won't be really happy until he wipes your
nose for you: that will come after you lose the use of your hands."

Once there was a war scare so serious that it stirred even the   9
lazy, profit-happy Corinthians. They began to drill, clean their
weapons, and rebuild their neglected fortifications. Diogenes took
his old cask and began to roll it up and down, back and forward. "When you are all so busy," he said, "I felt I ought to do *some-*
thing!"

And so he lived—like a dog, some said, because he cared noth-   10
ing for privacy and other human conventions, and because he

showed his teeth and barked at those whom he disliked. Now he was lying in the sunlight, as contented as a dog on the warm ground, happier (he himself used to boast) than the Shah of Persia. Although he knew he was going to have an important visitor, he would not move.

The little square began to fill with people. Page boys elegantly dressed, spearmen speaking a rough foreign dialect, discreet secretaries, hard-browed officers, suave diplomats, they all gradually formed a circle centered on Diogenes. He looked them over, as a sober man looks at a crowd of tottering drunks, and shook his head. He knew who they were. They were the attendants of the conqueror of Greece, the servants of Alexander, the Macedonian king, who was visiting his newly subdued realm.   11

Only twenty, Alexander was far older and wiser than his years. Like all Macedonians he loved drinking, but he could usually handle it; and toward women he was nobly restrained and chivalrous. Like all Macedonians he loved fighting; he was a magnificent commander, but he was not merely a military automaton. He could think. At thirteen he had become a pupil of the greatest mind in Greece, Aristotle. No exact record of his schooling survives. It is clear, though, that Aristotle took the passionate, half-barbarous boy and gave him the best of Greek culture. He taught Alexander poetry: the young prince slept with the *Iliad* under his pillow and longed to emulate Achilles, who brought the mighty power of Asia to ruin. He taught him philosophy, in particular the shapes and uses of political power: a few years later Alexander was to create a supranational empire that was not merely a power system but a vehicle for the exchange of Greek and Middle Eastern cultures.   12

Aristotle taught him the principles of scientific research: during his invasion of the Persian domains Alexander took with him a large corps of scientists, and shipped hundreds of zoological specimens back to Greece for study. Indeed, it was from Aristotle that Alexander learned to seek out everything strange which might be instructive. Jugglers and stunt artists and virtuosos of the absurd he dismissed with a shrug; but on reaching India he was to spend hours discussing the problems of life and death with naked Hindu mystics, and later to see one demonstrate Yoga self-command by burning himself impassively to death.   13

Now, Alexander was in Corinth to take command of the League of Greek States which, after conquering them, his father Philip had created as a disguise for the New Macedonian Order. He was welcomed and honored and flattered. He was the man of the hour, of   14 the century: he was unanimously appointed commander-in-chief of a new expedition against old, rich, corrupt Asia. Nearly everyone crowded to Corinth in order to congratulate him, to seek employment with him, even simply to see him: soldiers and statesmen, artists and merchants, poets and philosophers. He received their compliments graciously. Only Diogenes, although he lived in Corinth, did not visit the new monarch. With that generosity which Aristotle had taught him was a quality of the truly magnanimous man, Alexander determined to call upon Diogenes. Surely Dio-genes, the God-born, would acknowledge the conqueror's power by some gift of hoarded wisdom.

With his handsome face, his fiery glance, his strong supple body, 15 his purple and gold cloak, and his air of destiny, he moved through the parting crowd, toward the Dog's kennel. When a king approaches, all rise in respect. Diogenes did not rise, he merely sat up on one elbow. When a monarch enters a precinct, all greet him with a bow or an acclamation. Diogenes said nothing.

There was a silence. Some years later Alexander speared his best 16 friend to the wall, for objecting to the exaggerated honors paid to His Majesty; but now he was still young and civil. He spoke first, with a kindly greeting. Looking at the poor broken cask, the single ragged garment, and the rough figure lying on the ground, he said: "Is there anything I can do for you, Diogenes?"

"Yes," said the Dog. "Stand to one side. You're blocking the sun- 17 light."

There was silence, not the ominous silence preceding a burst of 18 fury, but a hush of amazement. Slowly, Alexander turned away. A titter broke out from the elegant Greeks, who were already beginning to make jokes about the Cur that looked at the King. The Macedonian officers, after deciding that Diogenes was not worth the trouble of kicking, were starting to guffaw and nudge one another. Alexander was still silent. To those nearest him he said quietly, "If I were not Alexander, I should be Diogenes." They took it as a paradox, designed to close the awkward little scene with a polite curtain line. But Alexander meant it. He understood Cynicism as the others could not. Later he took one of Diogenes' pupils with him to India as a philosophical interpreter (it was he who spoke to the naked *saddhus*). He was what Diogenes called himself, a *cosmopolitēs,* "citizen of the world." Like Diogenes, he admired the heroic figure of Hercules, the mighty conqueror who labors to help mankind while all others toil and sweat only for themselves. He knew that of all men then alive in the world only Alexander the conqueror and Diogenes the beggar were truly free.

Vocabulary

expounding (4)

conventions (4)

superfluities (4)

stylite (5)

discoursed (6)

contingent (6)

archives (6)

superscription (6)

suave (11)

supranational (12)

virtuosos (13)

Critical Inquiries

1. What are the bases of Highet's contrast? What characteristics do Diogenes and Alexander share? How are they different?

2. Which of the two men—Alexander or Diogenes—had a better chance for leading a contented life? Give reasons for your answer.

3. Reread paragraph 2. Do you agree with the idea that human beings should live naturally and that we have become far too elaborate? Give reasons for your answer.

4. How important are philosophy, poetry, and the principles of scientific investigation—all subjects taught Alexander by Aristotle—to a modern curriculum? What other subjects, if any, would you add for a balanced curriculum?

5. Paragraph 12 states that Alexander was far older and wiser than his twenty years. How is this maturity indicated? In your view, what are the aspects of life that tend to foster maturity most?

Rhetorical Inquiries

1. What method—alternating or block (see pp. 405–409)—does Highet use to develop his comparison/contrast? What does Highet's method require of the reader?

2. The opening paragraph contains a sentence characterized by balance and parallelism. What are the opening words of this sentence? What is its effect?

3. According to the essay, Alexander "understood Cynicism as the others could not." How is "Cynicism" defined for the reader?

4. What is the literary term for the phrase "to restamp the currency" in paragraph 5? What does the phrase mean?

5. What is the topic sentence for paragraphs 7, 8, and 9? How is it developed?

SOCIAL PSYCHOLOGY

Mark Zborowski

PAIN AMONG PATIENTS OF JEWISH AND ITALIAN ORIGIN

Mark Zborowski is a clinical psychologist with an interest in the biophysical aspects of pain. As part of a scientific experiment in this general area of study, he decided to focus on the cultural components of pain. His underlying assumption is that pain is the same for everyone, but contrasting reactions occur due to differing cultural experiences. The essay below was the result of research Zborowski conducted at the Kingsbridge Veterans Hospital in Bronx, New York. Three ethnocultural groups were selected: Jews, Italians, and "Old Americans." The main techniques used in the collection of the data were interviews with patients, observation of their behavior when in pain, and discussion of the individual cases with doctors, nurses, and other people directly or indirectly involved in the pain experience of the individual. We have excerpted the section entitled "Pain among Patients of Jewish and Italian Origin," which contrasts the reactions to pain of two different cultural groups.

Jews and Italians were selected mainly because interviews with medical experts suggested that they display similar reactions to pain. The investigation of this similarity provided the opportunity to check a rather popular assumption that similar reactions reflect similar attitudes. The differences between the Italian and Jewish cultures are great enough to suggest that, if the attitudes are related to cultural pattern, they will also be different, despite the apparent similarity in manifest behavior.   1

Members of both groups were described as being very emotional in their responses to pain. They were described as tending to exaggerate their pain experience and being very sensitive to pain. Some of the doctors stated that, in their opinion, Jews and Italians have a lower threshold of pain than members of other ethnic groups, especially members of the so-called Nordic group. This statement seems to indicate a certain confusion as to the concept of the threshold of pain. According to people who have studied the problem of the threshold of pain—for instance, Harold Wolff and his associates—the threshold of pain is more or less the same for all human beings regardless of nationality, sex, or age.   2

From "Cultural Components in Response to Pain," *Journal of Social Issues,* vol. 8, no. 4, 1952. Reprinted by permission of Society for the Psychological Study of Social Issues.

In the course of the investigation, the general impressions of   3
doctors were confirmed to a great extent by the interview material
and by the observation of the patients' behavior. However, even a
superficial study of the interviews has revealed that, although reactions to pain appear to be similar, the underlying attitudes toward
pain are different in the two groups. While the Italian patients
seemed to be mainly concerned with the immediacy of the pain
experience and were disturbed by the actual pain sensation that
they experienced in a given situation, the concern of patients of
Jewish origin was focused mainly upon the symptomatic meaning
of pain and upon the significance of pain in relation to their health,
welfare, and, eventually, for the welfare of the families. The Italian
patient expressed, in his behavior and in his complaints, the discomfort caused by pain as such, and he manifested his emotions
with regard to the effects of this pain experience upon his immediate situation in terms of occupation, economic situation, and so
on; the Jewish patient expressed primarily his worries and anxieties as to the extent to which the pain indicated a threat to his
health. In this connection, it is worth mentioning that one of the
Jewish words to describe strong pain is *yessurim,* a word that is also
used to describe worries and anxieties.

Attitudes of Italian and Jewish patients toward pain-relieving   4
drugs can serve as an indication of their attitude toward pain.
When in pain, the Italian calls for pain relief and is mainly concerned with the analgesic effects of the drugs that are administered
to him. Once the pain is relieved, the Italian patient easily forgets
his sufferings and manifests a happy and joyful disposition. The
Jewish patient, however, often is reluctant to accept the drug, and
he explains this reluctance in terms of concern about the effects of
the drug upon his health in general. He is apprehensive about the
habit-forming aspects of the analgesic. Moreover, he feels that the
drug relieves his pain only temporarily and does not cure him of
the disease that may cause the pain. Nurses and doctors have reported cases in which patients would hide the pill that was given
to them to relieve their pain and would prefer to suffer. These reports were confirmed in the interviews with the patients. It was
also observed that many Jewish patients, after being relieved from
pain, often continued to display the same depressed and worried
behavior, because they felt that, although the pain was currently
absent, it may recur as long as the disease was not cured completely. From these observations, it appears that, when one deals
with a Jewish and an Italian patient in pain, in the first case it is
more important to relieve the anxieties with regard to the sources

of pain, while in the second it is more important to relieve the actual pain.

Another indication as to the significance of pain for Jewish and   5
Italian patients is their respective attitudes toward the doctor. The
Italian patient seems to display a most confident attitude toward
the doctor, which is usually reinforced after the doctor has succeeded in relieving pain; whereas the Jewish patient manifests a
skeptical attitude, feeling that the fact that the doctor has relieved
his pain by some drug does not mean at all that he is skillful
enough to take care of the basic illness. Consequently, even when
the pain is relieved, he tends to check the diagnosis and the treatment of one doctor against the opinions of other specialists in the
field. Summarizing the difference between the Italian and Jewish
attitudes, one can say that the Italian attitude is characterized by a
present-oriented apprehension with regard to the actual sensation
of pain, and the Jew tends to manifest a future-oriented anxiety as
to the symptomatic and general meaning of the pain experience.

It has been stated that the Italians and Jews tend to manifest   6
similar behavior in terms of their reactions to pain. As both cultures allow for free expression of feelings and emotions by words,
sounds, and gestures, both the Italians and Jews feel free to talk
about their pain, complain about it, and manifest their sufferings
by groaning, moaning, crying, etc. They are not ashamed of this
expression. They admit willingly that, when they are in pain, they
do complain a great deal, call for help, and expect sympathy and
assistance from other members of their immediate social environment, especially from members of their family. When in pain, they
are reluctant to be alone and prefer the presence and attention of
other people. This behavior, which is expected, accepted, and approved by the Italian and Jewish cultures, often conflicts with the
patterns of behavior expected from a patient by American or
Americanized medical people. Thus, they tend to describe the behavior of the Italian and Jewish patients as exaggerated and overe-
motional. The material suggests that they do tend to minimize the
actual pain experiences of the Italian and Jewish patients, regardless of whether they have the objective criteria for evaluating the
actual amount of pain that the patient experiences. It seems that
the uninhibited display of reaction to pain as manifested by the
Jewish and Italian patients provokes distrust in American culture
instead of provoking sympathy.

Despite the close similarity between the manifest reactions   7
among Jews and Italians, there seem to be differences in emphasis,
especially with regard to what the patient achieves by these reac-

tions and as to the specific manifestations of these reactions in the
various social settings. For instance, they differ in their behavior at
home and in the hospital. The Italian husband, who is aware of his
role as an adult male, tends to avoid verbal complaining at home,
leaving this type of behavior to the women. In the hospital, where
he is less concerned with his role as a male, he tends to be more
verbal and more emotional. The Jewish patient, on the contrary,
seems to be more calm in the hospital than at home. Traditionally,
the Jewish male does not emphasize his masculinity through such
traits as stoicism, and he does not equate verbal complaints with
weakness. Moreover, the Jewish culture allows the patient to be
demanding and complaining. Therefore, he tends more to use his
pain in order to control interpersonal relationships within the family. Although similar use of pain to manipulate the relationships
between members of the family may be present also in some other
cultures, it seems that, in the Jewish culture, this is not disapproved, while in others it is.

In the hospital, one can also distinguish variations in the reactive
patterns among Jews and Italians. Upon his admission to the hospital, and in the presence of the doctor, the Jewish patient tends to
complain, ask for help, be emotional even to the point of crying.
However, as soon as he feels that adequate care is given to him, he
becomes more restrained. This suggests that the display of pain reaction serves less as an indication of the amount of pain experienced than as a means to create an atmosphere and setting in
which the pathological causes of pain will be best taken care of.
The Italian patient, on the other hand, seems to be less concerned
with setting up a favorable situation for treatment. He takes for
granted that adequate care will be given to him, and, in the presence of the doctor, he seems to be somewhat calmer than the Jewish patient. The mere presence of the doctor reassures the Italian
patient, while the skepticism of the Jewish patient limits the reassuring role of the physician.

To summarize the description of the reaction patterns of the
Jewish and Italian patients, the material suggests that, on a semiconscious level, the Jewish patient tends to provoke worry and
concern in his social environment as to the state of his health and
the symptomatic character of his pain, while the Italian tends to
provoke sympathy toward his suffering. In one case, the function
of the pain reaction will be the mobilization of the efforts of the
family and the doctors toward a complete cure, while, in the second case, the function of the reaction will be focused upon the
mobilization of effort toward relieving the pain sensation.

On the basis of the discussion of the Jewish and Italian material,   10
two generalizations can be made: (1) *Similar reactions to pain manifested by members of different ethnocultural groups do not necessarily reflect similar attitudes to pain.* (2) *Reactive patterns similar in terms of their
manifestations may have different functions and serve different purposes in
various cultures.*

Vocabulary

manifest (1)

symptomatic (3)

analgesic (4)

apprehensive (4)

skeptical (5)

criteria (6)

stoicism (7)

manipulate (7)

reactive (8)

pathological (8)

semiconscious (9)

mobilization (9)

ethnocultural (10)

Critical Inquiries

1. How would you summarize the essential difference in attitude toward
   pain between Jewish and Italian patients, as portrayed in this essay? State
   the difference in one sentence. If you have had experience with other ethnic or cultural groups facing pain, what was their general attitude? Give
   specific examples.

2. Which of the two attitudes toward pain described seems more rational?
   Support your answer with reasons.

3. What does the Jewish husband's concern with health indicate about his
   self image?

4. How do you react to the Jewish as well as Italian patients' habit of moaning, groaning, or even crying about his pain? Do you consider such a response immature and ignoble? Why? or why not?

5. How valid do you consider the investigation conducted in order to come
   up with the discoveries presented in this essay?

Rhetorical Inquiries

1. Although the study does not specifically describe the patients studied as
   male patients, the reader sees them as male. Why?

2. The opening sentences of paragraph 1 and 2 use passive verbs. Since writing instructors tend to laud active verbs over passive ones, what rationale can you supply for using two passive verbs to establish the context of this essay?

3. Where in the essay does the author begin to focus on the essential difference found in the investigation of Jews and Italians? Refer to the specific passage.

4. In paragraph 2, why does the author refer to studies on the threshold of pain? Is this an unnecessary digression or is it relevant to the current study? Give reasons for your answer.

5. What are some rhetorical strategies used in paragraph 7 to highlight the contrast between Italian and Jewish patients?

NEUROLOGY

Lee Dembart

BEAUTY IS IN THE EYE OF THE BEHOLDER, ALONG WITH EVERYTHING ELSE

Lee Dembart (born July 25, 1946, in New York City) graduated with a B.A. cum laude from Queens College in 1966. She has worked primarily as a journalist on such newspapers as The New York Post, The New York Times, *and* The Los Angeles Times *and has been a senior lecturer at the University of Southern California, Los Angeles.*

Everyone knows how the eye works. Light passes through the   1
lens and strikes the retina behind it, which tickles the optic nerve
and sends an electrical signal to the brain. Presto, we see.

I don't know about you, but I don't see electrical signals or any-   2
thing like that when I look out through my eyes. I see a scene—a
picture—before me, people and furniture and cars and buildings
and trees and whatnot. A constantly changing scene.

Where—and how—does that scene get put together?   3

Somewhere in the brain, the physical sensation is turned into a   4
mental sensation. But how it happens is a mystery. One thing is
certain: Vision is not a replication of the image on the retina.

The question of where vision comes from is an example of a   5
larger philosophical question that has concerned thinkers and sci-

Reprinted from the *Los Angeles Times,* June 20, 1988, part II, p. 3. Copyright, 1988, *Los Angeles Times.* Reprinted by permission.

entists for centuries: the mind-body problem. What is the relationship between our thoughts, which are "mind," and our brains,
which are "body?"

In the example of vision, the eye, the retina, the optic nerve and   6
its complex electrochemical activity are body. The scene we see is
mind.

Asking where vision comes from is like asking where conscious-   7
ness comes from. The little voice in your head that talks to you—
what is its source? The brain is not like other organs of the body,
whose outputs are physical substances. It would be a mistake to
say, for example, that the brain is like the pancreas: One secretes
insulin and the other secretes thoughts. You can collect insulin and
measure it. But where are the thoughts?

To simplify, there are basically two approaches to the problem   8
of understanding the relationship between mind and brain, neither
of which is altogether satisfying. On the one hand, there is the reductionist position, which says that mind and brain are the same,
that every thought, emotion, memory and nuance of experience
corresponds to a physical state of the brain. We are far from understanding what that correspondence is, of course, but someday it
will all be worked out.

Or, on the other hand, one could say that mind represents some-   9
thing else, something left over, the soul perhaps. The gray matter
is not all there is. The trouble with this explanation, which is favored by many researchers, is that all it does is give a name to
what we don't know. What is the something else and, more important, where is it?

I favor the reductionist position, which collapses mind to brain,   10
though I admit that it seems that there is something else involved.
But much of what neuroscientists discover points in this direction.

Consider, for example, one famous experiment in which elec-   11
trodes were placed on the heads of human subjects so their brain
activity could be monitored. They were then told, "When you feel
like it, bend your finger."

Sooner or later, the subjects bent their fingers. But in each case,   12
there was activity in their brains before they were aware of any
conscious decisions to move.

Brain activity comes first. Consciousness comes second. It is   13
simply how we experience the electrochemical activity in our
brains.

This finding casts doubt on our cherished notions of free will.   14
We may simply be deceived in thinking that we are free agents. If

thoughts follow brain activity, and brain activity is a matter of physics and chemistry, we have much less freedom than we imagined.

This is no idle philosophical issue. If mind and brain are the same, then people who are smart shouldn't be praised or rewarded for it. They can't help themselves.   15

Similarly, if free will is in question, our notions of punishment are on shaky ground. Is it proper to punish people for doing things for which they are not responsible?   16

The predominance of the brain over our mental life seems overwhelming. In some experiments, certain patients who are awake have had parts of their brains electrically stimulated. They report feeling sensations in various parts of their bodies. Not in their brains, mind you, but in their hands, for example. Stimulate the brain, and the patient feels it elsewhere.   17

Or take various studies of the perception of color. It turns out that there is no physical quality that enables you to determine what color is. Color is not a physical property. It is a property of brain. "The world is very much a matter of our own creation," says Richard Cytowic, a neurologist in Washington.   18

However, there is something out there. We don't just make up the world out of whole cloth. But it is fair to conclude that most of what we say about the world says more about us than it does about the world.   19

But as to how the brain works, our knowledge is, to be generous, rudimentary. In neuroscience, "We don't have a feeling for much at all," says Jack D. Cowan of the University of Chicago. "Physics is easy compared to biology."   20

Perhaps the 20th-Century philosopher Ludwig Wittgenstein said it best: All the interesting things can't be written down and described.   21

Vocabulary

replication (4)

retina (6)

optic (6)

electrochemical (6)

pancreas (7)

secretes (7)

insulin (7)

reductionist (8)

nuance (8)

neuroscientists (10)

electrodes (11)

predominance (17)

rudimentary (20)

Critical Inquiries

1. Does the author provide a complete understanding of the difference between mind and body? Summarize her views into two or three key sentences.

2. How does the author differentiate the brain from other organs of the body? Why is the distinction important?

3. How does the author view the soul? What is your opinion on the subject? Is the subject worth probing?

4. What does the author mean when she states that "if free will is in question, our notions of punishment are on shaky ground"? Do you agree? Give reasons for your answer.

5. What social problems, other than punishment and reward, do you see arising from the mind-body connection? Give specific examples.

Rhetorical Inquiries

1. If "everyone knows how the eye works," why does the author insist on reviewing the process in paragraph 1?

2. How does the author use the question posed in paragraph 3?

3. What rhetorical strategy does the author use in paragraphs 8 and 9? How is the strategy rendered coherent?

4. Where in the essay does the author introduce an illustration by using an introductory phrase? Point to a specific paragraph. Comment on the effectiveness of such an introduction. What does it contribute?

5. How does the author marshal support for her controversial position that the brain's control over one's mental life is overwhelming?

ADVERTISING

Barbara Lippert
SEND IN THE WIMPS

Barbara Lippert (b. 1954 in New York City) is a television commentator and critic of advertising copy. Since graduating with an M.A. from Mount Holyoke College in Massachusetts, she has become the recognized inventor of advertising criticism, a field that analyzes advertising imagery and links it to trends in pop culture. In addition to appearing on numerous television

Reprinted by permission of the author from *Vogue,* Nov. 1988, p. 414. Copyright © 1988 by The Conde Nast Publications, Inc.

shows, Lippert has written columns and essays for Manhattan, Inc., Vogue, Saturday Review, Money, U.S. News and World Report, Premiere, *and the* Washington Post. *Presently she is working in New York as the official* Adweek *critic.*

A much-talked-about ad for Benson & Hedges cigarettes shows five women and one older man sitting in business clothes, eating and smoking around a dining-room table, while a bare-chested man in pajama bottoms holds a cigarette and talks to them from the corner of the room. This peculiar scenario has drawn much conjecture about what's going on here. So much so that it generated a second campaign based on the original that asked just that: "What's going on here?" To me, it suggests aggressive defiance of the current taboos about smoking and sex: he holds the classic postcoital cigarette, and those are five satisfied women.

Advertising, with its long tradition of depicting half-naked, half-witted women to push its message across, has come up with a new stereotype — man in all his unglory, the hunk as bimbo, the he-man as wimp, and preferably as undressed as possible.

Of course, modern man as designer sex object moved into the mainstream with the Calvin Klein underwear ads of the early eighties. Bruce Weber's provocative photographs of a gorgeous young man clad only in a pair of white briefs became an instant print sensation: his billboard Adonis, trim, tan, muscular, and exposed, immediately elevated sex in advertising to a new art form.

This new graphic look — of redefining and objectifying male beauty — grew out of a gay aesthetic, but once its power to sell was proven, it became another household image. Concurrently, the women's movement changed sexual politics; it was okay for the women to be the new sexual hunters and gatherers and, as a result, naked men started showing up in ads outside the sophisticated realm of fashion and fragrance. In a TV spot for Fab detergent — that's the wash-a-day world of soapsuds — a man does a reverse-strip, bumping and grinding his way into his freshly washed clothing, accompanied by stripper music in the background. A commercial for Drano shows a young hunk bathing alone at dusk to the tune of "Splish Splash." His energetic rub-a-dubbing is stopped by a clog, but he hops out, pours in the Drano, and is so happy to be having germ-free fun on a Saturday night that he kisses a bathroom pipe. Marshall Blonsky, who teaches communications at New York University, says the spot shows that "women are angry. This ad makes men look kind of silly. A guy who kisses a pipe is not to be trusted — he's *sick.*"

Martha Farnsworth Riche, senior editor of *American Demograph-*   5
ics, attributes the male-bashing in advertising to the fact that "economically, men have been demystified" in society. "Essentially,"
she says, "women have fired men—they feel they don't need
them in their lives."

"Male-bashing in advertising hasn't anything to do with the real   6
world," says Carol L. Colman, a partner at Inferential Focus, a creative firm that spots trends "The women's movement has been dying since President Reagan was elected, and men are still following
the Hulk Hogan tradition. But the macho man who had been getting all the attention is losing out to the wimp—at least in the
media."

Advertising often relies on the device of making someone dumb   7
get a lot smarter with the help of the right product. Now, that
someone is a wimp. Marshall Efron, a screenwriter and actor who
appears in many commercials, notices that in the wimp department, there seems to be one actor who gets most of the work.
"This same guy is having a false heart attack in a Fleischmann's
Margarine commercial and then in a Dr. Scholl's commercial, he
thinks the problem is his back, but it turns out he only needs shoe
inserts. What is it with him?"

What's with him is that he's the perfect wimp type so much in   8
demand right now throughout the industry. Take the previously
innocuous category of cereal advertising, where rugged-individual/
hickory-nut heroes used to reign. These days we see men getting
knocked on the head by tennis balls or being told that they're not
kissable or marriage-material, even being humiliated by their own
kids, and all because they're eating the wrong breakfast.

The rise of the wimp would seem to be a crude role-reversal, an   9
action that advertisers are taking as a response to the fear of the
perceived Emergency Feminist Broadcast System. After forty years
of sexist ads, some advertisers realize that the standard male/
female images no longer apply. The culture right now is a peculiar,
complicated, postfeminist, postmacho wasteland. Advertising, by
its nature, must simplify and exaggerate.

Many spots reverse the age-old *Honeymooners* shtick, with the   10
wife coming up with an equivalent of the "to the moon" phrase. A
Diet Pepsi commercial managed to do that and reverse standard
locker-room mentality at the same time. It gave us bare-chested
Mike Tyson coming out of the shower as his wife, actress Robin
Givens, snaps a towel at him. "Hey, Champ, let's get the lead out,"
she says. "Yeth, dear," he lisps, winking to the camera.

Even the new sensitivity in men results in an insidious form of   11 sexism as men enter new territories, like bra commercials. Bra ads used to be women showing their breasts under sweaters like missiles parading through Red Square, or full-figured gal Jane Russell hanging the bra off her arm, shopping-basket style, talking about support. A revolutionary campaign for Maidenform shows no underwear at all; rather, it features men talking about lingerie and the women who wear it. The first spot used sensitive actor Michael York; now, there's one with *L.A. Law's* bad-boy Corbin Bernsen and super-gentle Superman Christopher Reeve. There's something at once creepy and kinky about these ads which update Frederick's of Hollywood as Frederick's of Malibu. While they're more contemporary looking than the standard bra ad, they trade on the same throwback manipulation of age-old advertising: with the right hair spray, the right soap, or the right underwear, a woman will attract a man.

The latest definitive symbol of the sensitive, multidimensional man in advertising is a bare-chested chap with that trendiest of accessories—a baby. Perhaps the baby is there just to cover the chest hair, but this image has popped up in everything from Chevrolet commercials to spots for a fragrance called "Man of Iron."   12

The interest in babies is an obvious nod toward simple demographics: the baby boom is aging and producing its own boomlet. That's why movies like *Three Men and a Baby* and TV shows like *thirtysomething* are successful. And it does reflect a clear social change. "Men are still not doing housework or laundry, but they are very involved in babies and baby care," says Baila Zeitz, Ph.D., a New York City psychologist. "It's a very humanizing thing for men, and socially, it's just about the best thing that's happened."   13

Advertising is not a subtle medium. And, with sex roles as complicated as they've gotten, most attempts to show change or progress just seem to be another sales device. But in the logic of contemporary advertising, what is new for the moment gets attention. Men as fools or bimbos will pass, too.   14

Vocabulary

scenario (1)	graphic (4)
conjecture (1)	aesthetic (4)
taboos (1)	concurrently (4)
postcoital (1)	demographics (5)
stereotype (2)	demystified (5)
Adonis (3)	inferential (6)

innocuous (8)   kinky (11)
shtick (10)   multidimensional (12)
insidious (11)

Critical Inquiries

1. The entire essay is centered on the term *wimp,* a word not defined in most dictionaries since it is contemporary slang. What is your definition of this term? Supply specific examples to illuminate meaning.

2. What assumption forms the base of the argument in paragraph 4? Do you agree with this assumption? Why or why not?

3. What social effects, if any, do you project from the rise of the wimp in advertising? Give specific examples.

4. In paragraph 13 the author suggests that the new interest in babies on the part of men may be the result of demographics—that is, the baby boom babies are now creating their own babies. Is this answer satisfactory or can other, perhaps more important, causes be identified? Support your answer with evidence from contemporary society.

5. In paragraph 14, the author argues that "advertising is not a subtle medium." What is meant by this statement? What evidence would you use to argue the opposite point of view—that advertising *is* a subtle medium.

Rhetorical Inquiries

1. How effective is the opening paragraph in catching your attention? Invent another opening paragraph and compare its effectiveness with that of Lippert's.

2. Where in paragraph 3 does the author use allusion? What is the purpose?

3. In paragraphs 4, 5, and 6, how does the author aim for credibility?

4. What is the purpose of the question at the end of paragraph 7?

5. What level of writing do you consider this essay—formal, informal, regional, slang, or what? Support your answer with evidence from the essay.

Exercises

1. List the similarities and differences between the following pairs:
   a. fast-food chains/gourmet restaurants
   b. persuasion/force
   c. white-collar work/blue-collar work

    d. pathetic/tragic

    e. love/romance

    f. the attitudes of liberals and conservatives toward welfare assistance

2. Write two brief outlines for the separate development of the following subjects—within and between paragraphs.

    a. the advantages of a small sports car over a large sedan (or vice versa)

    b. the superiority of classroom discussion over lecturing as a pedagogic tool (or vice versa)

    c. a contrast of the main street in your hometown during the day and night

    d. the difference between civil disobedience and breaking the law

    e. the difference between being prejudiced and being choosy

Writing Assignments

1. In a 500-word essay, compare and contrast the lives and/or careers of any two significant figures of history. Use either the "within" or the "between" paragraphs method. Be sure to reveal the bases of your comparison/contrast and to deal with both sides.

2. Write a 500-word essay contrasting two societies or cultures (past or present) based on their geographical locations, their systems of government, and their general lifestyles. Be sure to state each basis of contrast and to deal with both sides. Here are a few possibilities, but many others exist: ancient Greeks and Romans, present-day Jews and Arabs, London and Paris in the eighteenth century, poor urban blacks and affluent urban blacks.

3. After studying "Diogenes and Alexander" (pp. 405–409), write a 500-word essay in which you contrast the two men with the purpose of proving that one is superior to the other. Your thesis statement should sumarize this superiority in one sentence.

4. Using "Pain among Patients of Jewish and Italian Origin" as a model, write an essay in which you contrast the attitudes of two other cultures toward something—physical fitness, male machoism, the elderly, or anything else you consider significant.

Chapter

14

Analyzing Cause

*T*he end of our foundation is the knowledge of causes.

FRANCIS BACON (1561–1626)

Of all the modes of development, causal analysis is the most abstract and therefore the most difficult. The paragraph or essay developed in this mode focuses on explaining either the causes or effects of some occurrence. Exactly how that is done depends as much on the ability to think as to write (although it is arguable that the two go together). Good writing can sometimes compensate for bad thinking, but not when the subject is cause and effect.

To begin with, let us be clear about the difference between them. Consider, as our example, the awesome hurricane. Its *cause* is heat energy generated when warm ocean winds meet the cool upper air, forming a low-pressure trough behind which winds circulate in an accelerating spiral. Its *effects* may include uprooted trees, leveled houses, scuttled boats, downed power lines, flooded beachfronts, and loss of life. As you can see from the example, cause precedes an occurrence; effect succeeds it. Cause always refers to some motivating event, while effect always refers to some outcome. The difference between the two is illustrated in this diagram:

Cause (before) ← Situation → Effect (after)

Rhetorically, you are analyzing cause when you set out to explain why something happened, as this paragraph does. The writer is trying to decipher why the nation went mad on October 30, 1938, during and shortly after a broadcast of the radio program "The War of the Worlds." In some cities and towns, utter panic ensued. People armed themselves and went out hunting for aliens. Men and women huddled in basements and cellars, dreading capture and death at alien hands. Some families swore suicide pacts rather than be taken alive by Martian captors. Why, the writer asks? And then he answers with this analysis of cause:

At least one book and quite a pile of sociological literature has appeared on the subject of "The Invasion from Mars." Many theories have been put forward to explain the "tidal wave" of panic that swept the nation. I know of two factors that largely contributed to the broadcast's extraordinarily violent effect. First, its historical timing. It came within thirty-five days of the Munich crisis. For weeks, the American people had been hanging on their radios, getting most of their news no longer from the press, but over the air. A new technique of "on-the-spot" reporting had been devel-

426

oped and eagerly accepted by an anxious and news-hungry world. The Mercury Theater on the Air by faithfully copying every detail of the new technique—including its imperfections—found an already enervated audience ready to accept its wildest fantasies. The second factor was the show's sheer technical brilliance. To this day it is impossible to sit in a room and hear the scratched, worn, off-the-air recording of the broadcast, without feeling in the back of your neck some slight draft left over from that great wind of terror that swept the nation. Even with the element of credibility totally removed it remains a surprisingly frightening show.
—"Why the Radio Program 'The Invasion from Mars' Caused Panic," John Houseman

On the other hand, you are analyzing effect when you try to explain the consequences or results of a certain action, as this writer does in the paragraph below. Instead of explaining why we talk to babies, he is telling us what happens to a baby when we do talk to one.

When you talk to a very young baby, a curious thing is happening. Along with the arm-waving, the gurgling, and the engaging stare that can coax a smile from even the most solemn adult, the baby's body ripples with tiny coordinated muscular movements that can be detected only with specially sensitive electronic equipment. This extraordinary response, only recently discovered, is a powerful demonstration of just how firmly language is rooted in the human brain. In that baby the whole constellation of tiny, almost imperceptible movements have been generated by the brain as a result of the sound uttered by the admiring adult. More astonishing still—but also, on reflection, inevitable—is the discovery that exactly the same phenomenon occurs, whatever the permutation of nationality in baby and adult: that is, an American infant responds to the sounds of Chinese, Russian, and French exactly as it does to those of the English language.
—from *Origins,* Richard E. Leakey and Roger Lewin

Writing assignments requiring the analysis of cause/effect are common in academic departments, work and business, and even personal life. The chemistry instructor who asks you to explain what happens when mercury chloride is mixed with mercury metal is asking for an analysis of effect. The boss who demands to know why a certain product is not selling wants an analysis of cause. So, for that matter, does your best friend who writes to ask why you have finally split with the one you once loved. And no matter what the exact topic, there are certain common pitfalls to guard against when writing on such an abstract subject as cause and effect.

Be Cautious about Drawing Cause–Effect Connections

Do you believe that divorce is caused mainly by people watching too much television? Or that the world would be automatically made right if only everyone went to church? Or that the effects of violent movies is to make future warmongers of children? We have read these and other similarly farfetched assertions of cause and effect. Do not dogmatically assert a cause unless you have solid proof to back it up. We know of no proofs that qualify any of the above assertions as more than a belief. But belief is not cause. It is only belief.

The hard fact about the world of causation is that much more is unknown than known, and what is known is always subject to revision with later evidence. Take, for example, the ongoing debate about the fate of dinosaurs. Dinosaurs were the undisputed lords of the world for eons before they mysteriously vanished during the Mesozoic era. Some scientists blame their disappearance on the draining of swamps, the dinosaurs' natural habitat; some on the onset of colder climates, to which reptiles could not adapt. Others allege that the large, clumsy dinosaur perished in competition with the hordes of small and fleet-footed mammals from which we descended. And, most recently, the theory has been proposed that a comet or an asteroid collided with the earth setting off continental wildfires whose soot killed the plant life and ultimately starved the dinosaur. All of these causes seem to make sense; yet, none can be dogmatically asserted without argument.

Our advice, then, is that you write cautiously about cause. We do not mean that you should shilly-shally or hedge your bet or give here while taking away there as tentative writers are likely to do. We mean only that you should do your homework, dig for the evidence, and set down with conviction what is truly known. You may qualify your causal speculations with such phrases as "it seems," "appearances indicate," or "the evidence points to." However, if your analysis is grounded in uncontested truth, you should say so plainly. For instance, state firmly that, "A recent study by the Palomar Corporation indicates that the amount of smoke and dust raised as a result of a nuclear war is far more extensive than anticipated by current civil defense plans." Or, "Studies have found that a major cause of obesity among Americans is overeating and lack of activity."

In particular, beware of drawing illogical cause-effect links that are circular or ideological. Here is an example of what we mean by circular reasoning:

Original: `Heart infarctions are caused by a necrosis of blood`

`artery tissue.`

By definition, an "infarction" is a "necrosis" (death) of the blood arteries; thus, all you have really said is, "An infarction is caused by an infarction."

Revision: Heart infarctions, that is, the sudden collapse of
blood artery tissue, are caused when the arteries
clog up and no longer allow blood to flow through.

Here is an example of an ideological pronouncement:

Original: Women slave in the house because they are trapped
there and cannot get out owing to their excessive
dependency on a man. That is the only reason why
any woman would want to stay home and clean and cook
all day.

This is entirely based on an ideological point of view, and a reader would have to share the writer's values before agreeing with this belief. It is not unreasonable to believe that some women may be trapped in the home by circumstances, but common sense also tells us that many are there by choice. Here is a more acceptable version:

A generation ago, the women in my family
were trapped in a cycle of excessive dependency
on their men from which there was no escape
because there was no choice open to them other
than the drudgery of cooking and cleaning all
day.

This is less sweeping because it is grounded in specific examples the author intends to offer, namely, the women of her own family. She is no longer making a blanket and insupportable charge against all women. Causation is a complex force that should be written about with restraint and caution. If you have the facts to back it up, you can boldly state an assertion of cause. But it you do not have the facts, you should either get them or moderate your claim.

Use Connectives to Indicate a Cause or Effect Relationship

This simply means that you should say outright whether you are talking about cause, effect, or both. Do so by using the right connectives—those phrases and words that make your meaning clear to a reader. Here are some examples along with the revisions:

Original: `A corporate executive trying to close a sale in`
`Peking should not wear white.  In China, white is`
`the symbol of mourning.`

Revision: `A corporate executive trying to close a sale in`
`Peking should not wear white` <u>`because`</u> `in China white`
`is the color of mourning.`

Original: `Word processors have changed the complexion of`
`writing techniques.  It is easy to make a variety of`
`editorial changes.`

Revision: `One major` <u>`effect`</u> `of the computer is to make writing`
`easy through word processing software that can`
`quickly execute a variety of editorial changes.`

In an analysis of several causes or effects, you might even number them as follows:

> The first cause is . . . .
> The second cause is . . . .
> The third cause is . . . .
>   OR
> One effect is . . . .
> Another effect is . . . .
> A third effect is . . . .

Focus on Immediate Rather than Remote Causes

In a philosophical sense, cause and effect constitute an infinite chain. Remember this rhyme?

For want of the nail the shoe was lost.
For want of the shoe the horse was lost.
For want of the horse the rider was lost.
For want of the rider the message was lost.
For want of the message the battle was lost.
For want of the battle the war was lost.

If we believe the premise of this jingle, we might fall into the trap of searching infinity for the cause lurking right under our noses.

But causal analysis rarely requires you to probe the philosophical mists. What is required is an analysis of proximate cause—the one nearest and most significant to the analyzed event. For example, let us say that your history instructor gave this assignment: "List two main causes leading to the adoption of the Monroe Doctrine." Among the immediate causes of the Monroe Doctrine were (1) the disagreement with Russia over the colonization of the northwest coast of the American continent, and (2) the fear that reactionary European countries would not acknowledge Latin America's newly won independence from Spain. To go beyond these to remote causes such as George Washington's policy of noninterference, or, even more remote, the notion of human freedom embodied in the Constitution, is to journey by unicycle when you might have gone by car. A sophisticated essayist can no doubt do it, but it is above and beyond the call of the assignment and, if botched, might earn you a poor grade accompanied by the comment, "Vague causal connection."

Occasionally, however, an assignment may require you to trace origins, and you will need to examine the remote. For example, if you were asked to explain the origin of the world-famous Oktoberfest, held each year in Munich, you would have to cite the celebration of the wedding between Crown Prince Ludwig of Bavaria to Princess Therese of Saxon-Hildburghausen in the nineteenth century, which evolved into the annual festival. Such special assignments aside, you should focus your analyses of cause on the immediate rather than on the remote.

Exactly how skilled writers manage to focus on immediate rather than on remote cause is one lesson taught by the analyzing essays that follow. Barbara Holland explains why we like to wear bathrobes; Martin Seligman, why so many baby boomers are restless and discontent. Nicole Duplaix reaches into history to reconstruct the cause of the calamitous bubonic plague of the fourteenth century. And Marvin Harris probes the dreariest mystery of all—why nothing ever seems to work as it should. Our student writer analyzes the cause of a common but mysterious occurrence that enriches our daily lives—laughter. While she did an admirable job in her first draft, she made revisions that decisively bettered and tightened her second.

Original:

Your opening question hints at definition more than cause. Begin with immediate focus on cause. Use the word "cause" in your topic sentence.

What is laughter? Dogs, birds, or lizards don't laugh. Thus, we must assume that laughter is the result of a higher, more developed intelligence. Let us focus on some typical example involving laughter. A pompous, oversized, somber man, dressed in a spotless pinstripe suit and vest, sits down in the lobby of a luxury hotel to read the newspaper. But he misjudges the distance between him and the sofa, accidentally landing spread–eagle on the floor, with a foolish look on his face. People run to his aid, but it is obvious that they are more amused than concerned. Several onlookers turn away to keep from having their laughter discovered. Now, if it had been obvious that the *Elaborate on this point with more examples.* man intended to sit on the floor, the desire for laughing would not have surfaced. The fact that *Your conclusion needs to be more definite.* the man's sitting down was involuntary is what *Conclude with summary of the causal relationship you are analyzing. In other words, let your reader know what causes laughter.* makes him the target of laughter.

Revision:

What strange impulse causes human beings to laugh? After all, dogs, birds, or lizards don't laugh. Thus, we must assume that laughter is the result of a higher, more developed intelligence. But what exactly will cause in humans this sudden reaction of a chuckle, a giggle, a guffaw? Let us focus on some typical example

involving laughter. A pompous, oversized, somber
man, dressed in a spotless pinstripe suit and
vest, sits down in the lobby of a luxury hotel
to read the newspaper. But he misjudges the
distance between him and the sofa, accidentally
landing spread-eagle on the floor, with a
foolish look on his face. People run to his aid,
but it is obvious that they are more amused than
concerned. Several onlookers turn away to keep
from having their laughter discovered. Now, if
it had been obvious that the man intended to sit
on the floor, the desire for laughing would not
have surfaced. The fact that the man's sitting
down was involuntary is what makes him the
target of laughter. Humans laugh when a pie
lands in some bungler's face, when a stuck-up
snob of a lady gets her skirt caught in the door
as she attempts to waltz away in a snit, when a
bucket of sewage water is poured on an
absent-minded professor daydreaming as he passes
under some putzfrau's window. The ridiculous
element in each of these cases is a certain
mechanical inelasticity where one would expect
to find living pliability. The cause of
laughter, in short, is clumsy obstinacy in a
situation that calls for skillful flexibility.

The revision more clearly spells out the causal connection, adds some specific examples as evidence, and gives a sense of purpose to the paragraph by
ending on a clear topic sentence.

LITERATURE

Barbara Holland
NOW IS THE TIME FOR BATHROBES, THE CLOTH OF SLOTH

Barbara Holland (b. 1925 in Portland, Me.) is an author, poet, and freelance journalist. After graduating with an M.A. from the University of Pennsylvania, she worked as a lexicographer for G. & C. Merriam Co., John C. Winston, and Funk and Wagnalls in New York. Among her published works are Return in Sagittarius *(1965),* A Game of Scraps *(1967),* Autumn Wizard *(1973), and* Crisis of Rejuvenation *(1975). Holland is also in demand for readings of her own poetry. The essay below is reprinted from a June, 1988, issue of the* Los Angeles Times.

I do my best thinking in a bathrobe. I'm ashamed of it, naturally, 1
and if anyone catches me at it I fake a sneeze; when you're sick you can wear a bathrobe. Otherwise you're supposed to be dressed for action.

America has never been a nation of bathrobe wearers. Paul Re- 2
vere, Annie Oakley and General Custer all slept with their boots on. We're a frontier people and proud of it. Even now we feel we ought to be clothed to fight off Comanches at all times, and if the mailman catches us bathrobed we mumble and blush.

It has nothing to do with modesty, since a bathrobe covers us 3
generously. It's the shame of being thought inactive. Bathrobes, the cloth of sloth.

Everyone says we live in an age of increasing leisure, defined in 4
the dictionary as the "state of having time which one can spend as one pleases." But we shouldn't please to sit around in a bathrobe. We should go skiing. We wouldn't apologize to the meter reader if he caught us in our ski pants, but wearing a bathrobe isn't a proper use of free time. To be decent, American leisure must be vigorous. If we were out jogging we'd be considered a useful member of society, but in a bathrobe we're a leech, a slug, a parasite.

Bathrobes restrict activity. You can't mow the lawn or do aero- 5
bics in them—that's their charm and their shame. In the full-length female model you can't even walk up the stairs without tripping, though most male bathrobes stop at the knee, no one knows why. Perhaps men are thought to have more need of their legs: if a fire starts, they can carry their swaddled wives to safety.

By limiting movement, the bathrobe releases the mind, like go- 6

Reprinted from *Smithsonian* magazine, May 1988, by Barbara Holland.

ing into the lotus position but less painful. Enfolded in fabric, unable to bustle about, we can still read the Sunday paper, listen to music, sort old photographs or paint watercolors, absentmindedly wiping the brush on our laps. We probably won't muse over the budget deficit because you need proper clothes on to pay serious attention to current events. That's why the Sunday paper should be read in a bathrobe; it softens the hard edge of happenings. We can contemplate the arms race and a recipe for asparagus soufflé with equal detachment. Bathrobes encourage the long view and a sense of the durability of a civilization more likely to include soufflés than the arms race.

7   The bathrobe keeps us home, excused from dealing with the world. Feet on the coffee table, we are draft exempt from the battles of business and daily life. "I'm not dressed," we reply when people suggest that we drive them to the airport or put up the storm windows. Outside, time grinds through its endless events, large and small, but we can't be expected to take part: we aren't dressed.

8   The bathrobe keeps us gentle. It's possible to sulk in a bathrobe, but not to rage. A furious person in a bathrobe would be a joke, commanding neither respect nor fear, and when we feel a fit of temper coming on we instinctively go put on street clothes in which to have it. Habitually bad-tempered people never wear bathrobes—in order to stay prepared. You can make love in a bathrobe, but not war. Statesmen should wear bathrobes at all times.

9   Statesmen are probably afraid of them, though. A lot of people are. They won't admit it, but they think the bathrobe mindset, once yielded to, might weaken them forever. The soft folds, the easy sleeve, would soak through to the muscle and decay it. The taut bow of their determination would be quite unstrung. They would—perish the thought—relax, and this would be followed immediately by chronic unemployment and beer for breakfast.

10   You can tell bathrobe-phobics because they never oversleep, and always dress and tie their shoes before they drink their coffee. They often say "I like to keep busy." They say this whenever they see someone in a bathrobe.

11   Accomplishment means scurrying around with your shoes on. The prophets tell us about a future in which the modern executive will stay home and do it all by computer hookup, but I don't believe it—the American people would never stand for it. I mean, what's to stop him from getting through an entire day's work in his *bathrobe?* What would Daniel Boone say?

A friend of mine has cleverly replaced her bathrobe with a sweat   12
suit. She's still lounging around over coffee at noon, but she
doesn't look it; she looks as if she got up at 5 to jog. People in real
clothes see her and feel guilty, instead of asking scornfully if she's
sick. Still, a sweat suit just isn't the same. It doesn't impart the
same peaceable viewpoint. Sweat suits are involved, bathrobes are
detached.

Besides, you can go outside in a sweat suit, so it doesn't get you   13
out of doing things. True, I've driven people to trains in my bathrobe, but it isn't decent and I always hoped the robe would pass
for a coat. I tried to put a coat expression on my face instead of a
bathrobe expression. The brisk, dressed expression.

Surely, surely, it's time America packed in all this booted-and-   14
spurred business, barging out to shoot buffalo or clean the gutters.
Must we always stay dressed to chase cattle rustlers? Can't we put
on our bathrobes now?

Bathrobe wearers of the nation, stand tall. Open the door freely   15
and proudly, even to your in-laws, and let them see what you're
wearing. The frontier is closed. It is time now for philosophy, for
contemplation for bathrobes.

Perhaps even for an afternoon nap.   16

Vocabulary

sloth (title)

leech (4)

swaddled (5)

muse (6)

soufflé (6)

taut (9)

chronic (9)

phobics (10)

rustlers (14)

Critical Inquiries

1. What is the author's explicit thesis? Where is it stated? How does she support it?

2. The author takes considerable trouble to convince us of the value of wearing bathrobes. Do you believe that turning the bathrobe into a popular fashion item is what this essay is all about? Or does the author have something else, more important, in mind? Explain your answer.

3. Why does the author suggest that statesmen are probably afraid of bathrobes? (See paragraphs 8, 9.) Do you agree? Why or why not?

4. Reread paragraph 11. Do you agree with the author that executives will never stay home while computers do their work for them? Explain your answer.

5. Do you think women's clothes should be different from that of men? Or do you look forward to a time when clothing will simply be unisexual? Give reasons for your answer.

Rhetorical Inquiries

1. The author uses the bathrobe literally as well as symbolically. On the symbolic level, what does the bathrobe signify?

2. What do the allusions to Paul Revere, Annie Oakley, General Custer, and Daniel Boone have in common?

3. What is the tone of Holland's essay?

4. How does the author keep from sounding like a cranky judge who is patronizing the reader?

5. How is the humorous effect of paragraphs 15 and 16 achieved?

SOCIOLOGY

Martin E. P. Seligman
BOOMER BLUES

Martin E. P. Seligman (b. 1942) is a professor of psychology at the University of Pennsylvania. The essay below is reprinted from the October, 1988, issue of Psychology Today *and is based on Seligman's G. Stanley Hall Lecture to the American Psychological Association during its 1988 annual meeting. It will appear in adapted form in* Learned Optimism, *a book soon to be published by the author.*

The rate of depression over the last two generations has increased roughly tenfold, according to two recent studies on mental illness in our country. Why have we become more depressed, and what, if anything, can be done to prevent the trend from continuing?   1

The answer to the first question comes from studies suggesting that something about our society has made us increasingly vulnerable to depression—not just the blues but serious clinical problems. For years people have looked at the rate of depression in   2

From *Psychology Today*, Oct. 1988. Reprinted by permission of the author.

non-Western, developing cultures and have noted that they usually have few symptoms of depression as we know it—hopelessness, giving up, passivity, low self-esteem and suicide. Typically, when depression appears, as it does occasionally in China, its symptoms are physical rather than psychological. And among less technologically advanced cultures, depression is almost nonexistent.

Recently, anthropologist Edward Schieffelin tried to find the equivalent of depression in New Guinea among a primitive tribe called the Kaluli. But none of the psychological symptoms was there. This lack of depression may be related to their interesting way of solving problems of loss. A person who loses something valuable, such as a pig, has a right to compensation. The society has rituals for dealing with loss (such as dancing and screaming at the neighbor who presumably killed the pig). When someone demands recompense for the loss, either the neighbor or the whole tribe acknowledges the person's condition and provides compensating action. The Kaluli culture provides strong buffers against having loss turn into helplessness, hopelessness, sadness and despair. In so doing, it breaks up the process of depression.

We do not need to look at Stone Age tribes to see examples of a society with a low rate of depression. There is one in our own back yard. For the last 20 years, researcher Janice Egeland has led a monumental study of the mental health of the Old Order Amish of Pennsylvania. There are 10,000 of them living in Lancaster County, Pennsylvania. The Old Order Amish are a mid 19th-century farming culture; they use no electricity, no automobiles and no alcohol or drugs. Their community is very religious and closely knit.

When the lifetime rates of depression in the Amish reported by Egeland and her colleagues are compared with those of Baltimore residents, the rates of bipolar depression (manic-depressive disorder) are about the same: 1 or 2 percent. But the Amish rate of unipolar depression (depression without mania) is about one-fifth or one-tenth that of Baltimore residents; in fact, it's about the same rate found in our culture two generations ago.

So why the boom in depression? Why are today's young people about 10 times as likely to be depressed as were their parents and grandparents? Let's look at psychology itself as a factor. When I was a graduate student in psychology almost 25 years ago, the explanations for people's behavior were different from those we now use. In the early '60s we usually assumed that people were pushed or pulled by their environment. The details of this pushing and pulling depended on the theory you held—biological, ethological, Skinnerian, psychodynamic—but the common thread was the assumption that people act because they are driven largely by external forces.

Starting around 1965, our explanations of human behavior underwent a sea change. The site of action shifted from outside the self to within the self. In other words, psychologists now say that at least some of the time people decide, prefer, plan and choose their own course of action. This change seems to be intimately related to a new exaltation of the individual which, I believe, creates fertile ground for a rise in depression.   7

We live for the first time in an age of personal control, or, as Ronald Reagan dubbed it, "The Age of the Individual." At least four historical forces have converged to make this happen. The first two—the rise of "personalized" mass production, and general prosperity—have exalted the self; the other two—the assassinations of public leaders and the loss of faith in God and the family—have weakened our commitment to larger social institutions. And one untoward consequence of this convergence has been a huge increase in depression.   8

When the assembly line was created at the turn of this century, it was profitable to paint every Ford black. In the 1950s, changes in manufacturing technology made it just as profitable to paint cars every color of the rainbow. Automation—later abetted by the computer—opened an enormous market for customization, personalization and individual choice. Even blue jeans are no longer all blue; they come in dozens of colors and hundreds of varieties. If you include optional equipment, color and models, you can now buy any of several million "unique" cars. To tap this market, advertising has inflated—indeed exalted—individual choice. The deciding, choosing, hedonically preoccupied individual has become a profitable target.   9

And the money is there. America is a Croesus-rich [1]country. Even if some groups have been left out of this prosperity, the fact is that, on average, Americans now have more buying power than ever before in history. Wealth today means something different than it did in centuries past. Unlike the wealth of a medieval prince, who could no more sell his land and go out and buy horses than he could sell his title, our wealth means purchasing power—of a bewildering array of items. We have more records, clothes, education, concerts and books to choose from than ever before.   10

Our soaring expectations went beyond consumer goods into   11

---

[1]Croesus, last King of Lydia, was defeated and killed by the Persians in 546 B.C. He was known for his great wealth.

nonmaterial matters. We came to expect our jobs to be more than a way to make a living. Work now needs to be ecologically innocent, comforting to our dignity, a call to growth and excitement, a meaningful contribution to society—and deliver a large paycheck. Married partners once settled for duty, but today's mates expect to be ecstatic lovers, intellectual colleagues and partners in tennis and water sports. We even expect our partners to be loving parents, a historical peculiarity to anyone versed in the Victorian child-rearing model. It's as if some idiot raised the ante on what it takes to be a normal human being. We blindly accept this rush of rising expectations for the self. What's remarkable is not that we fail on some but that we achieve so many.

What follows from these changes is what I call the "California   12
self," a new self that has largely replaced the "New England self," its predecessor for generations. The traditional New England self is a minimal self, more like our grandparents than us. It's a nose-to-the-grindstone, duty-bound self that works hard to earn its rewards; it is certainly not preoccupied with what it feels—if it acknowledges that it feels at all. The California self, by contrast, is the self taken "to the max," a self that chooses, feels pleasure and pain, dictates action and even has things like esteem, efficacy and confidence. In our therapy-oriented society, psychotherapies that work on depression exploit the California self. Cognitive therapy and interpersonal therapy let the self reflect upon itself, talk to itself and find out what it's doing wrong, change and improve the self—and participate in an act of self-creation.

Our wealth, coupled with a market geared to individuals, has   13
produced the California self—an entity whose pleasures and pains, whose successes and failures occupy center stage in our society. Such rampant individualism, alone, might be positive, bringing with it sweet freedoms; at worst it might be merely innocuous. But the rise of the California self coincides with events that have weakened our commitment to the larger, traditional institutions of our society.

Many people probably sensed what I did on November 22,   14
1963, when our vision of the future was destroyed by gunfire. We lost hope that our society could cure human ills. And a generation altered its commitment from careers of public service to careers of self-service; at least, we felt, we can make ourselves happy as individuals. More bullets sent us scurrying from public to private concerns as Martin Luther King Jr., Malcolm X and Robert Kennedy also fell.

Still more killing—in the Vietnam War—taught those a bit   15 younger a more global lesson: America cannot be in the service of the world. Indeed, those who believed that it could—or should— were scorned. The futility of 10 years of war eroded youth's commitment to patriotism and America; it shattered almost completely with Watergate. Being committed to the nation no longer gave people hope.

Other institutions, such as religion and the family, could, in theory, replace the nation as a source of hope and identity, keeping young people from turning inward to themselves. But just as belief in the nation was crumbling, belief in God was also fading, and the skyrocketing divorce rate eroded belief in family as well. When people no longer believe that their country is powerful and benevolent, that the family can be a source of enduring unity and support or that a relationship with God is important, where else can they turn for identity, satisfaction and hope? Many people turn to a very small and frail unit indeed: the self. 16

Belief in the self—individualism—need not lead to depression as long as we can fall back on large institutions—religion, country, family. When you fail to reach some of your personal goals, as we all must, you can turn to these larger institutions for hope. When the Kaluli fail, their integration within their tribe prevents loss from becoming hopelessness. But in a self standing alone without the buffer of larger beliefs, helplessness and failure can all too easily become hopelessness and despair. 17

This is the link to the current epidemic of depression. I have argued for a number of years that depression is a disorder of the self. In particular, I believe depression can happen when people find themselves helpless to achieve personal goals or to escape frustrations. When people face failures that they cannot control, they feel helpless. This "learned" helplessness expands to become hopelessness and full-blown depression when people attribute their failures to causes that are stable (that is, enduring), global (likely to affect many outcomes), and internal (something about themselves). People who think this way are likely to say, for example, "I'm an unlovable person" when a relationship goes awry instead of saying, "Maybe he/she just had a bad day." Along with my students, I have done several years of experiments showing that the way we attribute blame for our failures can drive us into depression. 18

In this age of soaring expectations, life is inevitably full of personal failures. Our stocks go down, people we love reject us, we write bad papers, we don't get the job we want, we give bad lectures. When larger, benevolent institutions (God, nation, family) 19 are available, they help us cope with personal loss and give us a framework for hope. Without faith in these institutions, we interpret personal failures as catastrophic. They seem to last forever and contaminate all of life. The new emphasis on the self raises the chances that we will blame these misfortunes, losses and disappointments on ourselves and thus depress ourselves.

Either the emphasis on individualism alone or the loss of faith in [20] institutions alone would increase our vulnerability to depression. The recent combination of the two, I believe, is a surefire recipe for an epidemic of depression.

Will this epidemic continue or grow worse? I doubt it. Rampant [21] individualism carries with it the seeds of its own destruction. Individualism without commitment to the common good produces widespread depression and meaninglessness. A society cannot tolerate for long these painful and unrewarding byproducts of its obsession with self.

Surely one necessary (although hardly sufficient) condition for [22] finding meaning in our lives is an attachment to something larger than the lonely self. To the extent that young people now find it hard to take seriously their relationship with God, to care about their relationship with the country or to be part of a large and abiding family, they will find it very difficult to find meaning in life. To put it another way, the self is a very poor site for finding meaning.

How might the situation change? One possibility is that individ- [23] ualism will wane, that the California self will revert to the New England self. Another, more frightening possibility is that we will rashly surrender the sweet freedoms that individualism brings, giving up personal control and concern for the self so we can shed depression and find meaning. In *Escape from Freedom,* Erich Fromm showed how Hitler's Nazis did just that. This century is riddled with other disastrous examples. The current appeal of many fundamentalist religions around the world may reflect today's escape from freedom.

There is a final possibility, a more hopeful one: We can retain [24] our belief in the importance of the individual but scale down our preoccupation with comfort and discomfort and make a renewed commitment to the common good. A balance between individualism, with its perilous freedoms, and commitment to the common good should lower depression and make life more meaningful. In this age of choice, this choice, surely, is ours.

Vocabulary

passivity (2)

recompense (3)

buffers (3)

monumental (4)

converged (8)

untoward (8)

abetted (9)

customization (9)

hedonically (9)

efficacy (12)

cognitive (12)

rampant (13)

innocuous (13)

plummeted (16)

catastrophic (25)

Critical Inquiries

1. What is the author's basic argument? Does he provide scientific evidence for it? Are you convinced of the truth of this argument? Why or why not?

2. According to the author, what serious drawbacks accompany our age of individualism? How would you defend the importance of personal freedom despite its drawbacks?

3. What connection does the author draw between living in a materialistic society and depression? What examples from your own experience can you cite to either support or contradict the author's view?

4. Would you rather go back to a more primitive time in history, when depression was not so prevalent, or are you satisfied to live in today's atmosphere, despite the attendant danger of becoming depressed? Give reasons for your choice.

5. Is the essay pessimistic or optimistic in its ultimate outlook for our society? What is your own outlook?

Rhetorical Inquiries

1. Two questions form the basis for the organization of Seligman's essay. What are the questions? Where in the essay are they answered?

2. What two symbols are used in paragraph 12? What is your own interpretation of these symbols? Do you consider these symbols useful? Why or why not?

3. How does the author make a smooth transition from his report on the Kaluli culture to his report on the New England Amish people?

4. How does the author support his view that our age is an age of "personalized" mass production?

5. What contrast is drawn in paragraph 10? What words are used to indicate contrast?

EPIDEMIOLOGY

Nicole Duplaix
PLAGUE

Nicole Duplaix is Director of Environmental Assessments for GeoServices, a Florida engineering firm whose primary concern is the solution of environmental, geotechnical, hydrogeological, and waste-management problems. Dr. Duplaix received most of her education in France, where in 1981 she was awarded a doctorat es Sciences degree from the Faculty of Sciences at the University of Paris. Among her many accomplishments are editing zoological manuscripts for publication; founding and directing TRAFFIC, an organization that obtains, verifies, collates, and disseminates data on all species of plants and animals and their products involved in international trade; and Director of the Communications Office for the South Florida Water Management District. Beginning in November of 1982, Dr. Duplaix spent a whole year photographing and writing a story about fleas and the plague for National Geographic Society magazine, from which the essay below is reprinted.

Our helicopter skimmed at treetop level, the desert beneath us a dizzying blur. "Keeps us off unfriendly radar screens," commented the South African pilot wryly, as the copter lurched to dodge a tall palm.

We had entered the troubled border area between Namibia and its northern neighbor Angola. But I had come to investigate a far older war—man's battle against plague. It stalked the Namibian sands below, one of many plague zones that survive worldwide, despite ceaseless efforts to control this disease.

I glimpsed a fenced cluster of huts. Flea-control teams under the protective eye of soldiers were dusting the kraal with clouds of DDT. Around it corn crops lay shriveled: Drought was inflicting its misery—and helping spread plague.

"Wild gerbils, starved by the drought, seek food stored in the kraals," explained Professor Margaretha Isaäcson, a doctor from

From "Fleas: The Lethal Leapers," *National Geographic,* May 1988. Reprinted by permission of the author.

neighboring South Africa. "The rodents bring plague with them, and fleas for spreading it."

In the hospital in Oshakati I leaned over 11-year-old Monica   5
Sherugeleni and smiled. Shyly she lifted her arm to show me a swelling the size of my palm in her armpit. Warm and firm to the touch, it was a bubo, the symptomatic growth that gives the name to bubonic plague.

"Cases number in the hundreds, and the season isn't over yet,"   6
said Maj. Neels de Villiers, head of South Africa's 58 doctors on the scene. "Young children, two to three years old, usually recover. Older patients sometimes develop septicemia or meningitis, and these may die. But our mortality rate is only 4 percent, lower than yours in the States."

Accomplices of plague, fleas evolved as highly specialized blood-   7
sucking parasites at least 60 million years ago, probably living on prehistoric mammals. Their ancestors may have had wings, but these would have tangled in the host's fur. Jumping provided an alternative means of reaching a passing host or evading enemies. Gradually muscles and tendons were modified to help power the formidable hind legs that make the flea a star performer, a true insect Olympian.

Fleas of various species can   8
- jump 150 times their own length—vertically or horizontally— equivalent to a man jumping nearly a thousand feet;
- survive months without feeding;
- accelerate 50 times faster than the space shuttle;
- withstand enormous pressure—the secret to surviving the scratchings and bitings of the flea-ridden;
- remain frozen for a year, then revive.

In the 17th century when the Dutchman Anton van Leeuwen-   9
hoek was perfecting the microscope, he chose the flea as a subject for scrutiny. His observations aroused such interest that the microscope became known as the "flea glass." To great merriment Leeuwenhoek discovered that these minute parasites had parasites of their own, a web of predation that evoked Jonathan Swift's sally:

> So, naturalists observe, a flea
> Hath smaller fleas that on him prey;
> And these have smaller still to bite 'em,
> And so proceed ad infinitum.

But for millennia the disease spread by fleas has been no laugh-   10
ing matter. Plague may have originated among burrowing rodents

of central Africa and central Asia. When plague broke out in a rodent population—quickly reducing the numbers—rodents from neighboring colonies moved in, picked up the infected fleas, and spread the disease.

When plague entered the human population, the consequences were catastrophic. The first outbreak may have been a scourge that struck the Philistines in the 12th century B.C.; the Old Testament account mentions "mice that mar the land." 11

Later three plague epidemics—so vast they were called pandemics—ravaged the world. The first struck in A.D. 541, swirling around the Mediterranean in a deadly maelstrom for more than two centuries, killing as many as 40 million people and weakening the Byzantine Empire. "The bodies of the sick were covered with black pustules . . . the symptoms of immediate death," wrote Procopius, historian of Byzantine Emperor Justinian. At its peak in Constantinople, he reported, the plague killed 10,000 people a day. 12

The second pandemic came in the 14th century, when lucrative trade routes opened across Asia. Caravans and ships brought more than silk and jewels. In October 1347 vessels sailed into Messina, Sicily, with crews dying from a mysterious disease. No one noticed that shipboard rats were also ill. 13

The next five years were so devastating that they became known as the time of the Black Death. By 1352, plague had killed 25 million people in Europe alone. 14

Feverish victims suffered excruciating swellings in the groin or armpit—the buboes. Most died within five days. Sometimes the infection spread via the bloodstream to the lungs; then death came in three days or less. This was pneumonic plague, the deadliest form then and today. 15

Looking for scapegoats, Europeans massacred Jews, suspected of poisoning the water. Neighbors turned on neighbors, parents turned on children. The sick were walled up in their houses and later quarantined on islands. To no avail. So many died so quickly that cities dug plague pits for the corpses. With no escape, no cure, "there was no one who wept for any death, for all awaited death," wrote Agnolo di Tura, a chronicler in Siena, Italy. 16

"The worst thing was finding no explanation for the greatest natural disaster Europe had ever known," Professor Henri H. Mollaret and Jacqueline Brossollet, plague historians at the Institut Pasteur in Paris, told me. 17

The church saw the plague epidemic as a manifestation of God's wrath. A committee of doctors at the University of Paris pronounced that it was the sinister result of the conjunction of Saturn, 18

Jupiter, and Mars. A common belief that plague was caused by "corrupt vapors" gave birth to the macabre doggerel that children still recite today:

> Ring around the rosies,
> A pocket full of posies,
> Achoo! Achoo!
> We all fall down.

A nursery rhyme? Hardly. Rosies were the pink rash associated with plague; posies were the nosegays carried to perfume the corrupt vapors. Sneezing was brought on by feverish chills; then all fall down, dead.

As the sweeping scythe of plague turned bustling towns into sepulchers and emptied the countryside, it reshaped European society. With few serfs left to till the land, survivors could negotiate for wages with landlords. The breakdown of manorialism and the evolution of an economy based on money sowed seeds of capitalism. [19]

Plague struck without pattern, skirting one area only to bludgeon another. Busy ports such as Venice, Marseille, and Barcelona endured dozens of outbreaks. England took 200 years to recover from its 14th-century death toll. In the Great Plague of 1665 at least 68,000 Londoners died. Survivors cowered behind shuttered windows as the body collector cried, "Bring out your dead!" [20]

In man, plague enjoyed an unwitting ally. Families crowded in houses where rats were tolerated and hygiene did not exist. People wore the same underclothes day and night. Fleas and lice thrived and went along when the clothes of the dead were sold or passed on. [21]

As the second pandemic raged and waned through the centuries, chroniclers came tantalizingly close to the mysterious cause of the disease. Observed Chinese poet Shih Tao-nan in 1792, shortly before succumbing to plague: "Few days following the death of the rats, Men pass away like falling walls!" [22]

In the late 1800s the third pandemic spread plague around the world. It lingers today. Carried out of China's Yunnan Province in 1855, plague traveled slowly east; by 1894 it reached Hong Kong, where it killed some 10,000 people. In this charnel house a young French bacteriologist unmasked the pestilence. [23]

Alexandre Yersin had been sent by the Institut Pasteur to investigate the epidemic. Examining a plague victim, he found in the [24] buboes "a swarm of microbes, all similar in appearance . . . short bacilli with rounded ends."

One part of the puzzle had been solved. But how was the guilty 25 bacillus transmitted?

As Hong Kong's death toll mounted, hundreds of ships docked 26 and departed with their familiar complement of rats. Steamships now carried the disease even faster, before unsuspecting crews became ill. Plague fanned out to where it had been unknown: Japan, Australia, southern Africa, and the Americas.

India, the site of earlier outbreaks, was especially hard hit; six 27 million died in a decade. Once again the Institut Pasteur sent help, this time Dr. Paul-Louis Simond.

Walking filthy city streets, he observed dead rats littering plague- 28 ridden neighborhoods—75 in one house alone. Humans who picked them up, he noted, soon fell ill themselves. In his makeshift Bombay laboratory, a tent pummeled by the monsoon, Simond dissected rats and found the plague bacillus. These plague rats, he observed, carried far more fleas than healthy ones. He also noted that, contrary to common belief, the rat flea readily bit man.

Rats . . . bacilli . . . fleas . . . . Simond had the connection. 29 Rats were plague's natural host but could not themselves transmit the disease to man. Fleas engorged with contaminated rat blood, however, could transmit plague from rat to rat—or rat to man.

"On June 2, 1898, I was overwhelmed," Simond wrote. "I had 30 just unveiled a secret which had tormented man for so long." Though his discoveries went generally unrecognized for a decade, they helped form the basis for modern plague control.

Today we suspect that of the more than 2,400 known species 31 and subspecies of fleas, perhaps only 120 can transmit plague. Fewer than 20 species readily bite man.

Transmission of plague requires precise meshing of a complex 32 chain of events. To give you plague, the right type of flea must first bite a rodent infected with plague and pick up the bacillus. The microbe incubates in the flea's digestive tract, where it multiplies and eventually blocks the gut. If the now starving flea bites you in a fruitless attempt to feed, it will inject countless plague bacilli into your bloodstream. Just one can lead to death.

To keep plague in wild rodents from spreading to man, our lead- 33 ing weapon is insecticides. Spraying for fleas with DDT, Burma, Vietnam, India, and southern African nations have scored major victories against plague. But war or social upheaval can interrupt these programs, giving fresh opportunity to what one doctor called "the enemy in ambush."

During the Vietnam War soldiers and civilians sought protection   34
from shellfire in underground mazes. Bandicoot rats and other rodents adopted these convenient burrows. Between 1965 and 1970
official reports listed 24,848 cases of plague. Thanks to antibiotics,
96 percent of the victims survived.

"Plague mistakenly still carries a terrible stigma, something gov-   35
ernments feel they should be ashamed of," said Dr. Norman G.
Gratz, the World Health Organization (WHO) official in Geneva in
charge of keeping tabs on plague control around the world. He told
me of a doctor who worked with one country's local health officials setting up a program to check rampant plague and then paid a
courtesy call on the minister of health.

"We used to have many cases annually," said the minister glibly.   36
"Thanks to our control measures, we've had none in 30 years." Officially plague did not exist.

The United States once did the same. When plague came ashore   37
in San Francisco on June 27, 1899, political leaders, protecting business interests at the expense of disease control, overrode health officials and denied its presence. The governor decreed it a felony to
publicize its existence. By 1904, more than 100 people had died of
"syphilitic septicemia," the official pseudonym of plague.

Western Americans still pay for that deceit. Infecting one wild   38
rodent population after another, the disease made a macabre
march inland. Today 13 states live under its cloud. A result: Forty
Americans contracted plague in 1983; six died. Last year there
were 12 cases; two victims succumbed. Most cases occur in Arizona and New Mexico. Here plague-prone ground squirrels and
prairie dogs live as close as one's backyard.

Because plague occurs infrequently in the U.S., it is not always   39
recognized.

"The disease is difficult to diagnose," explained Dr. Allan M.   40
Barnes, director of the Center for Disease Control's plague branch
in Fort Collins, Colorado. "Patients may be suspected of having flu
or some other virus and sent home with prescribed medication,
which has no effect. By the time they call the doctor again, they're
critically ill."

The peril is greatest if you come down with the disease in a   41
plague-free area. In 1983 a teenage girl who had petted a sick chip-
munk in Santa Fe died of pneumonic plague in South Carolina on
her way home to Maryland. Local doctors never thought of testing
for plague. Whereas an estimated 2 percent of plague victims die in
Burma and 8 percent in South Africa, in the medically advanced
U.S., due to this unfamiliarity, the death rate is 17 percent.

To predict where plague will strike next, Western health officials 42
keep a check on wild rodent populations.

"We are concerned about plague outbreaks among wild rodents 43
anywhere there is risk to humans," said Dr. Bernard Nelson, head
of California's plague-monitoring team. "The main threat is in urban settings. In recent years we have trapped 'positive' rodents in
Griffith Park, in downtown Los Angeles. Plague is endemic in the
San Bruno Mountains, right next to San Francisco International
Airport. But the flea species that live there don't bite people."

Like control, plague treatments have greatly improved. 44

"The slower bubonic form is easily cured with antibiotics," said 45
Dr. Thomas Kereselidze of WHO. "But pneumonic plague, infecting the lungs, is fatal 95 percent of the time. The patient must be
isolated and given antibiotics very quickly if he is to survive.
Worse, the patient only has to cough or sneeze to transmit it to
others."

No one believes that plague will ever be eradicated. 46

"There is a vaccine, but it is not totally effective and lasts only 47
six months," explained South Africa's Margaretha Isaäcson. Yet in
plague-rife Vietnam only a few vaccinated U.S. soldiers contracted
the disease.

Wiping out the rodents that harbor plague is impossible—and 48
undesirable during outbreaks of the disease. "If you killed all
plague-carrying rodents," said Dr. Isaäcson, "their fleas would seek
another host, and it could be you! Rodent control should be practiced when there is no danger of depriving infected fleas of their
hosts."

Three pandemics, killing more than 200 million people. . . . 49
Only disease-carrying mosquitoes have caused as much misery as
this fascinating order of insects aptly called Siphonaptera—"wing-
less siphons." Yet for generations we have not only tolerated these
pests, we have used them for entertainment.

Vocabulary

kraal (3)	macabre (18)
gerbils (4)	sepulchers (19)
septicemia (6)	serfs (19)
meningitis (6)	manorialism (19)
scrutiny (9)	bludgeon (20)
predation (9)	tantalizingly (22)
catastrophic (11)	charnel (23)
scourge (11)	engorged (29)

maelstrom (12)   incubates (32)
pustules (12)   endemic (43)
conjunction (18)   eradicated (46)

Critical Inquiries

1. What image of the flea is projected in this essay? Describe the flea in your own words.

2. Why did it take so many hundreds of years for science to discover the cause of plague? Were people stupid, uncaring, or in some other way to blame?

3. In your view, how does the present epidemic of AIDS compare with the medieval plague? Is it less or more lethal, less or more vicious in its attacks?

4. Why do you think that a committee of Parisian doctors—that is, well-educated men—blamed the plague on the conjunction of Saturn, Jupiter, and Mars?

5. Why did it take a decade before Dr. Paul-Louis Simond's discovery of the connection between rats, fleas, and the plague was generally acknowledged? Speculate on the reasons.

Rhetorical Inquiries

1. In this essay, how does the author establish a connection between the present and the past? Is her strategy rhetorically sound? Why or why not?

2. In which paragraph is the process of spreading the plague described most clearly yet succinctly?

3. What effect does the reference to the childhood song have on the reader? (See paragraph 18.)

4. Do you consider this essay a valid scientific study or just another superficial account of a disease? Give reasons for your answer.

5. How does the author make it easy for the reader to identify the three pandemics first mentioned in paragraph 12?

MANUFACTURING

Marvin Harris
WHY NOTHING WORKS

Marvin Harris (b. 1927) is an anthropology professor at the University of Florida. Among his best-known books are Cannibals and Kings *(1977) and* America Now *(1981), works that explore American life from the*

point of view of the anthropologist. In the essay below, excerpted from
America Now, *Harris illustrates Murphy's Law as applied to modern*
consumer goods.

According to a law attributed to the savant known only as Mur-   1
phy, "if anything can go wrong, it will." Corollaries to Murphy's
Law suggest themselves as clues to the shoddy goods problem: If
anything can break down, it will; if anything can fall apart, it will;
if anything can stop running, it will. While Murphy's Law can
never be wholly defeated, its effects can usually be postponed.
Much of human existence consists of efforts aimed at making sure
that things don't go wrong, fall apart, break down, or stop running
until a decent interval has elapsed after their manufacture. Fore-
stalling Murphy's Law as applied to products demands intelligence,
skill, and commitment. If these human inputs are assisted by special quality-control instruments, machines, and scientific sampling
procedures, so much the better. But gadgets and sampling alone
will never do the trick since these items are also subject to Murphy's Law. Quality-control instruments need maintenance; gauges
go out of order; X rays and laser beams need adjustments. No matter how advanced the technology, quality demands intelligent, motivated human thought and action.

Some reflection about the material culture of prehistoric and pre-   2
industrial peoples may help to show what I mean. A single visit to
a museum which displays artifacts used by simple preindustrial societies is sufficient to dispel the notion that quality is dependent on
technology. Artifacts may be of simple, even primitive design, and
yet be built to serve their intended purpose in a realiable manner
during a lifetime of use. We acknowledge this when we honor the
label "handmade" and pay extra for the jewelry, sweaters, and
handbags turned out by the dwindling breeds of modern-day
craftspeople.

What is the source of quality that one finds, let us say, in a   3
Pomo Indian basket so tightly woven that it was used to hold boiling water and never leaked a drop, or in an Eskimo skin boat with
its   matchless   combination   of   lightness,   strength,   and
seaworthiness? Was it merely the fact that these items were
handmade? I don't think so. In unskilled or uncaring hands a handmade basket or boat can fall apart as quickly as baskets or boats

From *America Now,* by Marvin Harris. Copyright © 1981 by Marvin Harris.
Reprinted by permission of Simon & Schuster, Inc.

made by machines. I rather think that the reason we honor the label "handmade" is because it evokes not a technological relationship between producer and product but a social relationship between producer and consumer. Throughout prehistory it was the fact that producers and consumers were either one and the same individuals or close kin that guaranteed the highest degree of reliability and durability in manufactured items. Men made their own spears, bows and arrows, and projectile points; women wove their own baskets and carrying nets, fashioned their own clothing from animal skins, bark, or fiber. Later, as technology advanced and material culture grew more complex, different members of the band or village adopted craft specialties such as pottery-making, basket-weaving, or canoe-building. Although many items were obtained through barter and trade, the connection between producer and consumer still remained intimate, permanent, and caring.

A man is not likely to fashion a spear for himself whose point will fall off in midflight; nor is a woman who weaves her own basket likely to make it out of rotted straw. Similarly, if one is sewing a parka for a husband who is about to go hunting for the family with the temperature at sixty below, all stitches will be perfect. And when the men who make boats are the uncles and fathers of those who sail them, they will be as seaworthy as the state of the art permits.   4

In contrast, it is very hard for people to care about strangers or about products to be used by strangers. In our era of industrial mass production and mass marketing, quality is a constant problem because the intimate sentimental and personal bonds which once made us responsible to each other and to our products have withered away and been replaced by money relationships. Not only are the producers and consumers strangers but the women and men involved in various stages of production and distribution—management, the worker on the factory floor, the office help, the salespeople—are also strangers to each other. In larger companies there may be hundreds of thousands of people all working on the same product who can never meet face-to-face or learn one another's names. The larger the company and the more complex its division of labor, the greater the sum of uncaring relationships and hence the greater the effect of Murphy's Law. Growth adds layer on layer of executives, foremen, engineers, production workers, and sales specialists to the payroll. Since each new employee contributes a diminished share to the overall production process, alienation from the company and its product is   5

likely to increase along with the neglect or even purposeful sabotage of quality standards.

Vocabulary

savant (1)

corollaries (1)

laser (1)

artifacts (2)

dispel (2)

durability (3)

projectile (3)

barter (3)

parka (4)

alienation (5)

sabotage (5)

Critical Inquiries

1. Does the author ever tell us why nothing works, as he promises to do in
   the title of his essay? If he does, what is the answer? State it in one sentence. If the answer is not provided, speculate on the reason.
2. What is Murphy's Law? Do you believe in it? If you do, give examples
   from your own experience of its existence.
3. What evidence, if any, can you cite to prove that in today's technological
   world some labors are performed with immense care despite the fact that
   the producer may not know the consumer?
4. What suggestions do you propose for improving the quality of mass
   production? Use cars as an example.
5. In the final sentence of the essay, the author refers to "alienation" as a
   cause of poor workmanship. What other effects might alienation have on
   someone working for a large company?

Rhetorical Inquiries

1. What strategy does the author use to prove that quality is not dependent
   on technology?
2. What rhetorical role does Murphy's Law play in Harris's essay?
3. In paragraph 2, why does Harris use the term "craftspeople" instead of
   the older term "craftsmen"? Do you approve of Harris's term? Why or
   why not?
4. Paragraph 3 opens with two questions. What purpose do they serve?
5. What transition does the author use to move from the past to the present
   and to show contrast between the two?

Exercises

1. List the causes and effects of the following situations:
   a. smog in industrial cities
   b. battered children (or spouses)
   c. increase in drug addiction
   d. growing interest in health
   e. the difficulty of reaching an arms agreement with the Soviet Union
   f. gravity
   g. the beauty or ugliness of a certain place

2. Using the lists you created for Exercise 1, formulate a clear and concise thesis for a paragraph developed either through analysis of cause or of effect, such as: "The main causes of smog in industrial cities are factory pollution, automobile exhausts, and air inversion layers" or "The most obvious effects of smog in industrial cities are respiratory diseases, plant pollution, and an ugly environment."

Writing Assignments

1. In a 500-word essay, respond to Seligman's "Boomer Blues" by suggesting some cures for the depressed state of our generation.

2. In answer to Harris's "Why Nothing Works" (pp. 451–54), write a 500-word essay entitled "How to Manufacture Products That Work." You will want to use Harris's criticisms as a basis for your corrective suggestions.

3. Focusing on a current economic, social, spiritual, or psychological problem in our society, describe the problem and write a 500-word analysis of either cause or effect. Here are a few possibilities, but many others exist: child pornography, the national deficit, lack of money for education, overcrowded prisons, excessively long and cumbersome court trials, unequal pay for women in the work force, serial marriages, apathy toward church affiliation.

4. Turn the following model into an essay developed by analysis. Only the skeleton of the model is provided. If necessary, go to the library and find your own details. Some reorganization of the details below may also be necessary:

   a. Dag Hammerskjöld gained an international reputation when he served as secretary general of the United Nations.
   In 1955 he went on a diplomatic mission to Peking.
   In 1956 he was instrumental in establishing a United Nations emergency force to keep the peace in the Middle East.
   From 1960 to 1961 he played a strong role in gaining independence for Zaire, formerly the Belgian Congo.
   USE CAUSAL ANALYSIS OF EFFECT

3

Writing and Rewriting Sentences

Chapter

15

Rewriting Sentences for Clarity and Conciseness

Of every four words I write, I strike out three.

Nicolas Boileau (1636–1711)

Joseph Grand, a municipal clerk, has an unusual ambition: It is to write the perfect sentence. But he finds the task to be enormously difficult. Once he has perfected this sentence, which is to be the start of a great work, he expects all other words and sentences to automatically follow. "Gentlemen, hats off!" the astonished publisher will cry after reading the manuscript—or so Grand fantasizes.

This odd clerk was never one of our students. He is a character from the novel *The Plague* by the French writer Albert Camus. His perfect sentence?

> One fine morning in the month of May an elegant young horsewoman might have been seen riding a handsome sorrel mare along the flowery avenues of the Bois de Boulogne.

"That's only a rough draft," admits Grand. "Once I've succeeded in rendering perfectly the picture in my mind's eye, once my words have the exact tempo of this ride—the horse is trotting, one-two-three, one-two-three, see what I mean?—the rest will come more easily and, what's even more important, the illusion will be such that from the very first words it will be possible to say: 'Hats off!' "

Perfect sentences are not written; they are rewritten, and Monsieur Grand was right in grasping this fact. That the perfect sentence must not only be grammatically exact, but should also use rhythm to underscore meaning was also another truth he correctly understood.

But perfect or imperfect, the sentence by itself is of little practical use to the working writer, and Monsieur Grand was wrong to overweigh its importance in isolation. The sentence is merely one small boxcar in the train of meaning and can bear only so much freight. To be useful, it must be linked to other sentences in a common purpose. For purpose is the locomotive that drives expository prose and shapes its individual sentences. Find your purpose and your controlling idea, and you will at least know what kinds of sentences you must write.

What is a perfect sentence? We confess that we cannot say because we do not know. Perfection is an ideal of art, and the writing we are trying to teach in this book is intended for the practical world, not the artistic. "Don't let it end this way. Tell them I said something," muttered the Mexican revolutionary Pancho Villa on his deathbed. He was trying to think of something perfect to say on this grim occasion, but nothing came to him.

459

The reach for perfection often has this cruel effect of making the writer or speaker mute and tongue-tied.

What, then, is a good sentence? It is a sentence that is clear, concise, and emphatic. If it is also memorable, then it is nearly perfect.

Rewriting the Sentence for Clarity

There are three basic principles for writing clear sentences: avoid mixed constructions, use parallel constructions, and make reasoned constructions.

Avoid mixed constructions

Implicit in every sentence is a certain grammatical pattern. Native speakers unconsciously use these patterns to anticipate the endings and meanings of sentences. For example, if I start off a sentence this way, "When I was a young boy growing up on an island," you automatically expect the second half to begin something like this, "I used to think it would be fun to live on a continent." When I was this, then I thought or did that is the pattern implicit in this sentence. If a sentence begins with the words, "Looking around the room, . . ." you expect a subject to immediately follow, as in, "Looking around the room, I saw a well-dressed, matronly lady standing in the corner." You do not expect this kind of pattern: "Looking around the room, a well-dressed, matronly lady I saw standing in the corner," or "Looking around the room, the corner showed a well-dressed, matronly lady." These examples make no sense.

A sentence that begins with one pattern then lurches off into another, is said to have a mixed construction. Its beginning leads us to expect a certain pattern; its ending serves up another. And since it is an ending we did not expect, we have to puzzle over its syntax to understand what the sentence says. Here are some examples of mixed constructions, along with their corrections.

Mixed: In this description of World War I focuses on the assassination of Archduke Francis Ferdinand of Austria–Hungary by a Serbian nationalist.

Rewritten: This description of World War I focuses on the assassination of Archduke Francis Ferdinand of Austria–Hungary by a Serbian nationalist.

Mixed: Many adolescents show hostility to authority figures, but who want to be authorities themselves.

Rewritten: Although they show hostility to authority figures, many adolescents want to be authorities themselves.

Mixed: When countries try to negotiate nuclear missiles engenders fear in the public.

Rewritten: When countries try to negotiate nuclear missiles, they engender fear in the public.

Mixed: The art critics noticed the impressionists who ridiculed Monet used his techniques.

Rewritten: The art critics noticed that those impressionists who ridiculed Monet used his techniques.

Mixed constructions rarely occur in a manuscript that has been reread. Such twisted sentences can nearly always be caught on a second reading.

Use parallel constructions

A parallel construction creates a smooth and expected rhythm by balancing word for word, phrase for phrase, and clause for clause in a sentence. Consider the following example:

Not parallel: What can society do about youngsters who go to school hungry, child abuse, and cruel neglect?

The sentence reads smoothly until we reach "child abuse," when a disruptive break in its rhythm occurs. It begins with a relative clause—"who go to school hungry"—which is then immediately (and unexpectedly) followed by two intrusive noun phrases, "child abuse," and "cruel neglect." Such an unparallel sentence, because of its departure from the normal grammatical rhythm, is harder to understand than a parallel one. Here are possible rewritten versions:

Parallel: What can society do about youngsters who go to school hungry, who are abused, and who are cruelly neglected?

OR

What can society do about hungry, abused, and neglected children?

OR

What can society do about children who suffer hunger, abuse, and neglect?

These sentences are parallel: they use the natural and expected grammatical rhythms and are therefore easier to understand than unparallel equivalents.

Here are some additional examples of unparallel sentences and their improved revisions. The unparallel element is underlined in each example.

Not parallel: Pope Paul gained popularity because of his outgoing personality and being tough on Communism.

Parallel: Pope Paul gained popularity because of his outgoing personality and his tough stand on Communism.

Not parallel: For most people—their bodies flabby, their muscles weak, and having bad posture—aerobics is an excellent exercise.

Parallel: For most people—their bodies flabby, their muscles weak, and their posture bad—aerobics is an excellent exercise.

Not parallel: An intimate relationship, a job that poses some challenges, and a purposeful life are ingredients everyone needs.

Parallel: An intimate relationship, a challenging job, and a purposeful life are ingredients everyone needs.

Not parallel: `Ivan the Terrible was autocratic, stern, and `<u>`he`</u>
` `<u>`had no mercy toward his foes.`</u>

Parallel: `Ivan the Terrible was autocratic, stern, and`
`merciless.`

Make reasoned constructions

A good sentence has not only a normal grammatical pattern and rhythm, but also an inherent sense of logic. Consider the following sentence:

Unclear: `The prime minister delivered a brilliant`
`parliamentary speech on the limits of world trade,`
`and the American tourists watched the tennis matches`
`at Wimbledon.`

Because no plain connection is made between the two events—the prime minister's speech and the tourists who watched the tennis matches—the sentence seems odd or even illogical. Notice the difference when the connection is made clearer:

Rewritten: `Although the prime minister delivered a brilliant`
`parliamentary speech on the limits of world trade,`
`the American tourists did not attend the speech,`
`preferring to watch tennis at Wimbledon.`

To the grammarian, the sentence may be defined as words arranged according to accepted rules of syntax. But to the writer, the sentence consists not merely of words but of ideas; the good sentence, of ideas expressed in clearly logical relationships. How can such clarity be achieved? "Mainly," wrote the noted stylist F. L. Lucas, "by taking trouble."

Below are some examples of sentences whose ideas and relationships were initially unclear. By taking trouble, the students improved them in revision.

Unclear: `Many elderly people need medical care, and what is`
`the government doing with all of our taxes?`

The connection between the medical needs of the elderly and the query about what is happening to the U.S. tax dollars is not clear:

Rewritten: One cannot help but wish that the government would
give some of its tax dollars to the elderly so
that they can receive needed medical care.

Unclear: A skirmish is when small bodies of troops clash in
a minor encounter during a war.

In defining a word or a concept, it is clearer to state *what* it is rather than *when* or *where* it is. Here is a better definition of a skirmish:

Rewritten: A skirmish is a minor clash between small bodies
of troops during a war.

Here is another example of this same flaw:

Unclear: To politicize an issue is where it is discussed
only in terms of its political framework.

Rewritten: To politicize an issue is to discuss it within a
political framework.

Sometimes the ideas of a sentence may be muddled by the use of a **dangling modifier**—a group of words that are either unconnected to any element in the sentence or that are mistakenly attached to the wrong word. Here is an example:

Dangling: At the age of six, Henry Adam's grandfather took
him to school.

"At the age of six" is a dangling phrase. Where it is positioned, it makes "grandfather" six years old when he took his grandson to school—clearly impossible. Here is a revision:

Rewritten: When Henry Adams was six, his grandfather took him
to school.

OR

```
Henry Adams was six when his grandfather took him
to school.
```

Here are further examples of danglers, followed by corrections:

Dangling: `Looking down in horror, a huge green lizard`
`slithered away.`

The dangling participial phrase makes it seem as if the lizard were looking down—"in horror." Here is the rewritten version:

Rewritten: `Looking down in horror, I watched a huge green`
`lizard slither away.`

Dangling: `Desperate from hunger, the government finally gave`
`the starving families barrels of rice.`

This dangling phrase "desperate from hunger," makes the government, not the people, hungry.

Rewritten: `Desperate from hunger, the starving families were`
`finally given barrels of rice by the government.`

For more on dangling modifiers, see the handbook.

Another kind of unreasoned absurdity is caused by the **misplaced modifier**—a word or phrase whose position in the sentence is too far removed from the word it modifies:

Misplaced: `Many psychiatrists deny that a young boy develops`
`unconscious sexual feelings for his mother in`
`Germany.`

Obviously it is the psychiatrists who are in Germany, not the young boy:

Rewritten: `Many psychiatrists in Germany deny that a young`
`boy develops unconscious sexual feelings for his`
`mother.`

Misplaced: In Tolstoy's famous novel, Anna Karenina flings
herself under an oncoming train which she had
decided to take.

It is her life, not the train, that Anna decides to take:

Rewritten: In Tolstoy's famous novel, Anna Karenina decides
to take her life by flinging herself under an
oncoming train.

See relevant sections in the handbook for more on misplaced modifiers and parts.

Similar to the dangling or misplaced modifier, the **squinting modifier** is awkwardly placed between two words and could modify either one:

Squinting: He said long ago he lost his honor.

"Long ago" is the problem. Did he lose his honor long ago, or did he say it long ago?

Rewritten: Long ago he said he lost his honor.

OR

He said he lost his honor long ago.

Awkward shifts (in person, number, voice, tense, or mood) can often muddy the logical relationships a writer means to express between the ideas of a sentence. Some typical examples follow:

Person shift: When one is jealous, you tend to act like a
child.

The sentence starts out with "one" as the subject, but then suddenly shifts to "you." Usually, the best way to correct a shift in person is to rewrite the entire sentence:

Rewritten: A jealous person tends to act like a child.

Number shift: After a cat wakes up from his nap, they lick
themselves all over.

The sentence begins with one cat, then shifts to many.

Rewritten: `When cats wake up from their naps, they lick`

`themselves all over.`

`                        OR`

`When a cat wakes up from his nap, he licks`

`himself all over.  (Also:  When a cat wakes up`

`from her nap, she licks herself all over.)`

Voice shift: `The farmers were angry about facing the same old`

`pollution problems, so their meetings were used`

`to plan new strategies.`

The shift here is from the active to the passive voice. If you start with the active voice, you should also finish with it. (It is also more forceful than the passive voice.)

Rewritten: `The farmers were angry about facing the same old`

`pollution problems, so they used their meetings`

`to plan new strategies.`

Tense shift: `Tom Sawyer recounts the adventures of a boy who`

`has been dominated by an aunt and hated`

`repression; consequently, he escapes with his`

`friend to find freedom from authority.`

Here the writer has giddily shifted tenses from the present ("recounts"), to the present perfect ("has been dominated"), to the imperfect past ("hated"), and then back to the present ("escapes").

Rewritten: `Tom Sawyer recounts the adventures of a boy who`

`was dominated by an aunt and who hated repression;`

`consequently, he escaped with his friend to find`

`freedom from authority.`

The only verb used in the present tense is "recounts" because the story of Tom Sawyer is still the same today as it was yesterday.

Mood shift: `When you write, make your subjects and verbs agree in number, and also you should not shift tenses unnecessarily.`

Even if you do not know the formal definition of mood, your ear should still tell you that something is wrong with this sentence. English verbs are said to have three moods: the indicative, imperative, and subjunctive. By mood is meant the manner in which a statement is intended. The indicative mood is used to make a statement or ask a question: the imperative, to give a command; the subjunctive, to express a wish or a condition contrary to fact ("If I were you . . ."). The shift here is from the imperative mood to the indicative.

Rewritten (in the imperative): `When you write, make your subjects and verbs agree in number, and do not make unnecessary shifts in tenses.`

Rewritten (in the indicative): `When you write, you must make your subjects and verbs agree in number, and you must also not make unnecessary shifts in tense.`

For more on shifts, see the handbook.

Most of the errors described in this section are commonly caused by hasty writing and no rewriting. Remember that your reader owes you only one reading; but you owe your reader several rereadings and rewritings of your own work.

Exercises

1. Identify the construction error (mixed, not parallel, illogical) of each sentence below. Then rewrite the sentence to correct it.
   a. In this incident affecting the hero of the story focuses on all of his selfishness and immaturity.
   b. He was beaten and robbed, and then they left him in the gutter to die.
   c. Their grandfather paid all of their bills even though he is living on a small pension.
   d. When the leaves turn gold, when the days get longer, and as soon as the sky is blustery, we know that fall is here.

> *e.* When people are insecure results in the worship of a supreme being.
>
> *f.* Burned and collapsed, the people of Columbia must rebuild their houses.
>
> *g.* Bertrand Russell argued for world peace in the fall of 1918.
>
> *h.* Tourists visiting Venice can see Harry's Bar floating down the Grand Canal.
>
> *i.* The jury deliberated for several weeks; then suddenly the case is dismissed.
>
> *j.* An "interdiction" is when something is placed under religious or legal sanction.

Rewriting the Sentence for Conciseness

Three essential principles of concise writing are: Don't repeat yourself. Don't use unnecessary words. Don't use big words.

Don't repeat yourself

Needless repetition, also called "redundancy," means that the writer unnecessarily says the same thing more than once. If you say something once, you do not need to say it again in the same sentence unless you are deliberately trying to be emphatic. Here are some examples, along with their more concise, rewritten versions:

Repetitious: Van Gogh was assiduous in making revised changes on his canvases.

"Revised" and "changes" mean the same; one or the other can therefore be cut.

  Rewritten: Van Gogh was assiduous in making changes on his canvases.

Repetitious: The artists of the Renaissance period delighted in and were pleased by fleshy women.

To delight in fleshy women is the same as to be pleased by them.

  Rewritten: The artists of the Renaissance period delighted in fleshy women.

Repetitious: `After the Civil War had come to an end and was`

`terminated, reconstruction was slow.`

In this sentence "end" and "terminated" are synonymous. Moreover, the phrase "after the Civil War" already signals that the war had ended.

Rewritten: `After the Civil War, reconstruction was slow.`

Repetitious: `For a long period of time, the sky was cloudy in`

`appearance.`

"Time" is already implied in "long period," and "appearance" in "the sky was cloudy."

Rewritten: `For a long time the sky was cloudy.`

Don't use unnecessary words

"Let thy words be few," admonishes the Bible. It is advice as applicable today as it was in the time of the prophets. Less is often more in the well-written work. But learning to prune your sentences of unnecessary words is a skill acquired mainly by doing. Eventually, you get a "feel" for how cutting a word here and there can actually sharpen your meaning. Nevertheless, there are some known kinds of wordiness that writers look for and, when they find, mercilessly cut.

The first is the **prefabricated phrase**—words that are packaged in a convenient clump. Some common examples are "a full and complete report"; "a dyed-in-the-wool Republican" (or anything else believed to be genuine); "first and foremost among them"; "based on various and sundry experiences"; "the consensus of their opinions"; "for all intents and purposes"; "It is incumbent upon us all"; "last but by no means least"; and "deserving of your most serious consideration."

Usually such phrases can economically be replaced by a shorter expression or even by a single word. A "dyed-in-the-wool Republican" is nothing more than a "true" or "authentic" Republican. "It is incumbent upon us all" can usually be replaced by a single "must." Instead of writing, "It is incumbent upon us all to try to be good citizens," you can write, "We must all try to be good citizens." Prefabricated phrases are ineffective blobs of words, and "it is incumbent on you" to avoid them "as if your life depended on doing so" lest your sentences become as serpentine and wordy as this one and others like it that are commonly found in corporate shareholder reports.

A second major source of wordiness is a **phrase taking the place**

of a word. Why any working writer would prefer a phrase to a word is beyond imagining. Phrases take longer to type, use more space, yet often say less than the aptly chosen word. But the lamentable truth is that dozens of phrases are nowadays used by some writers when a single word would be just as effective. Here are some examples:

> the reason being that
>
> due to the fact that   } because, since
>
> considering the fact that

Wordy: The Red Cross sent supplies to Columbia due to the fact that a volcano had erupted.

Rewritten: The Red Cross sent supplies to Columbia because a volcano had erupted.

> despite the fact that
>
> regardless of the fact that   } although, even
>
> though

Wordy: Despite the fact that the patient was well, she needed constant reassurance.

Rewritten: Although the patient was well, she needed constant reassurance.

> in the event that
>   } if
> if it should happen that

Wordy: In the event that the painting is sold, the museum will purchase another masterpiece.

Rewritten: If the painting is sold, the museum will purchase another masterpiece.

> has the opportunity to
>
> is capable of
>   } can
> has the capacity to
>
> is in a position to

Wordy: A nuclear war has the capacity to extinguish all
life.

Rewritten: A nuclear war can extinguish all life.

```
there is a chance that      ⎫
the possibility is that     ⎬  may, might, could
it could happen that        ⎭
```

Wordy: There is a chance that punk rock will go down in
musical history as an art form.

Rewritten: Punk rock may go down in musical history as an art
form.

Finally, there is wordiness caused simply by the writer's use of unnecessary words. Here are some examples:

Wordy: The city hall was painted yellow in color.

Better: The city hall was painted yellow.

Obviously, "yellow" is a color.

Wordy: The object was square in shape.

Better: The object was square.

Again, "square" is obviously a shape.

Wordy: The sun shone a bright light.

Better: The sun shone brightly.

The sun always shines a light, never darkness.

The lesson of this entire section can be nicely summed up in the
words of the German writer Goethe: "The master reveals himself in his
straint." Say what you have to say. And when you have said it, stop. For
more on phrases see the handbook.

Don't use big words

For the writer of expository prose, exactness should govern the
choice of words, not size. If the bigger word is the more exact, then use it.

But often it is not. English is rich in synonyms, and its vocabulary is peculiarly layered. The bigger word is layered over the smaller one under which lies the image, idea, or object that is its meaning. Consider, for example, a big word like "senectuous," as it is used in the following sentence:

> She [The Goliath] was a small, senectuous battleship which had been launched when Victoria was still Queen.
> —William Manchester, The Last Lion: Winston Spencer Churchill, 1874–1932.

"Senectuous" will evoke no image in most minds. It means, quite simply, "old," but even those readers who know this must first translate "senectuous" into "old" before visualizing the sort of battleship the author intends. Here is the same sentence without the big word:

> She was a small, old battleship which had been launched when Victoria was still Queen.

Now it is instantly clearer what kind of battleship The Goliath was.

Why smaller words should have this evocative power over our minds while bigger words do not is in part explainable by the way we learn language. We learn the smaller, commoner words first and always in association with specific sights or images. It is an odd parent, indeed, who would answer a child's question about why a certain man is wrinkled and bent with the explanation that he is "senectuous." Most likely, the parent would say that the man is "old," and this image would become associated with the word in the mind of the child. Similarly, we are urged from childhood to blow our "noses," never our "proboscises." It is only much later, after "old" and "nose" have become firmly associated with specific images in our minds, that we learn their synonyms of "senectuous" and "proboscis" from a dictionary. But words gotten from a dictionary cannot have the power of those whose meanings were impressed upon us by the images and scenes of life.

Edward Thompson, editor in chief of The Reader's Digest, defines a word that immediately brings an image to mind as a "first degree word," and all others as "second" or "third" degree words. First degree words are usually the simpler and better known. They are also the words most useful to expository writers. Here is a list of some big words, followed by their first degree, and shorter, synonyms:

initiate	start
terminate	end
inundate	flood
lugubrious	sad
habitation	home

impecunious	poor
utilization	use
visage	face
subsequent	after

Use the exact word you need. Never use a word merely because it is big and sounds impressive. That will only make your writing seem pompous. Here are some examples:

Pompous: To achieve economic independence, it is essential that students be cognizant of the fact that computing the number of dollars utilized each month is an essential aspect of budgeting.

Concise: To achieve economic independence, a student must budget by counting the number of dollars spent each month.

The second version is clearly the easier of the two to grasp. Here is another example—this one from the preface of a history book:

Pompous: Because certain historians were desirous of maintaining the pursuit of historical accuracy, they treated the Pilgrims and the Plymouth Colony in a nonidealized manner, not taking into account the role and impact of the idealized Thanksgiving story as it was contingent upon the formation and preservation of the American character or its values and goals.

Cleared of its bloated phrases and heavy nouns, the sentence has a rather straightforward meaning:

Concise: For the sake of historical accuracy, certain historians emphasized the faults of the Pilgrims and the Plymouth Colony, while discounting the impact

```
their idealized Thanksgiving story had on the

formation and preservation of the values and goals

in the American character.
```

The rewritten version is clearer because it uses fewer words.

Conciseness is rarely present in any first draft and is almost never the result of writing. But it is one of the happier effects of repeated rewriting.

Use words appropriate to your subject and audience

The writer in English is always faced with a cornucopia of word choices. For every one word we use, we often have a choice between a dozen equivalents. But street-smart writers do not simply grab the first word that pops into their minds. Instead, they choose the word they think will help make their case most effectively, given their subject matter and audience. A word that will fit one writing occasion can sometimes seem grotesque in another. For example, if you were writing an obituary in a newspaper you would never write that "so and so croaked last week." "Passed on," "expired," "died" are phrases and words you would most likely use. On the other hand, you might say that "so and so croaked last week" in mentioning so-and-so's passing in a letter to an intimate friend, especially if you didn't much care that so-and-so croaked.

That is an extreme example, but the lesson it teaches applies to all writing, whether formal or informal. For example, examine the paragraph below along with the student's editing. Notice the changes he made in diction. His paper on the dinosaur Brontosaurus was written for an anthropology class:

```
                     thrived
Brontosaurus was king of the hill during

the Jurassic period, which is the middle period

of the Mesozoic era, between 190—140 million

years ago.  As reconstructed from
                          excavated
paleontological evidence dug up from Como Bluff,

Wyoming, Brontosaurus was a humongous animal

weighing nearly twenty tons.  In life it was

fifty feet long, had a neck over thirty feet
        moderate abdominal cavity
high, a big belly, no dermal armature, and feet
```

whose soles were as large as a square yard.

unintelligent

That the animal was slow moving and ~~dumb~~ is

very small

inferred from its ~~pea~~ brain and thin neural

cord.

Here is the edited paragraph:

Brontosaurus thrived during the Jurassic

period, which is the middle period of the

Mesozoic era, between 190—40 million years

ago. As reconstructed from paleontological

evidence excavated from Como Bluff, Wyoming,

Brontosaurus was an enormous animal weighing

nearly twenty tons. In life it was fifty feet

long, had a neck over thirty feet high, a

moderate abdominal cavity, no dermal armature,

and feet whose soles were as large as a square

yard. That the animal was slow moving and

unintelligent is inferred from its very small

brain and thin neural cord.

Notice the writer's changes. "Thrived" is better than "king of the hill," which is slangy and unsuitable in an objective writing assignment. "Excavated" is more anthropologically precise and fitting than "dug up." "Enormous" is better than "humongous," which is slang. "A moderate abdominal cavity" is scientifically more descriptive than "a big belly." "Unintelligent" and "very small" are standard English equivalents of the slangy "dumb" and "pea brain."

In a personal writing assignment, you are free to use the words you please (within the boundaries of decency, of course). But in an objective assignment, you should stick to standard English words, avoid contractions such as "they're," or "they've," and never use slang. Check the dictionary if you are unsure about the standing of a word. Many words that were once considered slangy have earned a promotion to standard English. For example, "to civilize" was once considered so colloquial that the famous English lexicographer Dr. Samuel Johnson railed against its use. Now it is considered perfectly acceptable among mixed company.

The writer of objective assignments definitely labors under narrower standards of acceptability in his word choices than the writer of personal assignments. But the personal writer is also expected to sound personal rather than textbookish (with apologies to ourselves.) For example, if you wrote as your opening sentence to an essay about a childhood memory, "When I was a diminutive preadolescent male, I had a terrifying experience with a dog," and weren't trying to be funny, you would have badly missed the mark. One does not begin an essay about a childhood memory sounding like a sociologist. It is better to begin, "When I was a small boy, I had a terrifying experience with a dog" because that is exactly the tone your readers have every right to expect in a childhood reminiscence.

Exercises

1. Identify the cause of wordiness (repetition, unnecessary words, big words) in each of the following sentences. Then rewrite the sentence to make it more concise.

   a. Today it is almost virtually impossible to find a student who has memorized by heart even the first two paragraphs of the Declaration of Independence.

   b. In a recent *Scientific American* article, written in a highly critical manner of expressing oneself, the question was asked, "How much intense heat would be caused by a breach in the reactor vessel?"

   c. It is a fact that novelists are probably more sensitive to the atrocities of our age than are most of the rest of us.

   d. Psychologists have become cognizant of the fact that nowadays the word *stress* is enjoying a peak of popularity.

   e. It would appear that every avenue should be explored to make a conscious effort to reduce smog in all major cities.

   f. Many bureaucrats avoid and shy clear of the decision-making process by submitting a problem to their superiors without recommendation, knowing beyond the shadow of a doubt that the matter will be sent back for further study.

   g. Bertrand Russell was an atheist who did not believe in God.

   h. Since the time of the fifteenth century, medicine has advanced considerably in its ability to treat and manage the disease of syphilis.

   i. Every well-read botanist is cognizant of the fact that George Bentham was a pioneer in the field of systematic botany.

j. In its most genuinely pure form, *fresco* is the art of painting upon the material of damp, fresh lime plaster.

Writing Assignments

1. Make up a topic sentence for each of the following subjects, then write six sentences that support it. Rewrite each sentence for wordiness.
   a. when no answer is an answer
   b. a note asking your teacher permission to be absent during a test
   c. smoking in restaurants
   d. how eating crabs is a nuisance
2. Write a one-page paragraph about the dangers of peer pressure. Bring the paragraph to class and exchange it for a paragraph written by a classmate. Edit each other's paragraphs for wordiness.

Chapter

16

Rewriting Sentences for Emphasis

Then rising with Aurora's light,
The Muse invoked, sit down to write;
Blot out, correct, insert, refine,
Enlarge, diminish, interline.

JONATHAN SWIFT (1667–1745)

An emphatic sentence is one whose words are arranged in the strongest possible sequence so as to deliver meaning with the greatest possible impact. The emphasis of any sentence will vary greatly with its context. A sentence may be unemphatic because it is too similar in construction to the sentences before or after it. Or it may be unemphatic because its words are arranged in a weak sequence. In sum, emphasis is largely a relative judgment of style and not an absolute judgment of grammar.

Nevertheless, there are some known characteristics associated with emphatic sentences. Among them are appropriate balance, structure, sound, variety, and diction. We will consider each one in turn.

Write Balanced Sentences

A balanced sentence is one whose grammatical parts are parallel. We have already discussed parallelism as an aid to clarity in Chapter 15. But the parallel sentence is not only easier to understand, it is also more emphatic. Compare the following two passages:

```
We have plenty of statutes that forbid

people to kill each other and make it wrong to

maim or even just to be threatening with

weapons.

     We have plenty of statutes that forbid

people to kill, maim, or threaten each other

with weapons.
```

Part of the greater emphasis in the second sentence comes from the parallelism of its three infinitives: "kill," "maim," and "threaten." Here is another example of a nonparallel sentence, followed by a parallel version:

Not balanced: Simple signing can be observed in nature: dogs
bark at the door to be let in; rabbits thump to
call each other; the cooing of doves is an
expression of feelings; and when a wolf defends
his kill, he growls.

Balanced: Simple signing can be observed in nature: dogs
bark at the door to be let in; rabbits thump to
call each other; doves coo to express feelings;
and wolves growl to defend their kills.

The parallel version establishes a simple subject-verb structure ("dogs bark"), which is then balanced against others in the sentence ("rabbits thump," "doves coo," "wolves growl"). In the nonparallel version, the third example ("the cooing of doves is") and the last ("when a wolf growls") take the reader by surprise, upset the expected harmony, and dilute the emphasis.

Balancing the parts of a sentence can create a pleasing rhythm while underscoring emphasis. One useful principle to remember is that a sentence is better balanced, as well as more emphatic, if its coordinate parts are arranged in order of increasing length. Here is an example:

Balanced: Finally, it is important to remember that gun laws
are confusing, that statistics can be juggled to
distort the truth, and that passing the wrong kind
of legislation could be expensive as well as
counterproductive or useless.

The three parallel *that* clauses are arranged in climactic order of increasing length, adding to the balance and emphasis of the sentence. Moving from long to short would seem anticlimactic:

Not balanced: Finally, it is important to remember that
passing the wrong kind of legislation could be
expensive as well as counterproductive or
useless, that statistics can be juggled to

```
distort the truth, and that gun laws are

confusing.
```

Some uses of parallelism are admittedly complex, requiring balance between several elements of a single sentence. Here is an example:

Balanced:
```
These educated young women prefer to seek

independence through a satisfying career rather

than to settle for dependence through a stultifying

marriage.
```

In this sentence, the noun "independence" is balanced against the noun "dependence"; "through a satisfying career" is balanced against a prepositional phrase, "through a stultifying marriage." Here is the same idea unemphatically expressed without balance:

Not balanced:
```
These educated young women prefer to seek

independence through a satisfying career, but

being dependent on a marriage that stultifies is

not such a good idea in their view.
```

The use of correlative conjunctions ("either . . . or," "neither . . . nor," "not only . . . but also," "both . . . and," "whether . . . or") automatically encourages parallel phrasing in a sentence:

Balanced:
```
The ideal among American writers today is not only

picturesque and exhilarating expression, but also

correct and reassuring utterance.
```

Here the correlative conjunction "not only . . . but also" is the pivot on which "picturesque and exhilarating expression" is balanced with "correct and reassuring utterance." Here is another example:

Balanced:
```
The alternatives presented by modern technology are

either that we shall all be killed instantly or

that we shall all be bored to death slowly.
```

In this sentence, grammatical balance is partly due to the use of a correlative conjunction ("either . . . or"). The "either" side of the sentence stands in opposition to the "or" side; but both halves are phrased identically in clauses introduced by "that."

Structure Your Sentences to Be Emphatic

The most important idea of an emphatic sentence is usually saved for its ending. There, it is more conspicuous and climactic than when buried in the middle. Save your best for last, then, and your sentences will seem more emphatic. Study the following examples:

Weak ending: People who eat a high-salt diet over many years are predisposing themselves to hypertension the same way cigarette smokers predispose themselves to lung cancer, according to recent population studies.

The most important idea of this sentence is not that recent studies have been performed, but what they reveal. It is this idea that should come last:

Strong ending: According to recent studies, people who eat a high-salt diet are predisposing themselves to hypertension the same way cigarette smokers predispose themselves to lung cancer.

The grim warning words "lung cancer" are now in a highlighted position— at the end of the sentence. Here is another example:

Weak ending: Lin Yutang understood the enigmatic quality of artistic creation when he wrote that an oversupply of glandular secretions is what genius is due to.

Prepositions are among the weakest words and usually do not belong at the end of a sentence. Note that there is no grammatical rule against ending a sentence with a preposition. But to end a sentence on a preposition is to end it weakly. Here is the sentence revised:

Strong ending: `Lin Yutang understood the enigmatic quality of`
`artistic creation when he wrote that genius is`
`due to an oversupply of glandular secretions.`

Preferring the active over the passive voice is another good rule for ensuring an emphatic sentence structure. Here is a sentence, that overuses the passive:

Passive: `Special commissions, encounter groups, task forces,`
`and think tanks have been appointed by the government`
`in an attempt to achieve a better grade of collective`
`thought.`

Notice how the active voice quickens the pace of the sentence while instilling it with vigor:

Active: `In an attempt to achieve a better grade of collective`
`thought, the government has appointed special`
`commissions, encounter groups, task forces, and think`
`tanks.`

In the passive voice, the subject does not act; it is acted upon, with a resulting tendency toward wordiness. Here is an example:

Passive: `The museum will be owned by the city; the major art`
`works will be donated by wealthy patrons, and the`
`upkeep of the building will be supported by grants`
`from huge corporations.`

Here is a leaner version in the active voice:

Active: `The city will own the museum; wealthy patrons will`
`donate the major art works, and grants from huge`
`corporations will support the upkeep of the buildings.`

We do not mean that you should never write in the passive voice, only that you should do so rarely. In special circumstances when you wish to emphasize an action rather than an actor, when you wish to highlight the one acted upon rather than the act itself, the passive voice is indeed appropriate. But as a general rule, the active is the stylistically stronger. Here are three examples of the appropriate use of the passive:

Jesus was burdened by the sins of the world.
The whole town was neglected by the rich, who did not care.
The school was destroyed by an enormous billow of flame.

In the first two examples the one acted upon is more important than the actor; in the third, the action—the school was destroyed—is more important than what destroyed it. In all three cases the use of the passive voice is justified. These exceptions aside, the active voice is nearly always a stylistic better choice than the passive.

Eliminating slow sentence openers is another way to achieve an emphatic structure. Such slow openers include "There is . . . ," "There are . . . ," "It is interesting to note that . . . ." Cut them out and open directly on your main idea:

Slow start: There are many youngsters in America who are completely misunderstood because they do not act like their peers.

Direct start: Many youngsters in America are completely misunderstood because they do not act like their peers.

Slow start: It is essential to understand that gifted children are more prone to feelings of loneliness and depression than are normal children.

Direct start: Gifted children are more prone to feelings of loneliness and depression than are normal children.

Your own sentences will be more emphatic if you begin by getting straight to the point.

A string of prepositional phrases can also weaken the structure of a sentence and lessen its emphasis. Multiple *of's* are among the chief offenders. Here is an example, taken from a student paper on the great pyramid of Giza:

```
      The pyramid of Giza, the only remaining one
  of the seven wonders of the ancient world,
  proves to be the greatest and most enduring of
  all monuments of all times.
```

With a few simple deletions, we can eliminate two *of*'s:

```
      The pyramid of Giza, the only remaining one
  of the seven wonders of the ancient world,
  proves to be among the greatest and most
  enduring archaeological discoveries.
```

An *of* or *by* phrase that indicates possession or authorship can often be eliminated by the possessive form of the noun: "The people of the country" becomes "the country's people." "The poem by Shakespeare" becomes "Shakespeare's poem." But be careful here, for sometimes *of* phrases do not indicate possession. For instance, if you change "the murder of Julius Caesar" into "Julius Caesar's murder," you ambiguously imply that Caesar committed murder. Here is another passage laden with *of* phrases:

Original: The decision of the Cabinet and the general
consensus of the Senate of the United States of
America are of intense interest to scholars of the
diplomatic stance of our country of that time.

Rewriting this passage to rid it of its excess *of*'s meant recasting it into the active voice.

Revision: Scholars studying the diplomatic stance of America
then are intensely interested in the Cabinet's
decision and the Senate's general consensus.

The revision has reduced the sentence to one *of* phrase.

Write Sentences That Sound Emphatic

Words have sounds, and sophisticated readers who do not read aloud can still hear them. Poets deliberately use the sounds of words to emphasize meaning. Writers of expository prose, too, should develop an ear for how sentences sound. It is relatively common to find the emphasis of expository writing ruined by a clumsy combination of syllables. Here, for example, is a sentence overburdened with internal rhymes.

Awkward Rhyming: `Twain's preoccupation and obsession with`
`the indication that human beings were a`
`corruption of their original nature added`
`a cold and pessimistic tone to his later`
`writings.`

The repetition of the *-tion* sound in the first two lines detracts from the text's meaning. A slight rewording improves the passage:

Revision: `Twain's obsessive preoccupation with the idea that`
`human beings had corrupted their original natures`
`added a cold and pessimistic tone to his later`
`writings.`

In the following sentence, the writer was unaware of overusing the *-ought* sound:

Awkward Rhyming: `Without further thought, they bought`
`another parcel of arid land, which taught`
`them many hard lessons about the so-called`
`simple romantic life.`

But in a line-by-line editing of the work, the writer noticed the grating sound and corrected it:

Revision: `Without further thought, they purchased another`
`parcel of arid land, from which they learned many`

```
hard lessons about the so-called simple romantic

life.
```

Sometimes the problem is not with rhyme, but with alliteration—the repeated use of words that have similar initial sounds. Here is an example:

Awkward Alliteration:
```
                    In past periods, parents paid attention

                    to the plow and the pasture, being

                    pushed to pursue hard work because of

                    their fear of poverty and of possible

                    health problems.
```

The popping of these initial *p's* gives the passage an unintentionally comic overtone. Here is an improved version:

Revision:
```
            In ages past our forebears devoted their energies to

            the back-breaking labor of farming, being pushed to

            this hard work by constant fear of poverty and

            disease.
```

You can avoid unpleasant combinations such as these if, in one of your rewriting passes, you read your manuscript aloud.

Vary Your Sentences

Judged alone, a sentence may seem flawless, but set in a paragraph beside others of an identical length and construction, it will invariably appear colorless and unemphatic. To avoid writing monotonous paragraphs, a writer must therefore pay attention to the length and grammatical construction of sentences. A paragraph crammed with nothing but short sentences will strike any reader as boring. The same effect is likely to occur if all the sentences of a paragraph are of an identical construction, even if their length is varied. Here is an example of both flaws, sameness in sentence length and construction, in a single passage:

Original:
```
            After years of trial and error, Disney finally found

                the character he was looking for.  This character
```

was called "Mickey Mouse." Mickey Mouse was first
introduced in the cartoon <u>Plane Crazy.</u> The most
famous of the Mickey cartoons was <u>Steamboat Willie.</u>
It was the first sound cartoon made. It was a great
achievement for Disney. Mickey's fame spread all
over the world. By 1930, Mickey was established as
the cinema's most popular cartoon character. Mickey
was a moralist with a sense of fun. He was a
character loved by all ages. Walt Disney reached
his peak of success with Mickey Mouse.

This is cookie-cutter writing, with each sentence being pressed out of the same pattern. Here is the passage after the writer reworked it for sentence variety:

Revision: After years of trial and error, Disney finally found
the character he was looking for. This character,
called "Mickey Mouse," was first introduced in the
cartoon <u>Plane Crazy</u> and later found ultimate fame in
<u>Steamboat Willie,</u> the first sound cartoon ever made
and thus a great achievement for Disney. By 1930,
after his fame had spread all over the world, Mickey
was established as the cinema's most popular cartoon
character. Because Mickey was a moralist with a
sense of fun, he became a character loved by people
of all ages. In him, Walt Disney reached his peak
of success.

Four sentences were condensed into four participial phrases ("called 'Mickey Mouse' . . . first introduced . . . found ultimate fame . . . the first sound cartoon ever made"), and two were turned into adverbial clauses ("after his fame had spread . . . ." and "Because Mickey was a moralist . . . ."). These simple changes infuse variety into the syntax and rid the passage of its plodding gait.

Suddenly reversing the order of a sentence is another way to achieve syntactic variety in a passage. Here is an example:

Original: Churchill's unique personality made him highly respected among the allies. It also brought him considerable criticism. Churchill was often seen on German and Italian propaganda posters as a large pig, a fat cow, or an assortment of other animal shapes because of his rotund body.

Revision: Churchill's unique personality made him highly respected among the allies. It also brought him considerable criticism. Because of his rotund body, Churchill was often seen on German and Italian propaganda posters as a large pig, a fat cow, or an assortment of other animal shapes.

While the first two sentences share an identical subject-verb construction, the last reverses this order by opening with the subordinate clause, "because of his rotund body."

Use common sense in varying a paragraph's sentences. Don't use several sentences in a row that have the same subject-verb construction. That's boring. At the same time, don't write a series of sentences that are uniformly short (they're tedious) or uniformly long (they're hard to read). As a general rule, a short snappy sentence used after a series of long ones tends to add an emphatic punch. Here is an example:

A civilized classroom atmosphere is one in which both the teacher and the students have a profound respect for each other. The teacher, on one hand, greets the students politely at the start of the lecture hour, does not interrupt a student's question or commentary, and listens

```
attentively to all student reports--without
slouching in a chair, planting both feet on a
desk, or chewing gum at the lectern.  On their
side, the students respond by paying full
attention to the content of the lesson, without
whispering to each other, fidgeting restlessly,
or looking bored to death.  In a civilized
classroom, both teacher and students pay
attention to the ideas being discussed because
they want to further in each other what William
James called the "theoretic instinct"; that is,
our basic need to know reasons, causes, and
abstract concepts about life on our planet.
This classroom, in short, is a special
place.
```

Notice that the final sentence ends the paragraph with an emphatic ring merely by being strikingly short and therefore different. If you will look back to the student paragraph on page 486, you will see that in the revised version the final sentence was drastically cut to pack just such a punch. For more on sentences see the handbook.

Use Inventive Diction

A diction marked by clarity, accuracy, and conciseness should be the first concern of the expository writer. Beyond these basics, if you can also use words that are memorable and imaginative, your writing will be superior. But it is the rare writer to whom freshness and originality in diction come as natural gifts. For most of us, the imaginative image, the enlightening phrase or metaphor, do not spring readily to mind, but are found—if at all—only through the labors of rethinking and rewriting.

We have already discussed imaginative language in Chapter 7 under the techniques of narration (see pages 159–68), and everything we said there applies here as well. For the expository writer, a fresh diction can make the difference between a drab and a colorful passage. Compare the following two passages taken from a paper:

Original:

    Volcanoes constantly ~~attack~~ *pepper* the edge of the North American plate, from Chile to Alaska. Mount St. Helens, the most active of the Cascade volcanoes, rises 8,000 feet above sea level and sits dangerously close to the fault line that ~~lies~~ *makes a jagged subterranean crack* between two immense plates of the earth's ~~disconnected~~ *fractured* crust. On May 18, 1980, an earthquake caused Mount St. Helens to erupt with ~~great violence.~~ *a stupendous and violent bang* The most severe in a series of quakes had ~~forced the growing bulge on the north~~ *punched a hole in the swollen north* ~~side~~ *face* of the mountain, ~~to become loose, throwing~~ *hurling* tons of volcanic debris over the Toutle River Valley. Suddenly the shining blue sky above the serene Toutle River ~~turned into a dark~~ *became a suffocating gray* ~~gray sight~~ *nightmare choked to death by tons of ash and lava mud,* ~~Covered by tons of ash,~~ the once lush green forest was transformed into a ~~bare~~ *lunar* ~~place.~~ *landscape.* The ~~top~~ *peak* of Mount St. Helens had gone *been sheared off* ~~completely, and out of the decapitated mountain~~ leaving behind nothing but death and destruction. *an irresistible onrush of lava, fire, death, and destruction erupted.*

Revision:

    Volcanoes constantly pepper the edge of the North American plate, from Chile to Alaska. Mount St. Helens, the most active of the Cascade volcanoes, looms 8,000 feet above sea level and sits dangerously close to the fault line that

```
makes a jagged subterranean crack between two
immense plates of the earth's fractured crust.
On May 18, 1980, an earthquake caused Mount St.
Helens to erupt with a stupendous and violent
bang.  The most severe in a series of quakes had
punched a hole in the swollen north face of the
mountain, hurling tons of volcanic debris over
the Toutle River Valley.  Suddenly the shining
blue sky above the serene Toutle River became a
suffocating gray nightmare.  Choked to death by
tons of ash and lava mud, the once lush green
forest was transformed into a lunar landscape.
The peak of Mount St. Helens had been sheared
off completely, and out of the decapitated
mountain an irresistible onrush of lava, fire,
death, and destruction erupted.
```

The second version uses a decisively more colorful diction than the first. In the first sentence, the verb *attacks* is replaced with the more colorful verb *peppers*. The fault line is described as "a jagged subterranean crack" in the earth's "fractured crust." A "growing bulge" that had come loose on the north side of the mountain is changed to "the swollen north face of the mountain" through which a hole had been punched. Instead of erupting "with great violence," as it does in the first version, the volcano erupts with "a stupendous and violent bang" in the second. Other changes in diction are made here and there, all with the effect of making the revision more vivid and dramatic.

No one can be taught how to write vividly and colorfully. Knowing what a metaphor or a simile is might enable you to write one, but it will not necessarily be one that is unforgettable or even apt. But you can be taught the method by which it is possible, through sheer persistence, to write more vividly. That method is rewriting. Rework your text constantly, pore over your every verb and image, and eventually your diction will become livelier and sharper. What you are looking for is the striking word, the sharp image, the fresh figure of speech.

In trying to find the striking word, the hardest lesson for writers to learn is not to overdo. You can easily be too singular in your diction, with the result that the writing sounds bizarre and overworked. Never choose a word merely to impress. For instance, the underlined word in this sentence just does not fit:

```
    Anorexia nervosa is a serious, sometimes

jeopardous disorder that typically occurs in

adolescent women.
```

In the context of this sentence, *jeopardous* is fancy-pants writing; an expression such as *life-threatening* or *fatal* would better suit the tone of this sentence. Here is another misfit:

```
    A knowledge of three aspects of semantics

can beef up one's writing.
```

Here the opposite error has occurred: *beef up* is too slangy for this sentence. *Improve,* though not novel or exotic, is a better choice.

Unfortunately, no specific rule, if applied, will always lead you to choose the ideal word. Repeated rewriting with an ear to your context is our only suggestion. It is an unmagical formula, but it works.

Here are several examples of how students improved their word choice as a result of careful revising. The problem word is underlined, and the replacement used in the revision is, in every case, a better choice.

Original: Geologists perceived the lateral bulge from

strategic locations as it reached an extension of

320 feet.

Revision: Geologists observed the lateral bulge from strategic

locations as it reached an extension of 320 feet.

Perceived implies casual awareness rather than careful geological study.

Original: We cannot call any proposition "certain" as long as

valid arguments exist contra it.

Revision: We cannot call any proposition "certain" as long as

valid arguments exist to refute it.

The Latin word used in the original is pretentious.

Original: It is difficult to explain why in the United States 50 million cigarette smokers have not been scared enough to give up a habit that <u>massacres</u> 250,000 lives each year.

Revision: It is difficult to explain why in the United States 50 million cigarette smokers have not been scared enough to give up a habit that <u>snuffs out</u> 250,000 lives each year.

Massacre is an overstatement, implying violent bloodshed, which smoking does not cause.

Original: All prisoners were made to eat garbage until most of them started to <u>regurgitate.</u>

Revision: All prisoners were made to eat garbage until most of them started to <u>vomit.</u>

Regurgitate is a euphemism.

Original: American education is in very big trouble.

Revision: American education is in trouble.

Very and *really* are intensifiers, but their overuse in speech and writing has robbed them of their capacity to make any adjective more intense. Better to find a synonym that means exactly what you have in mind. For instance, instead of "very cold," you might write "freezing," "ice cold," or "bitter cold." Instead of "really stupid," use "inane," "doltish," or "brainless."

Original: We must keep in mind that every gifted child not allowed to enhance his or her <u>possibility</u> is a lost opportunity and a reckless waste of society's potential.

Revision: We must keep in mind that every gifted child not

allowed to enhance his or her <u>natural</u> <u>talents</u> is a

lost opportunity and a reckless waste of society's

potential.

Possibility is a meaningless catch-all word. Others like it are *thing(s), aspect(s),* and *factor(s).* These words are not wrong, just mushy. Whenever possible, use a more specific word.

Sometimes a good thesaurus will suggest a better, sharper word over the one that comes readily to mind. Beware, however, of choosing an unknown synonym merely because it seems impressive. Words have subtle connotations that can only be grasped from repeated encounters with them in a written or spoken context.

Memorable writing also consists of detailed observations made in sharp, apt images. Through the use of representative and unforgettable details, the writer conjures up a scene in the reader's imagination. Here are some examples, taken from famous works and writers:

> The louder he talked of his honor, the faster we counted our spoons.
> —Ralph Waldo Emerson

> People by the hundreds were flailing in the river. I couldn't tell if they were men or women; they were all in the same state: their faces were puffy and ashen, their hair tangled, they held their hands raised and, groaning with pain, threw themselves into the water. I had a violent impulse to do so myself, because of the pain burning through my whole body. But I can't swim and I held back.
> —Futaba Kitayama, giving an eyewitness account of the atom bomb exploding over Hiroshima

> The foxes barked in the hills and deer silently crossed the fields, half hidden in the mists of the fall mornings.
> —Rachel Carson

> I find some difficulty in describing what a "meatball" was. Meatballs were usually day students or scholarship students. We were at Harvard not to enjoy the games, the girls, the burlesque shows of the Old Howard, the companionship, the elms, the turning leaves of fall, the grassy banks of the Charles. We had come to get the Harvard badge, which says "veritas," but really means a job

somewhere in the future, in some bureaucracy, in some institution, in some school, laboratory, university or law firm.
—Theodore H. White

The untouched savage in the middle of New Guinea isn't anxious; he is seriously and continually *frightened*—of black magic, of enemies with spears who may kill him or his wives and children at any moment, while they stoop to drink from a spring, or climb a palm tree for a coconut. He goes warily, day and night, taut and fearful.
—Margaret Mead

The actual headache, when it comes, brings with it chills, sweating, nausea, a debility that seems to stretch the very limits of endurance. That no one dies of migraine seems, to someone deep into an attack, an ambiguous blessing.
—Joan Didion

What all of these examples have in common is a picturesque sharpness. Each passage unforgettably captures, with a grace and elegance that is never effortless, an exact idea. The best way to create sharp images is to be meticulous in your observations and faithful in your transcriptions of them on paper.

Finally, emphatic writing is frequently characterized by the use of fresh figures of speech. A **figure of speech** is the opposite of **literal language.** Literal language renders meaning factually: "He left quietly, without being seen or heard." A figure of speech renders meaning imaginatively: "He stole away like a thief in the night." The metaphor and the simile are the most common figures of speech (see the handbook for a definition), and appropriately used, add emotional intensity to writing. Here are some examples of apt metaphors, taken from the works of well-known writers:

Man was born free, and everywhere he is in chains.
—Jean-Jacques Rousseau

Wide is the gate, and broad is the way, that leadeth to destruction, and many there be that go in thereat.
—St. Matthew

Old religious factions are volcanoes burnt out.
—Edmund Burke

For frequent tears have run the colours of my life.
—Elizabeth Barrett Browning

Gossip is a sort of smoke that comes from the dirty tobacco pipes of those who diffuse it; it proves nothing but the bad taste of the smoker.
—George Eliot

[Robert E.] Lee was tidewater Virginia, and in his background were family, culture, and tradition—the age of chivalry transplanted to a New World which was making its own legends and its own myths.
—Bruce Catton

I wanted to live deep and suck out all the marrow of life, to live so sturdily and Spartan-like as to put to rout all that was not life, to cut a broad swath and shave close, to drive life into a corner, and reduce it to its lowest terms. . . .
—David Thoreau

From a mechanistic viewpoint, companies with many outlying plants and offices can be more efficient if their people "resources" become interchangeable cogs.
—Vance Packard

But even if we choose wisely in the light of an apparent alignment of mutual needs, the crack in the marriage foundation that splits wide open is, simply, ignorance—the appalling ignorance of the realistic obligations of marriage itself.
—Norman Sheresky and Marya Mannes

This is the way it is with the white man in America: He's a wolf—and you're a sheep.
—Malcolm X

And here are some similes—like metaphors except that the comparison is explicitly drawn through the use of *like* or *as:*

His words, like so many nimble and airy servitors, trip about him at command.
—John Milton

And then one or other dies. And we think of this as love cut short, like a dance stopped in mid-career or a flower with its head

unluckily snapped off—something truncated and therefore lacking its due shape.
—C. S. Lewis

He had an upper-class Hoosier accent, which sounds like a bandsaw cutting galvanized tin.
—Kurt Vonnegut

The great enemy of clear language is insincerity. When there is a gap between one's real and one's declared aims, one turns as it were instinctively to long words and exhausted idioms, like a cuttlefish squirting out ink.
—George Orwell

Good metaphors and similes that sound effortless are usually composed only with the most strenuous effort. They bring an element of surprise into writing that catches us off guard and makes us think.

Exercises

1. An excellent exercise to help you master a variety of sentence types is **sentence combining.** It will give you practice in combining simple sentences into larger, varied, and more complex ones. Each of the following clusters of short sentences, when properly combined, can make a single sentence. Study the model.

> **Short sentences:** (1) Benjamin Franklin was an American statesman.
> (2) He was a printer.
> (3) He was a scientist.
> (4) He was a writer.
> (5) He was born the son of a tallow chandler and soapmaker.
>
> **Combined sentence:** Benjamin Franklin, born the son of a tallow chandler and soapmaker, became a printer, scientist, writer, and American statesman.

Combine the following short sentences into a single long one.
a. *(1)* A hat provides considerable psychological security.
(2) It protects the face.
(3) A hat hides one's face.
(4) The hiding is from curious onlookers.
(5) These onlookers threaten one's identity.
b. *(1)* Buddhism arose in India in the sixth century B.C.
(2) It was a protest.

   (3) The protest was against the overdeveloped ritualism of the Hindus.

   (4) Sometimes these sacrificial cults even involved sacrificing human beings.

c. *(1)* The passage of liquor laws has always been prompted by a public desire.

  (2) The desire was to prevent immoderate use of intoxicants.

  (3) The passage was also prompted by the need to raise revenue.

  (4) Liquor laws are legislation designed to restrict, regulate, or totally abolish the manufacture, sale, and use of alcoholic beverages.

d. *(1)* Changes in table manners reflect changes in human relationships.

  (2) Such changes have been documented for Western Europe.

  (3) Medieval courtiers saw their table manners as distinguishing them from crude peasants.

  (4) By modern standards the manners of medieval courtiers were unrefined.

e. *(1)* Today, efforts to improve the drab conditions of army life are always thwarted.

  (2) Recruits could be permitted to personalize their sleeping quarters.

  (3) Recruits could be allowed to choose their own hairstyles.

  (4) But conditions of army life are not improved.

  (5) Efforts to do so are regarded by many senior officers as responsible for breakdowns in order and discipline.

f. *(1)* Mr. Simmons will be an excellent addition to top management.

  (2) He has been employed by Home Federal Saving for 20 years.

  (3) He is knowledgeable about all areas of banking.

  (4) These areas include foreign deposits.

g. *(1)* Television newscasters are victims of the rating game.

  (2) They are hired and fired on the basis of how entertaining they make the news.

  (3) The rating game is controlled by anti-intellectual viewers.

h. *(1)* The early Incas did not have the wheel.

  (2) They did not have paper either.

  (3) Nevertheless, their architectural and engineering achievements were spectacular.

  (4) They established an elevated network of roads.

  (5) They built beautiful palaces.

i. *(1)* Martin Luther was the German leader of the Protestant Reformation.

  (2) He was born in Eisleben, Saxony.

  (3) His family were small, but free, landholders.

  (4) His family encouraged him to attend the cathedral school at Eisenach and later the University of Erfurt. At the University of Erfurt he studied law.

j. *(1)* Toward the end of the nineteenth century, the Belgian sheepdog began to decline in population.

(2) This gradual decline was the result of several new factors.

(3) First of all, the widespread use of fencing became popular.

(4) Also, rail transportation became available.

(5) The threat of marauding animals no longer existed.

2. **Classical imitation** is one of the best exercises to help you write sentences that have balance and rhythm. In this exercise, you are allowed to change the content, but not the grammatical structure, of the sentence or passage you are imitating. If the original begins with a subordinate clause followed by a main clause, so must your imitation. If parallelism is used in the original, it must also be used in your imitation. Even figures of speech must be imitated.

a. Imitate the following sentence structures:

> **Model:** "Speak of the moderns without contempt and of the ancients without idolatry."
> —Earl of Chesterfield
>
> **Imitation:** Think of the poor without scorn and of the rich without envy.

(1) "The humorous story is strictly a work of art—high and delicate art—and only an artist can tell it; but no art is necessary in telling the comic and witty story; anybody can do it."—Mark Twain

(2) "The earth is filled with a vague, a dizzy, a tumultuous joy."—Anonymous

(3) "No one can be perfectly free till all are free; no one can be perfectly moral till all are moral; no one can be perfectly happy till all are happy."—Herbert Spencer

(4) "Let us therefore brace ourselves to our duties and so bear ourselves that if the British Empire and its Commonwealth last for a thousand years, men will still say, 'This was their finest hour.' "-—Winston Churchill

(5) "As he was valiant, I honour him; but, as he was ambitious, I slew him."—Shakespeare

b. Imitate the following figures of speech.

> **Model:** "The moonlight spread a wash of gauzy silver over the clear spaces of the garden, and the shadows were cobalt blue."
> —Katherine Anne Porter
>
> **Imitation:** The fog wrapped a mysterious cloak of gray over the city, and the lights became blurred halos.

(1) "She was created to be the toy of man, his rattle, and it must jingle in his ears whenever, dismissing reason, he chooses to be amused."—Mary Wollstonecraft

(2) "Russian winter in this new guise attacked them on all sides; it cut through their thin uniforms and worn shoes, their wet clothing froze on them, and this icy shroud molded their bodies and stiffened their limbs."—Count Philippe-Paul de Segur

(3) "She is the crown of creation, the masterpiece."—Germaine Greer

(4) "When he hung up his shirt to dry, it would grow brittle and break, like glass."—Isaac Bashevis Singer

(5) "The lake was quite black, like a great pit."—D.H. Lawrence

c. Imitate the following entire passages. You do not need to imitate slavishly. If a slightly different idea from the one in the original occurs to you, do not hesitate to write it down.

> **Model:** Piccadilly before dawn. After the stir and ceaseless traffic of the day, the silence of Piccadilly early in the morning, in the small hours, seems barely credible. It is unnatural and rather ghostly. The great street in its emptiness has a sort of solemn broadness, descending in a majestic sweep with the assured and stately ease of a placid river. The air is pure and limpid, but resonant, so that a solitary cab suddenly sends the whole street ringing, and the emphatic trot of the horse resounds with long reverberations.
> —W. Somerset Maugham
>
> **Imitation:** Laguna Beach at sunrise. Before the whirring noises of traffic or the youthful shouts of surfing fanatics rend the air, a delicious soft breeze wafting down Pacific Coast Highway past the old Victor Hugo Inn, seems especially enjoyable. The world is quiet and peaceful. The Pacific Ocean, seemingly stretching clear to the end of the world, curls over the sand like the soft hair of a flirtatious girl. The sky is a velvety aqua blue, but damp, so that three or four big marshmallow clouds floating in the West prophesy that the afternoon may witness a few unusual raindrops, and the mournful sound of a screeching sea gull fades away into the mysterious air.

Imitate the following passages.

(1) But that night after dinner and a whisky and soda by the fire before going to bed, as Francis Macomber lay on his cot with the mosquito bar over him and listened to the night noises, it was not all over. It was neither all over nor was it beginning. It was there exactly as it happened with some parts of it indelibly emphasized and he was miserably ashamed at it. But more than shame he felt cold, hollow fear in him. The fear was still there like a cold slimy hollow in all the emptiness where

once his confidence had been and it made him feel sick. It was still there with him now.
—Ernest Hemingway

(2) But if a man would be alone, let him look at the stars. The rays that come from those heavenly worlds will separate between him and what he touches. One might think the atmosphere was made transparent with the design, to give man, in the heavenly bodies, the perpetual presence of the sublime. Seen in the streets of cities, how great they are! If the stars should appear one night in a thousand years, how would men believe and adore; and preserve for many generations the remembrance of the city of God which had been shown! But every night come out these envoys of beauty, and light the universe with their admonishing smile.
—Ralph Waldo Emerson

(3) He did not feel weak, he was merely luxuriating in that supremely gutful lassitude of convalescence in which time, hurry, doing, did not exist, the accumulating seconds and minutes and hours to which in its well state the body is slave both waking and sleeping, now reversed and time now the lip-server and mendicant to the body's pleasure instead of the body thrall to time's headlong course.
—William Faulkner

Note: In imitating the passage above, try simply to imitate the stream of consciousness creating a feeling (in this case, languor); your imitation need not be exact.

(4) I believe a leaf of grass is no less than the journeywork of the stars,
And the pismire is equally perfect, and a grain of sand, and the egg of the wren,
And the tree-toad is a chef-d'oeuvre for the highest,
And the running blackberry would adorn the parlors of heaven,
And the narrowest hinge in my hand puts to scorn all machinery,
And the cow crunching with depressed head surpasses any statue,
And a mouse is miracle enough to stagger sextillions of infidels,
And I could come every afternoon of my life to look at the farmer's girl boiling her
iron kettle and baking shortcake.
—Walt Whitman

Note: Following Walt Whitman's form, make up your own list of nature's miracles.

3. The purpose of this writing assignment is to give you practice at **editing** sentences. Choose a topic from the list below and write a 500-word essay on it. Make sure that the first draft of your essay is controlled by a thesis, written in unified and logical paragraphs, and uses correct spelling and

punctuation. Next, rewrite each sentence to improve clarity and emphasis, and to eliminate wordiness. Finally, rewrite your sentences for liveliness and color. Bear the following questions in mind as you rewrite:

a. Is the sentence unmistakably clear?

b. Have I avoided repetitions, deadwood, prefabricated phrases, and pompous words?

c. Are all of my sentences balanced? Do they read well aloud?

d. Would an apt figure of speech add sparkle?

Topics to choose from:

(1) Describe the most painful change ever experienced in your life. State what brought about the change and how you handled it.

(2) Write an analysis of what spring (summer, fall, or winter) means to you. Describe emotions as well as landscapes.

(3) Choose a high school or college course that taught you something valuable or fascinating. Explain as clearly as possible, what the course taught you and why you consider this information exceptional.

(4) Write an essay on the major personality traits you would expect to find in a U.S. president. Explain why each trait is important and what could happen if it was missing.

(5) Describe the person who so far has had the most profound influence on your life. Use concrete details to create a lively portrait. Be specific about the exact nature of the person's influence.

Appendix: Proofreading and Marking Your Drafts

After revising your sentences and making appropriate corrections, you should also check your text for errors of misspelling, bad spacing, omitted letters or words, and so on. A knowledge of standard proofreaders' symbols will save you time and effort as you work to clean up your final copy. For your own use, then, here is a list of the most commonly used proofreading symbols:

Symbol	Meaning
fact_ry	insert a letter
antecedánt	replace a letter

One, make choices *must*	insert a word
In ~~Peking~~ *Beijing*	replace a word
in the west	capitalize
He is a bank President	use lowercase
recieve	transpose letters
to quickly move	transpose words
a display of dazzling light	move word(s)
the future of the world	insert a space
a birth mark	close up the space
dissappear	delete a letter and close up
every ~~last taxable~~ dollar	delete word(s)
a ~~treacherous~~ enemy	stet (restore what was deleted)
her own self-esteem. Her physical stress	run the line on (no paragraph)

What follows is a page from a student essay with proper proof marks:

When I was ten and living in florida, I
learned that dogs may not *always* be man's best friend.
    I liked to discover new places, and one
afternoon, while riding a ~~bycicle~~ *bicycle* on the out-
skirts of my neighborhood, I discovered a train
station. As I was leisurely rolling by the
~~wherehouses,~~ *warehouses* I noticed three large dogs about

fifty yards infront of me. Since I had a dog of
my own, and he wouldn't (without a reason) bother
anyone, I payed not attention to these canines.
But, as I got closer, the dogs started to
approch me with menaceing growls and barks. At
this point I began to feel uneasy, so I turned
around to ride in the other direction. As soon
as I turned, all three dogs started to chase me
and nip at my heals. I tried to pick up speed
in order to create some distance between me and
these malign creatures, but to no avail. One of
the dogs sunk his teeth into my leg deeply and
would let go, no matter how hard I pulled. Only
when I gave a violent yank he did finally let
go. At this point, I didn't think about pain; I
only though about riding for my life.

Part

4

Special Purpose Essays

Chapter

17

The Argumentative Essay

*W*ords can be more powerful, and more treacherous, than we sometimes suspect; communication more difficult than we may think. We are all serving life sentences of solitary confinement within our bodies; like prisoners, we have, as it were, to tap in awkward code to our fellow men in their neighboring cells.

F. L. LUCAS (1894–1967)

The purpose of an argumentative paper, pure and simple, is to persuade a reader to the writer's point of view. As the writer, your starting assumption is that your reader holds either a neutral or opposing belief from your own and must be rid of that mistaken conviction. To do so, it is useful to think of your argument as having three principal parts: its proposition, its sources of proof, and its logical links.

The Proposition of an Argument

The proposition of an argument is the stand it takes on an issue, the position it tries to prove or defend. This is its thesis, which is therefore governed by all the advice we have already given in Chapter 3 on how to write one effectively. But propositions are also different enough from ordinary theses to merit special attention.

First and most obvious, a proposition must be for or against some topic or issue. It should not straddle the fence, should not hem and haw (nor should any good thesis), but should boldly proclaim the writer's stand. Here is an example of a weak proposition:

Original: `Nuclear power should be banned from our midst.`

Readers of Chapter 3 will immediately recognize this sentence as too broad to be a good thesis. The reader knows that the writer is against nuclear power, but not why. For the writer's part, if this opposition is not grounded in well-rehearsed reasons, some will have to be immediately found or the argument must come to a dead stop. We think it smarter to decide on the supporting evidence and reasons and include them in the wording of the thesis. Here is a rewritten version:

Revision: `Because nuclear power plants have become too`
`expensive to build and have lost public acceptance,`
`they should be banned.`

509

Now the writer knows where the argument is going. And so do readers.

Second, a proposition should not be unprovable. Unprovable propositions are those based mainly on personal values or beliefs. Here is an example:

Original: Casual sex is wrong because it is against the moral

code given by God.

On the other hand, here is a more arguable proposition:

Revision: Casual sex involves one in an empty, risky, and

unfulfilling commitment usually based only on

physical attraction.

You now have at your fingertips varied sources of evidence. You could back up your allegation of emptiness with testimony and anecdote. You can prove risk by citing pregnancy statistics and rate of venereal infection. Where formerly it had only scripture on its side, the reworded thesis now enlists the support of psychology, statistics, and common sense. Arguing in favor of some cause or cherished belief is not wrong, it is simply harder to do than to defend a provable issue.

Below are two more examples of unarguable propositions:

Original: Fauvism was a clumsy, meaningless period of art.

This proposition is based on personal taste and would be discounted by serious art critics.

Original: The purpose of all life is to evolve from plant

existence to spiritual existence.

Again, this is an unprovable proposition that cannot be backed by any objective certainty.

Third, a proposition should not rest on a shaky premise. The premise of a proposition is any major assumption it makes or takes for granted. Here are some examples of what we mean:

Thesis: Abortion should be outlawed because it denies the

constitutional guarantee of life to the unborn.

Premise: The fetus is a human being entitled to
            constitutional guarantees.

Thesis: The reinstatement of capital punishment throughout
            the nation will be an effective deterrent against
            major crimes.

Premise: Capital punishment deters crime.

Both these take for granted the truth of a suspect premise. Yet, if the fetus is not a human being, it is not entitled to constitutional guarantees; and if capital punishment does not deter crime, deterrence cannot be an argument for its reinstatement.

Finally, if you have the choice, we advise you to choose an argumentative proposition that takes advantage of your own personal strengths and expertise. For example, let us say that you have had extensive experience working at a family planning clinic. This background gives you a rich source of testimonial evidence about the value of family planning that would be useless in an argument on the topic of air pollution. In that case, you'd be clearly better off writing your argument on some issue of family planning since it is always more prudent to argue about what you know firsthand than what you don't.

Sources of Proof

The usual sources of proof are facts, statistics, testimonials, experience, anecdotes, and reasoning. Taken together, these make up the backing or evidence for an argument.

Facts

A fact is a relationship, force, or law of reality whose effect is independent of human belief. Lack of vitamin C in the human diet causes scurvy, and whether or not you believe that will not prevent you from getting scurvy if you fail to take vitamin C. People do not always universally agree on what is a fact and what isn't, but a fact will have its own way regardless of its doubters.

A fact may strike you as the same as a truth, but the two are substantially different. A truth is some idea in which a large number of people, perhaps even a majority, believe. When most of its believers give it up, the truth is demoted to a myth. For example, there was a time when people believed that the world was flat. Now we know that the world is round, and that belief in the former "truth" of its flatness was mistaken. But the fact of the world's roundness remained unaltered during the rise and fall of this former "truth."

Facts and truths are the staples of argumentative papers, and all writers use them. For all your cited facts and truths, you should provide the reader with a context, an interpretation, and a traceable source. Resist the temptation to weigh down the page with every fact you uncover in your research. Quote and cite as necessary to prove your case, but never for mere show. Here are some ways students have properly used facts. From a paper arguing that gifted students are tragically neglected:

> Writing for Science magazine, psychologist
> Constance Holden states that gifted children are
> often labeled "obnoxious," "unruly,"
> "hyperactive," or "rebellious," because they are
> inquisitive, active, often need little sleep,
> and get into things.

From a paper arguing that the present high school diploma does not adequately prepare students for earning a living:

> According to a 1985 U.S. Census Bureau report,
> the high school dropout rate is steadily
> increasing despite the job problems encountered
> by those who lack a high school education.

From a paper arguing against drinking alcoholic beverages:

> One of the worst results of heavy drinking is
> cancer of the pancreas. In his book Alcohol
> Addiction, Who Is in Control? Dr. Joseph P.
> Frawley explains clearly how the high level of
> sugar in alcohol causes the pancreas to take a
> severe beating as it attempts to create enough

```
insulin to maintain a healthy chemical balance

within the body. Eventually, however, the

pancreas loses the battle and becomes cancerous.
```

Each of these examples consists of a fact along with a traceable source.

Statistics

A statistic is a mathematical expression of some trend or relationship. The spread sheets of bookkeepers, the research of scientists, and the forecasts of economists are typically based on statistics. Statistics do not occur in nature but are strictly man-made, which means that they must always be cited with an accompanying source. Here are two examples of how students have successfully used statistics:

```
Opponents of gun control argue that their right

to self-protection would be taken away if a gun

control law were passed. However, guns in the

home increase the danger of accidents and crimes

of passion. According to the FBI, 47 percent of

all murders in 1983 were committed by relatives

or persons acquainted with the victim.

Perhaps the most important argument supporting

the continuation of nuclear power is that if the

United States pulls back from the nuclear

industry and does not develop other energy

possibilities such as fusion power, the country

may find itself fighting over what little fuel

remains in 100 years. Alvin Weinberg reveals

that in a year's time a 1,000 megawatt nuclear

plant produces as much electricity as 8 million

barrels of oil or 2.5 million tons of coal. He

also states that if by the year 2000 the nation
```

```
replaced the originally planned 300 nuclear

plants with coal burning plants, it would need

an additional 750 million tons of coal per year.
```

These two examples of the use of a statistic we may take as models. They give the statistic both a source and a context, using it to make a point. The point of the first passage is that guns in the home increase the likelihood of accident and crimes of passion. The point of the second passage is that nuclear energy plants are a necessity for the future.

Testimonials

A testimonial is the account of either an expert or eyewitness that supports your case and is usually given in the form of a direct quotation. The formula for citing testimonial evidence is quite straightforward: Give the credentials of the expert or eyewitness, cite the source of the quotation if you have one, and add whatever interpretative comment you think necessary. Here is an example of expert testimony:

```
Proponents of nuclear power say nuclear

power is safe.  According to Lynn Weaver, Dean

of the School of Engineering, Auburn University,

"There is broad agreement that our current plans

for storing radioactive waste are prudent and

safe."
```

The speaker, as dean of engineering in a major university, we take to be a believable expert on this issue.

Note that being believable is not the same as being right. Naturally, you hope the opinions of your experts are right, especially when you quote them to back up your own argument. But the burden of choosing right experts is entirely on you. Some self-proclaimed experts turn out to be plainly wrong, while others are badly at odds with their own peers. Consult volumes of *Who's Who,* read magazines, journals, and books in the field, and you will soon find a core of recurring names favorably mentioned in different publications. This is the group from which a sterling testimonial can be gotten.

In citing an expert's credentials, use common sense. Cite the credentials in all their naked glory if the expert is not internationally known; leave them out if the expert enjoys global or historical fame. For example, Jesus needs no introduction as an expert on theology, neither does Aristotle on philosophy, nor Queen Elizabeth I on royalty. But other experts who are less recognizable should be touted. Here is an example from a paper on the proposed Star Wars missile defense system in which the writer should have touted his expert but didn't:

Original: The tiered strategy will make the total defense more

effective. Robert Jastrow explains this strategy in

simple terms in his article "The War against Star

Wars," which appeared in Commentary.

Since Jastrow's name is not likely to bring a light of recognition to every face on a bus, his credentials, briefly listed, would have made this quotation more impressive:

Revision: The tiered strategy will make the total defense more

effective. Robert Jastrow, noted astronomer and

author of many books, explains this strategy in

simple terms in his article "The War against Star

Wars," which appeared in Commentary.

On the other hand, it is perfectly acceptable to gloss over the credentials of an expert being quoted not for what he or she is presumed to know, but for what he or she has seen or done. Here is an example from a student paper arguing for gun control:

Gun control enforcement is needed because

handguns in the United States are too easily

obtained. In an article "Wretchedness Is a Warm

Gun," author Bill Lueders describes his going on

a gun-buying spree. He purposely dressed the

part of a fanatic with buttons that read "Smash

the State" and "Kill 'em All and Let God Sort

'em Out!" He then took five or six Vivarin, a

> legal stimulant, downed a six-pack of beer, and
>
> proceeded to see if anyone would refuse to sell
>
> him a gun. No one did.

Leuder's credentials are unmentioned because who he is and what he knows are less important to his testimony than what he did—and that is covered.

Properly used, testimonial opinion can give a persuasive boost to your argument. In effect, it says to your reader, "I'm not alone in this opinion. These experts agree with me." But you should also be certain that you quote only authentic experts, and then only on the subject of their acknowledged expertise.

Experience

In some arguments the evidence of experience has a definite place, if only to illustrate or dramatize a point. Here is an example, from a student paper advocating breast-feeding. The writer has already covered the physiological and biological benefits of breast-feeding. Now she dramatizes her case with her own experience.

> But these facts and statistics tell only
>
> part of the story. What no one can ever really
>
> tell is how personally fulfilling breast-feeding
>
> is to the infant and the new mother. When I put
>
> my baby to my breast, a feeling comes between us
>
> that it indescribable. Writers such as Diony
>
> Young and Mary K. White call it "bonding,"
>
> meaning that between me and my baby an
>
> attachment is being formed that will last a
>
> lifetime. But it is more than that. It is a
>
> feeling of closeness and satisfaction that is
>
> impossible to put into words.

Sometimes the experience of someone else may be useful, as in the following argument against dial-porn telephone recording services:

```
Last summer, a neighbor admitted that his

teenage son had wasted a whole week's paycheck

on dial-porn messages, introducing his less

sophisticated friends to them.
```

Granted, this is not a hardheaded fact such as one might use to crack open a closed mind. But it is just this sort of personal and enlivening touch that makes an argument persuasive.

Anecdotes

An anecdote is a brief story that drives home a point. Like experiences, anecdotes by themselves do not make a defensible argument, but they can and do add dramatic impact. Here is an example from a student paper:

```
He is 5'7" tall, and he weighs 96 pounds.

He has a poor appetite, has trouble sleeping, is

withdrawn--all the classic symptoms of

depression.  When I visit him, he rarely smiles,

sometimes cries, and answers my questions in a

flat monotone voice.  He is 13, and he is my

son.  He has been diagnosed as having a Major

Depressive Episode.  I have watched Ronnie go

steadily downhill since his father and I

divorced seven years ago.  Ronnie never adjusted

to the breakup of his family, to having a father

he rarely saw or heard from.  Ronnie doesn't

like living in a hospital, but he wasn't happy

at home, and doctors warned that he was

suicidal.
```

The thesis of this paper is that adolescent suicide is directly related to the high rate of divorce, and the writer uses the anecdotal example of her own son's depression to underscore that point. Anecdotes of this kind do not prove anything; but they do make an argument compelling.

Reasoning

Reasoning refers not only to the claims of evidence you make on behalf of your thesis, but to the logical strategies you use to present your case. A typical argument will state a thesis and then marshal evidence behind it. But the alert writer will also look for chinks in the armor plating of the opposition's case, and when one is found, pierce it with a counterclaim. In the example on pp. 513–14, for instance, the writer quotes the argument used by pro-gun advocates that guns are needed for self-protection, and then refutes it with a statistic.

Another useful strategy is to expose inconsistencies you uncover in the argument of the opposition. In the minds of reasonable men and women everywhere, there is an expectation that legitimate arguments will be consistent. If you can find an inconsistency in the views of the opposition, you should therefore blare it out for all the world to hear. Here is an example, from a student paper against abortion:

Now we have laws. We do not have any laws
which govern the lives of plants. We have but
one law which governs the life of an animal.
That animal is man. The law has been written
and rewritten down through the course of the
centuries--in stone, on leather, on parchment,
on paper, in languages that have been lost and
long forgotten. But the law has remained the
same. No man, it states, may take the life of
another man. Perhaps you would recognize it
this way: "We hold these truths to be
self-evident--that all men are created equal and
are endowed by their Creator with certain
inalienable rights--that among these rights are
<u>life</u>. . . ." Or this way, quite simply stated in

another book: "Thou shalt not kill." But
whatever their form, the laws are there. And
there were no qualifications written into these
laws on the basis of age. What the matter boils
down to it this: A human life has been
determined by us, for centuries, millennia, to
be sacred, and we have determined that it cannot
be taken away. And a fertilized egg is human
life.

       For any violations of these laws to occur,
especially on a grand scale as is happening
today, a mentality has to have been developed
through which those who are going to commit a
wrong can justify their actions and can appease
the guilt that they might feel—the guilt that
they might feel if they had to admit that they
were killing a living human entity. And this is
what we have done. This is what we are doing.
We have learned to call a flower a stone. . . .

The writer thinks he has found an inconsistency in the views of pro-abor-
tionists—namely, that they exempt the living fetus from the ancient law
against murder—and he is quick to expose it. Note that exposing an inconsistency in an argument is not the same as making an *ad hominem* attack (See
Chapter 4.) The first is directed against a weakness seen in the argument itself; the second, against its advocate's character.
       A third strategy writers can use to make their arguments compelling
is an ethos appeal—"ethos" being the Greek word for "character." In one
study a recorded speech was played back to three groups of students, who
were respectively told that it had been given by the surgeon general of the
United States, the secretary general of the Communist party in America, and
a college sophomore. The results showed that the group most impressed by
the speech was the one who thought it had been made by the surgeon general. Since the speech was the same one given to the less persuaded groups,

something other than literary merit was responsible for its superior effect. This factor has been labeled "ethos" and defined as the perception by an audience of a writer's or speaker's character.

Studies have isolated three characteristics linked with perceived character in a speaker: trustworthiness, competence, and dynamism. Trustworthiness and dynamism are plainly easier for a speaker to demonstrate than for a writer, but writers can put ethos to work in their essays by a display of competence. If you have some special experience or association with your topic, you should therefore tell it. Here is an example. The writer's thesis is that animal experiments should be banned because they are often unnecessarily cruel. In the paragraph below, he makes an "ethos" argument:

```
As a medical technician, I have worked for
the experimental lab of a major university and
seen for myself the treatment that animals
suffer.  When we receive a shipment of dogs, the
first thing we do is schedule them for
ventriculocordectomy.  We anesthetize the
animals and then surgically sever their vocal
cords so that they can make no sounds during the
experiments and bother the researchers.  I
myself have performed scores of
ventriculocordectomies and know that the
experience, which the university insists is
painless, is deeply traumatic to dogs.  Once the
animal revives and finds that it can make no
sound, its look of anguish and grief is
unbelievable.
```

We tend to believe this piece of writing not only because of its specific detail, but because of its ethos appeal—the competence we attribute to the writer because of his experience. This same opinion from the pen of one who has never set foot into a laboratory would simply not be as believable.

Finally, your choice of evidence to support your case can in itself be an important strategy of reasoning. Bear in mind that the battering ram of facts and statistics is not always the best proof of a point. Sometimes the brute force of facts will not persuade as effectively as the soft touch of an anecdote or the breath of an ethos appeal. Admittedly, some arguments can be proven only by the sheer weight of facts. For example, geological data are the only possible sources of proof for any theory explaining the extinction of dinosaurs. But other propositions are provable by anecdote, experience, and ethos just as readily as by facts. For example, if you were arguing that a long delay in bringing an accused person to trial is a harsh injustice, and if you yourself have suffered at the hands of a slothful court, your account could be more moving than a pure recital of facts.

Logical Links

In Chapter 4, we discussed possible inconsistencies in an argument, and we would urge you to review that material before writing your own argumentative essay. Here we wish to stress the importance of the logical links that tie your statements of belief, theory, and conclusion into a chain of reasoning.

All arguments consist of statements linked in logical relationships. A common example is the assertion that if this is so, then that is so. By this we mean that if the first half of the statement is true, then so must be the second. When the link is one of compelling necessity, an assertion of this kind is logical. For example, it is entirely logical to assert that if you fall from a 20-story building onto the street below, you will likely be killed, since experience teaches us that death is the most probable outcome of such a plunge. But it is more prejudicial than logical to say that if a person is a woman, she will automatically not understand debates about missile defense systems. That conclusion does not necessarily follow.

So heavily dependent is a logical argument on these links between its parts that it is possible to chart the exact steps in reasoning from proposition to conclusion. Here is an example of an argument whose statements are poorly linked:

Original: The evidence linking rock music at concerts with hearing loss in the audience is clearly established; therefore, rock music should be abolished. Medical doctors say that once hearing in the high frequencies is lost, it never returns during the lifetime of the individual. Hence, since

rock concerts cause permanent damage to the

listener's hearing, they should be banned. It has

also been demonstrated that some rock music contains

what is known as "backward masking," which is where

a hidden message is present in the song and designed

to influence listeners. Some authorities have shown

that backward masking has been used to promote

Satanism, unbeknownst to the innocent listener.

Therefore, since backward masking can be used to

exert influence over a listener, rock concerts

should not be allowed.

The argument is weak mainly because it implies a relationship of logical necessity between assertions and conclusions where none exists. Here is a sketch of the major parts of the author's arguments, showing the logical links between them:

1. Evidence exists that links exposure to rock music at concerts to hearing loss in listeners;
   therefore,
   rock music should be abolished.
2. The damage done to the hearing of listeners is permanent;
   hence,
   rock music should be banned.
3. Rock music uses "backward masking" to influence listeners;
   therefore,
   rock concerts should be abolished.

The weaknesses in this argument are readily apparent from this sketch. For example, common sense tells that it is not only rock music played at concerts that can cause hearing loss in an audience, but excessively loud music of whatever type. Classical overtures played loudly enough will just as surely lead to hearing loss in concert-goers. The second reason is no more logically linked to its conclusion than the first. Granted that high-frequency hearing loss is genuine among people who frequent rock concerts, but that is a better argument for turning down the volume of the amplifiers, not for banning the concerts. Finally, the "backward masking" the writer refers to is allegedly present only in recorded rock music, but technically impossible in live performances. It cannot therefore be cited as a logical reason for banning rock concerts.

Members of the writer's peer-editing session caught most of the weaknesses in this essay and made notes suggesting revisions the writer might make. A facsimile of the essay, annotated by the peer editing group for the writer's benefit, is given below:

> The evidence linking rock music at concerts with hearing loss in the audience is clearly established; therefore, rock music should be abolished. Medical doctors say that once hearing in the high frequencies is lost, it never returns during the lifetime of the individual. Hence, since rock concerts cause permanent damage to the listener's hearing, they should be banned. It has also been demonstrated that some rock music contains what is known as "backward masking," which is where a hidden message is present in the song and designed to influence listeners. Some authorities have shown that backward masking has been used to promote Satanism, unbeknownst to the innocent listener. Therefore, since backward masking can be used to exert influence over a listener, rock concerts should not be allowed.

[Handwritten annotations: More evidence is needed. What incidence of hearing loss exists among the population. What studies support your assertion of cause/effect?

Irrelevant. Backward masking cannot occur at a live concert. Delete this.]

Using the suggestions of his peer group, the writer revised the paragraph and substantially improved it:

Revision: The evidence linking rock music at concerts with hearing loss in the audience is clearly established and is a solid argument for turning down the volume of the amplifiers. According to some

writers, there are 13 million Americans who have
suffered permanent hearing loss, usually from nerve
impairment. The number one cause of this loss,
writes an expert in the April 1984 issue of <u>Glamour</u>
magazine, is prolonged exposure to loud noise. But
rock concerts are not the only damaging source of
loud music. Studies done in Sweden and summarized
in the June 12, 1982, issue of <u>Science News,</u> have
found that classical musicians also suffer hearing
impairment from pursuing their careers. Trombone
and French horn players were found to have suffered
the greatest hearing loss. Some classical concerts
monitored in Swedish opera houses have exceeded 85
decibels, which is a higher noise level than Swedish
national standards allow in the workplace. Rock
concerts can cause hearing loss in an audience, but
so can Beethoven concerts. What's at issue is not
the music itself, but how loudly it is played.

This argument is stronger not only because it cites evidence that is specific, but also because the links between its assertions are reasonable and logical.

The links between the assertions and conclusions of an argumentative essay should be forged with iron-clad logic. Yet it is easy to confuse or misstate them during the actual writing. One way to avoid this error is to sketch out the major points of your argument before you write it. For example, if you are writing an argument against capital punishment, a diagram of your major ideas and the links between them might look like this:

Capital punishment is wrong
   because
it does not deter crime
   because
it puts society on equal moral footing with the murderer
   because
it debases the value of human life

because

it is arbitrarily practiced

because

it can lead to a catastrophic mistake.

From this brief chart, you know the major parts of your argument as well as the logical links that must connect them.

The arguments that follow illustrate the effective use of logical links between assertions and proof as well as all the other principles of argumentation and persuasion discussed in this chapter and in Chapter 4. In "A Hanging," George Orwell graphically shows us why he thinks capital punishment is wrong. Karl Menninger takes a more reasoned and less dramatic tack but comes to similar conclusions about punishment in general. Carl Sagan, in "A Sunday Sermon," tackles the question about God and origins in a skillful argument against religious orthodoxy. And Peter Drucker convincingly contends that what employees need most is the ability to write and speak effectively.

In its final draft the student essay similarly mounts an effective argument for the abolition or reformation of Halloween as a traditional holiday.

The original draft used an impressive satirical touch and an exaggerated sense of horror to expose the dangers of Halloween. However, it did not include enough evidence to support its contention that sugar was unhealthy, nor did it take sufficiently into account the opposition's viewpoint. Its ending was also notably weak. Study the original draft, with the instructor's suggestions; then, notice how the student incorporated these suggestions into the revised copy. The second version features a clear proposition supported by facts, expert testimony, witness, and experience. It also acknowledges and then promptly destroys the opposition's point of view:

Original:

Your opening is too abrupt. Why not begin with a negative description of a Halloween scene?

           A Night to Forget

    Halloween, as a traditional American

festival, should be eliminated from our

calendars because it spawns crime and poor

health.

    Halloween today represents a conglomeration

of ancient customs and religious beliefs.

According to the Encyclopaedia Britannica, the

celebration of Halloween can be traced back to

the Celtic Winter Festival. On this occasion the
Celts would celebrate the autumn harvest and the
coming of winter. At this time, it was believed *wordy*
that ancestors who had died during the year
passed into the spirit world, and it was
customary to masquerade in order to frighten
away evil spirits who might try to stop them on *Use a*
their way. In the eighth century, Pope Gregory *more striking expression.*
III decided to give the event a more religious
thrust and declared it All Saints' Day, or All
Hallows' Day, to be celebrated on November 1. On
the eve of this day adults and children would go
from house to house offering to fast for the
saints in return for money or some other gift.
The Irish later added the superstition that
"little people" roamed the roads and played
pranks on All Hallows' Night, thus providing
practical jokers with a perfect opportunity to
be mischievous without consequences. In the
nineteenth century, the Irish brought this
wretched mess of customs to this country, where
it has been deteriorating ever since. *Here you do take into account the opposition, but some parents would be upset at the idea of arguing against Halloween. You should mention their views somewhere in this argument.*

　　Halloween has been a great commercial
success, and no doubt candy makers and costume
companies would hate to see it go. Confection
manufacturers sell huge quantities of their
packaged junk food during the month of October.
Costume designers of today create increasingly
elaborate disguises for the occasion.

Sophisticated kids of today reject the traditional, but far less expensive, ghosts and goblins of yesteryear. If the little darlings don't demand a Darth Vader cape and helmet for $49.95, they need other elaborate components in order to make a social statement. Last year I had at my door a playboy bunny, a Rubic's cube, a medfly, and a formal dinner table, complete with silver candelabra and white wine.

And the reward for this creative effort? Usually a 20-pound bag of assorted candy and gum that a parent wouldn't allow a child to touch during the rest of the year. *needs supporting evidence* Sugar is bad for the health and yet children are allowed nearly unlimited quantities of it during Halloween. Even more ludicrous is the tolerance of mass vandalism. Trick-or-treaters today leave home armed with toilet paper, spray paint, raw eggs and shaving cream—ready to do battle with the first helpless old lady to run out of candy, or the first kid they see dressed as a fairy princess or Mickey Mouse. No longer do homeowners dare to darken their houses, leave the car on the street, place pumpkins on the doorstep, or hand out apples, for fear of reprisals.

Support this assertion with some evidence The many incidents of property damage that occur during Halloween keep the police busy. It's time we took Halloween out of the hands of

adults or juvenile delinquents and returned it *Weak ending, needs more punch.*
to a harmless custom, or forgot it completely.

Revision:

A Night to Forget

Picture streets mobbed with wildly excited
children. Imagine these untamed urchins banging
on door after door in hideous disguises,
greedily demanding sweets. Consider what might
happen if the little beasts were armed with raw
eggs or shaving cream. It happens. Otherwise
conscientious parents encourage their offspring
to beg shamelessly in the streets and condone
mass consumption of useless sugar. Is it a
country gone mad? No, it's Halloween. Halloween
has become a night of terror for those unarmed
with goodies and a night of anxiety and torment
for police and many parents. It's time we
examine this festival of horror and either
revamp or eliminate it completely.

Traditionalists will no doubt gasp with
horror at the thought of abandoning such a
quaint celebration. They may contend that in our
rapidly changing world young people need to
cling to some form of tradition now more than
ever before. But what tradition is it? Most
adults agree that Halloween includes ghosts,
goblins, and goodies, but beyond that, just what
exactly are we celebrating?

Halloween today represents a conglomeration of ancient customs and religious beliefs. According to the <u>Encyclopaedia Britannica,</u> the celebration of Halloween can be traced back to the Celtic Winter Festival. On this occasion the Celts would celebrate the autumn harvest and the coming of winter. It was believed that ancestors who had died during the year passed into the spirit world, and it was customary to masquerade in order to frighten away evil spirits who might hinder them on their journey. In the eighth century, Pope Gregory III decided to give the event a more religious thrust and declared it All Saints' Day, or All Hallows' Day, to be celebrated on November 1. On the eve of this day adults and children would go from house to house offering to fast for the saints in return for money or some other gift. The Irish later added the superstition that "little people" roamed the roads and played pranks on All Hallows' Night, thus providing practical jokers with a perfect opportunity to be mischievous without consequences. In the nineteenth century, the Irish brought this wretched mess of customs to this country, where it has been deteriorating ever since.

Halloween has been a great commercial success, and no doubt candy makers and costume companies would hate to see it go. Confection

manufacturers sell huge quantities of their
packaged junk food during the month of October.
Costume designers of today create increasingly
elaborate disguises for the occasion.
Sophisticated kids of today reject the
traditional, but far less expensive, ghosts and
goblins of yesteryear. If the little darlings
don't demand a Darth Vader cape and helmet for
$49.95, they need other elaborate components
in order to make a social statement. Last year
I had at my door a playboy bunny, a Rubic's
cube, a medfly, and a formal dinner table,
complete with silver candelabra and white
wine.

And the reward for this creative effort?
Usually a 20-pound bag of assorted candy and gum
that a parent wouldn't allow a child to touch
during the rest of the year. For years, dentists
and doctors have warned parents and children
against the evils of sugar. Dr. John Yudkin, a
distinguished British physician, biochemist, and
researcher, has devoted his career to exposing
the ill effects of sugar in the diet. In his
book Sweet and Dangerous, Dr. Yudkin contends
that a high intake of sugar contributes to tooth
decay, diabetes, heart disease, and obesity. In
addition, recent studies done at Stanford
University suggest that a correlation exists
between sugar intake and behavioral problems in

children and adults. Yet, on Halloween everyone
overdoses on sugar.

Even more ludicrous than setting aside a
night for children to gather killer candy is the
tolerance of mass vandalism. Trick-or-treaters
today leave home armed with toilet paper, spray
paint, raw eggs and shaving cream—ready to do
battle with the first helpless old lady to run
out of candy, or the first kid they see dressed
as a fairy princess or Mickey Mouse. For fear of
reprisals, no longer do homeowners dare to
darken their houses, leave a car on the street,
pumpkins on the doorstep, or hand out apples.

Sergeant Moreno of the Glendale,
California, Police Department stated that the
police department switchboard is heavily engaged
on Halloween night. In recent years, each
November first issue of the Los Angeles Times
has reported at least one incident of acid-laced
cookies or razor-blade-embedded apples passed
out to an unsuspecting trick-or-treater. These
incidents don't begin to cover the property
damage that goes unreported. Last year I
shoveled my way out of my driveway strewn with
pumpkin carcasses, got into my car splattered
with eggs, to pick up my daughter covered with
shaving cream, and returned to my garage
plastered with spray-painted obscenities.

Enough is enough! Of course, who doesn't

love to see the little tykes with their cute
little faces peeking out of an adorable Snoopy
costume? And certainly, everyone gets a kick out
of peculiar expressions carved into pumpkins,
but the rest of this crazy celebration is out of
control! How about having a mandatory retirement
for trick-or-treaters? Twelve years, puberty,
facial hair, voice change, or the onset of
acne—whichever comes first. What if we were to
unite in refusing to give away useless, harmful
sugar products and passed out notepads, pencils,
or balloons instead? Since we are celebrating an
occasion with questionable merit, what's to keep
us from making up some new rules? It's time we
took Halloween out of the hands of hedonistic
adults or juvenile delinquents and returned it
to a harmless custom, or forgot it completely.

BIOGRAPHY

George Orwell
A HANGING

*George Orwell (1903–1950) was the pseudonym of Eric Arthur Blair, a British novelist and essayist, born in India and educated at Eton. He served with the imperial police in Burma and fought on the Republican side in the Spanish Civil War of 1936. He is best remembered for his two satirical novels—*Animal Farm *(1945) and* Nineteen Eighty-Four *(1949), which reveal his concern with the sociopolitical conditions of his time, especially the problem of human freedom. The master of a wonderfully lucid and engaging prose style, Orwell also published several collections of memorable essays, among them the one below. While "A Hanging" never explicitly*

"A Hanging" from *Shooting an Elephant and Other Essays* by George Orwell, copyright 1950 by Sonia Brownell Orwell, renewed 1978 by Sonia Pitt-Rivers, reprinted by permission of Harcourt Brace Jovanovich, Inc.

states that it is wrong to take a person's life, the narrative nevertheless argues eloquently against the death penalty.

It was in Burma, a sodden morning of the rains. A sickly light, like yellow tinfoil, was slanting over the high walls into the jail yard. We were waiting outside the condemned cells, a row of sheds fronted with double bars, like small animal cages. Each cell measured about ten feet by ten and was quite bare within except for a plank bed and a pot for drinking water. In some of them brown silent men were squatting at the inner bars, with their blankets draped round them. These were the condemned men, due to be hanged within the next week or two. [1]

One prisoner had been brought out of his cell. He was a Hindu, a puny wisp of a man, with a shaven head and vague liquid eyes. He had a thick, sprouting moustache, absurdly too big for his body, rather like the moustache of a comic man on the films. Six tall Indian warders were guarding him and getting him ready for the gallows. Two of them stood by with rifles and fixed bayonets, while the others handcuffed him, passed a chain through his handcuffs and fixed it to their belts, and lashed his arms tight to his sides. They crowded very close about him, with their hands always on him in a careful, caressing grip, as though all the while feeling him to make sure he was there. It was like men handling a fish which is still alive and may jump back into the water. But he stood quite unresisting, yielding his arms limply to the ropes, as though he hardly noticed what was happening. [2]

Eight o'clock struck and a bugle call, desolately thin in the wet air, floated from the distant barracks. The superintendent of the jail, who was standing apart from the rest of us, moodily prodding the gravel with his stick, raised his head at the sound. He was an army doctor, with a grey toothbrush moustache and a gruff voice, "For God's sake hurry up, Francis," he said irritably. "The man ought to have been dead by this time. Aren't you ready yet?" [3]

Francis, the head jailer, a fat Dravidian in a white drill suit and gold spectacles, waved his black hand. "Yes sir, yes sir," he bubbled. "All iss satisfactorily prepared. The hangman iss waiting. We shall proceed." [4]

"Well, quick march, then. The prisoners can't get their breakfast till this job's over." [5]

We set out for the gallows. Two warders marched on either side of the prisoner, with their rifles at the slope; two others marched close against him, gripping him by arm and shoulder, as though at [6] once pushing and supporting him. The rest of us, magistrates and the like, followed behind. Suddenly, when we had gone ten yards, the procession stopped short without any order or warning. A dreadful thing had happened—a dog, come goodness knows whence, had appeared in the yard. It came bounding among us with a loud volley of barks, and leapt round us wagging its whole body, wild with glee at finding so many human beings together. It was a large woolly dog, half Airedale, half pariah. For a moment it pranced round us, and then, before anyone could stop it, it had made a dash for the prisoner and, jumping up, tried to lick his face. Everyone stood aghast, too taken aback even to grab at the dog.

"Who let that bloody brute in here?" said the superintendent angrily. "Catch it, someone!"   7

A warder, detached from the escort, charged clumsily after the dog, but it danced and gambolled just out of his reach, taking everything as part of the game. A young Eurasian jailer picked up a handful of gravel and tried to stone the dog away, but it dodged the stones and came after us again. Its yaps echoed from the jail walls. The prisoner, in the grasp of the two warders, looked on incuriously, as though this was another formality of the hanging. It was several minutes before someone managed to catch the dog. Then we put my handkerchief through its collar and moved off once more, with the dog still straining and whimpering.   8

It was about forty yards to the gallows. I watched the bare brown back of the prisoner marching in front of me. He walked clumsily with his bound arms, but quite steadily, with that bobbing gait of the Indian who never straightens his knees. At each step his muscles slid neatly into place, the lock of hair on his scalp danced up and down, his feet printed themselves on the wet gravel. And once, in spite of the men who gripped him by each shoulder, he stepped slightly aside to avoid a puddle on the path.   9

It is curious, but till that moment I had never realized what it means to destroy a healthy, conscious man. When I saw the prisoner step aside to avoid the puddle I saw the mystery, the unspeakable wrongness, of cutting a life short when it is in full tide. This man was not dying, he was alive just as we are alive. All the organs of his body were working—bowels digesting food, skin renewing itself, nails growing, tissues forming—all toiling away in solemn foolery. His nails would still be growing when he stood on the drop, when he was falling through the air with a tenth-of-a-second to live. His eyes saw the yellow gravel and the grey walls, and his brain still remembered, foresaw, reasoned—reasoned even about puddles. He and we were a party of men walking together,   10

seeing, hearing, feeling, understanding the same world; and in two
minutes, with a sudden snap, one of us would be gone—one
mind less, one world less.

The gallows stood in a small yard, separate from the main   11
grounds of the prison, and overgrown with tall prickly weeds. It
was a brick erection like three sides of a shed, with planking on
top, and above that two beams and a crossbar with the rope dangling. The hangman, a grey-haired convict in the white uniform of
the prison, was waiting beside his machine. He greeted us with a
servile crouch as we entered. At a word from Francis the two
warders, gripping the prisoner more closely than ever, half led half
pushed him to the gallows and helped him clumsily up the ladder.
Then the hangman climbed up and fixed the rope round the prisoner's neck.

We stood waiting, five yards away. The warders had formed in   12
a rough circle round the gallows. And then, when the noose was
fixed, the prisoner began crying out to his god. It was a high, reit-
erated cry of "Ram! Ram! Ram! Ram!" not urgent and fearful like a
prayer or cry for help, but steady, rhythmical, almost like the toll-
ing of a bell. The dog answered the sound with a whine. The
hangman, still standing on the gallows, produced a small cotton
bag like a flour bag and drew it down over the prisoner's face. But
the sound, muffled by the cloth, still persisted, over and over again:
"Ram! Ram! Ram! Ram! Ram!"

The hangman climbed down and stood ready, holding the lever.   13
Minutes seemed to pass. The steady, muffled crying from the prisoner went on and on. "Ram! Ram! Ram!" never faltering for an instant. The superintendent, his head on his chest, was slowly poking the ground with his stick; perhaps he was counting the cries,
allowing the prisoner a fixed number—fifty, perhaps, or a hundred. Everyone had changed color. The Indians had gone grey like
bad coffee, and one or two of the bayonets were wavering. We
looked at the lashed, hooded man on the drop, and listened to his
cries—each cry another second of life; the same thought was in all
our minds: oh, kill him quickly, get it over, stop that abominable
noise!

Suddenly the superintendent made up his mind. Throwing up   14
his head he made a swift motion with his stick. "Chalo!" he
shouted almost fiercely.

There was a clanking noise, and then dead silence. The prisoner   15
had vanished, and the rope was twisting on itself. I let go of
the dog, and it galloped immediately to the back of the gallows;
but when it got there it stopped short, barked, and then retreated

into a corner of the yard, where it stood among the weeds, looking timorously out at us. We went round the gallows to inspect the prisoner's body. He was dangling with his toes pointed straight downwards, very slowly revolving, as dead as a stone.

The superintendent reached out with his stick and poked the bare brown body; it oscillated slightly. "*He's* all right," said the superintendent. He backed out from under the gallows, and blew out a deep breath. The moody look had gone out of his face quite suddenly. He glanced at his wrist-watch. "Eight minutes past eight. Well, that's all for this morning, thank God."   16

The warders unfixed bayonets and marched away. The dog, sobered and conscious of having misbehaved itself, slipped after them. We walked out of the gallows yard, past the condemned cells with their waiting prisoners, into the big central yard of the prison. The convicts, under the command of warders armed with lathis, were already receiving their breakfast. They squatted in long rows, each man holding a tin pannikin, while two warders with buckets marched round ladling out rice; it seemed quite a homely, jolly scene, after the hanging. An enormous relief had come upon us now that the job was done. One felt an impulse to sing, to break into a run, to snigger. All at once every one began chattering gaily.   17

The Eurasian boy walking beside me nodded towards the way we had come, with a knowing smile: "Do you know, sir, our friend (he meant the dead man) when he heard his appeal had been dismissed, he pissed on the floor of his cell. From fright. Kindly take one of my cigarettes, sir. Do you not admire my new silver case, sir? From the boxwalah, two rupees eight annas. Classy European style."   18

Several people laughed—at what, nobody seemed certain.   19

Francis was walking by the superintendent, talking garrulously: "Well, sir, all hass passed off with the utmost satisfactoriness. It was all finished—flick! like that. It iss not always so—oah, no! I have known cases where the doctor wass obliged to go beneath the gallows and pull the prisoner's legs to ensure decease. Most disagreeable!"   20

"Wriggling about, eh? That's bad," said the superintendent.   21

"Ach, sir, it iss worse when they become refractory! One man, I recall, clung to the bars of hiss cage when we went to take him out. You will scarcely credit, sir, that it took six warders to dislodge him, three pulling at each leg. We reasoned with him. 'My dear fellow,' we said, 'think of all the pain and trouble you are   22 causing to us!' But no, he would not listen! Ach, he wass very troublesome!"

I found that I was laughing quite loudly. Everyone was laughing. 23 Even the superintendent grinned in a tolerant way. "You'd better all come out and have a drink," he said quite genially. "I've got a bottle of whisky in the car. We could do with it."

We went through the big double gates of the prison into the 24 road. "Pulling at his legs!" exclaimed a Burmese magistrate suddenly, and burst into a loud chuckling. We all began laughing again. At that moment Francis' anecdote seemed extraordinarily funny. We all had a drink together, native and European alike, quite amicably. The dead man was a hundred yards away.

Vocabulary

sodden (1)

wisp (2)

desolately (3)

Dravidian (4)

magistrates (6)

aghast (6)

taken aback (6)

gambolled (8)

Eurasian (8)

servile (11)

abominable (13)

timorously (15)

oscillated (16)

pannikin (17)

snigger (17)

garrulously (20)

refractory (22)

genially (23)

Critical Inquiries

1. The narrator in this event acts both as observer and as participant. What reason can you offer for combining these two points of view?

2. What is your reaction—emotional as well as intellectual—to the hanging described by Orwell?

3. What insights about the political atmosphere of "A Hanging" did you glean from this essay?

4. How do you interpret the "enormous relief," mentioned in paragraph 17, and all of the laughing described in paragraphs 18–24? Were these people, including the narrator, insensitive brutes, or is there another possible reason for these reactions?

5. What would your reaction be if the essay had revealed that the prisoner had staged an assassination attempt against a minister representing the British government ruling Burma?

Rhetorical Inquiries

1. What general mood is created by the opening paragraph? Pick out those words that contribute most to this mood.

2. What is Orwell's purpose in narrating the incidents of the dog and the puddle in paragraphs 6 and 10?

3. Orwell has been praised for his use of fresh images. What are some excellent examples in this essay? Point to specific passages.

4. In what two paragraphs does the author draw attention to himself? What reason is there for these shifts from "we" to "I"?

5. Does Orwell's method—one of showing rather than of telling—prove as convincing as a strictly logical argument against capital punishment? Give the reasoning behind your answer.

CRIMINOLOGY

Karl Menninger
THE CRIME OF PUNISHMENT

Karl Menninger (b. 1893, Topeka, Kansas) is an American psychiatrist, who, together with his father Charles and brother William, founded the famous Menninger Clinic, conceived with the idea of collecting many specialists in one center. In 1941, the Menninger Foundation came into existence. Its purpose was research, training, and public education in psychiatry. Today it is still one of the nation's most successful psychiatric centers. Karl Menninger's writings include such books as The Human Mind *(1930),* Man Against Himself *(1938),* Theory of Psychoanalytic Technique *(1959), and* The Crime of Punishment *(1968). Menninger always took the position that punishment as a vengeful response to crime does not work because crime is an illness requiring treatment by psychiatrists and psychologists.*

Few words in our language arrest our attention as do "crime," "violence," "revenge," and "injustice." We abhor crime; we adore justice; we boast that we live by the rule of law. Violence and vengefulness we repudiate as unworthy of our civilization, and we assume this sentiment to be unanimous among all human beings. 1

Yet crime continues to be a national disgrace and a world-wide 2

Adapted from *The Crime of Punishment* by Karl Menninger, M.D. Copyright (c) 1966, 1968 by Karl Menninger. Originally published in the *Saturday Review*. Reprinted by permission of Viking Penguin, a division of Penguin Books USA, Inc.

problem. It is threatening, alarming, wasteful, expensive, abundant, and apparently increasing! In actuality it is decreasing in frequency of occurrence, but it is certainly increasing in visibility and the reactions of the public to it.

Our system for controlling crime is ineffective, unjust, expensive. Prisons seem to operate with revolving doors—the same people going in and out and in and out. *Who cares?*   3

Our city jails and inhuman reformatories and wretched prisons are jammed. They are known to be unhealthy, dangerous, immoral, indecent, crime-breeding dens of iniquity. Not everyone has smelled them, as some of us have. Not many have heard the groans and the curses. Not everyone has seen the hate and despair in a thousand blank, hollow faces. But, in a way, we all know how miserable prisons are. *We want them to be that way.* And they are. *Who cares?*   4

Professional and big-time criminals prosper as never before. Gambling syndicates flourish. White-collar crime may even exceed all others, but goes undetected in the majority of cases. We are all being robbed and we know who the robbers are. They live nearby. *Who cares?*   5

The public filches millions of dollars worth of food and clothing from stores, towels and sheets from hotels, jewelry and knickknacks from shops. The public steals, and the same public pays it back in higher prices. *Who cares?*   6

Time and time again somebody shouts about this state of affairs, just as I am shouting now. The magazines shout. The newspapers shout. The television and radio commentators shout (or at least they "deplore"). Psychologists, sociologists, leading jurists, wardens, and intelligent police chiefs join the chorus. Governors and mayors and Congressmen are sometimes heard. They shout that the situation is bad, bad, bad, and getting worse. Some suggest that we immediately replace obsolete procedures with scientific methods. A few shout contrary sentiments. Do the clear indications derived from scientific discovery for appropriate changes continue to fall on deaf ears? Why is the public so long-suffering, so apathetic and thereby so continuingly self-destructive? How many Presidents (and other citizens) do we have to lose before we do something?   7

The public behaves as a sick patient does when a dreaded treatment is proposed for his ailment. We all know how the aching tooth may suddenly quiet down in the dentist's office, or the abdominal pain disappear in the surgeon's examining room. Why should a sufferer seek relief and shun it? Is it merely the fear of   8 pain of the treatment? Is it the fear of unknown complications? Is it distrust of the doctor's ability? All of these, no doubt.

But, as Freud made so incontestably clear, the sufferer is always somewhat deterred by a kind of subversive, internal opposition to the work of cure. He suffers on the one hand from the pains of his affliction and yearns to get well. But he suffers at the same time from traitorous impulses that fight against the accomplishment of any change in himself, even recovery! Like Hamlet, he wonders whether it may be better after all to suffer the familiar pains and aches associated with the old method than to face the complications of a new and strange, even though possibly better way of handling things.

The inescapable conclusion is that society secretly *wants* crime, *needs* crime, and gains definite satisfactions from the present mishandling of it! We condemn crime; we punish offenders for it; but we need it. The crime and punishment ritual is a part of our lives. We need crimes to wonder at, to enjoy vicariously, to discuss and speculate about, and to publicly deplore. We need criminals to identify ourselves with, to envy secretly, and to punish stoutly. They do for us the forbidden, illegal things we *wish* to do and, like scapegoats of old, they bear the burdens of our displaced guilt and punishment—"the iniquities of us all."

We have to confess that there is something fascinating for us all about violence. That most crime is not violent we know but we forget, because crime is a breaking, a rupturing, a tearing—even when it is quietly done. To all of us crime seems like violence.

The very word "violence" has a disturbing, menacing quality. . . . In meaning it implies something dreaded, powerful, destructive, or eruptive. It is something we abhor—or do we? Its first effect is to startle, frighten—even to horrify us. But we do not always run away from it. For violence also intrigues us. It is exciting. It is dramatic. Observing it and sometimes even participating in it gives us acute pleasure.

The newspapers constantly supply us with tidbits of violence going on in the world. They exploit its dramatic essence often to the neglect of conservative reporting of more extensive but less violent damage—the flood disaster in Florence, Italy, for example. Such words as crash, explosion, wreck, assault, raid, murder, avalanche, rape, and seizure evoke pictures of eruptive devastation from which we cannot turn away. The headlines often impute violence metaphorically even to peaceful activities. Relations are "ruptured," a tie is "broken," arbitration "collapses," a proposal is "killed."

Meanwhile on the television and movie screens there constantly 14
appear for our amusement scenes of fighting, slugging, beating,
torturing, clubbing, shooting, and the like which surpass in effect
anything that the newspapers can describe. Much of this violence
is portrayed dishonestly; the scenes are only semirealistic; they are
"faked" and romanticized.

Pain cannot be photographed; grimaces indicate but do not con- 15
vey its intensity. And wounds—unlike violence—are rarely
shown. This phony quality of television violence in its mentally
unhealthy aspect encourages irrationality by giving the impression
to the observer that being beaten, kicked, cut, and stomped, while
very unpleasant, are not very painful or serious. For after being
slugged and beaten the hero rolls over, opens his eyes, hops up,
rubs his cheek, grins, and staggers on. The *suffering* of violence is a
part both the TV and movie producers *and* their audience tend to
repress.

Although most of us *say* we deplore cruelty and destructiveness, 16
we are partially deceiving ourselves. We disown violence, ascribing
the love of it to other people. But the facts speak for themselves.
We do love violence, all of us, and we all feel secretly guilty for
it, which is another clue to public resistance to crime-control reform.

The great sin by which we all are tempted is the wish to hurt 17
others, and this sin must be avoided if we are to live and let live. If
our destructive energies can be mastered, directed, and sublimated,
we can survive. If we can love, we can live. Our destructive energies, if they cannot be controlled, may destroy our best friends, as
in the case of Alexander the Great, or they may destroy supposed
"enemies" or innocent strangers. Worst of all—from the stand-
point of the individual—they may destroy us.

Over the centuries of man's existence, many devices have been 18
employed in the effort to control these innate suicidal and criminal
propensities. The earliest of these undoubtedly depended upon
fear—fear of the unknown, fear of magical retribution, fear of social retaliation. These external devices were replaced gradually
with the law and all its machinery, religion and its rituals, and the
conventions of the social order.

The routine of life formerly required every individual to direct 19
much of his aggressive energy against the environment. There
were trees to cut down, wild animals to fend off, heavy obstacles
to remove, great burdens to lift. But the machine has gradually
changed all of this. Today, the routine of life, for most people, requires no violence, no fighting, no killing, no life-risking, no sud-

den supreme exertion: occasionally, perhaps, a hard pull or a strong push, but no tearing, crushing, breaking, forcing.

And because violence no longer has legitimate and useful vents or purposes, it must *all* be controlled today. In earlier times its expression was often a virtue, today its control is the virtue. The control involves symbolic, vicarious expressions of our violence—violence modified; "sublimated," as Freud called it; "neutralized," as Hartmann described it. Civilized substitutes for direct violence are the objects of daily search by all of us. The common law and the Ten Commandments, traffic signals and property deeds, fences and front doors, sermons and concerts, Christmas trees and jazz bands—these and a thousand other things exist today to help in the control of violence.

My colleague, Bruno Bettelheim, thinks we do not properly educate our youth to deal with their violent urges. He reminds us that nothing fascinated our forefathers more. The *Iliad* is a poem of violence. Much of the Bible is a record of violence. One penal system and many methods of child-rearing express violence— "violence to suppress violence." And, he concludes [in the article "Violence: A Neglected Mode of Behavior"]: "We shall not be able to deal intelligently with violence unless we are first ready to see it as a part of human nature, and then we shall come to realize the chances of discharging violent tendencies are now so severely curtailed that their regular and safe draining-off is not possible anymore."

Why aren't we all criminals? We all have the impulses; we all have the provocations. But becoming civilized, which is repeated ontologically in the process of social education, teaches us what we may do with impunity. What then evokes or permits the breakthrough? Why is it necessary for some to bribe their consciences and do what they do not approve of doing? Why does all sublimation sometimes fail and overt breakdown occur in the controlling and managing machinery of the personality? Why do we sometimes lose self-control? Why do we "go to pieces"? Why do we explode?

These questions point up a central problem in psychiatry. Why do some people do things they do not want to do? Or things we do not want them to do? Sometimes crimes are motivated by a desperate need to act, to do *something* to break out of a state of passivity, frustration, and helplessness too long endured, like a child who shoots a parent or a teacher after some apparently reasonable act. Granting the universal presence of violence within us all, controlled by will power, conscience, fear of punishment, and other devices, granting the tensions and the temptations that are also common to us all, why do the mechanisms of self-control fail so completely in some individuals? Is there not some pre-existing defect, some moral or cerebral weakness, some gross deficiency of common sense that lets some people tumble or kick or strike or explode, while the rest of us just stagger or sway?

When a psychiatrist examines many prisoners, writes [Seymour] Halleck [in *Psychiatry and the Dilemmas of Crime*], he soon discovers how important in the genesis of the criminal outbreak is the offender's previous *sense of helplessness or hopelessness*. All of us suffer more or less from infringement of our personal freedom. We fuss about it all the time; we strive to correct it, extend it, and free ourselves from various oppressive or retentive forces. We do not want others to push us around, to control us, to dominate us. We realize this is bound to happen to some extent in an interlocking, interrelated society such as ours. No one truly has complete freedom. But restriction irks us. 24

The offender feels this way, too. He does not want to be pushed around, controlled, or dominated. And because he often feels that he is thus oppressed (and actually is) and because he does lack facility in improving his situation without violence, he suffers more intensely from feelings of helplessness. 25

Violence and crime are often attempts to escape from madness; and there can be no doubt that some mental illness is a flight from the wish to do the violence or commit the act. Is it hard for the reader to believe that suicides are sometimes committed to forestall the commiting of murder? There is no doubt of it. Nor is there any doubt that murder is sometimes committed to avert suicide. 26

Strange as it may sound, many murderers do not realize whom they are killing, or, to put it another way, that they are killing the wrong people. To be sure, killing anybody is reprehensible enough, but the worst of it is that the person who the killer thinks should die (and he has reasons) is not the person he attacks. Sometimes the victim himself is partly responsible for the crime that is committed against him. It is this unconscious (perhaps sometimes conscious) participation in the crime by the victim that has long held up the very humanitarian and progressive-sounding program of giving compensation to victims. The public often judges the victim as well as the attacker. 27

Rape and other sexual offenses are acts of violence so repulsive to our sense of decency and order that it is easy to think of rapists in general as raging, oversexed, ruthless brutes (unless they are conquering heroes). Some rapists are. But most sex crimes are 28 committed by undersexed rather than oversexed individuals, often undersized rather than oversized, and impelled less by lust than by a need for reassurance regarding an impaired masculinity. The unconscious fear of women goads some men with a compulsive urge to conquer, humiliate, hurt, or render powerless some available sample of womanhood. Men who are violently afraid of their repressed but nearly emergent homosexual desires, and men who are afraid of the humiliation of impotence, often try to overcome these fears by violent demonstrations.

The need to deny something in oneself is frequently an underlying motive for certain odd behavior—even up to and including crime. Bravado crimes, often done with particular brutality and ruthlessness, seem to prove *to the doer* that "I am no weakling! I am no sissy! I am no coward. I am no homosexual! I am a tough man who fears nothing." The Nazi storm troopers, many of them mere boys, were systematically trained to stifle all tender emotions and force themselves to be heartlessly brutal.   29

Man perennially seeks to recover the magic of his childhood days—the control of the mighty by the meek. The flick of an electric light switch, the response of an automobile throttle, the click of a camera, the touch of a match to a skyrocket—these are keys to a sudden and magical display of great power induced by the merest gesture. Is anyone already so blasé that he is no longer thrilled at the opening of a door specially for him by a magic-eye signal? Yet for a few pennies one can purchase a far more deadly piece of magic—a stored explosive and missile encased within a shell which can be ejected from a machine at the touch of a finger so swiftly that no eye can follow. A thousand yards away something falls dead—a rabbit, a deer, a beautiful mountain sheep, a sleeping child, or the President of the United States. Magic! Magnified, projected power. "Look what I can do. I am the greatest!"   30

It must have come to every thoughtful person, at one time or another, in looking at the revolvers on the policemen's hips, or the guns soldiers and hunters carry so proudly, that these are instruments made for the express purpose of delivering death to someone. The easy availability of these engines of destruction, even to children, mentally disturbed people, professional criminals, gangsters, and even high school girls is something to give one pause. The National Rifle Association and its allies have been able to kill scores of bills that have been introduced into Congress and state legislatures for corrective gun control since the death of President Kennedy. Americans still spend about $2 billion on guns each year.   31

Fifty years ago, Winston Churchill declared that the mood and   32 temper of the public in regard to crime and criminals is one of the unfailing tests of the civilization of any country. Judged by this standard, how civilized are we?

The chairman of the President's National Crime Commission, 33 Nicholas de B. Katzenbach, declared . . . that organized crime flourishes in America because enough of the public wants its services, and most citizens are apathetic about its impact. It will continue uncurbed as long as Americans accept it as inevitable and, in some instances, desirable.

Are there steps that we can take which will reduce the aggres- 34 sive stabs and self-destructive lurches of our less well-managing fellow men? Are there ways to prevent and control the grosser violations, other than the clumsy traditional maneuvers which we have inherited? These depend basically upon intimidation and slow-motion torture. We call it punishment, and justify it with our "feeling." We know it doesn't work.

Yes, there *are* better ways. There are steps that could be taken; 35 some *are* taken. But we move too slowly. Much better use, it seems to me, could be made of the members of my profession and other behavioral scientists than having them deliver courtroom pronunciamentos. The consistent use of a diagnostic clinic would enable trained workers to lay what they can learn about an offender before the judge who would know best how to implement the recommendation.

This would no doubt lead to a transformation of prisons, if not 36 to their total disappearance in their present form and function. Temporary and permanent detention will perhaps always be necessary for a few, especially the professionals, but this could be more effectively and economically performed with new types of "facility" (that strange, awkward word for institution).

I assume it to be a matter of common and general agreement 37 that our object in all this is to protect the community from a repetition of the offense by the most economical method consonant with our other purposes. Our "other purposes" include the desire to prevent these offenses from occurring, to reclaim offenders for social usefulness, if possible, and to detain them in protective custody, if reclamation is *not* possible. But how?

The treatment of human failure or dereliction by the infliction of 38 pain is still used and believed in by many nonmedical people. "Spare the rod and spoil the child" is still considered wise counsel by many.

Whipping is still used by many secondary schoolmasters in En- 39 gland, I am informed, to stimulate study, attention, and the love of learning. Whipping was long a traditional treatment for the "crime" of disobedience on the part of children, pupils, servants, apprentices, employees. And slaves were treated for centuries by flogging for such offenses as weariness, confusion, stupidity, exhaustion, fear, grief, and even overcheerfulness. It was assumed and stoutly defended that these "treatments" cured conditions for which they were administered.

Meanwhile, scientific medicine was acquiring many new healing   40
methods and devices. Doctors can now transplant organs and limbs; they can remove brain tumors and cure incipient cancers; they can halt pneumonia, meningitis, and other infections; they can correct deformities and repair breaks and tears and scars. But these wonderful achievements are accomplished on *willing* subjects, people who voluntarily ask for help by even heroic measures. And the reader will be wondering, no doubt, whether doctors can do anything with or for people who *do not want* to be treated at all, in any way! Can doctors cure willful aberrant behavior? Are we to believe that crime is a *disease* that can be reached by scientific measures? Isn't it merely "natural meanness" that makes all of us do wrong things at times even when we "know better"? And are not self-control, moral stamina, and will power the things needed? Surely there is no medical treatment for the lack of those!

Let me answer this carefully, for much misunderstanding accu-   41
mulates here. I would say that according to the prevalent understanding of the words, crime is *not* a disease. Neither is it an illness, although I think it *should* be! It *should* be treated, and it could be; but it mostly isn't.

These enigmatic statements are simply explained. Diseases are   42
undesired states of being which have been described and defined by doctors, usually given Greek or Latin appellations, and treated by long-established physical and pharmacological formulae. Illness, on the other hand, is best defined as a state of impaired functioning of such a nature that the public expects the sufferer to repair to the physician for help. The illness may prove to be a disease; more often it is only vague and nameless misery; but something which doctors, not lawyers, teachers, or preachers, are supposed to be able and willing to help.

When the community begins to look upon the expression of ag-   43
gressive violence as the symptom of an illness or as indicative of illness, it will be because it believes doctors can do something to correct such a condition. At present, some better-informed individuals do believe and expect this. However angry at or sorry for the offender, they want him "treated" in an effective way so that he

will cease to be a danger to them. And they know that the traditional punishment, "treatment-punishment," will not effect this.

What *will?* What effective treatment is there for such violence? It will surely have to begin with motivating or stimulating or arousing in a cornered individual the wish and hope and intention to change his methods of dealing with the realities of life. Can this be done by education, medication, counseling, training? I would answer *yes.* It can be done successfully in a majority of cases, if undertaken in time.

The present penal system and the existing legal philosophy do not stimulate or even expect such a change to take place in the criminal. Yet change is what medical science always aims for. The prisoner, like the doctor's other patients, should emerge from his treatment experience a different person, differently equipped, differently functioning, and headed in a different direction than when he began the treatment.

It is natural for the public to doubt that this can be accomplished with criminals. But remember that the public *used* to doubt that change could be effected in the mentally ill. No one a hundred years ago believed mental illness to be curable. Today *all* people know (or should know) that *mental illness is curable* in the great majority of instances and that the prospects and rapidity of cure are directly related to the availability and intensity of proper treatment.

The forms and techniques of psychiatric treatment used today number in the hundreds. No one patient requires or receives all forms, but each patient is studied with respect to his particular needs, his basic assets, his interests, and his special difficulties. A therapeutic team may embrace a dozen workers—as in a hospital setting—or it may narrow down to the doctor and the spouse. Clergymen, teachers, relatives, friends, and even fellow patients often participate informally but helpfully in the process of readaptation.

All of the participants in this effort to bring about a favorable change in the patient—i.e., in his vital balance and life program— are imbued with what we may call a *therapeutic attitude.* This is one in direct antithesis to attitudes of avoidance, ridicule, scorn, or punitiveness. Hostile feelings toward the subject, however justified by his unpleasant and even destructive behavior, are not in the curriculum of therapy or in the therapist. This does not mean that therapists approve of the offensive and obnoxious behavior of the patient; they distinctly disapprove of it. But they recognize it as symptomatic of continued imbalance and disorganization, which is what they are seeking to change. They distinguish between disapproval, penalty, price, and punishment.

Doctors charge fees; they impose certain "penalties" or prices, but they have long since put aside primitive attitudes of retaliation toward offensive patients. A patient may cough in the doctor's face or may vomit on the office rug; a patient may curse or scream or even struggle in the extremity of his pain. But these acts are not "punished." Doctors and nurses have no time or thought for inflicting unnecessary pain even upon patients who may be difficult, disagreeable, provocative, and even dangerous. It is their duty to care for them, to try to make them well, and to prevent them from doing themselves or others harm. This requires love, not hate. This is the deepest meaning of the therapeutic attitude. Every doctor knows this; every worker in a hospital or clinic knows it (or should).   49

There is another element in the therapeutic attitude. It is the quality of hopefulness. If no one believes that the patient can get well, if no one—not even the doctor—has any hope, there probably won't be any recovery. Hope is just as important as love in the therapeutic attitude.   50

"But you were talking about the mentally ill," readers may interject, "those poor, confused, bereft, frightened individuals who yearn for help from you doctors and nurses. Do you mean to imply that willfully perverse individuals, our criminals, can be similarly reached and rehabilitated? Do you really believe that effective treatment of the sort you visualize can be applied to people *who do not want any help,* who are so willfully vicious, so well aware of the wrongs they are doing, so lacking in penitence or even common decency that punishment seems to be the only thing left?"   51

Do I believe there is effective treatment for offenders, and that they *can* be changed? *Most certainly and definitely I do.* Not all cases, to be sure; there are also some physical afflictions which we cannot cure at the moment. Some provision has to be made for incurables—pending new knowledge—and these will include some offenders. But I believe the majority of them would prove to be curable. The willfulness and the viciousness of offenders are part of the thing for which they have to be treated. These must not thwart the therapeutic attitude.   52

It is simply not true that most of them are "fully aware" of what they are doing, nor is it true that they want no help from anyone, although some of them say so. Prisoners are individuals: some want treatment, some do not. Some don't know what treatment is. Many are utterly despairing and hopeless. Where treatment is   53 made available in institutions, many prisoners seek it even with the full knowledge that doing so will not lessen their sentences. In some prisons, seeking treatment by prisoners is frowned upon by the officials.

Various forms of treatment are even now being tried in some 54
progressive courts and prisons over the country—educational, social, industrial, religious, recreational, and psychological treatments. Socially acceptable behavior, new work-play opportunities, new identity and companion patterns all help toward community reacceptance. Some parole officers and some wardens have been extremely ingenious in developing these modalities of rehabilitation and reconstruction—more than I could list here even if I knew them all. But some are trying. The secret of success in all programs, however, is the replacement of the punitive attitude with a therapeutic attitude.

Offenders with propensities for impulsive and predatory aggres- 55
sion should not be permitted to live among us unrestrained by some kind of social control. *But the great majority of offenders, even "criminals," should never become prisoners if we want to "cure" them.*

There are now throughout the country many citizens' action 56
groups and programs for the prevention and control of crime and delinquency. With such attitudes of inquiry and concern, the public could acquire information (and incentive) leading to a change of feeling about crime and criminals. It will discover how unjust is much so-called "justice," how baffled and frustrated many judges are by the ossified rigidity of old-fashioned, obsolete laws and state constitutions which effectively prevent the introduction of sensible procedures to replace useless, harmful ones.

I want to proclaim to the public that things are not what it 57
wishes them to be, and will only become so if it will take an interest in the matter and assume some responsibility for its own self-protection.

Will the public listen? 58

If the public does become interested, it will realize that we must 59
have more facts, more trial projects, more checked results. It will share the dismay of the President's Commission in finding that no one knows much about even the incidence of crime with any definiteness or statistical accuracy.

The average citizen finds it difficult to see how any research 60
would in any way change his mind about a man who brutally murders his children. But just such inconceivably awful acts most dramatically point up the need for research. Why should—how can—a man become so dreadful as that in our culture? How is

such a man made? Is it comprehensible that he can be born to become so depraved?

There are thousands of questions regarding crime and public protection which deserve scientific study. What makes some individuals maintain their interior equilibrium by one kind of disturbance of the social structure rather than by another kind, one that would have landed him in a hospital? Why do some individuals specialize in certain types of crime? Why do so many young people reared in areas of delinquency and poverty and bad example never become habitual delinquents? (Perhaps this is a more important question than why some of them do.)

The public has a fascination for violence, and clings tenaciously to its yen for vengeance, blind and deaf to the expense, futility, and dangerousness of the resulting penal system. But we are bound to hope that this will yield in time to the persistent, penetrating light of intelligence and accumulating scientific knowledge. The public will grow increasingly ashamed of its cry for retaliation, its persistent demand to punish. This is its crime, *our* crime against criminals—and, incidentally, our crime against ourselves. For before we can diminish our sufferings from the ill-controlled aggressive assaults of fellow citizens, we must renounce the philosophy of punishment, the obsolete, vengeful penal attitude. In its place we would seek a comprehensive constructive social attitude—therapeutic in some instances, restraining in some instances, but preventive in its total social impact.

In the last analysis this becomes a question of personal morals and values. No matter how glorified or how piously disguised, vengeance as a human motive must be personally repudiated by each and every one of us. This is the message of old religions and new psychiatries. Unless this message is heard, unless we, the people—the man on the street, the housewife in the home—can give up our delicious satisfactions in opportunities for vengeful retaliation on scapegoats, we cannot expect to preserve our peace, our public safety, or our mental health.

Vocabulary

repudiate (1)   apathetic (7)
reformatories (4)   incontestably (9)
syndicates (5)   deterred (9)
commentators (7)   subversive (9)
obsolete (7)   traitorous (9)

vicariously (10)

stoutly (10)

scapegoats (10)

iniquities (10)

eruptive (12)

abhor (12)

impute (13)

metaphorically (13)

arbitration (13)

ascribing (16)

sublimated (17)

propensities (18)

retribution (18)

retaliation (18)

curtailed (21)

provocations (22)

ontological (22)

impunity (22)

genesis (24)

infringement (24)

retentive (24)

reprehensible (27)

impelled (28)

blasé (30)

diagnostic (35)

consonant (37)

dereliction (38)

incipient (40)

aberrant (40)

enigmatic (42)

appellations (42)

formulae (42)

therapeutic (47)

readaptation (47)

imbued (48)

antithesis (48)

punitiveness (48)

provocative (49)

penitence (51)

ingenious (54)

modalities (54)

propensities (55)

predatory (55)

ossified (56)

obsolete (56)

Critical Inquiries

1. According to Menninger, why is our system of punishing criminals itself a crime? Do you agree with the author's view? Give reasons for your answer.

2. What are some of the important facts or assumptions you must keep in mind when evaluating Menninger's argument?

3. What is your answer to the question posed at the end of paragraph 32? Before you answer, have in mind a clear definition of the term *civilized*.

4. What is the author's view of gun control? How do you respond to his opinion? Be as specific as you can.

5. Is it possible that secretly we *want* and *need* crime, as the author suggests in paragraph 10? What other reasons might exist to explain our seeming willingness to put up with crime?

6. Menninger states that violent crimes are romanticized in the movies. (See paragraph 14.) What does he mean by this statement? What other facets of life or society do the movies romanticize? Refer to specific motion pictures.

Rhetorical Inquiries

1. Why does the author repeat the question "Who cares?" so often in the opening paragraphs of the essay? What purpose does the repetition serve?

2. What is the analogy used in paragraph 8? How apt is it?

3. How is Menninger's essay organized? What are the major parts?

4. Why does the author spend so many paragraphs (see 24–29) explaining why certain offenders commit violent crimes?

5. What rhetorical strategy characterizes the final paragraph? How effective is it?

PHILOSOPHY OF SCIENCE

Carl Sagan
A SUNDAY SERMON

Carl Sagan (b. 1934) is Professor of Astronomy at Cornell University and directs the Laboratory for Planetary Studies. Sagan has received international praise for his ability to make the intricacies of the cosmos understandable and fascinating to the average person. Of the many books Sagan has written, his most popular is The Dragons of Eden *(1978); it won him a Pulitzer prize. Sagan has also written numerous essays and is much in demand as a conference lecturer and television personality. The essay below reveals his belief that exploration and inquiry are the gateways to truth and to the management of our human survival.*

Extinguished theologians lie about the cradle of every science as the strangled snakes beside the cradle of Hercules.
—T. H. Huxley, 1860

We have seen the highest circle of spiraling powers. We have named this circle God. We might have given it any other name we

From *Broca's Brain*, by Carl Sagan. Published by Random House, 1979, pp. 281–91. Copyright (c) 1979 by Carl Sagan. All rights reserved. Reprinted by permission of the author.

wished: Abyss, Mystery, Absolute Darkness, Absolute Light, Matter, Spirit, Ultimate Hope, Ultimate Despair, Silence.

—Nikos Kazantzakis, 1948

These days, I often find myself giving scientific talks to popular audiences. Sometimes I am asked to discuss planetary exploration and the nature of the other planets; sometimes, the origin of life or intelligence on Earth; sometimes, the search for life elsewhere; and sometimes, the grand cosmological perspective. Since I have, more or less, heard these talks before, the question period holds my greatest interest. It reveals the attitudes and concerns of people. The most common questions asked are on unidentified flying objects and ancient astronauts—what I believe are thinly disguised religious queries. Almost as common—particularly after a lecture in which I discuss the evolution of life or intelligence—is: "Do you believe in God?" Because the word "God" means many things to many people, I frequently reply by asking what the questioner means by "God." To my surprise, this response is often considered puzzling or unexpected: "Oh, you know, *God*. Everyone knows who God is." Or "Well, kind of a force that is stronger than we are and that exists everywhere in the universe." There are a number of such forces. One of them is called gravity, but it is not often identified with God. And not everyone does know what is meant by "God." The concept covers a wide range of ideas. Some people think of God as an outsized, light-skinned male with a long white beard, sitting on a throne somewhere up there in the sky, busily tallying the fall of every sparrow. Others—for example, Baruch Spinoza and Albert Einstein—considered God to be essentially the sum total of the physical laws which describe the universe. I do not know of any compelling evidence for anthropomorphic patriarchs controlling human destiny from some hidden celestial vantage point, but it would be madness to deny the existence of physical laws. Whether we believe in God depends very much on what we mean by God.

In the history of the world there have been, probably, tens of thousands of different religions. There is a well-intentioned pious belief that they are all fundamentally identical. In terms of an underlying psychological resonance, there may indeed be important similarities at the cores of many religions, but in the details of ritual and doctrine, and the *apologias*[1] considered to be authenticat-

---

[1]Formal defenses or justifications.

ing, the diversity of organized religions is striking. Human religions are mutually exclusive on such fundamental issues as one god versus many; the origin of evil; reincarnation; idolatry; magic and witchcraft; the role of women; dietary proscriptions; rites of passage; ritual sacrifice; direct or mediated access to deities; slavery; intolerance of other religions; and the community of beings to whom special ethical considerations are due. We do no service to religion in general or to any doctrine in particular if we paper over these differences. Instead, I believe we should understand the world views from which differing religions derive and seek to understand what human needs are fulfilled by those differences.

Bertrand Russell once told of being arrested because he peacefully protested Britain's entry into World War I. The jailer asked—then a routine question for new arrivals—Russell's religion. Russell replied, "Agnostic," which he was asked to spell. The jailer smiled benignly, shook his head and said, "There's many different religions, but I suppose we all worship the same God." Russell commented that the remark cheered him for weeks. And there may not have been much else to cheer him in that prison, although he did manage to write the entire *Introduction to Mathematical Philosophy* and started reading for his work *The Analysis of Mind* within its confines.

Many of the people who ask whether I believe in God are requesting reassurance that their particular belief system, whatever it is, is consistent with modern scientific knowledge. Religion has been scarred in its confrontation with science, and many people—but by no means all—are reluctant to accept a body of theological belief that is too obviously in conflict with what else we know. Apollo 8 accomplished the first manned lunar circumnavigation. In a more or less spontaneous gesture, the Apollo 8 astronauts read from the first verse of the Book of Genesis, in part, I believe, to reassure the taxpayers back in the United States that there were no real inconsistencies between conventional religious outlooks and a manned flight to the Moon. Orthodox Muslims, on the other hand, were outraged after Apollo 11 astronauts accomplished the first manned lunar landing, because the Moon has a special and sacred significance in Islam. In a different religious context, after Yuri Gagarin's first orbital flight, Nikita Khrushchev, the chairman of the Council of Ministers of the USSR, noted that Gagarin had stumbled on no gods or angels up there—that is, Khrushchev reassured his audience that manned orbital flight was not inconsistent with its beliefs.

In the 1950s a Soviet technical journal called *Voprosy Filosofii*   5
(Problems in Philosophy) published an article that argued—very
unconvincingly, it seemed to me—that dialectical materialism required there to be life on every planet. Some time later an agonized official rebuttal appeared, decoupling dialectical materialism
from exobiology. A clear prediction in an area undergoing vigorous
study permits doctrines to be subject to disproof. The last posture
a bureaucratic religion wishes to find itself in is vulnerability to disproof, where an experiment can be performed on which the religion stands or falls. And so the fact that life has not been found on
the Moon has left the foundations of dialectical materialism un-
shaken. Doctrines that make no predictions are less compelling
than those which make correct predictions; they are in turn more
successful than doctrines that make false predictions.

But not always. One prominent American religion confidently   6
predicted that the world would end in 1914. Well, 1914 has come
and gone, and—while the events of that year were certainly of
some importance—the world does not, at least so far as I can see,
seem to have ended. There are at least three responses that an organized religion can make in the face of such a failed and fundamental prophecy. They could have said, "Oh, did we say '1914'?
So sorry, we meant '2014.' A slight error in calculation. Hope you
weren't inconvenienced in any way." But they did not. They could
have said, "Well, the world *would* have ended, except we prayed
very hard and interceded with God so He spared the Earth." But
they did not. Instead, they did something much more ingenious.
They announced that the world *had* in fact ended in 1914, and if
the rest of us hadn't noticed, that was our lookout. It is astonishing
in the face of such transparent evasions that this religion has any
adherents at all. But religions are tough. Either they make no contentions which are subject to disproof or they quickly redesign
doctrine after disproof. The fact that religions can be so shamelessly dishonest, so contemptuous of the intelligence of their adherents, and still flourish does not speak very well for the tough-
mindedness of the believers. But it does indicate, if a
demonstration were needed, that near the core of the religious experience is something remarkably resistant to rational inquiry.

Andrew Dickson White was the intellectual guiding light,   7
founder and first president of Cornell University. He was also the
author of an extraordinary book called *The Warfare of Science with
Theology in Christendom,* considered so scandalous at the time it was
published that his co-author requested his name omitted. White

was a man of substantial religious feeling.[1] But he outlined the long and painful history of erroneous claims which religions had made about the nature of the world, and how, when people directly investigated the nature of the world and discovered it to be different from doctrinal contentions, such people were persecuted and their ideas suppressed. The aged Galileo was threatened by the Catholic hierarchy with torture because he proclaimed the Earth to move. Spinoza was excommunicated by the Jewish hierarchy, and there is hardly an organized religion with a firm body of doctrine which has not at one time or another persecuted people for the crime of open inquiry. Cornell's own devotion to free and non-sectarian inquiry was considered so objectionable in the last quarter of the nineteenth century that ministers advised high school graduates that it was better to receive no college education than to attend so impious an institution. Indeed, this Sage Chapel was constructed in part to placate the pious—although, I am glad to say, it has from time to time made serious efforts at open-minded ecumenism.

Many of the controversies which White describes are about origins. It used to be believed that every event in the world—the opening of a morning glory, let us say—was due to direct micro-intervention by the Deity. The flower was unable to open by itself. God had to say, "Hey, flower, open." The application of this idea to human affairs has often had desultory social consequences. For one thing it seems to imply that we are not responsible for our actions. If the play of the world is produced and directed by an omnipotent and omniscient God, does it not follow that every evil that is perpetrated is God's doing? I know this idea is an embarrassment in the West, and attempts to avoid it include the contention that what seems to be evil is really part of the Divine Plan, too complex for us to fathom; or that God chose to cloud his own vision about the causality skein when he set out to make the world. There is nothing utterly impossible about these philosophical rescue attempts, but they do seem to have very much the character of propping up a teetering ontological structure.[2] In addition, the idea

8

---

[1]White seems also to have been responsible for the exemplary custom of not awarding honorary doctoral degrees at Cornell University: he was concerned about a potential abuse, that honorary degrees would be traded for financial gifts and bequests. White was a man of strong and courageous ethical standards.

[2]Many statements about God are confidently made by theologians on grounds that today at least sound specious. Thomas Aquinas claimed to prove that God cannot make another God, or commit suicide, or make a man without a soul, or even make a triangle whose interior angles do not

of microintervention in the affairs of the world has been used to support the established social, political and economic conventions. There was, for example, the idea of a "Divine Right of Kings," seriously argued by philosophers such as Thomas Hobbes. If you had revolutionary thoughts directed, let us say, toward George III, you were guilty of blasphemy and impiety, religious crimes, as well as such more commonplace political crimes as treason.

There are many legitimate scientific issues relating to origins and ends: What is the origin of the human species? Where did plants and animals come from? how did life arise? the Earth, the planets, the Sun, the stars? Does the universe have an origin, and if so, what? And finally, a still more fundamental and exotic question, which many scientists would say is essentially untestable and therefore meaningless: Why are the laws of nature the way they are? The idea that a God or gods is necessary to effect one or more of these origins has been under repeated attack over the last few thousand years. Because we know something about phototropism and plant hormones, we can understand the opening of the morning glory independent of divine microintervention. It is the same for the entire skein of causality back to the origin of the universe. As we learn more and more about the universe, there seems less and less for God to do. Aristotle's view was of God as an unmoved prime mover, a *roi fainéant,* a do-nothing king who establishes the universe in the first place and then sits back and watches the intricate, intertwined chains of causality course down through the ages. But this seems abstract and removed from everyday experience. It is a little unsettling and pricks at human conceits.

Humans seem to have a natural abhorrence of an infinite regression of causes, and this distaste is at the root of the most famous and most effective demonstrations of the existence of God by Aristotle and Thomas Aquinas. But these thinkers lived before the infinite series was a mathematical commonplace. If the differential and integral calculus or transfinite arithmetic had been invented in Greece in the fifth century B.C., and not subsequently suppressed, the history of religion in the West might have been very different—or at any rate we would have seen less of the pretension that theological doctrine can be convincingly demonstrated by rational

9

10

---

equal 180 degrees. But Bolyai and Lobachevsky were able to accomplish this last feat (on a curved surface) in the nineteenth century, and they were not even approximately gods. It is a curious concept this, of an omnipotent God with a long list of things he is forbidden to do by the fiat of the theologians.

argument to those who reject alleged divine revelation, as Aquinas attempted in the *Summa Contra Gentiles*.

When Newton explained the motion of the planets by the universal theory of gravitation, it no longer was necessary for angels to push and pummel the planets about. When Pierre Simon, the Marquis de Laplace, proposed to explain the origin of the solar system—although not the origin of matter—in terms of physical laws as well, even the necessity for a god involved in the origins of things seemed profoundly challenged. Laplace is said to have presented an edition of his seminal mathematical work *Mécanique céleste* to Napoleon aboard ship in the Mediterranean during the Napoleonic expedition to Egypt, 1798 to 1799. A few days later, so the story goes, Napoleon complained to Laplace that he had found no mention of God in the text.[1] Laplace's response has been recorded: "Sire, I have no need of that hypothesis." The idea of God as a hypothesis rather than as an obvious truth is by and large a modern idea in the West—although it was certainly discussed seriously and wryly by the Ionian philosophers of 2,400 years ago.

It is often considered that at least the origin of the universe requires a God—indeed, an Aristotelian idea[2] This is a point worth looking at in a little more detail. First of all, it is perfectly possible that the universe is infinitely old and therefore requires no Creator. This is consistent with existing knowledge of cosmology, which permits an oscillating universe in which the events since the Big Bang are merely the latest incarnation in an infinite series of creations and destructions of the universe. But secondly, let us consider the idea of a universe created somehow from nothing by God. The question naturally arises—and many ten-year-olds spontaneously think of it before being discouraged by their elders—where does God come from? If we answer that God is in-

---

[1]It is a charming notion that Napoleon actually spent his days aboard ship perusing the highly mathematical *Mécanique céleste*. But he was seriously interested in science and made an earnest attempt to survey the latest findings (see *The Society of Arcueil: A View of French Science at the Time of Napoleon I* by Maurice Crosland, Cambridge, Harvard University Press, 1967). Napoleon did not pretend to read all of the *Mécanique céleste* and wryly wrote to Laplace on another occasion, "The first six months which I can spare will be employed in reading it." But he also remarked, on another of Laplace's books, "Your works contribute to the glory of the nation. The progress and perfection of mathematics are linked closely with the prosperity of the state."

[2]However, from astronomical arguments Aristotle concluded that there were several dozen unmoved prime movers in the universe. Aristotelian arguments for a prime mover would seem to have polytheistic consequences that might be considered dangerous by contemporary Western theologians.

finitely old or present simultaneously in all epochs, we have solved nothing, except perhaps verbally. We have merely postponed by one step coming to grips with the problem. A universe that is infinitely old and a God that is infinitely old are, I think, equally deep mysteries. It is not readily apparent why one should be considered more reliably established than the other. Spinoza might have said that the two possibilities are not really different ideas at all.

I think it is wise, when coming face to face with such profound mysteries, to feel a little humility. The idea that scientists or theologians, with our present still puny understanding of this vast and awesome cosmos, can comprehend the origins of the universe is only a little less silly than the idea that Mesopotamian astronomers of 3,000 years ago—from whom the ancient Hebrews borrowed, during the Babylonian captivity, the cosmological accounts in the first chapter of Genesis—could have understood the origins of the universe. We simply do not know. The Hindu holy book, the Rig Veda (X:129), has a much more realistic view of the matter:

> Who knows for certain? Who shall here declare it?
> Whence was it born, whence came creation?
> The gods are later than this world's formation;
> Who then can know the origins of the world?
> None knows whence creation arose;
> And whether he has or has not made it;
> He who surveys it from the lofty skies,
> Only he knows—or perhaps he knows not.

But the times we live in are very interesting ones. Questions of origins, including some questions relating to the origin of the universe, may in the next few decades be amenable to experimental inquiry. There is no conceivable answer to the grand cosmological questions which will not resonate with the religious sensibilities of human beings. But there is a chance that the answers will discomfit a great many bureaucratic and doctrinal religions. The idea of religion as a body of belief, immune to criticism, fixed forever by some founder is, I think, a prescription for the long-term decay of the religion, especially lately. In questions of origins and ends, the religious and the scientific sensibilities have much the same objectives. Human beings are built in such a way that we passionately wish to answer these questions—perhaps because of the mystery of our own individual origins. But our contemporary scientific insights, while limited, are much deeper than those of our Babylonian predecessors of 1,000 B.C. Religions unwilling to accommodate to change, both scientific and social, are, I believe, doomed. A body of belief cannot be alive and relevant, vibrant and growing, unless it is responsive to the most serious criticism that can be mustered against it.

The First Amendment to the United States Constitution encourages a diversity of religions but does not prohibit criticism of religion. In fact it protects and encourages criticism of religion. Religions ought to be subject to at least the same degree of skepticism as, for example, contentions about UFO visitations or Velikovskian catastrophism. I think it is healthy for the religions themselves to foster skepticism about the fundamental underpinnings of their evidential bases. There is no question that religion provides a solace and support, a bulwark in time of emotional need, and can serve extremely useful social roles. But it by no means follows that religion should be immune from testing, from critical scrutiny, from skepticism. It is striking how little skeptical discussion of religion there is in the nation that Tom Paine, the author of *The Age of Reason,* helped to found. I hold that belief systems that cannot survive scrutiny are probably not worth having. Those that do survive scrutiny probably have at least important kernels of truth within them.

Religion used to provide a generally accepted understanding of our place in the universe. That surely has been one of the major objectives of myth and legend, philosophy and religion, as long as there have been human beings. But the mutual confrontation of differing religions and of religion with science has eroded those traditional views, at least in the minds of many.[1] The way to find out about our place in the universe is by examining the universe

---

[1]This subject is rich in irony. Augustine was born in Africa in 354 A.D. and in his early years was a Manichean, an adherent of a dualistic view of the universe in which good and evil are in conflict on roughly equal terms, and which was later condemned as a "heresy" by Christian orthodoxy. The possibility that all was not right with Manicheanism occurred to Augustine when he was studying its astronomy. He discovered that even the leading figures in the faith could not justify its murky astronomical notions. This contradiction between theology and science on matters astronomical was the initial impetus moving him toward Catholicism, the religion of his mother, which in later centuries persecuted scientists such as Galileo for trying to improve our understanding of astronomy. Augustine later became Saint Augustine, one of the major intellectual figures in the history of the Roman Catholic church, and his mother became Saint-Monica, after whom a suburb of Los Angeles is named. Bertrand Russell wondered what Augustine's view of the conflict between astronomy and theology would have been had he lived in the time of Galileo.

and by examining ourselves—without preconceptions, with as un-biased a mind as we can muster. We cannot begin with an entirely clean slate, since we arrive at this problem with predispositions of hereditary and environmental origin; but, after understanding such built-in biases, is it not possible to pry insights from nature?

Proponents of doctrinal religions—ones in which a particular body of belief is prized and infidels scorned—will be threatened by the courageous pursuit of knowledge. We hear from such people that it may be dangerous to probe too deeply. Many people have inherited their religion like their eye color: they consider it not a thing to think very deeply about, and in any case beyond our control. But those with a set of beliefs they profess to feel deeply about, which they have selected without an unbiased sifting through the facts and the alternatives, will feel uncomfortably challenged by searching questions. Anger at queries about our beliefs is the body's warning signal: here lies unexamined and probably dangerous doctrinal baggage.

Christianus Huygens wrote a remarkable book around 1670 in which bold and prescient speculations were made about the nature of the other planets in the solar system. Huygens was well aware that there were those who held such speculations and his astronomical observations objectionable: "But perhaps they'll say," Huygens mused, "it does not become us to be so curious and inquisitive in these Things which the Supreme Creator seems to have kept for his own Knowledge: For since he has not been pleased to make any farther Discovery or Revelation of them, it seems little better than presumption to make any inquiry into that which he has thought fit to hide. But these Gentlemen must be told," Huygens then thundered, "that they take too much upon themselves when they pretend to appoint how far and no farther Men shall go in their Searches, and to set bounds to other Mens Industry; as if they knew the Marks that God has placed to Knowledge: or as if Men were able to pass those Marks. If our Forefathers had been at this rate scrupulous, we might have been ignorant still of the Magnitude and Figure of the Earth, or that there was such a place as America."

If we look at the universe in the large, we find something astonishing. First of all, we find a universe that is exceptionally beautiful, intricately and subtly constructed. Whether our appreciation of the universe is because we are a part of that universe—whether, no matter how the universe were put together, we would have found it beautiful—is a proposition to which I do not pretend to have an answer. But there is no question that the elegance of the universe is one of its most remarkable properties. At the same time, there is no question that there are cataclysms and catastrophes occurring regularly in the universe and on the most awesome scale. There are, for example, quasar explosions which probably decimate the nuclei of galaxies. It seems likely that every time a quasar explodes, more than a million worlds are obliterated and countless forms of life, some of them intelligent, are utterly destroyed. This is not the traditional benign universe of conventional religiosity in the West, constructed for the benefit of living and especially of human beings. Indeed, the very scale of the universe — more than a hundred billion galaxies, each containing more than a hundred billion stars — speaks to us of the inconsequentiality of human events in the cosmic context. We see a universe simultaneously very beautiful and very violent. We see a universe that does not exclude a traditional Western or Eastern god, but that does not require one either.

My deeply held belief is that if a god of anything like the traditional sort exists, our curiosity and intelligence are provided by such a god. We would be unappreciative of those gifts (as well as unable to take such a course of action) if we suppressed our passion to explore the universe and ourselves. On the other hand, if such a traditional god does not exist, our curiosity and our intelligence are the essential tools for managing our survival. In either case, the enterprise of knowledge is consistent with both science and religion, and is essential for the welfare of the human species. 20

Vocabulary

planetary (1)

cosmological (1)

anthropomorphic (1)

celestial (1)

resonance (2)

authenticating (2)

reincarnation (2)

proscriptions (2)

derive (2)

agnostic (3)

benignly (3)

circumnavigation (4)

dialectical (5)

rebuttal (5)

decoupling (5)

exobiology (5)

ingenious (6)

adherents (6)

sectarian (7)

placate (7)

ecumenicism (7)

microintervention (8)

desultory (8)

omnipotent (8)

omniscient (8)

causality (8)

skein (8)

ontological (8)

phototropism (9)

hormones (9)

oscillating (12)

amenable (14)

resonate (14)

discomfit (14)

catastrophism (15)

bulwark (15)

preconceptions (16)

proponents (17)

prescient (18)

cataclysms (19)

quasar (19)

decimate (19)

nuclei (19)

Critical Inquiries

1. How do you think typical mainline Christians react to reading Sagan's essay? What is your own reaction?

2. What is Sagan's view of people who insist on having definite and incontrovertible answers to the deep mysteries concerning the origins of the universe and God's role in it? What is your answer to Sagan?

3. Do you agree with Sagan that the fundamentals of any religion must constantly be questioned if the religion is to survive? Do you tend to be skeptical about fundamental beliefs—religious, political, social, or otherwise? Give examples from past experience of your attitude.

4. In paragraph 19 Sagan tells us that if we look at the universe "in the large," we shall find it beautiful as well as violent. What specific examples of beauty and violence in our own world can you provide?

5. What is your definition of "God"? How do you think Sagan might define "God"?

Rhetorical Inquiries

1. What is the purpose of Sagan's title? What is its appeal?

2. What tone do you detect in paragraph 6? Why do you think Sagan uses this tone?

3. What is the purpose of the footnotes at the bottom of several pages?

4. What is the topic sentence of paragraph 9?

5. What effect does the Hindu poem (paragraph 13) have?

MANAGEMENT

Peter Drucker
WHAT EMPLOYEES NEED MOST

Peter Drucker (b. 1909 in Vienna, Austria) is a prolific writer of articles and books on management and the economy. With a doctorate from the University of Frankfurt, he has been a professor of economics, social science, philosophy, and management at Sarah Lawrence College, Benington College, New York University, and Claremont Graduate School. Among his many books are The Future of Industrial Man: A Conservative Approach *(1942),* The New Society: The Anatomy of the Industrial Order *(1950),* The Practice of Management *(1954),* Managing for Results: Economic Tasks and Risk-Taking Decisions *(1964), and* The Age of Discontinuity: Guidelines to Our Changing Society *(1969). His numerous essays have been collected in three books*—Technology, Management, and Society *(1970),* Men, Ideas, and Politics *(1971), and* Management: Tasks, Responsibilities, Practice, *ed. Cass Canfield (1974).*

Most of you . . . will be employees all your working life, working for somebody else and for a pay check. And so will most, if not all, of the thousands of other young Americans . . . in all the other schools and colleges across the country. 1

Ours has become a society of employees. A hundred years or so ago only one out of every five Americans at work was employed, i.e., worked for somebody else. Today only one out of five is not employed but working for himself. And where fifty years ago "being employed" meant working as a factory laborer or as a farm-hand, the employee of today is increasingly a middle-class person with a substantial formal education, holding a professional or management job requiring intellectual and technical skills. Indeed, two things have characterized American society during these last fifty years: the middle and upper classes have become employees; and middle-class and upper-class employees have been the fastest-growing groups in our working population—growing so fast that the industrial worker, that oldest child of the Industrial Revolution, has been losing in numerical importance despite the expansion of industrial production. 2

This is one of the most profound social changes any country has ever undergone. It is, however, a perhaps even greater change for the individual young person about to start. Whatever he does, in 3

Reprinted by permission of the author.

all likelihood he will do it as an employee; wherever he aims, he will have to try to reach it through being an employee.

Yet you will find little if anything written on what it is to be an employee. You can find a great deal of very dubious advice on how to get a job or how to get a promotion. You can also find a good deal on work in a chosen field, whether it be metallurgy or salesmanship, the machinist's trade or bookkeeping. Every one of these trades requires different skills, sets different standards, and requires a different preparation. Yet they all have employeeship in common. And increasingly, especially in the large business or in government, employeeship is more important to success than the special professional knowledge or skill. Certainly more people fail because they do not know the requirements of being an employee than because they do not adequately possess the skills of their trade; the higher you climb the ladder, the more you get into administrative or executive work, the greater the emphasis on ability to work within the organization rather than on technical competence or professional knowledge.

Being an employee is thus the one common characteristic of most careers today. The special profession or skill is visible and clearly defined; and a well-laid-out sequence of courses, degrees, and jobs leads into it. But being an employee is the foundation. And it is much more difficult to prepare for it. Yet there is no recorded information on the art of being an employee.

The first question we might ask is: what can you learn in college that will help you in being an employee? The schools teach a great many things of value to the future accountant, the future doctor, or the future electrician. Do they also teach anything of value to the future employee? The answer is: "Yes—they teach the one thing that it is perhaps most valuable for the future employee to know. But very few students bother to learn it."

This one basic skill is the ability to organize and express ideas in writing and in speaking.

As an employee you work with and through other people. This means that your success as an employee—and I am talking of much more here than getting promoted—will depend on your ability to communicate with people and to present your own thoughts and ideas to them so they will both understand what you are driving at and be persuaded. The letter, the report or memorandum, the ten-minute spoken "presentation" to a committee are basic tools of the employee.

Of course . . . if you work on a machine your ability to express yourself will be of little importance. But as soon as you move one step up from the bottom, your effectiveness depends on your ability to reach others through the spoken or the written word. And the further away your job is from manual work, the larger the organization of which you are an employee, the more important it will be that you know how to convey your thoughts in writing or speaking. In the very large organization, whether it is the government, the large business corporation, or the military, this ability to express oneself is perhaps the most important of all the skills a person can possess.

Of course, skill in expression is not enough by itself. You must   10
have something to say in the first place. The popular picture of the engineer, for instance, is that of a man who works with a slide rule, T-square, and compass. And engineering students reflect this picture in their attitude toward the written word as something quite irrelevant to their jobs. But the effectiveness of the engineer—and with it his usefulness—depends as much on his ability to make other people understand his work as it does on the quality of the work itself.

Expressing one's thoughts is one skill that the school can really   11
teach, especially to people born without natural writing or speaking talent. Many other skills can be learned later—in this country there are literally thousands of places that offer training to adult people at work. But the foundations for skill in expression have to be laid early: an interest in and an ear for language; experience in organizing ideas and data, in brushing aside the irrelevant, in wedding outward form and inner content into one structure; and above all, the habit of verbal expression. If you do not lay these foundations during your school years, you may never have an opportunity again.

If you were to ask me what strictly vocational courses there are   12
in the typical college curriculum, my answer—now that the good old habit of the "theme a day" has virtually disappeared—would be: the writing of poetry and the writing of short stories. Not that I expect many of you to become poets or short-story writers—far from it. But these two courses offer the easiest way to obtain some skill in expression. They force one to be economical with language. They force one to organize thought. They demand of one that he give meaning to every word. They train the ear for language, its meaning, its precision, its overtones—and its pitfalls. Above all they force one to write.

I know very well that the typical employer does not understand   13
this as yet, and that he may look with suspicion on a young college graduate who has majored, let us say, in short-story writing.

But the same employer will complain—and with good reason— that the young people whom he hires when they get out of college do not know how to write a simple report, do not know how to tell a simple story, and are in fact virtually illiterate. And he will conclude—rightly—that the young people are not really effective, and certainly not employees who are likely to go very far.

Vocabulary

numerical (2)

dubious (4)

metallurgy (4)

wedding (11)

overtones (12)

Critical Inquiries

1. The author aims his essay at employees. What advantage, if any, does being an employee have over owning one's own business? Support your answer with specific examples.

2. In paragraph 2 the author states that "ours has become a society of employees." Why has this change occurred?

3. The author places high value on the ability to communicate. In your opinion has your schooling so far adequately prepared you in this important area? Why or why not? What skills, if any, should receive more emphasis?

4. What is your opinion of the author's suggestion that students take a course in writing short stories and poetry?

5. According to Drucker, where in the organizational system are communications skills most important? Why?

Rhetorical Inquiries

1. What technique does the author use to capture your attention from the beginning of his essay?

2. Why is paragraph 7 so brief, consisting of a single sentence?

3. What connection exists between paragraphs 6 and 7?

4. How does Drucker support his proposition that an employee's most important skill is the ability to communicate well?

5. For what audience do you think Drucker is writing?

Exercises

1. Give the following argument a careful reading. In view of everything you have read in this chapter, how does the argument measure up? Write a brief critical review.

THE LIBERTINE EQUATION

The programs and actions growing out of libertine thought and its ideologies, have put society in bondage to the indifferent with disturbing consequences. It strikes me in this manner.

Ultra liberal thought in its libertarian way, racing on its erratic course deep within the sanctuary of man and woman, soon bursts forth upon society. Confused, discontented, immoral, demanding, abusive, with no restraints and in their frenzy call it freedom.

This is not freedom, this is an abuse of freedom in which society becomes a slave to turbulent thought, shiftlessness and wanton desires.

It is a delusion, the leading of individuals the wrong way down a one-way street. It is an intellectually organized view and principle presented in such a way, even though it is misleading, to meet the permissive demands of the time. This sort of libertine equation has just about bankrupted society morally and financially.

Society and religion must find a way to unwind from this dangerous thought that knows no evil, sees no evil, hears no evil; that has no moral or financial balance; that plays upon the weaknesses of human nature to gain its popularity. This kind of speculative philosophy has been the scourge of nations down through the ages.

Every so often history repeats itself and moral society has had to deal with this type of thinking and behavior. If in this present day and time it is allowed to continue, everyone will be engulfed in this delusion. For when the bell tolls, it tolls for all.

May I say in all fairness, while we cannot condone disoriented, undisciplined runaway thoughts and actions, we also cannot allow narrowness and cynicism to govern our lives. Both can be ruinous and so cloud the mind to reality and sane thought.

—Robert J. Carley, letter reprinted from *Mobile Press-Register,*
October 3, 1981.

2. Quote two expert testimonies and cite three facts for each of the following arguments:
   a. pro or con gun control
   b. pro or con nuclear energy plants

    c. pro or con censorship

    d. pro or con animal experimentation

3. Narrate an experience (yours or someone else's) that would support one of the following arguments:

    a. A college education is not for everyone.

    b. Much of contemporary poetry cannot be explained.

    c. Most T.V. advertising is socially and culturally biased.

    d. The typical white wedding dress is a shameful waste of money.

    e. Certain customs followed by "gentlemen" relating to "ladies" should be maintained (or abolished).

Writing Assignments

1. Choose a social custom or tradition which you do not particularly like. Propose a change and defend it in an argumentative essay.

2. Write an argument for or against one of the following subjects:

    a. legalized pornography

    b. U.S. intervention in the affairs of third world countries

    c. restructuring of the income tax system

    d. censorship of song lyrics

    e. abstract art

    f. a national welfare system (as opposed to a statewide one)

    g. mandatory registration of known AIDS carriers

3. "Dictionary definitions should prescribe ideal usage rather than reflect the way words are actually used." Write an argument for or against this idea.

4. After studying Orwell's "A Hanging" and Karl Menninger's "The Crime of Punishment", write your own argument either for or against the death penalty. Use quotations from the two essays studied as support for your own views or as ideas that you repudiate.

Chapter

18

Literary Papers and Essay Exams

*K*nowledge is the foundation and source of good writing.

HORACE (65–8 B.C.)

Literary Papers

In writing a paper about literature, it is useful to imagine yourself as a lawyer and the analyzed work as your client. If you say that this is what your client meant, your client should be allowed to testify freely to that effect. We suggest this pretense to make it easier for you to support your interpretations with adequate references to the work. The emphasis of a literary paper should always be on the work itself, and not on any other unrelated event or memory it may call to mind.

For example, we had one student who interpreted a certain poem as being about alligators although no mention of that reptile was to be found anywhere in the text. Pressed to expose the beast, he mentioned some remembered episode with an alligator in his childhood. That literature can and does arouse such unique associations in each of us is part of its charm. But sober analysis calls for proof, and if your paper cannot support your interpretation with material from the text itself, you may be guilty of a misreading.

But can a work not have a valid but different meaning for everyone? This objection to the idea that an interpretation of literature can be right or wrong is often raised by students. And it is an undeniable truth that literature can and does evoke different meanings in different minds. But so can the Grand Canyon. Yet, writing a geology paper about how the Grand Canyon brought to mind an alligator, would doubtless be irrelevant. To do so is to focus not on the canyon itself, but on the associations it evokes in the student's mind. It makes the analyzer, rather than the analyzed, the central theme of the paper, which is not what either a geological or a literary paper requires. The first wants you to focus on the rocks in the canyon; the second, on the words on the page.

What a literary paper requires is analysis of the work itself. You state your interpretation of the work and you prove it. You show the thinking and evidence that led to your conclusions. You make a point about an author and you back it up with quotations from the author's work. Along the way, you may also find yourself doing one or all of the following tasks:

Finding the theme

The main idea of the literary work is called its theme, and understanding and expressing it is a basic function of any literary paper. Characteristically, bad literature will trumpet theme as crassly as a television de-

571

odorant commercial, while good literature will express it in the subtleties of real life.

So how do you find the theme of a literary work? You might begin by examining its title. In a longer work, title may give no hint about theme. For example, *A Passage to India* gives little inkling about the theme of culture conflict in that famous novel. But the titles of other novels such as *The Good Earth,* or *For Whom the Bell Tolls,* do hint of their themes—that owning land is important, and that war is a call to death.

In shorter works, a title can be as illuminating as a lightning bolt. Here is an example of a poem that is nearly meaningless without its title:

> Last night
> a snail
> crawled out
> my ear.
> I feel
> some bad
> times
> coming.

What does this mean? The title tells us:

Omen

> Last night
> a snail
> crawled out
> my ear.
> I feel
> some bad
> times
> coming.

Sometimes, especially in a play, the theme of a work will be expressed by one of its characters. We do not mean that the character will suddenly abandon his or her role and mount a pulpit. But he or she will nevertheless have the last word—in emphasis if not actual sequence—and it will be given with the finality of a summation. Here is such a speech from *Death of a Salesman.* It is delivered by Willy Loman's wife, Linda, and crisply sums up the compassionate theme of the play—that obscure or unimportant people may suffer immensely.

> . . . I don't say he's a great man. Will Loman never made a lot

of money. His name was never in the paper. He's not the finest character that ever lived. But he's a human being, and a terrible thing is happening to him. So attention must be paid. He's not to be allowed to fall into his grave like a old dog. Attention, attention must finally be paid to such a person.

However, you should not approach the business of finding and expressing a work's theme as if you were coring an apple. Novels, plays, or poems are likely to have several themes, and the one you uncover must not only be expressed, but also documented by references to the work itself.

Summarizing

To summarize does not mean to give a blow-by-blow recounting of what any reader of the work already knows. Rather, it means to condense in your own words the content and theme of the work and to add, as you do, your own comments and perspective on it. Here is an example of what we mean. Students were asked to summarize the theme of this verse:

"Yes," I answered you last night;
"No," this morning, sir, I say:
Colors seen by candlelight
Will not look the same by day.
—E. B. Browning

One student wrote this:

The poem tells us that candlelight has the
ability to hide all kinds of cracks and flaws in
a room. Because the candles cast such a soft
light, much of the room remains hidden in
shadows. Perhaps a woman is speaking to a real
estate salesman. She had dined in a certain
house by candlelight and loved the place so much
that when it went up for sale, she wanted to buy
it. But when she sees the place in the harsh
light of day, the color of the wallpaper looks
hideous and she does not want the house at all.

This summary is based on a too literal-minded reading of the verse and therefore leads nowhere. Here is a better summary:

> The poem warns us that romance must not be
> confused with true love. It tells us that a
> romantic setting, such as a candlelit dinner in
> a cozy little bistro, can cause infatuation and
> may even elicit promises of undying love from a
> lover. But such a feeling rarely passes the test
> of reality involving a daily routine of work and
> paying bills. This lighthearted verse is in the
> ancient tradition of poems that puncture the
> myth of romantic love by pointing out how it
> promises everything but delivers nothing.

The author of this second summary does not merely serve up the meaning of the poem on the platter of a prose summary—giving us her words instead of the poet's. Instead, she clarifies the theme by commenting on it; she identifies the tone of the poem; and she mentions the ancient tradition to which it belongs.

Paraphrasing

To paraphrase means to restate in your own words some event or happening in a literary work. The paraphrase has two aims in a literary paper. One is to firmly anchor the literary paper onto the analyzed work itself and so curb any inclination a writer might have to drift. Another aim is to prove that you have actually assimilated the work and know what you are talking about.

Primarily, accurate paraphrasing is part of the evidence necessary to prove any point you wish to make about the literary work. Here is an example. The student is making a point about foreshadowing in the short story "The Lottery":

> In the short story "The Lottery," by
> Shirley Jackson, there are definite hints and
> clues that someone will die. Black is the

symbolic color for death in our society, and
throughout Jackson's story it occurs numerous
times. The little black box which the people
draw their lots from is referred to over and
over again. Jackson also portrays Mrs.
Hutchinson as a very frightened woman. For
example, when she realizes that someone in her
family is going to be picked, she begins
screaming that the drawing was unfair and should
be done over again. Before we even find out
that she is going to be the one to die, we have
several inklings of that outcome.

What is the difference between a paraphrase and a summary? Mainly a technical one. The paraphrase restates incidents and events in the work more or less as they happened. A summary expresses broad themes or ideas of the work without necessarily recounting any of its actual details. Here is an example of a summary about "The Lottery":

"The Lottery" is about scapegoating and the
symbolic function it can serve in a community. It
recounts the annual tradition in a certain
community of stoning a member by drawing lots.
Implied in the story is the idea that even if not
deliberately elected, the scapegoat eases the
fears of a community by making one of its members
bear the brunt of misfortune and evil that all
dread.

The paraphrase can be convincing evidence of your grasp of plot and outcome in a work. There is, however, a tradition of misuse of the paraphrase: namely, as a padding device. Any one can stretch one page into two through a picky paraphrase. Here is an example. The student was asked to write a paragraph or two on a favorite book and to say what was appealing about it:

> Of the many books I have read, <u>The</u> <u>Stand</u> by
> Stephen King is my favorite. The story takes
> place in the United States in the present time.
> There had been an accident in a germ warfare
> plant. Some people escaped with the deadly
> virus and they accidentally infected men at a
> nearby gas station.
>
> Eventually, the virus spread, killing
> millions of people. Soon survivors split up
> into two groups. One group is led by a man who
> is the devil. The second group is led by an old
> woman who is very religious.
>
> The two sides organize, with the bad group
> wanting to destroy the other. The good group
> sends people to make peace but they are captured
> and held prisoner. When these people are about
> to be executed, one of the bad brings in a
> nuclear bomb. The bomb explodes with help from
> the good group destroying all the bad.
>
> This is my favorite book. It is long but
> quite enjoyable.

Using a paraphrase this way makes your paper trivial and waters down its impact. Moreover, it is a blatant case of padding. Paraphrase when you have to and only as necessary to prove your point.

Quoting

Quoting means copying exactly a passage from a written work. Every essay interpreting literature should include quotations from the analyzed work. Set a context for the quotation, cite it accurately, and relate it to the point you are making. The conventions on the use of quotations are easy to remember and practice: If the quotation is shorter than four lines, integrate it grammatically into your text and set it off within quotation marks. Here is an example of a quotation that is badly integrated within the text of the paper:

```
Hawthorne uses symbolic objects to convey his

theme that mankind is basically evil. He uses

the forest to show "no church had ever been

gathered nor solitary Christian prayer," as a

symbol for the essence of evil and places the

most goodly and respectable persons within the

confines of this dark and dreary world.
```

Although accurate, the quotation is not grammatically integrated within the sentence. Here is an improvement:

```
Hawthorne uses symbolic objects to convey his

theme that mankind is basically evil. He uses

one of nature's objects, the forest, "where no

church had ever been gathered nor solitary

Christian prayed," as a symbol for the essence

of evil and places the most goodly and

respectable persons within the confines of this

dark and dreary world.
```

A quotation longer than four lines is reproduced exactly without quotation marks and indented ten spaces from your left margin (assuming a typewritten page). If the quotation is of a single paragraph, its initial line need not be indented. But if it consists of two or more paragraphs, the initial line of each quoted paragraph is indented three spaces. Here is a example:

```
The following lines from "The Short Happy Life

of Francis Macomber" characterize Hemingway's
```

typical female—a combination of cruelty and
good looks:

How should a woman act when she
discovers her husband is a bloody coward?
She's damn cruel but they're all cruel.
They govern, of course, and to govern one
has to be cruel sometimes. Still I've seen
enough of their damn terrorism.

"Have some more eland," he said to her
politely.

That afternoon, late, Wilson and
Macomber went out in the motor car with the
native driver and the two gunbearers. Mrs.
Macomber stayed in the camp. It was too hot
to go out, she said, and she was going with
them in the early morning. As they drove
off Wilson saw her standing under the big
tree, looking pretty rather than beautiful
in her faintly rosy khaki, her dark hair
drawn back off her forehead and gathered
in a knot low on her neck, her face as
fresh, he thought, as though she were in
England.

In longer papers on literature, quotations from both primary and
secondary sources may be used. The distinction between the two is a simple
one: The work you are analyzing is the primary source; any other writing or
opinion about it is a secondary source. In support of your interpretation, you
may wish to cite such secondary sources as the views of other critics.
And for such quotations, you should use exactly the same format as for a
primary source.

Analyzing form

The form of a literary work is the sum of its physical characteristics—its language, imagery, diction, syntax, and grammar. When we speak of form we mean the way an idea is expressed, whether with rhyme, in prose, with repetition, in images, or plainly; when we speak of content, we mean the idea itself, its proposition, merit, consequences, or tradition. Form and content are not divisible in any practical sense, but literary criticism often treats each as if it were capable of standing alone. A critic may therefore write at length about the form of the poem, or more usually, its content, as if the one could exist without the other.

It is not always appropriate or necessary to analyze the form of a work in a literary paper. The work may have no distinctly recognizable form, or its uninspired use of form may be unworthy of comment. But occasionally, if you spot something significant in the form of a work, you should mention it in your paper. For example, the poem on page 000, "Omen," is a variation on the haiku, a Japanese poem of 15 syllables, and the student who knows and mentions this fact in a paper will likely make a stronger impression than the one on whom it is lost.

What follows is the first draft of a student paper analyzing a short story by William Carlos Williams. As the result of one tutorial session with her instructor, the student made the editorial changes indicated. They consist mainly of some additional summarizing and explicating. The final version is a considerable improvement over the original.

Original:

```
               Critical Analysis of

               "The Use of Force"

                      by

                   W. C. Williams
                 (William Carlos)

     "The Use of Force" written by W. C.
                              (William Carlos)
Williams, is the story of a frightened child who

attempts to hide a sore throat so as to avoid

being treated by the doctor. The story vividly
                    the universal truth --
illustrates that fear an unpleasant and often

strong emotion can lead to violence and

irrational behavior.
```

The narrator, ~~who is the doctor himself~~ *an old-fashioned country doctor making his rounds during a diphtheria epidemic,* is

the spokesman for the theme. It is through him

that we feel the ~~intensity of the~~ *anger, the rebellion, and the intense* fear that the

girl is experiencing; *through him we also experience* the apprehension of the

parents and ~~his~~ *the narrators* own inner fear of not being able

to help her as a doctor. "The child was fairly

eating me up with her cold, steady eyes" he

tells us, as he notices for the first time the

terror reigning within her. He also doesn't fail

to notice the nervousness and apprehension of

the parents, who were "eyeing [him] up and down

distrustfully" upon his arrival. Furthermore, we

realize from the information the narrator gives us, ~~are informed~~ that the parents of the child are

uneducated, ~~when~~ they ~~apply~~ *use* such ~~sentences~~ *language* *for* as

"it don't do no good" and "her throat don't hurt

her." From this we can conclude that one of the

reasons for the parents and the child being

apprehensive is their ignorance, ~~that has~~ *which in time has*

developed into a *deep* fear *fear of* ~~caused by the~~

~~anticipation of~~ *unanticipated* an unknown danger.

As the story builds ~~up~~ towards its

climac~~t~~ic ~~point~~, the narrator *'s fear grows and* ~~illustrates how~~

~~that fear is~~ *becomes* intensified ~~and~~ *until it is* eventually released

through violent and irrational behavior. The

doctor is at first *controlled and* reasonable when "speaking

quietly and slowly" he approaches the child for

a throat examination. But the ~~hesitant~~ child,

filled with fear and fury, "clawe~~s~~/*d*

instinctively" ~~for~~ *at* [his]/ eyes"/ in a sudden

outbreak of violent behavior. "Then the battle
began" the narrator tells us. Enraged with the
parents of the child for not allowing him to
handle the case himself, and frightened that the
child *might* ~~may~~ have diptheria, ~~he~~ *the doctor must* now ~~had to~~ examine
her no matter how ~~violent he himself became~~ *much she resists*. "In
a final unreasoning assault I overpowered the
child's neck . . . forced the heavy silver spoon
. . . down her throat till she gagged . . . now
truly she was furious . . . now she attacked."

The confrontation between doctor and patient turns into a fierce jungle combat as each side loses control. Ironically, the doctor, whom we normally think of as a detached and reasonable person, is filled with a violence similar to that of the child. He says:

In essence both the doctor and the child
were frightened, but for different reasons: One
feared the death of a small human being, and the
other feared the thought of being hurt by a
stranger. ~~But~~ ironically both feared each other,
and both turned ~~against each~~ *on the* other in violent
behavior to protect themselves from what they
thought was the danger. *The lesson is*
Clear: Even the most rational among us
may act irrationally when enough stress
is present.

Revision:

Critical Analysis of

"The Use of Force"

by

William Carlos Williams

"The Use of Force," written by William
Carlos Williams, is the story of a frightened
child who attempts to hide a sore throat so as
to avoid being treated by her doctor. The story
vividly illustrates the universal truth that

fear—an unpleasant and often strong emotion—can lead to violence and irrational behavior.

The narrator, an old-fashioned country doctor making his rounds during a diphtheria epidemic, is the spokesman for the theme. It is through him that we feel the anger, the rebellion, and the intense fear that the girl is experiencing; through him we also experience the apprehension of the parents and the narrator's own inner fear of not being able to help her as a doctor. "The child was fairly eating me up with her cold, steady eyes" he tells us, as he notices for the first time the terror reigning within her. He also doesn't fail to notice the nervousness and apprehension of the parents, who were "eyeing [him] up and down distrustfully" upon his arrival. Furthermore, we realize, from the information the narrator gives us, that the parents of the child are uneducated, for they use such language as "it don't do no good" and "her throat don't hurt her." We can conclude that one of the reasons for the parents and the child being apprehensive is their ignorance, which in time has developed into a deep fear—fear of an unknown, unanticipated danger.

As the story builds towards its climax, the narrator's fear grows and becomes intensified until it is eventually released through violent and irrational behavior. The doctor is at first controlled and reasonable when "speaking quietly and slowly" he approaches the child for a throat examination. But the child, filled with fear and fury, "clawed instinctively" at his eyes in a sudden outbreak of violent behavior. "Then the battle began," the narrator tells us. Enraged with the parents of the child for not allowing him to handle the case himself, and frightened that the child might have diphtheria, the doctor now must examine her, no matter how much she resists. The confrontation between doctor and patient turns into a fierce jungle combat as each side loses control. Ironically, the doctor, whom we normally think of as a detached and reasonable person, is filled with a violence similar to that of the child. He says: "In a final unreasoning assault I overpowered the child's neck . . . forced the heavy silver spoon . . . down her throat till she gagged . . . now truly she was furious . . . now she attacked."

In essence, both doctor and the child were frightened, but for different reasons: One feared the death of a small human being, and the other feared the thought of being hurt by a stranger. Ironically, both feared each other, and both turned on the other in violent behavior to protect themselves from what they thought was

```
eminent danger. The lesson is clear: Even the
most rational among us may act irrationally when
enough stress is present.
```

Exercises

1. In one sentence, summarize the following poem:

Not Marching Away to Be Killed

Peace is the men not marching away to be killed.
I never saw my father marching away to be killed.
He was killed before I was born. But my mother
Always spoke of the men marching away to be killed.
Not "marching to the war" or "into action"
Or even "marching to fight for this country."
Although she was a soldier's daughter and a soldier's
Widow, "Marching away to be killed"
Was the fundamental reality for her.

                       For me

Peace is the man I love not
Marching away to be killed.
—Jean Overton Fuller (b. 1915)

2. Choose three quotations from the story "Young Goodman Brown" by Nathaniel Hawthorne that illustrate the main character's original inno-cence. Then choose three quotations that illustrate his guilt. (A copy of this short story will be found in your college library.)

3. State the theme of Shirley Jackson's "The Lottery." Whom do the charac-ters represent? What is the tone of the story? Who is the narrator? Inter-pret the symbolic meaning of the lottery itself. (A copy of this short story will be found in your college library.)

The Essay Exam

What is an instructor looking for in the answer to an essay examination? First, **understanding** of the material. You are expected to demonstrate a grasp of the subject matter, not merely to plunk down the facts. An answer consisting of lumps of facts bobbing among watery sen-tences is only an answer, not an essay. The essay exam is forgiving of the student who knows the material, but does not know it exactly, and positively generous to the one who knows how to express ideas in coherent paragraphs. It requires an essay as its answer, which means that you must frame your topic in a thesis behind which you marshal your facts as support or proof.

Second, the **organization** of the essay is important. If you know your facts but present them in a jumble, your essay's disorganization might even be taken to mean that you have not mastered the subject. That is like being ticketed for speeding when you are only badly parked. Organization counts, whether you are writing for psychology or English.

Third, the **selection** of material you include in your essay counts. It is as important to leave out irrelevant material as it is to include the relevant. If you spent a Sunday cramming on a topic that doesn't appear on the exam, don't just throw it in anyway for good measure. Give only the answer that the question wants, not the one you have carefully prepared.

Finally, if your essay is between a middle and high grade, the inclusion of **factual knowledge** will swing the decision in your favor. You must be correct in your facts, cite authorities accurately, be precise in your recall of events, dates, and names.

That, more or less, is what instructors look for in an essay examination. So how do you go about giving them what they want? We have some suggestions for doing exactly that:

Read the question carefully

This advice may strike you as fresh as Mother's admonition to wear a coat in chilly weather. But it is a fact that many students answer essay exam questions badly because they have misread the question. For instance, here is a question from a class in European history:

```
Define the Yalta Conference of 1945, explaining
who the participants were and what role they
played, and analyzing the major effects of the
conference.
```

If you study this question carefully, you will realize that it asks you to accomplish three tasks: (1) to *define* the conference, (2) to *explain* the participants and their roles, and (3) to *do an analysis of the effects* of the conference. To answer it correctly, you must follow this exact order of topics in your essay. Most instructors can judge whether or not you have adequately answered the question by quickly scanning your answer. If any part has not been answered, your grade will be lowered. Before attempting to answer an essay exam, then, always ask yourself what the instructor is after, and if you can't tell, don't write a word until you can.

Think before you write

In other words, don't simply jump in and start writing. Think. Pre-write your answer. Jot down important subtopics and ideas you should cover. Put them side by side with the question and ask yourself if they really answer it. If the exam allows a choice of questions, use part of this pause to decide which question you can best answer in the allowed time.

Organize your essay

We grant that all writers do not equally benefit from advanced organization and that this particular wisdom may therefore not be for you. But many writers will write a better essay if they systematically choose an organizing pattern for it. The pattern you use will naturally depend on how the question you answer is worded. Here are some examples of actual essay questions, along with the organizing mode or pattern a writer might use to answer them:

From Humanities

To demonstrate your understanding of the Aristotelian concept of "hamartia," discuss an incident in which you or someone you know was guilty of this error.

Suggested mode: *narration*

"Discuss" is one of those catch-all terms with multiple meanings depending on the context of the question. The error in judgment committed by the central character of a tragedy and resulting in his or her downfall is called "hamartia." And what this question wants is a narrative instance of this frailty. Narration is therefore the mode you should use to write on this topic.

From Geography

You have been transported to a tropical forest area of the world. Discuss the kind of flora and fauna you see about you.

Suggested mode: *description*

In this case "discuss" really means describe. The clue is in the wording of the question, which is asking you to tell what you see. If we were answering this question, we would also explain why we should see what we say we do. Doing so tells the instructor that we understand the natural forces behind the formation of a tropical rain forest.

From Western Civilization

Your author writes, "If there was one primary factor which operated more than others to accomplish the downfall of Roman civilization, it was probably *imperialism*." What does he mean by *imperialism?*

Suggested mode: *definition*

As a general rule, any question that probes for "meaning" is fishing for a definition. But there's a catch here: The term we are asked to define is cemented to the context of Rome's downfall. All the examples and details we use to back up our definition of this word we would therefore draw from the Roman experience.

From Art History

Write an essay that discusses Picasso's "Blue Period."

Suggested mode: *example*

In fact, this question calls for a mixed mode response. You must first define Picasso's "Blue Period," but thereafter the essay should focus primarily on examples of paintings typical of it. Note that examples are usable in essays of all modes. However, once you have defined "Blue Period," this particular essay should concentrate on the discussion of successive examples.

From History

Write an essay describing the stages of the Hegelian dialectic.

Suggested mode: *classification*

A classification essay, as we learned in Chapter 7, focuses primarily on dividing a whole into its constituent parts. On the surface, this question seems to ask for a description. But what it is really after is a listing and discussion of the parts of a whole, which is the typical subject of the classification essay.

From Government

Write an essay detailing the steps a candidate must take to qualify for a congressional election.

Suggested mode: *process*
We have said elsewhere that the process mode is relatively easy to
write. You simply recount how a thing is done, usually detailing sequential
steps in time. Most "how to" questions implicitly call for a process answer.

From English Literature

Write an essay in which you state the major differences in subject matter and style between the English poets of the 18th century
and those of the Romantic era.

Suggested mode: *comparison/contrast*
Not all comparison/contrast essays will be so conveniently worded.
This one not only tells us what it wants, it also provides the bases for our
comparison/contrast. To organize the essay into its major topics, you need
merely to list how poetry of the 18th century and Romantic period differ in
subject matter and style.

From Sociology

What are some of the major reasons for the so-called "unrespon-
sive bystander syndrome" in densely populated urban areas?

Suggested mode: *causal analysis*
Although you will mainly be analyzing cause in answering this
question, you should begin by defining the syndrome and giving an example
of it. Doing so sets a context for the discussion of reasons that will follow.

From Political Science

Argue for or against this statement: "There is absolutely no
question that 110,000 Japanese Americans living on the west coast
of the United States should have been interned in concentration
camps during World War II."

Suggested mode: *argumentation*

This is an unambiguous assignment: You merely need to put on your argumentative cap, choose a side, and begin by prewriting the principal points of your essay along with the underlying logical links between them.

Our point, perhaps laboriously made, is that the most appropriate rhetorical pattern for answering a question will often be implicit in its wording. Yet it is also clear that not all essay questions can be answered in a pure rhetorical pattern. Consider, for example, this topic:

> What did Karl Marx mean when he said, "Freedom is meaningless without equality of opportunity"?

Writing an essay on it will require you to say what Marx meant and also show how the quotation reflects his overall philosophy. And doing so will involve a rhetorical pattern considerably more complex than a clear-cut definition. What we have already said in Chapter 4 bears repeating. Rhetorical modes are intended as an aid to the writer and are not usable in every conceivable assignment. However, the principle of concentrated focus they teach applies to all kinds of writing, even to a paragraph whose organizing pattern is as thoroughly mixed as this one.

Here is a sample question from an actual college essay examination in History of the Americas. First, we supply the question and then we give two student answers, one average and one excellent. Study both answers to see where the second is superior to the first.

Exam question: What was the Rowell-Sirois Commission of 1937–41? What important recommendations did it make concerning federal-provincial relations in Canada? What role did the Depression play in this report?

Average answer:

```
         The Rowell—Sirois Commission was

appointed by the prime minister of Canada to

study what relationship should exist between

the federal government and the local

provinces.  It was particularly important to

do so because Canada had suffered some

serious fiscal problems during the Depression

and a former prime minister had suggested

some dramatic social and economic changes
```

that were thought by some Canadians to be
unconstitutional because they gave too much
power to the provinces. The main idea of the
report was to invest the federal government
with more power by giving it the right to
collect taxes and to be in charge of all
welfare programs.

This answer received only an average grade because it did not deal
adequately with all three parts of the question. First of all, the essay never
fully defines what the commission was. Second, it tells only superficially
what role the Depression played, and what little it does tell is not in the required order. Finally, the student offers only minimum facts and details, giving the impression of not having adequately studied for the exam. Now,
here is a superior answer to the same question:

Better answer: The Rowell–Sirois Commission was a special
task force appointed by Prime Minister William
Lyon Mackenzie King to study the role of the
federal government in relationship to the local
provinces. Two men chaired this commission:
First, Newton Wesley Rowell, chief justice of
Ontario, and later on, Joseph Sirois. In order
to combat problems brought on by the Great
Depression of the 1920s, Prime Minister Richard
Bedford Bennett had proposed sweeping social
and economic changes patterned after
Roosevelt's New Deal. Many of these proposals
were considered unconstitutional and led to
Bennett's ouster. When William Lyon Mackenzie
King became prime minister, one of his early
tasks was to appoint the Rowell–Sirois

Commission to study both the economic as well
as the constitutional problems of Canada.
Three years after its appointment, the
commission submitted its report, focusing on
two major points: (1) The higher courts had
been reversing the intentions of the founding
fathers of the confederation. (2) The powers
of the provinces had grown beyond proper
limits. In consequence of these two
points, the report suggested that a strong
central government was needed to guide
and control the economy. The following
specific recommendations were
made:

1. The federal government take over the debts
   of the provinces.
2. The federal government collect all taxes.
3. The federal government provide
   administrative and welfare programs.
4. The federal government make provisions for
   the unemployed.

Despite the fact that many Canadians objected
to these suggestions and that much of the
report was ultimately rejected, the commission
succeeded in convincing the people that the
government had a responsibility for the social
and economic welfare of the people. The
acceptance of this view gave unity to the
provinces.

This answer is superior because it is comprehensive and deals with the topics in their exact order in the question. It is evident that the student has not only studied but also mastered the subject.

Exercises

1. The questions below were questions actually asked in college exams. Suggest the proper mode(s) of development for each question. If more than one mode applies, list all appropriate modes.

   a. *From geology:*
   Discuss the major events that occur in plate tectonics. In your discussion explain how these events are responsible for the major features of the ocean floor seen today, as well as how they explain the formation of some important islands and shallow marine environments. (Use the appropriate terms in your answer and be complete in your explanation.)

   b. *From history:*
   What was the Yalta agreement of 1945? Who were the participants? How did the agreement affect China?

   c. *From literature:*
   In a 500-word essay, define the *nada* philosophy, indicating its source as a dominant theme in Ernest Hemingway's *Farewell to Arms.* Begin with a clear thesis and support this thesis through specific examples from the novel.

   d. *From psychology:*
   Bruno Bettelheim has made the following statement: "Every child believes at some point in life . . . that because of his secret wishes, if not also his clandestine actions, he deserves to be degraded, banned from the presence of others, relegated to a nether world of smut." In a brief essay, indicate how any one of the case histories studied this semester supports Bettelheim's contention.

Chapter

19

The Research Paper

Reading maketh a full man; conference a ready man; and writing an exact man.

Francis Bacon (1561–1626)

The research paper is aptly named, for it is a scholarly paper based on a systematic search. You search for a topic, for opinions that support your particular treatment of it, and for a narrowed thesis. You search for an organizing pattern for your ideas and for an appropriate style to express them.

From all this searching arise some measurable benefits. You learn to use the library, a skill which will prove useful no matter what your academic major or eventual employment. You learn the rules by which scholars work, the documenting forms they use to cite the works of others, and the standards of style and scholarship that they practice. And you learn these skills in the best and most memorable way of all—by doing.

You also learn to sift through contrary opinion, meld it with your own, and produce an original work. For that is what the research paper should be—your own original views on a topic backed by the supporting opinions of others. In writing the research paper you will play the dual role of editor and writer. As an editor, you find, extract, and edit the ideas and opinions of others that support your thesis. As a writer, you incorporate this material smoothly into the flow of your style and make it part of an original composition.

The Process of Writing a Research Paper

The process involved in writing a research paper is not markedly different from the one you would use to write any essay. You must find your topic, whittle it down to a controlling idea, and then frame it into a thesis statement. Next, you must research and uncover sources that support your thesis, arrange your ideas in their most emphatic order of presentation, and prewrite a formal outline or an abstract. The rough draft comes after, followed by successive revisions. The conscientious student would follow this agenda for any essay.

For the research paper, this process differs somewhat in degree and complexity. Research papers are longer than ordinary essays and therefore require more legwork, more time spent in writing, and a more formal style. Typically, they will range between a specified length of five to ten pages. Many instructors also require the citation of a minimum number of sources along with submission of note cards, an outline or abstract, and a rough draft. The schedule for writing such a paper will vary, but ordinarily it will

594

run over five weeks with submissions made by the student at specified intervals. That is the chronology we assume for the following discussion.

First Week: Finding a Topic

First, the topic you eventually settle on should be complex enough for an essay of some five to ten pages. This is probably as long an essay as you have to write in your first year or two of college, so be sure you base it on an appealing topic. Second, as you search for a topic, remember that instructors have their individual likes and dislikes too, and that it is only common sense for a writer to choose the topic most likely to please his or her reader. Finally, narrow your topic choice down to one that can be researched mainly at your local library. Since the collections found at most college libraries are substantial enough to support all but the most technical topics, this is not a severe limitation. Purely for practical reasons, however, it is smart to write on a topic that is convenient to research. Aside from being convenient, a narrowed topic also keeps you from ranging far and wide to provide support for your paper. Thus, a paper on Jacob Lawrence's contribution as a story-telling painter will provide better focus and direction than a paper on the contribution of Black American painters in general.

Using the library

The Card Catalog

The focal point of any search for a topic is the library, and your initial step should be a scan of the card catalog. Usually located in some central part of the lobby, the card catalog consists of alphabetized 3 × 5 cards that index every book in the library's collection. Books are listed separately under author, subject, and title headings. Translators, editors, and illustrators are jointly listed with the author on each card. If you have no idea at all for a topic to write on, rummaging through the card catalog might suggest one. Another useful source is the *Library of Congress Subject Headings,* a work that carefully lists most subjects and their subdivisions.

Microform Indexes

Microform is the name for systems of miniaturized storage. Many libraries store indexes of major periodicals on reels of microfilm that can be read by a special scanner. Others use film mounted on microfiche cards for condensed storage of college catalogs or other published information. Ask the librarian about the systems used in your own library.

Computer Searches

In some libraries, the computer has become a priceless tool for the researcher. Many libraries subscribe to on-line databases that can store and retrieve a vast quantity of information at the touch of a button. Thus, in a typical computerized library, all available works can be called up by title or author, with publication information displayed on the screen. For example, the best known database, DIALOG, stores published information on over 100 subjects ranging from government and education to the humanities and physical sciences. The service may provide topic headings or it may reproduce entire essays or books retrieved from original sources. Depending on library policy, students may or may not have free access to the terminals. Ask your librarian about the computer search facility in your own library. If it is there and available, take the time to learn how to call up the various databases. Once mastered, this latest research tool is the fastest and most convenient imaginable.

Periodical Guides

Much of the information you will cite in your paper is likely to be found in periodicals. Guides such as *The Reader's Guide To Periodical Literature* contain alphabetized listings of topics published in general periodicals. Similar guides are available for various subjects—for example, the *Social Sciences Index,* the *Humanities Index,* and the *Education Index.* In some schools, these or like indexes may be part of a computerized database.

The point of this initial visit to the library is to find a topic. You rummage through periodical indexes, scan the card catalog, browse through the book shelves until you find a topic you feel keenly about and would like to make the focus of your paper. By the end of the first week, you usually must have two topics ready for submission to the instructor, who will approve one.

Second Week: Assembling a Bibliography

The working bibliography is a list of promising sources turned up in an initial search. Eventually, this list will be narrowed down to a final bibliography, meaning those works you will actually use in the paper. On your first run through the library, you will most likely find many more sources than you can use and so must play the role of the selective editor. Here are some tips on separating usable from unusable sources:

1. Scan the indexes and tables of contents of books. If a chapter looks promising, leaf to its beginning and scan its thesis.
2. Scan the opening paragraph or two of articles. Finding the writer's thesis should tell whether the article might be useful.
3. Browse through book reviews found in references such as *The Book Review Digest,* whose articles summarize the contents of books.
4. Scan the preface of a book for the author's summary of its contents and emphasis.
5. Pay attention to the card catalog subject entry for any likely looking book. Books are classified on the cards under major headings such as "French Revolution," "Literary Criticism," "Medicine, History of," or "Archaeology."
6. Scan the bibliographical references listed at the end of articles or books for leads to other promising sources.
7. If you are doing a database search, scan the printout that summarizes the subject of an article or book (some databases offer this feature.)

Note that scanning is not the same as reading. You do not have the time to read through every likely source listed in the working bibliography. Scanning means running your eyes over the page, perhaps occasionally reading the initial sentence of a paragraph to grasp what it is about. Determining whether or not a source is usable should take you an average of no more than five minutes. Remember, too, that library workers have an uncanny knack for finding information stored in their collections, and most are eager to help. Get to know one of your friendly librarians and enlist his or her help in assembling a bibliography.

At the end of the second week you should have a working bibliography with each usable source listed on a 3 × 5 card. The card should contain information about where to find each source as well as a note about why it should prove useful. These cards should be submitted to the instructor for approval. Since you are unlikely to use every source in the working bibliography, the number of cards in it should exceed the minimum number of citations required. For example, if your instructor requires you to cite ten sources, your working bibliography should consist of at least fifteen to twenty cards. From this number, you can then choose the ten most applicable sources. Figures 19–1 and 19–2 are examples of bibliography cards.

Figure 19–1   Bibliography Card (personal library)

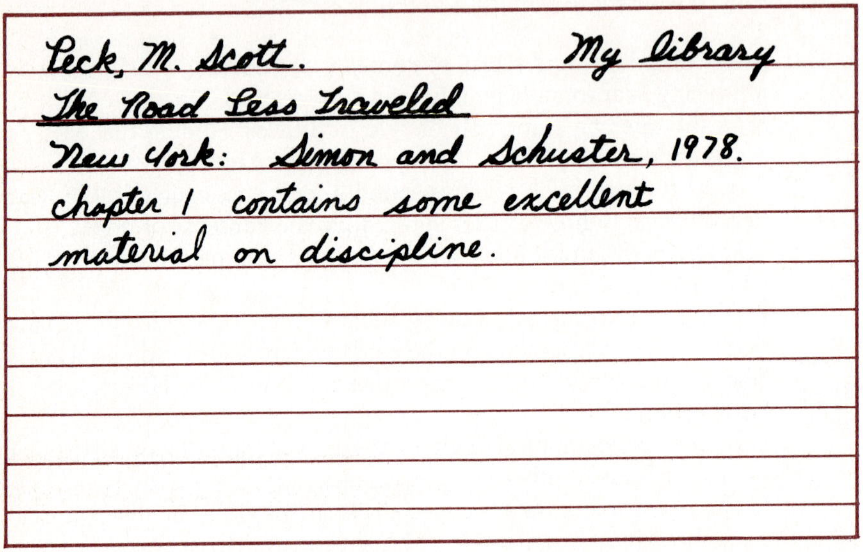

Peck, M. Scott.   My library
The Road Less Traveled
New York: Simon and Schuster, 1978.
chapter 1 contains some excellent
material on discipline.

Figure 19–2   Bibliography Card (college library)

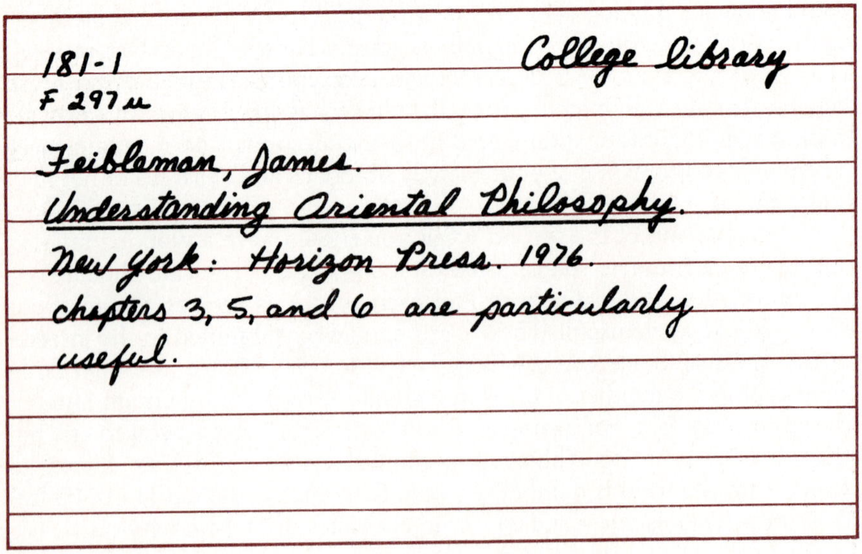

181-1   College library
F 297 u

Feibleman, James.
Understanding Oriental Philosophy.
New York: Horizon Press. 1976.
chapters 3, 5, and 6 are particularly
useful.

Third Week: Preparing Note Cards, a Thesis Statement, and an Outline (or Abstract)

Note Cards

Notes on each source should be made on 4 × 6 cards, written in ink rather than pencil, with only a single idea or quotation on each card. If the quotation takes up two or more cards, staple them together. In the upper left-hand corner of the card, identify the source of the idea or quotation with the author's last name or a key word from the title. In the upper right-hand corner, summarize the information the card contains. The idea is to be able to stack the cards in the order of their appearance in the paper and easily retrieve information from them.

There are four kinds of notes you can make on note cards:

The summary

The summary condenses useful information found in the source. In your own words, you faithfully sum up what is significant about the article or book. You state only major ideas. How much you condense depends on your paper. Some authors may sum up an entire book in one sentence or a chapter in one paragraph. Most student summaries, however, will consist of paragraphs condensed into sentences. Here is an original passage from a book about the ancient Egyptians. The summary of this passage appears in Figure 19–3.

> The manufacture of bricks gave employment to a great number of slaves and others, for almost every building in Egypt, with the exception of the temple, which was of stone, was made of un-baked bricks. The muddy soil of Egypt was particularly suitable for brick making, for it was free from stones and could be easily mixed with water and kneaded with the hands into a paste of the necessary consistency. A mass of paste was thrust into a wooden mold of the size of the brick required and the top of it smoothed with a flat stick, and when the brick was dry enough to take out of the mold, it was laid in a row with others on the ground to dry in the sun; in a day or two it was ready for use.
> —William O. Budge, *Dwellers of the Nile.*

The summary gets to the heart of a passage by including only its bare essentials while excluding minor points and details.

The paraphrase

To paraphrase is to put a passage in your own words while remaining faithful to the length of the original. Here is an example. The original

Figure 19–3   Summary Card

> Budge   Brick Manufacturing
> The manufacture of bricks was an
> important part of the Egyptian economy
> because it offered employment to
> slaves and other workers. The bricks
> were nothing more than mud formed
> into bricks and left to dry in the sun.

passage is below, with the paraphrase reproduced on the card in Figure 19–4.

> The Egyptians of the Neolithic Period believed that their exist-
> ence would not come to an end with the death of their bodies and
> they appear to have thought that the renewed life which they
> would live in some unknown region would closely resemble that
> which they were accustomed to lead in this world. This is proved
> by the fact that in the oldest known predynastic graves pots con-
> taining food, flint weapons for war and the chase, flint tools, etc.
> have been found in considerable numbers.
> —William O. Budge, *Dwellers of the Nile.*

The paraphrase is useful for incorporating the opinions of different writers into a single consistent style—your own.

The quotation

The quotation is an exact reproduction of an author's words. Slang, misspellings, even oddities of grammar are copied exactly as they appeared in the original. An example is shown in Figure 19–5.

Earlier, we cautioned against the overuse of quotations. Too many

Figure 19–4   Paraphrase Card

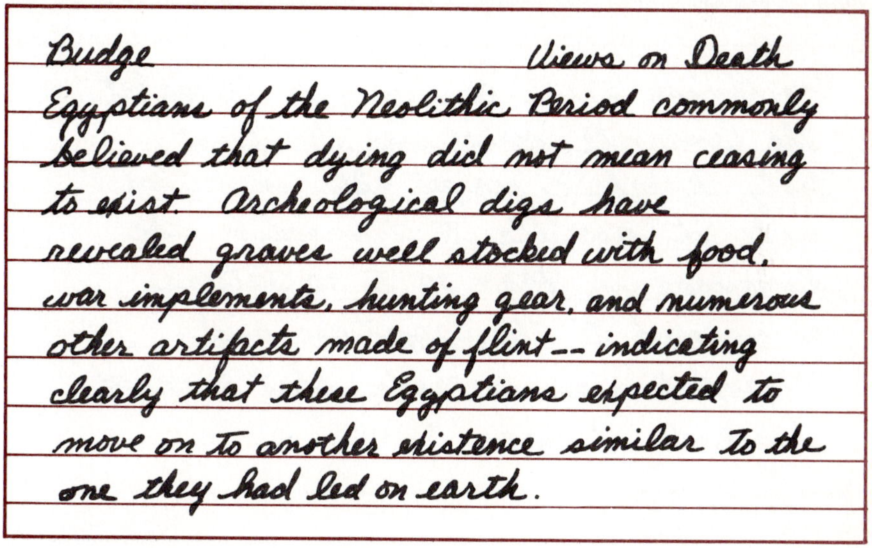

> Budge   Views on Death
> Egyptians of the Neolithic Period commonly
> believed that dying did not mean ceasing
> to exist. Archeological digs have
> revealed graves well stocked with food,
> war implements, hunting gear, and numerous
> other artifacts made of flint — indicating
> clearly that these Egyptians expected to
> move on to another existence similar to the
> one they had led on earth.

quotations cause a choppy style, called the "stringed pearls effect." A good rule to follow is to keep quoted material to under ten percent of the length of the paper.

The personal comment

The place for your own ideas, conclusions, or interpretations is the personal comment card. Use it to jot down any personal remarks about a source. An example is given in Figure 19–6.

Staple the actual source card to the card containing a personal comment about it. That way, you keep the two conveniently together.

The Thesis Statement

In Chapter 3, we explained at length about how to express your topic in a clear thesis statement. Everything we said there applies to the thesis statement of a research paper. There are, however, two main kinds of research papers: the report paper and the thesis paper. The first merely reports the writer's findings on a topic. It neither judges nor evaluates what the writer has found, and it is not argumentative for one point of view over another. Such a paper will contain a statement of purpose rather than a thesis. For example, a report paper on how a law is enacted in Congress might have this statement of purpose:

Figure 19–5   Quotation Card

Ben-Gurion 27   Origin of the Alphabet
" The Canaanite script was the first
truly alphabetic script. Its invention
made it possible to transcribe the
language in from 22 to 32 letters,
as opposed to the Egyptian and
Mesopotamian methods that involved
hundreds of signs. "

Figure 19–6   Personal Comment Card

It appears that the Canaanites
really had a more advanced literary
culture than did the Egyptians, who
in 1500 B.C. were still writing in
hieroglyphs, that is with primitive
pictures rather than with an alphabet
capable of transcribing sounds.

```
The purpose of this paper is to explain how a

bill is enacted into law by Congress from its

initial reading to final signing by the

president.
```

This is not a thesis in the usual sense. It is a summary of the paper's focus rather than an assertion of the writer's opinion on a debatable issue. Here are a few more examples of report paper theses:

```
Since the fifteenth century, medicine has

advanced considerably in its knowledge and

treatment of tuberculosis.
```

```
The completion of the first transcontinental

railroad brought various changes to the American

population.
```

```
The Indian caste system had its origin in

religion and resulted in an absolutely ordered

social structure.
```

On the other hand, if you were writing a research paper arguing against the influence of corporations on the passage of legislation in Congress, you would express that opposition in a thesis, following all the advice already given in Chapter 3. Your thesis might read this way:

```
Corporate America wields excessive influence on

the legislating function of Congress through

vigorous lobbying, the use of Political Action

Committees or PACs, and media campaigns.
```

Here are two more examples of theses for thesis papers:

```
Because of his futuristic views on the

wilderness and the preservation of forests,

Henry David Thoreau must be viewed as America's
```

```
first pioneer of conservation.

One of the main reasons for child abuse in our

society is drug abuse on the part of parents.
```

In both cases, the thesis implies an opposing point of view and therefore requires the writer to *defend* the position taken by the paper.

The Outline

(See p. 599 for treatment of an abstract.)

It is nearly a universal practice to require submission of a formal outline in advance of writing a research paper. Instructors can then pore over the student's plan and catch any evident structural flaw while it is easily corrected. But as we discussed earlier in Chapter 2, there are some writers who simply do not work well with an advance plan. If you are among them and your instructor will not exempt you from preparing an outline, you will simply have to make one.

But there are some convincing reasons for writing a research paper from an outline. In a long paper, it is easy for a beginning writer to lose sight of rhetorical purpose. The outline, however, tells you what you must do and guides your hand through successive pages. That a research paper must include material from other sources is another good reason for outlining it. Citing supporting sources at the right place in the paper is easier to do from a prepared outline than during the actual writing.

In preparing your outline, follow the format suggested in Chapter 2. (See also the sample student paper, pages 689–705.) Most likely, you will be required to do a three-level sentence outline such as the example from the student paper on pages 689–705. This detailed and therefore helpful kind of outline is especially useful to a writer for managing the flow of a complex paper.

The note cards, thesis statement, and outline are all due at the end of the third week. By now, you should have a solid grasp of your topic and know exactly what you have to do to write your rough draft.

Fourth Week: Writing the Rough Draft

You are now ready to write the rough draft. Your goal is to write a paper with emphasis on its thesis, to cite supporting opinion where necessary, and to make those citations as seamless and smooth as possible within your text. You must also acknowledge any use you make of the works of others.

In the past, this acknowledgement was given in footnotes or endnotes. Both forms of documentation have now been replaced by a new parenthetical style of documentation adopted recently by the MLA, the Modern Language Association. That style, which is characterized by simplicity and ease of use, is the one we shall feature. However, since some instructors insist that a paper dealing with aspects of the social sciences must follow the style recommended by the American Psychological Association (APA), we shall review this style also. We shall present sample student papers in both the MLA and APA styles.

Documenting the Paper with Parenthetical Citations

The idea behind documentation is simple. If you borrow from another's ideas or work, you must document the loan and give due credit to the source from which it came. If you do not, you create the false impression that the goods are your own when they were taken from someone else. This kind of theft is known among scholarly circles as **plagiarism.** Since the currency of scholarship is ideas, it is not farfetched to say that stealing a scholar's idea is the moral equivalent of stealing money from a bank. For this reason, if you use the work or idea of another in your paper, you must acknowledge the borrowing through the use of a certain documenting style.

The parenthetical style of documentation features a clean system of citations made within the text. You mention the name of the author whose work you are quoting and/or even the work itself, and you end by citing a page reference in parentheses. For example, let us say that you are borrowing from *Literature in Critical Perspective,* a book by a writer named Gordon. This is how you might handle it in your text:

```
Walter K. Gordon's Literature in Critical

Perspective offers evidence that literary

interpretation depends as much on the

perspective from which the analysis is conducted

as from the actual substance of the work itself

(10-22).

                      OR

Walter K. Gordon offers evidence that literary

interpretation depends as much on the
```

```
perspective from which the analysis is conducted

as from the actual substance of the work itself

(10-22).
```

And that's that. Within the text, the citation identifies either the writer and the book or the writer only, then ends with the page numbers in parentheses from which the quoted idea was taken. Be sure that each parenthetical reference is treated as a separate item, and that the surname (if not in the text), is included. Complete information about Gordon's book will appear in its alphabetical order on a separate bibliography page titled "Works Cited" (see page 000 for a sample of "Works Cited" entries). On that page it will look like this:

```
Gordon, Walter K., ed. Literature in Critical

      Perspective.  New York:  Appleton, 1968.
```

As you can see, this system has simplicity to recommend it. All actual citations are given within the text itself. A final "Works Cited" page (the new name for bibliography) gives complete publication information about each source.

The rules for using this system are simple to summarize:

1. In the first textual citation, give the full name of the authority:

```
Robert M. Jordon suggests that Chaucer's tales

are held together by seams that are similar to

the exposed beams supporting a Gothic cathedral

(237-38).
```

In subsequent citations, refer to the author by last name:

```
Jordon further suggests that . . . .
```

2. Wherever possible, say why the particular source is important by citing the author's credentials. Doing so is one way to add emphasis and variation to your introduction of a source:

```
Noam Flinker, lecturer in English at the

Ben-Gurion University of the Negev in Israel, an
```

authority on biblical literature, repeatedly

suggests) . . . .

3. If you do not introduce the source in your text, list the author's surname in parentheses at the end of the citation along with a page number:

Democracy is deemed preferable to monarchy

because it protects the individual's rights

rather than his property (Emerson 372).

Note that no comma separates the name from page number.

4. Handle material by up to three authors the same as material by a single author. The form for a textual citation is as follows:

Christine E. Wharton and James S. Leonard take

the position that the mythical figure of Ampion

represents a triumph of the spiritual over the

physical (163).

If the authors are not cited in the text itself, both should be listed in parentheses along with the page number at the end of the citation:

Some have argued that the mythical figure of

Ampion represents a triumph of the spiritual

over the physical (Wharton and Leonard 163).

If the work is by more than three authors, use the name of the first author followed by "et al." or "and others" (without a comma after the name).

(Smith et al. 51).

5. In using two works by the same author, mention the author's name in the text and then separately list each work and page number in parentheses:

Feodor Dostoevsky declares that the

"underground" rebel is representative of our

```
society (Underground 3).    He seems to confirm

this view in Raskolnikov's superman speech

(Crime 383-84), where he identifies . . . .
```

Or, if you don't mention the author's name in the text but are citing two works by the same person, make clear in parentheses which title is being cited and give the page number:

```
That the "underground" rebel is representative

of our society is an idea that has its roots in

the work itself (Dostoevsky, Underground 3).

This idea has been echoed in Raskolnikov's

superman speech (Dostoevsky, Crime 383-84.)
```

Note the use of abbreviations. The full title of the first work is *Notes from the Underground,* of the second *Crime and Punishment.* In your parenthetical citation, however, you need use only a key word from the title.

6. To refer to a specific passage in a multivolume work, give the author, volume number followed by colon and a space, and the page reference:

```
Other historians disagree with this view (Durant

2:25). . . .
```

If the reference is meant to include the entire volume rather than a specific passage in it, give the name of the author followed by a comma, and the abbreviation "vol." followed by the volume number:

```
This view of history has been rejected entirely

by some commentators (Durant, vol. 2).
```

7. For a double reference (a quotation within a cited work) use:

```
As Bernard Baruch pointed out, "Mankind has

always thought to substitute energy for reason"

(as qtd.  in Ringer 274).
```

"Works Cited" would contain the following entry:

```
Ringer, Robert J. Restoring the American Dream.

    New York:  Harper, 1979.
```

8. In citing a work by a corporate author: if you did not mention the name of the author in your text, the full or shortened name should appear in parentheses at the end of the citation:

```
That peanut butter is a good source of nutrients

is often overlooked by parents. Yet analysis has

shown that it is a rich balance of protein,

carbohydrates, and calories (Consumer Reports

69).
```

9. When quoting a short passage of poetry: if the passage is incorporated into your text, set it off with quotation marks; use a slash (with a space before and after) to mark separate lines; place the documentation in parentheses followed by a period immediately after the quotation. Here is an example:

```
Byron's profound sense of alienation is echoed

in canto 3 of Childe Harold's Pilgrimage:  "I

have not loved the world, nor the World me:  / I

have not flattered its rank breath, nor bowed /

to its idolatries a patient knee" (190-91).
```

10. For quoted material set off from the text: Quotations longer than four lines are indented ten spaces, double spaced, and set off from the text without quotation marks (unless the quotation itself uses quotation marks). Place the parenthetical citation after the last period. Here is an example:

```
According to an editorial in the May 1, 1981,

issue of Science, the air force, early on, had

designs on the shuttle:

        NASA officials, at least, have no regrets

        over redesigning the shuttle to accommodate

        military payloads or paying for the
```

```
construction of two shuttle orbiters (out

of four) intended for predominantly

military use. (520)
```

Shorter quotations of four lines or less are introduced in the text and reproduced with quotations marks:

```
According to Carl Sagan, some researchers

believe that one function of dreams may be "to

wake us up a little, every now and then, to see

if anyone is about to eat us" (151).
```

11. In citing a play by act, scene, and line: use Arabic numerals divided by periods to indicate major divisions in a play. For example, a quotation from Act 1, Scene 1, lines 146–53 of Shakespeare's *King Lear* would be treated as follows:

```
When Lear attempts to divide his kingdom among

his daughters, only the Earl of Kent, his

faithful friend, opposes him:

    Let it fall rather, though the fork invade

    The region of my heart; be Kent unmannerly,

    When Lear is mad. What wilt thou do, old

    man?

    Think's though that duty shall have dread

    to speak,

    When power to flattery bows? To plainness

    honour's bound,

    When majesty stoops to folly. Reverse thy

    doom;

    And, in thy best consideration, check

    This hideous rashness . . . .

    (Lear 1.1.146-53)
```

12. Use Arabic numerals for books, parts, volumes, and chapters of works; for acts, scenes, and lines of plays; for cantos, stanzas, and lines of poetry.

In-text citations:

Volume 2 of *Civilization Past and Present*
Book 3 of *Paradise Lost*
Part 2 of *Crime and Punishment*
Act 3 of *Hamlet*
Chapter 1 of *The Great Gatsby*

Parenthetical documentation:

(*Tmp.* 2.2.45–50) for Act 2, Scene 2, lines 45–50 of Shakespeare's *Tempest.* Notice that the titles of well-known masterpieces may be abbreviated.
(*GT* 2.1.3) for Part 2, Chapter 1, page 3 of *Gulliver's Travels* by Jonathan Swift.
(*Jude* 15) for page 15 of the novel *Jude the Obscure* by Thomas Hardy.
(*PL* 7.5–10) for Book 7, lines 5–10 of *Paradise Lost* by John Milton.
(*FQ* 1.2.28.1–4) for Book 1, canto 2, stanza 28, lines 1–4 of *The Faerie Queene* by Edmund Spenser.

13. Content notes: A content note is used to make a side remark about some assertion in your text without interrupting the flow of the writing. The note is placed at the bottom of the page and separated from the last line of the text by four spaces. Its initial line is indented five spaces with single spacing between the sentences. A superscript numeral in the text indicates the presence of the note. Here is an example from a student paper:

```
The centaur, being half horse and half man,

symbolized both the wild and benign aspect of

nature. Thus the coexistence of nature and

culture was expressed.¹
```

At the bottom of the page appeared the following content note:

```
    ¹It should be noted that the horse part is

the lower and more animalistic area whereas the
```

```
human portion is the upper, including the heart

and head.
```

Interruptions like these are rarely necessary in the typical paper, but when they are, the place for them is in a content note.

14. Vary your introductions. The parenthetical system is uncomplicated and easy to use. With the exception of the rare content note, superscript numerals have been eliminated along with the tiresome chore of counting and reserving lines on the bottom of a page for footnotes. But it is easy to become predictable in the introduction of each source, with the effect of giving the paper a wooden and stilted style. If you therefore cite one source this way:

```
Neeli Cherkovski argued that in 1958

Ferlinghetti began experimenting with newer

poetic forms and was influenced by the emerging

beat movement (91).
```

use an entirely different introduction for the next. Perhaps you might simply use a parenthetical citation without mentioning the author:

```
This attitude is central to the archetypal

approach used in interpreting poetry (Fiedler

519).
```

Our point is that you should vary the wording of your introductions as conscientiously as you would avoid writing several identically constructed sentences in a row.

Plagiarism

Earlier, we defined plagiarism. Citing without an acknowledged source is perhaps the most blatant instance of plagiarism. But there are more venial examples of it that can occur even when a source is cited. Consider, for example, this original passage:

> It is not necessary in a totalitarian dictatorship to be loved by the people. It is enough to be feared, as Stalin was in Soviet Russia. But that Hitler was beloved by the German masses—shocking as

that seemed to me and to the outside world—there could be no doubt. Goering was next in their affection. They loved his down-to-earth saltiness, his jovialness, his crude sense of humor, his common touch. To them he was a hail-fellow-well-met. It never seemed to concern them that he was a brutal, ruthless, unscrupulous killer.

—William L. Shirer, *The Nightmare Years: 1930–1940*, p. 191.

Here is an example of outright plagiarism.

```
There is no question but that Hitler was beloved

by the German people, even though this may seem

shocking to the rest of us. But next to Hitler

in the people's affection, came Goering. They

loved his down-to-earth saltiness, his

jovialness, his crude sense of humor, his common

touch. To them he was a hail-fellow-well-met. It

never seemed to concern them that he was a

brutal, ruthless, unscrupulous killer.
```

Altering a word here and there, the writer has lifted this passage nearly intact from the book by William Shirer but given it no credit. This conveys the impression that the idea is the writer's own rather than stolen property.

Plagiarism can also occur even when the reproduced passage is credited to a source. Here is an example:

```
It was well known to the world that the German

people loved Hitler. What the world did not know

then was that Goering was next in their

affection, that they loved his down-to-earth

saltiness, his jovialness, his sense of humor,

his common touch, and that to them he was a

hail-fellow-well-met (Shirer 191).
```

Even though a source is cited, this passage is still plagiarized because it takes words verbatim from the original without quotation marks to indicate the copying. The theft in this case is one of phrasing and style. Here is how this material should have been handled:

```
It was well known to the world that the German

people loved Hitler. But after Hitler, they also

loved Goering. As Shirer put it, they loved "his

down-to-earth saltiness, his jovialness, his

crude sense of humor, his common touch," and

seemed untroubled by the fact that he "was a

brutal, ruthless, unscrupulous killer" (191).
```

The quotation marks tell us that the writer has gotten these words from someone else.

Exactly what kinds of material do you have to document? The rule of thumb is based on common sense and fairness. If an assertion is repeated by a minimum of five sources, you may regard it as general knowledge and not give credit. But if an idea, no matter how well known, is memorably and cleverly phrased by another writer, you should not repeat it word for word without giving the originator credit. Play fair with your sources, be forthright in presenting your own opinions, and plagiarism will not be an issue in your paper.

Writing the Rough Draft

To write the paper, have your outline and thesis in front of you, arrange your note cards in the order of appearance in the paper, and begin. Remember that it is normal to have to make several stabs at a beginning. With a thorough outline and a stack of note cards to support all your major points, you should have a solid framework for the paper. Now it is merely a matter of bricking it in, word by word, sentence by sentence.

You are expected to write the paper in a formal style, using no colloquialisms or slang unless as part of quoted material. Don't refer to yourself as "I" unless your teacher has consented to your writing on an intensely autobiographical paper (which would be a most peculiar research assignment). Similarly, you should not refer to yourself with the royal "we," and you should never use "you" as a pronoun referring to an unspecified person. In short, you are expected to adopt a scholarly tone—not a pedantic one—and to use words and phrases that reflect your objectivity in dealing with the material. Review the discussion of voice and style in Chapter 2 if any of this is unclear to you.

The rough draft of the paper is due at the end of the fourth week. Happily, you are now almost done. The greatest labor is behind you, and what lies ahead are only the finishing touches.

Fifth Week: the Final Paper Complete with a Bibliography

At the end of the fifth week, you should submit a final paper containing the following: (1) an outline (or abstract), (2) title page, (3) text of the paper, (4) content notes (if any), and (5) bibliography ("Works Cited" or "References"). The facsimile on page 402 shows the layout of the title page of a student paper following the MLA style. Notice that no separate title page is necessary. The first page of the paper is the title page. Type the body of the paper double spaced with 1-inch margins. Number each page consecutively in the upper right corner. Number the outline with small Roman numerals; then number the main body of the paper with Arabic numerals. Beginning with page 2, precede the page number with your last name in case a page is misplaced. If your paper contains content notes, place them on a separate page entitled "Notes." Make sure that each content note is numbered and corresponds to the proper superscript in the text. For an APA-style paper, follow the format used in the student model.

Mainly, what will be left is to compile a "Works Cited" page in which you cite all the sources paraphrased, summarized, or quoted in the paper. Before we discuss the forms these citations should take, it is useful to summarize some basic conventions that apply to the "Works Cited" page:

1. Cited works must be listed on a separate page.
2. The title "Works Cited" must be centered one inch from the top of the page with two spaces between the title and the first citation.
3. Entries are listed alphabetically by the surname of the first author. Subsequent authors are listed with their names in normal order. Anonymously written works are entered alphabetically by the first word of the title, omitting all articles such as "a," "the," or "an."
4. Subsequent titles by an already listed author are entered in the line below on a separate line beginning with three hyphens and a period:

```
Lewis, Sinclair.   Babbitt.   New York:   Harcourt,

    1922.

—.Main Street.  New York: Harcourt, 1920.
```

5. Indent the second line of each entry five spaces.
6. Double space throughout.

I. General order for bibliographic references to books in "Works Cited" (MLA)

Bibliographic references to books list items in the following order:

a. Author

The name of the author comes first, alphabetized by surname. If more than one author is involved, invert the name of only the first and follow it by a comma:

```
Brown, Jim, and John Smith
```

For more than three authors, use the name of the first followed by "et al.":

```
Foreman, Charles, et al.
```

In some cases the name of an editor, translator, or compiler will be cited before the name of an author, especially if the actual editing, translating, or compiling is the subject of discussion (see next page).

b. Title

Cite the title in its entirety, including any subtitle, exactly as it appears on the title page. A period follows the title unless the title ends in some other mark, such as a question mark or an exclamation mark. Book titles are underlined; titles of chapters are set off in quotation marks. The initial word and all subsequent words (except for articles and short prepositions) in the title are capitalized. Ignore any unusual typographical style, such as all capital letters, or any peculiar arrangement of capitals and lowercase letters, unless the author is specifically known to insist on such a typography. Separate a subtitle from the title by a colon:

```
D. H. Lawrence:  His Life and Work.
```

c. Name of Editor, Compiler, or Translator

The name(s) of the editor(s), compiler(s), or translator(s) is given in normal order, preceded by "Ed.," "Comp.," or "Trans.":

```
Homer.  The Iliad.  Trans. Richard Lattimore.
```

However, if the editor, translator, or compiler was listed in your textual citation, then his name should appear first, followed by "ed(s).," "trans.," or "comp(s)." and a period:
TEXTUAL CITATION:

```
Gordon's Literature in Critical Perspective

     offers some . . .
```

"WORKS CITED" ENTRY:

```
Gordon, Walter K., ed.  Literature in Critical

     Perspective.  New York:  Appleton, 1968.
```

If you are drawing attention to the translator, use the following format:
TEXTUAL CITATION:

```
The colloquial English of certain passages is

due to Ciardi's translation.
```

"WORKS CITED" ENTRY:

```
Ciardi, John, trans.  The Inferno.  By Dante

     Alighieri.  New York:  NAL, 1961.
```

d. Edition (if Other Than First)

The edition being used is cited if it is other than the first. Cite the edition in Arabic numerals (3rd ed.) without further punctuation. Always use the latest edition of a work, unless you have some specific reason of scholarship for using another.

```
Holman, C. Hugh.  A Handbook to Literature.  3rd

     ed.  Indianapolis:  Odyssey, 1972.
```

Give the name of the series, without quotation marks and not underlined, followed by the number of the work in the series in Arabic numerals, followed by a period:

> Unger, Leonard. T. S. Eliot. University of
>
>   Minnesota Pamphlets on American Writers 8.
>
>   Minneapolis: U of Minnesota P, 1961.

f. Volume Numbers

An entry referring to all the volumes of a multivolume work cites the number of volumes *before* the publication facts:

> Durant, Will, and Ariel Durant The Story of
>
>   Civilization. 10 vols. New York: Simon,
>
>   1968.

An entry for only selected volumes still cites the total number of volumes after the title. The volumes actually used are listed *after* the publication facts:

> Durant, Will, and Ariel Durant. The Story of
>
>   Civilization. 10 vols. New York: Simon,
>
>   1968. Vols. 2 and 3.

For multivolume works published over a number of years, show the total number of volumes, the range of years, and specific volumes if not all of them were actually used.

> Froom, LeRoy Edwin. The Prophetic Faith of Our
>
>   Fathers. 4 vols. Washington: Review and
>
>   Herald, 1950–54, Vol. 1.

g. Publication Facts

Indicate the place, publisher, and date of publication for the work you are citing. A colon follows the place, a comma the publisher, and a period the date unless a page is cited.

You may use a shortened form of the publisher's name as long as it is clear: Doubleday (for Doubleday & Company), McGraw (for McGraw-Hill), Little (for Little, Brown), Scott (for Scott, Foresman), Putnam's (for G. Putnam's Sons), Scarecrow (for Scarecrow Press), Simon (for Simon and Schuster), Wiley (for John Wiley & Sons), Holt (for Holt Rinehart & Winston), Penguin (for Penguin Books), Harper (for Harper & Row). For example:

> Robb, David M., and Jessie J. Garrison. Art in
>
> the Western World. 4th ed. New York:
>
> Harper, 1963.

But list university presses in full (except for abbreviating "University" and "Press") so as not to confuse the press with the university itself: Oxford UP, Harvard UP, Johns Hopkins UP.

> Gohdes, Clarence. Bibliographical Guides to the
>
> Study of Literature of the U.S.A. 3rd ed.
>
> Durham: Duke UP, 1970.

If more than one place of publication appears, give the city shown first on the book's title page.

If more than one copyright date is given, use the latest unless your study is specifically concerned with an earlier edition. (A new printing does not constitute a new edition. For instance, if the title page bears a 1975 copyright date but a 1978 fourth printing, use 1975.) If no place, publisher, date, or page numbering is provided, insert "n.p.," "n.p.," "n.d.," or "n. pag.," respectively. "N. pag." will explain to the reader why no page numbers were provided in the text citation. If the source contains neither author, title, or publication information, supply in brackets whatever information you have been able to obtain:

> Photographs of Historic Castles. [St. Albans,
>
> England]: N.p., n.d. N. pag.
>
> Farquart, Genevieve. They Gave Us Flowers.
>
> N.p.: n.p., 1886.

Dickens, Charles. <u>Master</u> <u>Humphrey's</u> <u>Clock.</u>

    London: Bradbury and Evans, n.d.

h. Page Numbers

Bibliographical entries for books rarely include a page number; however, entries for shorter pieces appearing within a longer work—articles, poems, short stories, and so on, in a collection—should include a page reference. In such a case, supply page numbers for the entire piece, not just for the specific page or pages cited in the text:

Daiches, David. "Criticism and Sociology."

    <u>Literature</u> <u>in</u> <u>Critical</u> <u>Perspective.</u> Ed.

    Walter K. Gordon. New York: Appleton,

    1968. 7–18.

II. Sample bibliographic references to books (MLA)

a. Book with a Single Author

Brodie, Fawn M. <u>Thomas</u> <u>Jefferson:</u> <u>An</u> <u>Intimate</u>

    <u>History.</u> New York: Norton, 1974.

b. Book with Two or More Authors

Bollens, John C., and Grand B. Geyer. <u>Yorty:</u>

    <u>Politics</u> <u>of</u> <u>a</u> <u>Constant</u> <u>Candidate.</u> Pacific

    Palisades: Palisades Pub., 1973.

Allport, Gordon W., Philip E. Vernon, and

    Gardner Lindzey. <u>Study</u> <u>of</u> <u>Values.</u> New

    York: Houghton, 1951.

Brown, Ruth, et al. <u>Agricultural</u> <u>Education</u> <u>in</u> <u>a</u>

    <u>Technical</u> <u>Society:</u> <u>An</u> <u>Annotated</u>

> Bibliography of Resources. Chicago:
> American Library Assn., 1973.

c. Book with a Corporate Author

> American Institute of Physics. Handbook. 3rd
> ed. New York: McGraw, 1972.

NOTE: If the publisher is the same as the author, repeat the information, as shown here:

> Defense Language Institute. Academic Policy
> Standards. Monterey: Defense Language
> Institute, 1982.

d. Book with an Anonymous or Pseudonymous Author

No author listed:

> Current Biography. New York: Wilson, 1976.

If you are able to research the author's name, supply it in brackets:

> [Stauffer, Adlai]. Cloudburst. Knoxville:
> Review and Courier Publishing Assn., 1950.

The name of an author who writes under a pseudonym (or *nom de plume*) may also be given in brackets:

> Eliot, George [Mary Ann Evans]. Daniel
> Deronda. London: n.p., 1876.

e. Work in Several Volumes or Parts

When citing the whole multivolume work:

```
Wallbank, T. Walter, and Alastair M. Taylor.
     Civilization Past and Present.  2 vols.
     New York:  Scott, 1949.
```

When citing a specific volume of a multivolume work:

```
Wallbank, T. Walter, and Alastair M. Taylor.
     Civilization Past and Present.  2 vols.
     New York:  Scott, 1949.  Vol. 2.
```

When citing a multivolume work whose volumes were published over a range of years:

```
Froom, LeRoy Edwin.  The Prophetic Faith of Our
     Fathers.  4 vols.  Washington:  Review and
     Herald, 1950–54.
```

When citing a multivolume work with separate titles:

```
Jacobs, Paul, Saul Landen, and Eve Pell.
     Colonials and Sojourners.  Vol. 2 of To
     Serve the Devil.  4 vols.  New York:
     Random, 1971.
```

f. Work within a Collection of Pieces, All by the Same Author

```
Johnson, Edgar.  "The Keel of the New Lugger."
     The Great Unknown.  Vol. 2 of Sir Walter
     Scott.  3 vols.  New York:  Macmillan,
     1970. 763–76.
```

Selzer, Richard. "Liver." <u>Mortal</u> <u>Lessons.</u> New

York: Simon, 1976. 62–77.

NOTE: The MLA no longer recommends the use of the word "In" preceding the title of the collection or anthology.

---

g. Chapter or Titled Section in a Book

Goodrich, Norma Lorre. "Gilgamesh the

Wrestler." <u>Myths</u> <u>of</u> <u>the</u> <u>Hero.</u> New York:

Orion, 1960.

NOTE: List the chapter or titled section in a book only when it demands special attention.

---

h. Collections: Anthologies, Casebooks, and Readers

Welty, Eudora. "The Wide Net." <u>Story:</u> <u>An</u>

<u>Introduction</u> <u>to</u> <u>Prose</u> <u>Fiction.</u> Ed. Arthur

Foff and Daniel Knapp. Belmont:

Wadsworth, 1966. 159–77.

Cowley, Malcolm. "Sociological Habit Patterns

in Linguistic Transmogrification." <u>The</u>

<u>Reporter.</u> 20 Sept. 1956: 257–61. Rpt. in

<u>Readings</u> <u>for</u> <u>Writers.</u> Ed. Jo Ray McCuen

and Anthony C. Winkler. 2nd ed. New

York: Harcourt, 1977. 489–93.

i. Double Reference—a Quotation within a Cited Work

As Bernard Baruch pointed out. "Mankind has

always thought to substitute energy for reason"
(as qtd. in Ringer 274).

"Works Cited" would then contain the following entry:

Ringer, Robert J. Restoring the American
       Dream. New York: Harper, 1979.

j. Reference Works
(i) Encyclopedias

Ballert, Albert George. "Saint Lawrence
       River." Encyclopaedia Britannica. 1963 ed.
"House of David." Encyclopedia Americana. 1974
       ed.
Berger, Morroe, and Dorothy Willner. "Near
       Eastern Society." International
       Encyclopedia of the Social Sciences. 1968
       ed.

(ii) Dictionaries and annuals

"Barsabbas, Joseph." Who's Who in the New
       Testament (1971).
"Telegony." Dictionary of Philosophy and
       Psychology (1902).

k. Work in a Series
(i) A numbered series

Auchincloss, Louis. Edith Wharton. University of

Minnesota Pamphlets on American Writers 12.

Minneapolis: U of Minnesota P, 1961.

(ii) An unnumbered series

Miller, Sally. The Radical Immigrant. The

Immigrant Heritage of America Series. New

York: Twayne, 1974.

l. Reprint

Babson, John J. History of the Town of

Gloucester, Cape Ann, Including the Town of

Rockport. 1860. New York: Peter Smith,

1972.

Thackeray, William Makepeace. Vanity Fair.

London, 1847–48. New York: Harper, 1968.

m. Edition

Perrin, Porter G., and Jim W. Corder. Handbook

of Current English. 4th ed. Glenview:

Scott, 1975.

Craig, Hardin, and David Bevington, eds. The

Complete Works of Shakespeare. Rev. ed.

Glenview: Scott, 1973.

n. Edited Work

If the work of the editor(s)—introduction, notes, or editorial comments—rather than that of the author(s) is being discussed, place the name of the editor(s) first, followed by a comma, followed by "ed." or "eds.":

Rowland, Beryl, ed. <u>Companion</u> <u>to</u> <u>Chaucer:</u>
  <u>Studies</u>. New York: Oxford UP, 1979.

If you are stressing the text of the author(s), place the author(s) first:

Twain, Mark. <u>Letters</u> <u>from</u> <u>Earth.</u> Ed. Bernard
  DeVoto. New York: Harper, 1962.
Clerc, Charles. "Goodbye to All That: Theme,
  Character and Symbol in <u>Goodbye,</u> <u>Columbus."</u>
  <u>Seven</u> <u>Contemporary</u> <u>Short</u> <u>Novels.</u> Ed.
  Charles Clerc and Louis Leiter. Glenview:
  Scott, 1969. 106-33.

o. Book Published in a Foreign Country

Vialleton, Louis. <u>L'Origine</u> <u>des</u> <u>êtres</u> <u>vivants.</u>
  Paris: Plon, 1929.
Ransford, Oliver. <u>Livingston's</u> <u>Lake:</u> <u>The</u> <u>Drama</u>
  <u>of</u> <u>Nyasa.</u> London: Camelot, 1966.

p. Introduction, Preface, Foreword, or Afterword

Davidson, Marshall B. Introduction. <u>The</u> <u>Age</u> <u>of</u>
  <u>Napoleon.</u> By J. Christopher Herold. New
  York: American Heritage, 1963.

q. Translation

Symons, John Addington, trans. <u>Autobiography</u> <u>of</u>
  <u>Benvenuto</u> <u>Cellini.</u> By Benvenuto Cellini.
  New York: Washington Square, 1963.

r. Book of Illustrations

    Janson, H. W. History of Art: A Survey of the

        Major Visual Arts from the Dawn of History

        to the Present. With 928 illustrations,

        including 80 color plates. Englewood

        Cliffs: Prentice and Abrams, 1962.

s. Foreign Title

Use lower case lettering for foreign titles except for the first word and proper names:

    Vischer, Lukas. Basilius der Grosse. Basel:

        Reinhard, 1953.

Supply a translation of the title or city if it seems necessary. Place the English version in brackets immediately following the original, not underlined:

    Bruckberger, R. L. Dieu et la politique [God

        and Politics]. Paris: Plon, 1971.

III. General order for bibliographic references to periodicals in "Works Cited" (MLA)

Bibliographic references to periodicals list items in the following order:

a. Author

List the author's surname first, followed by a comma, followed by the first name or initials. If there is more than one author, follow the same format as for books.

b. Title of the Article

List the title in quotation marks, followed by a period inside the quotation marks unless the title itself ends in a question mark or exclamation mark.

c. Publication Information

List the name of the periodical, underlined, with any introductory article omitted, followed by a space and a volume number, followed by a space and the year of publication within parentheses, followed by a colon, a space, and page numbers for the entire article, not just for the specific pages cited:

```
Smith, Irwin.  "Ariel and the Masque in The

     Tempest."  Shakespeare Quarterly 21

     (1970):  213-22.
```

Journals paginated anew in each issue require the issue number following the volume number, separated by a period:

```
Beets, Nicholas.  "Historical Actuality and

     Bodily Experience."  Humanitas 2.1 (1966):

     15-28.
```

Some journals may use a month or season designation in place of an issue number:

```
2 (Spring 1966):  15-28.
```

Magazines that are published weekly or monthly require only the date, without a volume number:

```
Isaacson, Walter.  "After Williamsburg."  Time

     13 June 1983:  12-14.
```

Newspapers require the section or part number, followed by the page:

```
Rumberger, L.  "Our Work, Not Education, Needs

     Restructuring."  Los Angeles Times, 24 May

     1984, pt. 2:  5.
```

d. Pages

If the pages of the article are scattered throughout the issue (for example, pages 30, 36, 51, and 52), the following formats can be used:

```
30, 36, 51, 52 (This is the most precise method
and should be used when only three or four pages
are involved.)
30 and passim (page 30 and here and there
throughout the work)
30ff. (page 30 and the following pages)
30+ (beginning on page 30)
```

IV. Sample bibliographic references to periodicals (MLA)

a. Anonymous Author

```
"Elegance Is Out."  Fortune 13 Mar. 1978:  18.
```

b. Single Author

```
Sidey, Hugh.  "In Defense of the Martini."  Time
     24 Oct. 1977:  38.
```

c. More Than One Author

```
Ferguson, Clyde, and William R. Cotter.  "South
     Africa--What Is to Be Done."  Foreign
     Affairs 56 (1978):  254-74.
```

If three authors have written the article, place a comma after the second author, followed by "and" and the name of the third author. If more than three authors have collaborated, list the first author's name, inverted, followed by a comma and "et al."

Enright, Frank, et al.

d. Journal with Continuous Pagination Throughout the Annual Volume

Paolucci, Anne.   "Comedy and Paradox in

Pirandello's Plays."   <u>Modern Drama</u> 20

(1977):   321–39.

e. Journal with Separate Pagination for Each Issue

When each issue of a journal is paged separately, include the issue number (or month or season); page numbers alone will not locate the article since every issue begins with page 1.

Cappe, Walter H.   "Toward More Effective

Justice."   <u>The Center Magazine</u> 11.2

(1978):   2–6.

Mangrum, Claude T.   "Toward More Effective

Justice."   <u>Crime Prevention Review</u> 5 (Jan.

1978):   1–9.

Brown, Robert.   "Physical Illness and Mental

Health."   <u>Philosophy and Public Affairs</u> 7

(Fall 1977):   18–19.

f. Monthly Magazine

Miller, Mark Crispin.   "The New Wave in Rock."

<u>Horizon</u> Mar. 1978:   76–77.

Davis, Flora, and Julia Orange.   "The Strange

Case of the Children Who Invented Their Own

Language." <u>Redbook</u> Mar. 1978: 113, 165–67.

g. Weekly Magazine

```
Eban, Suzy.  "Our Far-Flung Correspondents."
        The New Yorker 6 Mar. 1978:  70-81.
"Philadelphia's Way of Stopping the Shoplifter."
        Business Week 6 Mar. 1972: 57-59.
```

h. Newspaper

```
Tanner, James.  "Disenchantment Grows in OPEC
        Group with Use of U.S. Dollar for Oil Pric-
        ing."  Wall Street Journal 9 Mar. 1978:  3.
```

List the edition and section of the newspaper if specified, as in the examples below:

```
Southerland, Daniel.  "Carter Plans Firm Stand
        with Begin."  Christian Science Monitor 9
        Mar. 1978, western ed.:  1, 9.
Malino, Emily.  "A Matter of Placement."
        Washington Post 5 Mar. 1978:  L 1.
```

i. Editorial

If the section or part is labeled with a numeral rather than a letter, then the abbreviation "sec." or "pt." must appear before the section number. For example, see the unsigned editorial below.
Signed:

```
Futrell, William.  "The Inner City Frontier."
        Editorial.  Sierra 63.2 (1978):  5.
```

Unsigned:

```
"Criminals in Uniform."  Editorial.  Los Angeles
        Times 7 Apr. 1978, pt. 2:  6.
```

j. Letter to the Editor

Korczyk, Donna. Letter. <u>Time</u> 20 Mar. 1978:   4.

k. Critical Review

Andrews, Peter. Rev. of <u>The Strange Ride of</u>
    <u>Rudyard Kipling: His Life and Works,</u> by
    Angus Wilson. <u>Saturday Review</u> 4 Mar.
    1978:   24–25.

Daniels, Robert V. Rev. of <u>Stalinism: Essays in</u>
    <u>Historical Interpretations,</u> ed. Robert C.
    Tucker. <u>The Russian Review</u> 37 (1978):
    102–103.

"Soyer Sees Soyer." Rev. of <u>Diary of an Artist,</u>
    by Ralph Soyer. <u>American Artist</u> Mar.
    1978:   18–19.

Rev. of <u>Charmed Life,</u> by Diane Wynne Jones.
    <u>Booklist</u> 74 (Feb. 1978):   1009.

l. Published Interview

Leonel J. Castillo, Commissioner, Immigration
    and Naturalization Service.   Interview.
    Why the Tide of Illegal Aliens Keeps
    Rising. <u>U.S. News and World Report</u> 20 Feb.
    1978:   33–35.

m. Published Address or Lecture

Trudeau, Pierre E. "Reflections on Peace and
    Security." Address to Conference on

```
Strategies for Peace and Security in the
Nuclear Age, Guelph, Ont., Can., 27 Oct.
1983.   Rpt. in Vital Speeches of the Day 1
Dec. 1983:   98-102.
```

V. Nonprint materials (MLA)

Since nonprint materials come in many forms and with varied information, the rule to follow when dealing with them is to provide as much information as is available for retrieval.

a. Address or Lecture

```
O'Banion, Terry.   "The Continuing Quest for
Quality."   Address to California Assn. of
Community Colleges.   Sacramento, 30 Aug.
1983.
Schwilck, Gene L.   "The Core and the
Community."   Lecture to Danforth
Foundation.   St. Louis, 16 Mar. 1978.
```

For how to handle the reprint of an address or lecture appearing in a periodical, see IV.m.

b. Art Work

```
Angelico, Beato.   Madonna dei Linaioli.   Museo
de San Marco, Firenze.
```

Notice that titles of works of art must be underlined.

c. Computer Source

A computer citation will refer to either: (1) a computer program, that is, information received directly from a data bank, or (2) a written publication retrieved by a computer base.

(i) Computer program

First, list the primary creator of the database as the author. Second, give the title of the program underlined, followed by a period. Third, write "Computer software," followed by a period. Fourth, supply the name of the publisher of the program, followed by a comma and the date the program was issued. Finally, give any additional information necessary for identification and retrieval. This additional information should include, for example, the kind of computer for which the software was created, the number of kilobytes (units of memory), the operating system, and the program's form (cartidge, disk, or cassette):

```
Moshell, J. M., and C. E. Hughes.  Imagination:

     Picture Programming.  Computer software.

     Wiley, 1983.  Apple II/IIe, 64KB, disk.
```

(ii) Source retrieved from a database

Entire articles and books are now being stored in huge databases, with companies like ERIC, CompuServe, The Source, Mead Data Control (Nexis, Lexis), and many others providing the access service. These sources should be listed as if they appeared in print, except that you will also list the agency providing the access service, preceded by "rpt." to indicate "reprinted by." If possible, list any code or file associated with the source:

```
Cohen, Wilbur J.  "Lifelong Learning and Public

     Policy."  Community Services Catalyst 9

     (Fall 1979):  4-5. ERIC; rpt. Dialog File

     1, item EJ218031.
```

d. Film

Film citations should include the director's name, the title of the film (underlined), the name of the leading actor(s), the distributor, and the date of showing. Information on the producer, writer, and size or length of the film may also be supplied, if necessary to your study:

```
Ross, Herbert, dir.  The Turning Point.  With

     Anne Bancroft, Shirley MacLaine, Mikhail
```

> Baryshnikov, and Leslie Brown.   Twentieth
>
> Century-Fox, 1978.

e. Interview

Citations of interviews should specify the kind of interview, the name (and, if pertinent, the title) of the interviewed person, and the date of the interview:

> Witt, Dr. Charles.   Personal interview.   18 Feb.
>
> 1984.
>
> Carpenter, Edward, librarian at the Huntington
>
> Library, Pasadena.   Telephone interview.   2
>
> Mar. 1978.

f. Musical Composition

Whenever possible, cite the title of the composition in your text, as for instance:

> Bach's <u>Well-Tempered</u> <u>Clavier</u> is a principal
>
> keyboard . . .

However, when opus numbers would clutter the text, cite the composition more fully in "Works Cited":

> Grieg, Edward. Minuet in E minor, op. 7, no. 3.

g. Radio or Television Program

Citations should include the title of the program (underlined), the network or local station, and the city and date of broadcast. If appropriate, the title of the episode is listed in quotation marks before the title of the program, while the title of the series, neither underlined nor in quotation marks, comes after the title of the program. The name of the writer, director, narrator, or producer may also be supplied, if significant to your paper:

<u>Diving</u> <u>for</u> <u>Roman</u> <u>Plunder</u>. Narr. and dir.

    Jacques Cousteau. KCET, Los Angeles. 14

    Mar. 1978.

"Chapter 2." Writ. Wolf Mankowitz. <u>Dickens of</u>

    <u>London.</u> Dir. and prod. Marc Miller.

    Masterpiece Theater. Introd. Alistair

    Cooke. PBS. 28 Aug. 1977.

<u>Dead</u> <u>Wrong.</u> CBS Special. 24 Jan. 1984.

h. Recording (Disk or Tape)

For commercially available recordings, cite the following: composer, conductor, or performer, title of recording or of work(s) on the recording, artist(s), manufacturer, catalog number, and year of issue (if not known, state "n.d."):

Beatles, The. "I Should Have Known Better."

    <u>The</u> <u>Beatles</u> <u>Again.</u> Apple Records, SO-385, n.d.

Bach, Johann Sebastian. Toccata and Fugue in D

    minor, Toccata, Adagio, and Fugue in C

    major, Passacaglia and Fugue in C minor;

    Johann Christian Bach. Sinfonia for Double

    Orchestra, op. 18, no. 1. Cond. Eugene

    Ormandy. Philadelphia Orchestra.

    Columbia, MS 6180, n.d.

Eagle, Swift. <u>The</u> <u>Pueblo</u> <u>Indians.</u> Caedmon, TC

    1327, n.d.

<u>Shakespeare's</u> <u>Othello.</u> With Paul Robeson, Jose

    Ferrer, Uta Hagen, and Edith King.

    Columbia, SL-153, n.d.

Dwyer, Michael. Readings from Mark Twain. Rec.

    15 Apr. 1968. Humorist Society. San

    Bernardino.

Wilgus, D. K. Irish Folksongs. Rec. 9 Mar.

    1969. U of California, Los Angeles,

    Archives of Folklore. T7-69-22. 71/2 ips.

Burr, Charles. Jacket notes. <u>Grofe: Grand</u>

    <u>Canyon Suite.</u> Columbia, MS 6003, n.d.

i. Theatrical Performance

Theatrical performances are cited in the form used for films, with added information on the theater, city, and date of performance. For opera, concert, or dance productions you may also wish to cite the conductor (cond.) or choreographer (chor.). If the author, composer, director, or choreographer should be emphasized, supply that information first.

<u>Getting Out.</u> Dir. Gordon Davidson. By Marsha

    Norman. With Susan Clark. Mark Taper

    Forum, Los Angeles. 2 Apr. 1978.

This citation emphasizes the author:

Durang, Christopher. <u>Beyond Therapy.</u> Dir. John

    Madden. With John Lithgow and Dianne

    Wiest. Brooks Atkinson Theater, New York.

    26 May 1982.

This citation emphasizes the conductor:

Conlon, James, cond. <u>La Bohème.</u> With Renata

    Scotto. Metropolitan Opera. Metropolitan

    Opera House, New York. 30 Oct. 1977.

This citation emphasizes the conductor and the guest performer:

```
Commissiona, Sergiu, cond.  Baltimore Symphony

     Orchestra.  With Albert Markov, violin.

     Brooklyn College, New York.  8 Nov. 1978.
```

This citation emphasizes the choreographer:

```
Baryshnikov, Mikhail, chor.  Swan Lake. American

     Ballet Theatre, New York.  24 May 1982.
```

VI. Special items (MLA)

No standard form exists for every special item you might use in your paper. Again, as a general rule, arrange the information in your bibliographic entry in the following order: author, title, place of publication, publisher, date, and any other information helpful for retrieval. Some examples of common citations follow.

a. Art Work, Published

```
Healy, G.P.A.  The Meeting on the River Queen.

     White House, Washington, DC. Illus. in

     Lincoln:  A Picture Story of His Life.  By

     Stefan Lorent. Rev. and enl. ed. New York:

     Harper, 1957.
```

For how to handle an art work you have actually experienced, see page 633.

b. The Bible

When referring to the Bible, cite the book and chapter within your text (the verse, too, may be cited when necessary):

```
The city of Babylon (Rev. 18.2) is used to

symbolize . . .
```

OR

```
In Rev. 18:2 the city of Babylon is used as a

symbol of . . .
```

In "Works Cited" the following citation will suffice if you are using the King James version:

```
The Bible
```

If you are using another version, specify which:

```
The Bible, Revised Standard Version
```

c. Classical Works in General

When referring to classical works that are subdivided into books, parts, cantos, verses, and lines, specify the appropriate subdivisions within your text:

```
Ovid makes claims to immortality in the last

lines of The Metamorphoses (3. Epilogue).

Francesca's speech (5.118-35) is poignant

because . . .
```

In "Works Cited" these references will appear as follows:

```
Ovid. The Metamorphoses.  Trans. and introd.

        Horace Gregory.  New York:  NAL, 1958.

Alighieri, Dante.  The Inferno.  Trans. John

        Ciardi.  New York:  NAL, 1954
```

d. Dissertation

Unpublished: The title is placed within quotation marks and the work identified by "Diss.":

```
Cotton, Joyce Raymonde.  "Evan Harrington:  An
```

```
          Analysis of George Meredith's Revisions."

          Diss. U of Southern California, 1968.
```

Published: The dissertation is treated as a book, except that the entry includes the label "Diss." and states where and when the dissertation was originally written:

```
     Cortey, Teresa.   Le Rêve dans les contes de

          Charles Nodier.   Diss. U of California,

          Berkeley, 1975.   Washington, DC:   UP of

          America, 1977.
```

e. Footnote or Endnote Citation

A bibliographical reference to a footnote or endnote in a source takes the following form:

```
     Faber, M. D.   The Design Within:   Psychoanalytic

          Approaches to Shakespeare.   New York:

          Science House, 1970.
```

In other words, no mention is made of the note. However, mention of the note should be made within the text itself:

```
     In Schlegel's translation, the meaning is

          changed (Faber 205, n. 9).

     The reference is to page 205, note number 9, of

          Faber's book.
```

f. Manuscript or Typescript

A bibliographical reference to a manuscript or typescript from a library collection should provide the following information: the author, the title or a description of the material, the material's form (ms. for manuscript, ts. for typescript), and any identifying number. If possible, give the name and location of the library or institution where the material is kept.

```
Chaucer, Geoffrey.   Ellesmere ms., E126C9.
        Huntington Library, Pasadena.
The Wanderer.   Ms. Exeter Cathedral, Exeter.
Cotton Vitellius.   Ms., A. SV. British Museum,
        London.
```

g. Pamphlet or Brochure

Citations of pamphlets or brochures should conform as nearly as possible to the format used for citations of books. Give as much information about the pamphlet as is necessary to help a reader find it. Underline the title:

```
Calplans Agricultural Fund.   An Investment in
        California Agricultural Real Estate.
        Oakland:   Calplans Securities, n.d.
```

h. Personal Letter

Published:

```
Wilde, Oscar.   "To Mrs. Alfred Hunt."   25 Aug.
        1880.   The Letters of Oscar Wilde.   Ed.
        Rupert Hart-Davis.   New York:   Harcourt,
        1962.   67-68.
```

Unpublished:

```
    Thomas, Dylan.   Letter to Trevor Hughes.   12
        Jan. 1934.   Dylan Thomas Papers.   Lockwood
        Memorial Library.   Buffalo.
```

Personally received:

```
Highet, Gilbert.   Letter to the author.   15 Mar.
        1972.
```

i. Plays

(i) Classical play

In your text, provide parenthetical references to act, scene, and line(s) of the play:

> Cleopatra's jealousy pierces through her words:
>
> What says the married woman? You may go;
>
> Would she had never given you leave to
>
> come: Let her not say 'tis I that keep you
>
> here; I have no power upon you; hers you
>
> are.
>
> (1.3.20–23)

The reference is to Act I, Scene 3, lines 20–23. In "Works Cited" the play will be cited as follows:

> Shakespeare, William. <u>Antony and Cleopatra.</u> <u>The</u>
>
>   <u>Complete Works of Shakespeare.</u> Ed. Hardin
>
>   Craig and David Bevington. Rev. ed.
>
>   Glenview: Scott, 1973. 1073–1108.

NOTE: When the play is part of a collection, list the pages that cover the entire play.

(ii) Modern play

Many modern plays are published as individual books:

> Miller, Arthur. <u>The Crucible.</u> New York:
>
>   Bantam, 1952.

However, if published as part of a collection, the play is cited as follows:

> Chekhov, Anton, <u>The Cherry Orchard.</u> 1903. <u>The</u>
>
>   <u>Art of Drama.</u> Ed. R. F. Dietrich, William
>
>   E. Carpenter, and Kevin Kerrane. 2nd ed.
>
>   New York: Holt, 1976. 134–56.

NOTE: The page reference is to the entire play.

j. Poems

(i) Classical poem

Lucretius [Titus Lucretius Carus]. Of the
Nature of Things. Trans. William Ellery
Leonard. Backgrounds of the Modern World.
Vol. 1 of The World in Literature. Ed.
Robert Warnock and George K. Anderson.
Chicago: Scott, 1950. 343–53.

Or, if published in one book:

Dante [Dante Alighieri]. The Inferno. Trans.
John Ciardi. New York: NAL, 1954.

(ii) Modern poem
Modern poems are usually part of a larger collection:

Moore, Marianne. "Poetry." Fine Frenzy. Ed.
Robert Baylor and Brenda Stokes. New York:
McGraw, 1972. 372–73.

NOTE: Cite pages covered by the poem.

Or, if the poem is long enough to be published as a book, use the following format:

Byron, George Gordon, Lord. Don Juan. Ed.
Leslie A. Marchand. Boston: Houghton,
1958.

k. Public Documents

Because of their complicated origins, public documents often seem difficult to cite. As a general rule, follow this order: Government. Body. Subsidiary bodies. Title of document (underlined). Identifying code. Place, publisher, and date of publication. Most publications by the federal government are printed by the Government Printing Office, which is abbreviated as "GPO":

(i) The Congressional Record

A citation to the Congressional Record requires only title, date, and page(s):

Cong. Rec. 15 Dec. 1977, 19740.

(ii) Congressional publications

United States. Cong. Senate. Permanent
        Subcommittee on Investigations of the
        Committee on Government Operations.
        Organized Crime--Stolen Securities. 93rd
        Cong., 1st sess. Washington: GPO, 1973.
United States. Cong. House. Committee on
        Foreign Relations. Hearings on S. 2793,
        Supplemental Foreign Assistance Fiscal Year
        1966--Vietnam. 89th Cong., 2nd sess.
        Washington: GPO, 1966.
United States. Cong. Joint Economic Committee
        on Medical Policies and Costs. Hearings.
        93rd Cong., 1st sess. Washington: GPO,
        1973.

(iii) Executive branch publications

United States. Office of the President.
        Environmental Trends. Washington: GPO,
        1981.
United States Dept. of Defense. Annual Report
        to the Congress by the Secretary of
        Defense. Washington, GPO, 1984.

> United States. Dept. of Education. National
>
>> Commission on Excellence in Education. <u>A</u>
>>
>> <u>Nation</u> <u>at</u> <u>Risk:</u> <u>The</u> <u>Imperative</u> <u>for</u>
>>
>> <u>Educational</u> <u>Reform.</u> Washington: GPO,
>>
>> 1983.
>
> United States. Dept. of Commerce. Bureau of
>
>> the Census. <u>Statistical</u> <u>Abstracts</u> <u>of</u> <u>the</u>
>>
>> <u>United</u> <u>States.</u> Washington: GPO, 1963.

(iv) Legal documents

When citing a well-known statute or law, a simple format will suffice:

> US Const. Art. 1, sec. 2.
>
> 15 US Code. Sec. 78j(b). 1964.
>
> US CC Art. 9, pt. 2, par. 9–28.
>
> Federal Trade Commission Act. 1914.

When citing a little-known statute, law, or other legal agreement, provide all the information needed for retrieval:

> "Agreement Between the Government of the United
>
>> States of America and the Khmer Republic
>>
>> for Sales of Agricultural Commodities."
>>
>> <u>Treaties</u> <u>and</u> <u>Other</u> <u>International</u>
>>
>> <u>Agreements.</u> Vol. 26, pt. 1. TIAS No.
>>
>> 8008. Washington: GPO, 1976.

Names of court cases are abbreviated and the first important word of each party is spelled out: "Brown v. Board of Ed." stands for "Oliver Brown versus the Board of Education of Topeka, Kansas." Cases, unlike laws, are italicized in the text but not in "Works Cited." Text: *Miranda v. Arizona.* "Works Cited": Miranda v. Arizona. The following information must be supplied in the order listed: (1) name of the first plaintiff and the first defendant, (2) volume, name, and page (in that order) of the law report cited, (3) the place and name of the court that decided the case, (4) the year in which the case was decided:

```
Richardson v. J. C. Flood Co.   190 A. 2d 259.
     D.C. App. 1963.
```

Interpreted, the above means that the Richardson v. J. C. Flood Co. case can be found on page 259 of volume 190 of the Second Series of the *Atlantic Reporter.* The case was settled in the District of Columbia Court of Appeals during the year 1963.

For further information on the proper form for legal citations, consult *A Uniform System of Citation,* 12th ed. Cambridge: Harvard Law Rev. Assn., 1976.

l. Quotation from a Secondary Source

Whenever possible, use primary sources. However, if only a secondary source is available, place the abbreviation "qtd. in" ("quoted in") before the secondary source cited in your parenthetical reference:

```
Samuel F.B. Morse said, "I cannot be happy

unless I am pursuing the intellectual branch of

art" (quoted in Eliot 45).  "Works Cited" will

then contain this entry:


Eliot, Alexander.  Three Hundred Years of

     American Painting.  New York:  Time, 1957.
```

m. Report

Titles of reports in the form of pamphlets or books require underlining. When a report is included within the pages of a larger work, the title is set off in quotation marks. The work must be identified as a report:

```
The Churches Survey Their Task.  Report of the

     Conference on Church, Community, and

     State.  London:  Allen & Unwin, 1937.

Luxenberg, Stan.  "New Life for New York Law."

     Report on New York Law School.  Change 10

     (Nov. 1978):  16-18.
```

n. Table, Graph, Chart, or Other Illustration

If the table, graph, or chart has no title, identify it as a table, graph, or chart:

```
National Geographic Cartographic Division.

    Graph on imports drive into U.S. market.

    National Geographic 164 (July 1983):  13.
```

NOTE: The descriptive label is not underlined or set off in quotation marks.

```
Benson, Charles S.  "Number of Full-Time

    Equivalent Employees, by Industry,

    1929-1959."  Table.  The Economics of

    Public Education.  Boston:  Houghton,

    1961.  208.
```

This time the table has a title, so it is set off in quotation marks.

NOTE: All tables, graphs, charts, and other illustrations should be numbered for easy reference.

o. Thesis

See VI. d., "Dissertation," (page 374).

Sample Student Paper (MLA Style)

The following sample research paper graphically illustrates the extent to which a conscientious student must be prepared to rewrite and revise a work. We include a draft of the paper, showing the corrections the student made in her own hand during rewriting. Also included is the finished paper along with the student's outline and "Works Cited" page. The note cards incorporated into the text are reproduced on the facing left-hand pages.

Meticulously researched and written in a clear and unpretentious style, this paper can serve as a model for your own efforts at writing and rewriting a research paper.

Bullard 9   Introduction
Cassatt was born on May 22, 1844, in
Allegheny City, Pennsylvania. Full name:
Mary Stevenson Cassatt.

Bullard 90   Introduction
Cassatt is described as "America's
foremost woman painter," who entered "the
male dominated art world "at a time when
most women were still restricted to
household duties and motherhood.

Sweet 154   Introduction
Cassatt received recognition as an
art advisor for prestigious art
collectors in the years after 1889.

Sweet XIV   Childhood Years
As a child she traveled extensively
throughout Europe with her family.

Bullard 11   Childhood Years
In 1851, Cassatt and her family moved
to Europe, settling in Paris, then
Heidelberg then Darmstadt, Germany.
(altogether four years).

Draft:

Annette Mikailian

Professor McCuen

English 101

20 November 1985

Mary Cassatt and Impressionism

Born on May 22, 1844, in Allegheny City,
Pennsylvania, Mary Stevenson Cassatt, "America's
foremost woman painter", _daringly_ entered the male-
dominated art world" at a time when most women
were still _restricted_ ~~expected only to aspire~~ to household
duties and motherhood (Bullard 9, 90). This
liberated and fascinating ~~liberated~~ woman became accepted as
the only American female artist ever to be
accepted in the Impressionist group. In addition
to her _fame_ ~~notability~~ as an artist, Cassatt also
received recognition as an art adviser for
prestigious art collectors in the years after
1889 (Sweet 154).

~~Being~~ _B_born the fortunate daughter of a
wealthy businessman, Mary Cassatt was _able_ ~~fortunate~~
~~enough~~ to travel extensively, ~~and~~ spending _weeks and months_ ~~much~~
of her childhood in Europe ~~with her family~~
(Sweet xiv). Mary was only seven years old when
~~in 1851~~, she and her family moved to Europe, _for a period of four years_
settling first in Paris, then Heidelberg and

Breeskin 8   Influences
"The fact that she was taken to live in
Europe during her childhood, was in all
likelihood, important in the formation of her
determination to become an artist."

Bullard 11   Academic Background
In the fall of 1861, Cassatt enrolled at the
Pennsylvania Academy of the Fine Arts for
a period of four frustrating years.

Hale 31   Academic Background
Lack of parental support:
"I would almost rather see you dead" her
father had said to her when she announced
her determination to become a professional
artist.

Bullard 11   Academic Background
Mary, dissatisfied with her studies at the
Pennsylvania Academy, decided to leave for
Europe to conduct an independent study of the
old masters.

Bullard 9   Apprenticeship in France
In the summer of 1866, Mary Cassatt went
to Paris. She attended classes in the workshop
of the prominent French painter Charles Chaplin.

Bullard 12   Apprenticeship in France
Cassatt studied the old masters in the
great museums of Paris.

Darmstadt ~~Germany, for a period of four years~~ (Bullard 11). On their return to America in ~~late~~ *the winter of* 1855, the Cassatt family stopped in Paris to see the Exposition Universelle, the art section of which featured large exhibitions of such ~~very~~ *famous* ~~well-known~~ artists as Ingres, Delacroix, and Gustave Courbet (Bullard 11). "The fact that she was taken to live in Europe during her childhood," declares the art critic A. D. Breeskin ~~(Graphic Art 8)~~, "was in all likelihood important in the formation of her determination to become an artist," *(Graphic Art 8).*

Eager to learn, and despite her family's opposition to her pursuit of the Arts, young ~~and~~ ambitious Mary began her extensive artistic studies ~~when~~ *when* in the fall of 1861, she enrolled at the ~~Pennsylvania~~ Academy of the Fine Arts, *in Pennsylvania for* *where she spent* ~~a period of~~ four frustrating years *trying to adjust to the restrictions* (Bullard 11) *of fossilized* "I would almost rather see you dead" her father *teachers determined to* had said to her when she announced her *keep Mary from* determination to become a professional artist *trying her own* (Hale 31). But Mary, dissatisfied with her *artistic wings.* studies at the Academy, shocked her father even further when she informed him of her decision to leave America for Europe in an attempt to study the old masters independently (Bullard 11).

Her decision to go to Europe was most likely based upon the fact that Europe at that time was the leading art center in the world.

Bullard 12   Apprenticeship in France
Mary, who possessed an "inquiring mind,"
probably attended the Paris World's Fair of 1867,
where a private collection of Gustave Courbet's
and Edouard Manet's paintings were exhibited.

Bullard 12   Apprenticeship in France
This was an important factor in her development
as an artist, because her works in the years before
1895 were influenced by these two leading exponents
of Realism, who challenged the "artificial" style
of the French Art Academy.

Rugoff 103   Back home in the U.S.
With the outbreak of the Franco-Prussian
War in 1870, Cassatt was forced to return
home. She began selling some of the paintings
she had created in Paris.

Mathews 73   Back home in the U.S.
Cassatt was terribly unhappy in the U.S.:
"I am in such low spirits over my prospects
that although I would prefer Spain, I would
jump at anything in preference to America."

Rugoff 104   Academic Training in Italy
In 1872, Mary returned to Europe, settling
in Parma, Italy, for a period of eight months.
She attended classes at the Art Academy.

Bullard 12   Academic Training in Italy
In Italy, Mary studied Antonio Correggio's
depictions of the Madonna and Child, which
greatly influenced her later impressionistic
works.

Where else but in the beautiful city of Paris could Mary find so many large collections of masterpieces? ~~in art~~. *Thus, in the summer of 1866,* ~~With this in mind, she embarked~~ the streets of Paris *became Mary's daily haunts. There, art historian* ~~in the summer of 1866, where for a short time~~ *John Bullard tells us,* she attended classes in the workshop of the prominent French painter Charles Chaplin (Bullard 9). *However, these studies did not last long. Mary, too much of a free spirit and* ~~But Mary,~~ ~~being~~ too independent to be confined to any type of academic restrictions, decided to conduct independent studies in the great museums of Paris, by copying the great works of the old masters ~~on her own~~ (Bullard 12). Mary, who possessed an "inquiring mind," must have attended the Paris World's Fair of 1867, where a private collection of Gustave Courbet's and Edouard Manet's paintings were exhibited (Bullard 12). This was an important factor in her development as an artist, because Cassatt's works in the years before 1875 were largely influenced by these two leading exponents of Realism, who challenged the "artificial" style of the French Art Academy (Bullard 12).

With the beginning of the Franco-Prussian War in 1870, Cassatt returned home to Philadelphia where she began selling some of the paintings she had created in Paris (Rugoff 103). However, soon *dissatisfied* ~~frustrated and unhappy~~ with her accomplishments here in the United States, Mary decided to return to Europe where she could

Bullard 12   Growing Success
In the spring of 1872, Cassatt sent her first
acceptable painting to the Paris Salon.
The painting is entitled _Before the Carnival_.
Due to her parents' opposition, Mary submitted
this painting under the name "Mlle. Mary
Stevenson."

Fine 130   Growing Success
In 1874, Mary sent her second acceptable
salon entry entitled _Madame Cortier_.
Edgar Degas remarked: "It is true, there
is someone who feels as I do."

Rugoff 104   Success at last
From 1875-1876, Mary exhibited at the
Paris Salon, but her fifth entry in 1877 was
denied because her paintings had become
Impressionistic in style. Degas, however, was
impressed by her 1874 salon entry and asked
her to join the Impressionist group.

Bullard 13   Cassatt joins Impressionist
"I accepted with joy. Now I could work
with absolute independence without considering
the opinion of a jury. I had already recognized
who were my true masters. I admired Manet,
Courbet, and Degas. I took leave of conventional
art. I began to live."
(Cassatt's reply to Degas' offer).

truly continue her artistic training free of any restrictions. In *a* letter addressed to her closest friend, Emily Sartain, Cassatt wrote: "I *reveals Cassatt's enormous disappointment over her artistic career in america* am in such low spirits over my prospects that although I would prefer Spain I should jump at anything in preference to America" (Mathews 73). Hence, in 1872 Mary returned to Europe, only this time settling in Parma, Italy, where she attended classes at the Art Academy (Rugoff 104). There she studied Antonio Correggio's depictions of the Madonna and Child, which greatly influenced her later Impressionistic works and led her to develop her own famous "mother and child" theme (Bullard 12).

As she progressed in her academic studies, Mary *gradually developed* ~~soon began developing~~ her own artistic style. In the spring of 1872, ~~Cassatt~~ *she* sent her first acceptable painting, ~~to the Paris Salon,~~ entitled Before the Carnival, *to the Paris salon* (Bullard 12). However, due to her family's disapproval of her artistic career, the painting was submitted under the name "Mlle. Mary Stevenson" (Bullard 12). A year later, Mary decided to settle in Paris for the rest of her life. In 1874, she sent her second acceptable Salon entry. This painting, entitled Madame Cortier, captured the attention of the famous Impressionist painter, Edgar Degas, who, upon seeing the painting,

Bullard 14   Degas and Cassatt
Degas was one of the biggest influences
on Cassatt. This influence caused her to
change her style.

Rugoff 104   Degas and Cassatt
Both Degas and Cassatt exhibited in the
Impressionist exhibitions of 1877, '79, '80,
'81, and '86.

Bullard 24   Degas and Cassatt
Degas' influence is most apparent in the
painting called Little Girl in a Blue
Armchair.
  "extensive use of pattern"
  "brushwork"
  "asymmetrical composition"

Personal Comment   Cassatt's Personal Style
Gradually Cassatt developed her own original
style. free from specific influences. she
focused on a "mother and child" theme __
probably making up for the fact that she
had no children of her own.

remarked: "It is true. There is someone who feels as I do" (Fine 130).

For two consecutive years (1875—76) Mary exhibited at the Paris Salon, but was denied her fifth Salon entry in 1877 because her paintings had become Impressionistic in style (Rugoff 104). In the same year, Degas, who was impressed by her 1874 Salon entry, asked her to join the Impressionist group, and Cassatt accepted the offer (Rugoff 104). According to her first biographer, Achille Segard, Cassatt had said:

> I accepted with joy. Now I could work
> with absolute independence without
> considering the opinion of a jury. I
> had already recognized who were my
> true masters. I admired Manet,
> Courbet, and Degas. I took leave of
> conventional art. I began to live
> (qtd. in Bullard 13).

From that moment on, Mary Cassatt's artistic career took a leap forward ~~changed for the better~~. As Cassatt and Degas began working together, a close professional and personal relationship developed between the two artists. Together, they participated in the Impressionist exhibitions of 1877, '79, '80, '81, and '86 (Rugoff 104). Cassatt's artistic style also began to change, as a result of Degas' influence on her works (Bullard 14): she began to apply

Bullard 15   Height of Cassatt's Career

"Her work in the 1870 exhibition was
noticed favorably by several critics, including
Edmond Duranty and J.K. Huysmans."

Breeskin 16   Japanese Influence

Cassatt visited the great Japanese art
exhibition in 1890, held at the Ecole des
Beaux Arts in Paris. Cassatt's works began
to show a strong Oriental influence.

Bullard 52   Japanese Influence

Techniques used in The Bath:
1) rich patterns
2) strong contours
3) solid forms
The Bath is known for its Japanese
influence.

Bullard 16   Final Success

On June 10th of 1891, Mary held her first
one-woman show at Durand-Ruel's, and was
praised by such famous painters as Pissarro
who referred to her works as "rare" and
"exquisite."

Bullard 20   Cassatt's Final Years

In her final years, Cassatt became inactive
as an artist.
She turned bitter due to the loss of her
closest friends.
She began to lose her eyesight.
Mary Cassatt died of diabetes in 1926, at
Chateau de Beaufresne, her summer
palace in France.

paint in a brushy-tonal style, her palette
became colorful, and she began drawing subjects
from everyday life. One of the best examples, in
which Degas's influence is most apparent, is the
painting entitled <u>Little</u> <u>Girl</u> <u>in</u> <u>a</u> <u>Blue</u> <u>Armchair</u>
(1878). The "extensive use of pattern," "the
brushwork," and "the asymmetrical composition"
of this painting are largely attributed to
Degas' influence on Cassatt (Bullard 24).

However, in the 1880's, Cassatt ~~made~~ as advanced
~~obvious advancements~~ noticeably in her career, ~~and~~ her
paintings began to show more originality in
design, and in ~~depicted~~ that subject matter. It was
during this period of time ~~when~~ that Cassatt
developed her famous "mother and child" theme.
~~It is a widely held belief~~ It seems reasonable to conclude that because Cassatt
never married and was unable to have any
children, of her own, she her desire to be a mother ~~was in a way~~
~~gratified~~ gratified through her paintings of mothers with
their children.

Cassatt ~~also~~ began to receive ~~considerable~~ more and more
recognition for her paintings showed at the
Impressionist exhibitions. According to E. J.
Bullard, "her work in the 1879 exhibition was
noticed favorably by several critics, including
Edmond Duranty and J. K. Huysmans" (15).

Mary Cassatt reached the height of her
career in the years between 1890 and 1900. After
she visited the great Japanese art exhibition in

Personal Comment   Conclusion

An outstanding artist and an exceptional woman, Mary Stevenson Cassatt died without even knowing she contributed more than just her paintings to the world. She gave birth to new hopes for all the women in the world who were afraid of reaching the horizons beyond the boundaries of their comfortable homes.

1890, held at l'Ecole des Beaux Arts in Paris, Cassatt's works began to show a strong Oriental influence (Breeskin, Graphic Art 16). For example, the painting entitled The Bath (1892), wherein compositional devices such as solid forms, "rich patterns," and "strong contours" are highly emphasized, shows the Japanese influence on Cassatt (Bullard 52). On June 10th of 1891, Mary Cassatt held her first one-woman show at Durand-Ruel's and was praised by such famous painters as Pissarro, who referred to her show as being "rare" and "exquisite" (Bullard 16). At last, Mary Stevenson Cassatt received the recognition which she deserved so very much as a true professional artist.

Her final years were not productive for Mary Cassatt. She slowly became more and more inactive artistically, moribund and turned bitter due to the loss of her closest friends, and of her eyesight (Bullard 20). Mary Cassatt died of diabetes in 1926 at Chateau de Beaufresne, her summer palace in France (Bullard 20). The art world now treasures her work as belonging to the history of art.

An outstanding artist, and an exceptional woman, Mary Stevenson Cassatt died without even knowing that she contributed more than just her paintings to the world. She had given birth to new hopes for all the women in the world who were afraid of reaching the horizons beyond the boundaries of their comfortable homes.

Works Cited
~~Bibliography~~

Breeskin, Adelyn D., and Donald H. Karshan. The
    Graphic Art of Mary Cassatt. New York:
    Smithsonian Institution P, 1967.

Bullard, E. John. Mary Cassatt New York:
    Watson—Guptill, 1976.

Fine, Elsa H. Women & Art. Totowa, N.J.: Rowman
    and Allanheld, 1978.

Hale, Nancy. Mary Cassatt. New York: Doubleday,
    1975.

Matthews, Nancy M. Cassatt and Her Circle. New
    York: Abbeville, 1984.

Rugoff, Milton. "Cassatt, Mary." Encyclopedia of
    American Art, 1981 ed.

Sweet, Frederick A. Miss Mary Cassatt. Norman,
    Okla.: U of Oklahoma P, 1966.

Final version:

Annette Mikailian

Professor McCuen

English 101

20 November 1986

Mary Cassatt and Impressionism

THESIS: At a time when most women were still in
the kitchen, Mary Cassatt entered the
male—dominated art world and received
recognition as America's foremost woman
painter.

I. The daughter of a prosperous businessman,
Mary Cassatt spent much of her childhood
in Europe with her family.

A. In 1851, the Cassatt family moved to
Europe, settling in Paris and Germany
for the next four years.

1. During her two—year stay in Paris,
Cassatt was exposed to the
artistic life of the French.

2. In 1853, the family moved to
Heidelberg and then Darmstadt,
Germany.

B. Late in 1855, the family returned to
America, stopping in Paris to see the
Exposition Universelle.

663

1. The art section of this world's fair featured large exhibitions of Ingres, Delacroix, and Gustave Courbet.

2. Such an experience at the age of eleven could well have aroused Mary's own desire to become an artist.

II. Mary Cassatt's official artistic studies began when she was seventeen.

A. In the fall of 1861, she enrolled at the Pennsylvania Academy of Fine Arts.

    1. For four years she followed a frustrating academic course of study.

    2. Dissatisfied with her studies at the Pennsylvania Academy, she decided to go to Europe to study the old masters independently.

B. After overcoming the resistance of her parents, Cassatt left for Paris in the summer of 1866.

    1. For a short period of time, Cassatt studied in the atelier of the academic painter Charles Chaplin.

2. But she soon left for independent study in the great public art collections of Paris.

C. As a young student of the Arts, Cassatt was influenced by the many famous artists of that time.

1. In the years before 1875, Manet and Courbet influenced the works of Mary Cassatt.

2. Corregio's depictions of the Madonna and Child influenced Cassatt's later impressionistic works.

3. Degas, the very famous impressionist artist, was the strongest influence on Mary Cassatt.

4. After the Japanese exhibition of 1890, her works began to show the influence of Japanese prints.

III. In 1873 Mary Cassatt decided to settle in Paris for the rest of her life.

A. The decision to settle in Paris proved crucial to Cassatt's development as an artist because Paris was the center of all that was new in art.

      1. Mary first met Degas in 1877, at the third Impressionist exhibition, where she was asked to joint the Impressionist group.

      2. She participated in all five Impressionist exhibitions with Degas.

      3. With Degas' influence she developed her Impressionistic style.

B. Cassatt's most famous works are noted for their "mother and child" theme.

      1. She developed this theme during the 1880s as she began developing her own independent style.

      2. It is said that her love for children was immense, but because she never married, she had no children of her own.

C. Cassatt's most productive years were the 1890s.

      1. She developed a new style, influenced by the Japanese prints.

      2. She was praised by many famous art critics.

D. In her last years, Mary Cassatt turned bitter, due to her partial loss of eyesight.

    1. She became inactive and lonely.

    2. Mary Cassatt died a famous artist, at Chateau de Beaufresne on June 14, 1926, at the age of eighty-two.

Annette Mikailian

Professor McCuen

English 101

20 November 1985

Mary Cassatt and Impressionism

Mary Stevenson Cassatt, "America's foremost woman painter," daringly entered the male-dominated art world at a time when most women were still restricted to household duties and motherhood (Bullard 9, 90). Born on May 22, 1844, in Allegheny City, Pennsylvania, this liberated and fascinating woman became recognized as the only American female artist ever to be accepted in the Impressionist group. In addition to fame as an artist, Cassatt also received recognition as an art adviser for prestigious art collectors in the years after 1889 (Sweet 154).

Born the fortunate daughter of a wealthy businessman, Mary Cassatt was able to travel extensively, spending weeks and months of her childhood in Europe (Sweet xiv). Mary was only seven years old when she and her family moved to Europe for a period of four years, settling first in Paris, then in Heidelberg and Darmstadt (Bullard 11). On their return to America in the winter of 1855, the Cassatt family stopped in Paris to see the Exposition Universelle, the art section of which featured large exhibitions of such famous artists as Ingres, Delacroix, and Gustave Courbet (Bullard 11). "The fact that she was taken to live in Europe during her childhood," declares art critic A. D. Breeskin, "was in all likelihood important in the formation of her determination to become an artist" (<u>Graphic</u> <u>Art</u> 8).

Eager to learn, and despite her family's opposition to her pursuit of the Arts, ambitious young Mary began her extensive artistic studies in the fall of 1861, when she enrolled at the Academy of Fine Arts in Pennsylvania where she spent four frustrating years trying to adjust to the restrictions of fossilized teachers determined to keep Mary from trying her own artistic wings (Bullard 11). "I would almost rather see you dead," her father had warned her when she announced her determination to become a professional artist (Hale 31). But Mary, dissatisfied with her studies at the Academy, shocked her father even further when she informed him of her decision to leave America for Europe in an attempt to study the old masters independently (Bullard 11).

Her decision to go to Europe was doubtless
based upon the fact that Europe at that time was
the leading art center in the world. Where else
but in the beautiful city of Paris could Mary
find so many large collections of masterpieces?
Thus, in the summer of 1866, the streets of
Paris became Mary's daily haunts. There, art
historian John Bullard tells us, she attended
classes in the workshop of the prominent French
painter Charles Chaplin (Bullard 9). However,
these studies did not last long. Mary, too much
of a free spirit and too independent to be
stultified by academic restrictions, decided to
conduct her own independent studies in the great
museums of Paris by copying the great works of
the old masters (Bullard 12). Mary, who
possessed an "inquiring mind," must have
attended the Paris World's Fair of 1867, where a
private collection of Gustave Courbet's and
Edouard Manet's paintings were exhibited
(Bullard 12). This was an important factor in
her development as an artist, because Cassatt's
works in the years before 1875 were largely
influenced by these two leading exponents of
Realism, who challenged the "artificial" style
of the French Art Academy (Bullard 12).

With the outbreak of the Franco-Prussian

War in 1870, Cassatt returned home to
Philadelphia, where she began selling some of
the paintings she had created in Paris (Rugoff
103). However, soon dissatisfied with her
accomplishments here in the United States, Mary
decided to return to Europe, where she could
continue her artistic training free of any
restrictions. A letter addressed to her closest
friend, Emily Sartain, reveals Cassatt's
enormous disappointment over her artistic career
in America: "I am in such low spirits over my
prospects that although I would prefer Spain I
should jump at anything in preference to
America" (Mathews 73). Hence, in 1872 Mary
returned to Europe, only this time settling in
Parma, Italy, where she attended classes at the
Art Academy (Rugoff 104). There she studied
Antonio Correggio's depictions of the Madonna
and Child, which greatly influenced her later
Impressionistic works and led her to develop her
own famous "mother and child" theme (Bullard
12).

    As she progressed in her academic studies,
Mary gradually developed her own individual
artistic style. In the spring of 1872, she sent
her first acceptable painting, entitled <u>Before
the Carnival,</u> to the Paris Salon (Bullard 12).

However, due to her family's disapproval of her
artistic career, the painting was submitted
under the name "Mlle. Mary Stevenson" (Bullard
12). A year later, Mary decided to settle in
Paris for the rest of her life. In 1874, she
sent her second acceptable Salon entry. This
painting, entitled <u>Madame Cortier,</u> captured the
attention of the famous Impressionist painter,
Edgar Degas, who, upon seeing the painting,
remarked: "It is true. There is someone who
feels as I do" (Fine 130).

For two consecutive years (1875-76) Mary
exhibited at the Paris Salon, but was denied her
fifth Salon entry in 1877 because her paintings
had become Impressionistic in style (Rugoff
104). In the same year, Degas, who was
impressed by her 1874 Salon entry, asked her to
join the Impressionist group, and Cassatt
accepted the offer (Rugoff 104). According to
her first biographer, Achille Segard, Cassatt
had said:

> I accepted with joy. Now I could work
> with absolute independence without
> considering the opinion of a jury. I
> had already recognized who were my
> true masters. I admired Manet,
> Courbet, and Degas. I took leave of

conventional art. I began to live.

(qtd. in Bullard 13)

From that moment on, Mary Cassatt's artistic career took a jump upward. As Cassatt and Degas began working together, a close professional and personal relationship developed between the two artists. Together, they participated in the Impressionist exhibitions of 1877, '79, '80, '81, and '86 (Rugoff 104). Cassatt's artistic style also began to change, as a result of Degas' influence on her works (Bullard 14): She began to apply paint in a brushy–tonal style, her palette became colorful, and she began drawing subjects from everyday life. One of the best examples, in which Degas' influence is most apparent, is the painting entitled <u>Little Girl in a Blue Armchair</u> (1878). The "extensive use of pattern," "the brushwork," and "the asymmetrical composition" of this painting are largely attributed to Degas' influence on Cassatt (Bullard 24).

However, in the 1880's, as Cassatt advanced noticeably in her career, her paintings began to show more originality in design and in subject matter. It was during this period of time that Cassatt developed her famous "mother and child" theme. It seems reasonable to conclude that because Cassatt never married and was unable to have any children of her own, she gratified her desire to be a mother through her paintings of mothers with their children.

Cassatt began to receive more and more recognition for her paintings displayed at the Impressionist exhibitions. According to E. J. Bullard, "her work in the 1879 exhibition was noticed favorably by several critics, including Edmond Duranty and J. K. Huysmans" (15).

Mary Cassatt reached the height of her career in the decade between 1890 and 1900. After she visited the great Japanese art exhibition of 1890, held at l'Ecole des Beaux Arts in Paris, Cassatt's works began to show a strong Oriental influence (Breeskin, Graphic Art 16). For example, the painting entitled The Bath (1892), wherein compositional devices such as solid forms, "rich patterns," and "strong contours" are highly emphasized, shows the Japanese influence on Cassatt (Bullard 52). On June 10, 1891, Mary Cassatt held her first one-woman show at Durand-Ruel's and was praised by such famous painters as Pissarro, who referred to her show as being "rare" and "exquisite" (Bullard 16). At last, Mary

Stevenson Cassatt received the recognition she deserved as a true artist.

Her final years were not productive for Mary Cassatt. She became more and more artistically moribund and turned bitter due to the loss of her closest friends and of her eyesight (Bullard 20). Mary Cassatt died of diabetes in 1926 at Chateau de Beaufresne, her summer home in France (Bullard 20). The art world now treasures her work as belonging to the history of art.

An outstanding artist and an exceptional woman, Mary Stevenson Cassatt died without even knowing that she had contributed more than just her paintings to the world. She had given birth to new hopes for all the women in the world who were afraid of reaching the horizons beyond the boundaries of their comfortable homes.

Works Cited

Breeskin, Adelyn D., and Donald H. Karshan. <u>The</u>
    <u>Graphic Art of Mary Cassatt.</u> New York:
    Smithsonian Institution P, 1967.

Bullard, E. John. <u>Mary Cassatt.</u> New York:
    Watson-Guptill, 1976.

Fine, Elsa H. <u>Women & Art.</u> New Jersey: Rowman
    and Allanheld, 1978.

Hale, Nancy. <u>Mary Cassatt.</u> New York:
    Doubleday, 1975.

Matthews, Nancy M. <u>Cassatt and Her Circle.</u> New
    York: Abbeville, 1984.

Rugoff, Milton. "Cassatt, Mary." <u>Encyclopedia</u>
    <u>of American Art,</u> 1981 ed.

Sweet, Frederick A. <u>Miss Mary Cassatt.</u>
    Oklahoma: U of Oklahoma P, 1966.

Using the APA (American Psychological Association) Style

The pointers about doing research offered in this chapter so far apply to all papers, regardless of the style required. Once you know the MLA style of parenthetical documentation, you will find it easy to shift to the APA style, the standard for research papers in the social sciences, especially psychology. The main difference between the two styles is a matter of emphasis and mechanics. For example, whereas the MLA emphasizes author and work, the APA emphasizes author and date (probably because research in the social sciences quickly becomes outdated). Moreover, APA stresses certain mechanical requirements in such matters as capitalizing or underlining, deleting quotation marks from titles, listing only the initials of authors' first names, and other idiosyncrasies explained in the following pages. Furthermore, APA papers require an abstract, rather than an outline, preceding the body of the paper (although some instructors may require both). Careful attention to the following rules and to the sample student paper provided will ease your task of converting to the APA style.

A. APA style for parenthetical documentation

Date
Place the year immediately after the author's name:

```
Madsen (1986) discovered that people seeking

political power reveal certain biochemical

characteristics.
```

Single author
If you do not mention the author's name in the text, insert the surname and year within parentheses:

```
People seeking political power reveal certain

biochemical characteristics (Madsen, 1979).
```

The surname and years are separated by a comma. Subsequent references would be as follows:

```
Madsen further discovered that . . . .
```

Two or more authors
When citing two authors, use both surnames joined by "and":

```
In their early studies, Kinder and Rutherford

(1921) found that retarded children faced

numerous problems in social adjustment.
```

NOTE: When placed within parentheses, the "and" joining two authors becomes an ampersand.

```
Early studies (Kinder & Rutherford, 1921) found

that retarded children faced numerous problems

in social adjustment.
```

When citing more than two authors, give all surnames for the first reference:

```
One important study (Dickey, Loewen, & Phraser,

1978) disagreed with previous findings.
```

In subsequent references, just use "Dickey et al."

When citing more than five authors, use the surname of the first author followed by "et al." for the first as well as subsequent references:

```
One particular study (Abrams et al., 1986) found

a strong correlation between people's

occupational success and their facial

attractiveness.
```

NOTE: The parenthetical documentation is always placed as close as possible to the mention of the study.

More than one work by the same author with the same date
Use small letters to list two or more works by the same author with the same publication date:

```
Meister (1986a) describes three studies showing

that mentally retarded children demonstrate

particular problems in their maturational

growth.  Later (1986b) he corroborates his

original study.
```

The studies will be ordered alphabetically by their titles in "References."

Corporate author
When a work is authored by a committee, a corporation, an institution, or a governmental agency, use the full name of the corporate author when it is cited for the first time.

```
(National Institute of Health, 1986)

(Association for Research in Nervous and Mental

Diseases, 1978)
```

In subsequent citations, abbreviate the name:

```
(NIH, 1986)

(ARNMD, 1978)
```

Short names of corporate authors should be written out each time:

```
(Stanford University, 1986)

(Bendix Corporation, 1984)

(Brookings Institute, 1978)
```

Anonymous work
An anonymous work should be cited in text as follows:

```
(Anonymous, 1986)
```

In the final reference list, this work will be listed under "A" for "Anonymous."

Work without an author
A work without an author is listed by key words from its title:

```
("Subjective Measures," 1985)
```

The full title is "Subjective Measures for Stress Computation." In the final reference list, a work without an author is alphabetized according to the first significant word in the title. Articles *(the, a, an)*, prepositions *(from, under, behind)*, and pronouns *(this, those, that)* do not count.

B. APA style for "References"

Note the following differences between MLA and APA styles:

1. APA uses the term "References" instead of "Works Cited."
2. APA uses an author's full surnames but only the initials of his or her first and middle name (for example, "Adorno, T. W."). In entries with multiple authors, all names are inverted (for example, Davis, M., McKay, M., & Eshelman, E. R.).
3. For names connected with "and", APA uses the ampersand (for example, Adams, L. & Lenz, E.).
4. APA places the date of a work in parentheses immediately following the author's name, rather than at the end of the entry:

```
Baron, R. A. (1971).  The tyranny of noise.  New

    York:  Harper.
```

5. APA indents the second and succeeding lines of an entry three spaces, not five. (See Baron entry above.)
6. APA capitalizes only the first word in the title of a book or article and does not place within quotation marks the titles of articles in journals or magazines. However, APA does capitalize all words in the titles of journals or magazines:

```
Anderson, R. A. (1978).  Stress power:  How to

    turn tension into energy.  New York:  Human

    Sciences, 1978.

Erikson, J., Pugh, W. M., & Gunderson, E. K.

    (1972).  Status congruency as a predictor of

    job satisfaction and life stress.  Journal of

    Applied Psychology, 56, 523-25.
```

7. APA underlines the volume number of a periodical and sets it off with commas. (See Erikson entry above.)

8. While both MLA and APA include the issue number of periodicals paginated separately in each issue, APA includes the issue number in parentheses, immediately following the volume number, with a comma separating the issue number from the page number(s):

Rosenthal, G. A. (1983). A seed-eating beetle's

adaptations to poisonous seed. Scientific

American, 240(6), 56-67.

9. APA uses the abbreviation "p." and "pp." for page(s) in magazines or newspapers, but does not use these abbreviations when citing journals:

Thurston, H. (1986, May). Newfoundland: The

enduring rock. National Geographic, pp.

667-700.

Books

Book with a single author

Cousins, N. (1979). Anatomy of an illness. New

York: Bantam.

Book with two or more authors

Friedman, M., & Roseman, R. H. (1974). Type A

behavior and your heart. Greenwich, CT:

Fawcett.

Davis, M., McKay, M., & Eshelman, E. R. (1980).

The relaxation and stress reduction

workbook. Richmond, CA: New Harbinger.

With two names, use an ampersand before the second name and use a comma to separate the names. With three or more names, use an ampersand before the last name and use commas to separate the names. For works with multiple authors, regardless of how many, list all names in "References," reserving "et al." for your text. If the place of publication is not well known, the way New York or London is, give both the city and state (or country). (See Friedman and Davis examples above.) If the publisher is obscure, supply the full name.

Book with a corporate author

```
Committee of Public Finance.  (1959).  Public
    finance.  New York:  Pitman.
```

When the corporate author is also the publisher, place the word "Author" in place of the publisher:

```
Commission on Intergovernmental Relations.
    (1955).  Report to the president.
    Washington, DC:  Author.
```

Book with editor(s)

```
Hambling, J. (Ed.).  (1959).  The nature of
    stress disorder.  Springfield, IL:  Thomas.
Rapoport, R. N., & Rapoport, J. M. (Eds.).
    (1978).  Working couples.  New York:  Harper.
```

When citing an article or chapter from an edited book, use the following form:

```
Poulton, E. C.  (1978).  Blue collar stressors.
    In C. L. Cooper & R. Payne (Eds.), Stress at
    work (pp. 23–30).  Chichester, England:
    Wiley.
```

Give the surname and initials of all editors appearing in the author's position, regardless of how many. Show "Ed." or "Eds." in parentheses after the name(s), followed by a period. When an editor's name is not in the author position, do not invert his or her name. Place "Ed." or "Eds." in parentheses after the name(s), followed by a comma. Give inclusive page numbers for the article or chapter, in parentheses after the title of the book. Precede the page number(s) by "p." or "pp."

Translated book

```
Rank, O.  (1932).  Psychology and the soul
    (William Turner, Trans.).  Philadelphia:
    University of Pennsylvania Press.
```

Place the name of the translator (not inverted) within parentheses after the book title, followed by "Trans." with a period after the end parenthesis.

Multivolume book
Citing two entire volumes:

```
Selye, H.  (1971).  Hormones and resistance
    (Vols. 1-2).  New York:  Springerverlag.
```

Citing an article in one particular volume:

```
Ruesch, J.  (1980).  Communication and
    psychiatry.  In H. I. Kaplan, A. M. Freedman,
    & B. J. Sadock (Eds.), Comprehensive textbook
    of psychiatry (Vol. 1, pp. 129-35).
    Baltimore:  Williams & Wilkins.
```

Use the word "In" to indicate a separate title. Place the number(s) of the volume(s) actually used in parentheses immediately following the title of the book and supply inclusive page numbers of the article. Use Arabic numerals. If a multivolume book has been published over more than one year, list years:

```
Brady, V. S.  (1978-1982). . .
```

Magazines, journals, and newspapers

Journal with continuous pagination

```
House, R. J.  (1971).  A path-goal theory of

    leader effectiveness.  Administrative Science

    Quarterly, 16, 321-38.
```

For listing multiple authors, use the same system as for books. (See number 2, page 679.)

Journal with renewed pagination in each issue

```
Rosenthal, G. A. (1983).  A seed-eating beetle's

    adaptations to poisonous seed.  Scientific

    American, 249(6), 56-67.
```

For journals with separate pagination in each issue, supply the volume number (underlined), followed immediately by the issue number within parentheses, a comma, and the inclusive page numbers for the article.

Magazine issued monthly

```
Weaver, K. F.  (1985, September).  Stones,

    bones, and early man:  The search for our

    ancestors.  National Geographic, pp.

    560-623.
```

Place the year—followed by a comma—and the month in parentheses after the author's name. Place a comma after the magazine title and write "p" or "pp.," followed by the page number(s).

Magazine issued on a specific day

```
Friedrich, O.  (1986, July 7).  On preventing

    useful activity.  Time, p.  68.
```

Place the year—followed by a comma—and the month and day within parentheses.

Newspaper article

```
Peterson, J.  (1970, July 20).  Assault on heart
    disease.  National Observer,  sec.  1, p.  1.
```

Give the section or part before the page (for example, "pt. 1, p. 4."; "sec. 4, p. 2"; "p. Bl.")

NOTE: If the journal, magazine, or newspaper article has no author, begin with the title of the article, followed by the date:

```
Rebirth of city.  (1977, September 6).
    News-Times  (Danbury, CT), pt. 1, p. 2.
```

NOTE: For an unfamiliar newspaper, give the place of publication.

Special sources

As with the MLA system, we cannot supply you with a sample of all possible sources, but only with the most common. Some of the sources you might commonly cite in a humanities paper you would probably not cite in a paper for the social sciences. Among the unlikely citations, for example, are theatrical performances, musical concerts, or visits to an art gallery. The following, however, are examples of citations you might need to use.

Editorial

```
Guion, R. M. (1983).  Comments from the new
    editor [Editorial].  Journal of Applied
    Psychology, 68, 547.
```

Following the title of the editorial, place the word "Editorial" in brackets, followed by a period. If the editorial has no title, place the bracketed "Editorial" following the date:

```
. . .  (1983).  [Editorial] . . .
```

Review

```
Ashton, S.  (1982, July/August).  [Review of

    Death and dying, by D. L. Bender & R. C.

    Hagen].  Times Literary Supplement, p.  785.
```

Place "Review of," followed by the title of the work being reviewed, in brackets. If the review has a title, which the preceding sample does *not,* place it immediately following the date:

```
Boorstein, J. K.  (1983, November/December).  On

    welfare [Review of . . .
```

Computer source

Computer citations refer to material of two kinds: (1) Computer programs (information received directly from data banks) and (2) written publications retrieved by a computer base. Examples of both kinds follow:

Computer program:

```
Poole, L., & Barchers, M.  (1977).  Future value

    of an investment [Computer program].

    Berkeley, CA:  Adam Osborne & Associates.

    (Basic for a Wang 2200).
```

List the primary creator of the database as the author, followed by the date (in parentheses) when the program was produced. Then give the title of the program, followed by "Computer program" in brackets. Give the location and name of the publisher of the program. Finally, enclose in parentheses any additional information necessary for identification and retrieval. This additional information should include the kind of hardware for which the software was created.

Source retrieved from data bank:

```
Ulmer, C. (1981).  Competence based

    instruction.  Community College Review, 8(4),

    51–56; rpt.  Los Angeles:  ERIC, Dialog File

    1, EJ27541.
```

Sources retrieved from data banks are cited the way you would the original source. Follow the original source citation with a semicolon and "rpt.," followed by the city and company providing the computer source service. Add a code, file, or record number when applicable.

Government document—Congress

U.S. Cong. House. (1977). <u>U.S. assistance</u>

<u>programs in Vietnam.</u> 92d Cong., 2nd sess.

Washington, DC: U.S. Government Printing

Office.

U.S. Cong. Senate. (1970). <u>Separation of powers</u>

<u>and the independent agencies:</u> <u>Cases and</u>

<u>selected readings.</u> 91st Cong., 1st sess.

Washington, DC: U.S. Government Printing

Office.

Government document—Executive branch

Executive Office of the President. (1981).

<u>Environmental trends.</u> Washington, DC: U.S.

Government Printing Office.

Government publications are incredibly complex and varied. In general, follow this order:

1. Person or organization responsible for the work
2. Year the work was published, produced, or released
3. Title of the work
4. Identifying code, if applicable
5. Place of origin or publication
6. Publisher (usually the U.S. Government Printing Office—spelled out)

C. APA style for "Abstract"

Papers in the social sciences are typically preceded by an *abstract,* that is a brief summary of the main findings of your research. It is written in coherent paragraph form but leaves out the details of the paper. Most abstracts are approximately one-half typewritten page long. The word "Abstract" appears centered at the top of the page, followed by double-spaced typing. (See the student sample.)

D. APA style for running head

An abbreviated title, called a running head, appears in the top right-hand corner of each page, including the title page. Do not use more than 50 characters (including spaces) for the running head. For example, if this were your full title: "The Elements of Depression: A Study of High School Victims," your running head might be as follows: "Elements of Depression." The page number is placed one double-spaced line below the running head.

E. APA style for title page

The first page of the paper is the title page. It includes the title of the paper, the name of the student, the name of the class, the name of the institution, and the date. All of this information should be centered in the middle of the page. (See sample student paper.)

Sample Student Paper (APA Style)

The following sample student paper was written for a philosophy class; however, since it focuses on the relationship between mind and body, using psychological as well as philosophical sources, it properly follows the style recommended in the *Publication Manual of the American Psychological Association.*

The Mind and the Body:

Do They Interact?

Pauline Huzau

Philosophy 101

Glendale Community College

June 6, 1989

Abstract

The modern field of psychosomatics has challenged and contradicted the traditional philosophy of dualism, which in varying degrees insisted that the mind and body are separate entities with little influence on each other. The purpose of this paper is to show how recent discoveries in medicine strongly support the idea that the mind does influence and control the body as well as vice versa. Specifically, Norman Cousins' personal experience refutes Descartes; biofeedback refutes Thomas Huxley; and recent studies on the immune system refute C. R. Broad.

The Mind and the Body:

Do They Interact?

Since the beginning of civilization, and
perhaps even earlier, no subject has captured
the human imagination more than knowledge about
self. One fascinating question seriously probed
throughout the centuries is this: How does the
mind affect the body and vice versa? Attempting
to answer these questions, the philosophers
Thomas Huxley, René Descartes, and C. D. Broad
developed a system of concepts that eventually
became known as dualism. Dualism holds that
humans are composed of two distinct substances,
mind and body. Different versions of this
theory claim different levels of separateness
between mind and body, but ultimately, dualism
refuses to see the mind and body as interacting
freely with each other. Dualism was the
accepted scientific view for many decades;
however, the advent of modern science, with its
emphasis on the scientific method and heavy
clinical research, has proposed another view:
the belief in the integrity and wholeness of
mind and body. In short, today we must take a
new look at the human mind and its connection

with the body to see whether new evidence incontrovertibly proves that the mind and body are not separate entities, but a unified whole.[1]

Recently, one particular field of study, psychosomatics, has most strongly contradicted the theories of dualism. Dorland's _Illustrated Medical Dictionary_ (1965) defines _psychosomatics_ as "having bodily symptoms of psychic, emotional, or mental origin." The etymology of the term can be traced to the Greek _psyche,_ meaning "soul," and _soma,_ meaning "body." In other words, psychosomatics is the study of the influence of the mind on the body as revealed in physical illness. Lewis and Lewis (1972) consider psychosomatics a total approach to health that views the person as a mind–body unity, taking into consideration one's whole way of life when health is scrutinized. According to these two scientists, the idea of a mind–body interrelationship is not really new, but can be traced back at least 4,500 years, to the Yellow Emperor of China, Huang Ti, who authored a famous manuscript dealing with internal medicine. In it he claimed that "frustration can make people physically ill" (cited in Lewis & Lewis, 1970, p. 5). Later on, in the fourth

century B.C., Socrates returned from military
service to tell his Greek countrymen that the
barbaric Thracians were culturally advanced
because they believed that "the body could not
be cured without the mind" (cited in Lewis &
Lewis, 1970, p. 5). Despite these early
historical views pointing toward an influence of
mind on body and body on mind, the dualistic
theories prevailed—with individual
modifications—until just recently, when a wave
of modern research has challenged them
seriously. This paper will present a brief
summary of the three major dualistic positions
and will show how each has been superseded by a
modern, clinically proven theory that renders
them outmoded.

One of the purest dualistic theories was
proposed in 1649 by René Descartes, whose
treatise "The Passions of the Soul" argued that
the physical world is mechanistic and entirely
divorced from the mind, the only connection
between the two being by intervention of God.
He proposed that since all emotions were
physical, if one would control the physical
expression of emotions, such as trembling, one
would control the emotion itself. While

Descartes agreed that bodily injury could cause mental pain and that mental pain could cause the body to respond, he insisted that the two entities operated separately. For example, if the foot was injured, the mind would immediately become excited "to do its utmost to remove the cause of evil as dangerous and hurtful to the foot" (cited in Hall & Bowie, 1986, p. 149). In other words, Descartes limited his belief to an instinctive level of interaction between mind and body, insisting that the mind reacts instinctively when the body is in danger: "I have a body which is adversely affectived when I feel pain" (cited in Hall & Bowie, 1986, p. 147). Descartes did not attempt to hide the fact that at one point he was not even sure if he had a body. Thus, one can only imagine what difficulties he had in trying to philosophize about a relationship between something that he knew existed and something he was not sure existed at all.

Descartes' view that mind and body react to each other as mere reflexes is seriously challenged by occurrences of healing having taken place because of the will to heal oneself despite the actual physical incapability of the

body to do so. One well-publicized example is
the miraculous recovery from a fatal disease of
Norman Cousins, the influential essayist and
editor associated with the New York Post and
Saturday Review. His experience was published
in the December 1966 issue of the New England
Journal of Medicine. Cousins caused a national
sensation when he claimed he had used his mind
to heal his body. In 1964, after a trip to the
Soviet Union, where he was apparently poisoned
by jet exhaust, he was hospitalized and lay
dying from a collagen disease. He found the
hospital stay highly uncomfortable and felt that
it was contributing to his body's wasting away.
When told that he had only one in five hundred
chances of living, he decided that "it was time
to get into the act" (Cousins, 1966, p. 1459).
He diagnosed the cause of his illness and
researched its possible cures. "Assuming my
hypothesis true, I had to get my adrenal glands
functioning properly again" (Cousins, 1966, p.
1460). He found that adrenal exhaustion could
be caused by tension, frustration, or suppressed
rage. He then reasoned that if he could get rid
of these emotions, he could put his physical
body back in order. Thus, he went on to wean

himself from pain medication and other massive
doses of drugs by using an emotion——
laughter——and by checking himself out of the
hospital environment, which he found deeply
depressing. Norman Cousins claimed to have
cured himself of his terrible affliction by
using his mind to help his body (Cousins, 1966,
pp. 1460-1463). Such a life-threatening or
life-saving interaction between the mind and the
body is impossible to assimilate into
Descartes's reflex-action theory.[2]

Another theory of dualism is the theory of
epiphenomenalism, upheld by Thomas Huxley. This
theory suggests that a causal connection exists
between mind and body, but that it only goes in
one direction——from body to mind, not from mind
to body. After reporting in detail clinical
experiments involving several spinal cords in
animals and observing the results, Huxley
concluded that some physical events do indeed
cause mental states, but that mental states
themselves have no power whatsoever to cause
either mental or physical states. In "Evolution
and Ethics" (1893), Huxley declared that things
going on in the body, especially in the nervous
system, do give rise to conscious mental states,

but that mental states exert no influence on the
body.

Today, Huxley's view is being strongly
challenged by supporters of biofeedback, a
quickly growing clinical method that is being
used to reduce the effects of stress on the
body, especially in patients with severe
migraine headaches. Biofeedback is based on
three major principles: 1) any biological
function that can be monitored by electronic
instrumentation can be regulated by the
individual, 2) every change in the emotional
state is accompanied by a change in the
physiological state, and 3) the reduction of
stress can be achieved through relaxation and
visualization. Research on biofeedback has now
proven that many involuntary functions of the
nervous system, such as brain waves, body
temperature, or heart rate, can be brought under
control by the individual. An example of the
use of biofeedback in medical treatment is
revealed in the following case history,
documented by Pelletier (1977, p. 280): A
19-year-old male patient, almost completely
paralyzed on the left side of his body due to a
severe neck fracture, was found to have the

entire left side of his body 15 degrees lower in temperature than his right side, causing a severe reduction in the use of his muscles. Using biofeedback methods, the young man was eventually able to use his will to raise the temperature on the left side of his body to within 2 degrees of the right side--an increase of 13 degrees. He then experienced amazing success in the muscular coordination of his previously useless muscles. Now, according to Huxley's theory of dualism this change would be impossible; yet, it is a medically documented fact. Biofeedback is one area of study that clearly demonstrates that Huxley's claims are being questioned.

Somewhere between the thinking of Descartes and that of Huxley lies the philosophy of C. D. Broad, who propounded a modified version of dualism. He argued that indeed certain states in the mind and body _seem_ to coincide. For instance, when one steps on a pin, one feels pain. But for him, such incidences were simply a sophisticated, pre-established harmony between the separate mind and body, preset by God. He believed that perhaps this was God's way of keeping human beings informed of what is

physically going on in their bodies. Broad
appeals to common sense in his argument,
insisting that if minds or mental events and
bodies or bodily events are "just what
enlightened common-sense thinks them to be and
nothing more, the two are extremely unlike."
Going one step further, he concludes: " . . .
however closely correlated certain pairs of
events in mind and body respectively may be,
they cannot be causally connected" (cited in
Hall & Bowie, 1986, p. 151). Again, numerous
modern, well-documented case histories exist to
prove an action on the part of the mind before
an action on the part of the body, not
coinciding with it. For example, in Australia
during 1970 a Dr. R. W. Bartrop and his
associates studied the effects of bereavement on
the body's ability to fight off illness and
disease. They found that the immune systems of
spouses grieving over the deaths of their
marriage partners had weakened considerably
during this mourning period. Almost two decades
later, in 1987, Ornstein and Sobell confirmed
specifically that widows or widowers had
clinically proven lower activity levels of what
are known as "T cells"--blood cells that resist

intruders in the body (p. 48). The Ornstein and
Sobell study was one of the first scientifically
controlled experiments that showed a measurable
weakening of the body's defense system <u>following</u>
severe mental stress in a real—life situation.
Here one clearly sees that, instead of a
physical act being accompanied by a coincidental
emotional feeling, the emotions occurred first
and the action on the physical system followed.
Grief is only one of many other clinical
examples that directly contradict Broad's view
that the mind is totally separate from the body
and is simply God's way of keeping the human
being informed of what occurs in the body. Many
clinical experiments have concluded that the
mind is often the primary action.

Philosophers such as Descartes, Huxley, and
Broad are fascinating to study, but their
theories of dualism, once deemed profound and
sophisticated, now seem almost simplistic. They
have signalled scientists to go on and explore
further the true relationship between these two
remarkable entities we know as mind and body.
We live in exciting times, when scientific
exploration and medical research are at their
most advanced stages ever, and it is up to us to

use the abundance of information never before
available in philosophic research to expound
upon the mind-body theories of the past. The
heroes of tomorrow are those philosophers or
scientists who will discover new sources of
power and healing in the interrelationship
between the mind and the body--making the world
a better place in which to live.

Notes

[1]Due to space contraints and the complex
nature of the subject, this paper will not deal
with the recent field of functionalism, which
takes into account the latest research in
artificial intelligence and cognitive science.
For further information on this new area of
knowledge about the mind—body connection, see
the works of Jerry A. Fodor and Hubert Dreyfus.

[2]Similar experiences have been narrated by
a number of patients who claim to have cured
cancer by using positive thinking. Oncologist
Carl Simonton established a clinic in Houston,
Texas, and in Santa Monica, California, based on
the concept of imaging——imagining oneself being
cured. For instance, a cancer patient might
imagine a medieval knight on a white horse,
representing the immune system inside his body
physically doing battle with the destructive
cancer cells. The Simonton clinic has drawn
patients from all over the world. While not
accepted by all members of the medical
community, the idea of imaging has gained some
enthusiastic proponents. For more on this
subject, see Dr. Simonton's book, <u>Getting Well
Again.</u>

References

Cousins, N. (1966, December). Anatomy of an
illness. The New England Journal of
Medicine, 295, (26), 1458-1468).

Broad, C. D. (1986). The traditional problem of
body and mind. In H. Hall, & N. E. Bowie
(Eds.). The tradition of philosophy (pp.
150-158). Bellflower, CA: Wadsworth.

Descartes, R. (1986). The distinction between
the mind and body of man. In H. Hall, & N.
E. Bowie (Eds.). The tradition of philosophy
(pp. 146-149). Bellflower, CA: Wadsworth.

---(1958). The Passions of the soul. In N. K.
Smith (Ed. & Trans.). Descartes
philosophical writings (pp. 34-45). New
York: Modern Library.

Dorland's illustrated medical dictionary. 1965
ed., s.v. "psychosomatic."

Huxley, T. E. (1986). Animals as conscious
automata. In H. Hall, & N. E. Bowie (Eds.).
The tradition of philosophy. (pp. 159-166).
Bellflower, CA: Wadsworth.

---(1931). Evolution and ethics. In C. W.
Thomas (Ed.) Essays in contemporary
civilization (pp. 363-396). New York:
Macmillan.

Lewis, H. R., & Lewis, M. E. (1972).
Psychosomatics. New York: Viking.

Ornstein, R., & Sobel, D. (1987, March). The healing brain. _Psychology Today,_ pp. 48–52.

Pelletier, K. R. (1977). _Mind as healer, mind as slayer._ New York: Delacorte.

Simonton, C. (1978). _Getting well again: A step-by-step self-help guide to overcoming cancer for patients and their families._ New York: Tarcher.

Checklist for Completed Research Paper

_____ 1. My introduction captivates and
includes my thesis.

_____ 2. My paper follows my outline (or
abstract).

_____ 3. My paragraphs are coherent.

_____ 4. The language sounds like me.

_____ 5. I have not quoted excessively.

_____ 6. I have documented all ideas from
sources other than myself.

_____ 7. I have not plagiarized.

_____ 8. My thesis and every major idea are
supported by evidence in the paper.

_____ 9. My documentation is accurate in
content and form.

_____ 10. I have proofread for mechanical
errors.

Abbreviations

Use abbreviations often and consistently in your notes and bibliography, but avoid them in your text. In notes you should abbreviate dates (Jan., Feb.) and institutions (Inst. Assn.). The following are abbreviations commonly encountered or used.

A.D.	*(Anno Domini)*. Refers to years after Christ's birth, as in "A.D. 200."
anon.	Anonymous.
art., arts.	Article(s).
B.C.	Before Christ. Refers to years before Christ's birth, as in "50 B.C."
bk., bks.	Book(s).
ca.	*(Circa)*. About, used to indicate an approximate date, as in "ca. 1730."
cf.	*Confer*. Compare one source with another.
ch., chs.	Chapter(s).
col., cols.	Column(s).
comp.	Compiled by, compiler.
diss.	Dissertation.
ed., eds.	Editor(s), edition, or edited by.
e.g.	*(Exempli gratia)*. For example—preceded and followed by a comma.
enl.	Enlarged, as in "enl. ed."
et al.	*(Et alii)*. And others, as in "John Smith et al."
f., ff.	Page(s) following, as in "pp. 8 f." meaning page 8 and the following page.
i.e.	*(Id est)*. That is—preceded and followed by a comma.
l., ll.	Line(s).
MS, MSS	Manuscript(s).
n.d.	No date.
no., nos.	Number(s).
n.p.	No place.
p., pp.	Page(s).
passim	Here and there throughout the work, as in "pp. 67, 72, et passim."

pseud.	Pseudonym.
pt., pts.	Part(s).
rev.	Revised, revision, reviewed, review.
rpt.	Reprint, reprinted.
sec., secs.	Section(s).
sic	Thus—placed in brackets to indicate that an error exists in the passage being quoted, as in "sevral [sic]."
st., sts.	Stanza(s).
trans.	Translator, translated, translation.
vol., vols.	Volume(s).

Acceptable shortened forms of publishers' names include the following:

Abrams	Harry N. Abrams, Inc.
Acad. for Educ. Dev.	Academy for Educational Development, Inc.
Allen	George Allen and Unwin Publishers, Inc.
Allyn	Allyn and Bacon, Inc.
Appleton	Appleton-Century-Crofts
Ballantine	Ballantine Books, Inc.
Bantam	Bantam Books, Inc.
Barnes	Barnes and Noble Books
Basic	Basic Books
Beacon	Beacon Press, Inc.
Benn	Ernest Benn, Ltd.
Bobbs	The Bobbs-Merrill Co., Inc.
Bowker	R. R. Bowker Co.
CAL	Center for Applied Linguistics
Cambridge UP	Cambridge University Press
Clarendon	Clarendon Press
Columbia UP	Columbia University Press
Cornell UP	Cornell University Press
Dell	Dell Publishing Co., Inc.

Dodd	Dodd, Mead, and Co.
Doubleday	Doubleday and Co., Inc.
Dover	Dover Publications, Inc.
Dutton	E. P. Dutton, Inc.
Farrar	Farrar, Straus, and Giroux, Inc.
Feminist	The Feminist Press
Free	The Free Press
Funk	Funk and Wagnalls, Inc.
Gale	Gale Research Co.
GPO	Government Printing Office
Harcourt	Harcourt Brace Jovanovich, Inc.
Harper	Harper and Row Publishers, Inc.
Harvard Law Rev. Assn.	Harvard Law Review Association
Harvard UP	Harvard University Press
Heath	D. C. Heath and Co.
HMSO	Her (His) Majesty's Stationery Office
Holt	Holt, Rinehart, and Winston, Inc.
Houghton	Houghton Mifflin Co.
Humanities	Humanities Press, Inc.
Indiana UP	Indiana University Press
Johns Hopkins UP	The Johns Hopkins University Press
Knopf	Alfred A. Knopf, Inc.
Larousse	Librairie Larousse
Lippincott	J. B. Lippincott Co.
Little	Little, Brown, and Co.
Macmillan	Macmillan Publishing Co., Inc.
McGraw	McGraw-Hill, Inc.
MIT P	The MIT Press
MLA	The Modern Language Association of America
NAL	The New American Library, Inc.
NCTE	The National Council of Teachers of English
NEA	The National Education Association
New York Graphic Soc.	New York Graphic Society

Norton	W. W. Norton and Co., Inc.
Oxford UP	Oxford University Press, Inc.
Penguin	Penguin Books, Inc.
Pocket	Pocket Books
Popular	The Popular Press
Prentice	Prentice-Hall, Inc.
Princeton UP	Princeton University Press
Putnam's	G. P. Putnam's Sons
Rand	Rand McNally and Co.
Random	Random House
Rizzoli	Rizzoli Editore
St. Martin's	St. Martin's Press, Inc.
Scott	Scott, Foresman, and Co.
Scribner's	Charles Scribner's Sons
Simon	Simon and Schuster, Inc.
State U of New York P	State University of New York Press
UMI	University Microfilms International
U of Chicago P	University of Chicago Press
U of Toronto P	University of Toronto Press
UP of Florida	The University Presses of Florida
Viking	The Viking Press, Inc.
Yale UP	Yale University Press

Postal abbreviations

Alabama	AL	Guam	GU
Alaska	AK	Hawaii	HI
Arizona	AZ	Idaho	ID
Arkansas	AR	Illinois	IL
California	CA	Indiana	IN
Colorado	CO	Iowa	IA
Connecticut	CT	Kansas	KS
Delaware	DE	Kentucky	KY
District of Columbia	DC	Louisiana	LA
Florida	FL	Maine	ME
Georgia	GA	Maryland	MD

Massachusetts	MA	Oregon	OR
Michigan	MI	Pennsylvania	PA
Minnesota	MN	Puerto Rico	PR
Mississippi	MS	Rhode Island	RI
Missouri	MO	South Carolina	SC
Montana	MT	South Dakota	SD
Nebraska	NB	Tennessee	TN
Nevada	NV	Texas	TX
New Hampshire	NH	Utah	UT
New Jersey	NJ	Vermont	VT
New Mexico	NM	Virgin Islands	VI
New York	NY	Virginia	VA
North Carolina	NC	Washington	WA
North Dakota	ND	West Virginia	WV
Ohio	OH	Wisconsin	WI
Oklahoma	OK	Wyoming	WY

Exercises

1. Write a one-sentence summary of the following passage:

> A failure in learning should *never* be punished by blows. Learning is difficult enough. To add fear to it simply makes it more difficult. Fear does not encourage, it drives on blindly. It blocks the movement of the mind. It produces the opposite effect to that of true education, because it makes frightened pupils dull and imitative instead of making them original and eager. And it is useless to object: "Boys don't fear physical punishment, they laugh at it and forget it": for it can always be made tough enough, by a brutal master, to make most of them secretly afraid and some of them paralyzed with terror.

> —Gilbert Highet, *The Art of Teaching.*

2. Write a paraphrase of the following passage:

> Eventually, a condition of learning any art is a *supreme concern* with the mastery of the art. If the art is not something of supreme importance, the apprentice will remain, at best, a good dilettante, but will never become a master. This condition is as necessary for the art of loving as for any other art. It seems, though, as if the proportion between masters and dilettantes is more heavily

weighted in favor of the dilettantes in the art of loving than in the case with other arts.

—Erich Fromm, *The Art of Loving.*

3. Find three different ways to introduce the following quotation by Samuel Johnson about Joseph Addison:

> As a describer of life and manners he must be allowed to stand perhaps the first of the first rank.

4. Arrange the following information into the proper form for "Works Cited":

   a. The first volume of a work edited by G. B. Harrison and the following other editors: Walter J. Bate, Bertrand H. Bronson, Reuben A. Brower, Douglas Bush, Herbert Davis, William C. DeVane, Elizabeth Drew, Charles W. Dunn, Northrop Frye, C. S. Lewis, Maynard Mack, George W. Meyer, I. A. Richards, Lionel Trilling, Mamie Van Doren, and Basil Willey. The title is *Major British Writers.* Published in New York by Harcourt, Brace & World in 1959.

   b. "High Spirits in the Twenties," an article in the July 1962 issue of *Horizon,* a magazine. The article is found on pages 33–40 of volume IV, issue number 6. The author is John Mason Brown.

   c. A review of the book *The Building,* authored by Thomas Glynn. The reviewer is R. Z. Sheppard, writing for *Time,* Dec. 30, 1985, page 76. *The Building* is published in New York by Alfred A. Knopf, 1985.

   d. The Cambridge University Press edition of the Bible.

   e. C. S. Lewis's novel *Perelandra,* put out by Macmillan Publishing Company in New York, 1944.

   f. An entry from the 1963 edition of the *Encyclopaedia Britannica* under "Pottery and Porcelain." The section referred to is by Sir Edgar John Forsdyke.

5. Arrange the sources in exercise 4 to conform with the APA style for "References."

Practice Essays to Revise, Edit, and Proofread

The following essays, submitted by students exactly as shown, vary in quality as well as subject matter. With revision, editing, and proofreading, each could be markedly improved. Your assignment is to revise each essay until you think it is strong enough to merit an "A." Using the techniques of revising you have learned from this book, tamper with the essays at will, adding, deleting, or rephrasing passages to improve the overall quality. The questions below are intended as guidelines to help you with this task:

1. Is the main point of the essay clear? Is it stated as a thesis somewhere in the first paragraph?
2. Is the pattern of organization obvious and helpful? (For example, progressing by order of importance, by space or time orientation, or by simple logic.)
3. Does each paragraph make a clear point? (Is it unified and coherent?)
4. Do the paragraphs reflect appropriate modes of development?

Narration: Can the reader instantly tell *when* the action happened, *where* it happened, and *to whom* it happened? Is the narration well paced, stressing the important events while glossing over the unimportant? Are sufficient details included? Is the point of view clear and consistent?

Description: Are the details focused on a dominant impression? Are the details specific and concrete rather than vague? Does the description come to life through colorful images and figurative language?

Examples: Are the writer's examples relevant to the point being made and are they effectively developed? Are the examples clearly introduced so that it is contextually clear what they mean?

Definition: Is it clear what term the writer is defining? Does the definition clearly answer the question "What is it?" Has the writer provided a dictionary-type definition first and then extended it?

Process: Does the writer tell the reader what process is being explained? Are all steps of the process included? Is the order of the steps clear and easy to follow? Can you understand the writer's explanation without confusion?

Comparison/Contrast: What items are being compared or contrasted? Are the bases of the comparison/contrast made clear? Are both sides of the question treated completely? Is the comparison/contrast clearly organized—either within or between paragraphs? Does the writer use plain indicators of comparison or contrast (*like, similarly, however, on the other hand,* and so on) to underscore the essay's purpose?

Causal Analysis: Does the causal connection make sense? Does the writer focus on the nearest rather than the most remote cause? Does the writer avoid circular reasoning about cause? (For example, "Swearing is bad because it means using profane language.") Is the writer's reasoning impartial or is it biased?

Classification: Is it clear what subject the writer is classifying? Is the classification based on a single principle (looks, color, age)? Has the *entire* subject been divided without the omission of any important part? Do the categories overlap or are they clearly separate? Are all of the categories treated with equal emphasis?

5. Does the essay have a strong beginning? Does it grab and hold your attention with a punchy statement, a quotation, an anecdote, a dramatization of the topic, or some other memorable opening?

6. Are clear transitions made between the paragraphs?

7. Does the essay conclude with some finality? (Make sure that it does not weakly peter out, move away from the subject, or abruptly stop, leaving the reader hanging.)

8. Are the individual sentences within the paragraphs clear and concise? (Check for errors of mixed constructions; lack of parallel construction; unreasoned sentences; dangling or squinting constructions; misplaced elements; shifts in person, number, voice, tense, or mood.)

9. Are the individual sentences within the paragraphs concise? (Check for the following errors: repetitiousness, unnecessary words, pretentious overuse of big words.)

10. Are the sentences emphatically written? Are they balanced? Has the writer overused the passive voice? Have multiple *of's* been eliminated? Have fragments and comma splices been corrected? Have jarring sounds, such as unintentional rhyme or alliteration, been avoided? Are the sentences varied in structure and in length?

11. Is the writer's diction effective? Does the language strike you as sincere? Are the writer's images vivid rather than stale?

12. If the essay is a formal argument, is its proposition stated clearly and forcefully? Has the opposing point of view been addressed? Is the evidence persuasive and varied, consisting of facts, witness, experience, and expert testimony?

13. Is the manuscript free from typographical or spelling errors, from grammatical mistakes, from poorly punctuated sentences, and from all other mechanical problems that are the result of careless proofreading?

Student Essay 1

Inner Beauty

The word beauty can be defined as "a beautiful person or thing, especially a beautiful woman." Modern day beauty is described in physical terms--pretty features and a slim figure. But there is a different kind of beauty. An inner beauty that comes from kindness, generosity, courage, and love. Eleanor Roosevelt, wife of Franklin Delano Roosevelt, who was President of the United States during the discordant years of World War II, was a woman who possessed this inner beauty irregardless of the fact that she did not have physical beauty judged by today's standards. She revealed her inner beauty to the world many times.

Mrs. Roosevelt was deeply committed to civil rights and to human dignity. She was the first wife of a President to openly support the civil rights of Blacks. Oftentimes she tried to include Blacks where they would normally not have been included. She invited the National

Council of Negro Women to hold meetings at the
White House, and unlike other First Ladies
allowed herself to be photographed regularly
with Blacks. She set a standard for courage in
welcoming Blacks to participate at national
levels.

Mrs. Roosevelt had an incredible love of
humanity. After her husband took office during
the Depression, her calling became to give
encouragement to the poor and helpless of
America. She went everywhere misery could be
found. She visited everything from rural slums
to the dying mines where men were out of work,
to the soup lines in the inner cities. She was
avid in combatting poor housing unemployment.
She gave many empassioned speeches criticizing
the crumbling stairways, grimy kitchens, and
rat-infested cellars of New York's tenements.

Eleanor Roosevelt fought for peace all of
her adult life. After her husband died in 1945,
President Truman appointed her to the American
Delegation of the United Nations General
Assembly. She is quoted as saying, "We face
today a world filled with suspicion and
hatred. . . . We can establish no real trust
between nations until we acknowledge the power
of love above all the other powers. . . . " One
of Eleanor's greatest talents, it seems, was the
ability to take the arguments of established

views and opinions and turn them into human situations that could be discussed in human terms.

She also wrote a immensely popular syndacated column called "My Day."

Student Essay 2

The Sumo Wrestler

I envision the Sumo wrestler as Rueben did his Renaissance women, voluptuous in proportion. The Sumo wrestler exhibitions many corporeally physical deformities and infirmities not ubiquitous on an ordinary figure. Let me illustrate: His steatopygous abundant buttocks, smooth as a fetal pig, glistens under spotlights; his Alpine thighs vibrate with potentiality. The Sumo wrestler's fortification, his elephantine belly, is the epicenter of power.

This Oriental combantant, thick set and squat, is a worthy adversary. He approaches his adversary as if he were walking on broken glass, with great caution. His flatulent limbs reach out to tease the opponent. His pudgy fingers perform calisthenics in anticipation of contact. Beads of sweat adorn his massive brows.

The Sumo wrestler is dressed in unique attire. A loin cloth for him is de regueur in this sport. Dating back to the Greco-Roman empire and used on through the centuries of professional wrestling, it has been upgraded to its present form. The wrestler's imposing behind is highlighted by the severe lines of the garment draped from his shoulders. The jutting cut of the loin cloth accentuates his spacious hips. To minimize the wrestler's cyclopean girth, a thick belt, made of cloth, is attached to the garment--minimal wear for an apish gargantuan.

I admire the Sumo wrestler's physique, he is so amply endowed. He is one of art's treasures.

Student Essay 3

Female Beauty in Renaissance Paintings

The Renaissance--the rebirth of all that was glorious in ancient Greece and Rome--inaugurated various concepts of beauty portrayed by the painters of that period. The ideal females in Early Renaissance paintings were slim, young beauties on the brink of maturity, and the madonnas and graces of the High and Late Renaissance gradually began to present a more robust figure.

One of the earliest of an Early Renaissance beauty is <u>Venusu</u>, painted by Sandro Botticelli.

Fresh, blooming, and young, this vision of
beauty stands tall and nude. Her wiry long
flowing hair, draped behind her softly rounded
thin neck, appearing to be soft yellow color
turning brown. Her eyes, tender and a deep blue,
exude an tensile gaze, gentle as a zephyr on a
summer day. Her lips, a shade of rose, are round
and small above a chin with a button in the
middle. Furthermore, in Botticelli's hands this
classical seductress takes on a virtuous
quality.

Let us take Leonardo Da Vinci's Mona Lisa.
Her enigmatic face genuinely reflects the taste
of the period. Her hair, as thin as the veil
spread on her head, is a dark brown. Her eyelids
are round like the vaulted ceilings of a Gothic
Cathedral. Her gaze is as soft and delicate as
her subtle and mysterious smile. And her nose,
long and angular, makes her even more unique. In
addition, this astonishing High Renaissance
beauty embodies a quality of maternal
tenderness, which was to High Renaissance men
the essence of virtuous womanhood.

From all the different Neo-Classical
concepts of beauty, a new Renaissance ideal
evolved. Among the most famous painters
representing this Late Renaissance ideal was
Michelangelo Buonarroti. The enticing goddesses
depicted by Michelangelo are all full-figured

women--generously endowed--and displaying
muscles a male might be proud of. The bodies of
these females are as big as those of the giants
in Greek and Roman mythology. And their eyes
flash with passion and anger, as if they wanted
to pass the last judgment on mankind.

Student Essay 4

Microwave Ovens Versus Conventional Ovens

In terms of time, expense, and convenience,
the microwave oven is superior to the
conventional oven.

First of all, the microwave oven can save
the cook a great deal of money. Not only does
the cook save money on the initial purchase, but
he or she also saves money while actually using
the microwave. The microwave cooks food two to
three times faster than the conventional oven
and requires no preheating, which saves on the
amount of electricity or fuel used while
cooking, and in turn saves money.

Secondly, the microwave can save time. One
of the microwave's biggest assets is the speed
at which it cooks, and of course any time saved
in the kitchen can be applied to liesure. In our
world of today, most people do not have time to
prepare meals in the time-consuming traditional
manner. An example of the time saved when

cooking with the microwave can be seen in baking a potato. The conventional oven requires at least forty-five minutes to one hour before a potato is thoroughly baked. The microwave, on the other hand, requires no more than eighteen minutes. A beef roast that requires two hours of baking in a conventional oven will require only one third that amount of time in a microwave (and will be juicier). Time can also be saved by warming food or defrosting frozen foods in the microwave.

Last, the microwave oven offers convenience. It can be extremely helpful in serving up meals quickly. Soup, casseroles, vegetables, or hot drinks can be heated up in a matter of minutes. Water can be boiled almost instantly. Furthermore, the amount of dishes to be washed can be reduced when cooking with a microwave since one can heat several food items in one dish whereas a conventional oven requires that each type of food be placed in a separate piece of cookware. The automatic timer on the microwave rings to alert you when the food is cooked, and then the oven will automatically shut off. Unlike the microwave, the conventional oven goes right on burning your food once the intended time is up. The microwave is also wonderfully easy to clean. One need no longer bother with messy oven cleaners or scraps of steel wool. Most microwave ovens come with a glass plate that protects you from spills and will easily slide out for fast cleaning. Also it has no greasy oven racks to clean.

Student Essay 5

Prison Rehabilitation Does Not Work

In the past, convicted criminals were automatically sentenced to death. Needless to say, crime was not as much of a growing problem then as it is now. As time went on, the punishment of criminals convicted of serious crimes became lighter as a result of compassionate sociologists and psychologists whose research concluded that harsh punishment was no deterrent to crime. These well-intentioned people wanted to focus attention on rehabilitating the criminal rather than on punishing him more and more severely. "Afterall, the human mind is a terrible thing to waste," was their altruistic attitude. Unfortunately, this altruistic attitude has gotten our nation into the grave situation it is now in. Prison rehabilitation is a lovely idea, but so is a Utopian society. Both are easy to talk about, but difficult to achieve.

The rehabilitation notion implies that the inmate needs to be changed. His whole idea about life, along with his attitudes, his values, and

self-concept has to be changed. This is as far-fetched an idea as trying to convince a zebra to be a leopard. Hardened criminals have a whole different concept about how to live life and what it should be lived for.

If the inmates need to change, the prison is the best place for rehabilitation programs. What rubbish! The environment in which these programs are to be instituted--of aggression, fear, totalitarianism, and exploitation--is what makes the idea of rehabilitation so preposterous.

Many studies of inmate treatment programs have reported that they have failed. For four years Dr. Robert Martinson analyzed and researched all of the different data connected with studies made of prison reform programs between 1945 and 1967. A total of 231 programs designed to rehabilitate convincted criminals were examined critically. Martinson writes, "There is very little evidence in these studies that any prevailing mode of correctional treatment has a decisive effect in reducing the recidivism of convicted offenders." (The Public Interest, p. 49.)

Two different studies came to the conclusion that inmates who were not involved in rehabilitative programs actually did better when released than those who remained involved in the programs. In a Florida study, 193 randomly

selected inmates were given work release
therapy, in which they were released to work in
the outside world and then returned at night. At
the end of the study, the inmates that had the
"benefit" of the experience had less favorable
answers to an attitude test than those who did
not participate. (Criminology, Vol II, No. 3,
pp. 345-381). In another study, 1,252 Florida
inmates released from prison due to a decision
by the United States Supreme Court concerning
"the right of indigent felons to counsel"
(Murton, The Dilemma of Prison Reform, p. 64),
were observed for 30 months. The 1,252 inmates
that had been released under the Supreme Court
decision did not complete their treatment
programs and went without the supervision of
parole officers. Another group of inmates (the
same number), who had completed their treatment
programs and were released under the supervision
of parole officers, were also studied and
compared with the control group. The results
indicated that of those released with
supervision and counseling, 15.4% returned to
prison whereas only 13.6% of those released
without supervision or counseling returned to
prison. To sum it up, those who received
rehabilitative treatment were twice as likely to
return to prison! (Murton, p. 64.)

    This seems to be convincing evidence that

rehabilitation efforts are pointless and even
detrimental to the prisoner's attitudes.
Rehabilitation is a great idea, but next to
impossible as far as achieving it is concerned.
I agree with the statement that "a mind is a
terrible thing to waste," but we're going at it
the wrong way. I feel that we must dig into the
psychological reasons for this behavior. If we
find out what goes wrong early, we may be able
to discourage crime.

Student Essay 6

Boat People

The day was coming to an end on a remote
island as beautiful as a painting. The brisk
clean wind went past me refreshingly as I sat on
the earth-colored sand to admire the lovely
natural scenery. I could hear the roar of the
crashing waves breaking upon the shore, smell
the fresh salt in the air, and felt the moisture
in the atmosphere. The orange fiery lines from
the sun were radiating away from the horizon.
Suddenly the appearance of a small sailboat was
looming on the horizon.

The white spot appeared far way on a vast,
blue sea surface. The tattered sails fluttered.
The seacoast became crowded and animated with
people. Suddenly the boat was within reach.

Together they tried to pull it in. We discovered
that it had sailed from a great distance. The
boat was very battered, and we wondered how it
could have endured a trip.

I saw nine skinny male survivors lying on
the planks of the boat. But one of them still
have strength to speak to our camp leader. His
weak voice came out through his parched, cracked
lips that barely moved, like those of a person
half frozen from the cold. I looked at his big,
glassy eyes. They spoke of such endurance and
fear. His skin was cold and clammy. He had the
look of a sick person who was barely alive. In
addition, his sunken cheeks made him look more
terrible than the face of a corpse. His cothes
were torn and grimy and spotted with dry blood
stains. The dirt and sweat mixed together
created an unendurable fetid odor which emanated
from him so strongly that I was inclined to
vomit. The rest of the survivors were in the
same awful condition. These nine men were
immediately carried to the emergency room in the
sick bay of our camp. They now had a chance for
life. They had survived.

After a while, I noticed that the seaside
became tranquil. The moon came up over the
mountain and shone on the sea like a bright new
light.

Part

5

Handbook

Basic Grammar

Punctuation

Mechanics

Effective Sentences

Basic Grammar

A command of basic grammar is as essential to writers as water is to fish. No matter how clever and creative a writer you are, if you cannot string coherent sentences together, use verbs and nouns properly, and make pronouns agree with their antecedents, your writing will inevitably appear amateurish. Yet the odd thing is that you are likely to receive little, if any, praise for mastering grammar. "Nobody ever admired an orator for using correct grammar," wrote Cicero. "They only laugh at him if his grammar is bad." So it is, too, with writers. They are expected to write grammatically, but get no glory for doing it.

It follows that the explanations of grammar, punctuation, mechanics, and style in this section may not help you to write exceptionally or even well. They will, however, help you to write correctly. To write well, you need to be grammatical and imaginative; to write exceptionally, you need to be grammatical, imaginative, precise, colorful, witty, and inspired. But no matter what level of excellence you hope to achieve in your writing, mastering grammar is an indispensable first step.

1. Parts of Speech

Words are the smallest grammatical parts of a sentence. Every word in a sentence performs a particular function by which it can be classified. These functions are carried out by eight parts of speech. Originally devised by Dionysius Thrax, a Greek grammarian, in 100 B.C., these categories have come down to us relatively intact.

The eight parts of speech are *verbs, nouns, adjectives, adverbs, pronouns, prepositions, conjunctions,* and *interjections.* Verbs, nouns, adjectives, and adverbs comprise almost all of the words in the dictionary. But even though the other four account for less than one percent of all words, they are used again and again in sentences.

1a. Verbs

The verb is the most crucial word in the sentence since it expresses an action, a process, or a state of being and since without it no sentence is complete. Verbs express commands, make statements about subjects, or link the subject to some idea about the subject.

> Sit   }   Verbs express commands.
> Stop! }   (The subject *you* is understood.)
>
> God loves   }
> Serpents hiss.}   Verbs make statements about the subjects.
> Fish swim.   }
>
> John is hungry.   }   Verbs link the subject to
> The children feel tired.}   some idea about the subject.

Most verbs express action or process. Linking verbs express a state of being. In addition to all forms of the verb *be,* they include *seem, feel, grow, look, sound, taste.*

> **Action:** The cow *jumped* over the moon.
> **Process:** The clock *ticked.*
> **State of being:** He *is* happy.
>   We *felt* sick.

The verbs in the examples above are complete in a single word, but others include one or more auxiliary (helping) words, thus forming a verb phrase:

> The clouds *had disappeared.* (*had* is an auxiliary word.)
> I *should* never *have taken* the money. (*Should* and *have* are auxiliary words.)

NOTE: Neither gerunds nor participles function as complete verbs, but more about them in 2c (2). *Verbal phrases.*

---

(1) Tense

Because actions take place at different times—in the present, past, or future—verbs can be adjusted to reflect this fact. The six tenses are:

Present tense expresses actions that happen now or that seem forever true:

> I *am eating* breakfast.
> John *likes* to eat.
> Roses *are* beautiful.

Past tense expresses an action happening sometime in the past:

> Nan *ate* all the cherries.
> Jack *sent* me these roses.

Future tense expresses an action that will happen sometime in the future.

> *Will* you *buy* some more cherries?
> The roses *will die* soon.

NOTE: It has become popular to use *shall* and *will* interchangeably. Nevertheless, purists of the English language make the following distinctions. To express a future action:

> I *shall* eat
> You *will* eat
> He/she/it *will* eat
>
> We *shall* eat
> You *will* eat
> They *will* eat

To express determination:

> I *will* eat
> You *shall* eat
> He/she/it *shall* eat
>
> We *will* eat (We are determined to eat)
> You *shall* eat
> They *shall* eat

In the case of questions in the first person, *will* and *shall* are not interchangeable:

> *Shall* we stay till 9:00 or *shall* we leave now?

> **but**

> Tomorrow we *will* (or *shall*) stay till 9:00.

Present perfect tense indicates that the action has taken place in the past but lasted until now.

> Nan *has eaten* all the cherries.
> The roses *have lasted* ten days.

Past perfect tense indicates that an action in the past took place before another past action:

> Nan *had eaten* all the cherries before the guests arrived.
> The lawyer *had gone* to court before June 15.

The *future perfect tense,* which is not often used, indicates a future action that will take place before another future action:

> Nan *will have eaten* all the cherries by lunch time.
> The roses *will have died* before the gardner arrives.

NOTE: Most verbs form the past tense and past participle by adding *ed* or *d* to the infinitive: *walk, walked, walked; believe, believed, believed.* Many verbs, however, form their principal parts through an internal vowel change *or* a final consonant change (*drink, drank, drunk; build, built, built*) or by not changing at all (*let, let, let*). If you are in doubt, check the dictionary, where you will find the principal parts of verbs listed. The principal parts of the following verbs are commonly misused:

> lie, lay, lain (I *lie* in the sun.)
> lay, laid, laid (He *laid* the book on the table.)
> sit, sat, sat (The baby *sits* in her crib.)
> set, set, set (John *has set* the vase on the shelf.)
> rise, rose, risen (We *rise* for prayer.)
> raise, raised, raised (Two men *raised* the flag.)

---

(2) Voice

Voice indicates who or what is doing the acting and who or what is receiving the action. Voice is either *active* or *passive.* In the active voice the subject always performs the action:

> Helen drank a gallon of water. (*Helen* is the subject.)

In the passive voice the subject always is acted upon:

> A gallon of water was drunk by Helen. (*Gallon* is the subject.)

Sometimes the passive voice omits the doer of an action:

> A gallon of water was drunk.

NOTE: Only transitive verbs (see next section) have voice.

(3) Forms

Verb forms are *transitive* or *intransitive*. A verb is transitive if it requires an object:

> Maria *discovered* an error. (*Error* serves as direct object.)

Occasionally a transitive verb will take a direct, as well as an indirect, object:

> She gave her sister a sandwich. (*Sandwich* is the direct object; *sister* is the indirect object.)

A verb is *intransitive* if it does not need an object to complete its meaning:

> The orchestra *played* beautifully.

NOTE: Some verbs are transitive only (*take, enjoy*), while others are intransitive only (*frown, giggle*). However, many verbs can function either way:

> He sang loudly; he sang an opera.

1b. Nouns

A noun is the name of a person, place, thing, idea, or event:

Persons: Dr. Wells, girl, Becky
Places: Chicago, heaven, school, world, park
Things: table, rice, chess, history, politics
Ideas: love, fear, humility, patriotism, stinginess
Events: war, trip, Christmas, Monday

Common nouns represent the names of general classes of persons, places, or things:

> boxer, state, writer, cereal

Proper nouns are always capitalized and name a particular person, place, or thing:

> Mohammed Ali, Michigan, the Constitution, Lake Tahoe

Compound nouns are proper nouns or common nouns that consist of more than one word and function as a single unit:

> South Africa, exchange rate, sunset, headache

1c. Pronouns

A pronoun is used in place of a noun. It is clearer and more concise to say "The man took off *his* coat" than "The man took off *the man's* coat." The antecedent of a pronoun is the word it replaces. Every pronoun must be in the same gender (masculine or feminine), case (subject of the sentence or object of the verb), and number (singular or plural) as its antecedent. Thus, "We saw the girl" will become "We saw *her*" because *girl* is feminine, object of the verb, and singular.

Pronouns may be grouped into seven categories:

Personal pronouns stand for someone or something specific: *I, you, he, she, it, we, you, they.*

Demonstrative pronouns point to nouns: *this, that, these, those.* They can be used as pronouns or as adjectives.

Pronoun: I reject *this.*
Adjective: I reject *this* idea.

Indefinite pronouns are unspecific: *anyone, everyone, each, someone.*

Interrogative pronouns ask a question: *who? what? which?* (Who destroyed the tree?)

Relative pronouns relate back to an antecedent (the banker *who,* the table *that,* the story *which*): *who, whom, those, which, that.*

Intensive pronouns emphasize: *myself, yourself, himself, ourselves, yourselves, themselves.* (I drove it *myself.*)

Reflexive pronouns function as objects or complements. They always refer to the person or thing named in the subject:

She drives *herself* to work every day.
The hot-water heater blew *itself* to smithereens.
I shall buy myself a car.

To use personal pronouns correctly, it is necessary to distinguish among their *subjective, objective,* and *possessive* cases. (See also 7. *Pronoun Case.*) The following table makes these differences clear:

SUBJECTIVE	OBJECTIVE	POSSESSIVE
I	me	mine
you	you	yours
he, she, it	him, her, it	his, hers, its
we	us	ours
you	you	yours
they	them	theirs

NOTE: A special case is *it* or *their* used as an expletive to postpone the sentence subject:

It is best that John be present.
There will be two books on the shelf.

1d. Adjectives

The adjective describes or limits nouns or pronouns. This describing or limiting is referred to as *modifying*. Generally, adjectives appear next to the nouns they modify:

> The *green* sweater cost *twenty-five* dollars.

However, adjectives used with linking verbs (see 1a. *Verbs*) may occur after the noun and verb and are called predicate adjectives:

> Dr. Jones is so *competent, thorough,* and *kind*.

Many adjectives are formed by adding suffixes such as *-al, -able, -ible, -ative, -ish, -ous,* or *-ic* to certain verbs or nouns:

VERB	ADJECTIVE
digest	digestible
communicate	communicative

NOUN	ADJECTIVE
fame	famous
penny	penniless

NOTES: 1. *A, an,* and *the* are special kinds of adjectives called articles.
2. Demonstrative pronouns often function as adjectives:

Pass me *that* napkin.
This book is Mary's.

1e. Adverbs

An adverb can modify verbs, adjectives, or other adverbs. Generally, adverbs are formed by adding the suffix *-ly* to an adjective:

The following examples illustrate how adverbs are used:

ADJECTIVE	ADVERB
normal	normally
quick	quickly
animated	animatedly

She moved *swiftly*. (*Swiftly* modifies the verb *moved*.)
It is an *exceptionally* boring game. (*Exceptionally* modifies the adjective *boring*.)
The queen whispered *very* softly. (*Very* modifies the adverb *softly*.)

The usual function of the adverb is to say *when, where, how,* and *to what extent* something happened:

> She came *soon.* (When did she come?)
> He put the book *there.* (Where did he put the book?)
> She fought *furiously.* (How did she fight?)
> Our love will last *forever.* (To what extent will our love last?)

See also 1g. *Conjunctions, conjunctive adverbs.*

NOTE: Both adjectives and adverbs can be used in three forms: *positive, comparative,* and *superlative.* The positive form is the unchanged adjective or adverb; the comparative form indicates *more* or *less;* the superlative form indicates *most* or *least.* Here are some examples:

> **Positive:** He spoke *loudly.* (adverb)
> She is a *loud* person. (adjective)
> **Comparative:** He spoke *louder.* (adverb)
> She is a *louder* person. (adjective)
> **Superlative:** He spoke *loudest.* (adverb)
> She is the *loudest* person. (adjective)

The following forms are irregular:

Adjectives

POSITIVE	COMPARATIVE	SUPERLATIVE
good	better	best
bad	worse	worst

Adverbs

POSITIVE	COMPARATIVE	SUPERLATIVE
well	better	best
badly	worse	worst

Be sure that you distinguish between *good* and *well, bad* and *badly:*

Wrong: He plays tennis *good.* (adjective)
 Right: He plays tennis *well.* (adverb)

Wrong: Sam burned his finger *bad.* (adjective)
 Right: Sam burned his finger *badly.* (adverb)

When discussing health, use *well* and *bad:*

> Jack feels *well.*
> John feels *bad.*

When discussing feelings, use *good* and *bad:*

> I feel *good* about my job.
> He feels *bad* about the misunderstanding.

1f. Prepositions

A preposition shows the relationship between nouns, pronouns, verbs, adjectives, and adverbs:

> John stood *behind* the doors. (*Behind* indicates relationship between John and the doors.)

A less complicated definition of the preposition is any word that describes what an airplane can do when approaching clouds. The airplane can go *by, across, above, below, into, between, over, through, inside, beyond, from, to* the clouds, among other things. However, not all prepositions qualify under this definition. *Concerning, regarding, of, for,* or *during* are examples of prepositions that do not.

A few prepositions consist of more than one word: *in spite of, because of, on account of, instead of, together with, in regard to.*

NOTE: A preposition and its object make up a *prepositional phrase:*

> They strolled *inside* the garden. (prepositional phrase)

1g. Conjunctions

A conjunction connects words, phrases, and clauses. Incoherent or mispunctuated sentences often result from misused conjunctions. There are three kinds of conjunctions: *coordinating, subordinating,* and *conjunctive adverbs* (also called *logical connectives*).

Coordinating conjunctions (and, but, nor, for) join words, phrases, and clauses of equal importance:

Words: Silk *and* velvet are my favorite materials.
Phrases: Living in pain *or* dying in peace was his choice.
Clauses: George continued to make money, *but* he was miserable.

NOTE: A special type of coordinating conjunction is the *correlative conjunction,* which also joins elements of equal importance but occurs only in pairs:

> *not only . . . but also*
> *neither . . . nor*
> *both . . . and*

Not only did he buy a Porsche, *but also* he paid cash for it.
Neither she *nor* her husband appeared at the reception.
Both my father *and* my grandfather agree with me.

Subordinating conjunctions (such as *if, because, when, since, where, while, whereas, after, before, until, as if*) are used to join subordinate clauses with independent clauses, as:

Felice studies *because* she is ambitious.
If it rains, we must buy an umbrella.

However, place a subordinating conjunction before an independent clause and you will have a *sentence fragment*—a transformation often overlooked by student writers:

The man stood at the door. (independent clause)
While the man stood at the door. (fragment caused by subordinating
    conjunction)

Such a fragment can be corrected by attaching it to an independent clause:

While the man stood at the door, the dog barked.
The dog barked *while* the man stood at the door.

See also 3. *Sentence fragments.*

NOTE: Relative pronouns can function as subordinating conjunctions to introduce adjective or noun clauses (see 2d):

We blamed the man *who* was driving without a license.
The house *that* she had just finished paying for burned down.

Conjunctive adverbs (such as *however, consequently, moreover, besides, on the other hand, that is to say, yet, furthermore, nevertheless, meanwhile, indeed, anyhow, hence, henceforth, then*) are adverbs used to connect independent clauses. Always place a semicolon before and a comma after a conjunctive adverb that connects two independent clauses:

The tickets are three dollars apiece; *however,* members of the club pay only
    two dollars.
The sky was dark and cloudy; *nevertheless,* we pressed onward.

NOTES: 1. A comma should be used before and after the conjunctive adverb when the conjunctive adverb is parenthetical:

My friend drove her car to the party; I, *however,* took the bus.
The other half of the restaurant, *meanwhile,* stood empty and forsaken.

2. The use of *yet* and *so* as coordinating conjunctions has been more or less accepted in informal writing. However, careful writers use *yet* only as a logical connective, and seldom use the anemic *so.*

1h. Interjections

An interjection is used to indicate emotion. Usually, interjections have no grammatical connection with other words in the sentence. Interjections may be either mild or forceful. If forceful, they are followed by an exclamation point.

    Mild: *Ah,* you kept your promise.
             Well, let's move ahead.
Forceful: *Oh!* I lost my wallet!
             Phew! That's hard work!

We began this discussion by saying that a part of speech can be classified according to the way it functions in a sentence. It follows that the same word may serve as a different part of speech in different sentences. Here are some examples:

The stairway contains one broken *step.* (noun)
Please do not let her *step* in the mud. (verb)

The man accompanied her *inside.* (adverb)
Her *inside* pocket is torn. (adjective)
The teacher disappeared *inside* the room. (preposition)

Exercise keeps a person limber. (noun)
They *exercise* every day. (verb)
We need an *exercise* room. (adjective)

Exercises

Exercise 1: Parts of speech
In the sentences below, name the part of speech of each italicized word.

    MODEL: The plum was *overly* ripe.

             Answer: **Adverb**

1. The priest picked up the book and *caressed* it.
2. The English tried to find a *northern* route.
3. The people were poor, *but* they wore fur pelts.
4. I don't care for *this.*

5. *If* he is allowed to dominate her, he will.
6. He had come on deck *without* notice.
7. There was not enough *space* for the food.
8. The breeze *had wafted* a strand of hair into her eyes.
9. In time, he *will explain* himself to all of us.
10. Her name was remembered *because of* her book.
11. My husband has five *living* sisters.
12. Why hurt a human being just to please *someone?*
13. The musket shot was aimed *directly* at the frigate's lower sails.
14. She was asked to stay *exactly* alongside.
15. *Wow!* What a beautiful pair of shoes!
16. *Not only* did he say the word in private, *but* he *also* repeated it in front of the crowd.
17. The *cold* was unbearable to anyone from the south.
18. The ballet dancers made one *final* effort before the curtain went down.
19. Mr. Thornburg swam *for* one hour and felt better.
20. *Proudly* she saluted the flag.
21. He blamed *himself* for all of the year's troubles.
22. The fish was white, slimy, and almost *tasteless.*
23. *Well,* perhaps he should take some Vitamin C.
24. The Japanese lady *had waved* her fan and had smiled encouragingly.
25. You have a terrible temper; *nevertheless,* you will make a good leader.
26. *Perhaps* she would suit another company better than mine.
27. Martha had remained thoughtful and *reserved.*
28. They discussed the *feasibility* of a full-scale war.
29. The old woman looked away *and* scowled.
30. In some countries, *it* is considered polite to sip soup from a bowl.

Exercise 1: Parts of speech

Identify the part of speech of each boldface word in the following paragraph.

It was **evening.** Around the low **fire, inside** the **paramount** chief's hut sat the **leading** men of the village, **each** swaying to the **rhythmic** tom-tom of the tribal drum. The wrinkled **witch doctor** squatted **near** the chief, **but** he seemed **totally unafraid as** his cunning, birdlike eyes restlessly **sought** the attention of **each** man. His hands were deftly arranging some tiger teeth **and** chicken bones; **however, he** was obviously **completely aware** of the **solemnity** of the occasion. "**Oh,** witch doctor, **we are listen- ing,**" a voice suddenly murmured. The **wrinkled old** man drew his basket of charms **close to** his crossed legs. He **then** threw some charms on the ground **while** he mumbled a monotonous formula in his untranslatable tribal dialect.

2. Sentences

The parts of speech, when put together in certain ways, constitute a sentence. All sentences have a *subject* and a *predicate*. A working knowledge of these components is useful to both the beginnng and the veteran writer.

2a. Subjects and predicates

The subject is what a speaker or writer makes a statement about; the predicate is what is said about the subject. A *noun,* or group of words functioning as a noun, makes up the core of each subject; a *verb,* or group of words functioning as a verb, makes up the core of each predicate. The essence of a sentence may then be said to consist—in its simplest form—of two words, a noun and a verb:

NOUN/SUBJECT	VERB/PREDICATE
People	think.
Bees	sting.
Dogs	bite.

In all three examples, a verb (predicate) makes an assertion about a noun (subject). This basic division applies even if a sentence is written as a question. *Where is my book?* can be divided into subject and predicate just as readily as the sentence *My book is there.* At the heart of both constructions are a noun and a verb—that is, a part about which something is said and a part that either asks or asserts something about a subject.

The three examples given above illustrate sentences in their most rudimentary form: a *simple subject* and a *simple predicate* with a single word functioning in each role. The *complete subject* and *complete predicate* consist of all those words that are a part of the subject and all those that are part of the predicate. Here are some examples:

SIMPLE SUBJECT	SIMPLE PREDICATE
People	think.

COMPLETE SUBJECT	COMPLETE PREDICATE
People of all creeds, ages and nationalities	think about life, love, and death.
People of all creeds, ages, nationalities, no matter what their life-styles or politics,	think about life, love, death, and other eternal questions.

SIMPLE SUBJECT	SIMPLE PREDICATE
He	ran.

COMPLETE SUBJECT	COMPLETE PREDICATE
Grabbing his overcoat and umbrella, he	ran away from the house as fast as he could.

The ability to recognize the complete subjects and complete predicates of sentences is especially useful in properly punctuating them.

2b. Complements

A complement is a word or group of words that completes the meaning of a verb. Complements are divided into the following categories: direct object, indirect object, subject complement, and object complement.

(1) Direct object

A direct object answers the question *What?* or *Whom?* in connection with a verb. In the following sentences, the direct object is italicized:

> The dog chewed the *rug*. (What did the dog chew?)
> He married *Cynthia*. (Whom did he marry?)

(2) Indirect object

The indirect object usually precedes the direct object, and tells *to whom* or *for whom* (or *to what* or *for what*) the action of a verb is done. In the following sentences, the indirect objects are italicized:

> The salesperson gave the *man* a blank look. (To whom did the salesperson give a blank look?)
> Her parents ordered *her* a Datsun. (For whom did her parents order a Datsun?)

(3) Subject complement

The subject complement completes the sense of the verb by further explaining the subject. The following qualify as linking verbs that can be completed by subject complements:

> Forms of the verb *to be: am, are, is, was, were, been*
> Verbs having to do with the senses: *smell, look, taste, feel, sound,* and so forth
> Certain other verbs: *seem, appear, become, remain, grow, prove,* and so forth

The subject complements are italicized in the following sentences:

> Most Spaniards are *Catholics*.
> That animal seems to be a *wolf*.

In addition to nouns, adjectives and pronouns can serve as subject complements:

> The blanket feels *warm* and *comforting.*
> My perfume smells *exotic.*
> He will not admit that it was *she.*

(4) Object complement

The object complement further explains the direct object. In the following example, the object complements are italicized:

> The mob called the criminal a cold-blooded *murderer.*

An adjective can also serve as an object complement:

> The thought of going home made her *depressed.* (*Depressed* modifies the
> direct object *her.*)

2c. Phrases

A phrase is a group of words, usually without subject and verb, that expresses a thought but is not a complete statement. Phrases can be classified as: prepositional, verbal, absolute, and appositive.

(1) Prepositional phrases

A prepositional phrase consists of a preposition followed by a noun (or pronoun) and any words that modify that noun (or pronoun). The prepositional phrase usually functions as an *adjective* or *adverb.* In the following sentences, the prepositional phrases are italicized:

> Jane left home *without a jacket.* (The prepositional phrase modified the verb
> *left* by specifying how Jane left home. It therefore functions as an
> adverb.)
>
> *Behind the bush* huddled a savage dog. (The prepositonal phrase modifies
> the verb *huddled* by specifying where the dog huddled. It therefore
> functions as an adverb.)
>
> The slipper *under the bed* was too big. (The prepositional phrase modifies
> the noun *slipper* by specifying which slipper was too big—the one *under
> the bed.* It therefore functions as an adjective.)

(2) Verbal phrases

A verbal phrase consists of a verbal and all the words immediately related to it. Do not confuse verbals with verbs. Verbals are derived from verbs, but make no statement about a subject. They function as *nouns, adjectives,* or *adverbs.* There are three kinds of verbals: *infinitive, gerund,* and *participle.*

An *infinitive* is used as a noun, an adjective, or an adverb and is usually made up of the construction *to* + the present form of the verb.

> *To study* is smart. (noun)
> This is the way *to study*. (adjective)
> John left *to study*. (adverb)

A *gerund* is used only as a noun and has an *ing* ending:

> *Skiing* is my favorite sport. (noun as subject)
> She hates *gardening*. (noun as direct object)
> Their goal is *making* money. (noun as subject complement)
> Before *stopping* he wants to finish. (noun as object of preposition)

A *participle* is used as an adjective. Participles are either present (ending in *-ing*) or past (commonly ending in *-d, -ed, -n, -en*. In the case of irregular verbs, vowels may change, as in *brought* and *clung*.) Participles and gerunds can be distinguished from one another by their functions in a sentence. The gerund functions as a noun; the participle, as an adjective:

> *Suffering* is a part of life. (gerund)
> The *suffering* child was hospitalized. (participle)

Like verbals, verbal phrases are either infinitive, gerund, or participle:

(a) **Infinitive** An infinitive phrase consists of an infinitive followed by its modifiers. The infinitive phrase may function as an adjective, adverb, or noun. In the following sentences, the infinitive phrases have been italicized:

ADJECTIVE	INFINITIVE PHRASE AS ADJECTIVE
The comedian used *appropriate* humor.	The comedian used humor *to match the occasion.*
ADVERB	**INFINITIVE PHRASE AS ADVERB**
The lecturer spoke *informatively.*	The lecturer spoke *to inform the audience.*
NOUN	**INFINITIVE PHRASE AS NOUN**
Larceny tempts many people.	*To steal money* is a common temptation.

(b) **Gerund** A gerund phrase consists of a gerund and its modifiers. The gerund phrase functions as a noun. (Although a gerund and a participle may share the same *-ing* ending, the gerund always functions as a noun.) In the following sentences, the gerund phrases have been italicized:

> *Chewing gum with her mouth open* was her worst habit. (The gerund phrase functions as a noun and as subject of the verb *was.* Notice that the entire phrase, like all nouns, may be replaced by a pronoun: *It* was her worst habit.)

> The reporter praised *the guitarist's loud and regular twanging.* (The gerund phrase functions as the object of the verb *praised.*)

(c) **Participial** A participial phrase consists of a participle followed by modifiers. It functions as an adjective. In the following sentences, the participial phrases have been italicized:

> *Crying in pain,* the football player limped away. (The participial phrase modifies the compound noun *football player.*)

> The windows of the car *parked in the driveway* were shattered to bits. (The participial phrase modifies the noun *car* by specifying which car was meant—the one *parked in the driveway.*)

> *Bent by old age,* the man struggled on. (The participial phrase modifies the noun *man.*)

(3) Absolute phrases

Absolute phrases stand grammatically independent ("absolutely" alone). They have no identifiable grammatical link to the rest of the sentence. Nor are they linked to an independent clause by a subordinating word. Absolute constructions are therefore difficult to identify and easy to misuse. Here are some examples:

> *The diver having finished his dive,* we left for tea.
> *All things being equal,* tomorrow will be our big day.
> *Considering the state of the budget,* the hearings should be continued.

An absolute construction should not be confused with a dangling participial phrase. Here are some examples to clarify the difference between them:

> *The meeting having gone as planned,* we broke for lunch. (absolute construction)

Wrong: *Having met for five hours,* lunch was then served. (Dangling participle implies "lunch" had met for five hours.)

Right: *Having met for five hours,* we were then served lunch. (Participial phrase modifies "we.")

See also 26. *Dangling modifiers.*

(4) Appositive phrases

An appositive phrase is a word or phrase placed beside another word whose meaning it expands or explains. The appositive must always be syntactically parallel to the word it stands in apposition to—that is, it must be the same part of speech and must fulfill the same grammatical function:

(a) Appositive as subject:

Paul's father, *a wealthy businessman,* was forced into bankruptcy. (*Father* and *businessman* are both subjects.)

(b) Appositive as object:

He rejected his first love, *oil painting.* (*Love* and *oil painting* are both objects.)

(c) Appositive as adjective:

He spoke in a paternalistic, that is, *authoritative,* manner. (*Paternalistic* and *authoritative* are both adjectives.)

(d) Appositive as adverb:

The essay was proofread carefully—*with utmost precision.* (*Carefully* and *with utmost precision* are both adverbials.)

Think of appositives as abbreviated or reduced clauses because they can be expanded into clauses by using some form of the verb *be:*

His father, *who was a wealthy businessman,* was forced into bankruptcy.
He rejected his first love, *which was oil painting.*
He spoke in a paternalistic manner, *which was an authoritative manner.*
The essay was proofread carefully, *meaning that it was proofread with utmost precision.*

2d. Clauses

A clause is a group of words containing a subject and a predicate. If the words make sense by themselves, they are said to constitute an independent clause. A clause that does not make sense by itself is called a dependent clause.

(1) Independent clauses

What makes a clause independent is its ability to stand alone and make complete sense. Here are some examples:

The man had bad breath.
People need to buy health insurance.
Fairy tales are important reading for children.

(2) Dependent clauses

A clause that does not make sense by itself is called a dependent clause since it must "depend" on an independent clause to complete its meaning. Here are some examples:

Who was standing next to me
Even though they have Social Security
That fairy tales teach about good and evil

Attached to appropriate independent clauses, however, these dependent clauses become grammatically complete:

The man who was *standing next to me* had bad breath.
Even though they have Social Security, people need health insurance.
That fairy tales teach about good and evil makes them important reading for children.

Dependent clauses can be recognized by the connectives binding them to independent clauses. These connectives are always subordinating words such as the subordinating conjunctions *although, even though, despite, what, that, who, which, when, since, before, after, if, as, because* that introduce adverbial clauses, or the relative pronouns *who, what, that, which* that introduce noun and adjective clauses. (See also 1g. *Conjunctions.*) Dependent clauses can also function as grammatical units in a sentence, playing the equivalent role of a noun, an adjective, or an adverb.

(a) **Noun clauses** A noun clause is a subordinate clause that acts as a noun.

Noun clause as subject:

What he demanded frightened the pilot. (The noun clause is the subject of the verb *frightened.* As with all nouns, a pronoun—in this case *it, this,* or *that* could be substituted for the entire noun clause.)

Noun clause as direct object:

I request *that you clean up your room.*

Noun clause as indirect object:

The government will give *whoever is hungry* food stamps.

Noun clause as objects of a preposition:

She longs for *whatever is right.*

Noun clause as subject complement:

Rest is *what he needs.*

Noun clause as appositive:

We suspected the object, *whatever it was.*

(b) **Adjective clauses** An adjective clause modifies either a noun or a pronoun in a sentence:

He remembered the place *where they had first kissed.* (The italicized adjective clause modifies the noun *place.*)

Look at the flower *she picked yesterday.* (The italicized adjective clause modifies the noun *flower.*)

(c) **Adverb clauses** An adverb clause modifies a verb, adjective, or adverb in the sentence. It may occur in various positions in a sentence, at the end, the beginning, or in the middle. An adverb clause is usually introduced by a subordinating conjunction:

ADVERB	**ADVERB CLAUSE**
She blew the trumpet *loudly.*	She blew the trumpet *so that everyone could hear.*
Later he made tea.	*When the water boiled,* he made tea.

ADVERB	**ADVERB CLAUSE**
Everyone *here* plays the guitar.	Everyone *where I live* plays the guitar.

As you can see from the above examples, the way to identify the function of a cluase is to see what part of speech may be substituted for it. A noun clause may be replaced by an equivalent noun or by a pronoun; an adjective clause may be replaced by an adjective; and an adverb clause may be replaced by an adverb.

2e. Kinds of sentences

Sentences are grouped into four types according to the number and kinds of clauses involved: simple, compound, complex, and compound-complex. A knowledge of the different sentence types is useful to anyone who aims for sentence variety and correct punctuation.

(1) Simple sentences

A simple sentence has one subject and one predicate:

Jim is getting married.
We will sail tomorrow.

NOTE: A simple sentence may have two or more nouns as subject and two or more verbs as predicate:

The *birds* in the sky and the *fish* in the sea add to life's beauty.
(*Birds* and *fish* form a compound subject.)

The entire town *praised* and *thanked* the mayor. (*Praised* and *thanked* form a compound predicate.)

(2) Compound sentences

A compound sentence consists of at least two independent clauses.

> The houses are tall, but the streets are narrow.
> Behind the fence is a garden, and beyond the garden lies a lake.
> We sang songs and offered prayers, and we waited for rescue.

(3) Complex sentences

A complex sentence consists of one independent clause and one or more dependent clauses. The dependent clauses are italicized in the following examples:

> Everyone arrived *when the sun came out.*
> *If he were to inherit a million dollars,* he would give it all to people *who work on farms.*

(4) Compound-complex sentences

A compound-complex sentence consists of two or more independent clauses and one or more dependent clauses. The independent clauses are in boldface and the dependent clauses are italicized:

> **He refused to enter the house** *unless I went with him;* yet, *while we were inside,* **he showed no fear.**
> *When they pay their gas bill,* **they will be happy** *that they bought the car,* but **they will never thank me for my advice.**

Exercises

Exercise 2a: Complete subjects and complete predicates

In the sentences below, separate the complete subject from the complete predicate by a vertical line.

> MODEL: The country road | stretched into the distance.

1. The traveler, a tall man in his late thirties, stood looking up into the branches of the oak tree.
2. Now old and bent, his father had loved to sit beneath the bridge.
3. Wandering about the campus with Francis, he remembered suddenly a particular summer morning.
4. The pattern of the coming year and of his behavior was set.
5. Like most religious fanatics, she had absolutely no sense of humor.
6. Its remarkable beauty did not lie only in its bright glitter.

7. Mrs. McClosky, a guest of the mayor, refused to ride in a car driven by a chauffeur.
8. Facing each other in front of the fire, two red sofas always waited for us every evening.
9. A hint of anger or coldness in his voice would keep her in the depths of despair for weeks on end.
10. The old man arose hurriedly and disappeared into the woods.

Exercise 2a: Simple subjects and simple predicates

In the following sentences, underline the simple subject once and the simple predicate twice.

> MODEL:　Moved almost to tears, I whispered back.

1. Perhaps his answer was an assent of the heart rather than of the mind.
2. Next year, too many people will visit the Vatican.
3. According to the Bible, "A prating fool will come to ruin."
4. The pilot was landing the plane during wind, rain, and hail.
5. Beside the president stood the secretary of state.
6. Gentlemen, please take your seats.
7. Did you remember the poem on the wall of the library?
8. John simply could not reject his past.
9. By jumping into the water first, he avoided being pushed by his friends.
10. There are always two sides to a question.

Exercise 2b: Complements

In the sentences below, decide whether the italicized words are direct objects, indirect objects, object complements, or subject complements.

> MODEL:　More and more, he appeared to be *alone.*
>
> Answer:　**Subject complement**

1. She had gone to bring the *eggs* from the henhouse.
2. Spring is a *time* of glorious magic.
3. The children considered him *king* of the block.
4. I had learned a great *principle* of the way grief affects people.
5. Because of its timing, the visit was *oppressive.*
6. Without further thought, Joanne labeled the teacher a *Communist.*
7. We could have simply given *him* a pile of money, but he needed attention and love.
8. To me, her thoughts seemed *nuggets* of gold.
9. Being a respectful man, he gave our *flag* a brisk salute.
10. While singing cheerfully, he stirred the *pot* of soup on the fire.

Exercise 2c: Phrases

In each of the sentences below, indicate what kind of phrase the italicized words are:

MODEL: *To own one's home in California* is extremely expensive.

Answer: **Infinitive phrase**

1. *Hoping not to be called on duty,* I snuggled up in my blanket.
2. *The cub meeting having adjourned,* the students trudged home.
3. He heard the sound *of boots marching down the corridor.*
4. The rain, *little more than a cool mist,* refreshed us immensely.
5. *To say goodbye without hope of seeing one another again* was heartrending.
6. *Cooking from scratch* is becoming a lost art.
7. More than anything else, we wanted *to know our neighbors across the street.*
8. *Playing poker* did not interest him in the least.
9. We looked at Sylvia, *a radiant young woman in her white gown.*
10. We lived *in the community of Whiting Woods.*

Exercise 2d: Independent and dependent clauses

In the sentences below, enclose the dependent clauses in parentheses and underline the independent clauses.

MODEL: (That Carl was not musical) <u>disappointed his parents; however, they bought a piano</u> (because they never lost hope.)

1. He had never doubted that the vessel was westward bound, nor had he ever believed that it would withstand a week of stormy waters.
2. The thought of that wonderful homemade bread conjured up images of a mother who worked day and night so that her family could be well fed.
3. Somehow her parents had instilled in her a clear idea of everything that is honorable.
4. If they wanted to remain allies, they were running a terrible risk.
5. At the same time, we met another friend, Bernard Townsend, witty, intelligent, handsome, who loved the poetry of John Donne.
6. We began, hardly knowing we were doing it, to revise our opinion of the strikers who had suffered so much.
7. Our fundamental assumption, which we had been foolish enough to consider intelligent insight, had been that all Christian church members were rigid and unwilling to think through important issues that affect a citizen's ethical commitments.
8. If they had been asked what they meant when they spoke of life on another planet, they would have answered with pure nonsense.

9. The Benedictine monks built the long, lovely buildings that are still part of one college quadrangle at Oxford University, where John received his degree in 1978.
10. Another reason for not skiing faster was that she was exhausted; however, her companions did not realize her fatigue and kept goading her on until she sat down in the snow and cried with frustration.

Exercise 2d: Identifying types of dependent clauses

In the sentences below, underline each dependent clause and indicate if it is an adjective clause, an adverbial clause, or a noun clause.

> MODEL: We decided to study the painting that had been shipped from New York.
>
> Answer: Adjective clause

1. The truth was that she had heard that tune before.
2. While he loved her desperately, he did not want to give up his job for her.
3. The problem that had been solved yesterday loomed up twice as big today.
4. It has been said that the fourth dimension is time and duration.
5. As a nun, she went where life would be calm and tranquil.
6. The disease, with all of its suffering, would return unless we could find the right specialist.
7. The friend from whom she had received the book never contacted her in the years to come.
8. The job was much more difficult and exhausting that she had expected.
9. The point is to admit candidly what bothers you.
10. Did you spend the entire day looking for the thief who stole your wallet?

Exercise 2e: Kinds of sentences

Identify each sentence below as simple, compound, complex, or compound-complex.

> MODEL: When the great tree came down, it left an empty space against the sky.
>
> Answer: Complex sentence

1. I was conscious of a sort of amazement that a steak could taste so good.
2. They had decided from the beginning to reach out and draw in all of the richness of this great university around them.
3. I did not admit it, but I was beginning to love poetry.

4. She stuck five-dollar bills into the drawer and then she escaped through the front door without leaving a note about where she was going.
5. His grandfather on his mother's side and his grandfather on his father's side were not at all the same, for the former was educated at Princeton whereas the latter had no formal education beyond the fifth grade.
6. When she looked up into those branches filled with rust- and gold-colored autumn leaves, she wanted to stay in New England forever.
7. War was no longer merely a rumor circulated by adventurers and fanatics in an attempt to get some attention.
8. It would seem that a career in the theater requires both an emotional and intellectual commitment.
9. He had not rejected the offer; he merely had not decided yet.
10. Our tacit understanding was that whoever went to the library would pick up the book.

3. Sentence Fragments (frag)

A fragment is a phrase or dependent clause capitalized and punctuated as though it were a complete sentence:

> An interesting book from the library.
> Who screamed in a loud voice.

These fragments are incomprehensible by themselves although they are written as if they were complete sentences. The easiest way to correct a fragment in your own writing is to add enough words to make the fragment into an independent clause. In the following examples, words have been added to make each fragment a complete sentence:

> I am reading an interesting book from the library.
> The child who screamed in a loud voice was frightened by a nightmare.

Sometimes, the correction can be made by adding the fragment to a preceding or a following independent clause:

Wrong: Ken might get a job. *If he will contact the manager of the store by Monday.* (The italicized phrase is a fragment.)

Right: Ken might get a job if he will contact the manager of the store by Monday.

In order to avoid sentence fragments in your writing, remember that dependent clauses cannot stand by themselves, and that the addition of any subordinating word to a sentence automatically makes it a fragment. Consider these examples:

Complete sentence: I was tired.
Sentence fragments: Because
               When
               Although
               Since   I was tired.
               Whereas
               Even though

Be alert to any construction beginning with a subordinating word. Make sure it is properly joined to an independent clause.

Writers sometimes use fragments for a stylistic effect. In the example below the writer used fragments to make a pair of climactic utterances about bones:

> Bones. Two hundred and eight of them. A whole glory turned and tooled.
> —Richard Selzer, "Bone."

This sort of writing, however, is not recommended for college students. Leave fragments to professional writers, and frame your own thoughts in complete, coherent sentences.

4. Comma Splices (cs)

A comma splice occurs when a comma is used to connect two independent clauses not joined by a coordinating conjunciton such as *and, nor, but,* or *for:*

Wrong: The nurse brought in the tray, Mr. Jones began to eat his breakfast.

4a. Correcting comma splices

(1) Comma and coordinating conjunction

Use a comma and a coordinating conjunction to connect independent clauses of equal strength:

> The nurse brought in the tray, <u>and</u> Mr. Jones began to eat his breakfast.

(2) Semicolon

Use a semicolon to connect two independent clauses that are closely related in thought:

> The nurse brought in the tray; Mr. Jones began to eat his breakfast.

(3) Period

Use a period between two independent clauses that require separate emphasis:

> The nurse brought in the tray. Without complaint Mr. Jones began to eat his breakfast.

(4) Subordination

Subordinate one idea to another:

> When the nurse brought in the tray, Mr. Jones knew it was time to eat his breakfast.

5. Run-on Sentences (ro)

A run-on or fused sentence, as the name implies, consists of two independent clauses improperly connected, with neither link or break between them.

Wrong: Robert stared at the screen he knew he had seen this fellow before.

5a. Correcting run-on sentences

The same methods of correction used on comma splices can be applied to run-on sentences.

(1) Comma and coordinating conjunction

Use a comma and a coordinating conjunction between clauses of *equal strength:*

> Robert stared at the screen, and he knew he had seen this fellow before.

(2) Semicolon

Use a semicolon between two independent clauses that are closely related in thought.

> Robert stared at the screen; he knew he had seen this fellow before.

(3) Period

Use a period between two independent clauses requiring separate emphasis.

> Robert stared at the screen. He knew he had seen this fellow before.

(4) Subordination

Subordinate one idea to another.

> As Robert stared at the screen, he suddenly realized that he had seen this fellow before.

Exercises

Exercise 3: Sentence fragments

Rewrite the following passages, correcting sentence fragments. If a passage contains no fragments, leave it alone. Add words if needed.

> MODEL: On the surface Jane appears to be a young woman. Struggling between a career and marriage.
>
> Answer: **On the surface, Jane appears to be a young woman struggling between a career and marriage.**

1. Randy is getting more decisive each day. Having promised himself to move in one direction.
2. Among married teenagers, one of the most popular routes out of the locked-in position is divorce. Because it supplies a quick and definite way out.
3. One part of him is searching for freedom. The other part desiring to be rooted and tied down.
4. Whereas the women seemed more mature than the men who entered college.
5. Although some parents offer glamorous opportunities to their children, they usually contaminate these offers with parental rules and values.
6. We each have our own set of ethics. The way we see and interpret right and wrong.
7. The simplest, and what appears to be the safest option, is for Mary to drive the car herself. Then Jack can pick it up from her.
8. On the other hand, if she were to sink all of her money into this publishing company, believing that eventually it would make her rich.
9. To be consigned to a life of boredom just because one wanted to please one's parents.
10. The older we get, the more we become aware of our mortality. Hoping against hope that we shall remain among the lucky few who live to a ripe and contented old age.

Exercises 3, 4, 5: Sentence fragments, comma splices, run-on sentences

Indicate whether the following are complete sentences, fragments, comma splices, or run-on sentences.

> MODEL: Marvin had a difficult time in life, he took himself too seriously.
>
> Answer: **Comma splice**

1. Three days passed, however, he still did not recognize anyone.
2. While the man was asleep, she had carefully gone through his belongings.

3. Her dresses were made from the most delicate silk her shoes were made from the softest leather.
4. Since the children were playing outside in the blizzard.
5. Of course, it would not pay to make that kind of man angry or jealous.
6. Attempting to make him forget his troublesome past in order to start a new life.
7. He bit his fingernails; his heart was beating rapidly.
8. She wished she could stay with him forever, she could not understand her own feelings about this simple man.
9. Is it possible to calculate the effect of a nuclear attack in our era?
10. Ginger eagerly swallowed her glass of champagne, her face was flushed and hot.
11. I want to be candid, our financial situation does not look good.
12. Jim balanced himself precariously, holding the book high in the air.
13. Confessing to the crowd that he had lied all along.
14. The poor girl is ill; she is not well at all.
15. We listened with great interest after all he was an expert in his field.
16. The message fell on deaf ears, ears that no longer responded to truth.
17. He was not a man to act on the spur of the moment, however, this telegram called for a response.
18. The lawyer called me into his office to explain all of the details involved in signing the papers.
19. While George was completely fascinated by the artist's bizarre use of black polka dots.
20. From now until tomorrow not eating another bite.
21. She felt sick, but the unkind words could not be recalled.
22. Having given directions to the nurse to prepare for the next operation.
23. He had had ten years of pain from the broken bones, ten years of suffering from that spreading ulcer.
24. It was a dark night, the children had walked silently along the dim path.
25. You look healthy you look strong.
26. Then addressing the group of amateur photographers who seemed to need a leader.
27. When he came to our town, he was young and strong.
28. The spots on his body disappeared his skin became healthy again.
29. His raised voice directed to the people who would take the long journey with him.
30. Sylvia Plath wrote depressing poems, she eventually committed suicide.

6. Agreement (agr)

A subject and its verb and a pronoun and its antecedent must agree in number.

6a. Subject-verb agreement

Once you have decided on a subject, it determines what form of verb you will use. For instance, you will write, "A fish swims," not "A fish swim," because *fish* in this instance is third-person singular. On the other hand, you will write, "Most fish swim" because in this instance *fish* is third-person plural. Agreement errors are primarily caused by the unusual word order of a sentence or by words intervening between a verb and its subject.

(1) Unusual word order

Unusual word order in a sentence may confuse you. Consider the following examples:

> The one fruit that I love *is* (not *are*) oranges. (The subject is *fruit.*)
>
> *Have* not (not *has*) the warm days of this lovely summer delighted your heart? (The subject is *days.*)
>
> Too many temper tantrums *were* (not *was*) the reason for their divorce. (The subject is *temper tantrums.*)
>
> Wrapped inside five blankets was (not *were*) a tiny white kitten. (The subject is *kitten.*)
>
> There *are* (not *is*) numerous ways to make good fudge. (The subject is *ways.*)
>
> There *remain* (not *remains*) many unsolved problems. (The subject is *problems.*)

(2) Intervening words

Intervening words may make it difficult to identify the subject. Study the following examples until you recognize the correct subject:

> Several of the students in Professor Smith's course *were* (not *was*) nominated for an award. (The subject is *several.*)
>
> The transportation of diamonds *is* (not *are*) dangerous. (The subject is *transportation.*)
>
> The discussions of that subject *are* (not *is*) necessary. (The subject is *discussions.*)
>
> Hunger, along with inadequate housing, *causes* (not *cause*) riots. (The subject is *hunger.*)
>
> Inner longings, as well as an outward goal, *drive* (not *drives*) ambitious people. (The subject is *longings.*)

(3) Special words and word connectors

To avoid some common agreement errors be alert to certain words and word connectors. Remember the following rules:

(a) A **relative pronoun** usually refers back to, and agrees with, the nearest noun:

Rod Laver is one of the greatest tennis players who *live* (not *lives*) in this country. (*Who* refers back to *players*.)

Tokyo is among those cities that *are* (not *is*) filled with smog. (*That* refers back to *cities*.)

Note the following exception:

This is the only one of the streets that *has* (not *have*) two-way traffic. (*That* refers back to *one*, emphasizing the fact that only one street has two-way traffic; the other streets do not.)

(b) Subjects joined by *and* require a plural verb:

Both his eyesight and his hearing *have* (not *has*) gone bad.

The boys and Elsa *were* (not *was*) caught up in the drug cult.

but

My best friend and confidante *is* (not *are*) having lunch with me. (*Friend and confidante* refers to the same person.)

(c) Singular subjects joined by *or, either . . . or, neither . . . nor* require a singular verb. However, if one of the subjects is singular and the other is plural, then the verb agrees with the nearer subject:

A large camera or a small computer *lies* (not *lie*) under that cover.

Neither the chair nor the couch *feels* (not *feel*) comfortable.

but

Neither his money nor his innumerable fans *make* (not *makes*) him happy. (*Make* agrees with the nearer subject, *fans*.)

(d) When used as subjects, **indefinite pronouns** like *either, neither, everyone, no one, anyone, each, everybody,* and *anybody* require singular verbs:

Everybody who is anyone *goes* (not *go*) to the ballet.

Each of the grandmothers *was* (not *were*) given a rose.

NOTE: *All, any, half, none, most,* and *some* are singular or plural, depending on the context:

Singular: Some of the wine *was* (not *were*) sour. (*Wine* is singular.)

Plural: Some of the stairs *were* (not *was*) terribly steep. (*Stairs* is plural.)

(e) Collective nouns (nouns that are singular in form but plural in meaning) require a singular verb unless members are acting individually.

Singular: The crew always *meets* (not *meet*) for a swim at sunrise.

Plural: The crew *are* (not *is*) coming to work in their overalls.

(f) Certain words are **plural in form but singular in meaning** and require a singular verb:

> Physics *is* (not *are*) difficult.
> Mumps *keeps* (not *keep*) children in bed for days.
> The news today *scares* (not *scare*) us all.

NOTE: If in doubt about whether a noun is singular or plural, check your dictionary.

(g) Words denoting **sums of money and measurements** take a singular verb when considered as a single unit, but take a plural verb when considered as separate units:

Singular: One hundred dollars *is* (not *are*) too much money for a wool sweater.
Plural: Three silver dollars *were* (not *was*) stacked on the game table.
Singular: Two miles *is* (not *are*) as far as I can jog.
Plural: Those two miles *stretch* (not *stretches*) into the distance like a snake.

NOTE: Problems in arithmetic can be plural or singular:

> Three and three *is* (or *are*) six.

(h) Titles of literary works, whether singular or plural, require singular verbs:

> *The Captains and the King is* (not *are*) Taylor Caldwell's best novel.
> *Myths of the Norsemen tells* (not *tell*) about the twilight of the gods.

6b. Pronoun-antecedent agreement

A pronoun always refers back to an antecedent (the word for which it stands) and must agree in person, number, and gender with that antecedent. The following words are singular and require singular pronouns: *person, each, either, neither, everyone, everybody, someone, somebody, one, anyone, anybody, no one, nobody.*

> The teacher asked, "Did anyone leave *his* (not *their*) workbook on my desk?"

Neither of the students gave *her* (not *their*) correct address to the police officer.

Anyone who loves *his* (not *their*) country must be willing to enlist in the army.

NOTE: Traditional usage has dictated that the masculine pronoun be used for words that include both sexes in order to avoid the awkward use of *he or she, him or her,* and *his or hers.* Many people, however, are offended by what seems an illogical exclusion of women in this construction. Recasting the sentence into the plural to avoid the generic is often possible.

Anyone who has his (not *his or her*) running shoes can use the gym.
All who have running shoes can use the gym.

Collective nouns acting as a single unit require a singular pronoun; those acting as individuals require a plural pronoun:

Singular: The faculty has posted *its* (not *their*) list of demands. (The faculty is acting as a unit.)

Plural: The faculty gave differing responses to *their* (not *its*) heavier teaching loads. (The members of the faculty are acting individually.)

Antecedents joined by *and* require plural pronouns:

Charles and Richard passed *their* (not *his*) exams.
The horse and buggy have had *their* (not *its*) day.

Antecedents joined by *or* or *nor* require a singular pronoun when the antecedents are singular; if one antecedent is singular and the other plural, the pronoun agrees with the nearer antecedent:

Singular: Either the custodian or a guest left *his* (not *their*) coat in the room.

Plural: Neither the guard nor the hostages were happy about *their* (not *his*) situation. (*Their* agrees with the nearer subject, *hostages.*)

but

Singular: Neither the hostages nor the guard was happy about *his* (not *their*) situation. (*His* agrees with the nearer subject, *guard.*)

NOTE: Be sure to use the noun *kind* or *kinds* with the right demonstrative pronoun:

I will not associate with *those kinds* (not *those kind*) of people.
The lecturer suggested *that kind of book* (not *that kind of books*).

Exercises

Exercise 6a: Subject-verb agreement

In the following sentences, choose the correct form of the verb.

> MODEL: The guild of carpenters and blacksmiths (*was, were*) important during the Middle Ages.
>
> Answer: **Was**

1. Americans belong to the nation that (*has, have*) always been vigilant about freedom.
2. A sack of gold coins (*is, are*) far more valuable today than a year ago.
3. There (*is, are*) dozens of rats in that old building.
4. The beautiful maple trees growing along Main Street (*keeps, keep*) the houses cool during summer.
5. Gymnastics (*was, were*) Alex's favorite sport.
6. An umbrella or heavy boots (*is, are*) what he needs.
7. The peasants were indebted to the king for one of the loans that (*was, were*) made.
8. War and peace often (*resides, reside*) side by side in a country.
9. The *Los Angeles Times* (*is, are*) news at a high professional level.
10. The Council of Venice (*was, were*) dogmatic about burial laws.
11. Love, along with strong family roots, (*helps, help*) to create a sense of identity.
12. Organized groups of 200 to 300 and possibly more (*is, are*) marching toward the city.
13. (*Does, Do*) everyone have an umbrella?
14. Measles still (*causes, cause*) permanent damage to some children.
15. Deceptive smiles (*was, were*) the weapon he used most often.

Exercise 6b: Pronoun-antecedent agreement

In the following sentences, choose the correct words in parentheses.

> MODEL: Each of the tenants is complaining about (*his, their*) rent.
>
> Answer: **His**

1. A person can count only on (*himself, themselves*).
2. If anyone gets three "C"s, (*she, they*) will have to resign.
3. A person should not have to worry about (*his, their*) health during adolescence.
4. Everyone spoke (*her, their*) mind.
5. Neither the sky nor the clouds revealed (*its, their*) famous silver lining.
6. Neither a German nor a Frenchman finds it easy to get rid of (*his, their*) accent.

7. Every woman on the staff thinks (*she is, they are*) not paid as well as the men.
8. I hate those (*kind, kinds*) of roving eyes.
9. The genuine belief in fairies and ghosts has seen (*its, their*) heyday.
10. No one who has lived alone in the wilderness for a week can consider (*his, their*) life immortal.
11. Through love and understanding the church wooed back (*its, their*) members.
12. The Chicago police made (*its, their*) legal view quite clear.
13. The long list of names spoke for (*itself, themselves*).
14. The Bible states that one should forgive (*his, their*) enemies.

7. Pronoun case (case)

According to their function in a sentence, personal pronouns can appear in three different case forms: subjective, objective, and possessive.

SUBJECTIVE	OBJECTIVE	POSSESSIVE
I	me	my, mine
you	you	your, yours
he, she, it	him, her, it	his, her, hers, its
we	us	our, ours
they	them	their, theirs
who	whom	whose

The *subjective* case is used for pronouns functioning as subjects and as predicate pronouns:

> *We* own this house.
> Is that Mike standing there? Yes, it is *he.*

The *objective* case is used for pronouns functioning as direct objects, indirect objects, objects of prepositions, and subjects or complements of an infinitive:

> The truck hit *her.*
> He gave *them* a package.
> The laugh came from *him.*
> To see *her* was to love *her.*

The *possessive* case is used for pronouns indicating possession:

> Nothing stood in *its* way.
> The money is *theirs.*
> That watch is *yours.*

Notice that possessive pronouns require no apostrophes.

Wrong: Nothing stood in *it's* way.
           The money is *their's.*
           That watch is *your's.*

7a. Using the subjective case

Ordinarily we naturally use the correct subjective pronoun. Few of us are tempted to write "Me want to eat" instead of "I want to eat." Nevertheless, some constructions require careful thought.

Treat a clause of comparison introduced by *than* or *as* as if it were written out in full and use the appropriate pronoun case.

> Richard is taller than *I* [am].
> No one plays as well as *he* [plays].

Pronouns that follow forms of the linking verb *to be* usually are in the subjective case:

> I swear it was *she* (not *her*).
> We expected that the winners would be *they* (not *them*).

NOTE: An exception is a pronoun functioning as an object complement of the infinitive *to be* (see 2b[4]. *Object complement*):

> We expected the president to be *her* (not *she*).

Pronouns used in apposition should be in the same case as the nouns or pronouns to which they refer:

> Two runners—*you* and *he*—were seen late at night.
> We—John and *I*—did our best.

A pronoun functioning as the subject of a subordinate clause must be in the subjective case even when the entire subordinate clause is used as an object:

> The flowers will be presented to *whoever* (not *whomever*) serves as
>   choreographer of the dance. (*Whoever* is the subject of the verb *serves.*)
> They never forgot *who* (not *whom*) had won the war. (*Who* is the subject of
>   *had won.*)

When intervening expressions like *I believe, you think, one supposes,* or *he says* come between the verb and its subject pronoun, the pronoun must be in the subjective case:

Who (not *whom*) does he say repaired the light? (*Does he say* is an
   intervening expression between *who,* the subject, and *repaired,* the verb.)
The woman *who* (not *whom*) the papers think committed murder has
   disappeared. (*The papers think* is an intervening expression between *who*
   and *committed murder.*)

NOTE: A noun in the possessive case cannot function as an antecedent for a
pronoun in the subjective case:

Wrong: At the very start of Julie's vacation, she sprained her ankle.
 Right: At the very start of her vacation, Julie sprained her ankle.

7b. Using the objective case

An objective pronoun must be used when a pronoun functions as a direct
or an indirect object, as the object of a preposition, as the subject or as the
object of an infinitive. The following is an example of a pronoun used as a
direct object:

   Everyone loved *him* (not *he*).

Special care needs to be taken with compound constructions:

   Everyone loved him and *me* (not *I*).

When a pronoun is the object of the verb in a subordinate clause, it requires
the objective case:

   He always hurts whomever (not *whoever*) he loves. (*Whomever* is the object
      of the verb *loves.*)

   but

   He always hurts *whoever* loves him. (Now *whoever* is the subject of the verb
      loves.)

NOTE: Always treat the *whoever* or *whomever* clause as if it were separate;
then you will use the correct case by judging whether the *whoever/whomever*
is subject or object.

A pronoun can also be used as an indirect object:

   Throw *them* (not *they*) a pillow.

Errors of this type by native English speakers are rare.

When a pronoun is used as the object of a preposition, some writers have trouble using the correct case:

The book was given to *him* (not *he*) and *me* (not *I*).

Do not yield to the popular temptation to say "between you and *I*." Although this error is often made by prominent people on television or on the lecture platform, it is ungrammatical. The correct form is "between you and *me*."

Pay special attention to the case of a pronoun combined or in apposition with a noun in the objective case:

Everyone spoke highly of *us* (not *we*) teachers.
The mayor invited two of us—Jack and *me* (not *I*)—to speak.

A pronoun serving as subject or as object of an infinitive is in the objective case:

Subject: They expect *him* (not *he*) to be discharged soon.
Object: We expected to see *him* (not *he*).

Avoid the common confusion of *who* and *whom*. *Who* is always a subject whereas *whom* is always an object:

Who has seen Jim? (subject)
Whom did Jim see? (object)
The girl *who* sold you the ticket is here. (subject)
The man *whom* you recognized has the ticket. (object)
To *whom* are you speaking? (object of preposition)

7c. Using the possessive case

The possessive case should be used before a noun or a gerund:

He will pay *his* son's tuition.
My parents denounce *our* (not *us*) seeing that violent movie.
I appreciate *your* (not *you*) lending me the money.

However, note this exception:

We noticed *him* (not *his*) playing the piano. (The emphasis here is on *him*, not on *playing*, which is a participle.)

NOTES: 1. *My, our, your, her, his, its,* and *their* are classified as adjectives when they modify nouns.
2. By all means learn the difference between:

it's (for *it is*) and *its* (the pronoun)
who's (for *who is*) and *whose* (the pronoun)

Exercises

Exercise 7: Pronoun case

Underline each pronoun used incorrectly and replace it with the correct form. If the entry is correct, leave it alone.

> MODEL: Give the money to the preacher and I̲.
>
> Answer: Me

1. The fence was taller than him.
2. Does the novel reveal who they killed?
3. The barons built their castles for whoever was within their vassalage.
4. My father gave us boys two dollars in addition to board and room.
5. Tom is certainly far stronger than they.
6. They—the landscaper and him—planted ten rose bushes.
7. Between you and I, the entire project isn't worth a dime.
8. The party was in honor of he and she.
9. The psychologists consider him to be a sociopath.
10. We hoped beyond hope that the victims would not be them.
11. Why doesn't the captain order either Luke or he to play center field?
12. I have just reread the story about them crossing the Rhine River.
13. The accident was caused by him, not I.
14. It was evident that whoever the mob controlled would become the next victim.
15. His father opened the door, expecting that the visitor would be me.
16. The table is ugly because two of it's legs are missing.
17. Regardless of who's wallet this is, the money is gone.
18. Most of the jury members found she to be mentally ill.
19. The community admired both he and she.
20. Whom do they say is the best candidate for the job?

8. Adjectives and Adverbs (ad)

Although adjectives and adverbs are both modifiers, they cannot be used interchangeably. Adjectives modify nouns whereas adverbs modify verbs (or adjectives or other adverbs).

Adjective: The pork chop is *good.*
  Adverb: I dance *well.*

Exceptions to this rule are certain linking verbs that require adjectives rather than adverbs because the modifiers following these verbs describe the subject rather than the verb. The most common of these linking verbs are *seem, be, appear, become, look, smell, sound, feel,* and *taste:*

> The fish smells *bad* (not *badly*).
> The patient feels *terrible* (not *terribly*).

8a. Adjectives and adverbs after sense verbs

Verbs of the sense (*look, smell, sound, feel,* and *taste*) are particularly tricky since they require either an adverb or an adjective, depending on their meaning in the sentence:

> The young man looked *eager*. (He is an eager man so an adjective is the appropriate modifier.)

> The young man looked *eagerly* into his lover's eyes. (The act of looking is described so an adverb is the appropriate modifier.)

8b. Don't confuse adjectives and adverbs

Don't use *sure, real,* and *good* when you should use *surely, really,* and *well:*

> The climb was *really* (not *real*) steep.
> I *surely* (not *sure*) enjoyed the concert.

8c. Comparative and superlative forms

See 1e. *Parts of speech.* Also, use the comparative degree when comparing two items and the superlative degree when comparing three or more items:

> Japan is the *stronger* of the two countries.
> Japan is the *strongest* of the Asian countries.

> Today I got the *highest* score of anyone in class.

> Is this your *best* effort?

Be sure to complete your comparisons:

Wrong: Marie is much healthier.
 Right: Marie is much healthier than she used to be.

8d. Don't convert nouns to adjectives

Don't make awkward conversions of nouns to adjectives. Nouns frequently function as adjectives, as in *torpedo boat, hospital care,* or *fut coat,* but avoid these forms if the resulting words sound confusing, ambiguous, or awkward:

Wrong: president bearing
 Right: presidential bearing

Wrong: jealousy results
 Right: results of jealousy

Exercises

Exercise 8: Adjectives and adverbs

Underline the correct modifier and identify it as an adjective or an adverb.

> MODEL: The moon shone (bright, <u>brightly</u>) through the clouds.
>
> Answer: Adverb

1. Before a large crowd she was told that she had done (well, good).
2. The apple tasted so (sour, sourly) that I threw it away.
3. The teacher looked (disapproving, disapprovingly) at her.
4. Speaking as (honest, honestly) as ever, he refused to be translated.
5. "He (sure, surely) was betrayed by you," they insisted.
6. "Did you do (well, good) on the final exam?" she asked him.
7. Of the three contestants, she was the (prettiest, prettier).
8. Offer him the (largest, larger) of the two rooms.
9. Most of us consider ourselves (real, really) fortunate if we haven't had surgery by the time we reach middle age.
10. The war continued (steady, steadily) for five years.
11. Drive (slow, slowly); someone is crossing the street.
12. That time he took an (awful, awfully) big chance.
13. She played the violin extremely (soft, softly).
14. I found it difficult to determine which was the (worse, worst) pain of all.
15. At home he felt (capabler, more capable) than at school.

Punctuation

Punctuation marks help to clarify the meaning of sentences. Without punctuation, sentences and paragraphs would not be intelligible to the reader. Some punctuation marks tell when a statement ends, whether it states a fact or asks a question; others form groups of words and ideas for emphasis, or set off material written by someone else. Punctuation marks are not decorative symbols to be used at random. In order to write effectively, you must be familiar with punctuation conventions.

9. The comma (,)

The comma is the most difficult punctuation mark to use. It has so many uses that writers tend to add it everywhere on a page, often incorrectly. Commas are correctly used under the following circumstances.

9a. Commas before coordinating conjunctions

Use a comma before a coordinating conjunction (*and, but, or, nor, for, so, yet*) that links two independent clauses:

> The trees had delicate foliage, but no birds nested in the branches.
> I grew up among these people, and their language was familiar to me.
> The weather was warm, yet the crops failed.

NOTES: 1. Do not use a comma to separate a compound predicate:

Wrong: We put on out hats, and opened our umbrellas.
 Right: We put on our hats and opened our umbrellas.

2. The comma may be omitted between short independent clauses:

Wrong: It rained, and I wept.
 Right: It rained and I wept.

9b. After introductory elements

Use a comma after an introductory subordinate clause and an introductory phrase.

(1) Introductory clause

Before I received my diploma, my father gave me a car.

No comma is needed if the dependent clause *follows* the independent clause:

My father gave me a car before I received my diploma.

(2) Introductory phrase

In the exquisite house of his dreams, all colors of the rainbow would be
   represented.
Speaking of the Devil, there she comes.
To understand the French sense of humor, one needs to be sophisticated.
After paying all of his bills, he invested in an old Chevrolet.

No comma is necessary after short prepositional phrases:

From surgery he was taken to intensive care.

9c. Series

Use a comma after each item in a series except the last.

(1) Words in a series

We shall need ribbons, flowers, and balloons.

NOTE: Careful writers use a comma in front of the final *and* in a series;
otherwise, the last two items tend to be taken as a pair:

Confusing: He used different types of conveyances: train, camel, bicycle,
          horse and cart. (Is the horse separate from the cart?)

---

(2) Phrases in a series

We looked under the table, behind the desk, and above the fireplace.

(3) Clauses in a series

He arrived, he moved in, and he took over.

9d. Nonrestrictive clauses or phrases

Use commas to set off a nonrestrictive clause or phrase.

(1) Nonrestrictive clause

A nonrestrictive clause adds descriptive information but is not essential to the meaning of the sentence.

> Harvard, which is one of the most prestigious universities in the United States, has an excellent law school.

In the sentence above, the clause *which is one of the most prestigious universities in the United States* could be deleted without changing the meaning of the rest of the sentence. Consider, however, the following italicized restrictive clause:

> Sarah wants to attend the law school *that her father attended.*

The restrictive clause is essential to the rest of the sentence because it identifies which law school Sarah wants to attend. Therefore, the clause is *not* set off by commas. To decide whether a clause is nonrestrictive or restrictive, leave it out of the sentence. If the meaning of the sentence changes, the clause is restrictive; if the meaning does not change, the clause is nonrestrictive.

Nonrestrictive: The three couples, who all lived on Coldwater Canyon, sued the contractor.

Restrictive: Only the three couples who lived on Coldwater Canyon sued the contractor.

(2) Nonrestrictive phrase

Like the nonrestrictive clause, the nonrestrictive phrase adds descriptive but nonessential information to the sentence, as in the following example:

> Eldon Rogers, dying of cancer, still attends work regularly.

Nonrestrictive: My cousin, employed by the May Company, refuses to buy an insurance policy.

Restrictive: Every person employed by the May Company must buy an insurance policy.

9e. Appositives

Use commas to set off appositives:

> Albert Einstein, one of the most brilliant men of the twentieth century, permitted his brain to be dissected after his death.
> Charles Benjamin Witt, Ph.D., will give a piano recital in March.
> Lone Pine, home of Mt. Whitney, is a popular fisherman's resort.

Appositives are almost always nonrestrictive, but in the following examples they are restrictive and therefore require no commas. The appositives are italicized:

> The movie actor *John Wayne* was on the cover of a magazine.
> I was counting on my cousin *Harry*.
> Edward *the Confessor* died before the Battle of Hastings.

9f. Parenthetical expressions

Use commas to set off parenthetical expressions, which are words or phrases that supply supplementary information and interrupt the flow of the sentence.

> Rembrandt, I suppose, loved his work more than he loved his wife.
> Walking under a ladder, for example, is said to bring bad luck.

Quite often, conjunctive adverbs serve as parenthetical expressions that help make a smooth transition from one sentence to the next. (See 1g. *Conjunctions, conjunctive adverbs.*)

> She did, nevertheless, graduate from nursing school.
> We wondered, furthermore, whether or not he would admit the truth.

9g. Miscellaneous elements

Commas are used to set off a variety of other elements in a sentence. Use commas after *yes* and *no* when they begin a sentence:

> Yes, he did return the sweater.

Use commas to set off words of direct address:

> My dear, he warned you not to touch the water pipe.

Use commas after mild interjections:

> Well, why didn't you say so?

Use commas to set off absolute phrases (see 2c[5]. *Absolute phrases*):

Their prayers recited, they left the mosque to go back to work.

Use commas to set off certain expressions of contrast:

The pillow was embroidered by my aunt, not my sister.

Use commas to introduce brief quotations and to set off quoted material from the rest of the text;

> "Then God or Nature calmed the elements," wrote Ovid.
> The Bible tells us, "Judge not lest you be judged."

NOTE: When a quotation is interrupted by explanatory words use a comma before and after the interruption. Always place commas inside the quotation marks (see also 16. *Quotation marks*):

> "When you have been driven out of your homeland," said Jake, "you feel like a piece of drifting seaweed."

Follow convention in the use of commas for dates, addresses, and places:

Dates: Today is February 25, 1980.
On July 4, 1776, our nation was born.
The company will be solvent by June, 1985.

A comma goes between the day (or month) and the year and after the year if the sentence continues.

Addresses: 1500 North Verdugo Road, Glendale, California 91208 (Do not place a comma between the state and the zip code.)

A comma goes between the city and the state and after the state if the sentence continues.

Use a comma before examples introduced by *such as* or *especially*:

> A writer should avoid using trite figures of speech, such as "big as a bear" or "white as a ghost."
> Americans love spectator sports, especially football.

Use a comma when it will prevent misreading a sentence:

Confusing: As soon as the airplane lifted the gauges began to fluctuate.
Clear: As soon as the airplane lifted, the gauges began to fluctuate.
Confusing: After Friday afternoon classes will be filled.
Clear: After Friday, afternoon classes will be filled.

NOTE: For fear of omitting commas, many students overuse them. In a number of places commas are not needed:

1. Don't separate a subject from its verb with a comma:

Wrong: All of the elderly people, expected the tax vote to fail.
  Right: All of the elderly people expected the tax vote to fail.

2. Don't separate a verb and its object with a comma:

Wrong: He loudly demanded, all of the money.
  Right: He loudly demanded all of the money.

3. Don't use a comma before the first or after the last item in a series:

Wrong: St. Paul gave Christianity, a theology, a church organization, and a sense of purpose.
  Right: St. Paul gave Christianity a theology, a church organization, and a sense of purpose.

10. The Semicolon (;)

The semicolon is a weak period and cannot be replaced by a comma. Use the semicolon between independent clauses to replace the coordinate conjunction:

> The days were dreary; the nights were unbearable.
> The people gathered in the streets and in the market places; they seemed to crawl out of nowhere.

Use the semicolon between independent clauses joined by a conjunctive adverb (*however, consequently, moreover, besides, on the other hand*):

> Everyone demands more and more services from the government; *consequently,* taxes are sky high. (It is customary, although not technically necessary, to place a comma after the conjunctive adverb.)

NOTE: A conjunctive adverb, used parenthetically, is enclosed by commas:

> My sister sings beautifully; my brother, *however,* sounds like a fog horn.

Use semicolons between items in a series when the items contain commas, and between independent clauses joined by a coordinate conjunction if the clauses contain commas:

For our clothing we wore bathing suits, shorts, and overalls; for our shelter we had tents, caves, and sleeping bags; for our food we ate nuts, dates, and bananas.

During the Middle Ages the average person believed in ghosts, magic spells, and omens; but today he believes in television, computers, and stock-market reports.

11. The Colon (:)

A colon is used to indicate that something is about to follow. It can be used to introduce a list preceded by *as follows, following, follows:*

The following officers were elected: president, secretary, and treasurer.

NOTE: Use the colon only at the end of an independent clause. Do *not* use it between a verb or preposition and its object:

Wrong: England has produced: Chaucer, Shakespeare, and Milton.
  Right: England has produced Chaucer, Shakespeare, and Milton.
Wrong: My three favorite cities are: Paris, London, and Rome.
  Right: The following are my three favorite cities: Paris, London, and Rome.
Wrong: Pam had a passion for: reading, writing, and traveling.
  Right: Pam had a passion for reading, writing, and traveling.

Use a main clause followed by a colon to introduce quotations of more than three lines:

This is how Sidney J. Harris defines a *jerk:*

A jerk, then, is a man (or woman) who is utterly unable to see himself as he appears to others. He has no grace; he is tactless without meaning to be; he is a bore even to his best friends; he is an egotist without charm.

Use a colon to direct attention to a summary, an explanation, or an appositive:

The entire problem can be summarized in one word: *poverty.*
Two passions have a powerful influence on men: ambition and avarice.
One thing he always remained: a gentleman.

Use a colon to separate the greeting in a letter from the body of the letter:

Dear Sir:

Use a colon to separate a title from a subtitle:

The Masks of God: Oriental Mythology

Use a colon between Bible chapter and verse:

Genesis 3:15

Use a colon between hours and minutes:

4:15 P.M.

Use a colon to separate the name of the speaker in a play from words spoken:

Hamlet: To be or not to be . . .

12. The Dash (—)

The dash should not be used for mere visual effect or as a substitute for a comma. Use the dash to show a sudden break in thought:

She was certain that he was dead and she—but no, his body moved.

Use the dash to signal an interrupted or unfinished dialogue:

"I want to be a farmer," he enunciated slowly.
"A farmer? But your father—"
"Don't ever mention my father again. For me, he no longer exists."

Use the dash after a statement, to explain or amplify it:

Barbara began to despise everything associated with the modern world—inflation, revolution, pollution.

Use the dash to emphasize parenthetical elements, particularly when they also contain commas:

She believes that there is nothing—no hell or paradise—after a person dies.
Four planets—Mars, Saturn, Jupiter, and Pluto—were embroidered on silk tapestries.

NOTE: The dash is typed as two hyphens with no space before or after; it is written as an unbroken line the length of two hyphens.

13. The Period (.)

The period is the first punctuation mark an elementary school student learns. It is most basic because it signals the end of a sentence.

Use the period to end a declarative statement:

The dinner was excellent.

Use a period to end a command:

Don't do that.

Use a period to end an indirect question:

We wondered when the truck would arrive.

Use a period to indicate an abbreviation or a contraction:

Dr.	Fed.	assn.
Mrs.	Co.	secy.
Ms.	M.D.	etc.
Mass.	Inc.	hwy.

NOTE: It is becoming increasingly popular to abbreviate well-known names without periods:

TWA, TV, NATO, HEW, CBS, YMCA

Use a period to indicate decimals:

$60.50   2.5%

A group of three spaced periods is used as an ellipsis to indicate that some words have been omitted from a quotation:

Original passage: "These gods, who do not die, cannot be tragic."
  With ellipsis: "These gods . . . cannot be tragic."

NOTE: If the omitted portion of the quotation follows a period, the period is retained, followed by the ellipsis:

Original passage: "The narrative is incomplete. And it may remain so. Nevertheless, it is one of the finest epics from any age."
  With ellipsis: "The narrative is incomplete. . . . Nevertheless, it is one of the finest epics from any age."

Ellipses are also used to indicate a pause:

"Listen to me," she said, trembling with fury. "Don't you ever . . . touch my brother again. If you do . . . I'll shoot you."

14. The Question Mark (?)

Use a question mark to end a direct question:

Do you love rain? Why?
The food was really good? (The question mark cues the reader that what would have been a declarative sentence is functioning as a question.)

NOTE: Do not follow a question mark with a comma or a period:

Wrong: "Do you like red hair?," she asked.
 Right: "Do you like red hair?" she asked.

Question marks can indicate uncertainty, especially in historical dating:

The clay tablets date back to 1750(?) B.C.
Antiochus II, king of Syria (261?–247 B.C.)

15. The Exclamation Point (!)

Use an exclamation point to indicate a strong emotion or an emphatic command:

Whew! You stink!
What a surprise!
Quick! Bring me some bandages!

Do *not* use an exclamation point to indicate a mild feeling or to emphasize an idea:

Wrong: I was surprised!
 Right: I was surprised.
Wrong: Milton is a better writer than Shakespeare!
 Right: Milton is a better writer than Shakespeare.

NOTE: Do not follow an exclamation point with a comma or period:

Wrong: "My God!," screamed the woman.
 Right: "My God!" screamed the woman.

---

16. Quotation Marks (" ")

The primary use of quotation marks is to set off the exact words of a speaker or writer. Quotation marks are always used in pairs to indicate the beginning and the end of a quotation. Do not enclose any introductory words within the quotation marks:

> He answered sarcastically, "You may be rich, but you're stupid."

Do not use quotation marks for indirect address:

Indirect: He told him that Thursday would be soon enough.
  Direct: He told him, "Thursday will be soon enough."

NOTE: Use commas to set off interruptions such as "he said" or "she observed":

> "As far as I am concerned," he said, "she is right."

When the quotation contains a question mark or an exclamation point, the question mark or exclamation point replaces the commas:

> "What does the master wish?" she asked.
> "A kiss at least!" he demanded.

Long quotations (four lines or more) are indented. They do not require quotation marks:

> Alan Simpson offers the following insight into our society:
>> The health of society depends on simple virtues like honesty, decency, courage, and public spirit. There are forces in human nature which constantly tend to corrupt them, and every age has its own vices. The worst feature of ours is probably the obsession with violence.

Quoted dialogue requires a separate paragraph for each speaker to stress the change from one speaker to another:

> After a long silence, Kevin muttered, "What's the use? Tomorrow I must leave."
> "But why must you leave?" Rosie asked.
> "Because I need money."

Quoted lines of poetry require no quotation marks since their stanza format already sets them off from the regular text. Quoted poetry should be double-spaced and centered between the left and right margins:

One equal temper of heroic hearts,
Made weak by time and fate but strong in will
To strive, to seek, to find, and not to yield.
—Alfred Lord Tennyson, "Ulysses."

Quotation marks are used to indicate the title of any subdivision in a printed publication: a chapter, an essay, a short story, a poem, a song, a lecture, a newspaper headline.

"Pharaoh and His Subjects" is the title of Chapter 3 in *The Dwellers on the Nile*.
"A New Year's Warning" is a *Time* magazine article on terrorism in Turkey.
"The Flowering Judas" is a short story by Katherine Anne Porter.
Robert Frost's poem "Design" questions God's providence.
"A Mighty Fortress Is Our God" is a marvelous hymn of confidence.
Professor Lang's lecture was entitled, "How to Sell Yourself."
The headline in Part II of the *Los Angeles Times* reads as follows: "FBI May Intervene in Athlete's Fraud Case."

Quotation marks can set off words used in a special sense:

Whenever my grandmother became schizophrenic, Grandpa said she was "exhausted."
What he called "art" had no more merit than did the scribblings of a child.

Quotation marks are used to enclose definitions:

The word *dulcet* means "gently melodious."

Definitions may also appear in italics:

Kinetics is *the study of motion.*

For a quotation within a quotation, use single quotation marks:

Thoreau once said, "I heartily accept the motto, 'That government is best which governs least.'"

17. The Apostrophe (')

Generally speaking, the apostrophe replaces *of* to indicate possession: "the people's choice" rather than "the choice *of* the people." It is also used to form contractions and certain plurals.

To indicate possession, add an apostrophe plus *s* to singular nouns:

Mabel's dress
someone's house

NOTE: Add only an apostrophe to singular words ending in an *s* sound:

Keats' "Ode to a Nightingale"
Jesus' words

Add an apostrophe plus *s* to plural nouns to form the possessive:

the children's hour
women's clothes

NOTE: Add only an apostrophe to plurals already ending in *s:*

three tigers' teeth
several teachers' lecturers

Place an apostrophe plus *s* after the last word in a hyphenated word to form the possessive:

mother-in-law's hat (not mother's-in-law)
sisters-in-law's hats (not sisters'-in-law)

Informal English allows writers to shorten words by omitting certain letters. Such shortened words are called contractions:

can't (cannot)	we're (we are)	In January of '55 (1955)
won't (will not)	there's (there is)	o'clock (of the clock)
who's (who is)	it's (it is)	ma'am (madam)

An apostrophe is used to indicate the plural of letters, numbers, symbols, and words referred to as words:

His *f*'s look like *t*'s.
Then they were hit by the Depression of the 1930's. (An acceptable
   alternative is 1930s.)
+'s and −'s often add nothing to a grade.
Delete all those innocuous *very*'s.

NOTE: Avoid the possessive apostrophe with inanimate objects:

Awkward: the chair's paint
  Better: the paint on the chair

18. The Hyphen (−)

Use a hyphen to form certain compound words:

> mother-in-law
> cave-in
> paste-up
> red-handed
> court-martial

Writers frequently construct their own compound words:

> All of us need to get rid of our I-don't-give-a-damn attitudes.

Rules for hyphenating compound words are varied. Check your dictionary to be sure you are following convention.

Use a hyphen to join two or more words used as an adjective before a noun:

> a home-grown tomato
> a well-known song

However, when the compound adjective follows the noun, no hyphen is necessary:

> The tomato is home grown.
> The song is well known.

Do not use a hyphen when the first word of a compound is an adverb ending in -*ly*:

> a dangerously long tunnel
> two badly hurt victims

Suspension hyphens are used in series:

> They ran two-, three-, and four-mile distances.

Use a hyphen after the prefixes *ex, self, cross, all, great;* before the suffix *elect;* between the prefix and a proper name:

> ex-football player
> self-educated
> cross-ventilation
> all-purpose glue
> great-uncle
> president-elect
> pro-Irish

The hyphen is used to avoid ambiguity:

He *recovered* from the shock of losing $10,000.
Mrs. Jones *re-covered* her sofa.

Aerobic dancing is good *recreation*.
The novel was a *re-creation* of his own childhood.

Use a hyphen with compound numbers from twenty-one to ninety-nine and with fractions:

twenty-two
three-fifths

A compound adjective that contains numbers is also hyphenated:

a thirteen-year-old boy

19. Parentheses ( )

Parentheses are used to enclose incidental information:

His home town (Bern, Switzerland) sent flowers to the funeral.
Brigham Young (1801–1877) was once territorial governor of Utah.

NOTES: 1. No capital letter or period is used when a sentence in parentheses is part of a larger sentence:

He believed in the efficacy of yoga (the term means *union*) as a way of uniting the body and the mind.

But a period is placed at the end of a sentence used independently within parentheses:

Earl Kemp Long was the brother of Huey Long and an important political figure in America. (See his biography by A. J. Liebling.)

The comma follows the closing parenthesis in sentences such as the one below:

Despite the emperor's warning (ten days prior to the festival), the soldiers continued the siege.

2. A question mark or exclamation point is placed inside the parentheses if it belongs to the parenthetical material, and outside if it does not:

Inside: She arrived (had she grown older?) once again to captivate him with her beauty.
Outside: Have you read Baker's *Practical Stylist* (latest edition)?

Use parentheses to enclose numerals or letters in enumerations:

> The babysitter was expected to (1) care for the children, (2) cook meals, and (3) wash the dishes.

Parentheses are used around a question mark to indicate uncertainty or doubt:

> In this frieze, the god Osiris (?) is seen seated on a throne.

20. Brackets ([ ])

Use brackets to insert editorial comments in quoted material:

> According to Campbell, "the Bull of Heaven seems to be the storm god [scholars do not clarify his exact identity] controlling the sky."

Use brackets to set off parenthetical material within parentheses:

> (See *The New Columbia Encyclopedia* [New York: Columbia University Press, 1975].)

Exercises

Exercise 9: Punctuation: The comma

Insert commas wherever they are needed. If the sentence is correct, leave it alone.

> MODEL: Try reading the poetry of Chaucer of Donne and of Dryden.
>
> Answer: **Try reading the poetry of Chaucer, of Donne, and of Dryden.**

1. As the proverb says "He that would bring home the wealth of the Indies must carry out the wealth of the Indies."
2. Were those teachers as all teachers before them preoccupied with trivial facts?
3. As Bill saw the case he had simply missed class.
4. There was obviously something missing in me.
5. I wanted to confront that ill-bred woman who hated Germans so much.
6. Yes we did have some moments of delight.
7. She was as efficient as a machine as friendly as a Dalmatian puppy and as beautiful as a movie star.
8. Doctors surgeons in particular have a god complex.
9. I promptly boarded the airplane that he had pointed out.
10. He would stand before us rejoicing in his sinewy body every inch an open air man.

11. We shall reside at 1344 Woodland Drive Detroit Michigan.

12. On March 13, 1950 her first child was born.

13. "But you are prejudiced" she insisted "because you hate him although you don't even know the person."

14. "Take a deep breath" he exhorted us.

15. Man is a gregarious animal but he does not always enjoy harmony with his fellow humans.

16. Hemingway's poignant war novel *A Farewell to Arms* reflects a pessimistic world view.

17. The judge having entered and the audience having risen, the trial began.

18. Because these boys were adolescents, they considered all adults brainless and stultifying.

19. If you set out to climb a mountain no matter how high you climb you have failed if you do not reach the top.

20. He had been on the quest so to speak from the beginning.

21. John Barrymore a member of the famous family of stage actors once played the role of Hamlet while he was drunk.

22. Many infirm lonely people prefer living in a convalescent hospital.

23. Before dying had been an irrelevant mystery to her but now it was a reality.

24. George Orwell said that political writing was often the defense of the indefensible.

25. The great enemy of concise writing one might say is a lack of politeness.

26. Before delving into his personal life let us study his doctrine.

27. Magnificent stately mansions leaned against the hillside.

28. Furthermore the word *science* has the ring of truth and authority.

29. An understanding of art requires that art be evaluated on more than just Aristotelian principles.

30. My little sportscar which has given me nothing but trouble was sold for twice as much as I paid for it.

Exercise 9, 10: Punctuation: The comma and the semicolon

In the following sentences, place a semicolon or a comma or no punctuation within the brackets.

> MODEL: The minister asked the audience to rise [ ] everyone stood immediately.
>
> Answer: **The minister asked the audience to rise [;] everyone stood immediately.**

1. I hated him for making so much money [ ] and keeping it all to himself.

2. By sunset the hunters retired [ ] however [ ] at dawn they continued with renewed vigor.

3. Because initiative and trust were sorely lacking [ ] the business went bankrupt within a year.
4. Here are the key people in this venture: Jack Jennings, chairman of the board [ ] Milton Le Cuyer, president of the overseas operation [ ] Dorothy Nibley, marketing supervisor.
5. The nights [ ] however [ ] seem long and cold.
6. Please give her the directions [ ] as soon as she asks for them.
7. As late as 1835 [ ] human sacrifices were performed in India.
8. The community college system in California [ ] without tuition and with open access [ ] is succeeding beyond the wildest and most hopeful dreams of its supporters.
9. All this was unsettling [ ] since I believed in democracy.
10. He had always been short of stature [ ] consequently [ ] he decided to make a success of himself.
11. The stars sparkled [ ] it was a lovely night.
12. Everything was finally in our hands [ ] we were completely in charge.
13. Either these few are considered to be innately superior [ ] or they are selected for special assistance.
14. Give her a telephone call [ ] as soon as you have received the grant money.
15. "It is fortunate that you live in a house [ ]" he stated [ ] "otherwise you might be paying an exorbitant rent."
16. She was a calm woman [ ] not one to be scandalized easily.
17. Ask any of the officials [ ] if you can catch them on duty.
18. The mad elephant had destroyed one of the bamboo huts [ ] it had also turned over the rubbish truck.
19. They stood in line clear around the block [ ] the news having reached the neighborhood that free tickets were being supplied.
20. In the rough [ ] the amethyst was worth $20 [ ] honed and polished [ ] it was worth $200.

Exercise 9–20: All punctuation marks

In the following sentences, supply any missing marks of punctuation. If the sentence is correct, leave it alone.

MODEL: The peoples choice is what counts thats how democracy works

Answer: **The people's choice is what counts; that's how democracy works.**

1. They were asked to supply the following items towels, sheets, and soap
2. He demanded to know when she was going to pay the rent.
3. Do you live in a politically active community he asked.
4. What remains but to spare him all of the unpleasant aspects of keeping house

 5. Caroline yelled Fire Get out
 6. His cat weighed so much that he called her tons of fun
 7. Everybodys a damnable liar he shouted with fury
 8. She is a well dressed beautifully groomed woman
 9. Our campus bookstore is student owned.
10. Have him read "The Last Ditch," an essay by Robert Coles.
11. Don't write your 7s and 9s so much alike.
12. Albert Schweitzer 1875–1965 was awarded the Nobel Peace Prize
13. He called me a let's see what did he call me
14. The question is this Where do we go from here
15. Poets philosophers hermits all are idealists
16. Jackies bloodstained suit now displayed in the Smithsonian Institution is a horrifying symbol of the vanished Camelot
17. My father in law is a loving grandfather
18. Will you come soon perhaps tomorrow
19. Boston, Massachusetts is his hometown
20. "The Lord is my shepherd. . . . He maketh me to lie down in green pastures."

Mechanics

Students often wonder whether mechanics will count as much toward their grade as content. The answer is that the mechanics of writing are often inseparable from content and therefore must exert a nearly equal influence on the grade. A manuscript that abides by the rules is like a city whose traffic flow is controlled by lights, signs, and regulations; a manuscript that ignores the rules is like a city whose traffic has run amok. You will increase the readability of your writing and make your reader immeasurably happier if you observe proper mechanics.

21. Capitalization (cap)

Capitalization is a way of drawing attention to certain words. Observe the following conventions of capitalization in your writing. Whenever you are in doubt about whether or not a word should be capitalized, consult your dictionary.

21a. First words

Use capitals for the first word in a sentence:

> Above all else, we want peace.
> How did life on our planet begin?

Use capitals for the first word in a line of traditonal poetry:

> The sun does arise,
> And make happy the skies;
> The merry bells ring
> To welcome the spring.
> —William Blake

Much modern poetry is in free verse, and the first word in a line is not always capitalized.

NOTE: If the quotation fits grammatically into a sentence, the first word need *not* be capitalized:

> William Faulkner once said (in a *Paris Review* interview) that "if a writer has to rob his mother, he will not hesitate; the 'Ode on a Grecian Urn' is worth any number of old ladies."

21b. Proper nouns

Capitalize proper nouns, words that are part of proper nouns, and adjectives derived from proper nouns, as well as names of specific people, races, nationalities, languages:

Abraham Lincoln	French
Levite	Asian
Russian	Latin

21c. Names

Capitalize names of continents, countries, states, cities, neighborhoods, streets, buildings, parks, monuments, oceans, lakes, rivers:

Africa	Union Oil Building
Sweden	Central Park
Michigan	Statue of Liberty
London	Atlantic Ocean
Morningside Heights	Lake Louise
Brand Boulevard	Tigris River

21d. Other capitalization rules

The following rules are to be used as guidelines for the use of capitals in your writing.

(1) Specific organizations and institutions

the Lakers
Daughters of the American Revolution
Smithsonian Institution
Federal Reserve
Democratic Party (or Republican)

(2) Historical periods, events, or documents

Middle Ages
Renaissance
Battle of Hastings
Bill of Rights

(3) Members of national, political, or religious groups

Rotarian
Democrat
Methodist

(4) Religions and sacred religious works or terms

Islam   the Virgin
Hinduism   Allah
Catholicism   the Bible
God   the Torah

Some people capitalize pronouns referring to the deity: His, He, Him, Thee,
Thou.

(5) Names of days, months, and holidays

Wednesday
August
Thanksgiving
Valentine's Day

(6) Names of academic degrees and specific courses

Ph.D.
Doctor of Jurisprudence
Biology 135
Advanced Typing

Usually if the course is a general course, it is not capitalized: psychology,
biology, mathematics.

(7) Names of stars, planets, constellations

Pluto
Mars
North Star
Milky Way

Unless they are personified, *earth, sun,* and *moon* are not capitalized.

(8) Names of ships, trains, and aircraft

the Queen Elizabeth II
the Lark
Air Force One

(9) Personifications

Father Time
Mother Nature

(10) Abbreviations indicating time, government divisions, or media stations

A.M., P.M. (also a.m., p.m.)
HEW
FHA
NBC
KNXT

(11) Titles preceding names

Dean Katz	President June Willard
Reverend D. L. Smith	Governor Mario Cuomo
Mr. Eric Reese	Chief Justice Rehnquist

NOTES: 1. Do not capitalize a title when it is not part of the name:

a former senator, Harold Berman
Gail French, director of personnel

2. An abbreviated title, used before or after a name, is capitalized:

Dr. Sigmund Freud
Fernando Garcia, Esq.
Richard Bauer, M.D.

3. Titles of distinction are capitalized when they take the place of the person's name:

The President spoke on TV.
The Archbishop offered the prayer.

---

(12) First word of each outline entry

1. Advantages of credit cards
   A. Instant money
   B. Delayed payment

(13) Titles of literary works

Capitalize all words except articles, conjunctions, and prepositions unless they are the first word in the title:

> *For Whom the Bell Tolls*
> "Ode on a Grecian Urn"
> *The Taming of the Shrew*

NOTE: Conjunctions and prepositions of five letters or more are sometimes capitalized:

> *War Against the King*
> "Comin' Through the Rye"

---

(14) Points of the compass

Capitalize when they refer to a specific area, but not when they refer to direction:

> My aunt lives in the East.

> **but**

> Turn west on Broadway.

(15) Titles of relatives

Capitalize when they are not preceded by an article or a pronoun, when they are followed by a name, and in direct address:

> Give the rose to Grandmother, my dear.
> I owe Aunt Margaret twenty dollars.
> Please, Mother, pay no attention.

> **but**

> My mother has arrived.
> They told us that the aunt was wealthy.

(16) The pronoun *I* and the interjection *O*

> As far as I am concerned, he might as well go home.
> How many crimes, O Liberty, have been committed in your name?

NOTE: *Oh* is not capitalized unless it appears at the beginning of a sentence.

Exercises

Exercise 21: Capitalization

In the sentences below correct all capitalization. Underline small letters that should be capitalized and strike through capital letters that should be in lower case. If the sentence is correct, leave it alone.

> MODEL: Many <u>A</u>ncient <u>s</u>umerian myths, such as the *epic of gilgamesh,* were found in <u>a</u>shurbanipal's Library at <u>n</u>ineveh.

1. If we need money for the First Mortgage, I can always borrow some from uncle charlie.
2. Because dr. Lewis, my English professor, lived in the south for many years, he has remained a baptist.
3. The Monarch butterfly has wings that resemble dead autumn leaves.
4. Anton Chekhov's short story "the new villa" portrays a clash between two cultures, the Aristocracy and the Serfs.
5. When we take our cruise to alaska, we shall go on the olav, a scandinavian Vessel.
6. I am sending grandmother some Violets for her Birthday.
7. The tiv, an african tribe, began their stories, "not yesterday, not yesterday."
8. During the Middle Ages, London had no sewers; consequently, the plague broke out from time to time.
9. After Adam and Eve had eaten of the tree of the knowledge of good and evil, they were expelled from eden.
10. Helen likes to be addressed as "ms. Griffith" rather than "miss Griffith."
11. My grandfather watched Charles Lindbergh land the spirit of St. Louis at orly airport in paris.
12. He will be made a fellow of the royal academy of surgeons next Spring.
13. How many more American Embassies will be attacked by Foreign countries who want to be our enemies?
14. We sat down and listened to the president's state of the union address on tv.
15. The Lincoln Memorial in Washington, D.C. will always remind us that civil war is possible.

22. Italics (ital)

In handwritten or typewritten manuscripts, italics are indicated by underlining. In printing, *italic* type is used.

Use italics for the titles of books, magazines, and newspapers:

> One of the most thoroughly American books is *Tom Sawyer* by Mark Twain.

Occasionally I don't understand *Time* magazine's choice for "Man of the Year."

He relies on *The Wall Street Journal* for news about economic trends.

NOTES: Copy the title of a newspaper as it appears on the masthead:

Los Angeles Times (not *The Los Angeles Times* or *The Times*)

Use italics for the titles of pamphlets or bulletins, musical compositions, plays, films, television programs, and long poems:

MacDowell Musical Society News Bulletin
Rock Climbing in the Sierras
Verdi's *La Traviata* (opera)
Beethoven's *Concerto No. 2*
My Fair Lady (musical comedy)
Neil Simon's *Chapter Two* (play)
All That Jazz (film)
60 Minutes (TV broadcast)
Byron's *Don Juan* (long poem)

NOTES: 1. Titles of brief musical pieces or songs are usually placed within quotation marks:

"Scaramouche" by Milhaud
"I Could Have Danced All Night" (from *My Fair Lady*)

2. Titles of short poems are placed within quotation marks:

"Journey of the Magi" by T. S. Eliot

Use italics for the names of ships, aircraft, spacecraft, and trains:

USS Missouri (ship)
Spirit of St. Louis (aircraft)
Apollo 17 (spacecraft)
Orient Express (train)

Use italics for titles of visual works of art:

Discus Thrower by Myron (ancient Roman sculpture)
Girl Pouring Perfume (detail from a wall painting)
Alexander at Issus (second century Greek mosaic)
Leonardo da Vinci's *Mona Lisa* (painting on canvas)

Use italics for foreign words not yet absorbed into the English vocabulary:

Schopenhauer had a gloomy *Weltanschauung.* (world view)
When I entered the room, I had a feeling of *déjà vu.* (already seen)
This day is certainly *bellissimo.* (most beautiful)

Latin abbreviations are not italicized:

etc., i.e., viz., et al., e.g.

Use italics for words, letters, figures, or symbols referred to as such:

Words like *superannuated* instead of *old* sound overblown.
The French have a way of gargling their *r's.*
Move those *10's* over to the next column.
Students should avoid using the *&* sign in formal essays.

NOTE: Quotation marks are sometimes used for cases such as those listed above, but we recommend italics.

Use italics for emphasis when it cannot be achieved by choice or placement of words:

Which of the following is *not* a fairytale:
    a. "The Descent of Ishtar into the Netherworld"
    b. "Snow White and the Seven Dwarfs"
    c. "The Frog and the Prince"
    d. "Sleeping Beauty"
(to draw attention to the direction in a multiple-choice examination)

I said that she should com*pli*ment, not com*ple*ment him. (to emphasize the distinction in meaning between the two words)

Exercises

Exercise 22: Italics

In the following sentences underline all words that should be in italics. If the sentence is correct, leave it alone.

> MODEL: On my flight to New York, I read Belva Plain's <u>Evergreen</u>, a charming novel.

1. If I had the money, I would subscribe to The New Yorker.
2. When you say you saw Gerald Ford, do you mean the Gerald Ford?
3. My history professor is constantly using the phrase coup d'état.
4. Does it bother you when someone misuses the word disinterested?
5. One television commentator gave the movie The Last Married Couple in America a bad review.

6. My favorite hors d'oeuvre is stuffed mushrooms.
7. The Dome of the Rock in Jerusalem is a holy shrine for both Jews and Moslems.
8. I have Van Gogh's Sunflowers hanging on my office wall.
9. Some of Toulouse-Lautrec's best paintings feature La Goulue, a cabaret dancer whom the artist befriended.
10. Numerous tourists each year take a Mediterranean cruise aboard the Royal Viking Sea, a luxury ship.

Exercise 16, 22: Quotation marks and italics

In the following sentences, underline words that should be in italics, and use quotation marks where needed.

> MODEL: Although poetry has never been my favorite literary genre, I am deeply touched by Edwin Markham's "Man and the Hoe."

1. The chapter entitled China: War and Resistance in Theodore H. White's book In Search of History is informative.
2. Although it has almost become commercialized, Michelangelo's famous David never fails to impress me with its youthful courage and zeal.
3. Ain't Misbehavin' is a zesty, jazzy musical.
4. The literary term used to describe stories that begin in the middle of the action is in medias res.
5. No television show has surpassed the Show of Shows in pure comic effect.
6. The Catbird Seat by James Thurber is a short story about a meek little office clerk who gets even with an overbearing female coworker.
7. In his article Why I Am an Agnostic Clarence Darrow tries to make some Christian beliefs look absurd.
8. John Ciardi's translation of Dante's Inferno keeps the complex gestalt of the original twenty-seven cantos.
9. A tragic loss of lives and property took place when the Titanic sank on April 10, 1912.
10. You Ain't Nothin' But a Hound Dog was one of Elvis Presley's earliest successes.

23. Numbers (nu)

In the following circumstances numbers are usually written out.

Numbers that can be spelled out in two words or less:

> seventy-thousand years ago
> forty-five senators
> three fourths of the country

A hyphenated number is considered as one word:

>   thirty-five thousand voters

Numbers used as compound adjectives:

>   a ten-year-old refrigerator
>   a three-wheel electric car

In the following circumstances numbers must be written as figures.

Numbers expressed in more than two words:

>   Much had changed in 225 years.
>   a list of 3,250 people
>   not more than 56¼ inches

Dates:

>   November 19, 1929
>   19 Nov. 1929
>   11/19/29
>   55 B.C.
>   A.D. 105

"B.C." follows the year, but "A.D." precedes the year. The day of the month may be written out when the year does not follow:

>   On the sixth of October

Decades may be written out or expressed as figures:

>   In the nineteen sixties
>   In the sixties
>   In the 1960's (or 1960s)

Centuries are expressed in lower-case letters:

>   Following the seventeenth century

Addresses:

>   245 Earlham St.
>   Apt. 15
>   Pasadena, California 91106

Time of day:

>   4:14 P.M.

If the expression "o'clock" follows, then the hours should be written out:

>   three-thirty o'clock

Exact amounts of money:

> $15.98
> $1,350
> $2.5 million (or $2,500,000)

Mathematical scores and statistics:

>   20¼
>   ⅝
>   3.5% (or 3.5 percent)
>   a median score of 48

Number of books, volumes, pages, acts, scenes, verses, and lines:

>   Book 3 (or Book III)
>   Volume 4 (or Volume IV)
>   page 23 (or p. 23)
>   Act 3, Scene 2, lines 15–18 (or Act III, Scene 2, lines 15–18)
>   Verse 3

NOTES: 1. The documentation for research papers follows a special format, as explained in Chapter 14 "The Research Paper."

2. Never begin a sentence with a figure. If necessary, rewrite the sentence:

Wrong: 36 was the score.
 Right: The score was 36.

3. If you are writing a paper that contains many numbers, use figures throughout for consistency.

Exercises

Exercise 23: Numbers

Correct all numbers used incorrectly. If the sentence is correct, leave it alone.

>   MODEL: That pound of chocolates costs $5.23

1. She swam 3 full miles.
2. Louis XIV was born in 1638.
3. Flapper girls were a product of the nineteen twenties.
4. 1980 was a year of strained relations between the U.S. and Iran.
5. Our flight leaves at three-thirty A.M.
6. The score was 30 to 1.
7. If 48% of the product sells, we shall profit.

8. The bridge cost three million and a half dollars.
9. Volume Three is the most difficult of all.
10. A foot has twelve inches.

24. Abbreviations (abb)

In general, avoid abbreviations. Under the following circumstances abbreviations are correct:

Titles preceding proper names:

> Dr. Strangelove
> Mr. Sebastian Peters
> Mrs. Reinbolt
> Ms. Balucci
> St. Theresa

The following titles are written out:

> President Harding
> Senator Baker
> Professor Fiedler
> The Honorable George Lundquist
> The Reverend Jesse Jackson

Titles following proper names:

> Marcel Ford, Jr.
> Christopher J. Marsh, Esq.
> Frances Moore, M.D.
> Henry A. Look, Ph.D.
> Gilbert Blaine, LL.D.

Names of well-known organizations and a few countries:

FBI	YMCA
CIA	OPEC
HEW	USA
IBM	USSR
CBS	NBC

Words used with dates or figures:

> 23 B.C. (or A.D. 23)
> 8:00 A.M. (or 8:00 P.M.)
> I answered No. 4 wrong.
> See Fig. 17.

Incorporated, Company, Brothers, and the ampersand when they are part of the official name of a business:

> Doubleday & Co., Inc.
> Cotton Bros., Inc.

Abbreviations used in footnotes, endnotes, or bibliographies:

e.g.	for example
i.e.	that is
etc.	and so forth
et al.	and others
ed.	edited by, editor, edition
trans.	translated by, translator
p., pp.	page, pages

The English versions of the first four abbreviations above are preferred for writing not related to formal research.

NOTE: Do not abbreviate the following:

1. Names of geographical areas, months, days:

Wrong: The cruise left for the Med. last Wed.
  Right: The cruise left for the Mediterranean last Wednesday.

2. Names of people:

> Will Matthew (not *Matth.*) pay the bill?

3. The words *volume, chapter, page* unless used in research-paper documentation or technical writing:

> He fell asleep after reading three pages (not *pp.*) of the first volume (not *vol.*).

4. Names of courses of study:

> She failed chemistry (not *chem.*).

5. The word *Christmas:*

> Christmas (not *Xmas*) will be here soon.

6. The words *street, avenue, road, park, mount, drive, lane, river,* and similar words when they are used as essential parts of proper names:

> Maiden Lane is filled with charming shops.
> The club climbed Mount Whitney.
> Their summer home is on the Colorado River.

Exercises

Exercise 24: Abbreviations

Strike out the version that would be incorrect in formal writing:

> MODEL: Give Geo. a call. / Give George a call.

1. Please consult Doctor Smith. / Please consult Dr. Smith.
2. Senator Cranston was interviewed. / Sen. Cranston was interviewed.
3. In the year 55 before Christ's birth, Rome controlled Palestine. / In 55 B.C. Rome controlled Palestine.
4. Terrence Belford, Junior, was in town. / Terrence Belford, Jr., was in town.
5. They returned $3.58. / They returned three dollars and fifty-eight cents.
6. His largest class was Eng. lit. / His largest class was English literature.
7. The Federal Bureau of Investigation was forced to investigate. / The FBI was forced to investigate.
8. Park Ave. is beautiful at Xmas. / Park Avenue is beautiful at Christmas.
9. The first payment is due in Nov. / The first payment is due in November.
10. The men are stationed in Switz. / The men are stationed in Switzerland.

Effective Sentences

Now that you have studied basic grammar, punctuation, and mechanics, you are ready to use your knowledge of all these elements to write effective sentences. A study of the principles in this section will help you to write an essay, a research paper, or a report that is made up of clear, concise sentences.

25. Subordination (sub)

Subordination is the use of dependent elements to give focus to a main clause or a kernel sentence. Subordination is one way of combining short, choppy sentences into a longer, smoothly integrated one—a technique that requires an understanding of the different types of phrases and clauses explained at the beginning of this handbook. Consider, for example, the following sentences:

> Caedmon was an ignorant herdsman.
> He believed that his poetic powers came from God.

These two sentences may be combined:

> Caedmon was an ignorant English herdsman who believed that his poetic powers came from God.

The second sentence (or independent clause) has been turned into a dependent clause and subordinated to the first. The result is a sentence that is smoother and longer yet still includes all the original information found in its constituent parts.

Many sentences can be subordinated without changing their original sense. Others, however, cannot be subordinated because they express ideas that are equal in value:

> Today, schools provide an education.
> Today, schools do not guarantee jobs.

To subordinate one of these sentences to the other would be to change the original meaning of both:

> Today, schools provide an education because they do not guarantee jobs.

A causal connection, not originally intended, has been established. Sentences such as these should be combined by placing a coordinate conjunction between them:

> Today, schools provide an education, but they do not guarantee jobs.

Subordination can be used only between ideas of unequal importance. Learn to assign the correct value to each sentence and reflect it through a subordinated structure. Consider the following independent clauses:

> 1. Lake Como is a tourist resort.
> 2. It is situated in the foothills of the Alps.
> 3. It is one of the most beautiful spots in Europe.

Through the process of subordination, these three independent clauses can be integrated into one clear and logical sentence:

> Lake Como, a tourist resort situated in the foothills of the Alps, is one of the most beautiful spots in Europe.

The most important independent clauses are 1 and 3, while 2 acquires a less prominent position by becoming a participial phrase and being squeezed into the middle as a parenthetical statement. If we had decided that 1 and 2 were the more important, then the subordinated sentence would have read as follows:

> Lake Como, one of the most beautiful spots in Europe, is a tourist resort situated in the foothills of the Alps.

To subordinate logically as well as coherently, you must decide which ideas are more important and which less, and construct your new subordinated sentence to mirror this decision.

Here are some further examples of subordination. Examine them carefully to see how the combining process works:

Choppy: 1. English architecture evolved in the twelfth century.
2. It began with the Norman style.

3. It was especially noticeable in the Norman churches.
4. These Norman churches have long naves.
5. They also have rectangular east ends.

Better: English architecture evolved in the twelfth century with the Norman style, which was especially noticeable in the Norman churches with their long naves and rectangular east ends.

Here, sentences 2, 3, 4, and 5 are subordinated to sentence 1. Notice, however, that 4 and 5 are combined with the coordinate conjunction *and* because they express ideas of equal value.

Choppy: 1. In ancient Greece, fire was considered one of the four basic elements.
2. It was considered a substance from which the other elements were composed.
3. The other elements were earth, water, and air.

Better: In ancient Greece, fire was considered one of the four basic elements, a substance from which all other elements—earth, air, and water—were composed.

In this combination, 2 is subordinated to 1, while 3 is inserted parenthetically into 2.

Choppy: 1. The speaker raised his hands to silence the audience.
2. The applause continued.
3. It was punctuated by boos.
4. The boos were isolated.

Better: Although the speaker raised his hands to silence the audience, the applause continued, punctuated by isolated boos.

Here, 1 is subordinated to 2; 4 is merged into 3 as an adjective and then attached to 2 as a participial phrase.

In sum, subordination can be achieved in three ways:

Subordinating a clause:

The beggar played his guitar.
He was hungry.

The beggar played his guitar because he was hungry.

or

The beggar, who was hungry, played his guitar.

Subordinating a phrase:

The mountains reach into the sky.
Their peaks are covered with snow.

Their peaks covered with snow, the mountains reach into the sky.

Subordinating a word:

The atmosphere was damp.
It was marked by darkness.

The atmosphere was damp and dark.

NOTE: Beware of the reverse subordination that results when the less important of two ideas is expressed as an independent clause:

Reverse subordination: Although Alex was accepted into Harvard, her entrance examination showed some weakness in vocabulary. (The fact that Alex was accepted into Harvard is the more important fact and should be expressed in the independent clause.)

Correct subordination: Although her entrance examination showed some weakness in vocabulary, Alex was accepted into Harvard.

Reverse subordiation: His legs paralyzed for life, he was stricken with polio when he was twelve. (The fact that his legs are paralyzed for life is the more important idea and should be placed in the independent clause.)

Correct subordination: Stricken with polio when he was twelve, he suffered paralysis of the legs for life.

Exercises

Exercise 25: Subordination

By careful subordination, combine the ideas in each of the following sets of sentences into one effective sentence.

MODEL: Marcia was highly intelligent.
Nevertheless she suffered from extreme timidity.
She never learned to hide this timidity.

Answer: **Although Marcia was highly intelligent, she suffered from extreme timidity, which she never learned to hide.**

1. My father died.
We moved into a small town.
It was outside of Boston.
It was called Reading.
There was almost no intellectual life there.

2. Mary Todd Lincoln longed desperately for Willie's presence.
   She longed for him so desperately that one night she awoke.
   It was midnight.
   She had the impression that Willie was standing at the foot of her bed.
3. He was lying on the bare earth.
   He was shoeless, bearded, and half-naked.
   He looked like a beggar or a lunatic.
4. The frightened hawk lay there for a long minute.
   He had no hope.
   He did not move.
   His eyes were still fixed on that blue vault above him.
5. Ulysses S. Grant and Robert E. Lee met on April 9, 1865.
   They met in the parlor of a modest Virginia house.
   They met to work out the terms for the surrender of Lee's Army of
   Northern Virginia.
   At this meeting a great chapter in American life came to a close and a
   great chapter began.
6. The mockingbird took a single step into the air.
   His wings were still folded against his sides.
   He accelerated thirty-two feet per second.
   Just a breath before he would have been dashed to the ground, he un-
   furled his wings.
   He then gracefully floated onto the grass.
7. Cleopatra worked diligently to learn coquettishness and flattery.
   She was the most famous courtesan of the ancient world.
   She reportedly practiced on slaves.
8. It was a cold, bright December morning.
   It was far out in the country.
   An old Negro woman came along a path through the pinewood.
   Her name was Phoenix Jackson.
   A red tag was tied around her head.
9. The priest nodded.
   Then I surprised the audience.
   I recited a sixteenth century poem about love and commitment.
   The poem caused my bride to burst into tears.
   I was amazed.
10. I refused many prestigious jobs.
    One job I refused was clerking for a judge
    Another job I refused was joining a wealthy law firm.
    I favored the public service sector.
11. Most primitive mythologies contain a flood story.
    In each of these stories the gods decide to destroy all human beings.
    However, they make an exception for one favored family.

This family survives the catastrophe.
Such a family was Noah and his brood.

12. My brother's face remains scarred for life.
When he was a mere baby, he was bitten and scratched by a Siamese cat.

13. There are thousands of marvelous summer resorts in the world.
There is Monte Carlo.
There is Bermuda.
There is Hawaii.
However, I prefer Miami Beach.

14. The highland wind blows steadily from north to northeast.
It is the same wind that blows down on the coasts of Africa and Arabia.
Down there they call it the "monsoon."
"Monsoon" was the name of King Solomon's favorite horse.

15. I have a vivid picture in mind.
It is a picture of Dr. Albert Schweitzer.
I see him at the age of eighty-four spending most of his time answering his correspondence.
It often consisted of silly questions.

26. Dangling Modifiers (dm)

A dangling modifier is a word or a group of words that does not modify anything in the sentence:

> Jogging along the beach, the sun set in a blaze of crimson glory.

A reader who took this sentence literally would think that the setting sun was jogging along the beach. The dangling participle, "jogging along the beach," appears to modify "the sun." Here is one way to correct the sentence:

> As I was jogging along the beach, the sun set in a blaze of crimson glory.

Now *I* is the subject of *jogging* and the phrase becomes a dependent clause. Here are some more examples of dangling modifiers:

Dangling: After our fight, she walked toward me while sitting on a bench. (How can she simultaneously walk and sit?)

Better: After our fight, she walked toward me while I was sitting on a bench.

Dangling: Crying her heart out, I was deeply moved by the sound. (How can the speaker cry another person's heart out?)

Better: I was deeply moved when I heard her crying her heart out.

Dangling: Looking to the far end of the football field, there he was. (The participle *looking* has no logical subject at all.)

Better: Looking to the far end of the football field, they saw him.

Dangling modifiers are usually corrected in two ways: by leaving the dangler as is but recasting the remainder of the sentence; or by expanding the dangling part into a complete dependent clause.

NOTE: Certain absolute constructions are exceptions to these rules (see 2c[3]. *Absolute phrases*):

> *Generally speaking,* men are taller than women.
> *To sum up,* cocktail parties are boring.

Exercises

Exercise 26: Dangling modifiers

Indicate which sentences are correct and which contain dangling modifiers. Rewrite the sentences that contain dangling modifiers.

> MODEL: While sneaking into our house through the back door, my father confronted me.
>
>   Answer: **While I was sneaking into our house through the back door, my father confronted me.**

1. When looking toward the sky, the enormous white clouds sailing across the deep blue are a breathtaking sight.
2. After complaining in two letters, the client finally received his rebate.
3. By showing respect for my teachers, they respected me in return.
4. After gaining her employer's confidence, doors began to open, and opportunities came her way.
5. Coming from a Persian background, her complexion is a lovely deep olive.
6. To be successful, a person must be willing to persevere despite failures.
7. Barking and snarling, the guests were scared by our big German shepherd dog.
8. Having pimples and lacking self-confidence, my grandmother reassured me that someday I would be beautiful.
9. Realizing that a course in western civilization would broaden his political views, Jack enrolled at UCLA.
10. Grease-stained and covered with dust, Margie rediscovered her diary.
11. The wind began to blow immediately after opening the windows.
12. Never having met the instructor, it seemed foolish of her to be so nervous.

13. Truthfully speaking, Miami, Florida, has a *nouveau riche* atmosphere.
14. Before entering the water, the scuba diving equipment should be checked.
15. Sitting in a sidewalk cafe listening to lovely violin music, San Marco Square seemed utterly romantic.

27. Misplaced Parts (mp)

A well-constructed sentence raises no uncertainty about which words belong where. Modifiers should stand as close as possible to the words they modify. Notice how each sentence below takes on a different meaning, depending on where the word *only* is placed:

> *Only* I loved her. (No one else did.)
> I *only* loved her. (I didn't hate, pity, or envy her.)
> I loved *only* her. (I loved no one else.)

A writer must be careful to place modifiers in positions that most clearly convey the meaning intended. The following is an example of a misplaced part:

> The United States has seen its President burned in effigy *on the living room TV.*

The writer has created an absurdity by having the phrase *on the living room TV* modify the verb *burned.* The following version makes clear the writer's intentions:

> *On the living room TV* the United States has seen its President burned in effigy.

Some modifiers, if ambiguously placed between two elements, will seem to modify both:

> The waiter who had served them *swiftly* disappeared.

The meaning of the sentence is unclear because it is impossible to know whether the waiter served swiftly or disappeared swiftly. Here are two clearer versions:

> The waiter who had served them disappeared *swiftly.*

> **or**

> The waiter who had *swiftly* served them disappeared.

Diligent proofreading is a good defense against misplaced parts.

Exercises

Exercise 27: Misplaced parts

Indicate which sentences are correct and which contain misplaced parts. Re-write the sentences that contain misplaced parts.

MODEL: It only takes Wally ten minutes to clean his room, whereas it takes me one full hour.

Answer: **It takes Wally only ten minutes to clean his room, whereas it takes me one full hour.**

1. Self-esteem is someone's own sense of his value and strength.
2. I almost love everyone of my neighbors.
3. Those men who had snored loudly greeted the morning.
4. Darwin wrote his famous book on the origin of the species in England.
5. All of the old people may be exposed on this trip to diseased water.
6. Because Marie believed in complete abstinence, she ordered merely a bottle of Perrier water.
7. To our amazement, the man almost spent half of his time collecting buttons from all over the world.
8. Some threadbare woman's underwear lay in the middle of the alley.
9. I discovered a sweater knit by my sister under the snow on the roof of our mountain cabin.
10. Last year, our publishing business grossed nearly a million dollars.
11. No one was allowed to use the condominium tennis courts except people living in the Northridge development.
12. A life of luxury was the only kind of life she knew.
13. All students will not be required to register for the draft.
14. One pedestrian got struck down by a truck emerging from the bus.
15. The carpet was laid on the parquet floor, which was made of silk and tied by hand.

28. Parallelism (//)

Parallelism enables a writer to express equal thoughts by using equal grammatical structures. In a parallel sentence, the writer balances noun against noun, adjective against adjective, infinitive against infinitive to emphasize the equality of ideas. Faulty parallelism upsets this balance of ideas in a sentence:

Awkward: My plan was to fish, hunt, and hiking.
  Parallel: My plan was to fish, hunt, and hike.

In short sentences such as the one above the preposition need not be repeated, but in longer sentences it shoud be.

Parallel prepositional phrases:

He talked to us about devotion ‖ to our family,
to our neighborhood, and
to our country.

Parallel subordinate clauses:

All of us knew ‖ that he was petty,
that he was jealous, and
that he was vain.

Parallel gerunds:

What I despised about him was his ‖ drinking,
gambling, and
cursing.

Parallel independent clauses:

‖ We counted our losses;
we cared for the wounded;
we advanced once again.

28a. Basic rules

There are some basic rules to follow when using parallelism. Do not use *and who* or *and which* unless preceded by another *who* or *which* clause.

Awkward: Pope John Paul II is a man with charisma *and who* is admired throughout the world.

Parallel: Pope John Paul II is a man ‖ who has charisma and
who is admired throughout the world.

When using correlative conjunctions (*either . . . or, neither . . . nor, not only . . . but also, both . . . and*), use parallel constructions to complete the sentence.

Awkward: Either you pay the fine or jail is where you will go. (*Either* is followed by a pronoun, whereas *or* is followed by a noun.)

Parallel: Either ‖ you pay the fine
or ‖ you go to jail.

Awkward: They not only invaded our privacy, but also our time was taken by them. (The *but also* part is in the passive.)

Parallel: They ‖ not only invaded our privacy,
       ‖ but also wasted our time.

To emphasize parallelism in a sentence, it is sometimes necessary to repeat a preposition, an article, or words in a phrase.

Awkward: She rummaged about in the kitchen, in the basement, and the attic.

Parallel: She rummaged about ‖ *in* the kitchen,
          ‖ *in* the basement, and
          ‖ *in* the attic.

(The preposition *in* is repeated.)

Awkward: Love is a gift as well as responsibility.

Parallel: Love is ‖ *a* gift as well as
        ‖ *a* responsibility.

(The article *a* is repeated.)

Awkward: Where he works and the place he lives are two completely different places.

Parallel: ‖ *Where he* works and
       ‖ *where he* lives
are two completely different places.
(*Where he* is repeated.)

Exercises

Exercise 28: Parallelism

Indicate which sentences are correct and which have faulty parallelism. Rewrite the sentences with faulty parallelism.

MODEL: Most of the students in my art class are youths of talent and who want to make a living from their art.

Answer: Most of the students in my art class are youths who have talent and who want to make a living from their art.

1. The pleasure of snow skiing comes from the thrill of speeding downhill and that it is out in nature.
2. She told Marie either to clean her fingernails or cut them shorter.
3. His rise had been predicted by astrology, prophecy, and dreams.
4. The crowds at the Olympic games seemed relaxed and enjoying themselves.

5. The father wanted to work rather than have free handouts.
6. He underwrote the cost of the journey, guaranteed revenue to the workers, and promising decent shelter for families with children.
7. My two favorite sports are fishing and to hike.
8. After attending the literature class, Leonard did not feel so much informed on issues as that he had increased his sensitivity to human needs.
9. The assignment was to create a myth about the edges of the universe and read it in class.
10. The bird flew above the tree, beyond the horizon, and into the blue yonder.
11. My salary is not as big as my sister.
12. The king demanded expulsion of the bishops, annihilation of all taxes, and burials.
13. All six of us agreed that we would ride the gondola to the top of the mountain but to hike back.
14. He came; he saw; he conquered.
15. The buildings of our city are black from soot and old age has cracked them.

29. Illogical Constructions (ill)

The illogical construction is inexact, confusing, or vague, and may be so for a variety of reasons, a few of which are cataloged below.

29a. Illogical comparisons

Comparisons require that the items being compared be similar and that the comparison be complete. Study the following sentences:

> The rose is prettier than any flower in the world.

Since the *rose* is included in the classification of flower, the sentence is really saying that the rose is prettier than the rose. Here is the comparison logically stated:

> The rose is prettier than any *other* flower in the world.

Another common error is ambiguity resulting from a badly stated comparison:

> He loves me more than his son.

Does he love me more than he loves his son? Or does he love me more than his son loves me? The comparison must be reworded to specify the intended meaning.

Perhaps the most common error in comparisons is incompleteness. Here is a typical example:

> Anacin gives more relief.

More relief than what? Copy writing is replete with this sort of carelessness. Here is an improvement:

> Anacin gives more pain relief than does any other analgesic sold over the counter.

If not marketable, this comparison is at least logically complete. Here are some more examples of comparisons that are illogical and vague because of incompleteness:

Illogical: Women are more aggressive today.
  Better: Women are more aggressive today than they were twenty years ago.

Illogical: French chefs cook better meat sauces.
  Better: French chefs cook better meat sauces than do American chefs.

or

> French chefs cook better meat sauces than they do cream pies.

29b. Mixed constructions

A mixed construction is a sentence that begins in one grammatical pattern but ends in another. Here is an example:

> It was because all members of the firm stood by time-honored moral values that enabled them to survive.

The sentence develops logically until it reaches the word *enabled,* when it takes a sudden lurch into another pattern for which the reader is entirely unprepared. Confusion and misreading will inevitably result. The correct version starts with and ends on the same grammatical pattern thus fulfilling reader anticipation:

> It was because all members of the firm stood by time-honored moral values that they were able to survive.

Here are additional examples of mixed constructions followed by corrected versions. Some of the shifts are subtle variations on the grammatical pattern one would ordinarily anticipate.

Mixed: When the stock market crashed and Sully couldn't get help from anyone, not even Joseph, therefore he committed suicide.

Better: When the stock market crashed and Sully could not get help from anyone, not even Joseph, he committed suicide.

Mixed: As for the effects the large city had on Nancy were typical of what happened to many young people abroad.

Better: As for the effects the large city had on Nancy, they were typical of what happened to many young people abroad.

Mixed: His free will is limited to the circumstances by which his destiny has forced upon him.

Better: His free will is limited by the circumstances his destiny has forced upon him.

Exercises

Exercise 29: Illogical constructions

Indicate which sentences are correct and which contain illogical constructions. Rewrite the sentences that have illogical constructions.

> MODEL: The weather in California is far better than New York.
>
> Answer: The weather in California is far better than the weather in New York.

1. The first play concerns the blacks and how they maintained their dignity and facing difficulties caused by the whites.
2. It was in my ability to look past the bad in people to the good that helped me to like my classmates.
3. His mother's judgment of financial investments and real estate values is much sharper than his father.
4. Edmund's job pays better than Mark's.
5. A tragic hero is when a tragic flaw causes his downfall.
6. The reason for the decline of Rome was because the Romans had become morally flabby.
7. Mt. Everest is higher than any mountain in the world.
8. It was not until Antony died before Cleopatra realized how much she loved him.
9. The reason education in the United States seems to have become mediocre is that our schools have been asked to educate more illiterate people than ever before.
10. The emphasis on human rights makes America more democratic.
11. When he dissected a frog in biology lab was the experience he remembered years later.
12. We bought an old cabin which by repairing the roof we could use it for camping in during the summers.

30. Shifts (shift)

It is very important to be consistent in your use of tense, mood, person, voice, and discourse. If you shift your point of view, you will confuse your reader.

30a. Tense (shift/t)

Tense is the form of a verb that expresses the time of its action. The correct tense for a verb is normally dictated by the chronology of the situation being written about. Most of us use the proper tense out of habit. However, here are a few general rules:

Use the present tense to express timeless, general truths or prevailing customs:

> Copernicus pointed out that the world *is* (not *was*) not the center of our universe. (Copernicus' discovery was in the past, but the truth of it still applies today.)

> The rabbi reminded everyone that the Sabbath *begins* (not *began*) Friday at sunset. (The rabbi's warning was given in the past, but the Jewish Sabbath still begins on Friday.)

Indicate differences in time by using different tenses:

Wrong: Eric admitted that he *used* all of the wood.

Right: Eric admitted that he *had* used all of the wood. (Eric must have used up the wood before making the admission.)

Wrong: *Getting* permission from my boss, I will take a day of vacation next week.

Right: *Having gotten* permission from my boss, I will take a day's vacation next week. (The permission has to be granted before the vacation can be taken.)

Indicate simultaneous happenings by using the same tense:

Wrong: Mark waxed his skis while George *gazes* at the mountains.

Right: Mark waxed his skis while George *gazed* at the mountains. (Both the waxing and the gazing happen simultaneously and must therefore be expressed in the same tense.)

Wrong: Because my girlfriend remained at home alone, she *writes* me this melancholy letter.

Right: Because my girlfriend remained home alone, she *wrote* me this melancholy letter. (Both the remaining and the writing took place in the past and therefore require the same past tense.)

Wrong: We had packed our suitcases as well as *ate* our lunch before the train arrived.

Right: We had packed our suitcases as well as *eaten* our lunch before the train arrived. (The packing and eating both took place before the arrival of the train; they therefore require the same past tense.)

30b. Mood (shift/m)

Mood (or mode) indicates under what conditions a statement is being made. In English we have three moods: *indicative, subjunctive,* and *imperative.* The indicative mood is used for the majority of declarations ("The fields are blossoming.") or questions ("Do you feel any better?"). The subjunctive mood is used to express a wish ("I wish I *were* wealthy."), a necessity ("It is necessary that he *see* his children."), or a condition contrary to fact ("If she had taken the medicine, she *would be* alive today."). It is also used for a request or an indirect command ("He insisted that the suitcase *be* checked for drugs."). The imperative mood is used for direct commands (*"Give* me liberty or *give* me death!"").

When you are writing, make sure you don't shift from one mood to another:

Wrong: They insisted that the money *be* collected and that a receipt *is* given in return. (shift from the subjunctive to the indicative)

Right: They insisted that the money *be* collected and that a receipt *be* given in return.

Wrong: *Pay* your taxes and you *should* also *support* your representatives in Congress. (shift from the imperative to the indicative mood)

Right: *Pay* your taxes and *support* your representatives in Congress.

Don't use *would have* when *had* is sufficient:

Wrong: If I *would have* been born in this country, I *would have* to enlist in the army.

Right: If I *had* been born in this country, I *would have* to enlist in the army. (The *if* clause requires only *had,* not *would have.*)

The subjunctive mood should be used in certain idiomatic expressions:

> *Come* (not *comes*) hell or high water, we'll be there.

NOTES: 1. Study the following rules on how to form the subjunctive.

The present subjunctive of *to be* is invariably *be:*

I demand that he *be* on time.

In all other forms, the subjunctive differs from the indicative only in that in the third person the third-person ending is dropped:

I suggest that she *listen* (not *listens*).

2. *Should* or *would* are often used to indicate suppositions as well as contrary-to-fact conditions:

Should an enemy attack, we *would* go to war.

3. You may prefer to avoid the subjunctive altogether by rewording the sentence:

Subjunctive: Suppose she *were to resign.*
   Rewrite: Suppose she *resigns.*
Subjunctive: Let's require *that he sign.*
   Rewrite: Let's require *him to sign.*
Subjunctive: It is necessary *that we be* kind.
   Rewrite: We *must be* kind.

30c. Person (shift/p)

A writer who doesn't write from a consistent point of view will bewilder the reader. Consider the following:

Basically each individual creates your own psychological self-portrait; however, others do contribute factors we use in evaluating oneself.

Like surprise flashes of lightning, the writer has struck from four different points of view: *each, your, we, oneself.* This fractured sentence is easily corrected if a single, consistent point of view is established:

Basically we each create our own psychological self-portrait; however, others do contribute factors we use in evaluating ourselves.

Most point of view errors occur when a writer attempts to speak about people in general. Here is a typical example:

Wrong: *Their* first thought is that *you* can't get the job. (The writer has shifted from *they* to *you.*)
Better: *Their* first thought is that *they* can't get the job.

See also 31. *Pronoun reference,* for the use of *one* and *you.*

30d. Voice (shift/v)

The voice of a verb tells you whether or not the subject acts or is acted upon:

> The boy ate the doughnut. (Here the subject *boy* is acting; he is eating the doughnut. Therefore, the voice is *active*.)

Now consider this version of the sentence:

> The doughnut was eaten by the boy. (In this case, *doughtnut* is the subject and it is being acted on by the boy. Therefore, the voice is *passive*.)

The choice between active or passive voice depends on whether you wish to emphasize the actor or the receiver of an action. As a general rule, the active voice is preferable because it is stronger and more direct than the passive. But whichever you use, don't shift unnecessarily from one voice to another:

Wrong: Although the Black Plague killed thousands of anonymous poor, the rich were attacked by it also.

Better: Although the Black Plague killed thousands of anonymous poor, it also attacked the rich.

Wrong: Jerry devoured a steak, and an entire half gallon of ice cream was eaten by him.

Better: Jerry devoured a steak and ate an entire half gallon of ice cream.

30e. Discourse (shift/d)

Discourse means conversation. Discourse can be direct, as:

> The flight attendant told the passengers, "Fasten your seat belts."

Or it can be indirect, as:

> The flight attendant requested that all passengers fasten their seat belts.

In the first example, the exact words of the speaker are used and enclosed in quotation marks. In the second example, the speaker's exact remarks are paraphrased. You may use either direct or indirect discourse, but you must not shift from one to the other:

Wrong: All of us wondered how the highjacker had boarded the plane and why didn't the security guards catch him? (shift from indirect to direct)

Better: All of us wondered how the highjacker had boarded the plane and why the security guards had not caught him.

Wrong: The salesperson informed me that she was collecting money for the blind and would I buy a broom.

Better: The salesperson informed me that she was collecting money for the blind and asked me if I would buy a broom.

or

The salesperson said, "I am collecting money for the blind. Would you buy a broom?"

Exercises

Exercise 30: Shifts in tense, mood, person, voice, discourse

Identify the kind of needless shift in each of the sentences below and then rewrite the sentences from a single point of view.

> MODEL: Their first thought is that we will never learn the dance step.
>
> Answer: **Shift in person**
> Their first thought is that they will never learn the dance step.

1. In those early days the primary reason for my happiness lay in the ability I possess to take people for what they are.
2. Henry asked if he could accompany us and would we reserve an airline ticket for him?
3. She swayed back and forth and her body was swung from side to side.
4. When one feels accepted by a peer group, you become a stronger individual.
5. Look for some yeast and you should also pick up a newspaper.
6. His leg was fractured, his face was cut, and he looks like an inflated beach ball.
7. Fine athletes function as role models. If one can measure up, fine; if you can't, you are consigned to the uglies.
8. She held her trophy high, and her medal was worn with pride.
9. As the motorcycle hit the wall, the crowd screams in fear and delight.
10. The crusaders exposed themselves to every peril, and their bodies were given up to the adventure of life in death.
11. The treasurer testified that she just finished her report when the phone rang.
12. Years later she wondered why her youth had been so miserable and how could it have been improved.
13. If he wasn't such a monster of conceit, I would admire him for his talent.
14. The young man declared that he was in love and would she please marry him.
15. The corpses are dragged to the courtyard of the palace and were left there for all to see.

31. Pronoun Reference (ref)

Every pronoun must have an antecedent. To avoid faulty pronoun reference, make sure that the antecedents of your pronouns are clear.

Do not use a pronoun that could refer to more than one antecedent:

Wrong: The bartender yelled at Harry that *he* could lose his job. (Is it the bartender or Harry who could lose his job?)

Better: The bartender yelled at Harry, "You could lose your job!" (Recasting the sentence is better than creating an awkward repetition, such as "The bartender yelled at Harry that Harry could lose his job.")

Avoid pronouns that refer to entire clauses or sentences:

Wrong: His room is cluttered; his clothes are wrinkled; and even the pages of his books bear stains of grease. *This* really bothers me. (Three full clauses form the antecedent of *this;* the reference is too broad.)

Better: His room is cluttered; his clothes are wrinkled; and even the pages of his books bear stains of grease. *This sloppiness of his* really bothers me.

Avoid pronouns that have no antecedent:

Wrong: In *Oedipus Rex* there is no free will; *it* was predestined by Apollo. (*It* has no antecedent.)

Better: In *Oedipus Rex* there is no free will; *all of the tragic events* were predestined by Apollo.

Avoid pronouns whose antecedents are only implied by context:

Wrong: John lived in Italy during the first eight years of his life; consequently, he speaks *it* fluently. (The antecedent *Italian* is only implied.)

Better: John lived in Italy during the first eight years of his life; consequently, he speaks *Italian* fluently.

Avoid using *it* or *they* without a clear antecedent:

Wrong: In the *Los Angeles Times* it expressed the opposite point of view. (*It* has no antecedent.)

Better: The *Los Angeles Times* expressed the opposite point of view.

Wrong: *They* say that migraine headaches are often caused by repressed anger. (Who are *they?*)

Better: *Some neurologists* say that migraine headaches are caused by repressed anger.

Notice the following correct uses of the impersonal *it* when referring to weather, time, or distance:

> It is foggy today. (weather)
> It is precisely two o'clock. (time)
> Is it much farther to your house? (distance)

Avoid using *you* and *your* except when addressing the reader specifically.

Wrong: If *you* want to be happily married, *you* have to be willing to sacrifice *your* own pleasure.

Better: People who want to be happily married must be willing to sacrifice their own pleasure.

NOTE: To refer to all human beings or people in general, use general terms like *we, one, a person,* or *people.* Notice, however, that throughout this book we often use the pronoun *you* because we are addressing you, our reader, specifically.

Exercises

Exercise 31: Pronoun reference

Indicate which sentences contain a faulty pronoun reference. Then rewrite those sentences to correct the error.

> MODEL: She seemed so young and innocent, which made Helene jealous.
>
> Answer: **Her apparent youth and innocence made Helene jealous.**

1. As serious as our differences may seem, it is a common case of dissimilarities.
2. At midnight the doctor came out and told us that he had survived the surgery.
3. Deprecating comments are made all of the time, and it makes the victim have a low opinion of himself.
4. The nurse's aide lied by writing on the chart that she had been given a bath.
5. She had a house which survived her only three years.
6. The senator squirmed in his seat and avoided the question, which amused the reporters.
7. His best friend warned him that he might get an "F."
8. Many youths feel that their environment is prejudiced against them, and this increases their hostility.

9. If I'm having a boring time, it shows on my face.
10. If a person wants to make money, he must learn how to take risks.
11. Although my brother is taking pre-med courses, I doubt if he will ever be one.
12. How far is it to the main library?
13. In Islam they believe that Jesus was a prophet.
14. I was stood up on two separate occasions, which embarrassed me.
15. Since the children want to make some animals out of apple cores, I need to buy some at the store.

Index

A 9
B 0
C 1
D 2
E 3
F 4
G 5
H 6
I 7
J 8

Proofreading Symbols

Symbol	Meaning
fact_ory	Insert a letter
antecedᵉnt	Replace a letter
One *must* make choices	Insert a word
In ~~Peking~~ *Beijing*	Replace a word
in the west (underlined to capitalize)	Capitalize
He is a bank President	Use lowercase
rec͡ieve	Transpose letters
to ⌐quickly move⌐	Transpose words
a display of ⟨dazzling⟩ light	Move word(s)
the future of#the world	Insert a space
a birth͡ mark	Close up the space
dis͡appear	Delete a letter and close up
every ~~last taxable~~ dollar	Delete word(s)
a ~~treacherous~~ enemy	Stet (restore what was deleted)
her own self-esteem. Her physical stress	Run the line on (no paragraph)